SOCIAL WORK PROCESSES

Revised edition

Social work processes

BEULAH ROBERTS COMPTON
University of Minnesota, Minneapolis

BURT GALAWAY
University of Minnesota, Duluth

1979 **The Dorsey Press** *Homewood, Illinois 60430*
Irwin-Dorsey Limited *Georgetown, Ontario L7G 4B3*

ISBN 0-256-02194-5
Library of Congress Catalog Card No. 78–70957

Printed in the United States of America

1 2 3 4 5 6 7 8 9 0 K 6 5 4 3 2 1 0 9

Dedicated to those
from whom we have learned much—
our families, the clients with whom we have worked,
and the students we have known.

Preface

As we complete this revision of our work, we have little to add to our earlier preface. While we have attempted to make changes and additions, including two new chapters, that will clarify our earlier notions and enrich the ideas presented, the purpose, structure, and focus of the book remain the same.

Perhaps the most significant change we have made, and one that we feel is important to call to the reader's attention, is our effort to eliminate sexist terms and language from the text. In our attempt to present to the student a consistently nonsexist approach we requested permission of authors of earlier works to edit their articles. All authors, except as specifically noted in the text, generously gave their permission for these desired changes. We recognize that such changes may do some damage to the material in that the authors were working at a particular time in our history and thus the editing of the material may result in some loss of historical value. And we recognize that some articles may seem to carry a less personal message to the reader when singular personal pronouns are changed to the plural. However, we are presenting the material in the text as an aid to students in today's world; thus we thought the historical context was not critical, and, while the use of such phrases as "the worker . . . he . . . ." may seem to focus more directly on the person of the reader, they also may seem to today's feminine readers to exclude them. We do wish to thank the authors of the reprinted material who were willing to let us tamper with their writing in this way.

We do want to express our great debt to those individuals who have made comments about the book, especially the teachers whose suggestions came from their use of the text in their classes. Such comments have been invaluable to us in our work on this revision. In addition we wish to thank the students in our own classes whose questions and comments about the material have helped to clarify both our own thinking and our explanations.

We must express a very significant debt of gratitude to Joan Velasquez who has used the text in her classes at the University of Minnesota School of Social Work in Minneapolis and has been willing to conduct a running dialogue with the authors about her experience. This feedback over the last year has helped us immeasureably in rethinking what we had written three years ago. Joan also reviewed most of our changes and supported them as being worthwhile. Finally, in spite of the generous help of others we must accept the sole responsibility for this text.

Diane Anderson, Maxine Brown, and JoAnne Martz of Minneapolis, and the office staff of the School of Social Development, University of Minnesota, Duluth, deserve special recognition and thanks for their help in typing the manuscript and taking care of many of the details necessary in producing this revision.

March 1979   BEULAH ROBERTS COMPTON
                                                 BURT GALAWAY

Preface to the first edition

This book is intended for those who are beginners in the process of learning to be competent social workers. This may include B.A. students, individuals who have entered practice without an undergraduate preparation in college and are now anxious to learn about the work they are doing, or M.S.W. students who are beginning their graduate preparation.

Our purpose in developing this text is to present to the beginning social work student, or to the beginning practitioner, a basic set of concepts and principles from which he or she may be able to develop a foundation of general practice knowledge. It is our belief that what is presented here is both basic enough and realistic enough that, once integrated by the student, it will serve as the foundation for a more elaborate and sophisticated structure of social work competence as the beginner accumulates more experience as both a learner and a practitioner. Our goal is to present a text that describes and analyzes the elements of practice—organized within a problem solving framework—in such a way that the student not only intellectually grasps the nature of social work processes, but also gains some knowledge of the trials and tribulations, joys and satisfactions of social work practice in today's world.

The selection and organization of knowledge in the field of social work is a perennial problem, and probably will continue to plague the profession. We believe that there are at least four large areas of knowledge that the competent social work practitioner will have integrated into his own practice formulations: (1) theories of people and society and their interaction which will help to answer such questions as how individuals and their social systems grow, develop, stabilize, change, function and dysfunction, and what is the effect of each upon the other, (2) knowledge of social work as a profession, and something of its history that takes into consideration the societal context within which it has developed and functioned over time, (3) knowledge of social welfare agencies, institutions, delivery systems, or other organized structures within which social work services have, over time, been lodged; and the effect of the structure and function of these delivery systems upon the way problems have been defined and the way social work practice has been shaped, (4) the nature of social work practice itself which includes some historical perspective of the development of the various practice modalities, general concepts, and principles of the practice processes, and a more sophisticated and specialized practice competence. It was our decision, in keeping with our purpose, that we would focus on the nature of the basic social work processes within this fourth area of knowledge, recognizing that this one volume will not "a social worker make."

The text is organized into 14 chapters. Each begins with the authors' development of the notions and concepts to be dealt with in that particular chapter. This material is followed by two or three reprints of the works of other authors that relate to the issues of that chapter. Each chapter ends with a brief annotated bibliography. The first six chapters of the text deal with the basic concepts of all social work processes. The last seven chapters present a specific model of social work practice and the processes that make the model work.

The readings at the end of each chapter are not presumed to be a representative sample of the literature. They were selected to complement the authors' statement so that the book would stand as a text built upon the authors' approach to social work processes. We attempted to select reprints that would contribute to the richness or the sense of complexity of the issues developed in each particular chapter. From the vast amount of material available, our goal was to select examples that would (in combination with the authors' work) give students a realistic, intellectual grasp of the nature of social work processes and that might serve to raise questions for further work or discussion.

We cannot predict the future of the profession, or the knowledge and skill that the future will demand of those who would practice in the name of social work—so we have developed this text to present what we see as the processes of the profession in today's world. It is precisely because we do not know what problems the future will present to the workers of tomorrow that we believe in the problem solving framework for practice. Such a model recognizes the inherent uniqueness of each problem while recognizing the function of knowledge. It is a relatively open framework which not only allows for use of current knowledge but allows for the integration of new knowledge, and, in fact, encourages seeking after the new. It demands the careful consideration of problem definition and goals in such a way that client system and practitioner become partners, and it demands a continual monitoring of service outcomes and client goal achievement. We have tried to present the material, and have selected and organized the readings and bibliographies, to stimulate the beginning of a journey toward professional competence rather than to present an arrived at destination.

We are indebted to so many people who have helped us in our own professional development, challenged our thinking, and supported us in the development of this book that we cannot possibly mention them all. So we must select only a few. First, we must recognize the contributions of our families, the social work professors we have had, the clients and others with whom we have worked professionally, and the students we have known. All of these persons, individually and collectively, have served as a source of learning and stimulation for us.

We wish to thank our colleagues of our two schools of social work who offered many insights and ideas and gave generously of their time in reading and commenting on the manuscript. We especially wish to thank professors Helen Yesner and Annalee Stewart who used the manuscript in their classes during this last year, and thus could give us live and objective feedback from both undergraduate and beginning graduate classes as to its utility.

We want to thank our own students of the last three years who have reacted with both criticism and support to the bits and pieces of the manuscript as they have appeared in their assigned readings, and especially the beginning graduate students of this last year who have read and discussed the completed manuscript with us.

We owe special thanks to the reviewers who commented on the manuscript as it was in process and on the finished document: Rhonda Connaway, School of Social Work, Washington University; Sheldon Gelman, School of Social Work, Pennsylvania State University; Gwendolyn C. Gilbert, School of Social Work, The Ohio State University; H. Wayne Johnson, School of Social Work, University of Iowa; Sylvia Krakow, School of Social Work, Boston University; and Louis Lowy, School of Social Work, Boston University. Their willingness to take time to read and share their thinking about the work resulted in strengthening the manuscript. Those who generously gave us permission to reprint their articles or to quote from their writings deserve acknowledgement and gratitude. Their generosity has contributed greatly to the strength of the text. Without their willingness to share, the book would be quite different. In spite of such generous help from others, we must accept the final, sole responsibility for the content of this text.

Wendy Gaskill as the chief typist, Jan Goodno, Sue Nelson, and Sue Newlin who ably assisted her deserve special recognition and our most heartfelt thanks, not only for typing the manuscript, but for taking care of the myriad of details with cheerfulness, calmness, and efficiency. Alice Chen, a social work teaching assistant, was most efficient in locating fugitive materials, supervising reprint reproduction, and in helping in any way she could. We also wish to acknowledge the contribution of Georgia Ann Guevara, Larry Ray, Pamela Jones and Elsie Fairchild, teaching assistants at the School of Social Work, University of Southern Mississippi, who assisted with the indexing.

The book is the result of our collaborative efforts as fellow faculty members at the University of Minnesota Schools of Social Work. We have found both teaching and writing together to be a fruitful venture in cooperation in the fullest sense of the word. The fact that one name precedes the other in the listing of the two authors does not in any way indicate that one member of the team is a senior author and one member a junior. The listing of the names is simply the result of an accident of the alphabet.

Together we have 15 years of practice experience representing the fields of public assistance, child welfare (with emphasis on foster care and protective services), corrections, day care, and private family agencies. We have held positions ranging from beginning B.A. workers to M.S.W. workers to supervisor to associate executive. Between us we have had 25 years of teaching experience in both class and field. The classroom experience includes continuing education courses and numerous institutes and workshops for employed practitioners, undergraduate teaching in the fields of social work practice and social welfare policy, M.S.W. classes in both general practice and specific practice modalities, and Ph.D. seminars. This book has come from this experience and from our desire to introduce others to a profession that we have found so challenging and stimulating.

BEULAH ROBERTS COMPTON
BURT GALAWAY

Contributors

ATTNEAVE, CAROLYN L.   Professor of Psychology and Adjunct Professor of Psychiatry and Behavioral Science, University of Washington, Seattle, Washington.

AUERSWALD, EDGAR H.   Chief, Maui Community Mental Health Center, Wailuku, Maui, Hawaii.

BENAVIDES, EUSTOLIO.   NIMH Project Assistant and MSW student, School of Social Work, University of Minnesota, Minneapolis.

COMPTON, BEULAH.   Professor, School of Social Work, University of Minnesota, Minneapolis.

CORMICAN, JOHN D.   Associate Professor of English, Utica College, Utica, New York.

DECKER, JAMES T.   Assistant Professor, School of Social Work, San Diego State University, San Diego, California.

DONOVAN, JOHN B.   Account Executive, Hill and Knowlton, New York.

DYAL, WILLIAM M.   President, Inter-American Foundation, Arlington, Virginia.

FEIT, MARVIN D.   Assistant Professor, School of Social Work, University of Tennessee, Memphis.

FORDOR, ANTHONY.   Head of Department of Social Work, Liverpool Polytechnic, Liverpool, England.

GALAWAY, BURT.   Instructor, School of Social Development, University of Minnesota, Duluth.

GARWICK, GEOFFERY.   Clinical Psychologist, St. Paul-Ramsey Community Mental Health Center, St. Paul, Minnesota.

GERMAIN, CAREL B.   Professor, School of Social Work, University of Connecticut, West Hartford.

GITTERMAN, ALEX.   Professor, School of Social Work, Columbia University, New York.

GORDON, WILLIAM E.   Professor Emeritus, George Warren Brown School of Social Work, Washington University, St. Louis, Missouri.

GROSSER, CHARLES.   Professor, School of Social Work, Columbia University, New York.

HALLECK, SEYMOUR L.   Professor of Psychiatry, University of North Carolina School of Medicine, Chapel Hill.

HARDCASTLE, DAVID.   Professor and Dean, School of Social Welfare, University of Kansas, Lawrence.

HARDMAN, DALE.   Professor of Social Work, University of Wisconsin, Oshkosh.

HARTMAN, ANN. Professor, School of Social Work, University of Michigan, Ann Arbor.

HOBBS, NICHOLAS. Professor of Psychology and of Preventive Medicine, Vanderbilt University, Nashville, Tennessee.

HOOYMAN, EUGENE. Assistant Professor, School of Social Development, University of Minnesota, Duluth.

HUDSON, JOE. Director of Victim Services, Minnesota Department of Corrections, St. Paul.

KADUSHIN, ALFRED. Professor of Social Work, School of Social Work, University of Wisconsin, Madison.

KIRESUK, THOMAS J. Chief Clinical Psychologist, Hennepin County Medical Center; Director, Program Evaluation Resource Center, Minneapolis, Minnesota.

KRAMER, RALPH M. Professor, School of Social Welfare, University of California, Berkeley.

LEWIS, RONALD. Associate Professor, School of Social Welfare, University of Wisconsin, Milwaukee.

LEVINSON, HILLARD L. Senior Supervisor, Foster Care Multi-Service Program, Illinois Children's Home and Aid Society and in private practice, Chicago.

LEVY, CHARLES S. Professor, Wurzweiler School of Social Work, Yeshiva University, New York.

McCLURE, MARILYN E. VIGIL. NIMH Project Director, School of Social Work, University of Minnesota, Minneapolis.

MALUCCIO, ANTHONY N. Professor, School of Social Work, University of Connecticut, West Hartford.

MARLOW, WILMA D. At time of death was Assistant Professor, School of Social Work, University of Connecticut, West Hartford.

PAWLAK, EDWARD J. Professor and Coordinator of the Planning, Policy, and Administrative Sequence, School of Social Work, Western Michigan University, Kalamazoo.

RED HORSE, JOHN G. Assistant Professor, School of Social Work, University of Minnesota, Minneapolis.

RUTMAN, LEONARD. Associate Professor, School of Social Work, Carleton University, Ottawa, Canada.

SCHWARTZ, WILLIAM. Professor Emeritus, School of Social Work, Columbia University, New York.

SPITZER, KURT. Professor, School of Social Work, Wayne State University, Detroit, Michigan.

TABER, RICHARD H. Assistant Minister, Wilton Congregational Church, Wilton, Connecticut.

TRADER, HARRIET PEAT. Professor, School of Social Work and Community Planning, University of Maryland, Baltimore.

TUCKER, SAMUEL. Associate Professor, School of Social Work, University of Southern Mississippi, Hattiesburg.

VELASQUEZ, JOAN. Lecturer, School of Social Work, University of Minnesota and Program Evaluator, Ramsey County Welfare Board, St. Paul.

WELSH, BETTY. Associate Professor, School of Social Work, Wayne State University, Detroit, Michigan.

Contents

Recapitulation. A look forward. Outline of problem-solving model—short form. Outline of problem-solving model—long form.

Readings

8. The contact phase: Problem identification, initial goal setting, and data collection   276

Giving and taking help. Getting started. The crossing of system boundaries. Defining the problem. Goal setting. Preliminary contract. Areas of data collection. Sources and methods of data collection. Skills in the contact phase. Recapitulation. A look forward.

Readings

9. The contract phase: Joint assessment, goal setting, and planning   317

Definition of the service contract. Joint assessment and decision making. Setting goals. Planning for intervention. Recapitulation. A look forward.

Readings

10. Interventive roles: Implementation of the plan   337

The concept of interventive roles. The role of social broker. The role of enabler. The role of teacher. The role of mediator. The role of advocate. Roles are not functional specializations. Recapitulation. A look forward.

Readings

Social work as a problem-solving process. Social work as a client-worker relationship. Social work as a rational process. The beginning.

Introduction

Climactic changes occurred in both social work and social work education during the late 1960s and early 1970s. For the first time since 1939 undergraduate social work education was officially recognized by the profession, standards were set, and accreditation of undergraduate programs by the Council on Social Work Education was instituted. Bachelor's degree social workers from accredited programs were afforded full membership rights in the National Association of Social Workers, and, reflecting the increasing social consciousness of youth, large numbers of students were enrolled in proliferating social work courses.

From these students has risen a frequent and reasonable demand to be taught something about how social workers engage in practice and serve as agents of change. What is the nature of social work intervention? What is its purpose? How is it carried out? And what are the processes through which social workers and clients move? In this book an effort is made to identify, conceptualize, and organize certain common elements of social work practice so that they can be logically and systematically examined by a student exploring the potentials of an exciting profession. This book rests on the assumption that common social work processes can be identified—processes which can be applicable to workers regardless of the setting (corrections, mental health, schools, public welfare, and so on) or the "relational system" (individual, family, small groups, community) in which they practice.

As used here, *process* may be defined as "a series of actions, changes, or functions that bring about an end or result." Thus the actions taken by the social worker in conjunction with clients to bring about planned change will be examined in text. *Client*, in this context, will take on a generic meaning and refer to those for whom the worker offers professional services, including individuals, families, small groups, and communities.

As a textbook-reader this book is an effort to combine the advantages of both textbooks and readers. In 15 chapters the authors present an explanation and application of selected theories, ways of thinking, and values and actions that are considered to be critical for the beginner in social work practice. The authors have also included a listing of other readings in an annotated bibliography to introduce the beginning student to related social work literature that should provide an additional perspective to that material offered by the authors. Some readings present a viewpoint different from that of the authors; others are in-

1

cluded because they broaden the material developed in the chapters they accompany.

A reference list is included at the end of the book to assist the student in locating all source material referred to in this book.

Underlying the authors' viewpoint are five assumptions:

1. As a human service profession, social work shares with other human service professions, as well as with many elements of the society at large, a common set of values concerning the dignity of man, the right to equal opportunity, and the qualities of justice. The different human service professions may, however, operationalize these values differently; in fact, the way in which they are operationalized for social work is the particular concern of this book.

2. The goals of social work intervention are the solving of specific, particular problems experienced by individuals, groups, or communities in their attempts to resolve discrepancies in their social existence or to achieve their social goals. The term *problem* is defined in the most basic sense as "a question or group of questions that need to be resolved" and does not necessarily carry implications of fault, blame, or weakness.

3. Self is the basic tool used by the worker in mobilizing resources within the client and the community in order to alter the interaction of the two.

4. The breadth of the social work profession requires that practitioners develop skill and knowledge in a wide range of content areas.

5. The problem-solving focus of social work is best carried out in a partnership arrangement between worker and client. This partnership arrangement holds major implications for the process of problem formulation, data collection, assessment, planning, and intervention.

Most social work practice occurs within the framework of an agency. This book, however, does not focus on agency services. The focus instead is on the actions of the social worker to bring about change, and this book is offered as an aid for learning basic practice skills in social work. These skills require the application of professional knowledge and principles to unique human situations. Because each situation is unique, the application of such knowledge and principles always involves the utilization of an elusive quality—judgment. For professional social workers, judgment develops with maturity, experience, and continued learning.

Judgment is to be distinguished from intellectual capacity and might be defined as the ability to make the most effective choice among alternatives which professional knowledge, perception as developed by knowledge and experience, and informed "hunches" present for one's decision. Professional judgment develops through personal maturity and continued learning from one's experiences, from exposure to new knowledge, and from encounters with a wide range of professional problems and relationships. The struggle toward professional judgment and professional skills in acting is a lifelong educational experience in which no one ever fully arrives. The authors certainly do not conceive of themselves as fully developed "knowers" but rather as "seekers after knowledge" who have mastered valuable concepts in their journey. This book is an attempt to share selected knowledge and principles related to basic social work processes. It is a beginning book that should provide students with a coherent framework for beginning practice. Whole books could be, and have been, written about information found in each of its chapters.

This is not a book of rules or an easy do-it-yourself manual. The authors do not believe that the student in social work can be supplied with a set of rules to be invariably followed. What is offered is a set of principles, processes in which the principles can be applied, and an opportunity to begin developing skill and judgment in their application. In this sense both this book and social work are in the best of the liberal arts tradition—a tradition which requires the disciplined exercise of judgment.

CHAPTER 1.

Nature of social work

What do social workers do? Where and how do they intervene? For most of us these are perplexing questions—questions made more perplexing by our lack of contact with social workers and the diffuseness of social work practice. From life experiences most of us have little difficulty identifying the job of the doctor as healing the body—mediating between the physical organism and environmental influences which threaten health. (The doctor's job becomes much less clear and less understood when it moves out of the area of physical illness and into the treatment of alleged mental illness.) Likewise, the lawyer's job as mediator between the individual and the legal institutions which have been developed to insure a reasonably orderly society is usually understood. And few of us, because of our life experiences, have any difficulty identifying the job of the teacher in transmitting the accumulated knowledge of the culture. But what about social workers? What is their job?

William Schwartz, in the article reproduced in this chapter, takes the viewpoint that "Every profession has a particular function to perform in society: it has received a certain job assignment for which it is held accountable." To Schwartz the social work job assignment is to "mediate the process through which the individual and . . . society reach out for each other through a mutual need for self-fulfillment." The Schwartz mediating model rests on the assumption that the interests of the individual and the interests of society are essentially the same, but that in a complex and changing society the individual's desire to belong as a full and productive member and the society's ability to integrate and enrich its people are sometimes blocked. Social work intervention is directed toward these blockages and toward freeing the "individual's impetus toward health, growth, and belonging; and the organized efforts of society to integrate its parts into a productive and dynamic whole."

This first chapter has three objectives:

1. The focus of social work intervention will be further explored in light of Schwartz's mediating model.
2. The organization of social work actions in the traditional format of casework, group work, and community organization will be considered in light of this focus of social work intervention.
3. An alternative view of social work actions will be identified and will become the focus for the balance of this book.

FOCUS OF SOCIAL WORK INTERVENTION

Martin Rein (1970, p. 15) suggests that one of the obstacles to the development of a professional social work creed has been the difficulty in defining the social work profession. Nevertheless, efforts have been made to define both the target and the nature of social work practice. The Commission on Practice of the National Association of Social Workers (1958, pp. 5–6) published a working definition which defined social work practice as a "constellation of value, purpose, sanction, knowledge, and method." The working definition identified three purposes of social work practice:

1. To assist individuals and groups to identify and resolve or minimize problems arising out of disequilibrium between themselves and the environment.
2. To identify potential areas of disequilibrium between individuals or groups and the environment in order to prevent the occurrence of disequilibrium.
3. In addition to these curative and preventive aims, to seek out, identify, and strengthen the maximum potential in individuals, groups, and communities (p. 6).

Werner Boehm (1958, p. 18) has also published a widely used definition of social work:

Social work seeks to enhance the social functioning of individuals, singularly and in groups, by activities focused upon their social relationships which constitute interaction between individuals and their environments. These activities can be grouped into three functions: restoration of impaired capacity, provision of individual and social resources, and prevention of social dysfunction.

More recently the West Virginia Undergraduate Social Work Curriculum Development Project conceptualized social work as

... concerned and involved with the interactions between people and the institutions of society that affect the ability of people to accomplish life tasks, realize aspirations and values, and alleviate distress. These interactions between people and social institutions occur within the context of the larger societal good. Therefore, three major purposes of social work may be identified:

1. To enhance the problem-solving, coping, and developmental capacities of people;
2. To promote the effective and humane operation of the systems that provide people with resources and services;
3. To link people with systems that provide them with resources, services, and opportunities (Baer and Federico, 1978, p. 68).

These definitions clearly place the focus of social work intervention on the interaction or disequilibrium between individuals and their environments. In this sense they are consistent with Schwartz's mediating approach, inasmuch as they consider social work as in some way intervening or mediating between people and their social environments.

Harriett Bartlett (1970, p. 116) writes of a social work focus on social functioning, which she defines as the "relation between the coping activity of people and the demand from the environment." For Bartlett the concept of social functioning does not refer to the functioning of individuals or groups, which she finds characteristic of earlier definitions, but "attention is now directed primarily to what goes on between people and environment through the exchange between them. This dual focus ties them together. Thus person and situation, people and environment, are encompassed in a single concept, which requires that they be constantly reviewed together."

William Gordon (1969, p. 6) with whom Bartlett is in agreement, finds that "the central focus of social work traditionally seems to have been on people in their life situation complex—a simultaneous dual focus on individuals and environment." Gordon further notes that

> Emphasis has been on individualizing the person-situation complex in order to achieve the best match between each person and the environment, in which either person-behavior or environmental situation may deviate widely from the typical or normative. We conclude, therefore, that the central target of technical social work practice is *matching* something in person and situation—that is, intervening by whatever methods and means necessary to help people be in situations where their capabilities are sufficiently matched with the demands of the situations to "make a go of it."

The focus of social work intervention is on the interaction between humans and their environments. In Schwartz's terms social workers mediate; in Gordon's terms social workers match something in environment to something in the individual; and in Bartlett's terms social workers seek to strike a balance between people's coping ability and environmental demands. Social workers may at times (1) direct change strategies toward individuals, (2) direct change strategies toward the environment, and (3) direct change strategies toward the interaction of individual and environment. But in all cases, these strategies are directed toward changing the nature of the person-situation interaction.

But does changing the nature of the interaction mean changing the individual or changing the environment? This is an old issue in social work which was enunciated at an early date by Porter Lee (1929) in his distinction between social work as cause and social work as function. Our contention is that social workers do both and that the debate as to whether the profession should focus primarily on individual change or on environmental change results from a largely incorrect formulation of the focus of social work intervention. The parties to this debate tend to perceive social workers as either focusing on the individual or on the environment and miss the central focus on the interaction of the two. Gisela Konopka (1958) has pointed out the inappropriateness of this dichotomous thinking in social work, and Martin Rein (1970, p. 19) notes that both individual and social change approaches can be used to either support or challenge contemporary standards of behavior. Recent research by Merlin A. Taber and Anthony J. Vattano (1970) finds no sharp distinction between clinical and social orientations among practicing social workers and suggests that most social workers are able to integrate both functions. Rein's concept of radical casework is particularly well suited to a social work focus on person-situation interaction. For Rein (1970, p. 19), "a radical casework approach would mean not merely obtaining for clients social services to which they are entitled or helping them adjust to the environment, but also trying to deal with the relevant people and institutions in the clients' environment that are contributing to their difficulties."

Alex Gitterman and Carel Germain, in the article in this chapter, suggest that a gap exists between new knowledge and social work practice; they offer a life model which "integrates the treatment and reform traditions." Social workers focus on problems in living which fall into three areas:

> (1) problems and needs associated with tasks involved in life transitions; (2) problems and needs associated with tasks in using and influencing elements of the environment; and (3) problems and needs associated with interpersonal obstacles which impede the work of a family or a group as it deals with transitional and/or environmental tasks (1976:602–603).

To recapitulate, the focus of social work activity is directed toward the interaction of people and their environments in accordance with Schwartz's view of the social worker as a mediator (1961, pp. 154–155). This process of mediation requires the ability to direct change strategies toward person and environment and the interaction between them. The debate as to whether social workers should be stretcher-bearers or social engineers fails to account for a dual focus on both person and situation. But this raises a central question. Are the actions and practice strategies of social work organized in such a way as to facilitate the focus on the person-situation interaction?

THE CASEWORK, GROUP WORK, AND COMMUNITY ORGANIZATION CONCEPTUALIZATION OF SOCIAL WORK ACTIVITIES

Traditionally, social workers have thought of themselves as caseworkers, group workers, or community organizers. Each group in this trinity is assumed to use methods characterized by distinctive skills and change strategies. The primary variable distinguishing these methods, however, is not related to what the social worker does but to the number of persons with whom the worker interacts, such as individuals and families. In the implementation of change strategies, group workers interact with members of groups, and community organizers with community representatives (Warren, 1966; Meenaghan, 1972).

Schwartz notes the inappropriateness of basing a definition of method on the number of persons with whom the worker interacts and suggests that the terms casework, group work, and community organization refer to the relational system in which the worker implements method. For Schwartz, method is "a systematic process of ordering one's activity in the performance of a function. Method is function in action." Thus method becomes a systematic way in which social workers carry out their function, that is, the systematic way in which they mediate between the individual and the social environment. Schwartz conceptualizes five essential tasks which constitute the social worker's method:

1. Searching for a common ground between the client's perception of need and social demand.
2. Detecting and challenging obstacles which obscure the common ground.
3. Contributing data to the client.
4. Lending a vision to the client.
5. Defining the requirements and limits of the client-worker system.

Herbert Bisno (1969) also considers casework, group work, and community organization a faulty conceptualization of social work method because "The inclusion of a quantitative attribute of the potential transactional unit and the designation of the method (without suggesting the nature of problem or appropriate problem solving technique) has led to an illicit bond between a given method and a given, but arbitrarily restricted and limiting, client system" (p. 8). Bisno is making the same objection as Schwartz: designation of method on the basis of the size of the client system is illogical. Methods, according to Bisno, "are techniques sufficiently generalized to be common to a discipline, practice, or range of disciplines and practice" (p. 7). As an alternative to the casework–group work–community organization model, Bisno conceptualized nine social work methods which may be utilized with any size of client system: adversary, conciliatory, developmental, facilitative-instructional, knowledge development and testing, restorative, regulatory, role-implementing, and rule making (pp. 9–12).

In addition to the illogic of basing a definition of method on the size of the relational system (Schwartz) or the client transactional system (Bisno), the casework, group work, community organization model has an additional major shortcoming. This approach encourages the dichotomous thinking of changing the individual or changing the environment instead of maintaining the primary focus of social work intervention on the person-situation interaction. Too often, for example, caseworkers are looked upon as changing the individual (that is, helping individuals adapt to the realities of environment) and community organizers are looked upon as the experts in environmental change. Group workers are divided into both camps, depending largely on the purpose of the group. Some groups are directed toward producing change within their own members (therapy groups, socialization groups, and so on) or toward providing opportunities for meeting normal developmental needs (club groups, and so on); others are directed toward change outside of group members (social action groups, neighborhood organizations, tenant groups, and so on).

Martin Rein (1970, p. 19) notes that the association of social change with community organization and of individual change with social casework may oversimplify social work inasmuch as work with individuals can be directed toward changing social standards and work with groups or communities can be and is directed toward helping people adapt to their current situations. We agree with the Rein formulation and think that this distinction has been largely missed in social work—the expectation remains that the community organizer will work to produce community change, the caseworker to produce individual change, and the group worker to do either, depending on the nature of the group. This expectation diverts the focus of social work from the person-situation interaction to either the person or the situation depending on the particular method in which the practitioner has been steeped.

A third problem relates to the organization of social work activities into casework, group work, and community organization. This has led to training specialists in each of these methods with very little effort to prepare people to assess a person-situation interaction except through the colored glasses of their particular methodological orientation. Thus community organizers see problems in terms of community change, group workers in terms of working with groups, and caseworkers in terms of individual intervention. Abraham Kaplan (1964, p. 23) noted this same problem in terms of research methodology and formulated a law of the instrument: "Give a small boy a hammer, and he will find that everything he encounters needs to be pounded. It comes as no particular surprise to discover that scientists formulate problems in ways which require for their solution just those techniques in which they themselves are especially skilled." In the same way the conceptualization if social work activities in terms of casework, group work, and community organization leads to a tendency to define problems for intervention in terms of the worker's particular methodological frame of reference rather than a careful assessment of the person-situation interaction.

In addition to the casework, group work, and community organization framework, two other conceptualizations of social work activities—the micro-macro approach and the setting of practice approach—require brief discusson.

Recently considerable attention has been given to efforts to reconceptualize social work strategies in terms of micro-macro approaches. This concept   lization is implied in Helen Harris Perlman's article "Casework Is Dead." Perlman (1967a) makes an impassioned plea for two kinds of practitioners—those skilled in the delivery of individualized services and those skilled in social change. Micro approaches focus on the individual either as an individual or as a member of a family or a small group and are directed toward assisting the person in coping with environmental stress. Macro approaches are directed primarily toward the community or larger social systems and toward producing change in these systems. Werner Boehm (1967) discussed the two approaches in terms of intervention in social situations (helping individuals as individuals or in small groups) and intervention in the social resource structure (efforts to bring about more adequate resources for individuals within the community). Micro strategies generally encompass most of casework, family counseling as done in social work, and group work activities directed toward helping individuals in a group setting. Macro strategies encompass community organization, policymaking, planning, and group work strategies directed toward change outside of the group members themselves. While the micro-macro formulation has the advantage of logically relating strategies within these two major categories, it suffers from the major limitation of the casework, group work, community organization conceptualization. The focus is on the individual or the situation, with two groups of experts being prepared—one to intervene with the individual and the other with the situation. This continues a basic dichotomy in social work, which detracts from the primary focus on the person-situation interaction.

A closely related issue is prevention versus rehabilitation in social work. Arguments are advanced that social workers may spend too much time dealing with the casualties of modern society instead of attacking root problems in efforts at prevention. This is an unacceptable dichotomy for two reasons. First, to a large extent, it is a renewed manifestation of the issue of work with the community versus work with individuals. Prevention is frequently assumed to require social change, with rehabilitation perceived as helping individuals to cope with immediate situations. We consider all social work activity as both preventive and rehabilitative. Helping a mentally ill person is rehabilitative, but it also prevents future distress. Efforts to provide deprived children with adequate nutrition, clothing, and in some cases substitute living arrangements, if effective, are both rehabilitative and preventive. The second objection relates to the matter of timing and client readiness. The social worker, as an agent of the client, does not intervene until the client (individual, family, group, or community) perceives a problem and is ready to engage in a process of problem-solving; for the social worker to act otherwise increases the danger of doing to or for rather than with. Once a client decision occurs, the actions of the social worker may be both rehabilitative and preventive. The social worker may at times be called upon to serve as an agent of society (as may occur, for example, in dealing with child abuse or delinquency); in such instances it is highly unlikely that either prevention or rehabilitation will occur until the client and the worker discover a mutually acceptable area for joint problem-solving. Rehabilitation is preventive and prevention may be rehabilitative; ideally neither occurs until a client has perceived a problem, after which client and social worker engages in a mutual problem-solving undertaking.

Another approach has been to conceptualize methods in relation to a particular setting or social problem area. Thus, we might think of social work in relation to mental health services, corrections, economic dependency, and so on. The integrating theme is not the relational system, for one can easily think of work with individuals, small groups, and large organizations in relation to any of these problem areas. Emphasis is placed on the unique characteristics of the social problem under consideration. This approach has merit, and certainly many social workers do wish to specialize in particular problem areas by developing advanced knowledge and skills in them. The approach does not, however, provide a useful basis on which to organize a book directed to social work students who are just entering education to prepare for professional practice. This book, therefore, deals with processes of social work practice found in all settings and leaves the specialized setting or problem-related component for further professional education or perhaps later learning at an agency in-service level.

We have argued that the traditional conceptualization of social work activity as casework, group work, and community organization has three major weaknesses: (1) This conceptualization of method is based primarily on the size of the client system in which the worker intervenes, rather than on activities utilized by the worker. (2) This formulation tends to encourage the dichotomous approach of changing the individual or changing the situation rather than a focus on the person-situation interaction. (3) The education of specialists in each method has resulted in a tendency to see problems in terms of the methodological skills of workers rather than in terms of complete assessment of the client-situation interaction.

Brief mention was made of the micro-macro conceptualization of practice, which is primarily a refinement of the casework, group work, and community organization formulation and which presents the same shortcomings. Similar difficulties are found in the prevention-rehabilitation dichotomy in social work. A setting-of-practice or social problem basis for organizing social work activity was briefly mentioned, and while this holds potential, it is not a practical basis for the organization of a book for the beginning student.

If these approaches do not provide a useful conceptualization of social work activity, what does? Can social work activities be organized and thought about in such a way that a focus is clearly maintained on the person-situation interaction, that method is defined in relation to worker activity, and that the impact of the law of the instrument is reduced?

THE ORIENTATION OF THIS BOOK

Herbert Bisno (1969, p. 9) sets forth a way of thinking about social work activities which may help avoid these difficulties. He suggests that there are basically two levels of skill involved in social work—skills in knowing what method to use (remember that Bisno does not use the term *method* in the traditional sense) and skills in the actual use of method. John Kidneigh (1969, p. 159) advances a similar formulation when he suggests that social workers must possess both the capability of "deciding what to do" and "of doing the decided." Kidneigh, using the tripartite division of powers in government as an analogy, suggests further that social workers must possess skill at resolving problems which arise in the doing of the decided. More important than his reference to this third activity, which will not receive attention here, is Kidneigh's contention that "social work practice in any of its recognized methods, in any of its programs or settings, consists of these functions of deciding why and what to do, doing the decided, and resolving questions which arise in the course of the doing."

The Kidneigh and Bisno divisions of skill provide a helpful guide to refining the more global Schwartz model of identifying the mediating function of the profession and conceptualizing the five tasks which may be necessary to accomplish the function. Operationalizing the mediating function and the associated tasks will involve processes in both areas suggested by Kidneigh and Bisno—arriving at decisions about how to mediate and implementing those decisions. These social work change processes include actions to define the problem, actions to collect information on which to base decisions, actions to engage the client in goal-setting and decision-making, actions to produce change, and actions to evaluate progress.

Our concept of social work practice is consistent with the ecological models which have been developing over the past few years (Baer and Federico, 1978; Germain, 1973; Meyer, 1970; Pincus and Minahan, 1973) and expressed in the Gitterman and Germain article reproduced in this chapter. These models focus on the transactions of individuals and their environments with both individuals and environments in a constant state of reciprocity with each shaping the other. Social work interventions are directed to the interface of the individual and environment or at problems of living generated from the person in situation interaction. The West Virginia Undergraduate Social Work Curriculum Development Project identified ten competencies which can be seen as necessary for social work practice within an ecological framework:

1. Identify and assess situations where the relationship between people and social institutions needs to be initiated, enhanced, restored, protected, or terminated.
2. Develop and implement a plan for improving the well-being of people based on problem assessment and the exploration of obtainable goals and available options.
3. Enhance the problem-solving, coping, and developmental capacities of people.
4. Link people with systems that provide them with resources, services, and opportunities.
5. Intervene effectively on behalf of populations most vulnerable and discriminated against.
6. Promote the effective and humane operation of the systems that provide people with services, resources, and opportunities.
7. Actively participate with others in creating new, modified, or improved service, resource, opportunity systems that are more equitable, just, and responsive to consumers of services, and work with others to eliminate those systems that are unjust.
8. Evaluate the extent to which the objectives of the intervention plan were achieved.

9. Continually evaluate one's own professional growth and development through assessment of practice behaviors and skills.
10. Contribute to the improvement of service delivery by adding to the knowledge base of the profession as appropriate and by supporting and upholding the standards and ethics of the profession (Baer and Federico, 1978, pp. 86–89).

Thinking of social workers as possessing these competencies is much different than thinking of skills for working with groups, individuals, or communities. The worker is expected to work with the person-situation interaction—to be able to broadly assess the nature of the interaction and the problems in living arising from it and to focus interventions in relation to the assessment which may involve efforts to change the person, the situation, and the interaction. Thus, skills can be classified in two broad areas—assessment or deciding what to do and intervention or doing the decided.

In this approach, a social work generalist can be thought of as a person who is skillful in deciding what to do. Such practitioners will not be limited in their vision by any preferred relational system or prior methodological commitment and will be able to focus their attention on the totality of the person-situation interaction. In the process of deciding what to do the practitioner is free to examine variables in the person, in the situation, and that relate to the interaction of the two. Abilities at data collection and assessment are essential for such a practitioner in order to both define the problem and arrive at a practical and workable decision as to what needs to be done.

At the second level of doing the decided the profession needs to provide its clients with a wide range of interventive strategies. Some strategies may require highly skilled specialists. In some situations the generalist practitioner will possess skills in the necessary interventive strategies and may implement the change decision. In other situations the generalist may call in a specialist for assistance. In some instances the specialist may carry most of the responsibility for the implementation of the service plan; in others more of the doing the decided will be the responsibility of the generalist, who will work as a team member with the specialist in meeting the objectives of the service plan.

The division of social work processes into the two broad categories—deciding what to do and doing the decided—represents the focus taken by this book. This contrasts with division according to the size of the relational situation in which the worker functions or the specific social problem with which the worker is attempting to cope. Deciding what to do requires that the social worker and the client engage in processes of problem definition, data collection, and contracting. Doing the decided involves the client and the social worker jointly in any of a great number of change strategies. Rather than attempt a cataloging and discussion of the types of change strategies, the authors will conceptualize doing the decided in relation to the process of evaluation and to worker interventive roles and change strategies available to the client and the worker.

RECAPITULATION

By now you have been introduced to the three basic ideas found in this book which will recur in various forms in subsequent chapters. First, the focus of social work intervention is on the person-situation interaction. A corollary of this approach is that a focus solely on the individual or the situation is inappropriate—

the long debate in the social work profession about individual services versus social reform loses sight of the basic focus of the profession. Second, thinking of social work activities in terms of casework, group work, and community organization is not a viable conceptualization; that approach stresses the relational system in which the worker functions rather than the activities of the worker, tends to maintain a focus on the individual or the situation rather than on the interaction of the two, and leads to analyses of client situations and interactions in terms of a worker's interventive skills rather than the needs of the client. Third, this book follows an alternative organization of social work activities into skills and actions needed to decide what to do and skills and actions in doing the decided.

A LOOK FORWARD

Let's take a short and a long look forward. Immediately following are articles by William Schwartz and Alex Gitterman and Carel Germain. Schwartz develops the concept of the mediating function of social work which is central to the position of this book, and Gitterman and Germain present an ecological or life model of social work practice.

In the long view, readers of this book will be introduced to the social work processes of data collection, assessment, contracting, intervention, and evaluation. Because of the importance of teamwork in human services and the fact that social work is practiced in agencies (some of which are highly bureaucratic), chapters are devoted to examination of each of these aspects of social work practice. Before moving to the processes (the problem-solving model) by which the focus of social work intervention is implemented, consideration will be given to three very important elements of social work practice—the knowledge base, the value base, and the use of relationship.

Reading
1-1 The social worker in the group*

William Schwartz

Professions have a way of moving periodically through eras of rediscovery in which an old truth comes alive with the vigor and freshness of a new idea. Such an occurrence seems to be taking shape in social work practice as we face the realization that the problems of people do not lend themselves easily to arbitrary divisions of labor among the various agencies of social welfare. In fact, this particular truth has been rediscovered several times, cutting deeply, in each instance, into established forms and calling for new institutional and professional alignments.

This stubborn fact has precipitated a reexamination of social work's historic system of designating the functions of agencies by reference to the number of people involved in the client-worker system at one time. Thus the casework agency, as we have known it, was one which derived its distinguishing

* Reprinted with permission of the author and Columbia University Press from National Conference on Social Welfare, *Social Welfare Forum, 1961* (New York: Columbia University Press, 1961), pp. 146–171.

characteristics from the fact that its workers talked to people one at a time; the group work agency (later called the "group service agency") worked with people in small, cohesive groups; and the community organization agency assumed the function of leadership with representative bodies and similar associations.

This typology emerged at an early stage of specialization and has remained relatively stable over the major course of social work history—not, however, without a certain marked degree of uneasiness throughout. Group workers have struggled for years with the need to "individualize," wondering whether they were "doing casework" when they dealt with individual problems, and continually raising the issue of whether individual or group problems should take priority. The agencies of social casework have been concerned about the reluctance of workers trained in the one-to-one relationship to carry these skills into committee work, multiple interviewing, group consultation, and other group constellations. And the community organization workers have been faced continuously with the vital connection between the tasks that people undertake and the uniquely personal ways in which they approach them.

These vague but pervasive concerns have now begun to crystallize into new conceptions about the appropriate client-worker systems through which agencies carry out their functions. The rapid development of social work services in the institutional therapeutic settings has created a community model which lends itself poorly to a type of specialization based solely on the number of people with whom the social worker interacts at a given time. In these settings, the caseworkers have been pressed into group service, just as the psychiatrists and the psychologists had before them (National Association of Social Workers, n.d.); and the group workers have found themselves involved in a degree of intensive individualization beyond anything they had ever experienced.

In general practice, the developing em-

phasis on the family as a unit of service has forced both caseworkers and group workers into new modes of activity. The former have been constrained to understand and work with the dynamics of family interaction; the latter, to replace the comfortable aura of friendly visiting with a more sophisticated and focused approach. In both agency types, the traditional forms have been changing, with caseworkers turning more and more to the group as a unit of service and group workers rekindling their old concern with ways of offering skilled individual guidance for those who need it (Family Service Association of America, 1959; National Association of Social Workers, 1958).

In the area of community organization, the picture is less clear. There seems to be little doubt, however, that its conceptualizers are recognizing another old truth, namely, that the only way to work with communities is to work with people, singly and together, and that skill in the helping process needs to be abstracted and formulated into teachable concepts. The newer theoretical attempts lean heavily toward organizing the experience of community workers into concepts that reflect the language and central concerns of social work method. Genevieve Carter (1958, p. 248), for example, has addressed herself directly to an analysis of the helping process in community organization, and her concept of "cumulative sequence" is an interesting attempt to relate the order of community change to that of individual growth and development.

Concurrently, the unification of social workers within a single professional association and the efforts of the social work schools to conceptualize the common elements in practice have dramatized the need to combine the learnings of workers from the various fields and settings into a functional scheme that can be taught and practiced under the name of "social work." Such a scheme would not eliminate specialization but would certainly redefine it; most important, it could create a new integration within which the component parts could be differentiated on a basis more consistent with the facts of life as they actually exist in the community.

The new conceptual framework would be built on the recognition that the function of a social agency is determined more realistically by the social problem to which it has been assigned than by the specific relational systems through which the social worker translates this function into concrete services. It would accept the fact that there is no known correspondence between a function such as child placement, or family welfare, or recreation, or social planning, and the exclusive use of the one-to-one or the one-to-group structure to carry it out. And it would become increasingly clear that any agency should be capable of creating, in each specific instance, that system of client-worker relationships which is most appropriate to its clients' requirements.

A significant corollary would then emerge quite naturally, namely, that the single variable embodied in the number of people one works with at a time is simply not significant enough to be endowed with the designation of "method." Not significant enough, that is, if we reserve the term "method" to mean a systematic mode of helping which, while it is used differently in different situations, retains throughout certain recognizable and invariant properties through which one may identify the social worker in action. In this light, to describe casework, group work, and community organization as methods simply mistakes the nature of the helping process for the relational system in which it is applied. It seems more accurate to speak of a social work method, practiced in the various systems in which social workers find themselves or which are established for the purpose of giving service: the family, the small friendship group, the representative body, the one-to-one interview, the hospital ward, the lounge-canteen, the committee, the street club, the special-interest group, and many others. Within this frame of reference, the task of safeguarding the uniqueness of the various so-called methods fades before the real problem of abstracting from all these

experiences the common methodological components of the helping process in social work.

This is partly why any serious attempt to define a unique entity called "social group work" begins to turn, under one's very hand, into a description of something larger and more inclusive, of which the worker-group system is simply a special case. Having now, after many years of shifting identification, found a resting place in social work function and the social agency network[1] group workers can indeed make a significant conceptual contribution to the theoretical problems involved in working with groups. But the context has changed, and the moment has passed, for a definition of "group work method." Rather, we must now search for those common elements in social work practice—the very elements which attracted group workers into the social work fold—from which social workers in all settings can draw the specifics of their own practice. The job can no longer be done most usefully by first defining social group work (or casework or community organization) and then trying to fit the description into the general framework of helping theory. The process is now rather the reverse: by laying the groundwork in a social work methodology, we may begin to analyze and clarify the activities of social workers as they work with people in groups.

To both of these endeavors—building the common model and describing the special case of the group system—those who have been schooled in the traditions of social group work have a rich store of experience from which to contribute. The task is, of course, rendered doubly difficult by the fact that workers who attempt it must break the bonds of their own training, since they themselves have been reared in the ancient fallacies. But, clumsy though these first efforts must be, it seems inevitable that they will be

---

[1] For a more detailed account of the developing integration of group work and social work see Schwartz (1959).

made, and in increasing numbers[2] for they represent an indispensable part of the still larger task of conceptualizing the generic framework of the social work profession as a whole. These larger issues are embodied in the Curriculum Study of the Council on Social Work Education (Boehm, 1959a) and in the work of the Commission on Social Work Practice of the National Association of Social Workers (Bartlett, 1958). The present segment of this overall task deals only with those activities through which the social worker functions in direct relationship with people of established or potential client status; the focus is on the helping process itself and on the factors which determine its nature and its variations. In what follows, we shall not presume to create a comprehensive theoretical statement but simply to highlight a few of the essential components around which such a statement will need to turn.

Let us begin, then, with three fairly simple propositions:

1. Every profession has a particular function to perform in society: it has received a certain job assignment for which it is held accountable.
2. This assignment is then elaborated in certain characteristic modes of activity—certain action patterns designed to implement the professional function.
3. These action patterns are further fashioned and developed within the specific systems in which they operate.

These propositions lead to a working definition of method as a systematic process of ordering one's activity in the performance of a function. Method is function in action.

This line of reasoning thus calls for three major lines of inquiry, each of which carries its own theoretical problems. The first line of inquiry is designed to produce an accurate

functional statement which formulates as precisely as possible the particular assignment drawn by the social work profession in the society which creates and sustains it. The second inquiry is designed to convert the functional statement into those patterns of activity through which the social work function is implemented. The third line of investigation is directed to seeking out the specific adaptations of the general methodological pattern in the various concrete situations in which social workers perform their jobs.

Requirements for a functional statement

The central requirement is to recognize at the outset that the very idea of function implies the existence of an organic whole, a dynamic system, in which the worker performs certain movements in relation to the movements of others. In Parsons's words (1937, p. 32):

The very definition of an organic whole is as one within which *the relations determine the properties of its parts.* . . . And in so far as this is true, the concept "part" takes on an abstract, indeed a "fictional" character. For the part of an organic whole is no longer the same, once it is separated factually or conceptually from the whole.

And Lawrence Frank (1957, pp. 10–12), in describing what he calls "organized complexities," speaks of the need for a field concept describing

circular, reciprocal relations . . . through which the component members of the field participate in and thereby create the field of the whole, which field in turn regulates and patterns their individual activities. This is a circular, reciprocal relation, not a serial cause and effect, stimulus and response relation.

This model of a dynamic system which surrounds and incorporates the movements of the worker provides specific clues for our statement of social work function. First, it helps us realize that function is itself *an action concept* and that it cannot be under

---

[2] Although not dealing specifically with the method component, an outstanding effort to develop a foundation for a unifying theory in social work has been made by Hearn (1958), Eaton (1959), and Bartlett (1959).

stood as a description of what social workers know, or feel, or hope to achieve. To say, as we often do, that the social work function is to "understand behavior," or "be sensitive to need," or "effect changes," is to beg the functional question entirely. Such statements remain fixed at the level of what the worker may need in order to carry out his or her function, or what they may envision as a result of having performed them well—they say nothing about the functions. The social workers' philosophy, social aspirations, attitudes toward people, and even knowledge about them are not unique to the profession and do not, in themselves, represent its assignment in society. Properly viewed, these qualities are simply prerequisite to the forms of action through which the profession justifies its social position.

Second, the model illustrates the need for the statement to reflect the activity of the social worker *as it affects, and is affected by, the activity of others* within the system. The failure to understand this feature of the helping system has created great difficulties in both the practice and the theory of social work. The inability to see the system as one "within which the relations determine the properties of its parts" has made it possible to imagine that one may deal with human beings by reference to certain discrete characteristics rather than to their movements within the relational system through which they seek help. To "diagnose" the client, to inventory "needs," and to recapitulate the life history leaves undone the task of understanding how these facts, if such they be, may be moving the client to act and react within the present field. Where the properties of parts are determined by their relations, the search for discrete characteristics is at best "interesting" and at worst produces a situation in which, in Merton's words, "Understanding is diminished by an excess of facts." It should be stated that the uneasy attempt to take over the language and the sequence-of-treatment concept of the medical profession has confused and retarded our own attempts to find terms and concepts which would truly describe the helping

process in social work. For the helping relationship, as we know it, is one in which the clients possess the only real and lasting means to their own ends. The worker is but one resource in a life situation which encompasses many significant relationships. And movement, at any given moment, is based on the movement of the preceding moment, as each new event calls for a reorientation of the worker to a new complex of demands for professional skill. Such a process is patently different from one in which the function of the person in difficulty is to supply information and the function of the worker is to create action based upon this information, by which division of labor a "treatment" or a "cure" is effected.

The third clue offered by the organic model is the need to represent the *limited field of influence* in which any part of a dynamic system operates. This involves acceptance of the fact that, within such a system, any single part affects only those with which it interacts; and, further, that it affects even these in a limited way, in accordance with its specific function. This recognition can help to scale down the grandiose, cure-all aspirations of any single profession, and to avoid couching its objectives in the language of absolutes—"achieving individual maturity," "fulfilling human needs," and the like.

Fourth, the model points to the fact that, within a dynamic relational system, the interplay of movements of the various actors is in effect an *interplay of functions*. Thus, as the worker is moved by the question "What am I doing here?" so are the others in the situation moved, consciously and unconsciously, by the same question. The worker-client interaction is one in which each needs and uses the other in order to carry out their own sense of purpose within the relational system.

Our next question must then be "What are the systems within which the social work profession in general, and the social worker in particular, derives and carries out the social work assignment?"

First, there is the general system of society itself, within which the profession has been set in motion and assigned to a given sphere of influence consistent with its ability to perform certain necessary tasks.

Second, there is the social agency system, within which the social worker translates agency function into concrete services. The agency situation represents a kind of partialization of the larger social system, from which it draws its own special assignment; and the agency creates, in addition, a unique subculture of its own, out of its own mode of living and working.

Third, there is the specific client-worker relationship—one-to-one or one-to-group— in which the social worker expresses both general function as professional and a specific function within the agency complex. The client-worker relationship, viewed from a distance, may thus be seen to be a system within a system within a system.

This is, of course, a simplified version of the relationship of parts to a dynamic whole. It is simplified precisely because we need to choose, from the immensely complex network of relationships in which social workers find themselves, those which exercise the most significant determining effects upon their movements.[3] We may say that these movements, within any specific helping relationship, reveal certain constant elements, which are derived from the professional identification, and certain variant elements, which are derived from agency identification and from the situations in which workers operate. The common components of social work function emerge from social work position within the social scheme; its adaptive components are those which express the specific ways in which the professional function is put to work.

Function: The professional assignment

Let us now venture a proposal for the functional statement itself. We would sug-

gest that the general assignment for the social work profession is to mediate the process through which the individual and society reach out for each other through a mutual need for self-fulfillment. This presupposes a relationship between people and their nurturing group which we would describe as "symbiotic"—each needing the other for its own life and growth, and each reaching out to the other with all the strength it can command at a given moment. The social worker's field of intervention lies at the point where two forces meet: the individual's impetus toward health, growth, and belonging; and the organized efforts of society to integrate its parts into a productive and dynamic whole.

More specifically, the social work assignment emerges from the fact that, in a complex and often disordered society, the individual-social symbiosis grows diffuse and obscure in varying degrees, ranging from the normal developmental problems of children growing into their culture to the severe pathology involved in situations where the symbiotic attachment appears to be all but severed. At all the points along this range, the social work function is to mediate the individual-social transaction as it is worked out in the specific context of those agencies which are designed to bring together individual needs and social resources—the person's urge to belong to society as a full and productive member and society's ability to provide certain specific means for integrating its people and enriching their social contribution. Placed thus, in Bertha Reynolds's old phrase, "between the client and the community," the social worker's job is to represent and to implement the symbiotic strivings, even where their essential features are obscured from the individual, from society, or from both.

It should be emphasized that this conception is different from that which places the social worker in a sphere of concern known as "dysfunctioning." While it is true that the profession operates in areas where the individual-social interaction is impaired, these areas are only part of the social work field of

---

[3] The interdependence of dynamic systems and the problems of abstracting one or another for analysis are discussed in Lippitt, Watson, and Westley (1958, pp. 5–11).

action. The problems of symbiotic diffusion are inevitable in any complex society and apply not only to social pathology but to the normal, developmental processes and to the ongoing social effort to order the relationship between needs and resources. The concern with developmental tasks has provided part of the traditional preoccupation of the leisure-time agencies, while the ordering of needs and resources has engaged those agencies concerned with social planning and action.

This is obviously only a brief outline of the symbiotic model; its rationale has been elaborated by Kropotkin (1925), Mead (1934), Sherif (1936), Murphy (1958), Bergson (1954), and many others. For our present purposes, the important points are the fundamental impetus of people and their groups carries them toward each other; this impetus is often blocked and diverted by a diffusion of the relationship between self- and social-interest; where the impetus can be freed to operate, it constitutes the basic motivation, for both individual and social change, with which social workers engage themselves.

This strategic location of social work as a kind of third force implementing the basic identity of interest between individuals and their groups creates its own problems when social workers fall prey to the very diffusion against which their function is set. It is at these times that we hear the controversies about whether the worker should be more concerned with social or with individual problems, with "content" or "process," "ends" or "means," and so on. This debate disregards the most essential characteristics of social work: that it stands on the meeting ground between the two; that it is inextricably involved with both; and that it sees no contradictions, even where the dualism looms large in the popular mind. The social work function is based on "the recognition of the fact that the individual's normal growth lands him in essential solidarity with his fellows, while on the other hand the exercise of social duties and privileges advances the high-

est and purest individuality" (Baldwin, 1911, p. 16).

Method: The professional tasks

The transition from function to method is essentially a problem in dividing a broad assignment into its component activities. For this purpose, we have chosen the term *task* as an organizing concept around which to gather up the various movements of the worker in any given client-worker system. The implication is that any function can be broken down into a number of tasks necessary to carry it out, and that any specific act performed should come under one or another of these headings. Our emphasis here is on categories of activity rather than on small discrete movements; for the latter may involve us in problems that lie outside the scope of method as we conceive it. While the concern with specific acts is important, the units of activity cannot be so small as to take us either into mechanical prescriptions for worker responses or into problems of personalized style and technique. The tasks are common and are based on a professional method held in common; but many of the helping acts in a given situation are heavily charged with the unique movements and personal artistry of the individual worker.

We envisage the following tasks as those required of workers as they carry out their social work function within the helping relationship:

1. The task of searching out the common ground between the clients' perception of need and the aspects of social demand with which they are faced.

2. The task of detecting and challenging the obstacles which obscure the common ground and frustrate the efforts of people to identify their own self-interest with that of their "significant others."

3. The task of contributing data—ideas, facts, value-concepts—which are not available to the client and which may prove useful in attempting to cope with that part of

social reality which is involved in the problems which are being worked on.

4. The task of "lending a vision,"[4] in which workers reveal themselves as people whose own hopes and aspirations are strongly invested in the interaction between people and society and project a deep feeling for that which represents individual well-being and the social good.

5. The task of defining the requirements and the limits of the situation in which the client-worker system is set. These rules and boundaries establish the context for the "working contract" which binds the client and the agency to each other and which creates the conditions under which both client and worker assume their respective functions.

The social worker in the group

As we move this methodological pattern into the worker-group situation, the first problem is to specify some of the salient characteristics of the small-group system which help create the social climate within which the worker functions.

First, the group is an enterprise in mutual aid, an alliance of individuals who need each other, in varying degrees, to work on certain common problems. The important fact is that this is a helping system in which the clients need each other as well as the worker. This need to use each other, to create not one but many helping relationships, is a vital ingredient of the group process and constitutes a common need over and above the specific tasks for which the group was formed.

Second, the group is a system of relationships which, in its own unique way, represents a special case of the general relationship between individuals and their society. The present group is, in other words, but one

of the many associational forms through which its members interact with social values, social objectives, and social resources. More specifically, the cultural climate of the group is drawn from three major sources: generalized social attitudes about what is good and bad, right and wrong, worthy and unworthy, permeate the group and form a part of its culture. The agency in which the group is embedded has drawn from the general culture its own characteristic and unique constellation of approved attitudes and behaviors. The group itself, by the nature of its central problem, by the activities in which it engages, and by the particular personalities it brings together, creates its own conditions for success and failure.

Finally, the group is, as we have indicated, an organic whole: its nature cannot be discerned by analyzing the separate characteristics of each component but by viewing the group organism as a complex of moving, interdependent human beings, each acting out a changing relationship to society in present interaction with others engaged in a similar enterprise. In this framework the worker is more concerned with what the member does and feels in the present situation than with what the member *is*. Further, the demands of society can be understood more clearly as they present themselves to the group member in the immediate situation than in abstract, holistic terms like "democratic responsibility" or "social maturity." It is, in fact, this very partialized and focused character of the present enterprise that makes helping and being helped possible and manageable. The implications for the worker are that the ability to help is expressed in action and that this action is limited, as in any functional system, to certain areas in which he or she has some control. One acts to help others act, and the emphasis on new ways of moving, of interacting, is more realistic and productive than the concern with total being, with discrete characteristics, and with totalistic conceptions of change.

With these observations in mind, let us examine the activities of the social worker

---

[4] For a discussion of this phrase borrowed from another context, see Kelman (1954, p. 113). "Goals of Analytic Therapy: a Personal Viewpoint," *American Journal of Psychoanalysis* 14 (1954), p. 113.

in the group, following the pattern of the five major tasks outlined earlier.

1. Searching for common ground, the worker's movements are fashioned by four major assumptions. The first is that the group member's main access to new ideas, new attitudes, and new skills lies through the ability to discern their usefulness and to invest affect in the tasks required to own them. The second assumption is that such connections —between individual aspirations and social objects—are always present, no matter how obscure they may seem to the members themselves. To conceive of a situation in which the connections do not exist would be to postulate a group in which the members are completely beyond the call of social demands—a situation in which the group itself would be a futile device since its members could exercise no effect upon each other. The third assumption is that these connections are both specific and partial. A gang of adolescents does not rush eagerly toward the ideal of "democratic values"; youngsters in a Jewish center do not respond quickly to the generalized notion of "Jewish identification"; hospital patients do not invest themselves equally and evenly in the tasks of rehabilitation. In each of these instances, the attraction between the individual's sense of need and the aspirations of society is present and inherent; but it is partial, elusive, and comes into the open only at certain significant points.

The final assumption is that these connections cannot be established in any permanent sense. From meeting to meeting, almost from moment to moment, the group members meet reality on new ground, with new connections constantly to be discovered as each member works at the job of building a bridge between past and present experience.

The worker's search for common ground is expressed in two major forms of activity. One is the efforts to clarify the function of the group and to protect this focus of work against attempts to evade or subvert it— whether by the agency, the group, or its individual members. The other is represented by consistent efforts to point up for the members those areas in which they feel, however faintly, an interest in the social objects which confront them. The clarification of group function represents an active demand by the helping agent that the agency, the group, and its members begin their working relationship with a clear "contract" and a common understanding of the issue: What are we doing here together? All of this is based on the worker's conviction that the search for common ground begins most auspiciously on a field where the members and their tasks have been, so far as possible, brought face to face. The endeavor to uncover and discover connections between individual goals and social realities is rendered infinitely more difficult when the terms of these realities are themselves shifting and unstable; as, for instance, when the worker "builds character" while pretending to teach basketball, or "improves social relations" when the group has enlisted a worker's skill in clay modeling. Further, these attempts to guard the focus of work do not end when the initial statement has been made and the terms of the agreement reached. The worker's activities in this regard persist as he or she continues to guard the focus of work or, where change in focus is feasible and permissible, to help the group to consider such changes openly and realistically.

The second complex of activity through which the worker searches for common ground begins with the workers' efforts to seek out the general lines of subject-object connection. This is a kind of internal process whereby one looks deeply into the characteristics of both subject and object, finds the elements of attraction, and is alerted to the possibilities of future engagement. What is the attraction between the gang member's hostility toward social norms and society's demand for conformity to these norms? Between the Jewish youngster's desire to be like others and the agency's emphasis on Jewish belongingness? Between the shock of diagnosis experienced by patients in an orientation group and the hospital's need for the patients to move smoothly into the necessary procedures, rules, and routines?

These are, in a sense, "diagnostic" attempts, but such preparatory insights cannot effectively be used to impose a series of prefabricated connections on a ready-made series of events. For the most part, this awareness of the general lines of connection is used in three ways: it enables the worker to be more responsive to subtle and covert requests for help; it compels the worker to focus on the here-and-now and to see through the members' evasions and denials to the strengths that lie hidden; and it helps structure the situation to favor strength rather than weakness.

2. As the search for common ground continues, the helping agent is constantly confronted with another task which, though it is a corollary of the first, is important enough to be considered on its own terms. This task evolves from the fact that the member's access to social reality is constantly impeded by obstacles which are thrown up in the course of the engagement. The existence of these obstacles is usually obscure to the group members themselves. Their awareness is limited by their incomplete vision of the common ground and by one's own subjectivity, which makes it difficult to recognize one's own defenses, to distinguish between internal and external deterrents, and to assess one's own productivity at any given moment. Thus, a force is needed within the learning group system that will challenge the obstacles as they appear, by calling attention to their existence and asking the group to come to grips with them. This is the second major task of the helping person.

These obstructions stem from many sources and appear in many forms. They originate in past experience and crystallize in the moment-to-moment events of the group situation. They are created by the attitudes of the members, the human image projected by the worker, the nature of the things to be learned, and the function of the agency. The origins of the obstacles are, in fact, so complex and interrelated that it is impossible for the worker to define causation as it appears in the context of the group experience.

Fortunately, it is unnecessary to do so. What is necessary is that one recognize these phenomena, accept them as relevant to the professional responsibilities, and offer help with the concrete learning problems they indicate. Whatever its underlying source, each obstacle always takes the form of a very specific struggle between the members and their present tasks: the group has a decision to make, has stressed its importance again and again, but falls into aimless chatting whenever the subject comes up; a member accepts a task with enthusiasm and repeatedly fails to perform it; a group proceeds, half-heartedly and unsuccessfully, on a course unanimously approved by the members but, in fact, subtly imposed by the worker, another group moves independently, but guiltily, along its "chosen" lines of action.

In these instances, there is an obstruction that lies between the group members and a valued objective, distorting their perception of what is valued and frustrating their efforts to act openly in their own self-interest. There is a path they need to take and cannot—because its entrance is blocked by taboo. The taboo may be present in the conditions that surround them; often, its complexity is such that it combines several factors. A discussion group may become dull and unproductive because it has built up a fund of resentment against a respected but authoritarian leader. Unable to deal with their need to conform, with the leader's unassailable correctness, or with the general subculture proscription against self-assertion, the members have no recourse but to express their resistance in listlessness and apathy.

The area of taboo may be painful enough to ward off recognition and remain buried in consciousness as it invisibly directs the actions of the members; or, the group may be aware of its existence but does not dare to enter an unsafe and risky region. Thus, in our example, the members' respect for the leader and worker and their need for his or her love can be so great that they cannot accept any flaw in the teacher but can feel only guilt for their own unexplainable lapse of ambition; or they may, on the other hand, feel their resentment against the beloved autocrat but shrink from inflicting hurt or from exposing themselves as rebels.

In either event, the effect is evasion of the obstacle that impedes their path to productivity. Consciously or unconsciously, the members withhold their energies from the task before them. Instead, they devote themselves to movements which reflect no real investment in content, but only their efforts to create the best imitation they can muster.

In the activities designed to carry out the task of dealing with obstacles, there are three major forms of endeavor. The first includes those actions in which the worker reveals the fact that an impediment exists and that this is permissible. This action is not "interpretive" in the usual sense; there is no way of "diagnosing" the nature of the difficulty, and the leader has no right to ask the members to deal with causative explanations, even if the worker were extremely intuitive in this regard. One asks them, simply, to recognize the fact that an obstacle exists, in the form of apathy, evasion, or inconsistency, between them and a desired objective.

The second category includes those movements by which the worker offers support and assistance as the members enter the area of taboo and seek to determine the nature of the impediment. This is to say that the worker helps them to examine the ways in which they are operating against their own interests in this situation. The attempt here is not to exorcise the taboo—that is, eliminates its power for all time—but to help the members identify it and examine its effects. It is important only that they recognize the source of their present frustration and free themselves to determine the direction of their self-interest. In this aspect the worker is asking the members to recapture control of their own impetus and to begin by dis-

countenancing the illusion of work where none exists.

In the third category of activities, the worker moves to keep the function of the group alive lest it be lost in the preoccupation with obstacles. The challenging of obstacles is based on the fact that they come between the member and the social product. When these impediments cease to be regarded as such and become objects of interest in their own right, the analytical process itself becomes an obstacle which needs to be dealt with. This calls for certain movements through which the helping person exercises a kind of "demand for work," an emphasis on performance; group members are asked to continue with their functional tasks even as they examine the obstacles to their achievement. This is still another way of saying that the examination of obstacles is part of the group function itself and that one does not cease as the other begins.

3. The third task encompasses those movements in which the helping agent makes a contribution of data in the group situation. The term *data* is used here to denote any ideas, facts, or value-concepts which the members may find useful as they involve themselves within the system. Whether the members' tasks are related to the specific problems of mastering facts and concepts in an established sequence, or to a less tangible complex of attitudes and feelings, the professionals have a responsibility to offer what can be used from their own store of experience. Their grasp of social reality is one of the important attributes that fit them to their function; while their life experiences cannot be transferred intact to other human beings, the products of these experiences can be immensely valuable to those who are moving through their own struggles and stages of mastery.

Thus, nothing can be more destructive to the worker's function than a decision to withhold knowledge on the sole grounds that members must make their own way. Such withholding is inevitably interpreted by the individual as deprivation, hence rejection; and the result is generally the very opposite of what the worker intends. It is common, for example, to find situations where the group members spend a major part of their energies in straining to find answers which lie hidden in the worker's questions; in this game of educational hide-and-seek, dependency increases as frustration mounts and as the members learn to search for hidden answers rather than to explore the nature of the problem itself.

In providing access to data, one is, in effect, providing access to oneself. The demand for a culture of work, and for a free sharing of ideas, can best be met if the worker and the clients become available to one another. What the worker knows should be accessible to the members of the group, not after they have tried to proceed "on their own," but in the course of their deliberations so that they may use this knowledge in their work. The need to withhold is generally felt by workers whose relationship to the group is too fragile to be sustained in a culture of work. Where the dependence on authority is already great—and not necessarily created by the worker—the reluctance to offer more information to be swallowed whole is a natural one. But the fear of creating dependency must be met in other ways. The worker who finds common ground is sensitive to the climate in which the subject-object engagement proceeds and prepared to challenge the obstacles as they appear will have no fear that the problem-solving process will be endangered by assuming full status as a knowing person in the group system.

As the worker contributes data, several major considerations guide the professional movements. The first is an awareness that this represents only a fragment of available social experience. If the worker comes to be regarded as the fountainhead of social reality, one will then have fallen into the error of presenting oneself as the object of learning rather than as an accessory to it. Thus, there is an important distinction to be made between lending knowledge to those who can use it in the performance of their own tasks and projecting oneself as a text to be learned. In the first instance, the worker is used as mediator of the subject-object relationship; in the second, the worker becomes the object.

The second consideration lies in the relationship between the information shared and the function of the group as this function is understood by the members and by the agency. Often, the worker is tempted to "expose" the group to certain facts and ideas which may, in some future context, be found useful. Such efforts generally serve to confuse rather than enlighten, since there is no frame of reference within which the data assume weight and significance. Where these acts of the worker constitute a series of ideological "plugs," the effect is to breed a vague distrust of the worker's purpose and stated desire to assist the group to carry out its own function.

The function of the group may be seen as a general frame of reference to be considered by the worker in selecting the data that will be shared with the members. Even more important as a factor is the specific working context. Again, this assumes the existence of a culture of work, within which the professional offering is but a single, important ingredient and only one of many sources of social reality; with this data, as with everything else, the test of utility will inevitably lie in its appropriateness to the demands of the current task. This is the sense in which the old group work injunction that "program is a tool" is important. It is a tool, not of the worker, but of the group and its members; and, like all tools, each fact, idea, or concept must be fashioned to the specific job for which it is to be used.

The final consideration is that, while each worker's own opinions represent important data, they are such only when presented honestly as opinion rather than as fact. There are many occasions where the member is at the mercy of the worker's power to disguise the distinction between the two. The temptation to becloud this distinction is strong, and often unconscious; culture-bound and ego-bound, the worker is often unclear in many important areas about the difference. But the struggle to distinguish between subjective perceptions and external reality is at the heart of all human learning and growing, and the worker who is not engaged in this struggle will find it impossible to help others in the same endeavor. As clients are helped to evaluate the evidence they derive from other sources—their own experiences, the experience of others, and their collaboration in ideas—so must they be helped to examine the evidence brought by the worker. When the worker understands that the helping person is but a single element in the totality of the member's experience, the first step has been taken toward helping the members free themselves from authority without rejecting it.

4. The responsibility for contributing data is related to the fourth task that expresses the function of the helping agent. This involves those activities through which the helper's own hopes and aspirations concerning the outcome of the group experience are frankly and directly revealed. Borrowing a phrase used by Norman Kelman, in another context, we would designate this task as that of lending a vision to the members of the group.[5]

In these activities, the worker is revealed as one whose own aspirations are deeply invested in the interaction between people and society, and who has, through personal struggles, developed a vision of what life can and should be like. In one's enthusiasm, sense of urgency, and capacity for empathy, the worker demonstrates that his or her own life experiences are involved here, that the professional has a stake in society and is not

here simply to dispense solutions to problems that are irrelevant to the worker's own concerns.

More specifically, the worker reveals emotional involvement in three important ways. The first is by the faith in the system itself and in the conditions under which the growing experience takes place. By acting to safeguard the function of the group, the professional expresses their respect for the dignity of the group itself and for the reasons which created it. And by refusing to trade identities with either the members or their materials, faith in the constructive power inherent in the relationship of one to the other is demonstrated.

The second aspect is the worker's attitude toward the relevant data of the group system. In this respect, the helping acts reflect something of the personal feelings toward the events of the group experience—its excitement, its depths, and its importance in the human scheme. As these feelings are shared, the worker is seen as a living example of the power to attract and intrigue the human mind. It is only in this sense that the helping agent is a salesperson and without the slightest intent to be one, but simply by virtue of one's role as a satisfied customer. Without this sense of enthusiasm, this vision of immense possibilities, and the status as models of mastery, the worker's contribution to the subject-object relationship resolves into a mechanical questioning and answering; with it, there can be a challenge, a driving curiosity, and a strong motive for work.

Finally, the workers' affect is a strong component in the professional relationship with each member of the group. This relationship can be described as a flow of affect between worker and member, combining the expectations and perceptions of the one with the other, as they work together—each on one's own tasks—within the group system. Their interaction is based on the circumstances which brought them together; and it is in the work itself that their feeling for each other grows. In this light, the worker's efforts

---

[5] Dr. Kelman (1954, p. 113) speaks of the necessity to "lend our vision to the patient" as the psychoanalytic process proceeds. Although his meaning here is slightly different from ours, his general intent is similar to the one we mean to convey.

to establish a relationship go much deeper than the kind of wooing used to gain the member's acceptance and approval through the exercise of one's personal warmth and attractiveness. The human qualities of the workers, however engaging they may be, should not be used to divert, to charm, or to build personal dependency.

Sensitized by the need to cope with the complexities of living and growing, the helper has a fund of feeling from which to draw in trying to understand the members' struggles in detail. This understanding is reflected not in a generalized "wanting to help," or "giving love," or "accepting them as they are," although these purposes provide an important ideological base from which to operate. Rather, the caring is communicated in the ability to empathize with the precise feelings engendered in the learner by the demands of a particular task in a specific situation. The ability to call up parts of one's own experience, to communicate feeling, and to demonstrate an active faith in the productive capacities of the member are important parts of the image of vitality that the worker projects.

In all, the worker's feeling involvement in the group system demonstrates better than words the conviction that the process of growing is complicated and difficult, but also challenging and rewarding if one is left free to conjure with it and to test one's experience under conditions where one can err without failing completely. The worker lends a vision to the members, not in order to exchange it for theirs, but because the aliveness, the faith in productivity, and the stake in work are inherent in the function of the helping person.

5. The agency, the worker, the group, and its members are related to each other by certain rules and requirements imposed upon them by the terms of their agreement. These requirements emerge first in the conditions under which the group is established, its function identified, and its procedures initiated. Later, the rules are modified, ampli-

fied, and reinterpreted as their concrete implications become clearer in the events of group life. These expectations are not limited to those imposed upon the members by the agency, or by the worker; they are reciprocal in that each actor imposes certain restrictions and is bound by others. Thus, while the group and its members are held to certain policies and procedures, the agency and the worker are also limited by standards such as equal treatment, consistency in approach, the members' concept of fair play, and so forth.

To the extent that the terms of the agreement are specific and unambiguous, the participants are free to pursue their tasks within the system in their own characteristic ways. Where the rules are, or become, obscure and vaguely defined, the major energies of both worker and members become diverted to exploring the boundaries and testing the limits of the group situation. This leads us to the final task of the helping agent, in which the participants of the learning group are called upon to face the necessities inherent in the conditions of their association. This definition of the requirements begins with the worker's first attempt to identify the specific responsibilities that have been undertaken by the agency, the group, and the worker; it continues as the helper monitors these realities and calls for clarification at those points where they become obscure.

The most important aspect of these requirements is that they emerge from the function of the group and the necessities of work rather than from the personal authority of the helping agent. As such, they are parts of a reality which is imposed by the nature of the setting, the conditions of group life, and the purposes for which the group has been assembled. The worker is often frustrated by an "inability to set limits," when the real difficulty arises from the failure to recognize that the task is to explain a situation rather than to create one. Club members find it a great deal easier to accept *situational* realities and limitations—dress requirements, bans on smoking, and so on—rather than those imposed by the worker for reasons which are ambiguous, or moralistic, or designed to build character. Since people do not join clubs to have their characters built, such taboos are not perceived as interpretations of reality, and in fact are not.

Science and art in the helping process

Because of our emphasis on viewing the social worker in action, we have concentrated our analysis on the worker's movements within the group system rather than on the personal and professional equipment that is brought to the job. Most attempts to identify the foundations of professional skill have resulted in an encyclopedic and somewhat frightening inventory of virtues. There is, after all, no sphere of knowledge, no personal strength, and no field of competence which is irrelevant to the responsibilities of the human relations worker. And yet we know that the tasks of helping are not performed best by paragons but by those who want to help, know what they are trying to do, and have sufficient mastery for themselves and of social realities to offer their strengths in the struggles of others. Thus, the central problem for helping agents does not lie in their nearness to perfection but in the extent to which they can mobilize the powers they do possess in the service of others. In order to find the common ground, they must use certain specific knowledge about human beings; in order to contribute data, to reveal their own stake in society, to define the rules, and to challenge the obstacles in the learner's path, they must be free to share what they have of sensitivity, science, and personal maturity. Where workers proceed from a clear sense of focus and function, their own strengths are tools they use in the specific tasks that they are called upon to face. As such, their powers are not pitifully inadequate replicas of a formidable ideal but full-blown strengths which they are free to own and to share.

There is nothing in the conception of a professional methodology which denies or subordinates the uniquely personal and artistic component which each worker brings to the administration of the helping function. On the contrary, the concept of a disciplined uniqueness is inherent in the definition of art itself. In a broad sense, we may view artistic activity as an attempt, by one innately endowed with extreme sensitivity to the surrounding world, to express strong personal feelings and aspirations through a disciplined use of materials. The analogy between the helping agent and the creative artist can be struck at several points. In both, there is an emphasis on feeling, on an empathic quality which is cherished as a tool of the craft; both feel a constant need for fresh insights into the nature of things and for new ways to express their view of the world; in both, there is a strong preoccupation with essences and basic principles; there is a high degree of subjectivity, of self-consciousness, which constitutes a major element in their ability to create new vistas and new perspectives; in both, the creativity is nourished by the continuous search for truth and is, in fact, an expression of this search; and both require an atmosphere in which one is free to explore, to err, to test reality, and to change.

If we add to these the powerful urge of both the artist and the social worker to communicate their view of life and to affect the experience of others through their artistry, then the sense in which the helping art is distinguishable from that of the painter, the musician, or the writer lies only in that which they are impelled to express, the nature of their materials, and the processes through which they move in order to carry out their functions.

Reading

1-2   Social work practice: A life model*

Alex Gitterman and Carel B. Germain

Over the years of its development, social work practice has had difficulty integrating two historical traditions: the emphasis on knowledge and skills to effect change in persons, and the emphasis on knowledge and skills to effect change in environments. Similarly, there has been difficulty in integrating method specializations of casework, group work, and community organization. In the past decade, new social conditions and new knowledge propelled social work to reexamine its formulations of practice and its technical interventions. Most efforts to reconceptualize the profession's practice manifest some common features: a view of human phenomena through a systems perspective, an emphasis on institutional and environmental structures, and the identification of various "target systems" as the loci for professional intervention (Goldberg and Middleman, 1974; Goldstein, 1973; Meyer, 1970; Pincus and Minahan, 1973; Siporin, 1975). Yet, quite naturally, a gap exists between the new knowledge and its use in everyday practice.

The life model integrates the treatment and reform traditions by conceptualizing and emphasizing the dysfunctional transactions between people and their social and physical environments. Through an ecological theoretical perspective and a reciprocal conception of social work function, people and their environments receive simultaneous professional attention. Needs and issues are reconceptualized from "personality states" and "environmental states" to problems in living.

Within the ecological perspective, human beings are conceived as evolving and adapting through transactions with all elements of their environments. In these adaptive processes the human being and the environment reciprocally shape each other. People mold their environments in many ways and, in turn, must then adapt to the changes they create (Germain, 1973).

Increasingly, industrial society has posed complex adaptive tasks to human beings at all stages of the life cycle. The structures and functions of familial, organizational, and other environmental systems have undergone dramatic change. The family's capacity for fulfilling its integrative functions has been taxed by its members' divergent opportunities, needs, responsibilities, and interests. At the same time, institutions are experiencing serious problems in managing their intended service functions. These dramatic changes and disjunctions between adaptive demands and the resources available for meeting the demands generate stress. People's styles of coping with stress emerge from their perceptions of environmental demands and resources and of their own response capabilities.

Social work's distinctive functions and tasks arise from its social purpose: to strengthen coping patterns of people and to improve environments so that a better match can be attained between people's adaptive needs and potential and the qualities of their impinging environments (Gordon, 1969; Schwartz, 1971b). Professional action is directed toward helping people and their environments overcome obstacles that inhibit the development of adaptive capacities. Assessment upon which action is based derives from a nonlinear view of causality. Assessment requires an understanding of the functions served by current transactions for the person and for the environment. In helping a person defined by self or others as depressed, for example, professional concern centers on the function of the depression for the person and his primary groups and on how it affects their reciprocal perceptions and transactions. Intervention then takes on the character of natural life processes that alter, use, or support properties of the environment, the coping qualities of the person(s), and the nature of the transactions between them.

Within this transactional focus, problems in living faced by individuals, families, and groups are further specified as: (1) problems and needs associated with tasks involved in life transitions; (2) problems and needs associated with tasks in using and influencing elements of the environment; and (3) problems and needs associated with interpersonal obstacles which impede the work of a family or a group as it deals with transitional and/or environmental tasks. Social work processes are directed to client problems and needs within one or more of these areas.

While these problems of living are interrelated, each comprises distinctive client tasks and professional interventions. For example, a sixty-five-year-old person may experience interrelated stresses arising out of the transition from employment to retirement, tensions within the immediate family, and unresponsive environmental institutions. The client and worker might contract to focus on the life transitional tasks, or the environmental tasks, or the maladaptive interpersonal processes among the family (or group) members. The focus might be on two or all three areas.[1] While the worker must pay attention to the complex interrelationships among these life forces, both the worker and the client must be clear at any given moment as to the specific problem-in-living receiving attention.

Emerging from the contracting process through which problems or needs are mutually defined, identified, and partialized, a division of labor evolves between client and worker (Gitterman, 1971; Kadushin, 1972; Mallucio and Manlow, 1974; Seabury, 1976). The client focuses on his life tasks; the worker seeks to assure the conditions necessary for the client to achieve the tasks (Studt, 1968). The worker remains continuously in tune with shifts in the client's concern from one area to another, drawing on knowledge and skill in the use of communication processes, actions to restructure situations, and environmental processes and resources.

Transitional problems and needs

Individual development occurs when internal, age-specific maturational phases transact with phase-specific environmental nutrients (Erikson, 1959). Thus every developmental stage represents mutual tasks for the individual and for the individual's environment. The individual must meet maturational and social demands that may require shifts in self-concept, new ego skills, and the relinquishment of customary coping patterns for novel strategies. At the same time, the environment must provide the required opportunities and resources. Incomplete or thwarted task resolution at one stage tends to create difficulties in task resolution associated with a later stage.

Similarly, there are status-role changes that occur over the life span, such as a new job, migration to a new environment, marriage, and parenthood. Some status changes coincide with developmental stages, as in retirement or entry into junior high school. Some do not necessarily coincide with developmental phases, for example, migration or a new job. These changes, too, pose demands for new ego skills, the replacement of familiar adaptive patterns by new coping mechanisms, and shifts in self-concept.

There are also changes to less valued and to stigmatized statuses when one becomes a foster child, a mental patient, a parolee or probationer, a welfare client, or a physically

---

[1] In these situations, it is essential that the client and worker work on the same problem in living at any moment in time. Otherwise, one might, for example, focus on an environmental definition while the other might focus on a psychological identity definition.

handicapped person. The tasks associated with these changes, however, are of a different order. In some instances, they are directed toward escaping the status, although the more stigmatized statuses have limited legitimized exits in our society.[2] In other instances, these changes place heavy coping demands in maintaining a positive self-image, controlling anxiety and depression, and taking effective action to escape the boundaries of these statuses. Moreover, occupants of these statuses are also dealing with the same developmental, status, and crisis tasks as other citizens. Hence, they carry an enormous adaptive burden, but with far less environmental nutriment.

Finally, there are the expectable and the exceptional crisis events of life, the threats and natural losses that come to everyone over time and those catastrophic threats and losses that come too early, or too "unfairly," or too profoundly to be considered expectable in all lives. Such situational crises have an immediacy and enormity of demand that distinguish them, in part, from the developmental and role transitions previously discussed.[3] They often require immediate mobilization of the environment and of the individual in order to prevent collapse.

It is not only the individual, however, who experiences such transitional challenges. Families have a life cycle of their own. They also move through identifiable stages of development, status changes, and crisis events, such as a new marriage, the birth of a child, unemployment, or illness, posing tasks for the collectivity that may not always mesh with the transitional tasks of individual members (O'Connell, 1972). Similarly, groups proceed through interactional phases of development (Bennis and Sheppard, 1956; Garland, Jones, and Kolodny, 1968), status

changes, and crisis events which threaten the life of the group.

In attempts to help individuals, families, and groups with developmental, status-role, and crisis tasks, certain practice principles become particularly relevant. Worker activity is directed toward exploration and mutual clarity of problem definition. People's stresses are legitimized as "normal" life processes appropriate for helping attention. Workers partialize problems into smaller, more manageable elements. At the same time, they search for patterns of behavior and for connections between past and present patterns. At times, it may be difficult for the worker to invite this elaboration. The content may be quite painful (for example, loss), or may touch upon social taboos (for example, sexuality), or may trigger the worker's own unresolved developmental issues (for example, ethnic identity). It becomes essential for the worker to sustain the content, carefully avoiding premature reassurance or interpretations. The worker and client together seek and use information, scan alternatives, and weigh costs and benefits. A central concern is to provide opportunity for resolution of life tasks in the life situation appropriate to the client's sense of time and space, lifestyle and aspirations. (Real life action, or even role play, can be helpful in working on adaptive tasks.)

In families and groups, the worker also helps members to separate out their individual developmental goals and tasks from the expectations exerted by the collectivity and by environmental forces. At the same time, the worker encourages family and group members to be responsive to one another as they seek areas of common developmental expectations and tasks. And people are always encouraged to use family, peer group, and environmental supports in pursuing their transitional tasks.

Environmental problems and needs

This area of help is concerned with adaptive issues arising from the nature of the

---

[2] Even though the formal role may be vacated, the person is assigned a similarly stigmatized status such as ex-mental patient or ex-prisoner.

[3] Developmental and social transitions occasionally take on the nature of crisis when the tasks are perceived by the person or the environment as insurmountable.

social and physical environments. The *social* environment, which man has created and to which individuals must then adapt, includes institutions, organizations, and social networks. The *physical* environment includes both natural and man-made structures and objects, and time and space.

A distinct feature of contemporary urban society is the existence of complex organizations and their impact on people's daily lives. As they become larger and more complex, organizations are more difficult to administer and coordinate. Out of necessity, they become preoccupied with the standardization of policies and procedures. Institutional homeostasis and administrative "peace and quiet" often take precedence over people's individualized service needs.

Within this context, people turn to organizations for essential services (health, education, welfare). At times, their contacts add to their distress instead of mitigating or alleviating it. Their encounters with organizational representatives may lead to a sense of personal inadequacy and stigma. While many organizational representatives are motivated to carry out their specialized functions at least initially, they sometimes build defenses against dehumanizing and frustrating conditions and a sense of failure. They may then become blind to the injustices and social inequities within their own and other organizations, and withdraw affect, zeal, and commitment to their service. Others may become overidentified with organizational need at the expense of client need. Still others may develop and rely on stereotyped characterizations of client behaviors.

Stigmatized by their client status and unaware of their rights and privileges, people often accept and resign themselves to these conditions. Hence, the social worker has a particularly critical function in helping people to use and to influence elements of their organizational environment. Knowledge and assessment[4] of organizational structures,

functions, and processes provide an important basis for professional influence.[5] Interventive strategies of influence[6] include differentially invoking or appealing to the formal organizational objectives, structures, roles, and policies favorable to the client's request but circumvented; the formal organizational and environmental accountability and sanctioning mechanisms; the organizational or individual representative's self-interest and self-esteem; the professional service ethic supportive of individualization; and the informal system in which favors are collected and exchanged (Dalbon, 1970; Gouldner, 1960). The effectiveness of these collaborative strategies are dependent on the worker's professional competence, credibility, zeal, and resilience. Within a host setting especially, professional visibility and reputation for competence provide an essential means for organizational involvement and influence. If these collaborative strategies prove ineffective, the worker may turn to more adversarial behaviors, for example, petition, public criticism, and use of mass media.

The concept of *social network* refers to important figures in the environment, including relatives, friends, neighbors, and peers. Such a network often meets the needs of human beings for relatedness; provides recognition, affirmation, and protection from social isolation; and offers the means for identification and for socialization to the norms, values, knowledge, and belief systems of the particular culture. It serves as a mutual aid system essential for adaptation and for coping with stress. Some networks, however, may reinforce deviance, be subject

---

[4] The depth and scope of an organizational assessment are dependent on such factors as client need, whether the worker is employed by the agency being negotiated, and previous contacts with the specific representative.

[5] Brager (1975) makes an important distinction between "helping" and "influencing" an organization.

[6] Prof. Irving Miller has been particularly helpful in identifying various practice strategies (for example, Miller's speech before the Alumni Conference of the Columbia University School of Social Work, November 3, 1973 [mimeographed]).

themselves to maladaptive interpersonal processes, or undermine the client's sense of identity and autonomy. Some social networks are too loosely organized and integrated to serve as a source of support. Some clients may be without any social network at all.

Since attachment behavior in the human being has adaptive importance across the life cycle, the social network is an important dimension of the social worker's attention. Client and worker action can be directed toward mobilizing or strengthening real life ties between the client and significant others in the life space, finding new linkages or reestablishing old ones. In the absence of natural networks, worker and client may consider the possibility of relational experiences through the use of other levels of social work personnel, volunteers, and friendly visitors. Together, worker and client may consider the use of organized groups (Parent-Teacher Associations, Parents Without Partners, tenant councils, consumer groups, and so on) to meet relationship (and task) needs, or the construction of mutual aid systems to meet adaptive requirements and to exchange resources. All of these actions are close to life processes and hence are likely to be of more adaptive value than major reliance on the time-limited relationship with the worker.

We are beginning to understand how people organize and use space in the physical environment and how, in turn, spatial variables affect behavior. Ward geography, for example, is an important factor in the social interaction of residents of a geriatric facility or patients in a mental hospital. Spatial arrangements in classrooms and treatment cottages may invite or discourage particular behaviors in children. Space, design, color, and decoration in social agencies communicate to users of services their differential statuses (Seabury, 1971). Social work interventions directed to spatial variables or to providing experiences in the natural world are used to enhance relatedness and increase the nutritiveness of the environment.

Whatever interventive strategies are used in helping people to deal with their social and physical environments, workers must take into account the consequences and implications of their actions on clients. At times clients can be hurt by professionals with benign intentions but dysfunctional interventions. Users of service need to be fully involved in the assessment and intervention processes. Through their full participation, users of service become educated to environmental structures, functions, and processes. They develop greater competence in negotiating their environment and in exerting control over achieving their life tasks.[7]

Maladaptive interpersonal problems and needs in families and groups

As the family or group works on the tasks associated with life transitions or with using and influencing the environment, it sometimes encounters impediments posed by maladaptive communication processes and relationship patterns. Such impediments may be poorly understood or altogether outside the members' awareness. Behaviorally they are expressed through patterned scapegoating, power struggles, interlocking hostilities, mutual withdrawal, double binds, and other distortions. While these patterned behaviors often serve a latent function in maintaining the family or group equilibrium, the consequences are usually maladaptive for some members. Thus, these interpersonal obstacles to individual and collective growth and adaptation become a third area of help.

Practice interventions, then, include an assessment of the factors which generate the

---

[7] Group services have a unique potential for achieving this objective. They possess an inherent advantage in that (1) people can gain strength, security, and relief from being with others in a similar situation; (2) perceptions of personal, psychological problems can be transferred into perceptions of collective, social problems; (3) collective action can gain greater institutional responsiveness; and (4) groups can be linked with other groups, thus representing a source for significant political action.

specific transactional obstacles. Our experience suggests that there are several repetitive sources of interpersonal conflict: (1) Discrepancy between an individual's and the collective's life transition tasks: A family may be preoccupied with its survival and maintenance, while its young adult member is striving for separation. Or a group in a late stage of its development may experience serious difficulty incorporating new members. (2) Dysfunctional accommodation to environmental pressures and inadequacies: In response to a hostile environment, some members may develop apathy that then interferes with mutual problem-solving. Others may cope by scapegoating one another. (3) Discrepancy among members' orientations to "power and love": One spouse may seek intimacy while the other requires emotional distance. Or the parents may disagree on matters of authority. (4) Normative conflicts among members, such as differing generational perceptions of right and wrong, attractive and unattractive, good and bad. (5) Compositional problems within the collective: A family or group may experience strain as a member leaves or a new or former member enters. Or a family or group may isolate a member because of deviant descriptive or behavioral characteristics.

When the focus is on helping families and groups to deal with such transactions as patterned scapegoating (Schulman, 1967; Vogel and Bell, 1968) or double-bind modes of communication (Haley, 1963), the worker invites and encourages the members to view the obstacle through a systemic perspective. The worker encourages mutuality among members by helping them search for common concerns and self-interests. At the same time, the worker reaches for and encourages the elaboration of differential perspectives. Strategically, it is often easier for members with the greater power and personal strength to begin the exploratory process. As work on the obstacle proceeds, the less powerful and more insecure members often require special support and encouragement to risk their perceptions and interpretations. Expression of members' divergent, discrepant perceptions needs to be partialized and the associated affect encouraged. If members attempt to avoid the content, the worker focuses, mediates, and guards the conditions of their agreed-upon contract. Throughout, the worker provides relevant facts, interpretations, and perceptions and lends professional strength, support, and faith in members' capacity to move beyond the painful obstacle.

In a similar way, interpersonal barriers can arise between worker and client(s) manifested in distorted communications and maladaptive relationship processes. Frequently such barriers are defined as client "resistance" when, in fact, they are transactional in origin. They arise from incongruencies in perceptions and expectations; feelings related to age, sex, race, and ethnic differences; transference and countertransference; and ambivalences, cognitive discrepancies, and ambiguities. The worker has the responsibility for continuous vigilance concerning the possible existence of such barriers and for bringing them into open discussion so that mutual work on them may take place, including assessing their source, nature, and consequences (Gitterman and Schaeffer, 1972).

Summary

The profession's social purpose has always referred to a dual interest in people and situations, but the lack of knowledge about their reciprocity made the practice application of social purpose difficult. This paper has attempted to present an integrated perspective on social work practice based on that reciprocity. The ecological perspective provides a means for capturing the transactional processes between human beings and their environments. The conceptualization of people's needs into three interrelated areas of problems-in-living transcends former methodological distinctions among casework, family therapy, and group work and provides a life model for intervention.

Selected annotated bibliography

Atherton, Charles. "The Social Assignment of Social Work." *Social Service Review* 43:4 (December 1969), pp. 421–429.

The author argues that the assignment of social work is to provide resources to individuals which will assist them in the performance of social roles.

Auerswald, E. H. "Families, Change, and Ecological Perspective," *Family Process* 10:3 (September 1971), pp. 263–280.

Auerswald illustrates a broader approach to working with families which includes working with the context or milieu in which the family functions.

Bartlett, Harriett M. *The Common Base of Social Work Practice.* New York: National Association of Social Workers, 1970.

Bartlett develops a common knowledge and value base for the profession and stresses the centrality of the concept of social functioning. She takes the position that assessment is a cognitive function preceding intervention and that a wide range of interventive approaches are required by the profession.

Bisno, Herbert. "A Theoretical Framework for Teaching Social Work Methods and Skills with Particular Reference to Undergraduate Social Welfare Education," *Journal of Education for Social Work* 5:1 (Fall 1969), pp. 5–17.

Bisno classifies social work change strategies in nine methods and suggests two levels of skill—skill in determining the method to use and skill in the use of specific methods.

Boehm, Werner W. "The Nature of Social Work," *Social Work* 3:2 (April 1958), pp. 10–18.

Boehm develops a definition of social work emphasizing the functions of restoration, provision, and prevention.

Boehm, Werner W. "Toward New Models of Social Work Practice," in *Social Work Practice, 1967.* New York: Columbia University Press, 1967, pp. 3–18.

Boehm agrees that social work activities can be organized into two broad groups to accomplish two types of change. One group of practitioners will be skillful at intervention in the social situation of individuals and small groups. A second group of practitioners will possess skills at intervening in the social resource structure.

Chambers, Clarke A. "An Historical Perspective on Political Action vs. Individualized Treatment," in Paul E. Weinberger (Ed.),

Perspectives on Social Welfare. New York: Macmillan, 1969, pp. 89–106.

Chambers offers a historical analysis of the individual treatment versus social reform dispute in social work.

Hearn, Gordon (Ed.). *The General Systems Approach: Contribution toward an Holistic Conception of Social Work.* New York: Council on Social Work Education, 1969.

Hearn's work is a collection of original papers developing the holistic or generalistic approach in social work.

Meyer, Carol. *Social Work Practice: A Response to the Urban Crisis.* New York: Free Press, 1970.

Meyer develops a model of practice calling for social workers to link clients to resources within urban settings and to assist institutions to deliver services in a humanizing manner.

Minahan, Anne. "Summary of the Report of the Undergraduate Curriculum Project," *Social Work* 23:3 (May 1978), pp. 183–184.

This brief statement summarizes the central issues of this latest report on social work—its nature, function, and the competency it demands for beginning professional practice.

Perlman, Helen Harris. "Casework Is Dead," *Social Casework* 48:1 (January 1967), pp. 22–25.

Perlman maintains that there is a continuing need for individualized services and suggests that the profession maintain a dual focus on individual service and social action.

Rein, Martin. "Social Work in Search of a Radical Profession," *Social Work* 15:2 (April 1970), pp. 13–28.

Social work change theories can focus on either individuals or social conditions. Rein believes that approaches in either area can support or challenge existing standards of behavior. He identifies four social work ideologies—traditional casework, community sociotherapy, radical casework, and radical social policy. He contends that radical casework may be the modality for accomplishing the central mission of social work.

Schneiderman, Leonard. "A Social Action Model for the Social Work Practitioner," *Social Casework* 46:8 (October 1965), pp. 490–493.

Schneiderman proposes a documentation model whereby the practitioner documents the need for action (generalizes beyond specific clients). He acknowledges that this is not a new proposal but notes that it is not being effectuated. He suggests that the professional association has the responsibility of responding to the documental needs in terms of action programs.

Schwartz, William. "Private Troubles and Public Issues: One Social Work Job or Two?" in *Social Welfare Forum, 1969.* New York: Columbia University Press, 1969, pp. 22–43.
Schwartz traces the dichotomous thinking that results in divisions of social work practice and suggests an alternative mediating approach which combines both foci of the dichotomy.

Taber, Merlin A., and Anthony J. Vattano. "Clinical and Social Orientations in Social Work: An Empirical Study," *Social Service Review* 44:1 (March 1970), pp. 34–43.
This survey of a national sample of 821 practicing social workers found that a clinical-social division does not characterize the attitudes of social workers. The study suggests that most social workers integrate the two orientations in their practice.

CHAPTER 2

Sources and functions of
knowledge for professional practice

Some of the sources and functions of knowledge in the professional practice of social work shall be discussed in this chapter. The meaning of the term *professional* and the importance of knowledge in professional practice will be of primary importance. The next task will be to define the various terms that will be found in this chapter. This chapter will also focus on the confusion between different types of knowledge and between knowledge and values that is often found in social work literature. Next, some of the very real and extremely complex problems involved in the selection and organization of knowledge for use as a base for practice actions will be presented. In conclusion, questions concerning the importance of knowledge, criteria for the selection of knowledge, and how to deal with ignorance when one is expected to be an expert will be examined.

WHAT IS A PROFESSION?

In the introduction to this book the authors speak of social work as "a human service profession." Schwartz also speaks of the role of a *profession* in society. What do social workers mean when they speak of social work as a profession? What common attributes do professional occupations possess which distinguish them from the nonprofessional ones? Literature on occupations generally lists the following elements as important distinguishing marks of a profession:

1. A high degree of generalized and systemic knowledge;
2. Community sanction;
3. A primary orientation to community interest rather than individual self-interest;
4. A high degree of skill involving responsibility and self-regulation of behavior that are internalized through formal education, work socialization, codes of ethics, and voluntary associations operated by the professionals themselves;
5. A culture including a value system;
6. A system of monetary and honorary rewards that are primarily an acknowledgement of work achievement and thus ends in themselves, not means to promotion of individual self-interest.

This book will contain a discussion, to a greater or lesser extent, of each of these criteria. Chapter 3 will deal specifically with values (Items 4 and 5), and Chapter 15 will deal with Items 2, 3, and 6. However, most of the text will be aimed at developing a general knowledge of practice theory and actions. Although a profession involves practice—a doing of something with a high degree of skill—the chief difference between a professional and a nonprofessional occupation is not in the degree of skill required. The crucial distinction is that the skills of the professional are based upon a fund of knowledge that has been organized into an internally consistent body of theory and that this theory plus values and ethics then directs the differential application of skill. Thus the use of skill in a profession is not directed by a set of rules, but rather by the practitioners' range of theoretical knowledge and their judgment in selecting from among the available theories one that is appropriate to the problem to be solved. It is this possession of knowledge, together with the capacity to organize and apply it differentially to individual situations, that marks the profession from other occupations.

Thus the important thing about professional knowledge is not only that it is generalized and systematic but that it must be available for use in unique human situations and congruent with the central values of the profession. This differentiates a profession from an academic pursuit. The acquiring of knowledge may be an end in itself in academic disciplines, but in a profession knowledge and theory is needed as a guide to action. For example, if one is to make some judgment as to what could be helpful to an adolescent with a problem of relationship to parents, one needs to have some knowledge of expected adolescent behavior, of parental responsibilities and feelings, and of the usual problems in the interactions of adolescents and their parents against which to assess this particular adolescent's problems.

In the last two paragraphs the terms *knowledge* and *theory* have been used as though they were interchangeable. And they are often used in this way in the literature. The next section will explore the meaning of these terms and will attempt to differentiate between knowledge and values which, because they both serve as the base of practice actions, are often confused.

DEFINITION OF TERMS

Perhaps a good beginning would be a discussion of what is meant by the term *knowledge* and by the phrase often met in social work literature, "the knowledge base of social work." Alfred Kadushin (1959, p. 39) states that the "knowledge base of social work is a comprehensive topic which encompasses the facts and theories, skills and attitudes, necessary for effective, efficient practice." In discussing the term *knowledge* as used in the working definition of social work practice (formulated by the National Association of Social Workers), William Gordon (1962), a social work educator who has long been interested in the problem of defining the scope of social work knowledge, states:

> Knowledge, in the working definition, designates generalized perceptions of individuals in their world which can be symbolized explicitly enough to be reliably communicated and are susceptible to testing and extension by the procedures of empirical science. Knowledge differs from value assumptions not only in the degree to which its propositions have already been verified . . . but

especially by the intent to verify them by scientific procedures. . . . A revised working definition should include under *knowledge* a wide range of propositions with respect to their degree of verification, but also exclude all assumptive preference rather than scientific necessity.

In this quotation Gordon attempts not only to define knowledge but also to differentiate it from another important base of social work practice which is discussed in Chapter 3—social work values. In a later article Gordon (1965, p. 34) elaborates more completely on this distinction:

> Thus knowledge refers to what, in fact, seems to be, established by the highest standards of objectivity and rationality of which people are capable. Value refers to what people prefer or would want to be . . . it becomes clear that the heart of continuity and professional utility lies in what social work wants for people (values) and what it knows about them (knowledge).

Bartlett (1970, p. 63), whose work was also referred to in Chapter 1, points out that "knowledge and value take priority over method and technique." She goes on to say:

> Values . . . refers to what is regarded as good and desirable. These are qualitative judgments; they are not empirically demonstrable. They are invested with emotion and represent a purpose or goal toward which the social worker's action will be directed. Knowledge propositions, on the other hand, refer to verifiable experience and appear in the form of rigorous statements that are made as objective as possible. Value statements refer to what is preferred; knowledge statements to what is confirmable.

Bartlett (pp. 63–64) also points out that the statement "There is interdependence between individuals in this society" has often been included under values in social work literature although it is a demonstrable fact and thus should be classified as knowledge:

> At any stage in the development of scientific knowledge there are some propositions that do not appear confirmable and thus must be regarded as value assumptions. In some instances, however, statements that are identical in form can be taken as either part of knowledge or as values. The idea that home is the best place for a child is an example; it can be taken as preferred or as a hypothesis for investigation. Here it is the intention regarding the proposition, rather than the actual substance, that makes the difference. There is also a long-range shift that will take place between a profession's body of knowledge and values. As scientific knowledge increases, some propositions that were at first preferred assumptions will become established as confirmed knowledge.
>
> . . . Knowledge and value play distinctly different roles, both of which are needed. . . . Proper use of knowledge and value rests not only on distinguishing those propositions that belong in different categories but also in recognizing that the user's intent—whether as a preferred or confirmable statement—also makes a difference as to how they should be classified. According to this approach, propositions regarded as verifiable by science and research—and that are intended to be verified—are considered knowledge.

Simply put, values answer the question of whether a proposition is right or wrong while knowledge answers the question as to whether something is true or false. This becomes very important to social work, both from the perspective of the worker and the client. If we believe we have tested evidence that a particular proposition is true and also believe that it is right there will be no desire to change it. In fact, there will be strong opposition to any proposal to change it. Some of our greatest conflicts in social work are found at the point where knowledge conflicts with value. For example, there are significant research findings that children who are treated violently often grow up to be adults who act violently toward others. However, there are people who believe that parents have a right to discipline children in any manner they please in order to control their behavior. A value cannot be challenged with another value, but it can be challenged with knowledge. Thus, one can ask that parents who believe differently about child care look at the evidence. There is significant evidence that living in abject poverty with too little food for adequate nourishment can be severely damaging both physically and psychologically to children, but we often confront a value system that says that people should "stand on their own two feet" and not take help from anyone "no matter what." In a democratic society all individuals have a right to their own value system. These values can only be challenged with empirical evidence that shows them to be damaging to human beings. We cannot demand that people change their values to conform to ours but, if tested knowledge showing a proposition to be true is available, people can be asked to consider this evidence.

Another example of the possible confusion between knowledge and value concerns the social work value of self-determination—the notion that people be allowed as far as possible to determine their own lifestyles (this concept will be discussed further in Chapter 4). If, in working with children, this value is not tempered with the knowledge that children need both freedom to grow and firm, consistent limits, we may be destructive to the child clients and/or to their families that come for help. Another important example of the confusion of value and knowledge is the way in which the knowledge that "clients will change with greater ease and less pain if they are actively involved in the process of deciding about change" is confused with the value that "clients as human beings have the right to make their own decisions about what they will do." In this instance knowledge and value support each other, but it is necessary to be clear in discussing work with the client whether one is acting primarily on the basis of knowledge, of value, or of both in some combination.

In earlier quotations Gordon (1962, 1965) discussed two kinds of knowledge: (1) knowledge that has been confirmed by empirical testing and/or observation and (2) knowledge that is accepted and acted upon as though it were true but has not yet been confirmed, although the intent is to confirm it eventually. This might be called *assumptive knowledge*. The important fact to note is that assumptive knowledge is open to efforts to test whether it is right or wrong. The only concern is that the person who engages in such testing follows the accepted guidelines of research design. If there is resistance to the effort to test a notion, it may be that a value is being dealt with and not a piece of assumptive knowledge. In the human services much knowledge is assumptive knowledge, notions that, given what tested base is available, seem to follow logically. The important thing for us as professional people is not so much the extent of the assumptive knowledge that is presently accepted but our willingness to expose it to exploration and the commitment to active attempts to test what is held as truths.

As pointed out earlier, in the beginning of this chapter the terms *knowledge* and *theory* are often used interchangeably. What is the difference between these two concepts? Generally, knowledge is considered to be discrete facts while theory is a set of related and logical propositions that orders and relates facts into some sort of meaningful whole. For example, in social work the knowledge of defense mechanisms is often spoken of as psychoanalytic theory. This is because the concept of defense mechanisms is found within psychoanalytic theory.

A *theory* is a coherent group of general propositions or concepts used as principles of explanation for a class of phenomena—a more or less verified or established explanation accounting for known facts or phenomena and their interrelationship. If one thinks of knowledge as discrete bits of truth or discrete facts and observations like a pile of bricks, theory can be likened to a wall of bricks. In a theory the observations of the real world are ordered and put together in a certain way and held together by certain assumptions or hypotheses as bricks in a wall are held together by a material that cements them in place. Thus theory is a coherent group of general propositions, containing both confirmed and assumptive knowledge, held together by connective notions that seek to explain in a rational way the observed facts of phenomena and the relationship of these phenomena to each other.

Thus when the knowledge base of social work is discussed, this may mean tested knowledge, but it is more likely to concern various theories such as theories about people, how they develop, and the genesis of dysfunctioning; theories about people and their institutions and how these grow and change, as well as how they are functional and dysfunctional for people and their society. A list of unrelated facts, no matter how well verified by empirical observations, seldom tells us what they mean. It is theory (something assumed to be true—taken for granted), constructed of known facts and phenomena held together by certain conceptual notions, that speaks to the meaning of facts.

Before leaving these definitions, one other word should also be explained. The term *principle* is often found in social work literature. This term can be used in two ways, and one should be aware of the context of the material to know which is meant. A principle may be an accepted or professed rule of conduct (often built on a value), or it may be a fundamental, primary, or general truth on which other truths depend. Used as an expression of a primary or general truth, a principle may have been empirically tested or it may be an assumption— a proposition taken as given.

To summarize: When one speaks of the knowledge base of social work, one usually is speaking of social work theory which is constructed partially of empirically tested knowledge and partially of assumptive knowledge which has not yet been empirically investigated but which can be subjected to such investigation. All this is in contrast to *values,* which are statements of what is preferred. Principles of action in social work rest upon both its values and its theories.

DEVELOPMENT OF KNOWLEDGE AND
THEORY IN SOCIAL WORK

Within a human services profession three levels of theory generally develop: (1) a general theory of humanity which includes growth, development, functioning, and interrelationships; (2) the profession's practice theory, which is a statement of the nature of the principles and processes (general guides to action) of the particular profession and of the responsibilities assumed by the practitioner in the lives of the people with whom one works; and (3) specific operational procedures and skills. In social work, *as in all other professions,* the individual practitioners use knowledge that comes both from their own profession and from other disciplines. In particular, much of social work theory about people and their organizations, about how they grow, change and function, is borrowed. All professions rely on borrowed knowledge generated and tested in the basic disciplines. And all human service professions borrow from each other. This is partly because practicing professionals, social workers included, are more interested in the application of present knowledge than in the creation of new knowledge, and partly because social workers in discussing their practice knowledge in the journals of the profession often write only of unique individual situations without making appropriate attempts to generalize their experiences and to connect them with what is already known and set forth in the literature.

In discussing the problem of the generation of new knowledge vis-à-vis the application of borrowed knowledge, Sidney Berkowitz (1969), a practicing social worker and agency executive, points out that the present-day heroes in the field of medicine are the surgeons who are engaged in organ transplants. Yet, these men are, strictly speaking, technicians who are largely dependent on borrowed knowledge supplied by research biologists, biochemists, geneticists, physiologists, and other scientists. Berkowitz reminds the reader that the majority of professional social work practitioners are largely concerned with practical and emotional motives rather than with intellectual drives; that, although they may have contributed little to theory building in the basic social, behavioral, or biological sciences, they have contributed much to the knowledge of the development and refinement of various social work methods and techniques. In addition they have developed, and passed on to others, a kind of wisdom about human behavior that can come only from skilled clinical practice over time.

It would appear that if social work is to expand its tested knowledge it needs to develop a group of social work researchers interested in the generation and testing of new knowledge; and the practitioner needs to internalize the discipline necessary to keep abreast of the literature so that there may be an orderly accretion of knowledge, a wall built gradually by the appropriate placing of bricks, rather than bricks scattered over the landscape without even a blueprint as to how they might fit together.

In his inquiry into behavioral science, Abraham Kaplan (1964, pp. 304–305), a philosopher of science, points out that "knowledge grows not only by accretion and replacement of dubious elements by more sound ones but also by digestion, by remaking of the old cognitive materials into the substance of a new theory." Although the growth of scientific knowledge is marked by the replacement of poor theories by better ones, if knowledge is to advance, each new theory must take account of the theory it seeks to replace. Each new theory must reshape and integrate the old so that there is a continuity of knowledge development, even in the most revolutionary of times.

Kaplan says that the problem in the behavioral sciences is that this is not done, that individuals do not steep themselves in the theories available before taking off on a charge of their own. He is concerned that the lag in the behavioral sciences comes because researchers or theoreticians are busily drawing their own "new" blueprints. The social and behavioral sciences are replete with low-level empirical findings, but these remain empirical bricks, unusable until someone can find the connection to hold them together. It is frustrating and troubling to read a piece of research in social work that would never have been undertaken if the researcher had done the proper literature search. To use precious time and money to test something that has already been tested because of ignorance of past efforts is almost criminal given the great needs in this field. Thus the first principle of attempting to develop new knowledge is to thoroughly know the old and the work that went into developing it and to build all present efforts on this foundation.

Actually, as pointed out by Kadushin (1959), there is an embarrassingly rich literature that details what the social worker needs to know, do, and feel. But that knowledge is not organized in a manner that allows one to readily specify what one will need to know about what. Thus, nowhere will you find a book on all knowledge necessary for social work practice.

There have been any number of attempts to organize social work knowledge in a manner that would allow it to serve as a base for social work practice. As long ago as 1917 Mary Richmond made the first major attempt to pull together this knowledge in a pioneering work called *Social Diagnosis.* In 1923 the Milford Conference brought together a panel of experts to examine and extract the common elements of social casework practice (American Association of Social Workers, 1929). In his review of the history of social work knowledge Kadushin (1959) points out that between 1929 and 1959 there were two major reviews of social work education throughout the world and five major studies of social work education in the United States. Since then there have been other attempts to specify the knowledge base of social work. Perhaps the most comprehensive and exhaustive attempt yet made is the Curriculum Study of the Council on Social Work Education (Boehm, 1959c). This study of 12 volumes can hardly be summarized in the space available in this text, or utilized by students in a discrete course. An Undergraduate Social Work Curriculum Development Project was just completed by the School of Social Work at West Virginia University. It was undertaken for the purpose of further developing both the educational objectives and the curriculum content essential for the Bachelor of Social Work degree. This is the most recent example of an attempt to set forth a knowledge base for social work practice (Baer and Federico, 1978). Kahn (1954, p. 197) who has studied the knowledge base of social work, gives us some notion of the possible range of data with which social work may be concerned.

> Social work knowledge is, at the present time, in fact, an amalgam of several different things: (1) propositions borrowed from or markedly like those of psychiatry and some branches of psychology; (2) propositions fewer than in (1), borrowed from, or markedly like those of, sociology, social anthropology, and a scattering from other fields; (3) apparently original propositions about how to do certain things in casework, group work, and community organizations; (4) methods, techniques, and attitudes, clearly derived from the fields of administration, statistics, and social research; (5) propositions about how to do things apparently derived from, or markedly like, those of progressive education.

Bartlett (1970, p. 152) says:

> These needed concepts and criteria to guide the social worker's use of knowledge come first from the core of the profession. A comprehensive concept concerned with people interacting and coping with their environment gives promise of

offering a central focus and a group of related subconcepts adequate to provide the necessary guidance. Here are to be found the ideas relating to life tasks, coping patterns, environmental demands and supports, exchanges, between people and their environment, and new concepts not yet perceived, all of which require disciplined examination and testing by the profession.

Recently the National Association of Social Workers—the professional organization of social workers, devoted an entire issue of *Social Work* (1977), to a consideration of the conceptual frameworks (theories) underlying social work practice. This gives evidence of the concern of the professional organization with the necessity to examine what social workers need to know in order to practice their profession.

The Council on Social Work Education, a body which speaks with some authority for schools of social work, from time to time issues statements on the council's official curriculum policy as an accrediting body of social work education which, among other issues, outline necessary curriculum for accredited schools. Since the membership of the council consists largely of social work educators, it could be assumed that this statement outlines the knowledge being taught, or seen as essential, by faculties of schools of social work. A copy of the council's latest curriculum statement is reproduced in this chapter (see Reading 2–2). At least three broad areas of knowledge are referred to in this statement: (1) knowledge pertaining to human behavior and the social environment of individuals, (2) knowledge pertaining to social welfare policy and services, and (3) knowledge pertaining to social work practice.

This list may not seem very helpful because it is so general. Yet these areas are the ones mentioned most in lists of social work knowledge. The problem is that these large chunks of knowledge need to be assembled and formed into some kind of meaningful whole in order to be useful. However, these large areas of knowledge have been very differently conceptualized, particularly as to principles that guide action, and there are no conceptual linkages. It is as though the profession had purchased an unfinished foundation in which different types of construction blocks were put together in different ways. This foundation cannot be built on until some way has been found to complete it so that the blocks not only fit together but can bear the weight of the structure being placed on top of it. Social workers are having much difficulty in finding what kind of construction blocks and what kind of construction can bring very diverse foundation walls together in such a way that they can be built on. Or perhaps some of the walls already built need to be torn down and, using the blocks of knowledge from the walls, constructed differently.

FUNCTION OF KNOWLEDGE IN SOCIAL WORK PRACTICE

Perhaps one of the reasons for the great problem in selecting and organizing knowledge has stemmed from the inability to define with any precision what social workers should be expert about in their practice. In the following quotation Meyer (1973, p. 38) speaks to the issue of the function of knowledge in social work practice: "Reliance upon empirical data has not been a hallmark of professional social work practice, partly because of our tools and objectives of research, but also, perhaps, because we have not yet agreed upon the goals and boundaries of social work practice." In the professions, in contrast to the basic sciences, knowledge is sought for use rather than for its own sake. What the social worker is supposed to be about dictates and according to Meyer (p. 97) "defines the boundaries of relevant knowledge as well as stimulating the search for new knowledge. Part of what makes a given profession distinctive is the nature of action or practice evolving from placing knowledge within a particular frame of reference."

This frame of reference is dictated by the purposes and values of the profession. Thus a profession does not seek to build knowledge outside of or beyond its purposes. However, knowledge and purpose have an interactive relationship in that, as purposes change, new knowledge is sought in order to deal with the new purposes, but also, as knowledge expands within a given purpose, it is sometimes found that the purpose itself is changed by the new knowledge (often more slowly than one would wish). But, remembering the earlier discussion on values, if only one solution is possible, or acceptable, there is no problem for empirical or experimental research. Thus "questions whose answers are dictated by the value system of our society and some questions that depend upon the value system of social work" are not researchable for purposes of knowledge building (Ripple, 1960, p. 28). So, values join purpose in setting a boundary to the knowledge that will be examined and incorporated.

Another problem in utilizing empirical research as a way of knowledge building in social work is the necessity we often face when making immediate choices in crisis situations. Since our society is not very good about planning ahead in relation to human services, problems often seem to arise with such rapidity that planning cannot be delayed while the relative merits of various solutions are investigated or empirical knowledge is acquired about the utilization of solutions. In such situations, social workers must act in the context of the knowledge already possessed, guided by how present knowledge is organized and evaluated in light of the problem.

It is well to remember that social work is a profession concerned with the impact of social problems on the lives of people, and the solutions that it can operationalize must fall within the value system and available resources of the times in which it acts. Thus, from the beginning, each generation of social workers has had to invest most of its energy in helping individuals, families, and institutions deal with the social crisis of the times, using the tools and knowledges available and improvising when these proved inadequate. One problem for today's social workers is the tendency to define one's problems and to take action based on one's tendency to hold previously accepted theory in awe instead of respecting the relevant knowledge that can be brought from the past while struggling to move beyond it in search of new knowledge in light of the new functions that confront the profession. In other words, unless social workers are constantly alert they will find themselves defining present problems in light of yesterday's knowledge base. As the needs and demands of practice change, the appropriate knowledge base changes; and as the knowledge base changes, grows, and develops, the functions and the value system of the profession also change. The constantly changing functions of social work, as dictated by our constantly changing and developing society and the constantly expanding knowledge of mankind in interaction with social institutions and the physical world, demand a constantly expanding and reorganized and reformulated knowledge base so that social workers will need to be active learners for their entire professional lives. The demand for a more adequate knowledge base always seems to move ahead as an unachievable goal.

But, before there is too much self-criticism about social work's slowness in developing an adequate tested knowledge base in human services, it might also be considered that people have, over the years, developed the wheel, the lever, and the pulley and have learned to know and use them as independent things before they put them together in complex configurations. In the same way scientists have sought to understand the components of systems before trying to deal with larger wholes. However, in human societies, by contrast, there existed functioning wholes (individuals, families, groups, organizations, societies, and even nations) long before one became aware of the need to analyze these phenomena in any systematic way. A human family cannot be torn apart to investigate its parts. Observations and collection of data have to be accomplished in the middle of a family's active life, dealing with a living thing that grows, develops, and changes even as it is examined. And even in the physical sciences, the precision of prediction declines rapidly as complexity increases, so that it is not the social sciences alone that suffer from the difficulty of making predictions in relation to complex phenomena (Kuhn, 1974, p. xvii).

However, that may be, as social workers struggle to understand human behavior for the purpose of being helping persons in planned change processes, they very rapidly become aware that in order to acquire such understanding they will need to have some grasp of the goals and purposes of the behavior. Take, for example, a friend who called one day to say that he had quit his job. He had been having a great many disputes with his supervisor and the supervisor had told him that he would not be recommended for the next raise for which he was eligible. In addition, his wife wanted the family to return to the state where they had lived previously and he had been offered a better job with a huge increase in salary in that state. Thus it was no surprise when he resigned. This behavior could have been predicted and, by any commonsense criterion of understanding, it could easily be understood. However, it is necessary to recognize that such prediction and understanding came from one's perception of this man, his circumstances, his preferences, and their interrelationships within him, which are "wholes," rather than from any analysis of specific impulses impinging on his nervous system and of the transformation of such impulses into others leading to the activation of effectors.

To carry this example further and make it more applicable to social work, let us suppose that Mrs. X came to you as a client requesting that you help her make a decision in a situation similar to the friend's described earlier. However, Mrs. X's situation is complicated by the additional fact that her husband is employed and doesn't want to move, their youngest child is both retarded and physically handicapped and the state in which the new job is located has no resources to continue the treatment and education the child has been receiving. Also, the new job does not provide health insurance under which much of the cost of treatment has been covered in her present employment. Feeling overwhelmed by the problem, Mrs. X really wants you to make the decision. What kinds of knowledge will you need in order to help this woman resolve her problem and come to a decision? And how do you select from and organize these knowledges to bear on this particular problem of this particular woman? Or consider the social worker in a large city high school located in a neighborhood in which there have recently been large population movements involving diverse racial groups. The social worker has been asked for help in handling the conflict between the school's black, Puerto Rican, and white students. What knowledge does the social worker need? Knowledge of the culture and social systems of the groups, knowledge of the problems in the larger community and its organizations, knowledge of the school system and its resources, and knowledge of community leaders as individuals and as leaders are all necessary. But how are these to be pulled together and utilized? Or consider the social worker employed by a federation of senior citizens' clubs who is asked to help the members obtain free public transportation during certain hours of the day, a privilege enjoyed by the aged in another city. What knowledge does this worker need? This will be further developed in Chapter 3.

IS KNOWLEDGE NECESSARY?

Given all the effort to identify the knowledge base of social work, and given the fact that it keeps eluding our grasp with such persistence, it might be asked whether knowledge and theory are necessary? The authors hold that it is. In the first place, as pointed out earlier in this chapter, although it has proven impossible to come up with a definitive statement of the knowledge base of the profession, all statements issued over the years are in remarkable substantive agreement at a generalized level. Thus there must be more grasp of a common knowledge base by social work practitioners than one might think. In the second place, the idea that one can operate without theory and knowledge is naive. Briar and Miller (1971, pp. 53–54) discuss this point:

> The choice for the practitioner is not whether to have a theory but what theoretical assumptions to hold. All persons acquire assumptions or views on the basis of which they construe and interpret events and behavior, including their own. These assumptions frequently are not explicit but are more what has been called "implicit theories of personality." Thus, the appeal for practitioners to be atheoretical amounts simply to an argument that theory ought to be implicit and hidden, not explicit and self-conscious.
>
> It is difficult, however, to defend an argument favoring implicit theory that, by definition, is not susceptible to scrutiny and objective validation and therefore cannot be distinguished from idiosyncratic bias. The weaknesses of implicit theory are particularly serious for a profession in which a significant portion of the practitioner's activity consists in forming judgments and impressions about persons on the basis of which decisions are made affecting their lives in critical ways. . . .
>
> Whether implicit or explicit, social workers' particular assumptions about human behavior can be expected to influence their professional actions, and therefore, to have important consequences for their clients.

As an example of their point, Briar and Miller (p. 30) indicate that the assumptions social workers hold about the possibilities of change in human nature will probably affect the degree of optimism with which they approach their clients and their problems; and that the premises about what can be changed will largely determine what one attempts to change. Perhaps the important things to keep in mind is that the interventive repertoire (what one does) of social workers grows out of and is dependent on knowledge based theory (what one assumes is the nature of the phenomenon and what one assumes will be of help) and values (what social workers see as desired ends) in interaction with the problems clients bring and the solution sought. The social worker's input into work with any client system depends on social work purposes and values; on how the worker understands the situation through the use of social work knowledge and theory; and on where one thinks "the client is" with the problem presented, based on what the practitioner hears the client say and how that is interpreted.

It is the social worker's responsibility to analyze and understand the situation before taking action. An essential of all professional practice is that it requires the rapid, continuous, expert selection and use of generalizations from the profession's body of knowledge, while remaining open to feedback from the client system that may force the abandonment of the first premise and the selection of another. Social workers put their professional knowledge to its first important use through their ability to "know where the client is," so that client and worker may be actively and appropriately involved in assessing the situation in which they are involved.

To summarize, social workers, particularly educators, are continually trying to identify the knowledge base on which the profession rests. However, the problems in such identification are almost overwhelming in that (1) the primary knowledge of the profession, empirically acquired, is drawn from the immense range of human problems as they are revealed by individuals in their situations and as they emerge in their cumulative aspects; (2) knowledge needed for many of the problem-solving activities of the profession has to be drawn from allied disciplines, with all the problems that this poses for selection, translation, and use; and (3) the relevant knowledge is changing constantly and advancing rapidly; (4) the profession is engaged in multiple functions and is uncertain as to what it should be expert about. For example, as the focus shifts from concern with the internal state of individuals and their adaptive functioning to a broader, and certainly more complex, view of individuals as participants in the interactional field of psychological and social forces, the knowledge base of social work begins to be organized differently than it was in earlier years, and an expanded range of approaches and techniques will have to be used. Helen Perlman (1957, p. 27) recognizes this point when she says, "Knowledge, no sooner grasped, leaps forward again to excite new pursuit, and this is both the gratification and the frustration of trying to work on problems-in-change.

It is reassuring to realize, however, that all the statements of the Council on Social Work Education, all the minutes of conferences, and all the books and articles on social work knowledge, which if laid end to end might well circle the world several times, are in general agreement on the three broad areas of knowledge important to the social worker: (1) people in interaction with environment, (2) policy and programs, and (3) practice actions. However, as already stated, the problem lies not in the task of finding a consensus on the broad areas of knowledge but in the task of selecting the critical concepts for use by the practitioner in social work from this immense range of knowledge and in the task of relating these concepts to one another.

CRITERIA FOR THE SELECTION OF THEORY

In *Problems and Issues in Social Casework,* Briar and Miller (1971, p. 180) discuss the requirements that any adequate theory of intervention should satisfy. They say that an adequate theory of intervention "must be explicit about the question of goals" (p. 183). They point out that theories holding an optimistic view of human change have the practical virtue of "orienting the practitioner to potentials for change and to searching for more effective and powerful ways of bringing it about." The theory should be clear about what its effective application would require of the client. If statements about what is required of the client are absent, there is danger that theories will be applied to systems for which they are inappropriate. And if this knowledge is not shared with clients, they are deprived of important decisions about their involvement.

Another point that Briar and Miller (1971, p. 184–185) make is that the theory should specify in behavioral terms what the practitioner needs to do to bring about changes. Some theories describe the practitioner's role in terms of what effect activities should produce rather than in terms of what the practitioner should do. Such theories leave the difficult task of translating theory into action to the practitioner. This makes actions difficult to evaluate. The theory should also specify what the practitioner needs to do in order to make sure that the changes that occur are carried over into the client's ongoing life situation. Finally, the theory should set forth some guides for the assessment of outcome.

In addition to Briar and Miller's formulation of the questions that theory should answer, the authors have included their own statement on the criteria for selection of the concepts that form the knowledge base of social work. To begin with, it should be recognized that since social work is a profession, social work's primary task is not to generate knowledge about people and human system per se, but to select and organize knowledge developed by researchers in psychology, anthropology, sociology, physiology, and so on in light of the nature of one's tasks and the ways people change. The knowledge base, therefore, must encompass concepts (largely borrowed from other fields) of how human systems develop, change, and dysfunction, and how the interrelationships between systems are formed, continue to operate, or dysfunction. Given the goals and purposes of social work in society, it is necessary to select from borrowed knowledge that which helps us determine (1) what in any given situation should be the unit of observation, (2) what events in this unit should be observed, (3) how they should be observed, (4) how they should be related to each other in meaningful ways for the selection of methods of intervention, and (5) how it should be determined whether this intervention produced the kind of change that was sought. (In other words, were social workers and clients able to achieve what had been jointly agreed on as a desirable goal?) In addition to the earlier criteria, Harriet Trader in an article reproduced in this chapter, quotes from the work of Charles Garvin (1972, p. 2) in which he says that in making choices among theories, social workers need to take into account the following issues:

1. Degree of worker responsibility for changes in the situation;
2. Whether society is viewed as a given with social order as a predominant goal or whether society is conceived as composed of conflicting classes with worker choices affected by and having effects upon such conflicts;
3. Degree of control which worker seeks to exert on the client situation, regardless of how much control is potentially possible;
4. Relative importance in ameliorating problematic behavior of cognitive, affective, and motoric elements.

Chapter 3, which is devoted to theoretical frameworks, shall deal in more detail with these points.

DEALING WITH INCOMPLETE KNOWLEDGE

The practitioner-to-be in the here and now is faced with a great deal of knowledge to master—knowledge that is not very well related or integrated. Some of this knowledge is supported by empirical evidence; and some of it is assumptive and supported, if at all, by only the roughest of evidence. Sometimes knowledge and value are all mixed up, and yet there never seems to be the appropriate interrelationships between bits of knowledge. The fact is that the amount of knowledge needed is so great and some of it is so uncertain that social workers are faced with the uncomfortable fact that they are constantly intervening in people's lives on the basis of incomplete knowledge (as are all other practitioners in the human services). This, however, raises some hard questions. How can we help people to feel some confidence in us as helpers while we remain tentative and often uncertain about what we know? How can we doubt our effectiveness and still be effective? How can we act as experts and yet be so constantly aware of our own ignorance?

The stress of acting on the basis of incomplete knowledge confronts all professionals in the human services, but it may bear heaviest on social workers because of their commitment to individuals and their worth. Some social workers handle it by trying to forget what they do not know, and they become very dogmatic people, certain of their own knowledge but unable to grow because one cannot learn if one already knows. Some social workers try to handle it by emphasizing what they do not know and how helpless they are. They often run around looking for authorities while their client suffers from the lack of a secure helper. Some practitioners try to handle it by blaming the profession for their discomfort. They then find themselves in the bind of representing a profession in which they have no confidence and with which they have no identification. That must be one of the most uncomfortable binds of all. Such workers have neither read nor considered enough literature of other professions to understand that all professions are woefully lacking in knowledge of human beings and their interacton. These workers never come to grips with their need to know.

The demand that we act on uncertain knowledge goes along with being a helping person in complex and everchanging situations. The best way of living with this is to commit ourselves (1) to becoming active learners all the time and (2) to the scientific method as a part of our equipment. We need to pledge to ourselves each and everyday:

I will try everything I know to help the client with which I am involved. In some aspects I may be too ignorant to truly know what way is best, but I will think carefully about my procedures, and I will be willing to assume the responsibility for my actions. I will neither be blinded by preconceptions nor will I be guilty of impulsively following a fleeting impulse or an easy answer. I will draw thoughtfully and responsibly upon every bit of knowledge that is available, and I will constantly and actively seek for more. I will be an insistent questioner rather than a passive taker, remaining identified with the profession while I vigorously question it. This is my solemn vow to my client. Thus, if my knowledge proves inadequate to the situation and the client's problem, my client and I will know that everything possible, given the present state of knowledge, has been done.

This book will offer some practice knowledge which we believe, from our study, our own questioning, and our own experience as both practitioners and teachers, will be helpful to people who are interested in beginning the challenging journey of becoming a truly competent social worker—a journey that no one ever completes. We believe that any other author, or even two, can offer only partial knowledge. For example, only a little knowledge about either the social services network or the human condition per se will be offered here. We have chosen to offer knowledge about professional social work practice itself, and believe that the other necessary knowledge (at least for now) can be acquired from other sources within the curriculum of the university and the social work major. We also believe that the knowledge given here will be the most valuable and the most immediately needed in fieldwork or on a first job. In some ways we are building the structure and trusting that you will be able to construct the basement from other sources. This may mean that for the time being your building is setting somewhat uncertainly on jacks without the underpinnings that will gradually have to be put in place.

RECAPITULATION

In this chapter we have looked at social work knowledge and the problems involved in the selection and organization of knowledge for professional practice. We have pointed out that the functions of a profession determine the parameters of the knowledge that helps in the delivery of services, the maintenance of organizations, and the effecting of change. We need to know more about the process of human and social change, the design of services responsive to the human systems that seek to utilize our help, and the final evaluation of what we do.

We have attempted to set forth some gidelines for the selection of theory, and have offered some ways of dealing with our feelings when we are aware of the need to act on incomplete knowledge. We would further remind our readers that all knowledge of human systems and their change is now and may be forever incomplete.

A LOOK FORWARD

The following readings deal with the two major issues discussed in this chapter. Gordon's article is a discussion of the difference between knowledge and values and of the purposes each serves. The areas of knowledge that the Council on Social Work Education thinks important in the education of social workers have been reproduced as an example of where the field is in its present thinking and as a statement of the areas of knowledge that are presently covered in the literature of the profession.

Chapter 3 will then briefly discuss a few selected theories that the authors of the text find important as a base to social work thought and practice.

Reading
2-1 Knowledge and value: Their distinction and relationship in clarifying social work practice*

William E. Gordon

Two of the five elements defining social work practice, as stated in the "Working Definition of Social Work Practice," are *value* and *knowledge*.[1] The relevant sections read as follows:

Value

Certain philosophical concepts are basic to the practice of social work, namely:

1. The individual is the primary concern of this society.
2. There is interdependence between individuals in this society.
3. They have social responsibility for one another.
4. There are human needs common to each person, yet each person is essentially unique and different from others.
5. An essential attribute to a democratic society is the realization of the full potential of each individual and the assumption of each person's social responsibility through active participation in society.

6. Society has a responsibility to provide ways in which obstacles to this self-realization (that is, disequilibrium between the individual and the environment) can be overcome or prevented.

These concepts provide the philosophical foundation for social work practice.

Knowledge

Social work, like all other professions, derives knowledge from a variety of sources and in application brings forth further knowledge from its own processes. Since knowledge of humans is never final or absolute, social workers in their application of this knowledge take into account those phenomena that are exceptions to existing generalizations and are aware and ready to deal with the spontaneous and unpredictable in human behavior. The practice of the social worker is typically guided by knowledge of:

1. Human development and behavior characterized by emphasis on the wholeness of the individual and the reciprocal influences of people and their total environment—human, social, economic, and cultural.
2. The psychology of giving and taking help from another person or source outside the individual.
3. Ways in which people communicate with

[1] The working definition is included in Bartlett (1958, pp. 3–9). The other three elements of social work practice are *purpose, sanction,* and *method.*

one another and give outer expression to inner feelings, such as words, gestures, and activities.

4. Group process and the effects of groups upon individuals and the reciprocal influence of the individual upon the group.

5. The meaning and effect on the individual, groups, and community of cultural heritage including its religious beliefs, spiritual values, law, and other social institutions.

6. Relationships, that is, the interactional processes between individuals, between individual and groups, and between group and group.

7. The community, its internal processes, modes of development and change, its social services and resources.

8. The social services, their structure, organization, and methods.

9. One's own self, which enables individual practitioners to be aware of and to take responsibility for their own emotions and attitudes as they affect their professional functions.

It can be seen that the working definition does not attempt to define *value* and *knowledge* except to refer under *value* to "philosophical concepts . . . basic to the practice of social work." The designers of the original definition apparently assumed that the meanings of *value* and *knowledge* were clear enough not to be confused.

Early in the work of the Subcommittee to Revise the Working Definition of Social Work Practice, however, it became clear that a distinction is not uniformly made between value and knowledge in social work. In the working definition itself, which purported to make such a distinction, assertions are listed under *value* that range from "The individual is the primary concern of this society" to "There is interdependence between individuals in this society." Even without benefit of formal definition, one immediately senses a fundamental difference between these two statements. The first is obviously an assertion of an ideal, the second of an empirically demonstrable fact. Similarly, there are in the literature consensual statements classified as "philosophy and principle" that range

from "Every human being is an end in him or herself and must not be used as a means to any other purpose" to "The human being as a social being grows, develops, and matures through relationships with others and needs these relationships to survive" (Oren and Kidneigh, 1961). Again, a difference between the two statements is obvious. The former asserts an ideal with its indicated action, the latter an empirically testable generalization.

The designers of the original working definition, as well as the subcommittee to revise it, saw fit to present two categories of propositions, one labeled *value* and the other *knowledge,* and to subsume under each some of what was thought to be definitive of social work practice. To complete this task obviously requires more clarification of what is intended to go under each heading and some examination of the rationale for separating them.

Distinction between value and knowledge

In their basic meaning, value and knowledge are quite distinct and run on quite independent meaning tracks. In its traditional meaning, to *value* something is to "prefer" it. A measure of the extent of a preference is what price, effort, or sacrifice one will make to obtain what is preferred, whether article, behavior, or state of affairs. To identify a value held by individuals or a society, therefore, requires a description of "what" is preferred and some measure of the extent of that preference, that is, the price in effort, money, or sacrifice individuals will pay to achieve their preference, or the provision a society will make or the positive or negative sanctions it will impose to enforce the preference. As pointed out by Muriel Pumphrey (1959), values

imply a usual preference for certain means, ends, and conditions of life, often being accompanied by strong feeling. While behavior may not always be consistent with values held, possession of values results in strain toward consistent choice of certain types of behavior whenever alternatives are offered. The meaning attached to values is of such impelling emotional quality that individuals who hold them often make personal sacrifices and work hard to maintain them, while groups will mobilize around the values they hold to exert approval and disapproval in the form of rewards and penalties (sanctions).

The idea of strongly preferring to the point of investment of self and goods to obtain or maintain what is preferred is clearly central in value.

Knowledge, on the other hand, denotes the picture man has built up of the world and individuals as it *is*, not as they might wish or fantasy or prefer it to be. *It is a picture derived from the most rigorous interpretation they are capable of giving to the most objective sense data they are able to obtain.*[2] An assertion of how things *are* that is found to hold when confronted with objective data rigorously interpreted is central to the idea of knowledge. Thus knowledge refers to what, in fact, *seems to be*, established by the highest standards of objectivity and rationality of which the human being is capable. Value refers to what individuals *prefer* or would *want to be* with a degree of attachment that may involve all the loyalty or devotion or sacrifice of which they are capable.

Some sources of confusion

While *valuing* and *knowing* in the sense given earlier are quite distinct when applied to real objects, behaviors, conditions and so forth, they are easily confused when applied to *statements about* such objects, behaviors, and the like. A statement of value and a statement of knowledge may be identical in form, and confusion arises, therefore, as to whether a given assertion should be taken as

---

[2] *Objective* is used here in the sense of data least influenced by the observer and most influenced by what is observed. *Rigorous* is used in the sense of following the rules of reasoning designed to reduce the incidence of erroneous conclusions.

a part of knowledge (generalization) or as a statement of preference (value). For example, the statement that "the inherent dignity and worth of the individual establish the individual's right to survive in terms which are satisfying personally as well as satisfying to the world" is not from its structure identifiable as a value or as a generalization (Oren and Kidneigh, 1961, p. 27).

A profession with pride in its orientation to the "real" world and to doing something about this world may be less concerned with its *statements* (generalizations, pronouncements, assertions, and the like) than it should be. Its statements, however, are the purveyors of its culture, except as it relies on example and demonstration for communicating and teaching. As social work is practiced in an increasing diversity of settings, with increasing fusion of methods, it becomes clear that the heart of continuity and professional utility lies in what social work wants for people (values) and what it knows about them (knowledge). To apply value and knowledge consciously and rationally, to communicate them in education, and to develop and extend them through research, all require their statement in some form. Social work's stance, therefore, toward these statements that constitute a large part of the profession's culture becomes critical to its practice, teaching, and research, and thus to its future. Social workers need to be aware of the extent to which they practice, teach, and research with these statements because of their preference for them or because of the statements' confirmation or confirmability.

With respect to statements purporting to describe values (what is preferred) and knowledge (what is thought to be), the distinction between value and knowledge lies largely in our sense of preference or sense of confirmation or confirmability concerning the statements. If this distinction is recognized, it is obvious that a statement may be:

1. Preferred and confirmed: "A democratic form of government leaves ultimate power in the hands of the people."

2. Preferred and not confirmed: "A democratic form of government permits individuals to reach the highest level of development of which they are capable."
3. Not preferred but confirmed: "Through the institution of war the human being has developed a socially sanctioned way of destroying millions of other human beings."
4. Not preferred and not confirmed: "Human beings are the only species to have evolved to their level in the universe."

Thus the problem of separating value and knowledge becomes in one sense a more precise location of our attitude and stance toward the statements describing our perception of the world, both as we would wish it and as we think it is. How we locate a statement with regard to preference and confirmation will determine what we will do about its implications. If, for example, we believe a statement is confirmed (corresponds to reality) and we prefer it (like it that way), we will be adherents to the status quo and will feel no impulse to modify our statements to bring them into conformity with reality (no urge to inquiry) and no impulse to change reality to conform with our preference (no urge to change the world). When we believe that a statement is not confirmed and we also have no preference for it, we have the ultimate flexibility with respect to new ideas and the greatest freedom, although not necessarily the greatest drive to inquiry.

Dysfunctional outcomes

The greater difficulty in social work, however, falls when confirmation and preference do not coincide (Items 2 and 3). Failure to distinguish between preference and confirmation or confusion of the two when they do not coincide is highly dysfunctional at two levels of professional activity.

At the practice level, where we try to use knowledge and value as guides to action, the dysfunctional result of confusion is read-ily obvious. The ineffectiveness of knowingly or unknowingly substituting a preferred for an objective view of a situation is well known. Equally ineffective is substitution of the preferred proposition for the confirmed generalization as a guide to action whether it is professional social work practice or any other activity. Knowledge and value play distinctly different roles, which, if not recognized or if mixed can greatly reduce the effectiveness of a profession and hence its ultimate development.

If a value is used as a guide in professional action when knowledge is called for, the resulting action is apt to be ineffective. If knowledge is called on when a value is needed as a guide to action, the resulting action may be unpurposeful. Both outcomes greatly reduce the potential for human welfare residing in the profession's heritage of both knowledge and values. People's ability over time to bring some aspect of the world into conformity with their preferences (realize their values) seems to be directly proportional to their abilities to bring their statements and perceptions into conformity with the world as it now is (develop the relevant science). As individuals develop and exercise their preferences for the confirmed, they increase their abilities over time to bring themselves and the world into conformity with their preferences. As they master the rules by which nature plays, they can increasingly influence the outcome of the game.

Dysfunctional results from failure to distinguish clearly between value and knowledge also express themselves in how the culture of social work itself is developed—that is, what is done about the statements that describe and delineate so much of that culture. Not separating clearly what is simply preferred from what is confirmed or confirmable restricts the active pursuit of knowledge and interferes with the constant adjustment required between preference and confirmation in any area where knowledge is expanding.

When confirmation is not clearly established for statements about *what is,* but preferences are strong for those statements, the difference between value and knowledge is expressed largely in one's intentions with respect to the preferred but not yet confirmed statement. Assertions that objective data rigorously interpreted offer the possibility of confirming can obviously be treated either as preferred states of affairs (values) or as putative knowledge (the assumptions and hypotheses of science), or both.[3] When assertions are preferred and unconfirmed but potentially confirmable, one's intentions toward them determine largely whether they are value or knowledge. For example, the proposition that the nuclear family is the best social medium for rearing mentally healthy children may be strongly preferred or valued or it may be treated as a hypothesis to be tested. Thus the difference between value and putative knowledge in this situation resides more in the stance taken toward the proposition—that is, in the intentions toward it—than in the proposition itself. These intentions involve considerable psychic interplay between preference (how we would like things to be) and reality insofar as it can be validly confirmed (the way things are). The fact that confirmation is especially tenuous in the social-psychological realm leaves far more room for interplay between the preferred view and that which purports to some confirmation than is the case in the physical or biological realms. The tension between preferred and thought-to-be-confirmed or confirmable propositions in the social and psychological sciences is therefore greater than in the physical and biological sciences.[4]

---

[3] The distinction is quite clear in scientific work. For the same person to treat a proposition both as preferred and as a hypothesis requires that the tester be doubly alert to bias in the testing procedures, and signs of such preferences are usually cause to raise questions about the investigator's objectivity or scientific neutrality.

[4] This tension is sometimes erroneously referred to as a clash between science and values rather than more precisely as a conflict between preference and confirmation.

Convergence of value and knowledge

Unconfirmed statements vary, of course, in their degree of confirmability, ranging finally into assertions that there is no reasonable expectation of confirming, and preference becomes the final arbiter of selection. It is here that all philosophies, scientific included, meet on equal grounds. The assumption that knowledge is good for all people competes on equal terms with the assumption that all people have worth and dignity. Neither is confirmable, but either or both can be strongly preferred. Once, however, there is a possibility of confirmation through objective observation rigorously interpreted, preference for the confirmed or confirmable statement over the unconfirmed or unconfirmable characterizes the scientific approach—that is, the confirmed or confirmable statement is valued more than others.

The ascendancy in a society of the scientific value (preference for propositions confirmed or confirmable) constantly narrows the realm of propositions held solely or largely by preference. Expanding scientifically derived knowledge, therefore, crowds propositions held largely by preference constantly in the direction of the presently unconfirmable. When expansion of knowledge confronts preferred explanations and assumptions with confirmatory or disconfirmatory evidence, the preference or value either becomes firm knowledge or loses its preference and ceases to be a value. For example, many pre-Copernican people actively preferred the proposition that the earth was the center of the universe and applied sanctions to those who did not hold with this proposition. The confirmed proposition that the earth is a minor planet in a minor galaxy is, however, the preferred one today. On the other hand, the value attached to a highly sacrificial life in which individuals "give" far more than they "get" is being thrown into considerable question by the nonvalued outcome to mental health and personality development.

Knowledge and value can thus converge

by two routes. One is the shifting of preference toward the confirmed, which is characteristic of a scientifically oriented society. The other is the modification of the reality on which confirmation is based so that the world, as it were, comes to be in accord with preference, which is characteristic of a change-oriented society.

Two approaches

For social work the minimum first step is the separation of what social work prefers or wants for people from what social work knows about people. A recasting of its propositions into those preferred or valued assertions about human beings, their behavior, and their society and those confirmed or confirmable by objective data rigorously interpreted would then follow. Two approaches are open for progress in this direction. One would begin with empirical data, and the other would move directly to formulations of choices openly and frankly made by the profession.

Empirical approach.   As Oren and Kidneigh (1961, pp. 27–30) demonstrated, it is entirely feasible to establish a list of assertions preferred by a defined group of social workers. An extended list of value assertions tested by consensus in the profession as a whole would yield an approximate value-set or profile for social work at the time it was established. Such a list of valued behaviors, conditions, relationships, and so forth might further be crudely distributed according to their degree of confirmation or confirmability, and thus throw some light on the extent to which preference and confirmation are congruent and the extent to which preference is for as yet unconfirmed or even unconfirmable propositions. One would look for those unconfirmed assertions that have a reasonable probability of being confirmed in the future by bringing reality into conformity with them as goals rather than as scientific propositions. One would also look for those unconfirmable propositions that attempt to rationalize conflict between prefer-

ence and emerging confirmed or confirmable or predictable states of human affairs. When personal values come into conflict with the yield of scientific endeavor, the offense to personal values may result in escape maneuvers that are more rationalizations than rational. It may result, for example, in casting what is really a preference as a putative knowledge assertion, but consciously or unconsciously designed to be unconfirmable by virtue of vagueness, structure, or reference to temporally and physically remote entities. The intentions one has toward a proposition —that is, to hold it notwithstanding or to modify it in accordance with objective data rigorously interpreted—are often revealed in the architecture of the proposition and its amenability to application of scientific procedures. In identifying and sorting out the propositions of social work into the value and knowledge categories, the profession needs to be aware of where it is rationally exercising its preference for things as they are or might be and where it is rationalizing its reluctance to submit its preferences to objective data rigorously interpreted.

Direct formulation of values.   A consensual approach to the identification of social work values and putative knowledge would be an illuminating exercise. Direct formulation, however, probably holds more promise for the reliable separation of values and knowledge, and especially for the selection of a value configuration of pervasive and enduring potential and the articulation of a science applicable to the attainment of the values.

Such a set of value assertions that the profession can accept and proclaim must meet several criteria. First, it must embrace, without fundamental contradiction, what the majority of the profession "feels is right" for social work and thus command practitioners' preference without reservation. Such a set must also be sufficiently basic and fundamental to remain useful over a substantial period of time in much the same way that the value implicit in the Hippocratic oath has served the physician over the ages. The focal value-set asserted by the profession should give the profession the highest possible sense of mission and suggest more immediate goals and objectives consistent with this purpose. Finally, the value-set ultimately selected should be so cast as to accommodate and encourage substantial growth of knowledge in the service of those values and encourage the treatment of preferred but unconfirmed assertions as hypotheses whenever they contain any elements of confirmability.

Value focus

Maximum realization of each individual's potential for development throughout that person's lifetime is a basic value that seems to meet the earlier criteria. As a value it may be treated as an unconfirmable assumption that it is "right" and "good" for each individual to continue to develop, grow, unfold, and attain the greatest possible elaboration of "humanness" in one's lifetime. While one might seek to rest authority for accepting the assumption in some higher ethic or value, it should need to appeal to a metaphysic to be accepted as fundamental in itself for anyone who fully appreciates people even as simply the most remarkable outcome of evolutionary history on this planet.

The core idea of human realization—unfolding of potential, continued growth in the human dimension, and so on—leaves ample room for adherence to the idea of self-determination. The faith that people when freed can be trusted to grow and develop in desirable directions is probably the highest expression of a belief in human dignity, and thus an encompassing value for social work to proclaim and use as an ultimate criterion to judge that which is good and desirable for people.

Knowledge focus

In conformity with the distinctions made earlier between value and knowledge (preference and confirmation), the knowledge base of social work must be formulated toward confirmed and confirmable propositions—that is, knowledge formulation must deal in generalizations that, even if preferred, are intended to give way to objective data rigorously interpreted. While the basic knowledge formulation must relate to present social work perspective sufficiently to utilize and build on social work wisdom, there are other important criteria to be met:

1. High relevance or applicability to the achievement of the values is essential if the knowledge formulation is to yield a science of social work to serve the values of social work.
2. Theoretical interest and potential for development are essential in the knowledge formulation if it is to provide the intellectual stimulation for research and the conceptual structure to formulate such research.
3. Commitment to knowledge-building further requires the selection of an area of phenomena and the selection of a few prime variables on which to focus and concentrate the scientific knowledge-building effort.

To meet these criteria it is proposed, therefore, that the central phenomenon of social work science is "social transactions," or the action interface between people, activity in the boundary between the human organism and one of the currently most important parts of the environment—other people. Theoretical interest would attach to *the relationship between the quality and the amount of this transaction and its effect on human realization* on the one hand, *and on the nature of the social environment* on the other.

Social functioning, for some time considered the ultimate concern of social work, becomes the beginning, not the end of social work interest, an interest fed by the impact of functioning patterns on both human growth and the social environment. Knowledge pursued and formulated along the feedback lines of social functioning to the individual and to the environment is a neglected area of inquiry largely untouched by psychologies and sociologies that are intent on explaining the causes of social functioning rather than its consequences.

Value-knowledge alignment

The location of the ultimate social work value in human realization and the focus of its contributing science on social functioning separate social work value and knowledge into distinct and separate dimensions—value in the growth or outcome dimension and knowledge in the pattern-of-functioning dimension. By shifting the major emphasis in valuing to outcome in the human realization realm, the behavior realm is open for scientific evaluation against that outcome. Behaviors evaluated scientifically against outcomes rather than valued according to current preferences would clearly separate the social worker's role of scientific professional from the role as social norm enforcer, a separation not always clearly made in the present mixing of values and knowledge. With the development of a science describing the relationship between social transaction patterns and outcomes both for human realization and social environment, social work would for the first time be in a position to evaluate scientifically rather than simply on the basis of preference the proposed social arrangements and behaviors thought to be good for people. Consequently, social work would place the foundation for its knowledge base clearly in the realm of a science and in the service of an emerging value of growing appeal.

Reading
2–2 *Social work curriculum**

Council on Social Work Education

The professional curriculum for social work draws broadly and selectively from the humanities, from other professions and scientific disciplines, as well as from the knowledge and experience developed by social work. Application of this content to social work involves ethical as well as scientific commitment. The study and analysis of ethical considerations is an important component of social work education.

The curriculum is developed as a unified whole and achieves its coherence by viewing all courses as presenting knowledge to throw light on several broad components related to human problems and needs: social welfare policy and services, human behavior, and the social environment and social work practice. These terms merely denote areas of substantive knowledge but are not intended to delineate the structure of the curriculum or the categorization of courses. It is expected that schools will provide systematic instruction relevant to the content of these spheres and that each school will develop an appropriate schema for the ordering of its particular courses. The general kinds of substantive knowledge and the major instructional objectives to be pursued within the total curriculum are described below.

* Reprinted with permission. From *Manual of Accrediting Standards for Graduate Professional Schools of Social Work, April 1971* (New York: Council on Social Work Education, 1971), pp. 56–60.

Content pertaining to social welfare policy and services

Opportunity should be provided all students to acquire knowledge of the general policies, conditions, legislative bases, institutions, programs, and broad range of services relevant to social welfare in contemporary society. Similarly, all students should be informed about the characteristics, functions, and contributions of social workers and of the profession in connection with social welfare problems and programs. Further, each student should have an opportunity, consistent with the school's objectives and resources, to concentrate study on a sector of social welfare having particular pertinence to one's professional career interests.

The major aims of study pertinent to social welfare policy and services are to prepare professionals to act as informed and competent practitioners in providing services, and as participants or leaders in efforts to achieve desirable change. Instruction should be directed toward developing both analytic skills and substantive knowledge, with a focus on the acquisition of competence required for the development, implementation, and change of social work policies and programs.

Attention should be given to the historical as well as current forces which generate social policies and contribute to social problems. Of particular importance is knowledge and ability to make choices about the social policies that condition authorization, financing, and programming of social welfare services, and development of a broad appreciation of the human values and social norms which shape both policies and services. Students should be provided with a basis for identifying and appraising the programs and agencies characteristically involved in dealing with problems of the individual and society, as well as those which contribute to the enhancement of personal experience and of social opportunity. Study should also be addressed to the changing nature of problem conceptions, to deficiencies in contemporary programs, and to emerging forms of service or expressions of need. Specific foci for study should include agencies' structural and administrative patterns, their service-delivery systems, the populations served by agencies, their linkages with related programs and other organizations, and their social and political environments.

Provision should be made for helping students to acquire an ability for critical analysis of the problems and conditions in society and its major institutions which have warranted or now require the intervention of social work. Study should be given to the characteristics and structures of social work as a profession, with particular attention to the roles its members have served, historically and currently, in the development and implementation of social welfare policies and programs. With respect to the fields of service within which they are practitioners, students should be helped to develop the capacity to raise relevant questions and to read and evaluate research reports bearing upon these questions.

Education in this area should aim at development among students of commitment to the profession's responsibilities to promote social welfare goals and services, to work toward prevention of social problems, and to contribute to positive social change. To be fostered are motivation and competence to participate effectively in the formulation and implementation of policies, in the improvement of programs, and in the progressive change of service agencies.

Content pertaining to human behavior and the social environment

The body of content relating to human behavior is designed to contribute to the student's understanding of the individual, group, organizational, institutional, and cultural contexts within which human behavior is expressed and by which it is significantly influenced. This objective is achieved through the retrieval, specification, and extension of those theories and bodies of knowledge derived from the biological, psychological, and social sciences as well as from the humanities which are needed for an understanding of social work values and practice.

Ultimately, all sciences are concerned with and contribute, directly or indirectly, to an understanding of human behavior. There is no generally accepted unified theory of human behavior, nor is there any single theory or formulation of relevant content which is sufficient for all social workers. Rather, there are many theories and systems of knowledge which have been developed for a variety of purposes and within a wide range of perspectives. These theories and perspectives, as well as their interrelationships, should be recognized and reflected as specifically as possible in the curriculum design and modes of instruction.

While it is expected that all social work students achieve a basic understanding of individual and collective dynamics, the particular specification of the content of this component of the curriculum and the design within which it is executed should derive from and be consistent with the educational objectives and program of the individual school, the range and quality of its educational resources, the needs and composition of the student body, and the functions of social work. Opportunities should be provided for social work students to develop the capacity to identify and master those aspects of this body of content which are relevant to the social work roles for which they seek competence and to the tasks which they expect to perform.

Equal in importance to the mastery of relevant content for social work students is the development of the capacity to assess critically the state of this theory and knowledge as it relates to social work practice, the assumptions which have influenced its development, and, finally, to begin to develop the skills and capacities which will ultimately permit them to fulfill their obligations to contribute to its development.

Content pertaining to social work practice

This area of the curriculum is designed to help the student learn and apply the knowledge and principles of social work practice in accordance with the values and ethics of the profession. The components of knowledge and competence to be fostered in this area of the curriculum may be combined differently in several areas of intervention for a variety of purposes and to meet diverse needs.

The development of competence in the practice of social work is a primary curriculum objective and requires provision of opportunities designed to help each student:

- Understand the relation of knowledge, value, and skill to each other and their utilization in the appraisal of problems or situations for social work intervention and in the provision of professional service.
- Develop the self-awareness and self-discipline requisite for responsible performance as a social worker.
- Recognize and appreciate the similarities and differences in the helping roles of various professionals and other personnel and in the problem-solving processes associated with service to individuals, groups, organizations, and communities.
- Understand the responsibility and functions of the social worker in contributing from professional knowledge to the prevention of social problems and to the improvement of social welfare programs, policies, and services.
- Develop a spirit of inquiry and a commitment throughout the professional career to seek, critically appraise, contribute to, and utilize new knowledge.

Social work practice is conducted through particular professional roles, generally in organizations providing social services. These roles require practitioners to exercise their knowledge and skills. Preparation for these roles necessitates acquisition of specialized learning and competence. To assure the provision of both basic instruction and specialized study, the graduate curriculum must include one or more concentrations. A concentration presents a distinctive pattern of instruction that organizes experiences appropriate to a specific range of professional roles and functions. Each concentration should be developed so that the student can attain a level of competence necessary for responsible professional practice and sufficient to serve as a basis for continuing professional development.

Schools may identify a variety of modes or dimensions of competence and service as their basis for development of concentrations within the curriculum. Programs of graduate education, in addition to their conservation function, must react to and encourage consideration of new or expanded roles, the changing nature of professional roles, and the conditions bearing upon practice. The pattern of concentrations within the curriculum is intended to organize instruction in preparation for competence practice, not to define or govern the nature of professional roles.

Responsibility rests with each school for definition and development of its concentration(s) for instruction in social work practice. In view of the profession's scope, no single concentration, and probably no school's composite of concentrations, should be conceived as providing instruction sufficient for the full range of social work roles. But no concentration should be so narrowly conceived that it focuses primarily on specific competencies, specific positions, or on career lines within particular service organizations.

For each concentration it offers, the school is expected to formulate explicitly the following:

1. Aims and rationale of the concentration including its relevance to social work.
2. Identification of existing or emerging professional roles suitable for and available to those who complete the concentration.
3. Specific educational objectives including the professional knowledge and competence to be fostered.
4. The specific arrangement of educational experience, including courses and practice skill components.
5. Relation of each concentration to the total curriculum and to its several components including other concentrations.

It is anticipated that there will be diversity among schools in the kinds and number of concentrations offered, as well as in their designations, and in the instructional activities and learning experiences provided. Each school is expected to formulate, develop, and justify its concentration(s) oriented to the responsibilities of the profession and commensurate with the school's resources and capabilities.

Reading
2–3 *Survival strategies for oppressed minorities**

Harriet P. Trader

Even in the present period, which has been described as the era of the welfare state, so-

* Copyright 1977, National Association of Social Workers, Inc. Reprinted by permission of author and publisher from *Social Work* 22:1 (January 1977), pp. 10–13.

cial work practice designed to promote the general welfare does not necessarily promote the welfare of members of oppressed minority groups. It may be that the requirements for the general welfare and those for the welfare of the oppressed are not always identical. Also, certain contradictions are inherent in the nature of social work practice. One such potential contradiction is that although the profession is committed to helping minority groups, it is also being financed for the most part by a majority society whose primary interests may be opposed to minority-group interests. Thus, the social worker must act as both social reformer and as an agent of social control. Despite these contradictory roles, however, practitioners have continued to balance the two requirements and have succeeded in helping individuals, families, groups, and communities of the oppressed minorities.

The status of minority groups in American society has been a source of continuing and increasing concern. The term *minority* has several implications and is applied differentially to various groups. For the purposes of this discussion, the term *oppressed minorities* refers to nonwhites who are assigned to a castelike social status irrespective of class. Although there are several such groups, including black Americans, Mexican-Americans, and American Indians, the observations presented here are based on experiential knowledge of and practice with black Americans. These observations may be applicable to members of other nonwhite minorities, but further exploration is needed to determine whether such generalizations would be appropriate.

Criteria for theories

The use of theoretical frameworks to support models of practice might be viewed as both a strength and a weakness of social work. Since no single theoretical formulation has been universally accepted within the profession, the opportunity for the input of new knowledge still exists. This opportunity must not be lost, especially as it relates to the application of new knowledge about minority groups in American society. As yet, the data are not all in, and there is still a chance to reexamine existing theories to determine what is meaningful and useful for practice with oppressed minorities.

It is important to remember that most, if not all, theories underlying practice are culture-bound. Theoreticians, however, have primarily used their own reference groups as a basis for conceptualization. Some practitioners find the idea of the cultural nature of theories acceptable if it is applied to theories they reject. Such an attitude is often taken toward broad philosophies, such as those of Freud, Rank, or Erikson. It is often more difficult for practitioners to accept theories based on cultural reference points that they not only agree with but use in daily practice. In addition, the theories that underlie practice are often selected largely because the practitioner feels professionally and personally comfortable with them. To overcome such tendencies, professionals should consider the extent to which the particular theory also fits the needs of the minority group to which their practice is directed.

This is not to suggest that a separate theory must be developed for each cultural group or that common human needs do not exist. It is strongly suggested, though, that the minority group status of clients should be one consideration in the selection of theory for practice. In this respect, some practitioners might argue that theory and practice should be color-blind, and perhaps they are right. A practitioner considering a theory that focuses only on the internal self would probably conclude that black and white psyches operate on the same color-blind principles. However, in a theory that attempts to link the internal self with the external world or social environment, it would be difficult to conclude that color could be irrelevant in the practice of social work when it is highly significant in all other social activities. To deny or to ignore the oppressed status of minority group clients is to ignore the reality of their external environment. The following criteria might be considered in selecting theory to support effective practice with oppressed minorities, particularly black Americans.

1. **Pathology–health balance.** Do the basic concepts on which the theory is developed focus either on illness rather than on well-being or on deficits rather than strengths? Are the definitions of pathology and health based solely on the expectations of the dominant group in society? Do standards for health include a range of potentials that allows for minority group differences? Are class differences implied or stated in the models for either normality or abnormality?

2. **Practitioner–client control balance.** Does the theory suggest that the worker carries more responsibility than the client in the process of changing the client's situation? Are clients perceived even subtly as being inferior to practitioners? Are practitioners seen as being obliged to use their knowledge and skills to increase clients' coping abilities? Does the theory view human beings as primarily dependent, interdependent, or independent? Can the theory allow for shared control? From what source does the practice derive its legitimacy?

3. **Personal–societal impact balance.** In assigning causation for problems, does the theory embody a personal-deficit model rather than a societal model? Does the theory take into account historical as well as current societal conditions? Can the theory account for political-economic influences on behavior? Does the theory assign importance to variations in socialization experiences among oppressed minorities? Does the theory allow for linking of the personal to the social and environmental aspects of behavior?

4. **Internal–external change balance.** Does the theory emphasize internal, psychic change in preference to changes that occur in society? Does the theory assume that the nature of society is primarily punitive rather than supportive? Are the definitions for change based essentially on the dominant societal patterns, or do they allow for a variety of patterns? To what extent is the view of change synonymous with adjustment?

5. **Rigidity–flexibility balance.** Does the theory allow for the adjustment of concepts to the needs of particular groups? Do the abstract principles lend themselves to creative and differential application in practice? Can the theory accommodate new information about oppressed minorities? Does the theory relate to a view of the class structure of society? Does the theory demand an uncritical adherence to its postulates? Are there built-in criteria for continual assessment of the utility of the theory?

Although these criteria might well apply to the selection of a theory for practice with any group of people, there is a particular need to apply them in practice with people in oppressed minority groups. This is vital in avoiding conscious, unconscious, or unrecognized tendencies to imitate society's negative relationship to and treatment of the oppressed. The questions in each criterion are meant to encourage practitioners to reconsider the process of theory selection for practice with oppressed minorities. Based on the application of the above criteria, the following incomplete model for practice is suggested as one that might be useful in such work.

An emerging model

The practice model being developed and used by the author in clinical practice with blacks is in a rough stage of conceptualization as well as practice. The framework for this model is a transactional teaching-learning process. It requires the practitioner and client to share responsibility for both teaching and learning, a process that is viewed as a unified activity and the primary mode for change. In the philosophy underlying this model, it is assumed that a great disparity exists between the reality of life for the oppressed minorities in this society and the goals to which they aspire.

This ideological base grows out of Black Liberation themes that emphasize the need for extensive changes in the American social systems and that see limited opportunities for change for black individuals and groups within the current political and economic climate. One of the major goals of this model is the achievement of independent control of self through the development of essential resources and the elimination of constraints.

The transactional teaching-learning model is based on the assumption that both individually and collectively blacks possess unique and varied knowledge and skills. The model depends on a horizontal rather than a vertical transmission of such knowledge and skills. It implies a shared experience in the teaching-learning process, and it rejects the traditional vertical transmission of knowledge from the "expert" practitioner to the "inexpert" client. Rather, the role of the "expert" is seen as shifting between worker and client, not only from one contact to another but also within the same contact. Thus, the transactional nature of the process demands a planned sharing of information.

The emphasis in this practice model is on the production of observable changes in coping behavior geared to the survival of blacks, and its primary goal is to provide blacks with the skills essential for independent and productive survival in a capitalistic society. One way in which the practitioner can help clients achieve this is to teach them the knowledge and skills she or he possesses and to learn from them the knowledge and skills that they possess.

The conceptual framework for this model is eclectic. However, it is possible to specify the nature of this eclecticism in terms of three theoretical orientations. First, from the field of ego psychology, the concepts of competence and mastery are considered relevant. As defined by White (1963, pp. 185–86):

Competence is the cumulative result of the history of interaction with the environment. Sense of competence is suggested as a suitable term

for the subjective side of this, signifying one's consciously or unconsciously felt competence—one's confidence—in dealing with various aspects of the environment.

As interpreted by Bennett (1973, pp. 54 and 291):

Mastery is the result of experiences of competense and is a belief, based upon these feelings, that one can change one's environment by obtaining knowledge of how to change it.

The second theoretical orientation underlying this model for practice is role theory, which focuses on a network of positions with various expectations regarding behavior and represents the point of articulation between the individual and society. Perlman's view (1968, p. 50) regarding role theory is useful:

In action within any one of their vital roles, individuals may feel themselves whole as acting-feeling-thinking-relating personalities. At the same time the nature of role structures and standards will affect their inner selves in several different ways.

The third relevant theoretical orientation is derived generally from a systems approach that includes systems of practice with the view of the practitioner as a mediator between systems. A more political systems approach is that which considers the client's as well as the practitioner's position in the class system of society as having an effect on practice. Such an orientation is represented in the works of Fanon (1965) and of Winston (1973). As Winston (1973, p. 297) observes:

Two societies do not and cannot exist in the United States. The segregation and triple oppression of Black people occur within a single system, a system that lacks all forms of class and racist oppression into one society based on the same economy.

The three theoretical frameworks summarized above are complex and varied, and it may not be easy for a practitioner to use such an array of orientations. However, similar complexities are found in many of the other theories supporting social work practice. As Garvin (1972, p. 2) observes, "The task is further confused—as if the variation among the stated theories were not enough—by the differences which exist within theoretical schools." He suggests a way in which the tasks of selecting and integrating theories can be partialized as a basis for practice propositions. It is his contention that the making of choices among and within theories can be facilitated if the practitioner takes into account the following four issues:

1. Degree of worker responsibility for changes in the situation
2. Whether society is viewed as a given with social order as a predominant goal or whether society is conceived as composed of conflicting classes with worker choices affected by and having effects upon such conflicts
3. Degree of control which worker seeks to exert on the client situation, regardless of how much control is potentially possible
4. Relative importance in ameliorating problematic behavior of cognitive, affective and motoric elements.

These issues might prove applicable to the practice model under consideration here, although the specific principles and the practice process for this transactional teaching-learning model cannot be adequately discussed until further testing has been completed. For example, some educational principles are still being considered, and the nature of the client-worker situation is being further formulated. Because the model has been tested only in clinical practice with blacks, there is a need to determine whether it can be adapted to general practice. It is also possible that this model may prove useful in more than one area of practice with blacks. The model's utility in such applications, as well as its relevance for practice with other oppressed minorities, has yet to be evaluated. However, even in its present rough stage of development, it can function as a supplement or alternative to the practice strategies already available.

Summary

Social work, like other professions, has recently become more sensitive to the need to develop practice strategies that can help oppressed minority groups in their struggles with personal and social problems. Although it may be that a theory of colonization based on patterns of racial stratification is most appropriate for understanding and helping oppressed minorities, it is recognized that there will be some practitioners, both black and white, who will find such a theory professionally untenable and personally discomforting.

Given the nature of the available theories, the practitioner might use the following criteria for the selection of approaches that might be of particular utility in working with blacks: (a) pathology-health balance, (b) practitioner–client control balance, (c) personal–societal impact balance, (d) internal–external change balance, and (e) rigidity-flexibility balance. These criteria, which might well apply to the choice of theories for practice with any group of people, need to become a more conscious and integral part of practice to be precisely applied in work with oppressed minorities. This is essential to avoid conscious, unconscious, or unrecognized tendencies to imitate society's negative relationship to and treatment of minorities.

In connection with these criteria, the author is developing a model for practice with blacks. This transactional teaching-learning model is based on the assumption that a sharing of "expert" knowledge and skills between practitioner and client is essential for the social survival of blacks. The model develops the resources essential to the achievement of the individual's control over his or her life. The theoretical base for this model is an eclectic one that uses ego psychology, role theory, and a systems approach. Although the principles and the practice process itself have been only tentatively formulated, this transactional teaching-learning model has been offered as another way of helping blacks in their personal and social struggles.

Society is constantly changing, and social work practice has demonstrated a degree of adaptability to such change. In a culturally diverse society such as ours, it can be ex-pected that practitioners will be required to continue the search for creative and helpful ways of selecting and adapting theories for meaningful practice. By meeting this challenge, they can advance the welfare of oppressed minorities and contribute to the advancement of the general welfare.

Selected annotated bibliography

Arkava, Morton L. "Social Work Practice and Knowledge: An Examination of Their Relationship," *Journal of Education for Social Work* 3:2 (Fall 1967), pp. 5–13.
This article is an examination of the nature and development of social work knowledge as it relates to the directions and limits of social work practice. Arkava, in discussing many of the same issues talked about in this chapter, takes the position that the parameters of social work practice are derived jointly from the profession's value base and from what is known about people and how the two are tied together.

Bartlett, Harriet M. *The Common Base of Social Work Practice.* New York: National Association of Social Workers, 1970.
The first two chapters of this text have quoted extensively from Bartlett's work. It is an important source from which students may learn about how social workers' think about their practice.

Briar, Scott, and **Miller, Henry.** *Problems and Issues in Social Casework.* New York: Columbia University Press, 1971.
While the authors would not agree with all the positions taken by Briar and Miller, they do believe that all social work students could profit by reading the first section of this text, especially chapters 3 and 4 that discuss the effect of views of the nature of human beings upon practice and the importance of the scientific method in practice.

Guzzetta, Charles. "Concepts and Precepts in Social Work Education," *Journal of Social Work Education* 2:2 (Fall 1966), pp. 40–47.
This article deals with the need to identify the principles of social work practice. Guzzetta points out that while many professions teach scientific concepts and other professions teach what essentially are philosophical precepts, social work must teach students both a commitment to competence in technical skill and a reliability of moral judgment.

Kadushin, Alfred. "The Knowledge Base of Social Work Practice," in Alfred J. Kahn (Ed.), *Issues in American Social Work.* New York: Columbia University Press, 1959.
Written 20 years ago, this statement might well be compared with the statement "Knowledge for Practice" in another book edited by Kahn, also listed in these references. In this earlier statement Kadushin makes a plea for a sounder knowledge base for the profession and sees it as coming from social work research.

Kahn, Alfred J. (Ed.). *Shaping the New Social Work.* New York: Columbia University Press, 1973.
This collection of original papers by leading social work scholars speaks to some of the challenges facing social work. The papers by Kamerman, Dolgoff, Getzel, and Nelsen ("Knowledge for Practice: Social Science in Social Work") and by Gurin ("Education for Changing Practice") and the "Epilogue" by Kahn bear on the issues discussed in this chapter.

Kidneigh, John C. "A Note on Organizing Knowledge," in *Modes of Professional Education*, Tulane Studies in Social Welfare. New Orleans: School of Social Work, Tulane University, February 1969, vol. 11, chap. 9.
This is a technical discussion of ways of organizing social work knowledge for teaching and learning in the profession.

CHAPTER **3**

Useful theoretical perspectives

As discussed in Chapter 2, the social worker makes judgments and decisions and takes action on the basis of two types of knowledge. Practice knowledge is concerned with interventive activities with individuals, groups, organizations, and communities and with research and administrative skills. Foundation knowledge is concerned with the development, interactions, and transactions of individuals, families, small groups, social organizations and institutions, communities, and cultures (and the transactions among institutions, communities, and cultures). The practice theory that deals with what social workers do in their professional roles will be the central focus of this book; but this chapter will present very briefly some foundation knowledge that the authors have found useful. Because we have found that the theories she suggests for practice with minorities are helpful as a base of practice with all people, much of what we say in this chapter will be an expansion of Trader's article (see Reading 2–3). It is appropriate to begin this discussion with a statement of criteria for the selection of foundation knowledge for social work.

CRITERIA FOR SELECTION

Given the fact, previously discussed in Chapters 1 and 2, that the assignment for the social work profession is to "mediate the process through which the individual and society reach out for each other in mutual need for self-fulfillment," the first requirement of a foundation theory is that it provide us with a conceptual formulation that views the essential feature of human life as the interpenetration of the self and the world. We need a theory that moves us away from the mental image of the person and the environment as billiard balls, which effect each other by striking one another but in which transaction only the course is changed still leaving the essential nature of each unaffected. In order to carry out society's charge, we must have a theory that helps us to be constantly aware that the structure of society, and transactions with others, is reflected in the self and the life structure of each individual. Yet, this theory must recognize that a person's life is individual and unique—a reflection of self and choices, that all human beings have their own particular world that presents them with opportunities, meanings, feelings, identities, and myths which each person individually and selectively uses and internalizes (Levinson, 1978, pp. 1–40). See

FIGURE 3–1
We, as individuals, are . . .

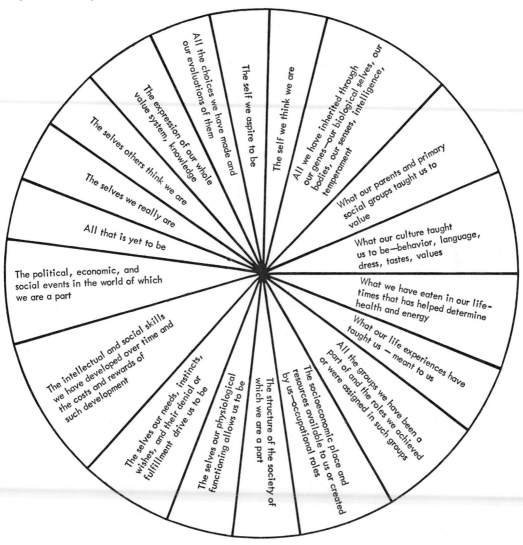

All the choices we have made and our evaluations of them

The self we aspire to be

The self we think we are

All we have inherited through our genes—our biological selves, our bodies, our senses, intelligence, temperament

What our parents and primary social groups taught us to value

What our culture taught us to be—behavior, language, dress, tastes, values

What we have eaten in our life-times that has helped determine health and energy

What our life experiences have taught us — meant to us

All the groups we have been a part of and the roles we achieved or were assigned in such groups

The socioeconomic place and resources available to us or created by us—occupational roles

The structure of the society of which we are a part

The selves our physiological functioning allows us to be

The selves our needs, instincts, wishes, and their denial or fulfillment drive us to be

The intellectual and social skills we have developed over time and the costs and rewards of such development

The political, economic, and social events in the world of which we are a part

All that is yet to be

The selves we really are

The selves others think we are

The expression of our whole value system, knowledge

Figures 3–1 and 3–2 for some diagrams showing the complexity of this interpenetration, interaction, and transaction.

Second, we need a theory that supports the importance of difference in the development of human societies, that recognizes that human organizations grow and develop through the expression of individual differences, and that demands respect for diversity. Such foundation theories would mean that our standards of health and/or normality would have to include a range of coping behaviors and value positions that would allow for individual diversity and for minority or ethnic group differences. Such theories are congruent not only with social work functions in society but with the core values of social work practice that demands respect for the individual and the unique ways people deal with their life situations. Figure 3–3 offers a very simple example of human difference. What

FIGURE 3–2
Factors that mutually influence each other in the development of the individual

do you see as you look at it? Do you see a vase or two faces? Both perceptions are correct, but could you imagine an argument between two people who see it differently over which view is "normal" or "correct" and, therefore, evidence of mental health or intelligence?

We believe the theories that serve social workers best as an adequate foundation for the understanding of human growth and human struggle are those theories that see human beings and their organizations as emergent or developing over time and that hold an optimistic view of human potential for growth and change. Their basic concepts should focus on the strengths of people rather than their weaknesses and on the needs and desires of people to cope with the tasks of life and grow from dependence to independence to interdependence. This view of human motivation and growth requires that we build a practice theory in which the worker joins the client system in its struggle toward its goals rather than one in which the practitioner carries the primary responsibility. This type of theory supports the primary social work belief in the right of people to

FIGURE 3–3
Do you see a vase? Or is it a
picture of two people facing
each other?

make their own life choices and furthers the deep respect for all human beings and for the growth struggle within each person that is such an important
social work value. The theory while recognizing the need of human systems
for stability and consistency should give primary weight to the internal push
in both individuals and the organizations they create toward growth and
change.

Social work practice theory must deal not only with the push toward growth
but with the nature of human change in both the individual and the human
groups created by human interactions and transactions. All basic theories of human and organizational development deal with the need of individuals and
groups for stability and the maintenance of some sort of inner integrity and most
theories account in some way for the change that inevitably takes place in individuals and groups. Early psychoanalytic theories and many theories of organizational functioning put heavy emphasis on the drive of the unit to maintain a
static equilibrium. Understanding certain resistances to change on the part of
any human system is necessary, but social workers also need a theoretical stance
that gives a place of importance to developmental growth and the human seeking for the new and the different.

All theories of human behavior embody some concepts of motivation. The
more useful theories for social work are those that hold that the significant force
in motivation is a feeling of mastery, of control over one's internal reactions and
relevant transactions with one's world. Theories that recognize that an individual's or a group's (social group, family, ethnic group, organization, or community) motivation to develop and use coping skills is significantly increased by
a feeling of competence and effectiveness in dealing with the tasks of living; and
that, when one is the helpless victim of forces beyond one's control, the result is
dejection, despair, and demoralization.

The importance of this type of theory demands that practitioners make available to their client systems all relevant knowledge and skills that will increase in

any way their coping ability. It makes the assumption that the progressive forces in human nature and human groups are stronger than regressive forces. This way of viewing human motivation supports a practice theory that sets forth ways of identifying the progressive forces within any human system and ways of identifying and removing blocks and obstacles that dampen these progressive forces. It means that practitioners no longer are so fearful of "creating dependency" but become primarily concerned with making all resources possible available to people for their use in coping and mastering. It means that theories of organizational behavior must recognize the push toward development as well as the importance of maintenance.

All theories of human functioning make some assumptions as to the cause of human dysfunctioning. Social workers need some concepts about what causes things to go wrong in the human condition. In order to serve social workers well the theories of human dysfunctioning cannot focus totally on the personal-deficit model. In order to be useful for social workers in carrying out their functions, theories about the genesis of human troubles must allow for problems of dysfunctioning to be lodged in the individual, in human organizations and groups, or in the transactions between the individual, the environment, and the groups and organizations. This type of foundation theory means that social work practice theory cannot deal exclusively with methods of individual internal change and adaptation but must include ways of dealing with change in individual coping skills, with change in organization and group, and with change in transactions between individuals and their groups.

GENERAL SYSTEMS THEORY AS A PART OF FOUNDATION KNOWLEDGE

It is the authors' proposal that ecological and general systems theory relating to open human systems may give us a conceptual framework which will allow us to organize our knowledge in ways useful to our professional functions. This is not a new idea. Others have made the same proposal in articles spanning the last 20 years. Therefore, our discussion will be essentially an integration of our understanding of the writings of other authors (Allport, 1964, pp. 39–59; Buckley, 1967; 1968, pp. 31, 304, 330, 354; Chin, 1961, p. 201; Goldstein, 1973, pp. 105–136; Hartman, 1970; Janchill, 1969; Koestler, 1968; Pincus and Minahan, 1973, pp. 530–564; Stein, 1974; Strean, 1971, pp. 123–195; von Bertalanffy, 1968). An article on systems theory has been reproduced in this chapter to give readers a second view of the use of this theory and to offer them another statement to help them develop further understanding of this complex theory (see Reading 3–1). The Forder article, other authors, and our own experience all serve to highlight the difficulty of grasping this highly abstract theory and its relationship to practice. However, we believe that the struggle to master systems theory is worth the effort. One of the confusions that confronts anyone seeking to understand systems theory is that there are many different theories that are discussed under the common ruberic of "systems theory." This discussion will deal primarily with the notions about open human systems as developed by general systems and ecological systems theorists. A further confusion in the use of systems theory is that it is used both as a conceptual model and as a description of empirical reality that has a predictive value. Both uses of the theory will be discussed in this chapter. For the conceptual model we shall use primarily the ecological systems model and shall discuss concepts of general systems theory as a description of empirical reality.

But first another problem in the literature on systems theory needs to be recognized and that is the difficulty of understanding systems theory because it uses a vocabulary different from that found in most social work literature. Terms, such as *input, throughput, output, entropy,* and *equifinality,* are strange and unappealing to social workers. These terms come from cybernetics and social science literature and usually seem very mechanical to social workers. This problem with language is of concern to us because we feel that any use of terms that tend to put distance between the client system and the social worker or that tend to introduce a mechanistic feeling—any terms that allow us to feel the client system as object rather than subject—is problematic for social work practice.

As a conceptual framework

A system is usually thought of as a whole consisting of interdependent and interacting parts, or as "a set of units with relationships among them" (Bertalanffy, 1956, p. 11). A system may also be described as "a complex of elements or components directly or indirectly related in a causal network, such that each component is related to some others in a more or less stable way within any particular period of time" (Buckley, 1967, p. 41). The interrelationships of the components creates a whole that is greater than the sum of its parts. The fact of interaction of the elements of the system imparts to it aggregate characteristics that are not only different from, but often not found in the components alone. Thus the "sum of the parts" does not refer to the particular parts of the units added together or summed but to the aggregate of the units and the transactions and relationships between them that creates a "whole" with some degree of continuity and boundary. The interrelationship of system parts gives rise to new qualities that are a function of the transactions within the system. Because of the wholeness of the system, a change in any part of the system affects the system as a whole and all of its parts.

In using the system as a conceptual model, it is important to specify both a frame of reference and a boundary. An individual may be considered as a psychological, a biological, or a physical system or as an element in a social system (group, organization, or community). Each frame of reference gives us a very different system and presents us with different elements and transactions. Yet, each system includes a human being. We also need to establish a boundary that will limit the field of concern. This conceptual boundary is very different from a recognition of empirical boundaries, such as the boundaries of a school system or the city limits or the boundaries of a family or organization that are established by transactions within the system being studied. Suppose, for example, we wish to study the interactions of two neighboring cities. A diagram such as the following might be drawn to illustrate the system being studied:

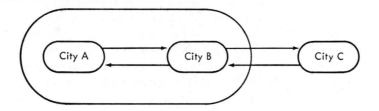

The system elements are the cities and the relationships are the interstate highways. It is also possible to study other transactions and lines of communication between these cities. But in order to study these two cities as a social system a boundary has been drawn around them and their relationships with other cities have been excluded as beyond our purpose. Such a conceptual model of systems theory requires that the system be defined to take in the elements and transactions of concern. Actually as one looks at this map and thinks about the relationships between the two cities, an infinite number of relationships and transactions can be identified between the two cities beyond the two drawn in.

The systems model, therefore, is proposed as a conceptual model in that it meets the first requirement for foundation knowledge for social work. It shifts attention from characteristics possessed by individual units to interaction and relatedness. Take the example of Maria in the Auerswald article reproduced in this chapter (see Reading 3–2). (The reader may want to read that article at this point.) The staff at the mental health center all regarded Maria as an entity bounded by her skin and used concepts of normality that had little relationship to the totality of this child and the transactions and relationships that were a part of her. To understand her and her uniqueness one had to draw a different picture. Let us compare the differences in the diagrams shown in Figures 3–4 and 3–5.

FIGURE 3–4
View of Maria from the perspective of the interdisciplinary team

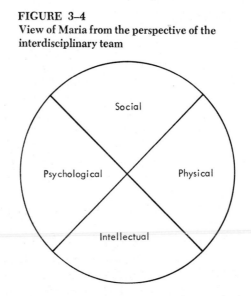

Figures 3–4 and 3–5 illustrate very clearly the radical difference between ecological systems theory as a knowledge base for social work practice and other approaches. It is far more than a difference in techniques; rather it is a whole different way of thinking that radically changes the basic approach of practitioners. In the first view of Maria various areas of her functioning were compared with "normal" functioning and from this view her functioning seemed pathological indeed. However, once the ecological map is drawn, it can be understood that Maria's behavior was a coping response to the transactions affecting her within her life space and was a result of the interactions between Maria and other system ele-

FIGURE 3–5
Maria's situation as seen from the perspective of the article

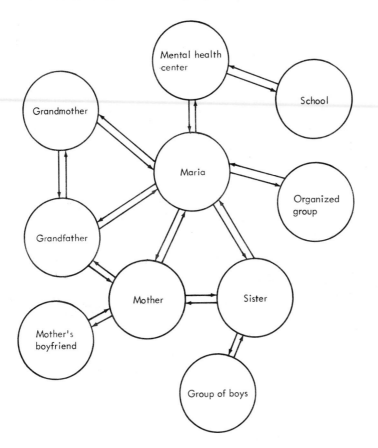

ments. What is important about this view is that different data are collected differently, analyzed differently, and lead directly to different interventive actions. There are other ways of viewing the system which would result in different maps. Maria's life space could have been diagrammed as shown in Figure 3–6.

This way of viewing Maria's situation comes from the drawing in of some empirical boundaries of certain subsystems within the larger systems picture. The boundaries of the overall map would be a conceptual boundary, but the map would recognize certain empirical subsystem boundaries found in the real world. Working from this map considerable data could be collected about the relationship between Maria's family and the school, or group, or mental health center, rather than Maria herself. In addition the grandfather and the grandmother could be seen as forming a subsystem together that transacts with Maria and her family as a system rather than individuals. Which map one would draw depends upon the notion of the importance of the interactions within the subsystems. It would depend upon whether we defined the central issue as one of Maria's family and its interrelations and its transactions as a unit with other system elements or of Maria and her transactions and interactions. There is still a third way that we could picture the application of ecological systems theory to Maria's life space. It might look something like Figure 3–7. This type of map attempts to picture the

FIGURE 3–6
Maria's situation seen from the perspective of large systems empirical boundaries

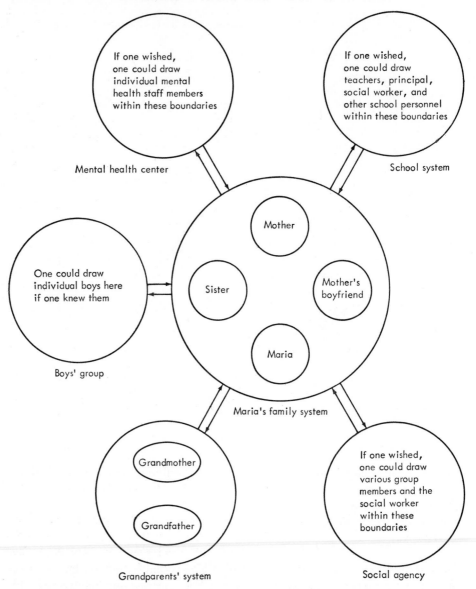

If one wished, one could draw individual mental health staff members within these boundaries

Mental health center

If one wished, one could draw teachers, principal, social worker, and other school personnel within these boundaries

School system

One could draw individual boys here if one knew them

Boys' group

Mother

Sister

Mother's boyfriend

Maria

Maria's family system

Grandmother

Grandfather

Grandparents' system

If one wished, one could draw various group members and the social worker within these boundaries

Social agency

different levels of systems, recognizing that there are larger and more encompassing systems and smaller systems that may be seen as subsystems of the larger systems. However, it is almost impossible to draw such a map on paper; one needs a three-dimensional model to picture this. It may be helpful to struggle with such representations if they sensitize us to all the elements in the life space of the human system with which we are working. One of the important elements of Maria's life that is highlighted in this map, but neglected in the others, is that of neighborhood. Maria is Puerto Rican and the family is part of a minority neighborhood which may have considerable significance for the way the social systems from the wider society intervene.

FIGURE 3–7
An attempt to picture Maria's situation from the perspective of system levels; primary sysems (intimate social groups) are drawn as circles, operating on same level. Here the community is seen as the largest social system.

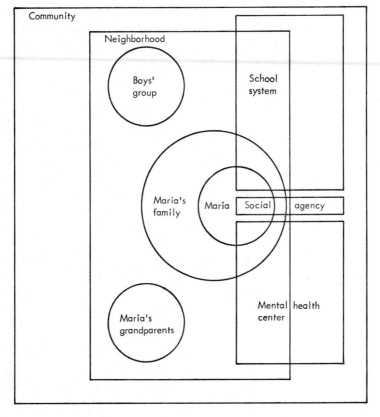

Systems theory is not in itself a body of knowledge, nor does it contain any prescriptions as to actions that a social worker might take. Rather, systems theory presents us with tools of analysis that may accommodate knowledge from many sciences. It is a way of thinking—a way of viewing and organizing data (Janchill, 1969, p. 77). Because it is a way of thinking that requires the abandonment of the linear approach to causation and the substitution of an understanding of the reciprocal relationships among all parts of the field (transactional approach) and an interactive focus, in which the effects of one system on another are dealt with, systems theory requires considerable study for any real understanding.

The use of systems theory is proposed as a conceptual framework for the organization of data about people and groups, as a way of originating more helpful questions and approaches to problem-solving. This is very different from proposing it as a model of empirical reality with a predictive capacity. Used in this way, systems theory helps us avoid the tendency, discussed in chapter 1, to focus on either the individual or on society as the primary locus of pathology or as the primary target of change. It reminds us that things are not so simple.

Systems theory offers a conceptual framework that shifts attention from discrete units (be those units either individuals or social groups) and their characteristics to the interaction and interrelatedness of units. Noting the success of the physical sciences in building knowledge by splitting "wholes" into pairs of smaller units (variables), establishing causal relationships between those variables, and attempting to understand a total phenomenon by the process of adding such understandings, the social sciences, too have tried to seek direct cause and effect relationships between paired variables. However, this appears to be an inappropriate method for explaining the complex behavior of living things. To demonstrate the inadequacy of this method, see how it would be used to explain the flight of birds. It would have no difficulty explaining the physical and chemical principles of the bird's ability to fly, but it cannot explain why the bird takes off in the first place (Rapoport, 1968).

The "wholes" concerned with in social work are more than the sum of their paired variables. That "more" is found in their purpose (or goal-directed behavior) and in their interactive complexity. The analytic method that breaks a phenomenon into its separate parts only gives us a vast number of items of information and leaves us without the ability either to make sense out of the information or to reassemble the system. The systems approach allows us to replace the older analytic orientation, in which the individual was observed on the one hand and the individual's environment on the other, with a more holistic orientation to the problem of complex organization, in which the individual and the social and physical environment are seen as an interacting whole. We are, thus, concerned with the laws of interactions and transaction rather than with the intrinsic qualities of the parts. The assumption is that the behavior of the parts is different when studied in isolation than when seen within the whole because of the dynamic interactions and organizing patterns that are only observable as a part of the whole.

A system may be described as a set of interrelated elements with a capacity for certain kinds of performance. Each component of the set is related to at least some others in a more or less stable way within a particular period of time and space (Buckley, 1967, p. 41). The assumption is that a system is a complex adaptive organization of parts which, by its very nature, continually generates, elaborates, and restructures patterns of meanings, actions, and interactions. Within a system something is continually going on, including a constant interchange with the environment across its boundary. Although a system is viewed as a constantly changing whole that is always in the process of movement toward a selected purpose, its parts are assumed to interact within a more or less stable structure at any particular point in time.

As a conceptual model the ecological systems model encourages transactional thinking and observations. It allows us to bring order into the massive amounts of data from all different frames of reference that we need to work with in social work practice. It increases our ability to consider the intricate patterns of interactions from many different perspectives. It also helps us to guard against the problem of reductionism, forcing us to a different method of data collection and thus making it possible to assess the impact of multiple factors that may bear on causation.

Another important point is that viewing reality as systems of related entities not only affects the way we collect and assess data but also presents us with multiple possibilities for intervention (see Figures 3–5, 3–6, and 3–7). When it is understood that affecting one component of a system affects all the other components, the possibilities for intervention are greatly increased. For example, Maria will be profoundly affected by what happens between her mother and the man in her mother's life and her life might conceivably have been altered by a change in the relationship between the grandfather and grandmother as a sub-system. If we operate from an ecological systems perspective, we come to understand that direct therapeutic intervention with Maria might not be the only or the most economical or even the best choice. Intervention with the mother, the grandfather, the family as a whole, or the group social worker might be more helpful. And it certainly would appear that one effective approach might be to the welfare board to assure that assistance for Maria would be continued even if her mother should remarry. Although we have suggested numerous possible avenues of intervention in Maria's situation, a systems view does not necessarily mean that intervention should always be more extensive because the worker uses systems theory. We may be able to make intervention more simple if we consider that a small change in one element of a system may change the total system.

There is one further conceptual formulation that needs to be developed in considering systems theory as a conceptual tool. In working with differing sets of subsystems, or different system levels, the worker must make three important decisions: (1) identify the client system, (2) identify the elements or subsystems that should be changed, and (3) determine what elements or subsystems will be involved in the change efforts. The activities of the practitioner can then be seen as involving a minimum of four types of systems (or subsystems)—the change agent systems, the client systems, the target systems, and the action systems (Pincus and Minahan, 1973, pp. 53–64). These concepts essentially relate to a practice model, but they will be discussed later in this chapter.

Empirical aspects of systems theory

Persons working with systems theory have gone beyond using it as a conceptual framework and have developed various concepts and principles about the way systems operate. These concepts are concerned with the functioning of open, living, or human systems. Living systems are seen as systems made up of matter and energy that are organized by and function through an exchange of information. They exist in space and time and have boundaries (empirical not conceptual boundaries) which are at least partially permeable, thus permitting transmissions of energy and information to cross them.

The open system. Perhaps the central concept in the theory of social systems is the view of the system as open, which means that an essential factor of a system's continuity and change is its engagement in interchanges with the environment. The open system receives input from and produces output to its environment. The environment and the transactions with it are basic to the existence of the system. It is because of this quality of openness that human systems grow and evolve toward increased order and complexity (negative entropy).

Closed systems. These systems do not interact with other systems; they neither accept input from them nor produce output to them. Such systems have a quality called entropy, which means that, over time, they tend toward less differentiation of their elements and toward a loss of organization and function. This notion brings us to the concept of boundaries.

Boundaries

A boundary may be defined as a closed circle around selected variables, where there is less interchange of energy or communication across the circle than there is within the circle. Open systems have, by definition, semipermeable boundaries. However, the relative "openness" or "closedness" of those boundaries will vary with the system. All of us are probably familiar with certain communities that are very conscious of themselves, of their entity, and are extremely unwilling to admit strangers or new behavior. Such communities have relatively closed boundaries and in time may well suffer some of the effects of entropy. We all have met families with such boundaries, boundaries well guarded by careful parents, and we may also know other families in which boundaries seem too open and unguarded to preserve the unit, in which social workers are allowed to intrude at will, with no challenge to their business there. To understand the boundary of a family is simple, but the concept of boundary itself is complex.

Social workers confronted with a problem involving the functioning of an individual, a family, or a social group will find that the definition of the problem and the definition of the boundaries of the social systems with which they will work are inextricably related. For example, when an individual brings a problem to a social worker, does the worker define the problem and the boundaries of the social system in such a way that the problem is seen as lying within the boundaries of the individual as a complete social system? Or does the worker define the problem in such a way that the system becomes the focus of concern and the individual is seen only as a component of the system? Or does the worker believe that the problem falls within the sphere of another institution? The boundaries of a system of concern are established by the practitioner, and it becomes the worker's task to determine what transactions are central to the solution of the problem (Klenk and Ryan, 1974, p. 21). Often social science definitions of social entities are used to set boundaries, for example, family, group, institution, organization, and so on.

A concept that may help in establishing the boundaries of the systems is that of *levels* of systems. Simon (1952, pp. 130–139) has called this notion *layering*, pointing out that the individual, primary groups, organizations, and so on can best be considered as "nests of Chinese blocks" in which any activity taking place in one system at one of these layers will obviously be operating simultaneously in at least one other system (the larger block) at another level.

Tension

Tension in human beings or in their organizations can be viewed as a pathological or disturbing factor that occurs only occasionally or residually. In contrast to this notion, systems theory conceives of tension as characteristic of, and necessary to, complex adaptive systems, though there is recognition that tension may manifest itself in either destructive or constructive ways. Thus systems theory does not attribute a positive or a negative value to tension per se, or even to conflict. Rather, such elements are seen as attributes of all systems simply because they are alive and open to transactions across their boundaries. It is the identification and analysis of how and to what purpose tensions operate within a system and between systems that are of major importance for social work practitioners. Rather than consider "inertia" as a given, or sought for, quality of complex, adaptive systems, with tension occurring as a "disturbing factor, some level of tension must be seen as characteristic of and vital to such systems although it may manifest itself as now destructive, now constructive" (Buckley, 1967, p. 53).

Feedback and purposive systems

A basic characteristic underlying purposive, goal-seeking mechanisms is that of *feedback*. By feedback is meant "a communications network which produces action in response to an input of information and includes the results of its own action in the new information by which it modifies its subsequent behavior" (Deutsch, 1968, p. 390). Feedback-controlled systems (and all human systems are thus controlled) are goal directed "since it is the deviations from the goal-state itself that direct the behavior of the system" (Buckley, 1967, p. 53). The goal-directed feedback loop underlying the self-directing human and social systems involves a receptor that accepts information from the outside, an element that imputes meaning to the information, a selector that establishes priorities of information processed, and a mechanism which measures or compares the feedback input against a goal and passes the mismatch information on to a control center which has the capacity of activating appropriate behavior to bring the system in line with its goal (p. 69). The meaning of the feedback is not something in it, or something in the system, but something in the interaction between the two. In the complex adaptve system there are "multistaged mediating processes" (p. 55) between the reception of feedback and the "output."

The question for the social worker is "Under what conditions does the information carried on the feedback loop promote change and under what conditions does it inhibit change?" Two kinds of feedback have been identified. It is generally held that negative feedback carries information that the system is behaving in such a way as to make it difficult to achieve its goal and that such feedback results in behavioral correction in line with goals. Positive feedback is generally held to mean that the system is behaving correctly in relation to its goal and that more behavior of the same quality is called for. Negative feedback is seen as deviation correcting since it results in behavioral change back to the goal, while positive feedback, since it calls for more of the same, is seen as moving toward ever greater deviation from the previous state.

Change and stability

Because of the openness of human systems and the interaction of elements within their boundaries, it is impossible to conceive of such systems as static. They are constantly in the process of change and movement. And such movements in a human system represent the system's attempt to take purposive, goal-directed action. Human systems strive for the enhancement and elaboration of internal order and for the ordering and selection of outside stimuli accepted across the system boundary in such a way that purposive movement toward a selected goal is maintained. At the same time that a system is constantly in a state of change, it must also maintain a dynamic equilibrium. This notion is expressed by the concept of *steady state* or *homeostasis*. This concept deals with the order and structure necessary for any effective movement—without these all is chaos and purposive movement becomes impossible. Thus, although the movement of systems toward some goal is essential to their continued existence, systems also have a need for a certain amount of order and a certain stability.

Equifinality and *multifinality* are two concepts relative to the change and stability of systems that are important to social workers. Equifinality is the capacity to achieve identical results from different initial conditons. If a system is open, it can be shown that the final state will not depend on those conditions. Such a system will have a goal of its own, and the end state will depend upon the interactions of the elements of the system and the transactions of the system with other systems in relation to that purpose. The concept of multifinality suggests an opposite principle: similar conditions may lead to dissimilar end states. Thus, similar initial conditions in any living system may or may not be relevant to or causally important in the establishment of the end state.

POTENTIAL VALUES OF SYSTEMS THEORY

Some potential values of systems theory as an organizing framework for social work knowledge are as follows:

1. Systems theory allows one to deal with far more data than does the analytical model, enabling one to bring order into a massive amount of information from all the different disciplines on which social work needs to draw. And it is the collection and ordering of the data that give structure to all else in the social work process, as all else is operational.

2. The concepts relating to systems and their development, function, and structure are equally applicable to the range of clients served by social workers, from the individual to society.

3. Systems theory provides a framework for gaining an appreciation of the entire range of elements that bear on social problems, including the social units involved, their interrelationships, and the implications of change in one as it affects all.

4. Systems theory shifts attention from the characteristics possessed by individuals or their environments to the transactions between systems, changing the vantage point of the data collector and focusing on interfaces and the communication process that takes place there. Social work has long been struggling to see individuals and their environments as complete units.

5. Systems theory sees people as active personality systems capable of self-initiated behavior and thus able to contribute and alter their behavior or even to create new environments. Adaptation of the environment is as much a property of human systems as is the tendency to be affected by or adapt to the environment. These concepts negate the tendency to see disturbances as pathology and move the worker into the present life of the system.

6. The concept of systems as purposive, combined with the concepts of equifinality and multifinality, radically changes the view of both causation and the possibilities for change, and supports the worker's concern with self-determination and with the client's participation in the change process.

7. The use of systems theory brings the purpose of the system into the center of the worker's consideration, engendering further concern with self-determination and the necessity of relating professional feedback to client purpose.

8. If a living, open system requires constant transaction with other systems

and its environment for its progressive development, it becomes evident that a major function of social workers becomes the provision and maintenance of such interchange opportunities for all populations.

9. Social workers need to be increasingly concerned with populations and systems heading toward isolation, with the strains in our society that result in isolation, and with our now isolated populations.

10. If change and tension are inherent in open systems, social workers need to direct their attention to why suggested changes may be resisted and why such changes become unbearable for a system. This further emphasizes the principle of meeting clients where they are and with self-determination. It removes the notion that tension or conflict is pathology.

11. The concept of system boundary speaks to social workers' concerns with client's rights and recognizes that social workers should be concerned with the ways they and their services move across the boundary of a social system.

12. The recognition that change in one part of a system can often greatly affect the whole means that one must be increasingly aware of the impact of intervention in the broader transactions of clients. In addition it speaks to the fact that it is not necessary to change a whole system to bring meaningful change but that the point of intervention must be chosen with care. It broadens the concept of the points at which a system can be entered, provides one with more ways of entering effectively, and may make the intervention simpler.

13. The systems perspective also places the agency as a social system and the worker and client in the same transactional field. Social workers are a social system and are involved as components of a social system network.

Basic conceptual systems in social work practice

At this point there will be a brief departure from the development of basic knowledge to insert some material related to a conceptual practice framework. We are inserting this material here because it has to do with systems theory and it will be refered to from time to time as the material in the next few chapters is developed. The notions to be discussed were developed originally by Allen Pincus and Anne Minahan (1973, pp. 54–74) as a model for teaching social work practice.

According to the discussion of systems theory, most of the examples used so far have involved what could be called client systems. However, social workers do some of their most important, time consuming, and demanding work with people other than those traditionally viewed as clients. In the case example of Maria, a social worker using systems theory would probably work with her mother, her sister, her grandparents, the income maintenance and the social service department of the county welfare board, personnel in the clinic, the group worker, and the school system. If the worker works in protective services for children, there will also be the necessity to work with court services, medical services, neighbors, police, attorneys, and perhaps the school system and foster parents or other child-care services. As a practitioner in a child-care agency, the worker may be involved with the children and their families, medical resources, the school, foster parents, and perhaps community centers and organized groups outside of the agency boundaries. If the agency has a residential center, the worker will be involved with others who have contact with their clients—the maintenance staff, child-care staff, teachers, and perhaps nurses inside the agency. In addition to the people they see outside of the agency, the workers are always a part of an organized structure in which they do their work. Even in private practice they will usually have a secretary and someone to answer the telephone with whom they interact as a system. Workers usually think first of their clients who they feel are the people they are there to help, but they may want to consider seriously who really benefits from their change efforts. Who is the client in the case of child abuse—the child, the parents, or the community who asked the worker to get involved? Who gives the worker the right to interfere in other people's lives? Who sanctions what the worker does? In daily transactions between themselves and others, workers find that they are working with many different people about different things and for different reasons in order to achieve some overall goal.

Pincus and Minahan (1973, pp. 54–74) suggest that the people with whom the worker interacts in practice actions can be classified into four types of social systems: the client system, the target system, the action system, and the change agent system. To this could be added two more systems: the professional system and the problem-identification system. The decision of the worker as to the purpose and the relationships that should be a part of each encounter will determine the definition of the system. The systems that make up social work practice may be described in the following ways.

The change agent system. Social workers may be viewed as change agents, who are specifically employed for the purpose of planning and working with the six systems toward the planned change. The agency or organization that employs them or of which they are a part can be thought of as the change agent system. Obviously, the change agent system heavily influences the worker's behavior through various policies and resources that represent sanctions, constraints, and resources. These will be discussed in greater detail in Chapter 15 on bureaucracy.

The client system. People may be considered to be a part of a client system when (1) they have either asked for or sanctioned the worker's services; (2) they are expected to benefit from those services; and (3) they have entered into an explicit or implicit contract with the worker (see the discussion on contracts in Chapter 9). This definition leads to a brief consideration of the nature of the first coming together of client and worker. There are clients who come to the agency voluntarily seeking the help of the worker, but there are large numbers of situations in which the worker approaches the client because the agency function calls for it to assume this type of responsibility in behalf of the community (which should be considered the client at this point), for example, corrections, child welfare, protection for the aged and incompetent, and so on. Also a neighborhood center staff (a change agent system) may identify what they see as a neighborhood need and ask a staff member to attempt to form an organization to deal with it. In all these instances the community or the change agent system itself may more appropriately be considered the client than the people the worker approaches "to help." The people identified as targets of the worker's efforts are more appropriately regarded as *potential clients* until some sort of agreement is reached in which potential clients sanction the worker's intervention in their lives and transactions. This principle will be discussed further in several parts of the text as it is a crucial one that is often not understood. An example of this is found in the Taber article included in Chapter 7. Taber discusses work as a community mental health worker in which the workers went out to offer help to a disorganized neighborhood. Another interesting example is found in Chapter 7 of a worker who attempted for several months to engage a potential client concerning care of her children, only to have the woman become a client when she needed financial help.

The target system.   The people that the change agents "need to change or influence in order to accomplish their goals" is the target system (Pincus and Minahan, 1973, p. 58). The target system and the client system often overlap when it is the client, or the client's part in an intersystem transaction, that needs to be changed. However, much of social work practice involves the social worker working with the client system toward some desired change in some other system (a target system).

The action system.   The term *action system* is used to describe those with whom the social worker interacts in a cooperative way to accomplish the purposes of the change effort. There are an endless number of different action systems in which the worker may be engaged. Chapter 14 will deal with the skills of teamwork which is essentially a discussion of the ways of working with action systems made up of professional or paraprofessional people. However, action systems may be a neighborhood group, a family group, or others that the worker works with toward bringing about a change helpful to the client. Readers will find two interesting examples in the Taber article of the worker asking an already established client system to serve as an action system for potential clients, helping the worker to influence the potential client to become an actual client and accept some needed services.

The professional system.   This system is made up of the professional association of social workers, the educational system by which workers are prepared, and the values and sanctions of a professional practice. The values and the culture of the professional system strongly influence both the required and the permitted actions of the worker as change agent. In working to change their own agency or in acting as an advocate of social change, practitioners often utilize the professional system.

The problem-identification system.   This system is the system that acts to bring a potential client to the attention of the worker. At the initiation of its contact with the worker, or the change agent system, it might be considered (as Pincus and Minahan discuss) the client system. However, it usually does not consider itself a client, and if, in the course of things, it should appear that it should be the focus of the helping effort, the worker will need to treat it more as a potential client until it makes a role transition.

These systems will be referred to throughout the rest of the text. We believe that the use of these concepts will result in the worker thinking more clearly about their practice decisions and actions.

COMMUNICATION THEORY AS FOUNDATION KNOWLEDGE

In the discussion of systems theory it was stated that the transaction and interactions between the elements or subsystems within the system and between the system and other systems are organized and structured by information and informational flow. Thus a critical factor in the functioning of the living system and/or its parts is the communication of information. Communication may be verbal or nonverbal and occurs at all levels of interaction and transaction. Communication may be direct or indirect, covert or overt. Verbal communication through the use of language is really a symbolic interaction in that words, and their organization are really symbols for facts, thoughts, and feelings. This area of foundation knowledge is so important to social work practice that Chapter 6 has been devoted to developing the conceptual knowledge base and discussing interviewing as a communication process.

ROLE THEORY AS FOUNDATION KNOWLEDGE

Another concept that helps us to understand and use systems theory is that of role. The structure of a social system may be described as a network of roles. The term *role* refers to the socially expected behavior prescribed for a person occupying a particular social status or position in a social system (Biddle and Thomas, 1966). Social norms for the position provide guides for the attitudes, feelings, and behavior that are permitted, expected, or prohibited for the individual filling that role. These norms will differ from culture to culture. In other words, the cultural environment in which the system finds itself will set different norms and expectations for role occupants. For example, all cultures have prescribed specific role behavior for a woman filling the role and status of mother within the family system. However, these prescribed attitudes and behavior may differ significantly depending upon the cultural environment of the particular family system. This fact has great importance for the activities of the social worker in problem definition, data collection, assessment, and interventions.

Three related concepts relating to role are the notions of *role set, role complementarity,* and *role conflict.* Important to the notion of role complementarity and reciprocity is the fact that role positions or statuses are usually paired. For every parent there is a child; for every wife there is a husband. If the position of husband is no longer filled in the family system, the role of wife changes to the role of widow, divorced person, or separated or abandoned woman. If a system is to enjoy some stability and integration, there must be some reciprocity of expectations between role partners. If an industrial organization is to be free to pursue its goals, there must be some agreement between those persons occupying management and policy-making roles and those occupying labor roles. If husbands and wives are to create a family system with some stability, there must be some agreement among them as to how their varying roles will be performed.

The patterns of expected role behavior grow from the need of social systems to have a steady state—to have the stability that comes from being able to predict within some acceptable limits the behavior of elements within the system. These patterns of expectation grow from two types of interaction. First, the opportunities, the deprivations, and the needs in the interactions between elements internal to the system will establish role expectations related to system maintenance and growth. For example, children need protection and nurture if they are to grow and make their contribution to life. The system must answer as to what position within the system will be given that job and what behavior from that element will assure effective care of the child. The second source of the expectations are found within the transactions the system has with other systems and environments. These come from the same sources as discussed earlier. For example, all individuals need food, clothing, and shelter, and depending on the geographic and climatic environment within which people find themselves, patterns of securing these needs will develop. When individuals group themselves into larger systems, certain differentiation of functions that are essential to the functioning of the system will develop. This differentiation will then result in assigned roles to system elements, and expected role patterns will develop. When other systems and environments change, there will be problems within the system as the various elements of the system continue previously patterned behavior. Thus today one sees conflict between parents and children—the aged and youth—which is largely a conflict between expected role patterns and the changing environment that appears to make certain of these patterns dysfunctional. This will be discussed further under role incongruity.

While there is always room in role expectation for certain individual interpretations and behaviors, when a role is either ascribed or achieved it is often found that certain aspects of the self are developed and brought out and certain aspects are neglected and often very consciously repressed. This is true of all choices of life. However, the more rigid and circumscribed the notion of role behavior, and the more certain characterstics of the person are tied to role position, the more stress individuals may feel in being placed in, or even in self-selecting, that role. At the moment many women in our society are very active in trying to change the woman's role. However, this is most difficult since all members of our society have been conditioned so strongly in sex-role differentiation. Consciousness may be raised, but conditioning is hard to deal with.

The construct of role set or role clusters, which is an array of roles that any one person may be filling at any particular time (Merton, 1957), is an important notion for social workers. Conflict between the various roles in any role set may be particularly painful for the individual or the system involved. For example, employers sometimes defend themselves against charges of discrimination against women by the statement that women are not as interested in advancement as men and will not fulfill certain prescribed behavior for management roles such as accepting night work or travel assignments. For the women involved, this type of demand may conflict in particularly difficult ways with the roles of wife and mother that may also be within their cluster of roles. What happens in this situation is that the woman involved suffers from role conflict. She is involved in two different role sets in two different systems and the expected behavior of the roles involved is defined so that the two roles cannot be simultaneously filled satisfactorily by one person.

The role expectations may conflict in at least three ways. The social system of which the woman is a part may provide no acceptable alternative for adequate child care. The woman's own internalized notions about the acceptable role of a mother and wife may not allow her to be away from husband and children. Third, the man who occupies the position of husband and father in the family system may hold role expectations that clash (role conflict to be discussed later) with the woman's wishes and generate conflicted interaction between these two primary elements of the family system.

Role incongruity, another construct in role theory, has been defined as a situation in which one's own perception of one's role is defined differently from the expectations of significant others in the system or the environment. The concept of the behavior expected of women who occupy the role of mother that has been held by our culture over the years has resulted in denying to women the resources of child care that would allow mothers to simultaneously occupy with some comfort the role of employee in occupational systems.

Another example of role incongruity is often found in the differing expectations for the behavior of the client system held by social worker and the client system, or conversely, the difference between the client's notion of the role of the worker and that held by the worker. There have been studies that show that there is often conflict between the client's expectations that the worker will tell them what to do and what actually happens in the interview which is directed by the social worker's notion of what is helpful. In correctional systems the worker may conceive of the role as that of "helper," while the client may conceive of it as one of surveillance and control (Perlman, 1961). There may be unrecognized but very painful and difficult problems when a social worker from one culture attempts to deal with role performances of an individual from another culture unless the worker understands the importance of role incongruity. The two cultures may hold very different and conflicting prescriptions about the attitudes and behavior that are appropriate to the role. For example:

> An Indian social work student was working with an Indian woman who desperately needed medical care but was too frightened to go to the clinic. In an attempt to act as a broker for her troubled client, the student went to talk to the doctor at the clinic. She felt very angry and upset because she felt that the doctor had been rude, suspicious, and rejecting. When she shared her perception with her field instructor, it was revealed that she came to this conclusion because of the fact that the doctor began immediately to question her about the client and continued to ask many very direct questions. This behavior was incongruent with her norms about the way strangers should behave with each other.

In this example the social worker (change agent), coming from a culturally defined role expectation as to the way strangers should interact, misinterpreted the meaning of the behavior of an element of an action system she was trying to construct for the client system. Incidentally, a very important principle here is that if the worker misinterpreted the doctor's behavior, how do you think the doctor would have related to the client's expectations?

Even the social scientists who originated the concept of role disagree on its definition and some of the basic constructs and propositions that surround it. However, since the authorities from which it is borrowed disagree, and since borrowed knowledge always needs to be reshaped to fit the function of the profession, this discussion on role will be pulled together with some notions of our own (Compton and Galaway) and some notions taken from the work of another social worker, Helen Harris Perlman (1961, 1962a).

Social roles are elements of all social systems and are generally assigned or achieved on the basis of the positions within the various social systems in which we all find ourselves. These expectations involve not only our overt behavior but what we are expected to be and feel like in interaction with what the other is expected to be, to act like, and to feel like (1961). In open systems there are two further principles that apply: (1) role prescriptions are very general and allow for certain changes in our behavior, and (2) changes in the way system elements fill their role (acting, feeling, and being) may result in significant system changes (see the discussion in Chapter 15 of the way the change agent may change the change agent system). Thus change in a system may be brought about by some change in the feeling, acting, or being of an element within the system, or by a change in the system's role behavior that affects the transactions of relating systems within larger social systems.

Perlman (1961, p. 375) writes as follows regarding the use of role in social work practice:

> We know it to be true of ourselves that, when we find ourselves in a social situation in which behavioral expectations (role) are not clear, we fumble in trial and error adaptation. When we are clear what the requirements are but find they run counter to our drives and needs, we feel conflicted. When our interpretation of requirements is different from the interpretation made by the person with whom we interact, both conflict and confusion may result. When requirements themselves are ill-defined or inadequately defined, we may feel and act in diffuse and inept ways.

To summarize, the following concepts from role theory are important to social workers:

1. Certain behaviors are prescribed (by us and by other elements of our social system) relative to our position within that system.
2. Every role involves both our own expectations and abilities and one or more others.
3. The notion of role expectation implies that there are certain social norms that set the outside limits for congruent, nonconflicted interactions, and transactions between positions within the system and between systems.
4. There are emotionally charged value judgments to how people carry out their roles both on the part of the person occupying the role position and others.
5. Social functioning may be seen as the sum of the roles performed by a human system (Boehm, 1959b, pp. 95–97).
6. The concept of role, role functioning, role expectations, and role transactions may be used to increase the knowledge base used for the assessment of the problem situation. Role failure and/or role conflict will tend to follow:
   a. The loss or absence of resources necessary to a system's ability to perform a role well.
   b. When systems are thrust into new roles without knowing the role expectations.
   c. When there is a conflict in role expectation on the part of interacting systems.
   d. When there is a conflict of role expectations within the cluster of roles carried by one system.
   e. When there is ambiguity on the part of other systems as to role expectations.
   f. When the individual as a system, or as a member of a social system, is deficient or handicapped in physical, intellectual, or social capacities demanded by the role.
   g. When high feeling or crisis situations suddenly and without warning disrupt previous effective role patterns (Perlman, 1961–62).

As an example, the Tucker article (see Reading 3–3) deals with the importance of a change agent understanding the roles of certain social systems in black culture and the effect of these notions on their functioning.

EGO PSYCHOLOGY AS FOUNDATION KNOWLEDGE

The most complete theory of human development is psychoanalytic theory as first developed by Sigmund Freud and further refined and expanded by countless disciples. There are several problems involved in any attempt to treat psychoanalytic theory briefly. First, there is the need to differentiate between the concept of human development found within psychoanalytic theory, the notion of how people get in trouble and how they change that is a part of this theory, and the method of treating human psychological disorders that was developed on the basis of this theory. Because of the complexity and volume of psychoanalytic theory, we will not try to present any coherent summary in this brief chapter. We suggest, instead, that students of social work may want to seek other sources of such understanding. The theory is introduced here only because it has been found that certain concepts from ego psychology, which rests on a psychoanalytic base about the development and functioning of the human personality, are extremely important to social work.

Psychoanalytic constructs

Psychoanalytic theory conceives of the human being as a dynamic energy system consisting of basic drives and instincts which in interaction with the environment serve to organize and develop the personality through a series of developmental stages. Individuals from birth are pushed by these largely unconscious and irrational drives toward satisfaction of desires which are largely unconscious and irrational. Because of the operation of an unconscious defense system and the structure of the mind, people go through life largely unaware of these irrational forces that have tremendous effect on their behavior and on the way they relate to others. The behavior that others observe, and our own knowledge of our behavior and our purposes, is actually a very incomplete view of what we are as individuals and what drives us. Most of the motivating forces of personality are thus beneath the surface and are available to our conscious and rational understanding and direction only through a careful exploration of these buried regions. Thus an individual's personality is seen primarily as an elaboration of the unconscious, irrational drives with which each of us are born and the early vicissitudes which lay down a foundation in early childhood. The personality system is viewed as primarily a semiclosed energy system which operates primarily to conserve energy by resisting stimulus and change. Because individuals are seen as being driven by these unconscious forces that tend primarily to struggle to maintain a homeostatic balance, real change in behavior after childhood can come only through an experience that is able to reach the deepest levels of one's personality. The environment and happenings in the world around us have an impact on us as individuals and on our behavior only through the meanings we assign such events as a result of our unconscious needs and defenses.

Freud held that the personality was structured into three divisions: "The id comprises the psychic representatives of the drives, the ego consists of those functions which have to do with the individual's relation to his environment, and the superego comprises the moral precepts of our minds as well as our ideal aspirations" (as related in Brenner, 1955, p. 45). The ego is expected to act as the executive officer of the personality dealing with impulses from the id and with moral signals of the superego as well as with the realities of the environment.

Over the years various individuals working with the concepts of psychoanalytic theory and observing human behavior began to focus primarily on the development of the rational, conscious processes in personality. They are given the name of ego psychologists, because, coming from a base in psychoanalytic theory, they have differed in that they have given the central place in human functioning not to the irrational and instinctual forces of the id but to the rational processes of the ego. They hold that the individual comes into this world with rational as well as irrational instincts and that the personality develops and becomes differentiated in relation to the environmental interactions, concerns, goals, and unconsicous needs rather than being almost entirely an elaboration of inner instinctual drives.

Ego psychology constructs

Eric Erikson, one of the earliest ego psychologists, held that, although early experience was significant, the personality system all through life was open to meaningful interaction with both the inner and outer life experiences. Throughout life, new tasks and new biopsychosocial demands bring human beings new opportunities for growth and change. However, the manner in which these opportunities are used will be reflective of the individual's success and failure in dealing with early life tasks (Hartman, 1970).

Ego psychologists began to challenge the earlier psychoanalytic view of the conservation of energy and the notion of a semiclosed system. They argued for the construct of an open personality system as they believed there was empirical evidence that human beings were born with an ego need to seek both difference and stimulus from the environment. Thus in ego psychology, personality development is seen as the result of interaction with the environment that is actively sought by the individual. Another earlier concept that was challenged was the notion of the personality's push toward static homeostasis. This concept was replaced by the notion that while the personality needs certain stability, people also seek and must have for appropriate growth and development new experiences and new transactions from the environment.

Competence and mastery.   Robert White's works (1960, 1963) further developed the notion that individuals are motivated from childhood on to interact actively with the environment not merely as a result of drives such as hunger, thirst or sex but because of a need to explore the world and to import new experiences and stimuli into the system. White has called this motive "effectance" by which he means a kind of general push from the ego to master the environment. When individuals master a new experience in line with their standards and with the approval of the real world (called competence by White), they are motivated to try new and more complex tasks. White called this motivational force a push toward mastery. This notion is discussed further by Trader in her article on the theories that form the base of effective work with minorities (see Reading 2–3).

White holds that as a result of experiences of competency, individuals grow to feel a sense of mastery—a belief that one can change one's environment by obtaining knowledge of how to change it and by the use of effective skills that one has developed. These concepts have tremendous significance for social workers in that they support the notion that, given a relatively benign environment, individuals actively seek control of their lives and welcome new experiences. Resistance toward change and apathy are seen as states resulting from environmental lacks and hurtful interactions and transactions over time. Thus the forces of growth and change are seen as stronger than the resistance to change provided the individual's transactions with the environment and other systems have provided experiences of effectance and mastery leading to a sense of competence.

In ego psychology the ego is seen to be that part of the personality that takes action in life situations—it is the executive officer of the personality. In the process of coping the ego develops both protective-defensive operations and seeking-discovering-learning operations. "The main categories of ego functions are its clusters of cognitive, affective, motoric, executive, and intergrative operations" (Perlman, 1975, p. 214). Cognitive functions are the thought processes that consist of facts, notions, concepts, memories, and beliefs and the way this material is acquired, stored, retrieved, organized, and reorganized. The affective functions of the ego have to do with our feeling processes: anger, guilt, hate, love, caring, and excitement. The executive function of the ego involves decision-making and action. Decision-making rests on the ability to integrate thinking, feeling, and a sense of mastery and on the possession of action skills with which to carry through with some satisfaction on the decisions.

All these functions of the ego are interrelated and each affects the other. Feeling affects thought; thought affects feeling. Action can bring significant change in both thinking and feeling. The feedback that a system receives from the environment as to its actions affects both thinking and feeling and future actions. Since this is true, it is equally true that individuals can intervene to change the functioning of any system by approaching anyone of the three functions. Thus we may begin work with either thinking, feeling, or action. Where we will begin depends on how we assess the client system, the problem, the goal, and the situation and on what the client wants. It is important to the selection of helping actions to remember that coping skills of the individual can be increased by starting with whichever function seems appropriate and our activity will affect all functions.

Motivation.   From these concepts of ego, competence, and mastery, there has developed some important work on motivation. A feeling of mastery, or control over one's internal reactions and relevant external events, appears to be a significant force in motivating human behavior (Liberman, 1978, p. 35). A number of laboratory investigations in the area of the importance of control is summarized by Lefcourt (1966, p. 188) as follows: "When individuals are involved in situations where personal competence can effect . . . outcomes, they tend to perform more actively and adequately than when . . . situations appear less controllable." Thus "insofar as individuals believe that their actions and inactions affect their well-being, the achievement of a sense of mastery becomes a major goal throughout their lives" (Liberman, 1978, p. 36). Liberman further points out that for an individual to acquire a sense of mastery, there must be a framework that links a person's performance to self-esteem. The link between performance and self-esteem is governed, among other things, by the person's background and current situation, task relevance, task difficulty, attribution of performance, and the attitudes of significant others.

The University of Chicago faculty developed a proposition (based on ego psychology and the work of Helen Perlman and Charlotte Towle) that the individual's use of social work services rests on some combination of motivation, capacity and opportunity. Lilian Ripple's attempt (1964) to test this formulation led to a further development of the concept of motivation by the Chicago faculty partly through integrating the work of Thomas French (1952). These notions may be summarized as follows: First, motivation is defined as what one wants and how much it is wanted. In other words, people will not move toward change unless that change is in line with their goals and purposes and there is a significant desire for the goal. Second, the two basic and necessary forces of motivation are the push of discomfort and the pull of hope. People do not have the courage and purposiveness necessary in goal-directed activities without a balance between these factors.

In order to move in a goal-directed way we need a certain amount of discomfort because we have to dislike where we are in order to see a reason for change, and a certain amount of focused discomfort about where we are helps us to withstand certain pressures to scatter our efforts rather than to focus and control them. There are two kinds of discomfort: (1) generalized and (2) focused. In order to move toward change, discomfort must be focused on the thing to be changed. A more generalized discomfort that relates to the whole of our life situation results in disintegration of goal-directed efforts and must be focused before effective planning can be done.

The pull toward goal-directed effort is provided by hope. Hope increases the amount of pressure that can be withstood before the disintegration of goal-directed efforts begin. When one is hopeful that one can effectively move toward what one wants, one becomes willing to forego other satisfactions and withstand other pressures from other needs and wants in order to realize the greater goal or want.

Based on the work of Perlman, Towle, French, and White and our own experience, we believe a sense of hope is based on (1) a sense of trust that there is some relationship between one's needs and the intentions of the world around one; (2) a sense that one has meaning for others—one's actions are important; (3) a sense of who one is; (4) a sense of competence built on evaluation of past efforts (past successes as one evaluates them); (5) perception of the opportunities in the environment around one; (6) one's experience with frustration in the past; (7) a generalized sense of mastery; and (8) relationship between one's perception of one's competence and one's perception of the skills needed to reach the goal.

Thus one's capacity to use the want and discomfort of motivation to change in a goal-directed way depends first upon hope and second upon how much one knows of how to achieve a purpose. This includes the ability to see the totality of the situation including the results of choices made in the process, the time factors, and the possible obstacles, reassurance from the real world, experiences with the real world including the pleasure in functional activity, substitute gratifications, and appropriate evaluation of achievement of subgoals or small steps.

In discussing motivation it is important to mention frustration. It is possible to avoid frustration by avoiding a commitment to a goal. Severe and repeated frustration will move an individual in this direction. Frustration is the realization that the goal to which one is committed is unattainable. The intensity of frustration is proportional to the degree of previous commitment to the purpose being thwarted. If goal-directed striving is frustrated after a particular quantum of pressure is committed to it, perhaps it is possible to find substitute goals so that the pressure can be rechanneled. If substitute goals are not found, it is possible that the pressure and desire may be discharged in destructive form and rage. If one has been pursuing a goal with confidence, and then it becomes unattainable, hope is destroyed and an overt rage reaction is produced. The experience of frustration over time is destructive of an individual's sense of competence and mastery. Frustration ends with the disintegration of goal-directed striving. The end phase of loss of hope is apathy.

Ripple's research (1964) attempted to assess the importance of the three constructs for the client's effective use of social work services: motivation, capacity, and opportunity. Her findings were that the client's level of hope plus the opportunities available were the critical factors in use of services. In spite of a belief that the personality functioning of the client and the type of problem is important, these factors did not appear to have a critical impact on the use of help. As a result of her research, Ripple recommended that in the initial explorations of the client's problem the worker make a careful assessment of the hope-discomfort balance. Ripple further recommended that workers should be concerned with the impact of their activities on this critical balance during the beginning stages of client-worker interaction.

SIGNIFICANT CONTRIBUTIONS OF EGO PSYCHOLOGY TO SOCIAL WORK KNOWLEDGE

1. The concept of the ego as having its own needs and drives and as being autonomous coupled with the belief in the human personality as emergent and developing over a life cycle gives importance to helping efforts directed to present life experiences.
2. The concept of the personality as an open system gives great weight to the importance of the day-by-day input from transactions with the environment. It joins with systems theory to support the importance of the active involvement of client system with a benign environment.
3. The construct of the individual's need for competence and mastery offers social work an optimistic view of the possibilities of human growth and change while it also demands that social workers be constantly concerned with input from networks of other social systems and environment.
4. Concepts from ego psychology focus on individuals as active, conscious participants in their own destiny rather than viewing individuals as reactors to stimuli or needs beyond their control. This leads to the concept of the relationship between the worker and the client system as a partnership.
5. The constructs of competence and mastery from ego psychology support the view of human beings as seeking active experiences and control of their

own destiny. This gives guidance in assessment and also demands that client systems be active participants in planning and change and supports social work values of self-determination and respect for the individual.

6. The notion that motivation is what the client system wants and how much it wants it joins with the concept of goal in systems theory to remind social workers of the importance of both client system goals and the value of self-determination.

7. The importance of hope as a stimulus for active problem-solving gives social workers a totally new view of the meaning of apathy and challenges many of the other concepts of what produces dependency.

CONCEPTS OF DIVERSITY AND DIFFERENCE

The last important piece of knowledge to be discussed in this chapter is the importance of social work's understanding of diversity and difference. Both systems theory and ego psychology point to the importance of diversity in the ongoing development of human systems. Without the stimulation of difference, human systems would not develop. However, the notion of patterned expectations, and the feelings and values attached to them from role theory, the construct of "steady state" from systems theory, and the formulation of homeostasis from psychoanalytic theory all posit a certain resistance to change, diversity, and difference.

Human systems need stability, the security of knowing that, at least in some dimensions of human life, their expectations of the behavior of others and transactions with others will be fulfilled and that the meanings they attach to that behavior will be accurate. This allows systems to shape and control their own actions through being able to predict both (1) the reactions of others to a contemplated action, and (2) what they may expect from others in the ordinary course of their transactions. The question for professionals working with human systems is the question of the balance between diversity and change, stability, and our purpose as a change agent. A strategy for change, particularly when we are concerned with an institution as the target system, is to induce crisis which deprives the elements of the system, and the system itself, of reference points in role behavior and will result in system change. "However, we need to remember that crisis resolution can go either way—toward the development of new adaptive modes or toward regression and defense through the closure of the system and the rigidifying of the structure" (Hartman, 1970).

A part of this need for stability of behaviors and meanings if workers are to make any predictive judgments about behavior and transactions with others results from the intolerance of difference on the part of human systems and their elements and part from the definition of "normal" behavior. As stated earlier, role expectations become internalized as value systems, thus there is a tendency of human systems to view difference in role behaviors as right or wrong rather than considering whether or not they are essential (given social work's present knowledge base from which to make judgments) to the existence and ongoing development of the system. This tends to be particularly true of the family system, so some examples from the operation of that system will be used to illustrate this point. But first, it must be recognized that the importance of the family system stems from the fact that society cannot exist without some form of reproduction of the elements of society (children) and their protection and socialization.

There is considerable evidence that children need certain protections which are usually furnished within the family system. However, family systems in different cultures will have different notions as to what member of the family system performs this role and what behaviors are necessary to such safeguarding of children. In white middle-class America this role is usually assigned to the position of mother, but it could be assigned just as effectively to an aunt, grandmother, uncle, father, or even to another system outside the family such as a nursery. The tendency, however, for human systems that assign this behavior to the role of mother is for members of that system to view the assignment of such tasks to any other position in the system, or particularly outside the system, as wrong, or abnormal, and needing change. In fact, in contemporary society, the grandmother, uncle, or another member of the extended family may be considered as properly belonging within another system. It is extremely important for social workers not to mix up their own internalized value expectations of role performance with their knowledge of what are the basic needs of human systems and what systems transactions are truly damaging to humanity.

The definitions of pathology and health seem to have developed solely from the expectations of the dominant groups in society as to role behaviors and the feelings and meanings attached to these behaviors. While it may be necessary to recognize that there is such a thing as health and well-being, definitions are also needed for pathology and health that are based on knowledge of the minimum required needs of individuals and systems and of the maximum allowable transactional behavior. It is also necessary to include a range of behaviors and feelings that allows for difference in the performance of necessary systems roles, particularly when that difference itself may stem from different cultural notions of expected role performance and different interpretations of the meanings of such performance. It is necessary to question the concepts of normality and pathology in relation to knowledge of what constitutes damaging deprivations and transactions and not measure them against the expected role patterns of the dominant society. It is also necessary to recognize that problems in system functioning often stem from a conflict in role expectations, which then leads to failure and conflict in role performance. Thus, social workers must become sensitive to the damage done minority groups, or other groups who live differently, when they are constantly confronted with role expectations through their necessary transactions with systems of the dominant groups in society that conflict with their own notions of expected role performance.

It is important that social workers have a broad knowledge of how cultures develop, of how opportunities and deprivation over time shape the culture of a people, and of how a given culture becomes a part of the human systems that transact with it. The Tucker paper reproduced in this chapter suggests some of the important considerations for workers concerned with the black experience (see Reading 3–3). The notions developed in the paper are important in attempting to assess the experience of any oppressed people.

RECAPITULATION

In this chapter some theoretical constructs have been presented which are identified as being valuable as a base for social work practice. Several selected concepts have also been presented about individual functioning as found in ego psychology and about social interactions as found in role theory. In addition, the systems theory has been proposed as a foundation that gives both theoretical perspective and empirical tools to work within or among all sizes of social systems from the individual to society and its institutions.

However, it is recognized that this is only a very brief look at the knowledge of human beings and their social systems that social workers need if they are to assess the needs of human systems and propose effective actions which will bridge the transactions within, between, and among such systems. The knowledge of the development of the individual, of the human family, of the development of various social groups, of group process, of organizational behavior, and of the sociological and anthropological base for understanding human systems are not included. These subjects should be found in the courses on human growth and social environment and cannot rightly be the subject of a beginning book on social work processes.

A LOOK FORWARD

Readers are urged to spend some time with the articles reproduced in this chapter. Each contributes further to the development of the knowledge outlined in this chapter. Two articles deal with systems theory; the other with knowledge needed to work across boundaries of systems different from that of the majority culture. While the Tucker article relates to black social systems, the basic concepts are applicable to working with any system across barriers of cultural difference.

The next chapter shall leave the knowledge base of social work practice and discuss the value base of the profession.

Reading
3-1   *Social work and system theory**†

Anthony Fordor

Social workers today are having to understand and use a range of social work methods instead of just one or two. Faced with the task of finding a model that will help them to do this, they are increasingly considering the possible contribution of general system theory. Both Goldstein (1973) and Pincus and Minahan (1973), whose works are recommended by the National Institute for

Social Work, make some use of system theory in their exposition of a unitary model. Anne Vickery (1974) has recently suggested ways in which it is relevant to the practice of casework. It is important for social workers to consider whether it is worth their while to master the theory and its jargon themselves, and for social work teachers to decide whether to subject students to it. This is particularly important when the theory is at such a high level of generality.

Faced with the complexity of a new approach like general system theory, there are

* British Journal of Social Work 6 (Spring 1976), pp. 13–42

† This reading retains British spellings.

a number of temptations that afflict writers and teachers in trying to fit their own theories into a new model. The first is to look at the new model quickly, decide that one's own theory is not essentially different or at least not incompatible, and carry on with a few oblique references that make one look more up-to-date. This is what Hollis (1970) appears to be doing when she describes the psychosocial method as a systems approach. She gives no further explanation of this claim although she knows well that the psychosocial approach developed quite independently of system theory.

A second temptation is to absorb the new jargon into one's theoretical presentation by renaming concepts, thus losing intelligibility without gaining precision. This was the impression left on the author by an article by Janchill (1969). This listed characteristics of systems taken from the general theory and related them to social work theory. It failed to put them into the context of the theory itself.

A third temptation is to take an eclectic approach, selecting aspects of the new theory and incorporating them into the old, but without fully relating the two models. This is what Goldstein (1973) appears to have done. Much of the material in his book, particularly in the early chapters, is not related to the system theory used elsewhere. This is more legitimate than the two previous approaches, but it is likely to be confusing to readers, both initially and subsequently as they try to follow it up with further reading.

It is my purpose in this article to give a brief explanation of general system theory and then to discuss its value for social work theory and practice in four areas. The first is its contribution at the philosophical level, the view it presents of humans and of society; the second, its contribution to social work perspective in making social workers aware of the range of systems they should be considering; the third, its contribution to practice in providing a model of the structure of systems which will indicate how to intervene; and the fourth, its contribution to understanding social work process.

General system theory

General system theory has been developed as a result of the needs of a number of different disciplines from engineering to sociology to find a way of analysing complex situations of interaction, in which, in common terms, "the whole is more than the sum of the parts"[1] The traditional physical sciences deal with "closed systems," which from the point of view of system theory are only one particular class of systems at one end of a continuum. In the typical experiment in the physical sciences, at least until recent years, the aim of the experimenter has been to exclude from the experiment as many variables as possible, and to concentrate on the interaction of a limited number of factors, ideally perhaps two. Subsequently additional variables may be added. The final interaction of these factors is represented by the sum of the individual effects. For example, Newtonian physics begins with a formula for the interaction of two bodies in isolation, and then considers the effect of additional factors, such as the presence of other bodies, atmospheric friction, and so on. The final behaviour of the bodies is the result of the combination of all these forces. This approach is called "reductionist," because its essence is the reduction of a situation to its constituent elements before adding them up. It assumes a deterministic causality in which the future and the past condition of an object can be deduced from knowledge of its present condition.

Biologists, psychologists, and social scientists have generally followed this pattern in developing their own theories and assumed that the difficulties presented to

---

[1] For further accounts see Von Bertalanffy (1971) *General System Theory*, and Buckley (1971). Von Bertalanffy, a biologist occupying an intermediate position between the physical and social sciences, has been an important figure in developing the theory.

them were due only to the complexity of the situations they were considering and their limited tools for analysis. But system theorists regard the model itself as inadequate. The closed system of the physical sciences are seen as one end of a continuum of increasing complexity in which there is still order.[2] Among the higher systems new characteristics emerge of dominating importance.

First, such systems are open, that is to say they maintain themselves by a constant flow of material in and out. A flame is a simple example of an open system. Its continuity is maintained by the input of fuel and oxygen and the output of heat, light, and the oxidized elements of the fuel.

Second, open systems may be goal directed. At its simplest the goal may be merely the maintenance of homeostasis within rigidly defined limits through devices such as thermostats. For more advanced systems homeostasis may be replaced by the concept of "the steady state."[3] In the steady state input and output are related in a way that not only maintains the system and adapts it to changes in the environment but allows work to be done and growth to take place. So as an embryo develops towards adult status, at any one time it is in a steady state that is itself in the process of change.

The steady state is not a condition of equilibrium, but a condition short of equilibrium, in which some degree of tension is a permanent feature. In an ecological system competing systems stand ready to expand their numbers as environmental conditions make this possible. In some animals given a situation in which all other needs are met, a condition of stress arises from lack of stimulation. In human beings, as one set of goals is reached new goals are specified, so that inner tension is maintained. Hence the continuation beyond childhood of such activities as play, exploration, and creation.

When systems are goal directed, the same goal may be achieved from different initial conditions. This characteristic is known as equifinality. An adult may develop from a single ovum, from a divided ovum as with identical twins, or from two fused ova. The marsupials of the Australian continent have developed a range of forms and ways of life very similar to the mammals of other continents from very different origins. Equally the same final condition may be reached by different routes. Physical maturity in animals and emotional maturity in humans may be achieved through different patterns of experience. Early deprivation, for example, gives no certainty of deformation in the adult. So it is impossible merely from knowledge of the final condition to deduce what happened earlier, nor to forecast the future from knowledge of the present.

Open, goal-directed systems may show a tendency towards increasing elaboration of organization. In the closed system of physical science, the tendency is towards an equilibrium of maximum entropy—entropy being defined as a measure of disorder. But living systems show "negative entropy"— they import into themselves not just enough to maintain themselves, but enough to enable them to grow and develop. The elaboration of the system involves increasing differentiation in its parts. This differentiation is not necessarily based on initial difference in the parts but on the needs of the system. So cells that are initially undifferentiated in the embryo give rise to cells that form different parts of the body. Similarly the same people will often change their behaviour in

---

[2] It is the combination of complexity and order that is significant. Physics is also concerned with systems of "chaotic complexity" like a cloud of gas. For a table giving a summary picture of the systems' continuum and the theories related at each stage see Von Bertalanffy 1971, pp. 26–27.

[3] The term *steady state* is derived from physics where it describes an essentially homeostatic condition which is reached after the initial changes have worked themselves out, for example, a thermostatic system that begins to operate in a steady state after the initial increase in temperature to the minimum limit of the thermostat. My explanation is based on Von Bertalanffy (1971, pp. 132–133). In some ways the term does not seem appropriate to the dynamic picture given by system theory, and Buckley (1971) manages to avoid the term.

quite striking ways when they are given new roles in an organization, for example through promotion, in order to fit in with the expectations of others in the system.

An essential prerequisite of goal-directed behaviour is some means of gaining information about changes in the condition of the system and its environment, and the capacity to modify behaviour in response. So for goal-directed systems, information replaces energy as the stimulus to activity and the link between parts. Information theory is concerned with this.[4] Given a wide range of information being transmitted from a changeable environment, the system needs some method of selecting and mapping the information that can be related to its behaviour. The more variable the environment, the greater the variety of patterns of behaviour that will be required for effective adaptation—that is, there is a need for "a pool of variety" within the system that can be called on as need arises to match the extent of variety in the environment.

In the extreme complexity of modern urban society, there is need for a very large pool of variety in terms of behavioural patterns. Some of these patterns may be defined as illegitimate or deviant and yet have value for the survival of particular groups and potential value for society as a whole in the event of a major change in the environment. For example "terrorist" activity is normally defined as deviant by the dominant groups in a state but may have importance for the survival of a minority group. The same activities may receive social sanction when a war allows them to be directed against a national enemy. The existence of this pool of variety itself complicates the environment of the subsystems of society and in turn increases the need of these subsystems for flexibility and responsiveness.[5]

---

[4] *Information* is in this theory interpreted broadly in a way in which it ultimately becomes synonymous with a measure of organization. Buckley (1971, pp. 82–89).

[5] It is worth noting recent concern with maintaining the pool of available variety through both

A central tenet of general system theory is that all systems but the largest are themselves subsystems of other systems and all systems but the smallest are environments for other systems. Thus to take part of the middle ground of the systems continuum, human beings, who are themselves composed of cells, organs, and members, are subsystems of families, small groups, organizations, communities, and states. Moreover the boundaries of open systems cannot be clearly defined. In considering a candle flame it is an arbitrary decision whether to include or exclude in the definition of the system the wick, the candle, and the surrounding atmosphere which both feeds the flame and receives its output. The same is equally true of human systems, as social workers are well aware. Even individual human beings, whose physical existence is contained within clear bounds, present problems of definition as soon as feelings are taken into account. For example, how can you disentangle what feelings belong to whom, when each child in turn in a family takes on the sick or delinquent role to accommodate the projections of the parents?

Philosophical implications

System theory, though starting from a mechanical model, is concerned with differences between more complex and simpler systems as well as with similarities between them. As a result it can provide a much less mean picture of people and society than is currently provided by most psychological and sociological theories.

Turning first to psychology, most psychological theorists treat human beings as superior robots, responding to environmental stimuli (Von Bertalanffy, 1971, pp. 217–218). This is most obvious in behavioural theory, which treats humans as though they were rats, not live rats, but ones that have been robbed of all their natural individuality by

---

the conservation of endangered biological species and, to a lesser extent perhaps, with the languages and ways of small tribal and national groups.

statistical averaging.[6] The reductionist approach of behaviourism can be seen in the early work of Eysenck (1953, p. 10) who, while recognizing that the personality might be more than the sum of individual traits, believes that the latter is all that can be validly known. Freudian theory is less reductionist in its approach, concentrating attention on the interaction of parts of the personality, and showing awareness of the importance of interpersonal interaction. It is in this sense that Hollis can claim that the psychosocial method of social work, which relies so heavily on Freudian theory, is a systems approach. Yet, for Freud, personality is no more than the product of external pressures on a primitive and devouring id, seeking gratification in a state of equilibrium or homoeostasis. Creativity and other aesthetic and altruistic aims are only sublimations of these basic primitive urges in the interests of psychic comfort.

A few psychologists, such as Rank, Rogers, and Maslow, have given more place to will and purpose, but only Rank has had a direct influence on social work theory through the functional school (Smalley, 1970). Here the concept of choice has been important but has been narrowed by a view of the environment including the social work agency itself, which at times seems to exclude intervention to change the environment.

In contrast to "robot" psychology, system theory is concerned with behaviour which may be directed towards growth and development and not just the achievement of equilibrium. This does not necessarily require the admission of freewill and conscious purpose within a system. Clearly the development of an ecological system does not imply that the living subsystems that compose it have the ability, either separately or together, to choose the course they

will take. Yet, given a self-conscious being like a person, capable of handling symbolic concepts, there is no reason in system theory why the goals should not be conscious and choice should not be a reality. Most system theorists accept that this is the case (Von Bertalanffy, 1971, pp. 45 and 230). So Maslow's concept (1954, chap. 11) of the self-actualizing person is consistent with system theory in a way that it is not with Freudian psychology or behaviourism.

In practice, of course, social workers have intuitively rejected the deterministic implications of psychological theories. They have recognized the existence of will, choice, and purpose as important influences on the outcome of behaviour. They have talked of "self-determination" even as they have used a Freudian interpretation of behaviour. Nevertheless the conflict between a determinist psychology and an intuitive belief in free will has often been a real problem for students.

In so far as social workers have in any case rejected a robot view of human nature, system theory adds nothing very new. But it does provide a scientific theory that is compatible with free will and therefore helps to give intellectual respectability to important values in social work.

Turning to sociology, much theory has again been based on an equilibrium model. This has been particularly true of the structural-functional theories associated with Parsons. These have been criticized as providing a spurious justification for the maintenance of the *status quo* (Buckley, 1971, pp. 23–31; Von Bertalanffy, 1971, pp. 207–208).

While sociology has been much less influential than psychology on social work practice, the consensus view of society supported by functional theory has probably given support to the natural bias of a casework approach towards conservatism in social organization. The only real alternative to this model is a conflict theory deriving from Marxism, which is in many ways antipathetic to social work ideals.

---

[6] My colleague John Mayhew has described to me vividly the individuality of rats in the test situation, which one would never guess from the description of experiments.

System theory by abandoning an equilibrium model leaves open the possibility of a much wider range of developments. It is true that it has sometimes been regarded by sociologists as providing support for the consensus view of society and rejected by them on that account. Some writers on system theory lend support to that view even using Parsonian theory in their examples. However, there is plenty of room within the theory for the inclusion of conflict, and for conflict to be seen as having a positive role. For example, in ecological systems conflict has a most important place, and mathematical formulae have been developed to provide a basis for prediction in this area (Von Bertalanffy, 1971, pp. 63–66). System theory accepts that subsystems within a system may have different objectives from one another and from the system as a whole, which may only partially cohere and thus make conflict possible. Such conflicting objectives have their part to play in the "pool of variety," which is regarded in system theory as one of the conditions for survival in an unpredictably changing environment.

Of theories at a less than societal level both exchange theory and role theory in their different ways present a very limited view of human nature if carried to extremes. Berger (1966), for instance, seeing roles as central to personality, considers that "the self is . . . a process, continuously created and recreated in each social situation that one enters, held together by the slender thread of memory" (Ruddock, 1969, p. 24). Similarly in exchange theory, symbolic goals can be regarded as no more than an extension of personal gratification in a social interaction governed by economic motives (Buckley, 1971, p. 112). System theory can integrate these theoretical approaches while providing some protection against such extreme interpretations. In using role theory to understand the interaction of people within a larger system, it accepts that for the person the adoption of a role may be a way of adapting to the environment within a more consistent pattern of goal-directed behaviour. Turner's concepts of role-making and

taking (as discussed in Buckley, 1971, pp. 146–149), which give a more positive role to the person in structuring his situation than Berger does, are more consistent with system theory. Similarly exchange theory provides a useful way of describing interpersonal transactions within systems, but if the transactions are seen as promoting growth rather than merely maintaining equilibrium, ideals can be seen as having a genuine motivating force. They need not be just rationalizations. In this way system theory provides a model that is at once less limited, and, one hopes, more realistic.

The systems perspective

One of the most obvious ways of using system theory in social-work practice is to draw attention to the multiplicity of systems at different levels of complexity that influence any particular situation. This, in turn, makes possible a review of a wider range of possible targets for intervention—referred to as "target systems." Goldstein (1973, pp. 108–119) provides an example in which an adolescent is involved in drug-taking. The situation is outlined with the aid of a diagram in a way which makes possible a choice of action between individual and family casework, small group action, influencing the school, getting a community group involved, and changing the program of the social worker's own agency—"the change agent system" as it is called.

Diagrams similar to Goldstein's are used by Hunt, Harrison, and Armstrong (1974, pp. 405–424) in an article on group dynamics in social work education. This shows the value of the systems perspective in the analysis of the relationship between social workers and their clients and also of the educational institution within which the social worker is being trained. Anne Vickery (1974, note 22), whose article appears in the same issue of *The British Journal of Social Work*, chooses an example too complex for diagrammatic presentation. Instead she lists more than 16 systems that might be potential targets for intervention.

It is hoped of course that the presentation of a wider range of potential target systems will make it easier for the social worker to select the most appropriate social work method to use in effecting change. However, as Baker (1975, pp. 205–209) points out, little guidance on this point has yet been provided by studies of social work.

In addition to the change agent system and target system, Goldstein also points out that the development of the social worker-client relationship involves the creation of a new system which he calls the "change system" (1973, pp. 120–153). Pincus and Minahan (1973, pp. 61–63) further refine the model by talking about "the action system." This includes all those who are actively working together to create change. This will normally, of course, include the social worker and a member or members of the client system. But it will frequently include members of other systems, too.

In family casework the action system will often be limited to the social worker and one or both parents. In community work it will typically be a committee. In residential work it might be a committee of staff and resident representatives, but it might include all the staff and residents.

The appraisal of systems

While the contribution of system theory to philosophical/scientific understanding and to social work perspective are useful,

the crucial issue is its applicability to the practice situation. Does it provide a model of the working of systems which gives guidance about where and how intervention should take place? Only if it does, will teachers feel justified in giving the time necessary to grasp system theory concepts, and to pass them on.

Anne Vickery (1974, p. 398) puts forward a diagram to illustrate the model (Diagram 1). This diagram has some serious limitations. First, goals and objectives have no place in it, although Anne Vickery's case analysis brings out the importance of these. Secondly, in the diagram the central feature is the box labelled "transformation." This feature is difficult to locate in either space or time. Is it an activity taking place in the client system alone or in both the client system and the envronment simultaneously? While "output" and "feedback" presumably follow input, it is not clear at all how feedback relates to output. There are answers to these questions, but the diagram does not reveal them.

A third problem is much more serious. Neither the diagram nor Anne Vickery's exposition of it allow any place for issues of power. This is a crucial element in community work and important, though often neglected, in other methods of social work. Its neglect is one of the major criticisms of social work, particularly from sociologists.

An alternative diagrammatic presentation is put forward by Buckley (1971, p.

Diagram 1

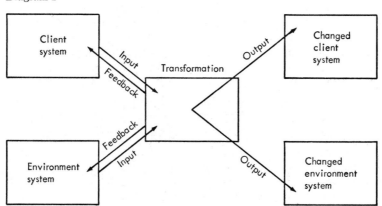

Diagram 2

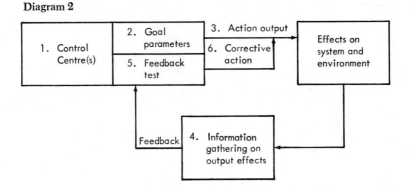

173) in Diagram 2. A control centre or centres (1) determine certain goal parameters (2) and the means to achieve them on the basis of information already gathered about its own internal situation and its environment both of which may be in the process of change. These decisions are translated into an action output (3) which results in certain effects on the system and its environment. Information about these effects (4) is gathered and fed back into the control centre where it is sifted, mapped, and interpreted (5). If the error leaves the system outside the goal parameters, corrective output action (6) is put into operation by the control system (or the goal parameters revised).

This very simplified model can be applied to any system including of course a social work agency, a client system, or a system created by the interaction of client and social worker. It is a model of a problem-solving process.

However, this diagram has two major limitations. First, it is confined to the transmission of information and ignores the physical resources that are available to the system internally and externally. Second, while it indicates that there may be more than one control centre, it does not demonstrate any of the implications of this. Diagram 3 is a refinement of Buckley's and is more explicit on both these counts. It shows that one of the effects of the action output of the system is to change the resource input into the

system and so affect the resources available to it. Internally the two ovals represent subsystems and the overlap indicates that there is only a partial sharing of resources, information, control, and goals of each. The different sizes of the ovals indicate differences of power in the subsystems. Although visually restricted to a dyad to simplify presentation, it is equally relevant to larger systems.

Before carrying on the argument further, it is necessary to say something more about the box labelled "information." Obviously it contains "information" about the system and its environment received through the senses. But this information has to be interpreted within a framework that gives it meaning. A smile for example only has meaning because we can relate the curve of the lips that we see to a sort of dictionary developed from past experience which indicates that this shape according to its context means happiness, or amusement, or disdain, or perhaps "I recognize you and am pleased to see you." This "dictionary," which is usually referred to as a "map," contains a series of propositions. Some of these are concerned with what is right or wrong, others with what is true or false. The former can be regarded as values, the latter as knowledge.[7]

The use of the model for analysing systems with a view to intervention can now be

---

[7] This is a simplification of a complex issue. See Gordon (1962).

Diagram 3   Goal-oriented behavior

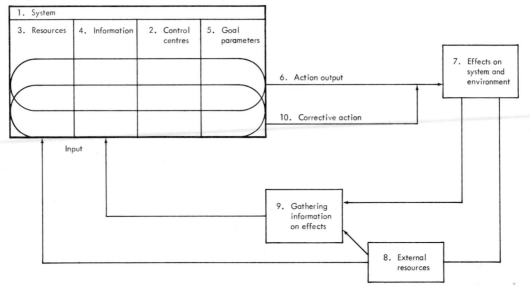

System (1) with certain control centres (2), on the basis of its current resources (3) and information (4) about its own condition and that of its environment determines certain goal parameters (5), and the means to achieve these goals. The resultant action output (6) has certain effects (7) on the system and its environment. Information is gathered on these effects (8). One of the effects may be a change in the resource input (9) into the system. The system selects and evaluates the information. If the action leaves it outside its goal parameters, it will institute corrective action (10) or revise its goals. Within the system different sizes of the ovals associated with the different decision-making centres is intended to reflect differences in power.

examined. The fact that a problem has been brought to a social worker generally indicates that the action output of a system has left it outside its goal parameters (or sometimes outside the parameters set by others). A steady state could be achieved by either a change in the goals, or a change in the action output. The model suggests that the latter can be changed either directly, by for instance an improvement in skills, or as a result of changes in the feedback process, in the knowledge map, or in the resource input. But the model also suggests the possible value of changes in the relations between the constituent subsystems. There may be a need for a more effective use of internal resources, possibly by changes in task allocation. Internal communication may need to be improved. The coherence of goals may have to be examined (with an implication that if coherence is not possible it may be in the interests of some that the system should break up). Above all consideration may have to be given to the relative influence of differ-

ent subsystems on the control of the system, in other words questions of power.

This analysis leads to the following list of areas in a system that may be the subject of intervention:

a. Internal use of resources (including skills) and task allocation.

b. The information "map" (including values and knowledge).

c. Internal communication.

d. The allocation of power.

e. The goal parameters.

f. The action output.

g. The improvement of information gathering with regard to the system itself and its environment.

h. The resource input (including the learning of new skills).

It may be helpful for purposes of comparison to reanalyse a case example presented by Anne Vickery.

The client is a 40-year-old bachelor, Mr. A., living alone in the suburban terrace house where he was born. His parents have been dead for 10 years. He is referred by the local housing department to the social services department. In order to make way for a large housing scheme his house is due for demolition. Mr. A. is refusing to cooperate with plans for his rehousing in council property. He will not open the door to housing department officals and has for some time exchanged acrimonious correspondence with the department. The worker offering help to Mr. A. discovers that he has worked for 20 years as a messenger and that he has very little verbal communication with anyone. He was an only child and his elderly parents used him as an almost constant companion. They discouraged him from forming outside relationships even while at school. His house is in ill-repair and very dusty inside. Mr. A. is thin, and he looks tired and undernourished. He is sleeping badly and complains of being miserable and anxious because of threats from the housing department and also because of seemingly sinister things done to him by neighbours' children playing outside his house.

In this example three potential target systems were presented: Mr. A., the housing department, and the potential system created by the interaction between these two. In addition new action systems could be created by the social worker's relationship with one or all of these systems.

In considering Mr. A., Vickery's model focuses on such items as his output of anxiety and depression, and his fear of the output of the housing department (is this an input for him?). The new model, however, begins from his goals and values which Vickery does not mention. What is the meaning of the house for him in terms of his goals? Are his anxiety and depression related to specific external threats to the goals and values enshrined in his way of life, or do they reflect a more general dissatisfaction with that way of life? Is his social isolation due to a lack of social skills, despite a conscious desire for more human contact, or does he prefer a relatively self-contained life? It is as the worker focuses on Mr. A.'s actual and possible goals, that the worker understands the significance of Mr. A.'s lack of skills, resources, and power and his disturbed perception of the outside world, which create barriers to these goals.

Looking at the housing department, attention is focused on possible inadequate goals (perhaps a policy that ignores the social needs of people like Mr. A.) or inadequate skills in communication and inadequate feedback.

If one takes the system that contains both Mr. A. and the housing department, in addition to the issues that concern each of them separately, one's attention is immediately drawn to the fact that there are two different control centres with conflicting goals. Between these two, there is a considerable imbalance of power. In this situation the worker may feel constrained to accept the inevitability of victory for the housing department, and therefore to help Mr. A. to achieve the best bargain he can in return for his capitulation. But the worker may also think it appropriate to seek to change the balance of power in Mr. A.'s favour.

Finally it is worth looking at the system created by the interrelationship of Mr. A. and the social worker. Again there are two different control centres whose goals are likely to be different, raising issues of power and authority. As the system is created, the contract is developed through agreement about goals and the methods of achieving them. The relative influence of each party on decisions such as these is a crucial philosophical issue for the social work profession and each social worker.

Two further examples may help to illustrate the value of this model for focusing attention on important diagnostic criteria. The first is from casework.

A wife comes to a social worker to complain about her husband's behaviour. They have been married about 18 months and have a baby of 6 months. He goes out almost every evening to his mates in the pub leaving her to stay in with the baby. Before the baby came, they used to go out together and were generally happy. Now she cannot manage on the money he gives her (which seems low to the social worker) so she has got in arrears with the rent. She does not know how much he earns and has not told him about the arrears. When she complains about him going out and leaving her and about the money, he laughs and takes no notice. Last night she got so angry she threw a plate of food at him. He gave her a black eye.

A preliminary assessment of the situation suggests the following hypotheses for exploration with implications for further action:

a. The arrival of the baby has changed a situation which may or may not have been as ideal as the wife pictures it ("spontaneous" change in the family situation).
b. The husband appears unwilling to change his behaviour in response to the new situation and leaves all the adaptation to his wife (corrective action in response to feedback).
c. He does not appear to be committed to the same expectations of family as his wife, obviously in the short run and possibly in the long run (conflicting values and goals).
d. He is using his control over the family income and his wife's commitment to the child to impose his will in the situation. She may be making inadequate use of whatever bargaining counters she has in this situation (power).
e. He does not appear to take his wife's views seriously. This may be because she cannot convey to him the depth of her feelings, or because she conveys them in a way that for whatever reason provokes a negative reaction in him (communication), or because he rightly or wrongly regards them as irrelevant to his goals (power or communication).
f. Financial resources may be inadequate as well as apparently being "misused" (resources).

An interview with the husband may of course produce a very different picture of what is happening. For example he may complain that the home is filthy and his wife never cooks him a meal and sits moaning at him all evening when he does stay in— which may of course be a manifestation of her inadequacy or of her attempts to communicate her feelings or use her power. The disparity in the account may be because either or both is deliberately misrepresenting the situation or because if genuinely different perceptions of the situation. But if their stories are in approximate agreement, the analysis gives clear indications of the most profitable lines of exploration with a view to promoting change.

Of course the fact that one is analysing this very personal situation in relatively impersonal terms does not invalidate the use of casework methods in involving clients in the solution of their problems. Nor does it mean that the feelings of clients are neglected in any way. The model does, however, provide the social worker with a guide to certain focal points which are of crucial importance in determining what can or cannot be done to improve the situation.

The second example involves possible community action. A social worker visiting a client on a council estate discovers that the house is in poor condition due to neglect of maintenance. The client says that several of the houses are in a similar condition. When the client and others have told the rent collector, the collector says it will be reported but nothing happens. Some of them have complained to the housing manager in the past. Workers have been sent, but their work has been poor and no permanent improvement has resulted. They have given up trying. There is no tenants' association.

Considering this information in relation to the housing department the following hypotheses emerge:

a. The housing manager may have come to accept inadequate standards of performance either generally or in relation to this estate, because the tenants are not sufficiently influential as compared with other tenants who are making competitive demands on the department (goals and values).

b. The manager may have inadequate means of gathering information (the feedback process).

c. The manager may be deploying the workforce inadequately (internal use of resources).

d. The manager may have inadequate resources, including skilled workers for the work required (resource input).

e. The lack of resources may be due tto inadequate communication or inadequate influence on higher levels of the Council system (power and communication).

In relation to the tenants the following hypotheses emerge:

a. As individuals they lack skills in communication and in influencing their environment (skills).

b. Past failures have given them a poor self-image, which may not be justified, and may have given them a misleading impression of the imperviousness of housing department and the council to outside pressure (information gathering about the system and its environment).

c. As a group they lack an organization that could make them into an effective countersystem (power).

Taking the tenants and housing department as a conjoint system the analysis focuses attention on the inadequate communication between them and the inadequate influence of the tenants.

This analysis leaves the social worker with a number of open options:

1. To focus on the housing department by collecting and presenting information on behalf of the informant alone or on behalf of several tenants. If this fails to achieve results, the worker may use personal skills in mobilizing other forms of influence and power.

2. To focus on the tenants, helping them to organize and develop their skills (or possibly to refer them to a community worker for help in this).

3. Some combination of these, for example, helping them to organize while at the same time taking up the individual case as a matter of urgency; or helping them to organize and becoming involved in their actions towards the housing department.

The congruence between the list derived from this model and one produced by Lippitt, Watson, and Westley (1958, chaps. 2 and 3) provides some independent evidence of the relevance of the model.

These authors examined the writings of a range of "change agents" using specialized techniques from psychoanalysts to management consultants and community workers. They did not use system theory, although they did use the term "client system" to provide a common term for the individuals, groups, organizations, and communities with which change agents might be engaged. They appropriately accepted the definitions of their client systems used by each type of specialist. So client systems were seen as having clearly defined boundaries (in contrast to the approach of system theory) and the change agent as only having sanction to operate within those boundaries.

As a result of their study, Lippitt, Watson, and Westley discerned six aspects of a situation on which different change agents focused in their interventions. These "diagnostic orientations," to use the authors' phrase, were

1. Internal power;
2. Internal mobilization of energy;
3. Internal communication (in which they included the self-image);
4. Correspondence between internal and external reality;
5. Skills and strategies; and
6. Goals and values for action.

Each of these items can be found in one form or another in the list derived from the model.

Moreover the model itself provides a basis for ordering these diagnostic orientations which in the original account appear as discrete items.

The process of social work

Turning to the process of social work, there has long been dissatisfaction with the simplistic casework formula "study, diagnosis and treatment." This dissatisfaction arises mainly because of the authoritative connotations of the medical model. But criticism is also made of the fact that these different stages cannot be readily separated. "Treatment" begins from the first contact, and study and diagnosis never end.

Functional casework rejected the medical model, and particularly the authoritative connotations of "diagnosis." Instead it pointed to the special characteristics of the beginning and ending of a relationship. So casework was seen as having three phases: the beginning, the middle and the end (Smalley, 1970, pp. 77–129).

Lippitt, Watson, and Westley (1958, chap. 6) found in the wider literature of change agents evidence for seven stages.

1. Development of a need for change;
2. Establishment of a change relationship;
3. Clarification or diagnosis of the client system's problem;
4. Examination of alternative routes and goals: establishing goals and intentions of action;
5. Transformation of plans into actual change efforts;
6. Generalization and stabilization of change; and
7. Achievement of a terminal relationship.

This still appears as a linear process but they add an appropriate warning: "Most change processes probably proceed by a kind of cyclic motion, starting over and over again as one set of problems is solved and a new set is encountered: hence the different phases become mixed up and the final objective may be achieved by a process which seems rather muddled to the observer who is looking for a clear-cut developmental sequence (chap. 6).

This account, which is probably readily recognizable to most practising social workers, has a very close relationship to Diagram 3 which offers a cyclical picture of a problem-solving process. Goldstein (1973, pp. 120–153) in fact uses this concept of a cyclical process to develop a model of social work practice involving six stages divided into three phases. The three phases are induction, core, and ending, corresponding to the three phases of functional theory. The induction phase is concerned with the development of the contract with the client-system; the core phase with the problem-solving action. In both these, information is gathered, an activity pursued, and the situation reassessed with a view to planning the next steps. The last phase of course is primarily concerned with reassessment. At every stage the possibility is written into the model that the client may withdraw or there may be a return to an earlier stage in the process, perhaps focusing on a new problem.

Goldstein (1973, pp. 136–137) talks about a contract between client and worker, and this is another way in which the diagram supports current thinking on the process of social work. Increasingly this has been seen as an essential element in the beginning phase (Roberts and Nee, 1970, pp. 45, 155, 196, 237, 244, and 291). The diagram gives a clear indication of what this involves. There is first a sharing of information about the situation as the client sees it, about the agency and about the resources available to both. There is a recognition of the power brought to the situation by all the parties concerned and agreement about how the power of the social worker will be used, for example how information given to the social worker will be used, and what conditions may be attached to any help that is given. All this should lead to the establishment of agreement about common goals and a broad indication of how these will be tackled. Thereafter there will be further exploration of means of achieving the goals and the roles to be taken by the different people involved.

Of course the idea of the contract has relevance to other systems with which the social worker is involved as well as the client system. Pincus and Minahan (1973, pp. 164–168) recognize this and discuss the nature of the contract that may be developed by a social worker with his agency, with an action system involving people other than members of the client system and also with target systems which may be different again.

Thus the same model that gives the basis for an assessment of systems also gives guidance on the process of social work in so far as that is concerned with the creation of systems and problem-solving.

Conclusions

In this article I set out to consider the relevance of general system theory to social work practice and the extent to which social workers would find it worthwhile making themselves familiar with system theory and its jargon. The material presented coupled with the wider reading from which it has been extracted seem to me to justify four conclusions.

First, it is important to recognize one serious limitation of general system theory. As far as human systems are concerned, it provides an "expository model" rather than a "research model," to use Lathrope's terminology (1969). That is to say it is a model that sets out to describe phenomena rather than to explain them. In engineering and biology its status as a research theory is justified because its mathematical formulations can be related to concrete systems and can be used to construct hypotheses and predict results. In the study of human systems the lack of adequate measurement scales for most relevant factors (except perhaps in economics) make the mathematical formulae irrelevant, and the precise formulation of hypotheses that can be proved or disproved very difficult. Nevertheless as an expository model, the approach may be acceptable as "an explanation in principle," as Bertlanffy (1971, p. 35) suggests and give guidance for both research and action.

Second, it is the capacity of system theory to provide a model of goal-directed behaviour which is relevant both to the assessment of human systems and to the process of social work which justifies its study by social workers. The philosophical issues are more relevant to the social science basis of social work than to social work practice itself. The system perspective is largely a matter of common sense, requiring little theoretical backing although it does provide the framework for a wider view of personal and social problems than has commonly been employed by social workers in their practice.

Third, from the point of view of most social workers there is probably no need to spend much time inculcating the elaborate jargon of general system theory which I have largely avoided in this article. Part of the need for the jargon is created by the attempt of the theory to cover such a wide range of systems. Social workers are only concerned with a limited range, and it is sufficient to make use of terms from the social sciences that can easily be applied to most human systems. Simple models can be derived from system theory and provide a framework for analysis, without necessarily having to study general system theory itself. Both Goldstein and Pincus and Minahan demonstrate this.

Fourth, for social work teachers the need for deeper study of the theory will be greater. If these models are to be used in social work courses, teachers will need a grasp of general system theory to give consistency to their teaching, to deal with the confusions that any students may meet, and to assist those students who wish to go deeper into the theory. Some practising social workers may also wish to make deeper study of the theory to extend their thinking.

Reading
3-2 Interdisciplinary versus ecological approach*

Edgar H. Auerswald

The explosion of scientific knowledge and technology in the middle third of this century, and the effects of this explosion on the human condition, have posed a number of challenges for the behavioral sciences that most agree are yet to be met. The overriding challenge is, of course, the prevention of nuclear holocaust, but such problems as crime and delinquency, drug addiction, senseless violence, refractive learning problems, destructive prejudice, functional psychosis, and the like follow close behind.

Practically all behavioral scientists agree that none of these problems can be solved within the framework of any single discipline. Most espouse a putting together of heads in the so-called "interdisciplinary approach." The notion is not new, of course. The "interdisciplinary team" has been around for some time. Some new notions have emanated from this head-banging, but there have been few startling revelations in the last decade or so.

However, a relatively small but growing group of behavioral scientists, most of whom have spent time in arenas in which the interdisciplinary approach is being used, have taken the seemingly radical position that the knowledge of the traditional disciplines as they now exist is relatively useless in the effort to find answers for these particular problems. Most of this group advocate a realignment of current knowledge and reexamination of human behavior within a unifying holistic model, that of ecological phenomenology. The implications of this departure are great. Once the model of ecology becomes the lattice-work upon which such a realignment of knowledge is hung, it is no longer possible to limit oneself to the behavioral sciences alone. The physical sciences, the biological sciences, in fact, all of science, must be included. Since the people who have been most concerned with constructing a model for a unified science and with the ingredients of the human ecological field have been the general systems theorists, the approach used by behavioral scientists who follow this trend is rapidly acquiring the label of the "systems approach," although a more appropriate label might be the "ecological systems approach."

These terms are currently being used metaphorically to describe a way of thinking and an operational style. They do not describe a well-formed theoretical framework as does the term "general systems theory." It is with the former, the way of thinking and the operational style, that I am concerned with in this paper.

The two approaches described above differ greatly. Let us examine why the difference is so profound. The ongoing accumulation of knowledge and its application to practice follows a well-known sequence. This might be broken down into steps as follows: the collection of information or data, the ordering of that data within a selected framework, analysis of the data, synthesis of the results of analysis into hypotheses, the formulaton of strategies and techniques (methodologies) to test the hypotheses, the construction of a delivery plan for use of these strategies and techniques, the implementation of the plan, and the collection of data from the arena of implementation to test its impact, which, of course, repeats the first step, and so on.

* Reprinted by permission of author and publisher from *Family Process* 7 (September 1968), pp. 202–215.

The key step in this sequence is the second one, the ordering of data within a selected framework, because it is this step, and this step alone, that gives structure to the rest, all of which are operational. Not only does the nature and outcome of subsequent steps depend on this structuring framework, but so does the prior step, the collection of data. What data among the infinite variety of available natural data are considered important, and are, therefore, collected in any given arena, will depend on the conceptual framework used. It is here that the difference between the two approaches is to be found.

The "interdisciplinary" approach maintains the vantage point of individual contributors within their own disciplines. While it has expanded the boundaries of the theoretical framework of each discipline to include concepts borrowed from other disciplines, only those concepts which pose no serious challenge or language difficulties are welcomed. More importantly, I think, the interfaces between the conceptual framework of different disciplines are ignored, and, as a result, the interfaces between the various arenas of systematic life operation (for example, biological, psychological, social or individual, family, community) represented by different disciplines are also ignored.

The structural aspects and the clarity of context of the data collected are lost as a result. The precise source, pathway, and integrating functions of messages passing between various operational life arenas in the ecological field cannot be clearly identified. Analysis of such data depends almost entirely on the *content* of these messages, and much distortion can and does take place.

The "systems" approach, on the other hand, changes the vantage point of the data collector. It focuses precisely on the interfaces and communication processes taking place there. It begins with an analysis of the *structure* of the field, using the common structural and operational properties of systems as criteria for identifying the systems and subsystems within it. And by tracing the communications within and between sys-

tems, it insists that the structure, sources, pathways, repository sites, and integrative functions of messages become clear in addition to their content. In my opinion, this, plus the holistic nonexclusive nature of the approach, minimizes the dangers of excessive selectivity in the collection of data and allows for much more clarity in the contextual contributions to its analysis. And the steps which follow, including prescription and planning of strategies and techniques, gain in clarity and are more likely to be rooted in concrete realities.

There are some very practical advantages that accrue as a result of the above. At the level of *theory,* for example, the ecological systems model, by clarifying and emphasizing the interfaces between systems, allows for the use of a variety of theoretical models which have to do with interactional processes and information exchange. These models form bridges between the conceptual systems of single disciplines. Information theory, crisis theory, game theory, and general communications theory, for example, represent some of the bodies of research and knowledge which become useable in an integrated way.

Knowledge that has been accumulating from the study of specific ecological systems, such as the family and small groups, the development of which lagged until recently because the systems did not fit neatly into the bailiwick of any one traditional discipline, can also be included without strain. And the developmental model of the life cycle of the individual and of various larger human systems as they move through time in the ecological field of their environment assumes meaning in a larger context.

In addition, the use of this model in planning has demonstrated its many implications for the design and operational implimentation of delivery systems, especially for community programs (for example, "comprehensive community health" programs). The ecological systems approach insures that the entire process of planning for a community is rooted in the realities and needs of that community. The organized identification of the ecological systems making up a target community allows for the planned inclusion of information collection stations in each key system and at primary interfaces which provide feedback to the planning arena, thus setting up a servo-system which assures that planning will remain closely related to changing need. Over a period of time, as a picture of a target community emerges from such data, it will emerge as an idiosyncratic template of the structural and operational configurations of that community. It will not, as in the "interdisciplinary" approach, emerge as a predetermined template of the theoretical structure of the dominant discipline.

As a result, program designs constructed in this manner are deeply imbedded in the target community. They will develop as another ecological system among the many, thus greatly clarifying the context in which any program can be integrated into the life of the community as a whole. Furthermore, the delivery organization itself becomes viewed as a system with assigned tasks made up of subsystems performing subtasks including intraorganizational tasks. This allows for more clarity in the selection of staffing patterns, in the definitions of staff role functions, in the construction of communication systems and data collection (record-keeping) systems, and of the assignment of tasks within the organizational structure to staff members best equipped to handle them. Of special import to community programs is the fact that with the clarification of specific tasks to be performed comes the increased possibility of identifying those tasks that can be carried out by staff members or volunteers who need relatively little training.

At the *operational* level the strategies of evolution and change can be more clearly designed. More important, perhaps, use of the ecological systems approach allows for the development of a whole new technology in the production of change. Many techniques have, as a matter of fact, already appeared on the scene, largely within orga-

nized movements aimed at integration in its broadest sense, such as the Civil Rights Movement and the "War on Poverty." Some community organization and community development programs, techniques using economic and political pressure, and techniques which change the rules of the game such as the nonviolence movement, all represent a new technology, and all have their relevance to the broadly defined health needs of socially isolated individuals, families, and groups.

In service programs working with individual people and families, this new technology is also emerging, more slowly perhaps. Many new ways of coping with familiar situations are being developed. Techniques of treating families as systems, for example, represent one advance. In particular, an emphasis which stresses the organization of events in time and traces the movement of the developing infant-child-adolescent-adult-aged individual's degree of participation versus isolation in relation to the family and to the flow of surrounding community life—such an emphasis makes it possible to determine with much more clarity in what life arenas the individual, the family, or a group of individuals needs assistance, and thus to more effectively combat the anomie and dehumanization characteristic of our age. The result is that the targets of therapeutic activity are much clearer and therapeutic work is more clearly focused on forces and situations that are truly etiological in a given problem situation. Techniques of producing therapeutic change can be brought to arenas much larger than the therapy room or even the home. I think that a single story will serve to illustrate more concretely what I mean.

In the story I wish to tell, two therapists, one a "systems" thinker, the other a member of an "interdisciplinary" team, became involved in the case of a runaway girl.

To give you some initial background, I should explain that I have been involved in designing and implementing a "Neighborhood Health Services System" for provision of comprehensive biopsychosocial care to a so-called "disadvantaged" community. The main aim in setting up this unit was to find ways to avoid the fragmentation of service delivery which occurs when a person's problem is defined as belonging primarily to that person, and the individual is sent to a specialist who is trained to deal primarily with that type of problem. The specialist naturally sees the problem not only as an individual matter but defines it still further according to the professional sector which is inhabited. The specialist is not accustomed to looking at the total set of systems surrounding the individual with the symptom or to noticing the ways in which the symptom, the person, the family, and the community interlock, and the specialist is often in the position of desperately trying to replace a fuse when it is the entire community power line that has broken down. Furthermore, the specialist's efforts to solve the problem are apt to be confined to arbitrarily chosen segments of time called "appointments." And finally, there is that unfortunate invention, the written referral, a process of buck-passing that sends many a person in trouble from agency to agency till the individual finally gives up or breaks down. As a beginning we decided that we would have to pilot some cases in order to gain some experience with the different approach we felt was needed.

At this point, a case providentially dramatizing the points we had in mind fell into our hands. (We have since found that almost every case that falls into our hands providentially dramatizes these points.) One of our psychiatrists was wandering about the neighborhood one day in order to become better acquainted with it and to explore what sort of crises and problems our neighborhood program must be prepared to serve beyond those we already anticipated. I should say here that this psychiatrist,[1] by virtue of several years of pioneer-

ing work with families, including the experimental use of game theory and games in diagnosing and treating them, was particularly well qualified to handle the situation I will describe. His explorations that day had brought him to the local police station, and while he was talking to the desk sergeant, a Puerto Rican woman arrived to report that her 12-year-old daughter, Maria, had run away from home. This was apparently not the first time. She described the child to the police, who alerted their patrols to look for her and assigned two men to investigate the neighborhood. Our psychiatrist, whom I will refer to from now on as our "explorer," was intrigued and decided to follow up the situation himself.

He first identified himself to the mother as she left the police station and asked if she would be willing to allow him to help her with her current difficulty. She agreed. He learned that she lived a few blocks away with her now absent daughter and another daughter, aged 14. Her own parents lived nearby, and she had a paramour who also lived in the neighborhood. The father of her two children had long since deserted his family, and she was uncertain as to his whereabouts. The exploring psychiatrist learned also that the runaway girl had been seeing a psychotherapist at the mental health clinic of a local settlement house. In addition, he ascertained the location of her school.

He then decided that his behavior might appear unethical to the child's therapist, so he proceeded to the mental health clinic, a clinic which prided itself on the use of the "interdisciplinary" team approach. The original therapist turned out to be a social worker of considerable accomplishment and experience, who agreed to cooperate with him in his investigation after he explained what he was up to and that he had the mother's permission. He read the child's case record and discussed the girl with the therapist at some length. He learned that at a recent team case conference, the diagnosis which was originally assigned to the girl,

---

[1] I am indebted to Dr. Robert Ravich for the case material reported.

that of childhood schizophrenia, was confirmed. The team also decided that in the light of repeated episodes of running away from home, her behavior was creating sufficient danger to indicate that she be placed in a situation where that danger would be alleviated while her therapy continued. For a 12-year-old Puerto Rican girl in New York City, especially one carrying a label of schizophrenia, this almost always means hospitalization in the children's ward of a state hospital. Accordingly, the arrangement for her admission to the state hospital covering the district had been made and was due to be implemented within a few days.

The next stop for our explorer was the school, where Maria's teacher described her as a slow but steady learner, detached from most other children in the class, vague and strange, but somehow likeable. The guidance counselor reported an incident in which she had been discovered masturbating an older boy under the school auditorium stairs. This behavior had led the school authorities to contemplate suspending her, but since they knew her to be in treatment they decided to hold off, temporarily, at least.

The exploring psychiatrist also learned at the school that Maria was involved in an afterschool group program at the settlement house. He returned there and got from the group worker a much more positive impression of the girl than he had previously encountered. She participated with seeming enthusiasm in the projects of the group and got along very well with the other children. The group worker, by way of providing evidence that Maria had much potential, showed the therapist a lovely and poignant poem she had contributed to a newspaper put out by the group. It was never ascertained whether the girl had written or copied the poem. She had, nevertheless, produced it, and there was general agreement that its theme of isolation was one which was expressive of her.

Back at Maria's home, our explorer talked to Maria's sister, who at first grudgingly,

but then with some relish, admitted that she knew where the girl had gone during her previous runaway episodes. She was the sometime mascot of a group of teenage boys with whom she occasionally traveled for two or three days at a time. The sister did not know where she went or what she did during the junkets, but she suspected that sex was somehow involved. She also volunteered the information that neither she or her mother had ever found it easy to communicate with her sister, and that if the therapist really wanted to talk to someone who knew her, he should talk to her grandfather. So off to the grandparents' apartment he went.

The grandmother turned out to be a tight-lipped, highly religious Pentecostalist who was at first unwilling to say much at all about the girl.

The grandfather, however, was a different kettle of fish. Earthly, ebullient, jocular, bright, though uneducated, his love for Maria was immediately apparent. He spoke of her warmly and bemoaned the lack of understanding that existed in her home. Remembering a passing reference in the case record at the mental health clinic to a suspicion that the grandfather may have engaged in seductive play with the girl, if not open sexual activity, our explorer raised the issue of the girl's emerging adolescent sexuality. This brought an outburst from the hitherto silent grandmother that confirmed the mutually seductive quality of the grandfather's relationship with the girl, followed by a return blast from the grandfather who revealed that his wife had refused to sleep with him for several years. He readily admitted his frustrated sexuality and the fact that he was at times aroused by his budding granddaughter.

I have presented only a sparse picture of the rich amount of information collected by our explorer up to this point. In a continuous five-hour effort, without seeing the absent Maria, he was able to construct a picture of her as a child who had grown up in relative isolation in a home where she received little support and guidance. Communication between herself and her mother had become more and more sparse over the years, most likely because of efforts of her older sister to maintain her favored position in the home. She had turned to her grandfather, who, feeling frustrated and himself isolated in his own marriage, brought his sexually-tinged warmth willingly into a relationship of mutual affection with her. Furthermore, it seemed clear that with someone like the group worker who liked her and who, because the group was small, could spend time with her, Maria could respond with warmth and exhibit an intelligence that otherwise remained hidden. But, and this was, of course, speculative, the tools she perceived as useful in her search for a response from others would most likely be limited to infantile techniques of manipulation developed in early years prior to the need for verbal communication or, based on the relationship with the grandfather, some form of seduction where the currency of acceptance was sex. And, at the age of puberty, having been shut out of the female world of her mother and sister, she was using this currency full blast in the world of boys.

The next day our explorer talked again to the mother, who told him that the girl had been found by the police on the street and had been hospitalized at a large city hospital on the adolescent psychiatric ward. Before visiting her, he briefly questioned the mother about her paramour. It turned out that the subject of marriage had come up between the two of them, but because he earned a limited income, both he and the mother had decided against living together or getting married. Either action would result in loss of the support the mother was receiving from the Department of Welfare for herself and her two children.

All that had been predicted the day before was corroborated when our explorer visited the girl in the hospital. Her behavior with him, and, as it turned out with the

resident physician on the ward, alternated between childish manipulation and seductive behavior of a degree which appeared bizarre in a 12-year-old. But she was, at the same time, a lithely attractive girl with a lively wit which blossomed once she felt understood. She was ambivalent about the alternatives of going home or of going to a state hospital, mildly resisting both.

Our exploring psychiatrist then returned to the mental health clinic to discuss what he had observed with the child's therapist and the consulting psychiatrist. He suggested a plan of action as an alternative to hospitalization. By targeting on key issues in various systems surrounding this child, it seemed theoretically plausible that the conditions which held her fixed in a pattern of behavior that had been labeled as sick and crazy might be changed, thus freeing her to accept new coping patterns which she could be helped to learn. An effort to reestablish communication between the child and her mother, who had shown with her other daughter that she could raise a child with relative success, would be one step. It might not be feasible to work with the grandparents' unsatisfactory marriage, but an explanation to the grandfather, who had already tentatively understood his contribution to the girl's dilemma, might be useful. If the Department of Welfare were willing, and if the boyfriend's income could be enhanced by at least a little supplementary public assistance, the mother and her boyfriend might be induced to marry. Teacher and guidance counselor could be helped to understand the girl's behavior more fully and might cooperate on a plan for helping the girl learn new ways of relating in school. The group worker's investment in the girl could be used to a good effect in this joint effort to help her grow. And the original therapist, instead of concerning herself with defense systems and repressed conflict could concentrate on helping the family provide the maximum of support and guidance possible, or, if she wished, could still work with the girl herself. With these suggestions, our exploring psychiatrist bowed out.

A month later, a follow-up visit to the mother revealed that the girl had been sent to the state hospital on the recommendation of the resident on the adolescent ward who agreed with the diagnosis and felt that, since she was "a schizophrenic," she should be in a hospital. No one had made any countermove and contact between all of the helping people except the state hospital doctor and the girl's family had been terminated. This outcome had occurred *despite the fact that the mother and her boyfriend had, after a conversation stimulated by our therapist-explorer, presented themselves at the mental health clinic and expressed their willingness to marry if it seemed wise, their wish to have Maria come home, and their hope that someone at the clinic would help them learn what they must now do for her as parents.*

I have, I realize, presented an unusual situation. Reasonable question could be raised, I suppose, as to how often this sequence could occur. And in my own bias is obvious in the manner of my presentation. But I think the case illustrates the radical difference between the two approaches under discussion. The approach of the therapist from the interdisciplinary clinic and that of our exploring psychiatrist are not merely two points on a continuum of techniques. The "ecological systems" approach literally changed the name of the game. By focusing on the nature of the transactions taking place between Maria and the identifiable systems that influenced her growth, it was possible for the "systems" psychiatrist to ascertain what strengths, lacks, and distortions existed at each interface. Two things happened when this was done.

The first was that Maria's behavior began to make sense as a healthy adaptation to a set of circumstances that did not allow her to develop more socially acceptable or better differentiated means of seeking a re-

sponse to her needs as a developing child. Thus, the aura of pathology was immediately left behind.

The second was that the identification of lacks and distortions in the transactional arena of each interface automatically suggested what needed to be added or changed. Thus the tasks of the helping person were automatically defined. Rigidity of technique in accomplishing these tasks could not, under those circumstances, survive. Flexibility, ingenuity, and innovation were demanded.

The implications of what can happen if this approach is used universally are obvious. If proper data is kept, it seems inevitable that new clusters of data will occur to add to our knowledge, and a new technology of prevention and change develop.

The case of Maria has a certain uniqueness that separates it from most similar cases across our country. The uniqueness is not to be found in the "interdisciplinary" approach used, but rather in the quantity of skilled people who were trying to help her. Despite their dedicated efforts, all they managed to accomplish was Maria's removal from the only system that could be considered generic in terms of her growth and socialization—her family—and her removal from the school and community which should provide the additional experience she needed if she were to become a participant in the life of her society. In addition, they succeeded in stamping a label on the official records of her existence, a label which is a battleground of controversy among diagnosticians, but which means simply to the lay public that she is a nut.

By chance, Maria wound up in a mental hygiene clinic where her behavior was labeled as sick. She might just as easily have joined the many girls showing similar behavior who wind up in court and are labeled delinquent. Either label puts her in a category over which various members of "interdisciplinary" teams are in continued conflict. The needs of the girl, which are not clearly apparent, in either arena, become hopelessly obscured. Decisions made by those charged with the task of helping her are likely to be made without cognizance of those needs, since they depend for their outcome too often on the institutionalized procedures and momentary exigencies in the caring organization or person.

As a final point, let me explore the nature of the communications breakdown that occurred between the two therapists.

In his explorations, our "systems" psychiatrist collected a good deal of data that was not known to the "interdisciplinary" therapist and team in order to insure that he understood the operations that had been going on at each interface in which he was interested. This additional data only supplemented the data previously collected and agreed with it in content. Thus the two agreed substantially as long as they confined their communications to content and to inferred construction of the internal psychodynamics of the persons involved, Maria and the individual members of her family. And, as it happened, this was all they discussed until the exploring "systems" psychiatrist returned for a final chat. At that time, having ordered his data in such a way as to clarify the transactions which had been taking place at the interfaces between Maria and the various systems contributing to her growth, his suggestions flowed from a plan designed to affect those interfaces. The "interdisciplinary" team, including the original therapist, had not ordered the data in this way. Since the dominant disciplinary framework used in their arena was psychiatric, they had ordered the data around a nosological scheme for labeling illness. The outcome of their plan of action, therefore, was to apply a label signifying the nature of Maria's illness, and to decide, reasonably enough within this framework, that since treatment of her illness on an outpatient basis had not been successful, the next step was hospitalization, a decision backed by the assumption that her runaways were dangerous.

It was literally impossible, at the final meeting, for the suggestions of our "systems" therapist to have meaning to the "interdisciplinary" team. They fell on ears made deaf by a way of thinking which could not perceive them as meaningful. They came across as a dissonance which had to be screened out. Communication between the two approaches thus broke down completely.

This instance of breakdown is characteristic of efforts of communication between people from the two arenas. Conversations I have had with a variety of people who take the ecological systems view, backed by my own experience, seem to add up to the following:

There seems to be no serious problem of communication between the systems thinker who emphasizes structure and the experimental behavioral scientist who does basic research in his laboratory or even the researcher who is attempting to deal with a wide range of natural data. Such researchers have selected and defined the structure of the theoretical framework in which they wish to work and are the first to admit that the outcome of their research carries the label of validity within that framework alone.

Clinical scientists, whose emphasis is more on the content of their data, are for the most part different animals. Most clinical theorists, planners, and practitioners, regardless of discipline, seem caught in the highly specialized sequence of their own training and intradisciplinary experience, upon which they seem to depend for the very definition of their personal identity. Generally speaking, a situation seems to exist in which the integration of the cognitive apparatus of clinicians is such as to exclude as a piece of relevant data the notion that their intradisciplinary "truths," which are carried to the interdisciplinary arena, are relative. They most often will hear and understand the notion when it is expressed. But, again speaking generally, they treat it as unimportant to their operations, as peripheral to the body of knowledge they invest with meaning. Why should this be?

I think it is because clinicians are products of the specialized fragmentation of today's world of science. To them, admission of this fact would mean that they would have to rearrange their cognitive styles, their professional ways of life, and, all too often, their total lifestyles as well, if they were to maintain a sense of their own integrity. Not only would they have to renounce their idols, but they would have to go through a turbulent period of disintegration and reintegration. They would have to be willing and able to tolerate the fragmentation of identity boundaries such a transition entails. They would have to leave the safety of seeming truths, truths they have used to maintain their sense of being in the right, their self-esteem, their sense of values, and their status in the vertical hierarchies of their society. They would have to give up the games they play to maintain their hard-won positions in their disciplines, games such as those which consist of labeling persons from other schools of thought

as bright but limited, misguided, or insufficiently analyzed. More often than not, they would rather fight than switch.

I imply, of course, that they should switch. Thus the question must reasonably be asked: "Why should they?" "Why should they attempt such a fundamental change?" After all, they can point with pride to the many accomplishments and successes of their disciplines and their own work within them.

But to rest on their laurels, in my opinion, is to abdicate responsibility. It is like crowing over the 70 percent or so of juvenile delinquents who become law-abiding citizens and ignoring the 30 percent who do not. The major responsibility of today's behavioral scientists is to those who don't or won't make it, not those who do, to Maria, not to Little Hans, whom they already know how to help.

The least they can do is examine their labels and how they are used. In the life-space of Maria's world, there is a serious question as to which system deserves the prefix, *schizo.*

Reading
3–3 *Minority issues in community mental health**

Samuel Tucker

The purpose of this paper is to build on the emerging knowledge of social structure and cultural differences as the basis of identifying and setting forth knowledge and skills for community mental health practices within minority communities and particularly black communities.

There are several assumptions upon which this practice approach is based; none of which will be elaborated on in this presentation.

* An original article prepared for this edition.

1. The term *community* added to mental health is a social structure designation, based on the awareness of the importance of the social structure implications for emotional adjustment.
2. This social structure designation makes possible the expansion of the mental health concept of treatment of individual dysfunctioning to include intervention into the social structure in which the client lives.
3. This expansion provides the basis upon which "community mental health" is

practiced with the primary purpose of social structural intervention, while mental health continues to focus primarily on individual dysfunctioning and treatment.

4. Intervention into the social structure and treatment of individuals and groups are complimentary and reinforce mental health activities.

These assumptions make it possible to discuss community mental health in relation to the peculiar social relationships of black Americans, without arguing the merits of a unique black psyche. Plus, it provides the natural basis of separation to talk about the social community needs of blacks, without arguing with whites about their needs or standards of acceptance, because of a different set of social relationships to the American society. And, it provides a basis of thinking of skills and knowledge in relation to the black community as it exists rather than the required standards established by the societal institutions.

I must constantly remind myself that the peculiar relationship of blacks to American society is constantly in flux, and any statement today could have no relevance under different social circumstances tomorrow. However, I will mention in passing that racism, historically practiced and institutionalized, is the social atmosphere by which majority rule has justified minority status and roles in society. And, it is the black psyche that has suffered this peculiar adjustment.

In popular community language—"to be black and well adjusted under current social circumstances is to be emotionally disturbed."

The basic theoretical frame is social structural conceptalization formulated by the 19th-century French sociologist, Emile Durkheim (1964). The selection of social structure conceptualization emanates from this writer's perception of the black community as an "internal colony." While I recognize the radical characterization Stokely

Carmichael and Charles Hamilton gave the concept of *internal colonialism* (Blauner, 1968), in their book *Black Power* (1967), Kenneth Clark in his book, *Dark Ghetto* (1965), demonstrated the colonial nature of Harlem in good acceptable sociological form.

Clark (1965, p. 38) describes the situation as follows:

The community can best be described in terms of the analogy of a powerless colony. Its political leadership is divided, and all but one or two of its political leaders are short-sighted and dependent upon the larger political power structure.

Its social agencies are financially precarious and dependent upon sources of support outside the community. Its churches are isolated or dependent. Its economy is dominated by small businesses which are largely owned by absentee owners, and its tenements and other real property are also owned by absentee landlords.

Under a system of centralization, Harlem's schools are controlled by forces outside the community. Programs and policies are supervised and determined by individuals who do not live in the community.

While Harlem is not typical of all black communities, the nature of external control differs only slightly. While internal colonialism is not a precise conceptualization, it has sufficient implications to merit serious research and testing as a valid model.

Community mental health practice in minority, and particularly black, communities must be characterized by a different orientation. This orientation requires additional information in problem identification, problem and need assessment, and a social system approach to causation and solution. To implement, such practice would require knowledge and skill in the areas of social structural change, positive assessment of community and cultural life, social structural support, community management, social structural building, and a needs and maintenance approach.

This should not be assumed to indicate a limit on knowledge and skills, but an additional dimension added to existing knowledge and skills. While this presentation will not deal with psychodynamic conceptualization, past personal experiences of individuals, individual support on the ego level, agency service, rehabilitation, problems, and treatment, it should be understood that these are necessary and important treatment activities in mental health. Community mental health is an added interventive arm of the mental health body.

Social structure change

The notion of social-structural change is rooted in the elementary ideas of one of the founders of modern sociology, Emile Durkheim. However, the works of Peter M. Blau (1976), Lewis A. Coser (1956), Ralph Linton (1936), Robert K. Merton (1968), Ernest Nagel (1957), and Talcott Parsons (1951) have legitimized the concept of social structure in theory. The basic idea of social structure change consists of a change in the combination of statuses or roles which make up the structure or change the types of people who occupy that structure. When this concept is applied to the Black community, described earlier as having many aspects of an internal colony, it is clear that the social relationship is such that one cannot change the colony without some change in the colonist—or more specifically—"colonial interest." Social work practice must enter such systems, being fully aware that the residual model is not appropriate, if the residual model is practiced, it must be perceived as a means of maintaining "colonial domination" or, to put it more mildly, a means of protecting the status quo.

Under such a social arrangement—internal colonialism—the mental health problems cannot be separated from the economic, political, and social life of the individual in such a relationship. The luxury of such separation is in itself traumatic to the black psyche and lends itself to the sick reality that "a well-adjusted black person in such a social system," is mentally ill.

Consequently, problem identification in a colonial social system requires that we add to community assessment a careful look at external power influences in black communities including:

1. Land ownership;
2. Housing;
3. Business;
4. Employment control;
5. Church affiliation and support;
6. Composition of boards in control of institutional policy that affect local community conditions. This includes social agencies, schools, city councils, political parties, labor unions, and financial institutions.

All of these forces must be looked at in terms of their influence on the health and well-being of local residents. Their actions must be weighed in direct proportion to their power and be credited with their share of the community climate that creates the atmosphere of emotional chaos—frustration, insecurity, lack of recognition, negative self-image, powerlessness, pessimism, double standard experiences of moral, legal, economic, and political behavior measures.

For example, the worker must be aware of the frustrations and mental agony suffered by minority communities over policy decisions to build roads, expressways, warehouses, halfway houses, drug abuse centers, and junk yards in black areas, rationalized by nonownership or cheap land, while attractive office buildings, universities, and hospitals are by necessity located elsewhere . . . while deliberate or expedient, black communities are constantly devalued . . . in a social atmosphere that determines the "self-image" on physical appearances.

Positive aspects of black community life

The assessment process in such a system by necessity should take into account the odds by which the local social structure must function. The functioning of the black institutions, such as the family, church, and community cannot start with identification of the problem but must first begin with an assessment of the strengths.

For example, the black family has managed to fulfill its socializing function to the society even more successfully in many cases than their white counterpart, given the proclaimed societal values (Olson, 1970) of the "work ethic, freedom, local autonomy, equal opportunity, and land ownership." In spite of the circumstances of a colonial system that limits the access of blacks to the fulfillment of those values, blacks unquestioningly hold these in high esteem.

The black family has functioned exceptionally well in spite of the exploitative labor practices committed against black males and the destructive social environment created for black women and children. The black family has functioned in spite of institutionalized dependency of the welfare system (National Advisory Commission on Civil Disorders, 1968) and an educational process that intimidates the black child and the family with opportunities that, in fact, can never exist under racism.

The black church, in spite of its unstable financial base, its often secondhand, converted buildings, its poor attempt at imitating Western rituals has produced from its shabbiness, moral leadership unmatched by the white churches. And, at a time when national morality is in a crunch, the white church has appeared to "leave the driving to us."

The black community has survived in spite of its segregated character. It has survived in spite of the violation of its privacy by police, bill collectors, "Johns," research surveys, and social workers. The community survives in spite of its unprotected residents who have been left powerless by a majority rule, handcuffed by an economic system based on free enterprise, and demoralized by a social system that teaches democracy and practices colonialism.

But, the black community has survived as a symbol of common goals, language, and experiences that are so nationally profound that "brother and sister" from every social class, geographic region, and age understands and are bound by the common heritage. This again, I suspect, has qualities unparalleled in the majority community.

If the assessment does not begin with strength, a sense of weakness and failure can be fed into the community and solutions on such bases become accommodations to weakness and failure.

Social structural support

In this model of practice, intervention begins at the level of community social structure. The support has to be deliberately designed to support the family structures as they exist; observing functions as a measure of adequacy rather than design. Those aspects of family function that provide biological needs, emotional needs, and support for acceptable values and goals, rather than the process by which they are achieved.

For example, the father role may be played by a grandfather, who enjoys, accepts, and is enhanced by the role. The child loves, accepts guidance, and turns to him for protection and help. The record should reflect this, rather than a long social monolog on illegitimacy, loose morals, absentee father, and weak parental involvement. The state of the family functioning must be reflected and supported.

The role of the black church and its influences must be recognized, accepted, and worked with to broaden its social structural involvement. Its institutional posture has historically evaded overt colonial interference to the degree that it has survived as a perpetuated institution over time. Since the interference with it is more pronounced and reacted to, it stands as a monument in the black community. Community mental health efforts must be tied to the spiritual and moral needs of the black community.

For example, the space available in black churches should be made use of when and on whatever conditions possible. They should be generously reimbursed for lending their community relations, moral sanction, and facilities to mental health services. The role of the minister in the leadership of the local congregation should entail a concentrated financially supported training program for black ministers in mental health leadership and a total congregational participation in a carefully designed, well-delivered membership training in community mental health and counseling knowledge. This is critical to insure the survival of mental health practice when the mental health funds are no longer available.

A deliberate program with local schools, businesses, and absentee vested interest to identify and plan their responsibility in local community mental health is necessary.

For example, the local movie theater owner who builds his business on the showing of "X"-rated movies in local neighborhoods might consider a matinee for the children as well as local residents on a continuous basis of human relations, community development, and black-oriented films on weekend afternoons. This is by no means a limit to local community support structures accessible to the community mental health practitioner.

Community management

Management as a task in intervention into community social structure appears most appropriate. Management is defined by this writer as "the judicious use of means to accomplish an end." Implied in management is activity around the resources of a system. If the system is a community, it means the resources of a community which is expanded beyond a discussion of "social services" or social agencies. However, this does not exclude these as resources to be included in the management effort. Workers must be conscious of their needs to bring all of the resources of a community together to accomplish the commu-

nity's mental health goal. And, in this instance, they are not seeking good mental adjustment in the presence of "unemployment," or self-actualization in the face of rank injustice. They seek these in an environment that is conducive to the nature and development of emotional stability and this currently does not exist for the majority of black Americans—and if I may speculate, this is becoming less and less available to all Americans (Olson, 1970).

For example, a community must look at the security measures used to protect individual property of absentee owners and expand that to protect local residents in the community. It might be better from a management point of view to use five security guards and two dogs to protect the entire community than to use them to protect five private businesses. Such an approach would serve to remove the hostile reminder of many communities that "colonialists prefer the protection of their property over the protection of the natives."

Construction

Construction in social structure intervention demands the ability to build new structures. These new structures are critical in colonial communities, not that they are new in the society but because of the power of external forces such social structures were not permitted to exist in the local community. Social workers now realize from the era of "sanctioned community participation" the attempt to imitate role performance can be chaotic and destructive. The construction of new social systems must be based on the natural behavior of the community. This requires new looks at boards, committees, and groups in terms of structure and operation. One can no longer mindlessly borrow from the standards of boards, committees, and groups that individuals have been socialized into accepting, but they must examine their use and operation in relation to the supportive cultural elements in the community. Every aspect of the decision-making apparatus would need to be explored, examined, and tested against community reality. The professional may have to take the responsibility for integrating these new functional models into the main stream of American thought.

For example, universities might provide "aid-ships" (grants) to outstanding teams of students in the areas of urban planning, social work, nursing, law, journalism, and business to assist local community organization in line with the goals of the community. Maybe they could be called "technical assistants."

External intervention

While this model of practice is interventive, the focus should be clearly social structural which is external to the individual members who compose the structure. The peculiar character of the colonial structure implies members who are invisible in the structure, but who have power in and over the structure. The reality has made it difficult to understand the black community without understanding the nature of white-vested interest who are invisible to both local residents and the white community, in general. Because of this quality, the worker will, by necessity, need to work with persons outside of the system in instances where those vested interests are moved to employ their system power against the interest of local residents.

For example, a community who approaches a local merchant about expanding the security resources, that is, a security guard and a dog, may find the merchant quite willing. But at the same time, a security company who profits from poor security management may view this move as "bad for business." If the security company refuses to permit the guards to engage in this more practical approach to community security, even though the local shopkeeper

has paid for their time, you may find that external force is sufficient to stymie social structural change. These external forces must be worked with. The current social work experience lends itself to a narrow view of work with individuals outside of the "client category." Social work with the "upper class" would be extremely helpful in this model of practice.

Needs and maintenance

Change in social structure which emanates out of social dysfunctioning often moves to meet the needs in ways that lead to further problems. To this end, the question for social structural change comes from the needs of the social system to function appropriately. The complexity of the black community experience is that the system is composed of alien parts—black needs and interest—white needs and vested interest. Such a system by its very structure is unhealthy in its totality of composition. When a service is moved to correct this hazard, the emotional health of the black community or any community can neither be promoted nor maintained.

The colonial system creates a social atmosphere that is alien to good community mental health. It is impossible to seriously consider community mental health without examining the social structure by which a healthy person is expected to exist—healthy people resist inequities.

Social workers have the opportunity to create new social structures with community mental health practice that can begin to respond to the needs of the black community. The black community can maintain those structures, but it is a task that requires serious resolve. Community mental health practice must meet this challenge if it is to relate itself to the issues of mental health in minority communities and particularly the black community.

Selected annotated bibliography

Allport, Gordon W. "The Open System in Personality Theory," *Journal of Abnormal and Social Psychology* 61 (1960), pp. 301–311.

This article is a classic for students on the meaning of systems theory for human systems. As the title indicates, Allport puts great emphasis on the difference between closed and open systems.

Buckley, Walter. *Sociology and Modern Systems Theory.* Englewood Cliffs, N.J.: Prentice-Hall, 1967.

Buckley presents a model in which the sociocultural system is seen as a complex, adaptive system.

Chin, Robert. "The Utility of Systems Models and Developmental Models for Practitioners," in Warren G. Bennis, Kenneth D. Benne, and Robert Chin (Eds.), *The Planning of Change.* New York: Holt, Rinehart and Winston, 1961, pp. 201–215.

This article on the meaning of systems theory for human service practitioners is an excellent one for beginning students of systems theory. Chin discusses the difference for the practitioner in the use of developmental theory and systems theory as a base for practice.

Frank, Jerome D. "Expectation and Therapeutic Outcome—Placebo Effect and the Role Induction Interview," in Jerome D. Frank et al. (Eds.), *Effective Ingredients of Successful Psychotherapy.* New York: Brunner/Mazel, 1978, pp. 1–35.

This excellent article expands and supports the material developed in this chapter on the importance of expectation and the concept of mastery.

Hartman, Ann. "To Think About the Unthinkable," *Social Casework* 58:8 (October 1970), pp. 467–474.

An excellent article dealing with systems theory from the perspective of the social worker. It is strongly recommended for use in increasing the understanding of this complicated theory.

Janchill, Sister Mary Paul. "Systems Concepts in Casework Theory and Practice," *Social Case Work* 50:2 (February 1969), pp. 72–84.

Sister Janchill's excellent article is an attempt, paralleling Hartman's article, to select and organize systems concepts for use by the caseworker.

Liberman, Bernard L. "The Role of Mastery in Psychotherapy: Maintenance of Improvement and Prescription Change," in Jerome D. Frank et al. (Eds.), *Effective Ingredients of Successful Psychotherapy.* New York: Brunner/Mazel, 1978, pp. 35–72.

This article expands the importance of expectation and the concept of mastery discussed in the chapter.

Polansky, Norman A. *Ego Psychology and Communication.* New York: Atherton Press, 1971.

A good text to supplement the author's statements on the use of ego psychology.

Social Casework. 53:5 (May 1972); 53:8 (October 1972); 54:2 (February 1973); 55:2 (February 1974); 55:8 (October 1974); 56:7 (September 1975); 56:8 (October 1975); 57:3 (March 1976); and 58:8 (October 1977).

These issues provide much knowledge in the important area of ethnicity.

Sotomayor, Marta. "Language, Cultural and Ethnicity in Developing Self Concept," *Social Casework* 58:4 (April 77), pp. 195–204.

An article that should supplement the chapter statements about the meaning of diversity and difference. It presents some interesting considerations of the meaning and interrelationships of language, culture, and ethnicity in social work practice.

Vickers, Geoffrey. "Is Adaptability Enough?" *Behavioral Science* 4 (1959), pp. 219–234.

Vickers discusses the concept of adaptation from a system theory perspective in which adaptation is seen as an endless process of give and take between the individual, society, and the physical environment.

White, Robert W. "Ego and Reality in Psychoanalytic Theory," *Psychological Issues* 3:3 (1963), monograph 11.

This basic work by White develops the notion of competence and effectance and is well worth reading in connection with the material in this chapter.

CHAPTER 4

Values in social work practice

No issue can be more troublesome for social work than that of values. Efforts to make definitive statements about social work values stir heated controversy. Is there a value base which all social work practitioners must accept? Does social work possess a set of values that are unique in our culture in some way? Are there interventive methodologies that social workers should not use because they may be inconsistent with what the profession believes about the nature of humanity? These questions are commanding the attention of many contemporary social work thinkers. Charles Levy (1973) takes a clear stand: "The social work profession is well advised to tolerate differences in diversity about some things but not about its ideology." Levy goes on to suggest a framework for conceptualization of the profession's ideology along the dimensions of preferred conceptions of people, preferred outcomes for people, and preferred instrumentalities for dealing with people. Henry Miller (1968) notes some of the value dilemmas encountered by contemporary social work practitioners and suggests the withdrawal of social work from settings in which treatment is imposed or coerced as one alternative. Elizabeth Salomon (1967) suggests the possibility of inherent conflict between the humanistic stance of social work and scientific methodology. In their book Scott Briar and Henry Miller (1971, p. 42) advance the intriguing suggestion that one of the profession's traditional values—client self-determination—might be conceptualized as a treatment technique rather than a basic value. They suggest that clients in one-to-one relational systems make faster progress when extended maximum opportunities for self-determination, and thus self-determination might be viewed as a treatment technique geared toward facilitating client progress rather than as a basic human value which the profession promotes (p. 40).

Rather than offer definitive answers to these questions, we will attempt to raise some of the issues for thought and consideration as well as to outline our own positions. The chapter will attempt to accomplish the following three purposes:

1. Arrive at a definition of the concept of social work value.
2. Examine two value premises that are considered essential to social work practice.
3. Note relationships between these value premises and practice.

WHAT IS MEANT BY SOCIAL WORK VALUE?

Webster's defines value as "something intrinsically valuable or desirable." As noted in Chapter 2, value refers to things which are preferred, whereas knowledge refers to things which are known or knowable (see Reading 2–1). Values might be thought of as things a profession prefers; to use Levy's suggestions, values might be further classified as to preferred conceptions of people, preferred outcomes for people, and preferred instrumentalities for dealing with people. Values can be thought of as beliefs which a profession holds about people and about appropriate ways of dealing with people. Paul Halmos (1966), an English sociologist who has devoted considerable attention to the study of helping professions, suggests from an extensive review of their literature that helping professions operate from tenets of faith concerning nature of people. This faith, Halmos argues, is accepted without proof and provides guidance and direction for the helping professions. Thus values can be considered as unproved (probably unprovable) beliefs which a profession holds about the nature of people. These beliefs are reflected in the day-to-day work of the practitioner and provide direction and guidance to professional practice.

But are a profession's values uniquely its own? Does a profession find its uniqueness and distinctiveness in the value premises underlying its work? We think not. The social work profession exists within a larger cultural context; it identifies and operationalizes value premises already existing in society and not held exclusively by the profession. Schwartz's concept of the sources of limitations on professional social work practice relates to this point. Schwartz identifies three sources of limitations—the norms of the overall society, the function of the agency, and the service contract with the particular client system (see Reading 1–1). The social work profession exists within a culture whose value premises provide a source of limitation to the profession. A complex culture, however, is characterized by diverse value premises—some of which may be in conflict with each other. Like other professions, social work selects from this diversity the premises it will support and builds its practice on. The profession may achieve a degree of uniqueness in the particular way in which it operationalizes value premises, but the premises themselves are shared with other components of the culture.

We have tried to establish that values can be construed as unproven beliefs which guide and direct the work of a professional. These beliefs however, are not uniquely the possession of the profession. They are elements of the overall culture and are shared with others in the culture. However, they may achieve a degree of uniqueness in the way they are operationalized by particular groups. What are the value premises with which the social work profession identifies, and how are these premises operationalized? Two essential value premises underlie the practice of social work: (1) belief in the uniqueness and inherent dignity of the individual and (2) belief in client self-determination. Before these premises are examined, a few comments are necessary concerning the levels of abstractness with which values are discussed.

One way of thinking of values is to picture an inverted triangle (see Figure 4–1). The top or wide part of the triangle can represent values in a remote, general, or abstract sense. Near the bottom and point of the triangle the values become more proximate, specific, and concrete. The challenge to practitioners

FIGURE 4–1
Values can be conceptualized at abstract or concrete levels

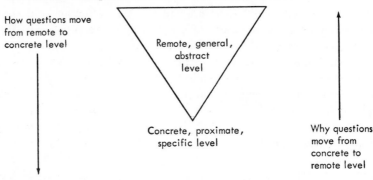

PRINCIPLES:
1. Agreement about values increases with remoteness.
2. It is important to know the level of abstraction when values are discussed.
3. The challenge to social work is to apply remote value concepts in concrete situations.
   Source: This diagram was suggested by Dr. Philip Heslin, Catholic Charities Bureau, Superior, Wisconsin.

is to take abstract value concepts, such as client self-determination or the innate dignity of the individual and to use these concepts in specific applied situations. When asking *how-to-do-it* questions, movement is implied in this direction, from the general to the specific; conversely, in asking a *why* question to seek justification or explanation of actions, movement is from the specific to the remote. In thinking of values at these two levels—remote and concrete—one must recognize that agreement generally increases with abstractness. Agreement, for example, to the abstract principle of client self-determination is readily secured; but at the specific level, say, in working with a 15-year-old who is bent on stealing cars, there may be considerable controversy over how to make this principle concrete. In talking about value premises, it is important to specify whether the discussion is about an abstract principle or is an attempt to apply an abstract principle in a concrete situation. The next task is to discuss two abstract principles—client self-determination and the innate dignity of the individual—and to identify ways in which they can be operationalized by the social work practitioner.

RESPECT FOR THE DIGNITY AND UNIQUENESS OF THE INDIVIDUAL

One of the central value premises consistently accepted and supported by the social work profession is that each person is a unique individual with an inherent dignity which is to be respected. People are sufficient ends in themselves and are not to be treated as objects or as means to other ends. Diversity and variety among individuals are to be welcomed and encouraged. Paul Tillich (1962), a theologian who has directed his attention to the philosophy of social work, refers to the uniqueness of every individual and situation as people's existential nature which he perceives social work as promoting. William Gordon derived his matching concept of the social work function (referred to in Chapter

1) from the same basic notion; Gordon (1969, p. 6) has suggested that the social work profession does not attempt to move either the environment or the person toward some ideal model but rather strives to establish linkages between individuals and their environment allowing for the widest possible diversity of both people and environments.

What are some of the implications of this principle for social work practice? This is the *how* question. How can the premise that every individual is unique and has the right to be treated with respect and dignity be applied in concrete social work situations? The potential for operationalizing the value premise will be considered in two areas—(1) sensitivity on the part of social workers to messages they are giving others; and (2) the relation of classification procedures to individualization.

Social psychologists have rather soundly established the theoretical position that people's image of themselves develops largely out of their communication with others (Rose, 1962). Specifically, people build and incorporate their self-image from the messages they receive from other people about themselves. Further, people who feel good about themselves, see themselves as persons of worth, and have a sense of their own strength and capability, tend to be happier and have the ability to deal constructively and appropriately with their environment.

Given these positions, social workers and other professionals intervening in the lives of people are well advised to be constantly sensitive to the messages they are extending to others about their worth. Do social workers, in the little things they do, communicate to other people that they are unique individuals to be highly prized? What, for example, is the message communicated when they safeguard time and provide a client with a specific time to be seen as opposed to a catch-me-on-a-catch-as-catch-can basis? Do appointments in advance communicate to the client a higher sense of respect than unannounced visits or hurriedly arranged telephone appointments? And, speaking of telephoning, how about the all too frequently overlooked return call? What message does the client get from the worker in terms of the client's worth when the worker does not have the courtesy or good sense to return telephone calls promptly? How about the ability to listen to the clients, to secure from them their own account of their situation, and to avoid prejudgments. And does not privacy, both in terms of how social workers conduct the interview and how they treat the material gained from interviews, communicate something to clients about the esteem in which they are held? Workers attempting to operationalize the premise of individual uniqueness and dignity may find it useful to repeatedly inquire of themselves: "What does this action on my part communicate to the client about my perception of the client?"

Another thorny problem confronting the social worker attempting to operationalize the value premise of individual uniqueness and dignity is that of striking a balance between classification and the responsibility to respond to persons as individuals. Classification refers to the need to generalize beyond individuals and to organize phenomena on the basis of common characteristics. This process is essential in order to make sense out of a mass of raw data and, as discussed in Chapter 2, is an essential part of the process of knowledge building. When the phenomena being dealt with are people, however, classification may cause social workers to respond to people as objects placed in a particular category rather than as individuals. The pitfalls of this process are being documented in a growing body of literature from sciologists studying deviance from a labeling perspective (Rubington and Weinberg, 1968; Simmons, 1969). Not only does labeling or classification lead to distortion of individual differences, but, as labeling theorists and their supporting research are noting, when a person is labeled deviant, those doing the labeling, and the surrounding audience frequently respond to the deviant on the basis of the label rather than on the basis of individual characteristics. This creates conditions for the development of a self-fulfilling prophecy in which the person becomes what the person has been labeled (Merton, 1957, p. 421–436). Current efforts to divert youth out of the juvenile justice system are recognition of the position that the very process of labeling a youngster a delinquent may contribute pressure toward additional delinquencies. Hans Toch (1970, p. 15) states the problem succinctly:

> Playing the classification game in the abstract, as is done in universities, is a joyful, exhilarating experience, harmless and inconsequential. Classifying people in life is a grim business which channelizes destinies and determines fate. A person becomes a category, is processed as a category, plays the assigned role, lives up to the implications. Labeled irrational, the person acts crazy; catalogued dangerous, the person becomes dangerous or stays behind bars.

Karl Menninger (1968, pp. 117–118), a noted psychiatrist, has reacted with strong words to the 1968 publication of a revised set of diagnostic (that is, labeling) categories for psychiatry:

> A committee of our worldly national body has just [1968] published a manual containing a full description of all the bewitchments to which all human flesh is err, with the proper names for each one, the minute suborder and subspecies listed and a code number for the computer. The colleagues who prepared this witch's hammer manual are worthy fellows—earnest, honest, hard-working, simplistic; they were taught to believe that these horrible things exist, these things with Greek names and Arabic numerals. And if patients show the stigmata, should they not be given the label and the number? To me this is not only the revival of medieval nonsense and superstition; it is a piece of social immorality.

Social workers who are sometimes prone to adopt psychiatric terms and classifications might pay special heed to Menninger's concern.

But is not classification necessary? Or, are we to agree with Salomon's position (1967) that there is an inherent conflict between the needs of science to order and classify and the humanism of social work? Toch (1970, p. 15) suggests that "the point of concern rests in any labels that lead to sorting or disposition." Toch takes the position that the labeling is necessary for thinking or theory building but is not particularly helpful in making dispositional decisions about people; concern should occur when decisions about what is going to happen to people are based on the individual's having previously been placed in a particular category. And yet it is precisely at this point that classification appears to be most useful. Generally classifications come into play when professionals are attempting to assess or diagnose a situation as a guide in selecting appropriate procedures for dealing with the problem. Our point of view on this will be more completely developed in

Chapter 9, in which assessment procedures will be discussed in terms of the participation of both the worker and the client. In general, however, we think it possible to develop assessment procedures which maximize individuality and minimize the need for categorization, yet maintain scientific rigor in dealing with valid and reliable data, vigorously pursuing facts, and conscientiously seeking alternative explanations.

We have attempted to identify one major value premise in social work— the individual is unique and should be treated with respect and dignity—and have suggested that this principle can be operationalized through careful analysis of our own behavior to be sure we are communicating messages to clients that indicate their worth and through minimizing the use of classifications which may both distort the individuality of the client and provide an impetus for the client and others to react to the classifications rather than the individual. We will now turn our attention to a second major value premise —client self-determination.

CLIENT SELF-DETERMINATION

The principle of client self-determination derives logically from belief in the innate dignity of the person. If people possess an inherent dignity, then it follows that they should be permitted to become what they wish—to determine their own lifestyles insofar as possible. The belief in client self-determination clearly implies that people should be permitted to make decisions for themselves. This carries with it the rather clear assumption that most of the time those decisions will be responsible—responsible in the sense that people in their decision-making will, for the most part, make decisions which are consistent with the welfare of the community. The social work stance has generally been to couple the concept of client self-determination with that of responsibility for the total community and to attempt to work out a balance between the two. Barring some clear-cut indication of danger to others, however, the social worker in day-to-day contacts with clients will generally attempt to maximize opportunities for client self-determination.

Inherent in the concept of client self-determination is the idea of alternatives. Self-determination implies decisions, or the making of choices between one course of action as contrasted with other courses of action. It is fraudulent to think of self-determination without alternatives. If there is only one course of action, how can there be self-determination? The client has no choice and thus no opportunity for self-determining. Much of social work activity with clients consists of a quest for alternatives in order to expand the client's opportunities for self-determination. The quest for alternatives may take various forms— helping the client develop new alternatives and resources within the environment or helping the client find and develop new ways to respond to environmental demands. Thus, interventive activity may focus on removing blockages within the environment which are limiting clients' opportunities or helping clients remove blockages within themselves which limit their abilities to see alternative courses of action. People whose range of responses to their environment are limited by their own stereotyped and patterned behavior are as much lacking in opportunity for self-determination as the ghetto client confronted with a lack of environmental opportunities.

Both the value premises of human dignity and self-determination imply respect and support of a wide diversity of client value orientations. But these values also raise many issues for the social worker. For example, if we believe in the self-determination of all people, what do we do when our clients coerce another or interfere seriously with the rights of a vulnerable person? Another issue in self-determination is inherent in the nature of choice itself. What is the meaning of self-determination if alternatives are so seriously limited as to be no choice at all? And, can one really exercise self-determination if one does not understand the consequences of the choice or if one does not have adequate facts upon which to base a decision? Certain laws to protect consumers, or laws relating to warranties and "truth in lending," are examples of society's actions in protecting those who must make certain decisions. If we believe that each person has a right to total self-determination with no limits, then they must support the notion that the race is always for the strong and the uncaring. Some of the most difficult jobs of the social worker are those involving conflicts between those who would exercise self-determination in ways that are destructive to themselves and others and those they damage. What is our responsibility when we take on the function that Schwartz discusses of representing the rights and needs of the individual but also the rights and needs of the human group (see Reading 1–1).

Does the principle of client self-determination require the social worker to support such value orientations among cultural groups in which they are dominant? It is our position that when client behavior results in damages to another individual or another group, damages that our knowledge of the needs of others tells us is severe, workers cannot support the hurtful action. However, this principle—that workers do not support the action—says nothing about what our action should be.

Charles Levy identifies a number of areas in which social workers valuing planned change have value conflicts with potential clients (see Reading 4–2). There may certainly be times in which a social worker's conception of how to operationalize the notion of human dignity and client self-determination may be inconsistent with value orientations held by clients; when this occurs these differences become a matter for discussion and negotiation between the worker and client. The differences must be clarified and a workable resolution achieved before intervention efforts occur. Client values may serve as a barrier to alternatives and a limit to self-determination. Hardman suggests that when the values of a client conflict with the welfare of others or the client's achieving the agreed upon goals, then the values themselves become an appropriate target for change.

Dale Hardman confronts the question of whether social work is always bound to support the self-determined actions of the client (see Reading 4–3). His unexamined belief in the client's right to self-determination leaves him uneasy but essentially uninvolved with the issue that the values of the client regarding sexual activity are likely to lead to illegal behavior and to damage the dignity and feelings of another. The rights of another only became a real problem for him when he realized that the person being damaged was his daughter. Suddenly the rights of the other became critical. Thus, Hardman was confronted with an issue not only of his own value system and its difference from the client's but with the issue of the responsibility of a professional person to be concerned with the rights of all people. Another intriguing example is the problem of wife battering which seems to be related to value orientations present in some groups of our society regarding the proper role of women as being subservient to the husband. And what about certain groups in our society that believe that "to spare the rod spoils the child?"

It is our position that social workers are not engaged in the process of forcing people to change behavior. Forced change of behavior is a matter for courts and the legal system. Therefore, any work to change client values or behavior in the interests of increasing life satisfactions of clients, or of others involved with clients, has to come from the engagement of client and worker in an agreed upon plan. Certainly client values may be such that actions that follow from them may hurt others, and certain values may also serve to limit the adequate choices of the client. However, any effort toward change must involve the client. Thus, to repeat, when the values of a client conflict with the rights of others or get in the way of the client achieving agreed upon goals then the values themselves become an appropriate target for change.

Thus the principle of client self-determination should always lead the social worker in the direction of engaging the client in three actions: (1) consideration of how these values may restrict progress toward the goals desired by the client, (2) consideration of all possible alternatives and their consequences for goal achievement, and (3) consideration of the rights and needs of others. The principle of client self-determination is seriously misunderstood if it is taken to suggest that the worker does nothing but put the total responsibility for considering choice upon the client with no offer of alternatives or consideration of the outcome of choice.

The client exercising decision-making is a key phrase in this formulation. The concept of client self-determination as operationalized in social work calls for maximizing opportunities for clients to make decisions for and about themselves. This is an area in which the social work profession may differ markedly from other professions. Clients generally go to other professionals for expert advice, that is, expecting to be told what in the view of the professional is best for the client. Patients expect the doctor to diagnose an ailment and to recommend a specific course of treatment, and clients expect the lawyer to advise them as to what action should be taken in dealing with a legal problem. In both of these situations there is, of course, an element of self-determination, inasmuch as the patient or client must ultimately decide whether or not to follow the expert's advice.

In most dealings with professionals in our culture the decision-making authority of the client is largely overshadowed by the expertise of the professional and, to a large extent, limited to the decision of whether or not to accept the professional's advice. But not so with the social work profession. The expertise of the social worker lies less in the substantive areas of knowing what is best for the client and more in the process area of assisting clients in developing alternatives for themselves, making a decision among the alternatives, and implementing the decision. To assume that one knows what is best for clients is to run the very grave risk of developing what Matthew Dumont (1968, p. 60) refers to as a rescue fantasy:

The most destructive thing in psychotherapy is a "rescue fantasy" in the thera-pist—a feeling that the therapist is the divinely sent agent to pull tormented souls from the pit of suffering and adversity and put them back on the road to happiness and glory. A major reason this fantasy is so destructive is that it car-ries the conviction that the patient will be saved only through and by the thera-pist. When such a conviction is communicated to patients, verbally or otherwise, they have no choice other than to rebel and leave or become even more helpless, dependent, and sick.

Sometimes the new or even the experienced worker feels frustration in com-ing to grips with the reality that the social worker cannot be the fountainhead of all wisdom who can masterfully assume and resolve the client's problems. A certain humility is necessary to recognize that the client is the chief problem-solver. This is not to deny that the worker plays a major part in assisting the client through the process and may at times serve rather forcefully as the client's agent.

Does the foregoing suggest that the social worker does not offer an opinion or make a suggestion? Emphatically not. Just as the extreme of taking over and making decisions for the client is to be avoided so is the extreme of never shar-ing a viewpoint with the client. Such action denies clients the benefit of the worker's judgment and may effectively deny clients alternatives that they may wish to consider in their own decision-making. As Charlotte Towle (1965, p. 26) has said: "The social worker's devotion to the idea that every individual has a right to be self-determining does not rule out valid concern with directing peo-ple's attention to the most desirable alternative." Workers have the obligations of sharing with clients their own thinking, perhaps their own experiences, not as a way of directing the clients' lives but rather as an additional source of information and input for the clients to consider in their own decision-making. It is imperative, however, that the social worker's input be recognized as in-formation to be considered and not as edict to be followed. Schwartz offers some very helpful suggestions in this regard (see Reading 1–1). He suggests that the worker has a responsibility to contribute data to the client and that the data might include facts, ideas, and value concepts. He goes on to argue that in contributing data the worker should inform the client that the worker is offering only part of the total available social experience and is not the source of all knowledge. Moreover, the data contributed should be clearly related to the purpose of work with the client, and opinions, while important data, should be clearly labeled as opinions and not represented as facts. Client self-de-termination does not imply worker nonparticipation; the skill, indeed, the mark, of successful practitioners lie in their abilities to share knowledge and thinking without imposing a judgment, but leaving the client free to accept or reject their views.

Another aspect of self-determination requires emphasis. Some workers con-fuse client self-determination with worker self-determination. We are not argu-ing for the latter. In taking on a professional responsibility, workers agree to limit their own self-determination in the clients' behalf. The National Associa-tion of Social Workers Code of Ethics clearly limits worker self-determination, especially in its seventh clause: "I practice social work within the recognized knowledge and competence of the profession" (see Reading 4–1). When a worker's communication style or dress style arouse the antagonism of clients or others who may influence clients, the worker's professional responsibility may call for the forfeiting of the worker's self-determination in the clients' behalf. This excerpt from an interview with a social worker functioning in a community organization capacity illustrates the frustrations which may be experienced by a worker unwilling to set aside personal self-determination in behalf of the clients.

> I remarked that it certainly must be satisfying to organize and be part of such an event. I was surprised when Alice shook her head slowly and said in a much more somber tone of voice, "No, 99 percent of the time there is very little glamour to organizing." I asked her to explain further, and she went on to say that it is hard, hard work and that one of the most discouraging things for her to realize is that oftentimes the people you are organizing aren't necessarily looking for a change in the system, but rather to become a part of that system. Usually that means playing the same games that those in power play. She talked further about the frustration she deals with constantly. I, too, began to feel that organizing was not the glamorous, romantic job I had pictured it to be.

Does this worker have an obligation to set aside her own goals of "changing the system" and work with clients who want to be successful within the system rather than produce more revolutionary change. We think she does.

In this section on client self-determination the authors have attempted to establish this concept as one of the value premises underlying social work. Five points have been made: (1) Self-determination commits the social worker and the client to a quest for alternatives. Without alternatives there is no opportunity to make decisions and no opportunity to engage in self-determination. (2) A major responsibility of the social worker is to maximize clients' opportunities for decision-making. Social workers are not experts in what is substantively best for clients and thus should avoid making decisions for clients; but social workers are expert in assisting clients in a process of joint decision-making. (3) Social workers have the obligation to offer their own viewpoints and suggestions to clients. These are offered as alternatives and input which a client may consider, and not as an edict or a "right" answer for the client. (4) Efforts to modify client's values are not necessarily inconsistent with the concept of self-determination providing the values interfere with the clients' efforts to attain their goals, or with the welfare of others, and clients concur with efforts to produce value change. (5) A differentiation must be made between client self-determination and worker self-determination. In assuming professional responsibility, workers sharply limit their own self-determination and become responsible for conducting themselves in ways which best meet the interests of clients and maximize clients' opportunities.

LEGAL AUTHORITY AND SELF-DETERMINATION

Fields of practice, in which the worker possesses legal authority that may be used to coerce the client, present some special issues in regard to the matter of client self-determination. Coercion is typically mandated for two different types of clients and for different reasons. One group of clients is perceived as being in need of protection because of their dependency status and thus coercion is justified as necessary to protect the client. Dependent children, developmentally disabled persons, and the aged are typically perceived as in need of protection. A second use of coercion is to force rehabilitation for those who have violated the norms of society—persons in this group typically include juvenile and adult offenders, chemically dependent persons, and mentally ill persons. We think the appropriate stance of a profession such as social work with a high commitment to the principal of client self-determination may vary in regard to the use of coercion depending on whether the coercion is used for the protective or the forced rehabilitative purposes.

William Reid and Laura Epstein (1972) make a distinction between the protective and helping functions of the social worker when they suggest that the practitioner must not only recognize these differences but also must make sure the client understands them. We have argued that available knowledge should direct our interventions (see Chapter 2). And our knowledge base confirms that dependent children, developmentally disabled persons, and aged persons may be victimized and harm themselves; responsible action would indicate that some limitations in client self-determination may be warranted in the interest providing protection to the client. Even within the limits imposed as necessary to protect the client, the worker has responsibility to develop as many practical alternatives as possible for client decision making thus increasing client self-determination. For example, our knowledge may indicate that a physically ill, aged person may no longer be able to live alone at home despite their wishes to do so. A need for protection may limit client self-determination in regard to this choice but the astute worker may well be able to engage the client in decision-making regarding the type of specific alternative living arrangement to be followed. Likewise, in child welfare children who must be removed from their homes because of extreme neglect or abuse may be provided considerable involvement in the decision-making regarding the alternative living arrangements; indeed, involving the children in this decision-making may open up resources such as relatives, neighbors, and others previously unknown to the social worker.

When coercive authority is being used and justified on the basis of protecting the client we think it is essential that the worker be clear as to the knowledge base which justifies the use of authority as well as the source and extent of the authority; these matters must further be clearly communicated to the client. The source and extent of authority is an example of agency function, Schwartz's second source of limitation on the worker's activity (see Reading 1–1). Because of possibilities of abusing protective authority we consider it appropriate for clients to have opportunities to request appeal and review of worker's decisions and consider the involvement of courts or guardians independent of the worker as an appropriate check and balance against possible abuses. Social workers in the profession have an obligation to continually reassess whether coercive authority is really necessary to protect the client or is being used unnecessarily to impose a particular standard upon a client. Marvin Silverman (1977, p. 177) addresses this issue in relation to coercion of children:

> If children's rights became a reality, there would clearly be a change in the
> nature of many social workers' professional relationships. These would become

largely voluntary—the kind of relationship most consistent with the traditions of social work. There would also be changes in specific roles. At the present time, there are large and expensive professional and bureaucratic structures which are organized to maintain children in nonvoluntary associations and to work with the problems such associations generate. They would no longer be needed. If schools were populated by willing students, there would be far less need for school social workers, school psychologists, guidance personnel, and administrators who deal mainly with discipline problems. There are children in residential treatment centers not because of family problems but because of inability to function in school. Police, courts, and probation officers spend a great deal of energy in dealing with truancy, status offences, incorrigibility, and runaways. With increased children's rights, social work roles would flow directly from children's needs rather than being filtered through structures which, to some extent, at least, are organized around social control. Similarly, teachers could concentrate on improving the educational program, and police could concentrate on true crime—juvenile and adult.[1]

The second use of legal authority—to attempt to force rehabilitation upon the client—creates a serious dilemma for the profession. There are at least two distinct directions by which this dilemma might be resolved. One direction is to attempt to integrate the authority and service roles and, within the limitations imposed by the setting, try to expand opportunities for client self-determination. A second alternative to be discussed later, would be for social work to withdraw from the coercive efforts to rehabilitate.

Typically social workers have attempted to integrate their authority and service functions (Hardman, 1960; Hatcher, 1978; Klockars, 1972; Overton, 1965). While the presence of legal authority may limit areas for client self-determination, it also leaves extensive areas for the exercise of client self-determination. These include determining how the authority will be exercised as well as noting areas in addition to the legal requirements in which self-determination may be emphasized. A probation agency, for example, may enforce the legal requirement that the probationer must report to the probation officer; this is not a matter for client self-determination. But the sensitive probation officer can allow for considerable client self-determination in the frequency of reporting, the length of the interviews, the time of reporting, and the content to be discussed during the interviews. Even in correctional settings clients can be extended considerable self-determination in how they utilize workers including, if they choose, only using them for the minimum mandated by the probation orders. Gerald O'Connor (1972) offers a very insightful position on the question of self-determination in corrections:

> The principle of self-determination, the freedom to choose one's own destiny is based on an assumption of individual dignity. . . . The recognition of people's right to free choice guarantees that they may choose to run their life as they see fit. This choice may run counter to society's welfare and even their own, yet essentially it is their choice and their prerogative. Society may censure, but it cannot take from them the right; nor should society strip them of personal dignity by a censure. The criminal then has a right to say "crime is my choice

---

and I am willing to pay the price. If you send me to prison, I am paying my debt to society and refuse to submit to your attempts to reform me." The principle of self-determination makes it incumbent upon society to honor such a plea.

There are large numbers of inmates in correctional institutions who recognize a need for rehabilitation and are willing to become involved in programs for that end. An inmate's voluntary recognition of a need for assistance does not, in turn, give officials a free reign in outlining the inmate's rehabilitation program. It is reasonable that the offender have input into the definition of the offender's own problem and have this included in the official assessment. The inmate should have the opportunity to say what type of program would be of assistance and who should provide the services. Further, it seems appropriate that the inmates have a right, in part, to determine the conditions under which the services are delivered.[2]

Even in situations involving legal authority, considerable latitude exists for clients to exercise self-determination. Skillful workers can maximize these opportunities with the client. At the very least, of course, the clients have the option of determining whether they are going to do anything more than the legal minimum as well as the option of ignoring the requirements of the authority and accepting the consequences.

Another response to the dilemma of self-determination vis-à-vis coercive services is the withdrawal of social work from these roles (Miller, 1968). The lack of evidence to support the effectiveness of coerced rehabilitation (Lipton, Martinson, and Wilks, 1975; Martinson, 1974) further supports this notion. Withdrawal of social work from coerced rehabilitative roles does not, of course, mean that social services should not be provided to offenders and others who are presently being subjected to forced efforts of rehabilitation. The services of social workers should certainly be provided to these populations but structures can be developed which permit the provision of these services on a voluntary basis.

Many offenders would certainly enter into agreements to work jointly with social workers to resolve problems the offender is experiencing in their personal situations and interactions. Silverman makes the same assertion for children. While this issue is certainly a very complex one and one which will undoubtedly be debated within the profession for quite some time, our inclination is to begin challenging the appropriateness of social work activity in coerced rehabilitative settings and to begin development of structures, policies, and programs to permit a more voluntary association and partnership between client and social worker. Such a process is more consistent with the principal of client self-determination. This does not, of course, exempt persons who are found guilty of violating laws from being negatively sanctioned or punished by the society. The authors only suggest that the role of the social worker should not be to carry out these sanctions but to provide social services within a partnership arrangement with clients, regardless of their status, who are defining problems in their day-by-day living and wish to engage in a partnership with the social worker for problem-solving purposes.

---

[2] Copyright 1972 by the University of Chicago. All rights reserved. Reprinted by permission of the University of Chicago Press from Gerald O'Connor, "Toward a New Policy in Adult Corrections," *Social Service Review* 46 (December 1972), pp. 485–486.

RECAPITULATION

This section has presented our views concerning social work values. Values were defined as things which a profession prefers but which cannot be proven to be true. Values are not unique to a profession but are adapted from the overall culture. The uniqueness and innate dignity of the individual and the principle of client self-determination were analyzed as two value premises underlying social work practice. The process of operationalizing these values—especially client self-determination—provides an opportunity for social work to find its distinctiveness among the professions.

Several implicit principles in the preceding discussion should be more explicitly stated: (1) Values are guides to action; they are principles which, whenever possible, are to be maximized. Values, however, are not straitjackets. They are to be used selectively and creatively, although the primary focus will be on maximizing them. (2) In situations where the value premise and knowledge are in conflict, opt for knowledge. In chapter 2 a potential conflict was noted between self-determination and a child's need for protection and stability in order to meet developmental needs; a lower priority was attached to the value of self-determination because of knowledge of the child's needs. (3) When knowledge is lacking, the value premises should become the prevailing standards. (4) Values limit the uses to which the profession's methodology can be placed. Group processes, for example, might well be used to subvert individualism or to stir up fear and hysteria which threaten diversity and self-determination. This use of group strategies is inappropriate because it is inconsistent with the value premises of the profession. Change strategies and methodology can be used for a variety of ends. Social work practitioners must be sure that their strategies are used to support the uniqueness of the individual and the client's right to self-determination.

A LOOK FORWARD

Two articles in addition to the Code of Ethics of the National Association of Social Workers are reproduced in this chapter. Charles Levy identifies a series of potential value conflicts between social workers committed to planned change and clients, but he does not offer suggestions for resolving these conflicts (see Reading 4–2). Our position is that they should be discussed and a working resolution developed as a part of the worker-client problem-solving process. Dale Hardman focuses on an intriguing issue: "Should social workers attempt to change client values?" His answer will provide considerable opportunity for discussion and debate (see Reading 4–3).

The National Association of Social Workers Code of Ethics provides a statement, at an abstract level, of the present values of the profession (see Reading 4–1). But there is not universal agreement that this statement reflects social work values appropriately. The authors do not necessarily expect agreement with these readings or with the foregoing material. This material is presented to stimulate thought and discussion about some of the difficult value questions confronting the profession.

The pages ahead will present an approach to social work practice which is believed to be both humanistic and scientific. Classification is minimized, clients are involved in a partnership undertaking with workers; and individuality is maximized. The problem-solving process which is to be outlined requires a high degree of rationality and discipline on the part of workers. In Chapter 5 the concept of relationship—the medium through which much of the problem-solving work may occur—is introduced. A discussion of communication and interviewing as basic skills is found in Chapter 6. Subsequent chapters outline the phases of the problem-solving model.

Reading
4-1 Code of Ethics*[1]

National Association of Social Workers

Social work is based on humanitarian, democratic ideals. Professional social workers are dedicated to service for the welfare of mankind; to the disciplined use of a recognized body of knowledge about human beings and their interactions; and to the marshaling of community resources to promote the well-being of all without discrimination.

Social work practice is a public trust that requires of its practitioners integrity, compassion, belief in the dignity and worth of human beings, respect for individual differences, a commitment to service, and a dedication to truth. It requires mastery of a body of knowledge and skill gained through professional education and experience. It requires also recognition of the limitations of present knowledge and skill and of the services we are now equipped to give. The end sought is the performance of a service with integrity and competence.

Each member of the profession carries responsibility to maintain and improve social work service; constantly to examine, use, and increase the knowledge upon which practice and social policy are based; and

to develop further the philosophy and skills of the profession.

This Code of Ethics embodies certain standards of behavior for the social worker in his professional relationships with those he serves, with his colleagues, with his employing agency, with other professions, and with the community. In abiding by the code, the social worker views his obligations in as wide a context as the situation requires, takes all of the principles into consideration, and chooses a course of action consistent with the code's spirit and intent.

As a member of the National Association of Social Workers I commit myself to conduct my professional relationships in accord with the code and subscribe to the following statements:

- I regard as my primary obligation the welfare of the individual or group served, which includes action for improving social conditions.
- I will not discriminate because of race, color, religion, age, sex, or national ancestry, and in my job capacity will work to prevent and eliminate social discrimination in rendering services, work assignments, and in employment practices.
- I give precedence to my professional responsibility over my personal interests.
- I hold myself responsible for the quality and extent of the service I perform.
- I respect the privacy of the people I serve.

---

* Reprinted by permission of the National Association of Social Workers.

[1] Adopted by the Delegate Assembly of the NASW, October 13, 1960, and amended April 11, 1967. The editors desired to have this article reflect neutral gender; however, permission to edit the article was denied by the publisher.

- I use in a responsible manner information gained in professional relationships.
- I treat with respect the findings, views, and actions of colleagues and use appropriate channels to express judgment on these matters.
- I practice social work within the recognized knowledge and competence of the profession.
- I recognize my professional responsibility to add my ideas and findings to the body of social work knowledge and practice.
- I accept responsibility to help protect the community against unethical practice by any individuals or organizations engaged in social welfare activities.

- I stand ready to give appropriate professional service in public emergencies.
- I distinguish clearly, in public, between my statements and actions as an individual and as a representative of an organization.
- I support the principal that professional practice requires professional education.
- I accept responsibility for working toward the creation and maintenance of conditions within agencies which enable social workers to conduct themselves in keeping with this code.
- I contribute my knowledge, skills, and support to programs of human welfare.

Reading
4–2 Values and planned change*

Charles S. Levy

Despite differences in views among social workers concerning the implications and consequences of planned change as an approach to social work practice, there is considerable agreement among them regarding its applicability to social work practice. This "process of giving help to people . . . who must change in order to improve their level of functioning" (Lippitt, Watson, and Westley, 1958, p. 4) has given to social workers in their professional orientations responsibility to clients at all levels of practice—work with individuals, with families and groups, and with representatives of organizations and communities.

The meaning of planned change has been extended, however (and here the extent of consensus is probably more limited), to imply not merely practice *with* various types of clients toward the end of improving their level of functioning, but direct action *on* the institutions, governments, and societies

around them in order to effect changes. The concept nevertheless applies to the social workers' professional role in that they encourage for their clients—whether individuals, families, groups, agencies, or communities—change in their functioning in order to manipulate and modify their social, community, and governmental environment more effectively. In such a case, the social workers' professional aim is to effect change in their clients so that they, along with social workers, may make the kinds of changes in the institutions around them which will net for them more of the available rewards and resources.

For example, social workers who work with welfare clients may, through the social work helping process, evoke in them a revised view of their rights and entitlements and of their own role in, and capacity for, realizing them. They, in turn, may effect change in the institutions which affect them. This process may necessitate the social workers' direct collaboration and reenforcement, depending on whether they also regard themselves as advocates.

* Reprinted by permission of Family Service Association of America, publisher, from *Social Casework* 54:8 (October 1972), pp. 488–493.

Prerequisites for planned change

When social workers are professionally oriented to apply the concept of planned change, a thorough grounding in the nature, process, components, and consequences of personal and social change, both historically and dynamically, is required. Conscious and deliberate use of themselves as intervening agencies (in this capacity they are often described as "change agents"[1]) require them to understand why and how persons, groups, organizations, or institutions change in their functioning, and under what circumstances.

For social workers such understanding is similar to their understanding of the growth and behavior of persons, social groups, and institutions in society. They base their judgments regarding the action they feel responsible to take, as well as their ultimate choices of action in relation to those they serve, upon this understanding. In addition, since social workers are but one species of change agents, their professional orientation to planned change requires elements which distinguish theirs from the professional orientation of other change agents, although not all of its elements are inevitably distinguishable from those of other professional orientations. They certainly need not be mutually exclusive or contradictory. Nevertheless, some differences are indicated for a sufficient determination of the division of labor among various change-oriented professions.

Bases for differentiation among change agents

One basis for differentiation among change agents is the professional functions they represent. Both the psychiatrist and the social worker may regard themselves as change agents with the shared aim of "giving help to people . . . who must change in order to improve their level of functioning." Nevertheless, they do represent different professional functions which would (or should) lead to differences in specific ends sought through professional intervention, differences in modes of intervention, and differences in knowledge, competencies, and skills relevant to these modes of intervention. There may be a great deal of overlap between psychiatrist and social worker in these respects, but the differences between them have to be sufficiently significant in order to reflect the division of professional labor and to justify differences of background education, and training. Some boundaries are necessary to define professions. Their functions as sanctioned by society, their methods, and the knowledge premises upon which their functions and methods are founded require some delineation.

Another basis of differentiation among change agents is the value orientations by which they are guided. The remainder of this article is devoted to a proposed value orientation for the social worker in relation to planned change. Such an orientation may be regarded as consistent with the social worker's professional function and with the codified values and ethics of the organized social work profession.

A comparison of this orientation with that ascribed to other occupations is not intended here. The formulation of such an orientation for social work would make a comparative study possible of course, but its main purpose is to suggest guides for professional practice in relation to planned change. The emphasis here, therefore, is not only on what social workers value but on the bearing their professional values ought to have on their choices of professional action (that is, strategies of intervention) in relation to planned change.

---

1 *"Planned change . . .* originates in a decision to make a deliberate effort to improve the system and to obtain the help of outside agents in making this improvement. We call this outside agent *change agents* (Lippitt, Watson, and Westley, 1958, p. 10). The "system" alluded to refers to the "client system" or "the specific system—person or group—that is being helped . . ." (p. 12).

The values of clients in relation to planned change

Using the relatively simple definition of values as the ideals and preferences of a group toward which its members have an affective regard,[2] one may understand the responses of clients to personal or social change, or to its prospect—planned or otherwise—on the basis of clients' values in relation to change. Clients at any level of social organization, to which the professional responsibility of the social worker happens to correspond, have value predispositions toward or against changing or being changed. These value predispositions constitute an important determinant of the social worker's professional activity or inactivity and thereby become a component of social workers' value orientation as they contemplate planned change. The issue is not the professional skill required, but whether social workers will honor the values of their clients and how they will take them into account in selecting their courses of professional action to affect their clients. Brief consideration of a few of these value predispositions of clients, which would affect their view of the prospect of planned personal or social change, should attest to their relevance to social work practice.

Valuation of idea of change

Clients often have specific inclinations in regard to change or its prospect. They may be highly motivated to change or very resistant to it. Their responses to the suggestion of, or the pressure to, change may be psychologically derived: Clients may dread different ways of coping with their situations and conditions. On the other hand, these responses may be practically moti-

---

[2] Compare the definition in *The Random House Dictionary of the English Language* (unabridged edition) which suggests that values may be either positive or negative—that is, affective regard may be *toward* or *against* an object or prospect depending upon one's values.

vated: Clients may dread the real consequences of changes they are asked to make in their mode of functioning. A youth being guided toward personal emancipation may struggle to remain dependent. A group may prefer to retain its restrictive admissions procedures because its members enjoy the superiority of status implied by these procedures and hence resist moves toward democratization. A community or society, out of zeal to preserve its history and identity, may block attempts at technological improvement.

Very often these inclinations are culturally reenforced. The charge has been made that in our time and place change is inherently valued in some circles. For many, what is new or different is *ipso facto* good. Contrariwise, in some circles change is devalued. Tradition is the guiding motif. Besides other reasons for welcoming or resisting change, clients have some kind of value predisposition to the idea of change—for, neutral, or against. Social workers can hardly ignore this predisposition. They must first evaluate their own, or their profession's, choices regarding change and their readiness to relinquish their aspirations to effect planned change should their clients prefer not to have it. They must also understand this predisposition in order to deal with it, even if dealing with it means overcoming value-based resistance to change. In short, such a value predisposition is a practical consideration for the social worker, as well as a value consideration.

Valuation of self-determination

To clients, even to those who acknowledge their need for the social worker's service and invite it, the option to determine their own course and destiny may be more highly valued than the need for change. Conversely, they may prefer to have others make decisions for them (Levy, 1963, pp. 416–419). Social workers, in their turn, must clarify their own value predispositions in relation to those of their clients. The predisposition to preserve one's own self-determination at all costs, even to the point of resisting the social worker's strategic interventions, is especially difficult for the social worker who is already identified with the value of self-determination. As expressed in the *Standards for the Professional Practice of Social Work*,[3] the social worker has "unswerving conviction of the inherent, inalienable right of each human being to choose and achieve his own destiny in the framework of a progressive, yet stable, society." If clients feel justified in resisting social workers and the prospect of change which they present, social workers will have to come to value terms with them, particularly if the planned change which they envisage represents a hard imperative for them.

Valuation of planned specific change

Clients may differ from social workers in their interpretation of what constitutes improvement. They therefore resist the idea of change not from their own value predisposition or from a threat to their own self-determination, but rather because they do not consider the social workers' planned change as valuable, regardless of their factual data and experience.

An individual's defenses may be too precious to them to subject them to modification. An ethnic group's comfort and security in the selective association of its members with one another may cause it to repel efforts to broaden the horizons of their association to include members of other ethnic groups. The rituals of a religious group (a snake sect, for example) may mean too much

---

[3] *Standards for the Professional Practice of Social Work*. Adopted by the 1951 Delegate Assembly, American Association of Social Workers, New York, 1951. Supplement to *Social Work Journal* (July 1952), p. 3. The last phrase sounds a bit like the AASW taketh away what it hath given, but since the only problem is a bit of ambiguity in the context and not in the principle, the value is cited as stated.

to it to permit consideration of alternatives, even in the interest of personal health. In each case, the change proposed or intended by the practitioner represents to the client something to be avoided. This feeling exists despite what the practitioner considers compelling evidence dictating change.

Valuation of the agent of change

Social workers must measure carefully the clients' responses to their role as change agents and to the change which they advocate. When their clients' estimation of them and their profession is low, social workers must evaluate carefully their responses to their role as change agents and to the changes which they advocate. They must also measure carefully their own responses to theirs. It is not enough for them simply to overcome their clients' resistances with expertise. They must also decide to what extent they will take into account the values which generate the resistance. Clients with a cynical view toward the commitments and loyalties of social workers may question their good faith in relation to changes espoused or promoted.

Comparison of changes

The priority ordering of changes by clients on the basis of their value predispositions may not always coincide with that of social workers. Though their priorities may, in fact, be more judicious than theirs and be more practically related to what is attainable or to what is a prerequisite for other changes, the clients may not think so. They may also be right. With this fact, too, social workers will have to make their value-oriented peace—not simply to know what to do, but whether to do it at all.

Valuation of timing of change

Although clients may value the prospect of change, they may prefer a different timing. If they are more radically oriented than the social worker, they will seek action "now." If workers are more radically oriented, they will press for immediate change while the clients will hold out for long-range change. Justice and opportunity may be on the side of the clients, and social workers may know it; therefore they will have to contend with their values. Their objective will be to arrive at a course of action that will seem right to them and compatible with the professional values to which they subscribe. In these instances the criterion for social workers cover what they regard as right and good, not what they regard as more efficient or successful, even in terms of the objectively verifiable benefits to be accrued to their clients.

Value-based actions of the social worker

It is also incumbent upon social workers to crystallize their own value orientations with respect to planned change. Some of their dilemmas in professional practice relate to the congruence or incongruence between their value orientations and those of their clients. Their resolution will depend in great measure on the values by which they are guided in their practice and their correlation with the values dictating their clients' responses to the personal or social change to which their practice is geared.

Brief consideration of some of the loci of the social workers' value predispositions in relation to planned change should suggest some of the sources of value conflicts they may have with their clients. It should also show some of the sources of value conflicts they may experience within themselves, as they select or discard modes of professional intervention which affect their clients.

Social workers, having taken stock of the internal and external conditions affecting their clients, charge them and their approaches to them with their own affective regard, and on that basis, they value change or stability. Their valuation of the need for change in their clients' functioning or circumstances may or may not coincide with

their clients' valuation. In any case, social workers' values require scrutiny before as well as when they are applied toward the end of effecting planned change.

Social workers who place a premium on role as change agents will tend to value change above adaptation and accommodation. They will orient their practice primarily to change either in their clients' functioning or in the functioning of institutions around them. The queasiness of social workers about the "adjustment" of clients may be explained by their relatively high valuation of change, particularly external or environmental change. A similar value attends resistance to internal change when clients' own functioning is viewed as in need of improvement. In both cases change is valued, although a debate among social workers might be precipitated concerning who or what should do the changing. Social workers' valuation of their roles as change agents go quite far in determining their choices of professional action as well as their experience in relation to their clients.

Clients' resistance to personal or social change and, therefore, to social workers' attempts to effect it may be viewed by social workers as a hindrance, an obstacle, or a nuisance to be surmounted. This resistance could also be viewed as a reflection of values which merit preservation and respect. The substantive merits of the planned change notwithstanding, the accreditation of the clients' resistance on the grounds of self-determination, or the sheer strength and identity which it represents, would depend upon social workers' affective regard for it—to the point, perhaps, of laying aside professional goals related to personal or social change.

Social workers may be so oriented to the attainment of goals related to the needs to which they assign high priority that they may not look beyond them to the chain of consequences and interactions that could be set off were the change effected. The effect of planned change on clients—their lives, their situations, their relationships—merits social workers' professional concerns. This concern is a matter of values as well as the rational consideration of the consequences of available alternatives. The degree of responsibility social workers feel for the aftermath of the change stimulated by their professional intervention, as well as for the change itself, becomes an integral part of their value orientation as change agents.

Translation of values into professional ethics

The values of their clients in relation to the personal and social change toward which social workers have positive affective regard discipline their choices of professional action. Similarly, social workers' values regarding the prospective impact and consequences of their intervention for their clients, not only as far as the contemplated change is concerned but also as far as the process of effecting it is concerned, also discipline their choices of professional action. These constraints amount to ethics for social workers in the role of change agents, for they are the behavioral expression of the values, their clients' and their own, to which they are oriented.

Social workers share values which shape their preferences with regard to the *ways* of fulfilling professional responsibility as well as the responsibility to fulfill it and to whom (National Association of Social Workers, 1971; 1958).

It is not only what social workers do that constitute a professional concern, but how they do it; it is also the effect they have on clients before they do it, while they are doing it, and after they have done it. A "good" (that is, practical) solution to a client's problem may be discarded or avoided by social workers if it is to be attained at the expense of the client's dignity or self-determination. It may not be discarded by the workers, but social work values press in that direction; if they do not press social workers firmly enough to influence their behavior, they may be adjudged unethical.

Emphasis has been placed here on value considerations affecting the role of social workers as change agents because the need for change at so many levels of society may be regarded as so imperative that it is easy to lose sight of the value-based responsibility of social workers toward the clients through whom, with whom, and for whom their professional efforts at planned change are designed. Fortunately, social workers' clients are not the exclusive channel for change, although they are a very important one. Other actions through which necessary changes can be effected, at other levels or in other capacities, are possible. To the extent that clients themselves are an important or necessary medium and locus of change, however, social workers who work with them must not so abandon themselves to their commendable quest for personal and social improvements that they abandon their clients, their values, and those values of their own and their profession which are calculated to preserve the integrity, the freedom, and the autonomy of their clients.

Reading

4-3 Not with my daughter you don't!*

Dale G. Hardman

It was a balmy spring afternoon at the Blintz County workhouse. The interviewing room was only half separated from the cell corridors. The inmate looked out the dirt-specked window for some time, then returned his gaze to the social worker. "Twelve more days. I could do 12 days on a bed of spikes. You're the reason I got 55 days knocked off my six months. I wouldn'ta got it without you went to bat for me."

Oscar De Curia only nodded, but inwardly he beamed because expressions of gratitude were infrequent among workhouse clients. "I would like," he said, "to get some idea of your plans when you get out. Most guys need some help getting into a job or school or. . . ."

"Nah. I work for my old man, putting up siding. I always got a job waiting."

"Good. What about school?"

"Can't work and go to school too."

"Some guiys do." De Curia bit his lip; he knew as soon as he said it. There he was, imposing his middle-class norms on a lower-class client.

"I quit when I was 15. Nine years ago—too late to go back now."

De Curia had an impulse to suggest some Voc-Ed courses, but instead he just nodded and said, "Okay then, what about your social life?"

"That's all I been thinking about since I got my commutation."

De Curia brightened a bit. At least here he didn't have to worry about imposing his own norms. Here he could relax, be more natural, more human.

"Chicks," said the inmate. He leaned back and clasped his fingers behind his thick black curly hair. "Chicks is my specialty. Take the average guy in here—for him sex is just quick service stuff: roll in the hay, be on your way. No art to it. No class."

"You're most artistic, then."

"That's it. I'm an artist. Most guys in here wouldn't know the difference."

"But you do. How would you go about it that's any different from anybody else?"

"Well see, same as me they've been locked up for six months to a year. Anything would look good to them, and they'll try to make up for the whole year in the first ten minutes they're out. First broad they see. But not me. Like the soup commercial says: 'To make the best you gotta begin with the best. Then prepare it tenderly . . . carefully . . . slowly.' So I begin with the best. Nothing but fresh meat for me—very fresh. A virgin."

"I see. Well, since there's not a lot of those around. . . ."

"Well, ya gotta know where to look. For one thing you gotta start young—maybe 14 or 15—so you find where they hang out."

"Hmm." De Curia opened his mouth to point out that a sex act with an adolescent would constitute a new violation, but he again bit his tongue and admonished himself that he must not be a moralist. And certainly this client was canny enough to know the law on this point.

"They hang out a lot around Whiffly Dip, especially on weekends. Skating rinks and bowling alleys is good hunting grounds. Always full of teeny chicks."

"Hmm." In truth, De Curia felt a bit more uncomfortable with each self-revelation of his client. But he knew that disapproval on his part would only serve to turn off his client's verbal spigot, and certainly the man needed to talk after four months in lock-up.

"There was one little chick I met at the Rollerama just before I got busted. A virgin, I'll bet my shirt. About 14. Real good skater."

"Hmm." De Curia resolved to be nondirective if it killed him, but his discomfort continued to rise.

"I only saw her two, three times before I got sent up. Skated with her each time. I know she likes me. I think she's the one I'll start with."

"I see." De Curia shifted uneasily as his tension mounted.

"Like I say, begin with the best. And she's the best. Long slender legs. Willowy. Little round bazoobs like ripe peaches. Long auburn hair, always in a pony-tail. Her name was Irma Jean something."

Every man has a sort of safety plug in his boiler; it melts at a lower temperature than the boiler and serves to prevent the boiler from rupturing. And here De Curia blew his plug. Out spewed his professional role, his persona, in a great gust and blast, and he stood before his client a very angry human being. "Hey, wait a minute! That's my daughter you're talking about, you lecherous bastard!"

Oscar's conflict

It was several hours later that Oscar De Curia sat in his office, pondering his misdirected interview at the workhouse. In ten years of practice he had held doggedly to the dictum of nondirection: the nonmoralistic listener, eschewing judgments, never imposing his own norms, never playing God, never setting himself up as an ethical model for his clients' emulation. For ten years, he had adhered to these fundamental premises, drilled into his skull in classrooms, in texts and journals, and in interaction with other social workers. He was, he believed, the epitome of Powers and Witmer's delineation (1951): "Modern casework is distinguished . . . by the fact that its practitioners seldom give advice, cite ethical precepts or the consequence of antisocial behavior, or urge particular courses of action." True, he constantly had to remind himself in those pesky situations that clashed against his own middle-class value system. He had come, in fact, to feel a bit apologetic for being middle class or subscribing to its norms. He felt as though he had been called a dirty name when he was referred to as middle class. But now, suddenly, when these norms were violated close to home, his carefully cultivated professional posture had disintegrated and he had blown his cool, the interview, and the case.

Although De Curia was not given to extensive self-contemplation, he was, in those brief and unaccustomed moments of introspection, essentially honest with himself. Perhaps these two facts were related: in introspection he usually came out loser, due to a basic trait of honesty, so he indulged in it rarely.

Oscar had experienced similar interviews in the past, listening with composure to expressions of sexual exploitation, tales of assaults on persons or property, and threats of vengeance or power or violence. He had often felt a rising discomfort and a need to protest, and always, until today, he had successfully repressed such unprofessional impulses. But now, with his treasured, auburn-haired teen-ager as the proposed object. . . .

At this juncture a new thought trekked across Oscar's synapses: suppose the name his client had dropped had not been Irma Jean; suppose instead it had been Sandra or Millie. Wasn't it conceivable that the fathers of other pony-tailed, knobby-kneed damsels might harbor feelings for them as tender as his? De Curia was struck by this thought much as Goliath encountered David's stony projectile: such a thing had never before entered his head. It jolted him in his tracks. A host of balding and paunchy middle-aged fathers arose in his mind's eye, like a legion of Banquo's ghosts, to ask: In how many hundred cases, have you said "Mm hmm" or "I see" and thereby given tacit asquiescence to illegal, immoral, or violent acts? It was well beyond closing time when the janitor found De Curia still at his desk pondering his conflict.

Upon his return home, De Curia was unusually attentive to his daughter, but otherwise his manner was, for him, exceptionally quiet and subdued. His wife reckoned that he had either been fired or out philandering but that in either case he would shortly tell her so. He hadn't and he didn't.

Generalizing the problem

During the ensuing week, Oscar De Curia resolved that he would, at whatever cost, resolve his newly mounted conflict. One of his first acts was to request that his supervisor transfer the client who had torpedoed his cool. As has been noted, Mr. De Curia was not a profoundly thoughtful man, but an honest one. His supervisor, on the other hand, was not a profoundly honest man, but a thoughtful one, and so he asked the reason for his subordinate's request. And within the next half hour De Curia had upended the whole wretched can of worms.

The supervisor had indeed encountered this knotty question before; he had mulled it over at considerable length and then shelved it. But Oscar would not be shelved. He was a persistent clod, and he insisted on answers. And answered he was. The supervisor said: "Mm hmm."

"Well, it's true, ain't it?" De Curia waxed ungrammatical only when he became emotional. "From the time we enter graduate school we're admonished against imposing our own values on people. So I don't and look what happens! My own daughter is up for grabs!"

"Mm," said the supervisor, thoughtfully.

"Tell me honestly, Jake," (the supervisor encouraged this bit of familiarity) "What would you do? You must have encountered this kind of incongruity before. How did you handle it?"

Jake could not admit that he had resolved the question by shelving it. So he said, "Hmm." Thoughtfully, that is.

"That doesn't exactly answer my question, you know," De Curia persisted.

Jake squirmed considerably, inwardly at least. Outwardly he was all concern and empathy, as a supervisor should be.

"Well, the problem is really much larger than you are recognizing here, Oscar. What you are saying applies to a lot of lower-class values besides sex behavior."

"So?" said Oscar De Curia.

"You have already mentioned one: you tried to get the guy back into school. Miller (1958, 1959) says that dropping out at about age 16 is the norm for lower-class culture. Riessman (1962) calls it anti-intellectualism —actual hostility toward eggheadedness. Yet the poverty experts had a truism: 'In the poverty battle, all roads lead to the schoolhouse.' How are we ever going to get kids —or young adults—back into the schoolhouse without changing their basic values?"

"That doesn't answer my question. Anyway, maybe we middle class do overvalue education. There are still thousands of blue-collar jobs, some with pretty good pay, that don't require literacy, much less a high school diploma."

"Oh, yes. But high school represents something else to an employer. I once went to a foundry to line up a job for a male parolee. The foreman's first question was: 'Has he finished high school?' I asked why a guy needed a high school diploma to tamp sand into a casting mold. His answer was a good one: 'To us, completion of high school means a guy has stick-to-it-iveness, that he'll stick with a job until it's finished, that he's more likely to be here all day every day than a guy who hasn't finished school.' You can't argue with that reasoning."

"Yeah. Now about my question."

"Patience. At least half our welfare bill can be traced directly to family breakdown. Yet it seems pretty clear that the lower class doesn't take family ties as seriously as does the middle class (Goode, 1964; Hollingshead, 1950; Udry, 1966). How are we ever going to crack the poverty cycle without family stability? And how do you get family stability without changing the cultural norms regarding families?"

"You're not giving me answers, you're giving me more questions. I need more questions like Noah needed more rain."

"Let me finish, please." Jake was merely stalling for time, of course. But sometimes if you talk long enough, a problem will go away—or the client will, which is functionally the same. "Sexual exploitation," continued Jake, "is only one corner of lower-class attitudes toward female status (Rainwater, 1960; Reissman, 1962). A general subordination of females is the norm. If you're an advocate of women's rights, or even if you subscribe to the social work Code of Ethics regarding sex discrimination, you're going to run afoul of a major lower-class value" (National Association of Social Workers, 1971, p. 958).

· "There is also an item in the Code of Ethics that says I will subordinate my personal interests to my professional responsibility. Like I have a professional responsibility not to impose middle-class values. Well, I'll be damned if I'm gonna subordinate my daughter's chastity to that or any other code of ethics."

"Of course. But I want you to look at the whole perspective, the whole panorama of lower-class norms."

"To hell with all that. Let's answer the question about my daughter first." Persistent as dysentery.

"But we can't answer for your daughter until we answer some of these broader questions first. They all gotta be answered." Jake immediately cursed himself for this slip. An entire shelf full of unresolved questions, like the contents of Fibber McGee's closet, tumbled down upon him in an avalanche of evaded issues. Damn my big flapping mouth, he thought.

"Okay, then let's answer them," said Oscar De Curia.

"I think we are never going to make a dent in the poverty problem until the anti-intellectual attitudes of the poor are changed. And their male chauvinism too."

"Okay, let's change them."

"But these attitudes are dependent on, related to, and interfunctional with a dozen other lower-class norms—maybe all of them, tied up together like a spider web."

"For instance."

"Masculinity, for instance. The poor emphasize masculinity much more than we do (Miller, 1958). And action—getting things done as opposed to theory and abstraction. Therefore, school is considered sissy-prissy and largely female-dominated."

"You think it would help to hire a few football players and prize fighters for teachers?"

"It would be a step toward the schoolhouse. But it would also reinforce their ideas of masculinity and chauvinism. Further, the poor crave excitement more than do the middle and upper classes (Rainwater, 1960; Reissman, 1962). Schools aren't noteworthy for excitement, you know."

"Judging from the slum schools I've been in, about half the teacher's time and energy is spent in trying to keep a lid on the excitement the kids generate. I think if they took the lid off for a minute the average slum classroom would erupt into bedlam."

"Right. And this leads into teaching methods. Student-centered education is based on the same assumptions as client-centered counseling: the students or clients must carry the ball, must be responsible for their own decisions, must set their own goals and limits, and so on. There is a mountain of research indicating that these student-centered teaching methods produce about the same level of retention of class material as do lecture-recitation methods. But when it comes to measuring such intangible traits as self-confidence, initiative, creativity, and leadership, the student-centered methods will win by ten lengths" (Cronbach, 1954; Blair, Jones, and Simpson, 1954).

"Seems like the answer is pretty obvious: use more student-centered teaching in slum schools."

"It would be nice if life were so simple. A guy in California ran off an experimental group project in a boys' club (Maas, 1963). He found that middle-class kids adapted quite readily to group-centered methods. But lower-class kids resisted them to beat hell. They'd stand around with their thumbs in their bums and say: 'Why don't somebody tell us what we're supposed to do?' "

"Mmm," said Oscar De Curia.

"So let me point out, there is nothing the poor need more than self-confidence, creativity, and leadership (Keller, 1963; Goff, 1954). Yet they consistently resist the methods that develop it."

"Hmm."

"And this leads directly to another point. The same guy who did the California study also found that the great majority of correctional workers prefer nondirective methods, even though most of their clients are of the lower class and don't dig them" (Maas, 1954).

"Hmm," said De Curia. "Maybe this is why most counseling agencies have better success with middle-class clients. We've always blamed the lower-class failures on the stratification gap; you know, middle-class social workers can't communicate with lower-class clients."

"Yes. And there's still more to this story. This same guy studied parents bringing kids into guidance clinics (Maas, 1955). He asked specifically about their expectations at the clinic. How long did they think it would take? How much would they, the parents, have to participate? How much would the parents have to change their ways? He found that middle-class parents had much more realistic expectations concerning both time and involvement. The poor usually expected that the treatment would take perhaps a few weeks and that the clinic would straighten the kid out without much parental responsibility."

"So maybe middle-class parents are better risks for therapy regardless of the therapist's socioeconomic background."

"At least you can stop your self-flagellation for being a middle-class caseworker."

"Okay, you have absolved my middle-class guilt. You have also given me a dozen more questions, when all I really wanted was one answer. So how about an answer: Do we or don't we impose middle-class norms on people?"

Imposing values

Jake knew when he had talked himself into a corner. He glanced at the desk phone, hoping that perhaps a call might spare him a confrontation with his untenable position. It didn't. He glanced out his window, hoping perhaps to see a tidal wave rolling across the midwestern prairie. There was not so much as a ripple. He glanced out his door, perchance to spot a client in need of his attention. A swatch of blue and a hank of white hair caught his eye. "Hey Dave!" yelled Jake, much as a man might yell when stranded on a sandbar by high tide.

Dave had been retired from the agency for several years now, but occasionally popped in "to see how things were going." These visits by the old warhorse at pasture were usually welcome and especially so today.

"Come in, Dave, and shoot the bull a spell," said Jake with an outward show of camaraderie and an inward sigh of relief. "Oscar and I were just talking about lower-class norms. How they often impede therapy or movement or progress, or whatever you wanna call it, but how we're not supposed to tamper with them."

"So what did you tell him to do?" asked Dave.

"Huh?"

"I imagine he asked you whether he should or shouldn't impose his own value system. What did you tell him?"

I'm stabbed in the back, thought Jake. He was desperate now. "First I'd like to hear your opinion. You must have run into this question in your 20-odd years here?"

"That's the biggest understatement since Genghis Khan was called unneighborly," said Dave. "Not a day went by that that question didn't pop up."

"Ever have a client make a pass at your daughter?" asked Oscar. "Your 13-year-old daughter?"

"That's how we got started," added Jake.

"So what did you tell him?" asked Dave persistently. But Jake was a skilled infighter. He would try a show of honesty to disarm them. When all else fails, a guy should consider being honest. Well, partially. "I really haven't answered it yet," said Jake. "We were just generalizing the problem, sort of."

"That's what I figured," said Dave. "So you want me to get you off the hook."

Jake grinned like a nauseated sailor demonstrating his seaworthiness, but he said nothing. He resolved never again to resort to honesty.

"My friend," said Dave, "there is nothing in social service more frequently encountered than interclass conflict regarding values. Every social worker I know runs into it daily, and most of them, like you, never really come to grips with the realities of the problem. And every social worker I know, consciously or unconsciously, overtly or covertly, imposes his norms on the poor every day of his working life."

"But you're different," said Jake, with a noticeable edge to his voice.

"Only that I'm honest about it," said Dave. "I do it intentionally. Deliberately. In cold blood. Further, a half dozen studies indicate that the more moralistic, value-imposing workers have better success with their clients" (Parloff, Iflund, and Goldstein, 1957; Powers and Witmer, 1951; Rosenthal, 1955).

"Then what about the advice of the experts? You can't pick up a journal today without some author jollyragging us about understanding the poor instead of trying to change them to our nasty middle-class way of life."

"Slop and hogwash," said Dave. "I suggest that the more you understand the poor, the more you will see the need for them to make some basic changes."

Oscar De Curia brightened noticeably. "For instance?" he said.

"For instance, take the time orientation of the Chicanos and Puerto Ricans (Clapp, 1966; Lewis, 1966). Half of them don't own a clock. A street-gang worker I know says a lot of his Chicano teen-agers can't even tell time. You say, 'Let's be ready to go at ten,' and they'll show up maybe at twelve-thirty. While you're at lunch, likely."

"Understandable, though," said Jake. "They come from an agrarian background where you get up when it's morning and go to bed when it's dark. So who needs a clock?"

"General Motors needs one. Bell Telephone and General Electric need one. And there ain't no way that Chicanos are ever going to adapt to an industrial society without getting clock wise. I've never heard of a factory that will let one guy come to work at eight, another at nine-thirty, and another at ten-fifteen. We either impose our middle-class time consciousness or let them remain forever in unemployment."

"Ah, ha!" Jake burst in. "Now you are blaming the victim."

"Ryan's point (1971), I believe. But Alinsky (1946) said it 25 years earlier."

"Well, were they wrong, both of them?"

"Let's pick one—Alinsky, since he had nothing good to say about middle-class values."

"Right."

"Alinsky would have screamed like a ruptured panther if he heard me say this, but I'll say it to you. I suggest that Alinsky made his living precisely by imposing middle-class norms on the poor. A better living, incidentally, than the three of us combined."

"Please go on."

"The poor have always been more comfortable in primary group relations: first names, informal buddy relations, that sort of thing (Barber, 1961; Brager, 1963; Gutentag, 1970; Reissman, 1962). They always shy away from formalized secondary groups, like titled officers, by-laws, committees, *Robert's Rules of Order*. Now, in themselves, a million people are powerless; they are nothing unless they are organized, whether in the military or in power politics. You can't cite an example in history of a primary group wielding any political clout. The major reason that the middle class carries a bigger stick is not their numbers but their organization. And Alinsky made his living teaching the poor to organize for power, to form secondary groups—a middle-class norm."

"Mm hmm," said Jake. Oscar merely said, "Hmm."

Fatalism and poverty

"Let me point up another lower-class norm that, in my mind, constitutes one of the biggest hang-ups the poor have to carry, maybe the biggest."

"What's that?"

"Fatalism. *Que sera sera.* A belief that what happens to you has already been decided by some capricious Fate (Lewis, 1966; Miller, 1958; Reissman, 1962). A conviction that it is not only a waste of time, but actually hazardous to take arms against a perverse and incontrovertible Fate, because she may stomp on you to straighten you out."

"For example?"

"For example, a hundred studies plus common sense confirm that the poor have too many kids. But to date no birth control program among the poor is even moderately successful as compared to middle-class family planning."

"Why?"

"Fatalism. Rainwater found that the number one cause of birth control failures among the poor is a belief that 'you're just gonna have the kids you're s'posed to have and you can't do nothin' to change it'" (Reissman, 1962).

"Seems kinda extreme."

"Not at all. My brother Gus was driving a truck for a mining company in Wyoming. He picked up a couple of hitchhikers and put them in back. 'Now for hell's sake don't you guys smoke,' he told them. 'I've got seven tons of dynamite on here.' They both agreed, but when he stopped for gas an hour later, there they both sat, smoking on top of a box of dynamite. Gus blew his

stack and kicked their cans off his truck. As they went stomping off down the highway he heard one mumble, 'Well, the way I figure, if it's gonna blow it's gonna blow.' Now there's extreme."

"But an isolated case."

"Okay, think back. In the years you've been handling offenders, how many times have you heard expressions like 'my luck ran out,' 'my number was up,' 'the dice were loaded against me,' 'it wasn't in the cards for me,' 'the Bear (bad luck) was after me,' 'I was fighting a stacked deck,' 'it wasn't my day,' and so on and on."

"Or, 'I'm a born loser,'" said Oscar. "Or, 'when my ship comes in.' Or 'Dame Fortune smiles on me.' Or 'some guy was born with a silver spoon in his mouth.' Or 'there's no oil on my dipstick.' Or 'I lucked out or crapped out.'"

"Right. Nobody in the hoosegow ever got there by goofing off. Always he fell. Or his foot slipped. Or, he 'landed behind the eight ball.' Or 'the old wheel came up on black.' Some day I'm gonna write a book. There must be a thousand such expressions."

"I think," said Oscar, "that these are defense mechanisms to rationalize getting busted. Like 'if I'm so damn smart, how come I'm locked up? Bad luck, that's why.'"

"Okay, but in no way is this limited to offenders. You find these same expressions among the poor everywhere. And for the same reason: it gets them off the hook for being poor. Fate is to blame."

"Well," said Jake, "without these defenses what do the poor bastards have? Isn't it better to leave them their defenses at least?"

"I suggest that a valid social service is to help them find or develop more realistic defenses—defenses that don't perpetuate the cycle of poverty."

"How do you mean?"

"The culture of poverty is self-perpetuating (Lewis, 1966; Miller, 1953). It forms a vicious circle that repeats over and over. Like kids believe that school grades are mostly a matter of luck. Incidentally, I think true-false exams reinforce this crap-game concept of grades. So they flunk out or drop out of school. They're unqualified for employment and grow up in poverty. The surrounding culture constantly reinforces their belief in fatalism, which they and the other poor pass on to their kids. And they in turn enter school expecting Luck or Fate or Chance to determine their outcome. Sure enough, it does, and the cycle repeats. And there are a number of others. McClelland (1961, 1969) says that father dominance—a lower-class norm—has gotta be decreased and that a number of other child-rearing practices of the poor have to be changed too. He also says we gotta push for the good old Protestant ethic and urge more creative and expressive fantasy production. Less traditionalism. All these things, mind you, require changes in lower-class values."

"So you think the place to break this poverty cycle is at the level of norms and values."

"It's all one place. Myrdahl (1948) says that it's not so important where we begin as that we begin somewhere. Consider this one. Mobilization for Youth workers found kids who would say: 'Why go down to the employment office? I'll be here; let the job find me.' At first they thought it was the kids' perversity. But it wasn't; the kids were dead serious. Being employed or unemployed, they believed, was a matter of being touched by the fickle finger of Fate. Hustling for a job may only make Fate mad at you. It seems to me this is a good place to make a dent in the poverty cycle."

De Curia pondered this a bit. "It seems to me this is the only place to make a dent."

"I think Hyman (1953) would agree. He says that 'the variable which keeps the poor poor is a system of beliefs and values ... which reduce the very *voluntary* actions which would ameliorate their low position.' My own view is that this is the best place to make a dent. But there are others: They gotta get back to high school, vocational school, college, on-the-job training. There's delinquency, medical and housing problems,

discrimination, exploitation. You name it and it's a good starting place. But working on any one of these will inevitably necessitate some value changes. If not—if no values are changed—we may as well take the poverty funds and dump them in the streets for grabs, because volitional behavior doesn't change if attitudes, values, and norms don't change. In fact, I think dumping our funds in the ghetto streets would be at least as effective as some programs I know of."

"Touché!" Oscar De Curia said, but without a smile. "However, you and Jake both mentioned the road to the schoolhouse. Harrison (1972) cites some pretty convincing figures that additional years of school won't affect the ghetto kid's lifetime income as much as dropping school and working a couple of extra years."

"Ah, yes, years of school. But he only gives passing acknowledgment that there may be a difference in quality of lower- and middle-class education. If this goes unrecognized, then the whole area of educational enrichment is meaningless. Yes, a kid can graduate from a ghetto school but be unable to write a purchase order, add up a grocery list, or understand directions on a can of spray paint. About a third of the kids on my caseload couldn't travel across town and find an address because they couldn't read street signs from a bus. Try listening to one of them giving directions to another. They memorize routes, not addresses. Half of them couldn't look up a number in a phone book. They were limited to the numbers they memorized or wrote down because they didn't dig alphabetical listing. And not one in a hundred could write an intelligible letter if the kid's life depended on it, even if they had a high school diploma. They were graduated, not educated. Now who's going to give one of them a job at anything better than tamping sand in a rathole?"

"To me the solution seems obvious—improve slum schools," Oscar said.

"My friend, I suggest that Jesus himself could not teach these kids as long as they retain their self-defeating attitudes. Yes, schools must change, but student attitudes must change also."

Scapegoating

"Dave old boy, you claim to be honest with yourself," Jake put in. "Aren't you really blaming the victim when the real blame lies elsewhere? In social injustice, unequal opportunity, exploitation, discrimination? You've said yourself that the criminal justice system screens out the poor predominantly."

"Right. And all social workers should redouble their efforts to correct all these inequities. But let's say they've all been corrected, no discriminating employers and so on. It's still a competitive job market, and the better trained, the aggressive job hustlers, and the pushers are the ones who'll get the jobs."

"Okay, you will easily find a hundred authors who assert that once these injustices are corrected and people begin to move upward into middle-class society, their cultural norms will change accordingly."

"I think it's true that whenever people are placed in another subculture, whether above or below their own, in time some of that culture will rub off on them. But the preponderance of evidence indicates that the social strivers, the upwardly mobile, change their values *before* they begin their upward mobility. Mobility is much more often a result than a cause of value change" (Berelson and Steiner, 1964; Hyman, 1953; McClelland, 1969).

Jake shook his head. "It still seems to me that by putting the onus on the poor, we lift the blame from the guilty ones."

Dave pondered this one for a few minutes. Finally: "Jake, if there's anything I've learned in 40 years of social work, it's that scapegoating—hunting up someone to blame for a social problem—is not only a gross waste of time, but it actually inhibits the solution of problems." Dave ran his finger across Jake's bookshelf. "Do you have any idea how many tons of pulpwood trees have been butchered in the past decade to make publications that are essentially given over to scapegoating?"

He hadn't, and Dave proceeded. "I have never heard of a social problem that was attributable to a single cause. There are always multiple causes if you bother to scratch the surface, so finding a suitable scapegoat merely focuses attention on one factor and ignores the others. As for me, I'm not going to burn up good mental energy either in blaming the poor for being poor or blaming the middle class for being middle class."

But Jake recalled another problem. "Did I misunderstand you when you admitted that you superimpose your own values?"

"That's right, deliberately."

"Then aren't you saying, in effect, that your values are better than those of the lower class?"

"Ah, now comes the stinger. I impose *some* middle-class values. There are quite a number of lower-class values that I prefer to middle-class ones."

"For instance?"

"Comradeship. Closer, more intimate interpersonal relations. More egalitarian views; more emphasis on person than on status. More interpersonal good humor. More freedom of expression. More open expression of affection" (Reissman, 1962).

"Affection?"

"Yes. Take one example: When I was a kid I worked on a string of blue-collar jobs: ranches, mines, factories, railroads, construction. It wasn't uncommon to see two guys who were buddies standing around the fire at night or around the bar or bunkhouse, with an arm slung over the friend's shoulder. No one thought anything of it. Now suppose that on some white-collar job —let's say in an insurance office—you spot two guys at the water cooler with their arms around each other. You'd nudge your neighbor and say, 'Hey, Fred! Lookit!' What a helluva culture when two people can't express honest affection without being considered gay."

"Maybe there are more gays in the lower class."

"Fewer (Kinsey, 1948). I'll tell you another trait of the poor that I'd consider keeping. When a husband and wife are at loggerheads, they are much more likely to have a good old hell-raising, whooping and hollering knock-down-drag-out battle. But in 20 minutes it's over and out of their systems. You and me, when we're on the outs with the old woman, we turn on the deep freeze for about a month. We never speak or look at each other for weeks on end. Now I ask you, honestly, which is better for mental health? And for kids?"

"Hmm."

"And I'll tell you another. I think there's more real honesty in the lower class."

"Aw, come off it, Dave. Nine-tenths of our correctional clients come from the lower class."

"I wasn't thinking of law violations specifically. However, since you've raised the point: a dozen studies of self-reported offenses show no significant class difference in crime and delinquency. Our legal machinery simply screens out more of the poor for processing" (Akers, 1964; Empey and Erickson, 1966; Meyerhoff and Meyerhoff, 1964; Short and Nye, 1957; and Voss, 1966).

"Then what do you mean by 'honesty?'"

"Interpersonal honesty. If a lower-class guy doesn't like you, he will say so. Or maybe punch your nose. But we middle class will rationalize it with some kind of mealy-mouthed double-talk. I invite you, for instance, to sit in on a college promotions committee if you want to observe some fancy verbal footwork. Like 'Now understand, I've got nothing personal against old Charlie. But . . .' A blue-collar worker would say, much more honestly, 'I can't stand the damn creep.'"

"Not footwork. Tonguework."

"Okay, I recall one college department of about 25 faculty. There were some faculty cuts coming up, so two sections of the department formed a coalition and voted to abolish the third section in order to save their jobs. I have never heard of this kind of job cannibalism among blue-collar workers."

Functional norms

"Dave, you're not being consistent," Jake said waving his hand. "A minute ago you were the champion of good old middle-class values. Now you've changed sides. You can't play both sides at once. What *do* you want?"

Dave pondered this one briefly: "First, I want social workers to be honest about it when they impose norms, whether middle- or lower-class. Second, I want them to forget the infantile quibble about norms to one class being better than those of another. I want. . . ."

"How do you decide which norms you are going to support, then? You gonna play God?"

"Functionality is how. First we gotta decide on objectives, social workers and clients in dialogue together. And this holds true whether it's one client and one caseworker or a project involving 50 workers and 10,000 clients. We can agree that employment is a goal, or marriage stability or family planning or whatever, but we have to thrash it out and arrive at some consensus regarding our objective. Once the objective is agreed upon, my job is clear. If a certain cultural norm is functional, if it aids in achieving the agreed-upon objective, I will support it. If it's dysfunctional, if it's thwarting our objectives, then it's gotta go, and I'll do my damndest to see that it goes. And I couldn't care less whether the norm comes from the lower, middle, or upper class."

"Meehl and McClosky" (1947), said Jake, "consider that our job definition is to help the client achieve the client's end. Period. That doesn't leave room for negotiation about objectives."

"I'll be damned if I'm gonna help that sonofabitch achieve my daughter's end," said Oscar De Curia hotly.

"And I'll venture no social worker worth his salt would," replied Dave. "In fact, I think they'd draw the line on about half the goals of our correctional clients. Plus a number of others. For instance, I won't help a client toward suicide, if that's his goal. Or to obtain heroin, or to bust out of jail or a hospital. Or to defraud the welfare office or desert his family or go AWOL. Or, in my case, to obtain an abortion. This is why I said we must first agree on objectives."

"And if you and the client can't agree?"

"My personal guideline is this: I will never help clients accomplish something that I consider morally wrong, harmful to them or to me or to others. And I won't help a client to rendezvous with any teenager, not your daughter or anyone else's."

"Okay, let's say we agree on a number of objectives in a certain poverty project," said Jake. "And we find certain lower-class norms that inhibit the achieving of these goals. Dysfunctional, you called them. Now how do you go about changing those norms?"

"That, my friend, is another can of worms. But it can be done and has been done."

"How?"

"Another time, Jake, another time. We've emptied enough worms for today."

Selected annotated bibliography

Aptekar, Herbert H. *An Intercultural Exploration: Universals and Differences in Social Work Values, Functions and Practice.* New York: Council on Social Work Education, 1966.
This volume is a summary of the highlights of a ten-day seminar undertaken by 22 social work educators from ten different countries. The primary focus of the conference was on values and their relationship to other social work issues. The volume allows students to explore values in international perspectives.

Glick, Peter M. "Individualism, Society and Social Work," *Social Casework* 58:10 (December 1977), pp. 579–585.
This article provides a thought-provoking discussion of the necessary balance between the pursuit of individualism, self-realization, social responsibility, and the desire for personal freedom.

Halmos, Paul. *Faith of the Counsellors.* New York: Schocken, 1966.
From an examination of the published literature from psychiatry, clinical psychology, psychiatric social work, and educational counseling, the conclusion is reached that these counseling professions operate from an unproven set of tenets of faith. The tenets are identified and discussed.

Kendall, Katherine A. (Ed.). *Social Work Values in an Age of Discontent.* New York: Council on Social Work Education, 1970.
This is a collection of lectures on social work values given over a period of three years in honor of Ann Elizabeth Neely.

Levy, Charles S. "The Value Base of Social Work," *Journal of Education for Social Work* 9:1 (Winter 1973), pp. 34–42.
Social work has an ideology which can be conceived along three basic dimensions—preferred conceptions of people, preferred outcomes for people, and preferred instrumentalities for dealing with people.

Levy, Charles S. *Social Work Ethics.* New York: Human Sciences Press, 1976.
Levy offers ethical principles regarding relationship of the social worker to clients, third parties, employers, colleagues, and society; he identifies and suggests guides for reconciliation of ethical dilemmas.

McLoed, Donna L., and **Meyer, Henry J.** "A Study of Values of Social Workers" in Edwin Thomas (Ed.), *Behavioral Science for Social Workers.* New York: Free Press, 1967, pp. 401–416.
Major value premises of social work were conceptualized from the literature. A scale was developed to measure these values, then used to compare students with experienced social workers and social workers with teachers.

Miller, Henry. "Value Dilemmas in Social Casework," *Social Work* 13:1 (January 1968), pp. 27–33.
Much of present casework is with involuntary clients which creates a dilemma for the social worker. Miller argues for withdrawal of social work from settings involving unsolicited treatment but the development of alternative ap-

proaches to make services available to these clients on a voluntary basis.

National Association of Social Workers. *Values in Social Work: A Re-examination,* monograph 9 in the series sponsored by the Regional Institute Program. New York: Author, 1967.

This excellent monograph for social work students is a collection of papers on values presented at the Regional Institute Program that focused on values. Among others, there are papers by Biestek, Perlman, Keith-Lucas, and Bernstein.

O'Connor, Gerald. "Toward a New Policy in Adult Corrections," *Social Service Review* 46:4 (December 1972), pp. 581–596.

Changes in adult corrections policy are suggested to increase self-determination and respect for client dignity while also protecting society. Specific suggested changes include the discontinuance of enforced therapy, the greater use of a determinate sentence, and the development of correctional communities, initiated by inmates, to achieve their own rehabilitation.

Otis, Jack. "Liberty, Social Work, and Public Policy Development," in National Conference on Social Welfare, *Social Welfare Forum, 1976.* New York: Columbia University Press, 1976, pp. 35–46.

Liberty is both freedom from authoritarian controls and ability to make choices. Social work in its effort to expand choices becomes an instrument of freedom.

Salomon, Elizabeth L. "Humanistic Values and Social Casework," *Social Casework* 48:1 (January 1967), pp. 26–32.

Salomon suggests the possibility of conflict between the humanistic values of social work and the demands of science for classification, objectivity of observations, and the tendency to oversimplify complex phenomena.

Silverman, Marvin. "Children's Rights and Social Work," *Social Service Review* (March 1977), pp. 171–178.

Misguided efforts to protect children have resulted in their being placed in a disabled status in which they lack political rights. Article offers suggestions for extending children's rights and explores implications for social work.

Tillich, Paul. The Philosophy of Social Work," *Social Service Review* 36:1 (March 1962), pp. 13–16.

Social workers individualize, listen with empathy, and are directed to the aim of helping all individuals find a place where they can consider themselves necessary.

Toch, Hans. "The Care and Feeding of Typologies and Labels," *Federal Probation* 34:3 (September 1970), pp. 15–19.

Toch offers four principles to avoid the harmful effects of classifying people-participant classification; no label should transcend its criteria; work with clients should facilitate declassification; and classification is of behavior and not people.

CHAPTER 5

The social work relationship

This chapter will focus on the social work relationship and will center primarily on the helping relationship that develops between practitioner and the client system. In this type of statement *client* may be read *client system* and *worker* may be read *change agent*. The terms *client* and *worker* are used because they lend themselves well in communicating the attitudes being discussed by authors. Readers should always be aware that every social work system is either an individual or composed of individuals.

Chapter 3 focused on systems theory and talked of the need of human systems, individuals, and human groups, as open systems, for input from the world around them if they were to grow and develop and to continue to cope with life tasks. As stated earlier, every human system needs input from relationships with others, although not all systems find it easy to accept the thought that they do. During our lifetime each of us has experienced the connectedness of emotion and intimacy with others that is called the "human relationship." When we cannot find these connections with other people, we often name and personalize trees and animals, or perhaps our car. Then we draw comfort from acting as if another human being were present. In fact, though individuals may rarely be conscious of what these relationships mean and what powers they contain (except at certain points in life when people are suddenly bereft of a meaningful relationship or are in the process of becoming involved in a new one), the most critical characteristic of our humanity is that lives are lived within relationships to other people. Thus "relationships" do not originate for any of us within the social work process, or the professional helping effort (and therein may lie the rub, as shall be discussed later). Nor can social work claim to have been the lone discoverer of this attribute of humanity or the only group interested in pursuing its investigation. Psychology and psychiatry, among other professions, have also been very active in attempting to research the helping relationship.

However, social work can take pride in the fact that from its earliest beginnings it recognized the importance of human interaction and attempted to employ the concept of relationship in a conscious and deliberate way for the benefit of the people it served. In the early formulations describing social work activity, the relationship between worker and client was given a special importance—and no concept appears more frequently in the literature of the profession. Although the goals toward which this early activity was directed were those which the worker thought desirable for society and personally redemptive for the client, there was a beginning of the principle of self-help and a very clear conviction of the power of personal influence in the stimulation of this process (Pumphrey and Pumphrey, 1961; Reynolds, 1963; Richmond, 1899).

Perhaps the outstanding author and teacher in the field of social casework at the beginning of the 20th century was Mary Richmond. Her writings contain considerable material about the social work relationship. She asserted that social casework stands for the "intensive study and use of social relationships." Richmond (1917, pp. 211–215) defined the focus of casework activity in terms of "skill in discovering the social relationships by which a given personality has been shaped; an ability to get at the central core of the difficulty in these relationships; power to utilize the direct action of mind upon mind in their adjustment." The importance of the effect of "mind upon mind" was recognized in the development of "friendly visitors" in early social work.

In spite of the early recognition of relationship as a basic concept in social work theory, and in spite of the years of concern with the development and use of relationship in practice, a clearly defined concept of the social work relationship has yet to be articulated. There is great unanimity about the importance of human relationships in the promotion of growth and change, but there is little common understanding about just how these relationships promote such development. In the professional literature authors often merely describe qualities of the relationship that they consider important, or they record very specific instances of their use of relationship in the helping process.

Being convinced that the concept of relationship is central to all of social work practice, we intend in this chapter to consider some attempts of selected social work authors to express the nature of social work relationships and to examine some of the notions, implicit or explicit, in such statements. We shall consider the roles that social workers carry and how these affect and shape social work relationships and the qualities of social workers who would work effectively with others.

A REVIEW OF THE LITERATURE

Felix Biestek (1957, p. 11) has collected a number of excerpts illustrating the attempts of social workers to express the nature of the relationship. He points out that relationship has been compared to an atmosphere, to flesh and blood, to a bridge, and to an open table.

> The essence of the relationship has been called an interplay, a mutual emotional exchange, an attitude, a dynamic interaction, a medium, a connection between two persons, a professional meeting, a mutual process. The concept "interaction" seems to be the most generic and it was most commonly described as "dynamic."
>
> The purpose of the relationship was described as creating an atmosphere, the development of personality, a better solution of the client's problem, the means for carrying out function, stating and focusing reality and emotional problems, and helping the client make a more acceptable adjustment to a personal problem.

Biestek (p. 4) sees the relationship between caseworker and client as the medium through which the knowledge of human nature and the individual is used. "The relationship is also the channel of the entire casework process; through it flow the skills in intervention, study, diagnosis and treatment." Biestek (p. 12) defines the casework relationship as

> the dynamic interactions of attitudes and emotions between the caseworker and the client, with the purpose of helping clients achieve better adjustments between themselves and their environments.

In a book on social casework Helen Harris Perlman (1957, pp. 65–66) says of *relationship* that

> It is a condition in which two persons with some common interest between them, long term or temporary, interact with feeling. . . . Relationship leaps from one person to the other at the moment when some kind of emotion moves between them. They may both express or invest the same kind of emotion; they may express or invest different or even opposing emotions or . . . one may express or invest emotion and the other will receive it and be responsive to it. In any case, a charge or current of feeling must be experienced between two persons. Whether this interaction creates a sense of union or of antagonism, the two persons are for the time "connected" or "related" to each other.

Perlman (1957, pp. 64–68) goes on to say that the identifying mark of a professional relationship "is in its conscious purposiveness growing out of the knowledge of what must go into achieving its goal"; that "all growth-producing relationships, of which the casework relationship is one, contain elements of acceptance and expectation, support and stimulation." She also identifies authority as an element of the professional relationship and clearly differentiates between the relationship and other aspects of the helping process. Perlman sees the caseworker as helping people to deal with their problems through (1) the provision of resources, (2) the problem-solving work, and (3) the therapeutic relationship, which she defines in another work (1971, p. 58) as the "climate and the bond" between workers and clients that "acts to sustain and free clients to work on their problems."

Social workers who attempted to help people through the use of groups were also concerned with the development and use of relationships. Grace Coyle (1948, p. 91), who was very influential in the early development of group work, defined relationship as "a discernible process by which people are connected to each other, and around which the group takes its shape and form." Gisela Konopka (1963, pp. 107–118), an international authority in group work theory, does not define the relationship in her writings. She does discuss it as one of the major helping media available to the social group worker and sets forth its elements as purpose, warmth, and understanding.

In her book *Social Work with Groups*, Helen Northen (1969, pp. 53–58) says:

> Relationship has been described as consisting "primarily of emotional responses which ebb and flow from person to person as human behavior evokes different affective reactions." The social worker in a group situation develops a unique relationship with each member, based on an understanding of the individual.

Writing about the giving and taking of help, Alan Keith-Lucas (1972, p. 47) defines the helping relationship as "the medium which is offered to people in trouble through which they are given the opportunity to make choices, both about taking help and the use they will make of it." Keith-Lucas (1972, pp.

47–65) identifies the qualities of the relationships as (1) mutuality, (2) reality, (3) feeling, (4) knowledge, (5) concern for the other person, (6) purpose, (7) takes place in the here and now, (8) offers something new, and (9) is non-judgmental.

Several years ago Pincus and Minahan (1973, pp. 69–73) wrote that a relationship "can be thought of as an affective bond between workers" and other systems with which they may be involved and that relationships may involve an "atmosphere of collaboration, bargaining or conflict." They classify all social work into three types: collaborative, cooperative, and conflicted. These authors go on to identify the common elements of all social work relationships as (1) purpose, (2) commitment to the needs to the client system, and (3) objectivity and self-awareness on the part of the worker.

SOCIAL WORK ROLES AND RELATIONSHIP

In studying this brief review of relationship, one will readily note that with the exception of Pincus and Minahan the concept of the professional relationship has been most thought about, and most written about, by persons concerned with the one-to-one or one-to-group *helping* relationship. However, as Pincus and Minahan point out, in addition to the direct helping relationship social workers carry many other types of relationships. They may be involved with landlords, teachers, employers, and even boards of directors and executives of other agencies on behalf of their clients. Or workers, noting that a number of the parents with whom they work are concerned about drug problems, may help their agency develop a special seminar for workers on the subject of drug use. Another worker may be helping agency representatives develop plans for increased agency coordination on the assumption that this will be helpful to clients. A third may be lobbying for a law requiring that all group insurance carried by employers for employees must cover the pregnancies of unmarried as well as married employees and the pregnancies of minor daughters of employees. In all of the above situations, the workers would be involved in relationships with others. However, these relationships are neither with clients nor are they helping relationships per se, in that the worker offers no services to the other persons in the relationship and carries no professional responsibility to help them with their personal problems or development.

Social workers engaged in administration, policy, planning, and organization activities often carry a client relationship with the system in which they are involved, but the responsibilities they assume within this relationship are quite different from those of the direct services helping relationship. In these relationships, too, they carry no responsibility to help the other system with personal problems or to provide personal growth experiences for any individual member or the group as a unit. Rather, they are involved in helping the client system to change another (target) system in regard to certain professional policies and programs.

It is our position that all social work relationships carry certain common elements, but that the mix and importance of the elements are different in different types of relationships. Relationships may be classified along two axis: (1) the role of the worker within the change agent system, for example, as helper, administrator, policymaker, and/or researcher and (2) the type of system with which the change agent is involved, for example, the action system, the target system, or the change agent system, as well as different composition and purpose of the client system. However, although relationships may differ with the interaction of elements along these axis, all social work relationships have purposes that have some common aspects because they embody the normative purposes and values of the profession although not necessarily the operational and the unique aspects. All social work relationships involve elements of power and authority, but these elements may be lodged in persons other than the social worker especially in situations involving policymaking or organizational change.

All professional relationships involve self-discipline and self-knowledge paired with the capacity for free, genuine, and congruent use of self. However, different types of relationships may involve different qualities of awareness and the use of different elements in the self. Some relationships may call for self-awareness in problems dealing with power and status, competitive feelings, and impatience with colleagues; others may call for awareness of one's fear of dependency or the need to do for others. One can deal with other persons and systems better if one has some sensitivity to their situation and goals and some empathy for them. However, the content of the empathetic understandings will vary greatly. All social work relationships are emergent and are affected by time and place. In all professional relationships social workers are representing something beyond themselves, either their agency or their profession, and all practitioners share a commitment to client welfare as a base for their professional activities. There are seven essential elements that are a part of social work relationships: (1) concern for others, (2) commitment and obligation, (3) acceptance and expectation, (4) empathy, (5) genuineness, (6) authority and power, and, overriding and shaping all the rest, (7) purpose. In order to carry their professional relationships with professional skill, workers will need to make the following qualities a part of their professional selves: maturing, creativity, the capacity to observe self, the desire to help, courage, and sensitivity.

Although it is our belief that all social workers need to have a grasp of the elements discussed in this chapter, we also believe that these elements of the professional social work relationship are used differentially and that the variables affecting their use may be expressed in the following model (Fraley, 1969, pp. 45–54):

1. The purpose of the relationship.
2. The position of the practitioner in the change agent system.
3. The role of the worker and the role of the other in interaction (remember the earlier description of the differing perceptions of role and their importance).
4. The role and position of the other in the larger social systems of which both worker and other are a part (the community, church, social groups).
5. The goal toward which the social worker is directing change activities.
6. The goal toward which the other systems are directing their activities. Note that in the relationship between client system and change agent system, it is assumed that the goal is to develop a relationship that allows for working together. However, relationships between the change agent and

individuals in the target system or the action system may involve relationships of cooperation, negotiation, or conflict.

7. The form of communication. In the direct, helping relationship between an individual client and the practitioner as the change agent, communication is usually verbal. However, in the relationship between practitioners and their own change agent system, or between the change agent and action or target systems, many other forms of communication may be used, such as letters, reports, and so on. It is important that the practitioner be skilled in the use of all methods of communication.

8. The skill of the worker in decision-making and the use of appropriate intervention methods.

9. The type of system with which the worker interacts—the practitioner may work toward change in a client system that consists of an individual, group, organization, or community; or workers may work with individuals or groups representing other than client systems.

As an example of these points, Gisela Konopka (1963, pp. 107–116) has written that the relationship between the social worker and the small, helping group differs from that of the social worker involved with an individual in the following ways: (1) members support each other and are not alone with authority, (2) there is greater informality, (3) members are surrounded by others in the same boat and there is a feeling of identification impossible in casework, (4) members are not bound to accept other members, (5) the worker is shared, and (6) there is a lack of confidentiality.

PURPOSE AS AN ELEMENT OF RELATIONSHIP

As was pointed out at the beginning of this chapter, all human beings have experienced connections with other human beings that we call relationships. Most of us are capable of, and most of the time are involved in, many sets of simultaneous relationships. In social intercourse many of us drift into "relationships" with others without being aware of just how or why they developed. However, few of us continue relationships with others without some reason; there is something that brings us into contact with them and some reason why the interaction is continued. When one becomes involved with another person, the nature of one's purpose, goals, or intent, together with one's perception of the other individual's purpose, goals, or intent will determine how one behaves toward that individual and how the relationship will develop.

If purpose is a part of all relationships, why does it need to be discussed as a special part of professional relationships? And how does purpose differ in professional relationships as compared with personal relationships? That the relationship is purposive and goal directed does not give the social work relationship its special mark. What makes the social work relationship special is that its purpose and goal are conscious and deliberate and come within the overall purpose and value system of the profession.

In chapter 1 the discussion centered on the purpose of social work practice—the changing or altering of something in the interaction of people and their environment so as to improve the capacity of individuals to cope with their life tasks in a way reasonably satisfying to themselves and to others, thus enhancing their ability to realize their aspirations and values. In Chapter 4 the main points dealt with how professional values limit and shape what we do as social workers. These two factors, the overall purpose of the profession and its value system, limit and focus the purpose of the social work relationship so that influence is not used capriciously. This is called the normative limits of purpose in the social work relationship—the normative purpose of all social work relationships is some kind of change in, or development of, a human or social system to the end that the capacity of individuals to cope with their life tasks and to realize their aspirations and values is improved.

In addition to being shaped by the normative purpose, each social work relationship will be deliberately and consciously shaped, in part, by the purpose of the given "type" of encounter. For example, the "helping relationship" is distinguished by a particular type of purpose—an increase in the coping capacity of the client system. However, a social worker may attempt to convince a legislative committee of the necessity for increasing state aid to school systems so that special education classes or open schools for dropouts may be established. The different purpose of this interaction will be critical to the way the relationship develops and is utilized. This aspect of purpose can be termed the operational purpose of the relationship. One of the critical differences among types of social work relationships is that they are governed by different operational purposes even though they share a normative purpose. Within the overall limits set by the normative purpose, the operational purpose determines the outer parameters of a relationship.

Besides the normative and operational purpose, each social work relationship will have a unique, individual purpose. And these unique purposes will be affected by time: the immediate, unique purpose of this particular interaction will differ from the long-range purpose of a series of interactions. Thus, Mrs. Jones may have become involved in a helping relationship because she wants to have an enduring and happy marriage (a longtime purpose), but when she comes in today she may want help about the way she responded this morning to her husband's criticism of her housekeeping (an immediate goal which is a step to the long-term goal). The outreach worker at a community center may be involved with a street group in discussions about using the center for its meetings. The worker's immediate purpose is to provide the group with a better meeting place, while the longtime purpose may be to help the group develop less destructive activities.

It is the position of the authors that, while the normative and operational purposes of any social work relationship may be implicit, the social worker needs to be able to clearly formulate the unique, immediate purposes of professional contacts with others and that such purposes should be verbally shared with them. (With some clients who have little acquaintance with the "talking therapies," it might be helpful to discuss the normative and operational purposes as well.) A study by Mayer and Timms (1972) shows that one difficulty in establishing a helping relationship with certain clients is their lack of understanding of the purposes and values of the professional person. Ideally, in the helping relationship, the unique purpose should come out of mutual consideration of what the client wants; but be that as it may, it is the worker's obligation to see that purpose is established. A professional relationship is formed for a purpose consciously recognized by all participants and ends when that purpose has been achieved or is judged to be unachievable. This understanding or perception of purpose sets certain norms for how persons will behave toward one another in the relationship and how the relationship will develop. (Purpose will be considered again in Chapter 7.)

DEVELOPMENT OF RELATIONSHIP

This brings us to a critical point. Relationship in a social work helping process does not emerge spontaneously and whole out of some mysterious chemistry of individuals in interaction but develops out of purposive interaction, out of the business with which the worker and the client (or other system) concern themselves. It can not be not presumed that the client is looking "for a helping relationship" when entering the social work situation, but rather that the client comes out of concern about a problem in which the professional relationship is instrumental in working toward a solution. This means that we do not speak of the worker's "establishing a relationship" or "offering a relationship"; neither do we speak of needing a good relationship before difficulties can be discussed. The relationship comes out of the communication about difficulties. It grows and develops out of purposive work. The professional relationship as an affective, experimental interaction should develop as necessary to the task. It is not necessarily pleasant or friendly; sometimes the problem is worked out in reaction and anger, in conflict as well as in collaboration or bargaining. A wise social worker writes that "the attempt to keep the relationship on a pleasant level is the greatest source of ineffectual helping known to people (Keith-Lucas, 1972, p. 18). Seek relationship as a goal, "and it will generally elude one." But in a helping situation a relationship will grow wherever people demonstrate to others by their actions and words that they respect the other, that they have concern for them and care what happens to them, and that they are willing both to listen and to act helpfully (Keith-Lucas, 1972, pp. 48–49).

The fact that the relationship develops out of purposive work means that it has motion and direction and emergent characteristics. It grows, develops, and changes; and when the purpose has been achieved, it comes to an end. The time structure is another variable which directly affects the nature and rate of the development of the relationship. Whether time limits are imposed on the process arbitrarily by outside forces or are imposed as necessary for task accomplishment, they have a deep effect on the emergent quality of the relationship. It is generally known that the frequency of meetings and the amount of time the participants spend together affects the climate of the relationship and the speed with which it develops. The authors believe that the imposition of individualized time limits consonant with a shared unique purpose will increase the effectiveness of the joint purposive work. The setting in which the worker and the other system find themselves will also affect relationship, since the setting interacts with time and purpose. In every instance the operational purpose will be affected by the setting and the worker's position within it; and in most instances the limits of the purpose will also be imposed by the setting and the worker's position within it. This is to be expected, since the unique purpose of the relationship must fall within the parameters of the operational purpose.

Relationship is subject to differentiation and differential use. The kind of relationship that develops between social workers and the system with which they are interacting will depend on the particular combination of a number of variables. The overriding variable is purpose, but other variables combine with purpose to form the relationship: the setting in which the worker and the system come together; the time limits of the process; the individuals or groups involved and the interests they represent; the capacities, motivations, expectations, and purposes of those involved; the problem which brings practitioner and system together and the goals each has for its resolution; the qualities of the workers and what they bring of themselves, their knowledge, and their skills; and the actual behaviors of the members of the relational system is transactions over time.

In the helping process the relationship may be used in one of two ways. The worker may use the relationship to sustain the clients as they and the worker work on the problem, or the consideration of the relationship itself may become the task, and the client and worker may focus on the way the client uses this as a protype of the problems they may have in other meaningful relationships and interactions. Certain problem-focused groups, too, may consist of individuals where the problem-to-be-worked is of their interpersonal transactions with each other, or where the relationship between the worker and the group or the relationships between various members may become the focus of the group's attention. In work with task groups, the relationship between the worker and group, and the relationships between the members, is used to sustain the members as they work on a problem common to all of them but external to their relationships with one another.

It is now time to turn to the workers and what they, as professional helping people, are expected to bring to the helping relationship. Both the worker and the client (or the other system, if this is not a helping relationship) bring to the relationship irrational elements, nonrational elements (emotion, feeling, affect), and rational elements (intellectual and cognitive qualities). In the case of both the worker and the other system these elements come from (1) past experiences that have affected and developed the ability of the individuals to relate to others; (2) the here and now physical and emotional state of those involved; (3) the here and now thoughts or mental images of each individual about him or herself, the process, and the problem; (4) each person's anxiety about the present situation and about the person in it; (5) each person's expectations of how one should behave and what should come out of the interaction; (6) each person's perception of the other, or others, involved; (7) the values and ideals shared in common by the participants in the process; and (8) the influence of other social and environmental factors (Goldstein, 1973, pp. 139–50). However, since workers present themselves as the professional people in the relationship, and because of this are often allowed to share in the most private and sensitive aspects of vulnerable people, they carry special responsibilities for what they bring to the helping process.

If readers will now reexamine the attempts of earlier authors to explain or describe what the worker should bring to the helping relationship, they will find that most of these attempts deal with the communication of certain affective attitudes. While through the years social workers have used different words to express what they saw as the nature of the helping relationship, the notions of what kind of worker behavior is necessary to that particular relationship have changed relatively little. They have simply been better elaborated and differentiated over the years. The literature of other human service professions also discloses that their professional helping persons have developed very similar concepts. Some of these concepts have been broken down into smaller units and have been the object of experimental study, some are very well established because they are based on the clinical observations of many professional helping people over many years with many clients (Truax and Mitchell, 1971). Thus most human service professionals use similar words to describe the emotional quality of the helping relationship. It is generally agreed among professional people in the human service professions that certain qualities are necessary within a human relationship for growth and change to take place.

We believe that all these various qualities can be classified into six groups of essential elements of all professional relationships: (1) concern for the other, (2) commitment and obligation, (3) acceptance and expectation, (4) empathy, (5) authority and power, and (6) genuineness and congruence. These elements will be used according to the purpose and type of relationship.

ELEMENTS OF THE RELATIONSHIP

Concern for the other

To put this as simply as possible, concern for the other means that the worker sincerely cares about what happens to the client and is able to communicate this feeling. In the helping relationship concern for the other involves "the sense of responsibilty, care, respect, knowledge of other human beings and the wish to further their lives" (Fromm, 1956, p. 47). It is an *unconditional* affirmation of the client's life and needs—wanting clients to be all they can be, and to do all they want to do, *for their own sake.* Those last four words are critical.

It is obvious that if we want to help others we must become deeply involved with them, and we need to want for them what they would want for themselves as we would want for ourselves what we want for ourselves. However, there is a danger in this, as the closer our emotional relationship with an individual the more likely we are to become overinvolved out of desire to see the trouble removed or the problem solved. When we feel that someone else's problem is our own problem, when we are unable to tolerate the thought of our own pain and need to have the client succeed because that is what we want, rather than to offer what the client wants or needs, then we are too involved.

True concern for another in the helping relationship means that we offer our skills, our knowledge, ourselves, and our caring to the client to be used (or not used, as the case may be) in the client's movement toward desired goals. It means that (within certain limits of purpose, time, and place) we respond as the client needs us rather than as our need to help demands, that we care enough for the other to leave him/her free to fail. For most of us it is so much easier and more satisfying "to do" than to stand and wait (but "he also serves who only stands and waits") that we convince ourselves that concern is expressed through "doing" rather than through "an active waiting." To be truly concerned means that we are willing to be the "agent of a process rather than the creator of it" (Keith-Lucas, 1972, p. 104).

Keith-Lucas (1972, p. 103) gives us an excellent summary of this notion when he writes that concern

> means the willingness to let the helped person decide to what extent and under what conditions he is willing to be helped. It does not mean necessarily agreeing to help under these circumstances, or even refraining from pointing out that help is not possible under them. Nor does it mean refraining from offering what help is available, or even, if the need is desperate, intervening in an attempt to get help started. But it does mean, ever and always, treating the helped person as the subject of the sentence, serving his interest, allowing him all possible freedom to be what he wants to be.

Sometimes workers equate this business of concern for others with "liking." It is the position of the authors that notions of "liking" or "disliking" are misleading, and that to ask workers to "like" everyone often results in the denial or repression of feeling rather than a change in it. What we are speaking of in the use of the concept of concern is a sense of so caring for the other (as the subject of our interactions together) that personal feelings of liking or disliking (which are, after all, related to the person as the object of the response) no longer have any meaning. Again according to Keith-Lucas (1972, p. 106):

> What the helping person develops is a feeling to which liking and disliking are wholly irrelevant. This is what is meant by concern. It means to care what happens to another person quite apart from whether one finds the person attractive or unattractive.

Under the rubric of the concept of concern we would place many descriptive words used by other authors in discussing the helping relationship, words such as *warmth, liking, support, nonjudgmental respect, expectation,* and *understanding.* Some of these words are descriptive of emotions and attitudes that also fall partially under other concepts; for example, *nonjudgmental respect* is also a part of acceptance and will be discussed in some detail when that concept is taken up.

Understanding may also be a part of other attitudes, but it should be pointed out here that it is an important part of this concept that workers seek understanding out of concern for the other person and out of desire to help in a way that can be used, not out of their own need to know, or understand, for their purposes. It is always disturbing to hear a social worker use the amount and extent of the material that the client "felt free to share with me" as the test of a helping relationship or the "success of an interview." Sharing oneself with a helping person is never an easy or an unmitigatedly positive experience. Knowing this, and being concerned for the privacy and rights of the client, workers seek knowledge about a person, or understanding of the person, only because they are concerned to help. Workers seek only so much understanding as is necessary for the process of helping. To seek knowledge for the sake of knowing, or in order to demonstrate skill at interviewing to others, is, again, to make the client the object rather than the subject of our efforts.

We communicate this attitude of concern and respect in any type of relationship to the people with whom we are working by, among other things, being on time for interviews or conferences; by making appointments before visting the home or office (which says that the worker respects them and their privacy and wants them to have the opportunity to present themselves as they wish to); by seeing that interviewing or conference space is as attractive as it can be made; by dressing in the way that their culture says is "appropriate to a helping person offering service to a *valued* person"; and by concerned listening.

For the worker, concerned listening is not a passive "hearing." It is an active search for the meaning in, and an active understanding of, the client's communication. One may well disagree with what is being said, but one must value the sharing that is going on. In a helping relationship particularly, the worker values the client's offering of feelings, thoughts, and ideas. The high feeling in a situation heavy with conflict should not obscure the worker's need to hear accurately. In the helping relationship the worker must, in one way or another, convey recognition of the value of the client's communication and the worker's desire to understand it. Responding to the content of the client's communication with relevant questions or comments in the search for understanding is one indication of responsive caring; an expressed desire to understand often conveys concern better than a statement of already achieved understanding.

Concern for the other means that workers view clients as uniquely valuable human beings and in a helping relationship this means that, in addition, workers transcend their own needs and view of the problem and lend themselves to the serving of the clients' interests and purposes of getting together.

Commitment and obligation

Persons cannot enter into interrelationships with others in a meaningful way without assuming the responsibilities that are linked to such interactions. These responsibilities may best be expressed in the concept of *commitment* and in its corollary, *obligation*. In the helping relationship, both client and worker must be bound by commitments and obligations if the purposes of the relationship are to be achieved. A commitment of the conditions and purposes of the relationship and to an interdependent interaction, built upon involvement and investment, allows the client to feel safe and thus to reduce the testing behavior and trial-and-error searching that usually mark the beginning of a relationship. This allows clients to turn their attention and energy to the task at hand rather than to employ this in self-protection. Once a commitment to the relationship has been established, and the limits of time, place, and purpose have been accepted, each participant is able to depend on the predictability of the other's behavior, attitudes, and involvement.

The earlier writings on the helping relationship seldom mention commitment and obligation, but recently there has been more and more social work literature that speaks of the helping contract. Usually, this phrase means that the expectations and terms of the commitments and obligations of both client and worker are explicitly shared. This defining of commitment and obligation, along with the clarification of purpose, time, and setting is an important process and will be discussed in greater detail in Chapters 8 and 9. However, whether or not commitments and obligations are explicitly defined, they are an important, and inescapable, part of every professional relationship involving the giving and taking of help.

Any person asking for help from another is acutely, if unconsciously, aware of the necessity for commitments and the taking on of obligations; and it is often the fear of what may be involved in the expectations and obligations of the commitments that keeps the person from seeking help. The general obligations that clients are usually expected to assume are an open and honest presentation of the problem, of their situation, and of their ways of coping that relate to the problem; an accommodation to the minimum procedural conditions of the helping relationship, such as coming to a certain place at a certain time for an interview and working as they can on the selected problem. Clients are expected to assume these obligations as they can, and their commitments can be renegotiated without penalty.

The worker assumes more binding commitments and obligations and cannot renegotiate the contract without the consent and participation of the client. The worker's obligations include the responsibility to meet the essential procedural conditions of the relationship in the fullest way—being present at prearranged times and places and in certain emergency situations as well; keeping the focus of the work together on the client's problem; offering a relationship that is conducive to sharing, growth, and change. If these commitments to the contract are violated without adequate reason and adequate explanation to the clients, it is certain that clients will question the worker's desire to help. Perhaps worse, clients may interpret such a violation as a message that we do not consider them important. Being present when we are needed carries a connotation that we think the client important, and being absent or late when we are obligated to be present carries a connotation of rejection.

Thus far the helping relationship has been the focus of discussion. However, in summary, we would broaden our comments to define commitment as an involvement with a client, a client system, or other systems that is unqualified by our idiosyncratic personal needs. It is a freely determined wish to further the purpose of the relationship without the expectation of returns that support a sense of worth, add to our self-esteem, or preserve our status. This commitment is communicated through a resolute consistency, constancy, responsible follow through, and the preservation of the other's dignity and individuality. This preservation demands more than an awareness of the other's dignity and individuality; it involves actions based on sensitive and thoughtful understanding of the other and the other's position. Commitment requires that the workers assume a simultaneous responsibility and accountability for what they say and do to the client, the client system, or other systems; to the professional system which sanctions their right to offer help; and to themselves (Goldstein, 1973, p. 74).

Acceptance and expectation

In most discussions of acceptance in helping relationships one finds notions to the effect that this means the communication of a nonjudgmental attitude as well as efforts to help workers differentiate between accepting the person and accepting the person's actions. We would prefer that workers regard acceptance as more than a refusal to judge and that they try not to distinguish between a person and the person's actions. We would like them to consider acceptance as an active verb—*to accept*—meaning to receive as adequate or satisfactory, to regard as true, to believe in, to receive what the other offers. To accept others means to receive what they offer of themselves, with respect for their capacity and worth, with belief in their capacity to grow and mature, and with awareness that their behaviors can be understood as attempts at survival and coping. Acceptance means acting in the recognition that the essence of being human is having problems, making choices (good and bad, wise and foolish), and participating in the shaping of one's destiny with the resources at one's command. Therefore, a better meaning than "to refuse to judge" would be "to actively seek to understand."

The basic elements in acceptance are perhaps knowing, individualization, and trust or expectation. *Knowing* relates to one's efforts to take in and understand other people's reality and experience. Their values, needs, and purposes; to acquire some idea of where other people come from, of their life and frame of reference. *Individualization* means the capacity to see the person as a unique human being with distinctive feelings, thoughts, and experiences. The individual must be differentiated from all others, including ourselves. Assumptions must not be made about others based on generalized notions about a group, a class, or a race, although there is a need to appreciate and understand the manner in which race, class, and sex influence client-worker transactions. *Trust* or *expectation* means that workers have a belief and faith in the capacity of individuals for self-determination and self-direction—that they consider it the right and responsibility of each individual to exercise maximum self-determination in the person's own life with due regard for the welfare of others.

Acceptance of the client does not just occur. It grows from the roots of a fundamental belief and faith that the inherent processes of individual development will lead a person toward greater maturity when such processes are fostered and matured, and it develops as one seeks to understand the feelings, thoughts and experiences, resources and lack of resources, opportunities and deprivations that have led the individual to making certain choices. In fact, it is our conviction that one finds it almost impossible to be judgmental when one is fully engaged in a cooperative journey to the understanding of another. One cannot understand if one is observing another through the lenses of what is right or wrong, good or bad. Most human behavior is purposive, and if one can understand the purpose of behavior, then it becomes understandable rather than right or wrong.

Acceptance does not mean that we always agree with the other person. It does not mean that we forgo our own values in order to agree with or support the client's values. It does not mean that clients are excused from the world in which they must live. It means rather that workers may present the importance of, and the belief in the importance of, behaving in socially appropriate ways in keeping with established laws and regulations at the same time that they seek to understand the intense anger that drives clients to act impulsively against certain limits and regulations and that workers can empathize with their need to strike out. True acceptance carries with it an assumption that people act as they must in the complexity of their particular human situation and that they are what their nature and their environment, coupled with their vision, permits them to be.

Thus it can be seen that self-determination, nonjudgmental respect, sensitivity, individualization, expectation of growth, and understanding are all part of the general notion of acceptance. One of the most effective ways to communicate acceptance is to try to understand the position and feelings of clients. This can be done by commenting on their communication in ways that indicate a desire to understand or to further understand what they are saying, or by asking questions that are related to the content they are trying to communicate and thus to reveal that you heard and are interested in understanding them.

"A unique characteristic of human beings is that their mental representations of the future powerfully affect their state of well-being in the present" (Frank, 1978a, p. 1). Not only does the type of expectations of the future affect the state of well-being in the present, but it also affects behavior in the present which in turn affects present and future sense of well-being and future behavior. Freud wrote: "Expectation colored by hope and faith is an effective force with which we have to reckon . . . in all our attempts at treatment . . ." (in Frank, 1978a, p. 1). Expectation is a potent force with which social workers have to reckon in all their transactions with other human systems. There are at least three elements of expectation that are important for social workers to consider: (1) how they feel about the system's ability or desire or willingness to change, and their ability to contribute effectively to the change in the situation of the client or target system, (2) the expectation of the social worker held by the system involved, and (3) the system, particularly the client system's expectation of the effect of the helping process.

There has been considerable research in support of the notion that the change agent's expectation that the client system is capable of growth and change, learning and problem solving has a powerful effect on that growth and change. Teachers given a class of students that had a history of learning problems were told that the class was very bright and capable. Not only did the class achieve far beyond what anyone knowing their history would have predicted but at the end of the year IQ tests showed a 20-point improvement. Psychology students told that a group of experimental rats had been specially bred to run mazes discovered that indeed this group of rats were unusually able in such behavior. The fact of the matter was that this particular group of rats was randomly selected from the shipment of rats that had arrived at the laboratory that day. The key to the difference in the performance of the rats lay in the students' expectations of their exceptional performance and the way the students' communicated their regard and expectation to these animals by their handling of their subjects.

In medical practice there have been numerous double-blind studies in which patients improve regardless of whether they are given placebos or medication. These improvements are powerful indicators of the importance of the attitude of the attending doctors. Because the physician believed that the placebo was a powerful medication, the physician expected improvement and showed increased interest in the patient's progress in treatment. Both these attitudes had tremendous impact on the patient's improvement.

This evidence would support the principle in our relationships to all social systems, to all human beings encountered in the professional life, that social workers need to be very aware of their inner feelings about the system with which they work. The social workers who are most effective in the helping process (or other change) will be those who expect that their clients (or other systems) can and will change in their own way given appropriate help and support. To go back to the concepts from ego psychology: social workers must be convinced of the power of the push toward growth in all of us if they are to be effective change agents.

The second element of expectation with which we must be concerned is the client's (or other system with which we are working) expectation of what we will do to help. Over and over again studies of the effectiveness of social work help point to the importance of the client's expectation of social workers' behavior. To quote a cogent example from Mayer and Timms (1970, p. 1):

> My husband's gambling was driving me around the bend and I thought maybe the Welfare could help me do something about it. But all the lady wanted to do was talk—what was he like when he gambled, did we quarrel and silly things like that. She was trying to help and it made me feel good knowing someone cared. But you can't solve a problem by *talking* about it. Something's got to be done.

While this woman received some help by her contacts with the social worker, she was "dismayed and perplexed by the worker's approach and . . . failed to return after several sessions" as she could not see that anything was being accomplished. Clients will probably not be helped from social work unless their expectations are in accord with what actually happens in their transactions with the practitioner. This principle can be stated another way by drawing from our earlier development of role theory: The more congruent the notions of client and worker are as to what will be going on between them in their work together, the more effective that work will be. If the expectations of the worker's behavior are highly discrepant with what actually occurs, the client will rapidly withdraw from involvement in the relationship.

This discussion points out the importance of exploring with the client in the initial contact what it is that the client (or any other system) expects. Is this expectation congruent with what can be done in the given situation? If it is not, what can be done, what is the worker prepared to do, or what is seen as what ought to be done. At this point it becomes critically important to both the helping process and the helping relationship that the matter be discussed. Through this discussion either the other system's or the workers' behavior must be altered and changed in such a way that they are congruent if workers are to be helpful.

The third important element in expectation is the client's (or other system's) belief that good results will follow from their interaction with the social worker. Expectations of the future that are critical to the change process are found in client attitudes of trust and faith. In trusting social workers the clients (or other systems) not only must perceive them as competent and helpful at the present moment, but they must also perceive the workers as competent and helpful over time. For example, in a group of clients seen for approximately six weeks in a mental health clinic, hope scores before treatment showed a positive correlation with improvement after their case was closed. (Gottschalk et al., 1973). There are many examples of this from medicine such as the finding that patients' scores on an acceptance scale before open heart surgery were considerably better predictors of poor postoperative recovery or death than the actual severity of their disease (Frank, 1978a, pp. 3–5).

Empathy

All the authors cited in the first section of this chapter agree that empathy is a necessary quality of the helping relationship. *Empathy* is the capacity to enter into the feelings and experiences of another—knowing what the other feels and experiences—without losing oneself in the process. The helping person makes an active effort to enter into the perceptual frame of the other person without losing personal perspective, but, rather, using that understanding in order to help the other person. In an article on "Being Understanding and Understood: Or How to Find a Wandered Horse" Wendell Johnson (1951) tells of how experienced western cowboys demonstrated an uncanny ability to find a lost horse:

> The experienced western cowboy was able to find a lost horse with uncanny ability. I understand that he did this by working at the job of trying to feel like a horse. He asked himself, "Now what kind of reason would I have for wandering away if I were a horse? With such a reason where would I go?" Apparently, it is possible to empathize with a horse a good deal—to feel like a horse to a surprising degree.
>
> At any rate, the cowboy would imagine that he was a horse, that he had the horse's reason for going, and then he would go to the place he would go if he were a horse—and usually he would find the horse.[1]

The cowboy found the horse because he was able to feel as if he were the horse—to feel and think as the horse might feel and think. However, since he was not a horse, having found the horse he brought it back.

Carl Rogers (1966, p. 409) defines empathy as "the perceiving of the internal frame of reference of another with accuracy, and with the emotional components which pertain thereto, as if one were the other person but without ever losing the 'as if' condition." Keith-Lucas (1972, pp. 80–81) points out that empathy is the worker's understanding of the feelings the other has about the situation, knowing inside oneself how uncomfortable and desperate these feelings may be for the client, but never claiming these feelings for oneself as the helping person. He goes on to differentiate between pity, sympathy, and empathy with a very cogent illustration:

> Consider three reactions to someone who has told us that he strongly dislikes his wife. The *sympathetic man* would say, "Oh, I know exactly how you feel. I can't bear mine, either." The two of them would comfort each other but nothing would come of it. The *pitying man* would commiserate but add that he himself was most happily married. Why didn't the other come to dinner sometime and see what married life could be like? This, in most cases, would only increase the frustration of the unhappy husband and help him to put his problem further outside himself, on to his wife or his lack of good fortune. The *empathetic person* might say something like, "That must be terribly difficult for you. What do you think might possibly help?" And only the empathetic person, of the three, would have said anything that would lead to some change in the situation.

Empathy requires what may seem to many beginning workers to be antithetical qualities—the capacity to feel an emotion deeply and yet to remain

---

[1] Reprinted from *ETC.* Vol. VIII, No. 3 by permission of The International Society for General Semantics.

separate enough from it to be able to utilize knowledge. Methods of reasoning are necessary if one is to make an objective analysis of the problem and the possibilities of solution. Even as workers let the full awareness of clients' emotions wash over them, they are aware that they are feeling, not as clients feel, but *as if* they were the clients. They must remember that the clients came to them, not to have someone share their feelings (although this is relieving) but to enlist aid in coping with a situation that feeling alone cannot resolve. If it could, clients would not need help, for they have feeling enough invested, and undoubtedly they have hard thinking and trying invested, too. They need a worker who, in standing apart, can bring some difference in feeling and thinking, and who is able, with a clear head, to manipulate or secure resources that were unavailable to the clients' influence, were unknown to clients or were not thought of by them.

In learning to be empathetic, workers have to develop the capacity for imaginative consideration of others and to give up any fixed mental image that may lead one to change reality to fit any preconceived expectation. In this workers are handicapped by two factors: (1) the set of stereotypes carried with them, which are useful in enabling them to quickly grasp the meaning of encounters in daily life but which block greater discernment; and (2) the limited symbols—words, gestures, and reports—available to them to convey another's reality. Thus the accuracy of interpretation is dependent on sensitivity and intuition; the ability to put this together in a dynamic way with all that is known about the clients (their experiences, behavior, problems, and associations), the conception of their potential and what is known about what they want and hope for; all the theoretical knowledge and helping experiences; and all the other experiences with similar kinds of people and situations—real or fantasied. Then, when workers have this mental representation of the other, they must hold it lightly, recognizing that there is always something unknown and unfelt about the other that makes any mental representation tentative, no matter how hard they have struggled to attain it, and no matter how much understanding is brought to it.

In speaking of work with handicapped children, Johnson (1951, pp. 178–179) continues:

> You simply ask yourself, "Now what are the possible reasons for behaving as this child does? If I were the child, what would be my reason for doing what I do? Just what would I be trying to achieve? What would I be trying to avoid?"
>
> You can go from there to ask a lot of questions, such as "How could I achieve my purposes differently? What other motives could I have? What other effects could I try to achieve, and by what other means? What changes would I have to achieve before I would be able to use other procedures, or work toward other goals?" And so forth.
>
> . . . you never see the child as a whole. You see only what you are prepared to see. You can understand only what you are prepared to understand. It does not matter what books you have read, either—at least, it does not matter as much as we think it does. You had a childhood in which conditions determined and limited what you are now going to do with the books you have read. The child will look different to you from the way he will look to any other worker. The net result is that the child somehow feels that he or she is being understood or evaluated only by one individual, and that he or she is not being evaluated in anything like a complete sense.

There is another reason why we do not understand these children better than we do, a very obvious reason. It is that we do not have their handicaps ... I wonder, however, whether it is possible for an individual who has never had a problem—if there are any individuals like that—to have any significant insight into the difficulties of individuals who do have serious problems. The point is that if you have not had a handicap, then all you can ever have in the way of knowledge of the individual that you are attempting to help is the kind of knowledge that is verbal.[2]

Full knowledge of another being is something forever beyond attainment by anyone; it can only be approached, never achieved. It is questionable whether any client wants to be fully and totally known. There is something very frightening about someones' knowing everything about us as an individual for in knowledge lies control; so in the ordinary course of living people reveal their intimate selves only to those they trust. Without the pain of the problem and the hope that the worker can offer some help toward coping with it, few clients would be willing to share themselves with an unknown other person.

The fact that workers can never fully know another except in a limited way, and that if workers felt like the client, workers would be unable to introduce the differences in thinking and feeling that bring change, all require that workers be able to maintain a certain detachment. This demand is often more difficult for the beginning worker than the demand to feel. Each worker maintains this balance differently. This is an area in which supervision can be of great help. By comments and questions the effective supervisor helps practitioners observe themselves and be aware of their contribution to the relationships they form with others. Thus self-awareness—an essential quality of all social work relationships—grows.

While some degree of empathy is needed at the very beginning of a relationship (and without this quality a relationship cannot be formed), it is a quality of the relationship and thus is not something which workers construct by themselves. It comes, grows, and develops from the process of interaction of client and worker in which the client can be encouraged to express personal feelings more and more specifically, fully, and precisely, and the worker grows in capacity to feel with the client and in understanding of what is expressed. What clients seek, especially at the beginning of the relationship, is not full understanding, but rather to enter a relationship with a helping person in which they sense that their feelings and thoughts are acceptable and that what they express is understandable as a possible human response to their situation.

Johnson shares his notion on how workers better understand a client:

And how can we do that? Well, I think we do it mainly in two ways. One is by never being dogmatic when it comes to how the other individual feels. We do not know for sure how another feels, and I think we ought frankly to face that. The other thing we tend to do, I think, if we have this point of view, is to be more ready to ask the child what she/he thinks about the problem and about our approaches to it.

Those who have attempted to help me have always wanted to ask me a good deal about how I felt about my speech problem, and about my mother and

---

[2] Reprinted from *ETC*. Vol. VIII, No. 3 by permission of The International Society for General Semantics.

father, and so on, but seldom, if ever, have clinical workers asked me how I felt about them, how I felt about what they were doing, how I felt about their ideas. There was always a feeling that the expert was attempting somehow to force on me a point of view, an interpretation, a kind of understanding. And almost always when I would ask questions, or say perhaps, "No, no you don't quite understand . . . ," there was a tendency on the part of the clinical worker to take that to be evidence of what the psychoanalysts call "resistance." It is a rare clinician who listens really effectively to what "the case" tries to share. It could be that as clinicians we are wrong and that "the case" has something to tell us, that they are not resisting at all. They may be trying to teach us something. Some of our methods, for example, sound very good to us and they are backed up by great authorities, but when applied to a particular individual, they do not work. Some of the children and adults on the other side of the desk might be trying to tell us why they do not work.

I had a very strong feeling, most of the time, when I was on the other side of the desk, that the clinician working with me was *interested in the work*. I hardly ever had the feeling that the interest was directed exclusively at me, and I think I have noticed that sort of thing in other cases. In my own clinical work I feel quite sure that I, too, have a tendency to get interested in the theory and the techniques and somehow to lose sight of the child. It is actually hard to stay interested in (the person).[3]

Acceptance and empathy are seldom discussed in social work literature dealing with the social worker's relationship with other than client systems. However, it would seem that such elements could be of help in either cooperative or conflicted relationships that involve purposive change in nonclient target systems. Resistance to change, and conflict will be prevented to the degree that the practitioner is able to help the target system develop its own understanding of the need for change as well as an awareness of how members of the target system feel about change and what change will mean to the target system. If conflict is the chosen method of bringing change, the practitioner's ability to empathize with the feelings of the other will facilitate choosing the most effective way to become engaged in the conflict. The practitioner who is able to accept the members of a client, or a target, system as individuals with both rational and nonrational positions and who can empathize with those positions will, other things being equal, be more productive than the practitioner who does not possess these skills. The way the worker uses these skills will differ in different situations. In the helping relationship the worker may communicate empathy directly. In other types of relationship workers may use it to shape other communications.

Authority and power

The two remaining elements of a helping relationship to be discussed are (1) authority and power and (2) genuineness and congruency. Not only are these perhaps the most difficult concepts to understand, but it is the misunderstanding of the element of authority and power in helping relationships that often affects a worker's genuineness with clients. Among other things,

---

3 Reprinted from *ETC*. Vol. VIII, No. 3 by permission of The International Society for General Semantics.

authority may be defined as a power delegated to the practitioner by client and agency in which the practitioner is seen as having the power to influence or persuade resulting from possession of certain knowledge and experience and from occupying a certain position. Thus there are two aspects of authority in the helping relationship. The first might be called the institutional aspect in that it comes from the social worker's position and function within the agency's purpose and program. The second aspect is psychological in that clients give workers the power to influence or persuade because they accept them as sources of information and advice—as experts in their field. A person in need of help seeks someone who has the authority of knowledge and skill to be of help. If workers accept the clients' assumptions that they carry this authority, the relationship may become infused with a sense of safety and security when the client's own powers of self-dependence fail them.

The primary characteristic of the concepts of power and authority in the helping relationship is that they are neither good nor bad in themselves. Some aspects of these elements are always present, and the attempt of social workers to abdicate their role and pretend that they carry no authority only leaves clients troubled by suspicions and doubts about why workers are unwilling to admit what they, the clients, are so aware of. This incongruence between what the client feels and what the worker says makes an authentic relationship impossible. The crucial significance of power and authority lies in how they are utilized for help.

Social workers have had a hard time with the concepts of authority and power. There has been too little examination of authority and power as factors that enter into all human relationships—all human relationships develop laws about acceptable behavior of the people involved within those relationships (Haley, 1972, pp. 1–68). This is one of the problems that workers often face in using professional relationships for other purposes than the direct helping process. The clients of the community organization worker, the research worker, and the consultant are in a different power relationship to the worker than are the clients in the helping relationship. If what this factor means for the workers and those with whom they work is unexamined (or, worse, even denied), they lack the needed knowledge to guide them. Social workers need to be able to deal with power and authority both when they exercise it and when others exercise it in relation to them.

In his discussion of authority in social work relationships, Goldstein (1973, pp. 84–86) points out that when persons require what another has to offer "that cannot be obtained elsewhere—whether one is seeking the adoption of a child, financial assistance, help with a personal problem, or professional services to assist in a social action enterprise—the relationship cannot be equalized." As the social worker's needs have no relevance to the task, "the seeker cannot reciprocate or supply the provider with any reward that can restore the balance. The fact that the seeker has limited alternatives to meet personal needs, is further heightened by the fact that workers are seen as having competence and knowledge." When social workers say, "We will meet once a week on a Monday, if that is convenient to you," or when they decide to include another family member in treatment, they are setting the conditions of the relationship. Or they may refer clients elsewhere. These are all examples of power and authority.

Genuineness and congruence

In the research that has been done on helping relationships (Truax and Carkhuff, 1967, pp. 1–2; Truax and Mitchell, 1971), it has been found that in an effective helping relationship the helping person needs to communicate four things: empathy, acceptance, unconditional positive regard (we have called this quality "concern for the other," as we find this phrase more expressive of the essential notion), and congruence. Congruence means that workers bring to the relationship a consistent and honest openness and realness and that behavior and the content of communications with, and in regard to, the client must at all times match each other (be congruent) and must match the underlying value system and the essential self as a professional person. (The qualities needed as helping people will be discussed later in this chapter.)

In order to be congruent and genuine, we must seek three things: (1) an honest knowledge of ourselves, of who and what we really are; (2) a clear knowledge of agency procedures and policies and of the professional role, both in their meaning to the worker and in their meaning to the clients; and (3) an internalization of the first two and our concern for the other, acceptance of clients, commitment to their welfare and to the authority aspects of the workers' role and position, so that these qualities are so much a part of us that we no longer need to be consciously aware of them and can turn our full attention to clients and their situation.

People who are real, genuine, and congruent in a helping relationship are ones who know themselves and are unafraid of what they see in themselves or what they are. They can enter a helping relationship without anything of themselves to prove or protect, so they are unafraid of the emotions of others. For example, unwillingness to be honest with clients about authority in a relationship, or about what will be done with the information they share (see Reading 5–1), may be a consequence of negative experiences with authority in one's own life. Therefore, we try to deny (to lie about) what the client sees so clearly is really there. To be congruent we need to have faced and examined our own feelings about many central life experiences that clients share with us, so that we know which feelings are ours and which are the client's. What are our feelings about the lies we encounter? We are angry about them and so we must be different? We want the client to see we are different and that we understand better than anyone else? Do we really? Can we free ourselves of certain behaviors and feelings we dislike? Will our being free of them help our client? Or is it better to admit that they are there so that the two of us can examine what they mean for the client? What are we afraid of, or what do we want, in denying to clients the facts about certain agency restrictions on service and about our capacity to skew these so that they do not bear so heavily on them?

This brings up the second half of the worker's awareness—the meaning of the agency role and position to the worker and to the client. Not how workers want the client to see them, but how the client does see them—as representatives of a particular agency or service. Workers and clients come together, as a rule, within some kind of bureaucratic structure. The client usually does not pay for the costs of service, or at least does not pay the full costs. So the worker is paid by someone other than the client. What do the structure of the agency, its position in the community, and the source of the funds to support its services mean to the client? Workers who have not honestly examined these questions and who have not faced what they mean both to themselves and their clients will often appear to the client to be somewhat divorced from the reality of the client's life. So being honest and real means that workers have examined their roles and tasks in relation to agency, client, and target systems and that they can assume them fully and honestly with an openness about all their parts and of their impact on the client.

Our popular culture tends to place emphasis on irrationality in caring relationships with others, to hold that true caring ought to be something impulsive and instinctive, from the heart as it may be as of this moment, uninhibited and "natural." There is a belief that to think about a feeling distorts it and makes it less an expression of what people are—as though the head were not a genuine part of the body; or as though only the heart were good, and the head must perforce be evil. This stance neglects the common theme of much of the literature of human emotion, in which the heart is held to be fickle and inconsistent, unwilling to be committed to another. Actually, congruent people need a warm and nurturing heart, an objective, open, aware, and disciplined mind, and an open channel of communication between head and heart so that they appear all of one piece to others.

There is a tendency to view *professionalism* and *objectivity* as though these qualities mean "coldness," "cautiousness," and an impersonal, restricted reaction to the expressed feeling of others. Actually, these ways of presenting oneself in a relationship are totally unprofessional and are related to one's own need to be self-protective, to be afraid of oneself and thus of others. Both this impersonal way of operating with others and the undisciplined, personal expression of one's impulses of the moment are self-serving modes of behavior that are destructive of the capacity to communicate congruence and genuineness in the helping relationship, which requires that the client be kept squarely in the center of concern.

Perhaps an example will illustrate this point. When a really competent woman figure skater is watched in a "free skating" program, the viewers do not feel that she is incongruent, or unreal, or dishonest. Instead they feel the spontaneity and creative force with which she puts her whole self into the performance. But the performance required years of slow and painful learning— it required more than a little of self-discipline and persistence, of hard, slow growth and change in the use of self. The creative, free movements of this skater are quite unnatural to the untrained beginner on ice skates. They are not in any way the "natural" movements of the skater the first time she put on skates and tried the ice. Yet, the skater does not think of each movement or gesture. In fact, if she does, she will not give a free performance. Her performance has the effect it does because she has so internalized the demands of the task that she can give herself to it entirely and can respond freely and spontaneously to what is in herself and in the here and now situation. And as viewers watch her, they are aware that she gets great satisfaction from the use of her competence in a disciplined yet free way. She knows herself and her capacity, and there is a joy in what she does. Workers, too, should enter all professional relationships with a clear knowledge of what can be and what cannot be done, a sense of competence and a belief in what workers are doing. Satisfaction can be received in helping others. How can workers believe that the creative use of self in helping others demands less time, work, and discipline, and knowledge of self and of the limits of action than does the performance of a figure skater?

Rational and irrational elements in the helping relationship

Obviously there are cognitive elements in the professional relationship. Both workers and those with whom they interact think as well as feel in a helping transaction. Both bring knowledge and values to their association. In all professional relationships social workers need to be actively cognitive—relating what is said and done to their knowledge—and making sense out of the interchange of feelings. Much of the rest of the text will be devoted, as have the first four chapters, to setting forth the values and knowledge that the worker needs to master. It is enough to mention here that cognition is an important element of the relationship.

The irrational elements of the relationship are those elements—feelings and attitudes, inherent patterns of behavior—which are not called forth by the present situation but are brought to it, relatively unchanged by the here and now and by reality, from earlier relational experiences. They are irrational in that they are usually unconscious (and thus not available to present awareness) and in that they are, in the form in which they appear, inappropriate to the present situation.

As an example of the power of the irrational: One of the authors was once involved in a helping relationship with a family which had been referred by the school social worker because a son was emotionally disturbed. Bob was one of two sets of twins. Besides the twins, there was one other child in the family. None of the other children showed any unusual difficulty in school. After some observation of the mother's relationship to her children it became obvious that she treated Bob differently from the others. She indulged him more than his brothers and sisters and was totally unable to limit him. When confronted with examples of the different way in which she reacted to Bob, she burst into tears and said she could not deny him because he was just like her. It seems that she had always felt "picked on" as a child, and she was sure Bob felt the same way. She had been the younger and smaller of a set of twins, as Bob was, and she was sure he felt just as she did, so she was trying to help him feel better. In reality, she had no evidence that Bob felt the way she assumed he did. Nor had she ever faced the fact that she and Bob were two very different persons with two very different childhood situations. Her response to Bob was an irrational one with roots in her own painful childhood.

A further, and also important, example of the effects of the irrational in all our lives is found in the attempt to create a congruent honest working relationship across racial, cultural, or social class barriers. Individuals may master all the knowledge about the history and culture of another race; they may plan rationally how to use themselves in the relationship; but, too often, when they actually come together with a member of another race, they find feelings and thoughts rising inside them that may be quite contrary to what they want to feel and think. They condemn themselves for these forbidden feelings and deny them both to themselves and to others, yet they persist. They persist because they are irrational responses that are learned as a part of culture. All individuals live and grow up in a racist society, so they all absorb, to a greater or a lesser extent, the irrational attitudes of that society in regard to race. These attitudes become a part of all persons and are all the more difficult to understand and eradicate because of the very fact that they are irrational.

It is important that workers recognize that such irrational elements are a part of the helping relationship (indeed, of all relationships) because such realization enhances their capacity to understand and accept the expressions of clients, and because it helps them to accept the importance of their own self-awareness. The presence of irrational elements in the most knowledgeable and thoughtful of individuals makes the demand for self-awareness a constant one. All people need to exercise all the care of which they are capable in order to keep such elements in themselves from intruding inappropriately into the helping relationship.

In the development and use of the professional relationship in the service of another there is the demand that workers know themselves. It is necessary to speak of the conscious use of self that carries within it the demand for self-awareness. As one considers the differences in the development and use of the relationship with different size systems and for different purposes, it would appear that these differences are significant enough to demand a differing self-awareness on the part of the worker.

It would appear that in work with client, target, or action groups, one must be self-aware not only in relation to the group as a whole but also to each individual in the group, who relating differently, may call up different responses. Favoritism, rejection, avoidance, demands for special attention—all present the group worker with special demands in self-awareness. In the one-to-group helping process, because group relationships are concurrent with the worker-to-group relationships, workers must be aware of their push to react in areas of power and status problems, sibling rivalries, competitions, and aggressions. It would appear that considerable self-awareness and self-discipline is necessary to maintain focus and purpose while weaving the many strands of individual needs and competitions into a meaningful process. The ability to keep focused on the needs of others in the face of the group's questioning of the worker's operations or authority is a difficult discipline to achieve. Workers with groups must develop an understanding and a discipline of their own status needs, their needs to preserve face before a group, and their innate responses to open conflict.

In the one-to-one relationship, workers can depend less on immediate feedback from clients in relation to inappropriate operations so there is a greater demand to be aware of feelings and responses that are aroused in the transactions with the client that will affect the helping process. Workers need to be particularly aware of their own dependency needs and how these needs affect their reactions to the dependency needs of others and of their feelings about authority. Workers need to be conscious of any feelings of omnipotence and the need for client approval. They need to be aware of their need to take too much responsibility or assume too little with their clients and of self-expectations and the ways these affect client relationships, both in terms of subtle demands for change, growth, and performance and in terms of the bearing this has on the psychic self-determination of the client. Workers need to be aware of the points at which the client's needs and problems touch off feelings in them that may not be helpful in work with the client and the kinds of self-discipline that are effective to control such feelings.

Because of its great overriding importance in all social work practice we want to introduce once again the problems caused in the effective use of relationship by a lack of self-awareness about feeling, thinking about, and attitudes toward racial/ethnic and sex difference. A recent study of work with women clients revealed that the theoretical position one espoused had little to do with the social worker's stereotyped reaction to women clients (Davenport and Reims, 1978, p. 306). The theories could be used flexibly. The critical variable that resulted in rigid and stereotyped reactions on the part of social workers came from the individual's biased belief systems. It is absolutely basic to social work practice that workers be aware of their belief systems, the impact of such systems on their use of self, and that they find ways to deal with themselves so that they can work without bias with all people.

THE HELPING PERSON

It is difficult to discuss "the helping person" because there are almost as many kinds of helpers as there are people who need help. There is probably no one person who is equally effective in creating helping relationships with all people. And there is probably no one person who is an ideal helping person, so that each of us will probably lack some of the qualities a helping person should have. There are, however, certain qualities, attitudes, and approaches toward life that are found to an uncommon degree among helping people—and, thus, among social workers. There are six qualities that are seen as central to effective social work functioning. Someone once wrote that "helping relationships are created by helping people, not by helping techniques." From this point of view, this means that social work practitioners bring about system change through their use of self—of what they are—of what they have made a part of themselves including their beings, their thoughts, their feelings, their belief systems, their knowledge. In other words, what they do must be congruent with what they are seeking to become as persons.

There are many people who do not have the capacity to help others—just as there are many people who do not have the capacity to design computers or perform surgery. And neither of these jobs is simply a matter of knowledge. Both require certain kinds of people with certain kinds of talents. Among the kinds of people who are not good helpers are those who are interested in knowing about people rather than in serving them (coldly objective students of humanity); those who are impelled by strong personal needs to control, to feel superior, or to be liked; those who have solved problems similar to the problems of the people in need of help but have forgotten what it cost them to do so; and those who are primarily interested in retributive justice and moralizing (Keith-Lucas, 1972, pp. 89–108).

Maturing people

The most effective helping people usually experience themselves as living, growing, developing people who are deeply involved in the process of becoming. They do not exclude themselves from the "human condition" but view all people, including themselves, as engaged in problem-solving. Not only are they unafraid of life, but they frankly enjoy the process of being alive with all the struggle that this may involve. They find change and growth exciting rather than threatening. Their anxiety and tension are at an optimum level, so they are free to take on new experiences. Thus they do not need to be "right" to defend where they are. Perhaps most of the other qualities to be discussed will stem from this quality.

Creativity

Helping people need to be nonconformist in that they need to hold most solutions to the problems of life as tentative. Conformity involves accepting prevailing opinion as fact, and this stymies openness to other solutions. However, it is necessary to distinguish nonconformity from "counterconformity," a term which has been used to characterize a person who is always "against" authority or accepted ways of doing. Such a person is not truly independent but is motivated by a need to defend personal identity and by hostile and/or aggressive needs. Intellectual openness and receptivity suggest a state of freedom to detach oneself from certain theoretical positions or systems of thought. Creative people can allow themselves to be dominated by the problem with which they are grappling rather than search for a known solution. It is not that creative people are not knowledgeable, that they have not given a great deal of themselves to learning what is known, but that they are able, in spite of the heavy investment they have made, to hold this knowledge tentatively. This seems paradoxical to many people, and it is indeed a heavy demand, for when people invest heavily in things they tend to hold them dearly.

This brings up another paradoxical quality of creative people. Although they are often deeply committed to a problem, they are at the same time detached from it. The creative person likes complexity. They do not seek premature closure but can maintain an openness and joy in the contradictory or obscure and have a tolerance for conflict.

Capacity to observe self

Capacity to observe self is usually discussed in social work literature under the rubric of self-awareness, and it has already been discussed as an element of genuineness and congruence. It is an important capacity for the social worker and is discussed in most material that deals with the helping relationship. Perhaps the two previously discussed qualities are an important part of this capacity, which really means to be sensitive to one's own internal workings, to be involved with oneself and one's needs, thoughts, commitments, and values, yet to stand back enough from oneself to question the meaning of what is going on. This means that the helping person must take a helping attitude toward oneself as well as toward others.

We have chosen not to use the term *self-awareness* for this quality because we think it is more than self-knowledge. There have to be other qualities. Self-love and love of others, self-respect and respect for others, self-confidence and confidence in others, acceptance of self and acceptance of others, faith in self and faith in others develop together or not at all. So the capacity to observe self probably requires the ability to care deeply about oneself and one's goals, to respect and to believe in oneself and yet to be able to stand back and observe oneself as an important piece of the complex activity of helping.

This way of regarding self leads to flexibility, a sense of humor, a readiness to learn, an acceptance of one's limitations, and an openness—all of which are important qualities of the helping person. And most of all, the capacity to observe self demands courage—we need to be unafraid of what we will find. All of us, to some extent, distort in one way or another feelings that we do not want to acknowledge, but the more this is true, the less we can help others. It is the need for self-protection, the fear for self, that gets in the way of sincerity, openness, genuineness, and honesty.

Like all other human beings, social workers cannot make themselves over simply because they wish to do so. Like all other human beings, they are the product of their intellectual and physical attributes, they are shaped by the range, expansiveness, and richness of their life experiences, including their educational experiences, and by how they have used those experiences in developing their basic beliefs, values, and attitudes. However, even if we cannot remake ourselves at will, it is important in observing ourselves that we have the capacity to see ourselves as growing and developing people.

Desire to help

A deep desire to increase the ability of people to choose for themselves and to control their own lives is an absolutely essential quality of a helping person. Effective helping relationships or other social work relationships simply cannot be created and sustained without this desire. Basically, the desire is a commitment to oneself rather than to others because it must be our desire, be related to us and a commitment to ourselves. It is this commitment that gives one the courage to know oneself and the willingness to risk oneself in the service of others.

Courage

It takes great courage—not the courage of the unaware and insensitive but the courage of the person who is thoroughly aware yet does what one knows needs to be done—to take the risks with oneself and others that social work relationships inevitably demand. Workers must be willing to assume the risks of failing to help, of becoming involved in difficult, emotionally charged situations that they do not know how to handle, of having their comfortable world and ways of operating upset, of being blamed and abused, of being constantly involved in the unpredictable, and perhaps of being physically threatened. "It is only the person who can be afraid and not be afraid of this fear who is in a position to help" (Keith-Lucas, 1972, p. 100).

It takes great courage to be able to think about ourselves and others as we are. And, even more, it takes great courage and strength to directly face clients with the reality of their problems when this reality threatens. And it takes courage to engage in honest thinking about others and yet to be basically for people—to be skeptical and inquiring in one's thinking, yet trusting in one's attitude toward others.

Sensitivity

Our methods of sharing ourself completely with others are awkward and imperfect even when we are committed to that sharing. For troubled people the ability to share themselves and their situation is incredibly more difficult because of all their feelings about their problems and about themselves as people with problems, and because of the threat of the unknown in the helping process. Therefore, the worker who would help needs a capacity for feeling and sensing—for knowing in internal ways—the inner state of others without specific clues. This quality probably depends on one's ability to observe even small movements and changes in others and to make almost instantaneous inferences from them, to put oneself into the feeling and thinking of others, and to avoid stereotypes. It is probably closely related to one's capacity to be open to the new and to one's readiness for change.

RACE AND THE SOCIAL WORK RELATIONSHIP

We cannot leave a discussion of the professional relationship without some mention of the impact of racial or cultural difference on the development and use of the professional transaction. It is particularly fitting that this discussion should follow the sections on rational and irrational elements in the change process and on the helping person. Racist attitudes and actions are so deeply embedded in American society that it is impossible for any individual to have escaped their impact on one's conscious and unconscious selves and on the ways one relates across racial lines. It is easy to underestimate the extent of the impact of racist attitudes on individuals of all races because of the multivarious sources which subject all individuals to both explicit and implicit negative stereotypes. Implicit negative messages are more insidious, hence more devastating and difficult to deal with, yet they affect every one and all relationships.

Shirley Cooper (1978, p. 78) expresses it well when she says: "Clearly racism bites deeply into the psyche. It marks all its victims—blacks and whites—with deep hurt, anger, fear, confusion, and guilt."

Cooper urges that workers examine their thinking with special care as "efforts to acknowledge and deal with racial factors are affected by highly emotional attitudes." She points out that white people "influenced by a culture rampant with racism and unfamiliar with the intricacies and nuances of the lives of ethnic people may, even with the best of intentions, fail to recognize when social and cultural factors predominate" in their professional attitudes. Cooper (1978, p. 78) notes that "ethnic therapists are vulnerable to the opposite form of clinical error. Because they are so centrally involved, they may exaggerate the importance or impact of ethnic factors." She goes on to say that in color blindness individuals tend to lose their particular richness and complexity; and that there is a danger of no longer relating to individuals as they are but rather of relating to individuals as though they were "only culture carriers" (1978, p. 78).

Cooper (1978, p. 78) discusses the unavoidable guilt experienced by white practitioners who live in a privileged and segregated society and says that in their struggle with this guilt they may deal with it through "unrealistic rescue fantasies and activities—a form of paternalism."

When white guilt remains unconscious, it can lead to overcompensation, denial, reaction formation, an intense drive to identify with the oppressed, and a need to offer the victim special privileges and relaxed standards of behavior no more acceptable to minorities than to the general population.

In the black practitioner, oppression produces its own personality and distortion. It may lead to costly overachievement at the expense of more normal development. Whether one achieves or does not achieve, there is the anxiety that hard-won gains, or battles lost, are not, in fact, the consequence of one's performance but rather the result of considerations based on race. With the actuality of one's own productivity in doubt, there are anxieties about self-worth and competence and there is no real way to measure one's own behavior (1978, p. 78).

In speaking of the white-black encounter within the professional relationship, Gitterman and Schaeffer (1974, pp. 154–156) say:

One direct consequence of the institutionalized racial positions of blacks and whites is social distance. . . . As a result of these conditions, there emerge two separate and distinct experiences, each somewhat unknown and alien to the other. It is this very quality of mutual strangeness which characterizes the initial black-white encounter. It may be camouflaged, denied, or rationalized. The void may be filled by stereotyped "knowledge" and preconceptions, but the essential unknownness remains. Not only are the two different, but, not having lived or known each other's differences, they can only speculate about them. They see each other and the world, and are in turn viewed . . . by the world, in different ways. . . .

Thus separated . . . white . . . and . . . black . . . come together . . . face each other and are confronted with the necessity of doing something together. . . . First, there is suspiciousness and fear between them. . . .

There is also anger between them. Once again, much has been written, especially in recent years, of the rage that is felt by black people. White workers also feel anger of which they may or may not be aware. They may be angry at the black client for being so troubled, or helpless, or dependent, or hard to reach. They may be angry at themselves for their inability to do very much to really help their clients, or they may be angry at the clients for being angry at them. The anger is there on some level. It is most likely that the client perceives it even if workers do not.

There is also pain between them. This pain is one of the most complex dynamics because it stems from so many different sources . . . pain and suffering connected with whatever presenting problems caused the client to seek service . . . pain at being black in America . . . pain felt by the worker in response to the client's pains . . . pain from the guilt felt by each party. . . . Most profoundly, there is guilt caused by repressed anger and other negative feelings experienced by both.

Gitterman and Schaeffer (p. 157) recommend some ways of dealing with the racial gap between worker and client. Essentially, their recommendations reflect the factors in the relationship that was discussed earlier in this chapter. They point out that the helping process is a mutual endeavor between active participants, that it takes both participants to do the job, and that they must listen to each other. They emphasize that the white worker cannot ignore or minimize the social factors that contribute to the plight of the racially different client.

Perhaps the best way to end this too brief discussion of race is to quote from the preface of the volume in which Gitterman and Schaeffer's contribution appears. Here the editor (Goodman, 1974, p. xiii) says:

> The profession of social work cannot afford to sustain practices that would diminish the humanity of any group. It must deny that only blacks can treat blacks, or only whites can treat blacks, or only people of the same culture can understand each other well enough to provide help.
>
> Social work must teach that different is not "better," nor is it "worse," it is *different.* And its technology must be developed, in every sense, to propagate a multiracial set of identities that will continue and extend the search for a common basis in humanity.

RECAPITULATION

In this chapter the professional relationship has been discussed. The chapter has been long and complex, but even so it does not fully express the richness and complexity of the professional relationship as it is known by workers and the other systems with which they interact in the daily struggle with human problems. We have attempted to summarize the development in social work literature of the concept of relationship, to identify the various components of relationship, to deal briefly with some of the differences in the use of these components in various types of relationships, to discuss workers themselves and their capacities, and to deal with the issue of racism in professional relationships.

A LOOK FORWARD

In this chapter are two articles that deal with special problems in professional relationships. These articles deal with the problem of dishonesty and considerations in establishing a relationship across racial/ethnic lines. They are presented to you as a means of increasing the richness of the chapter, but with no pretense that they are an adequate sampling of the rich, diverse literature on relationship. We would strongly recommend that you sample the selected bibliography for further reading in this important area. The following chapters will focus on what the worker does within the relationship.

Reading

5-1 *The impact of professional dishonesty on behavior of disturbed adolescents**

Seymour L. Halleck

The role of dishonesty on the part of those who treat the emotionally disturbed has

* Copyright 1963, National Association of Social Workers, Inc. Reprinted by permission of author and publisher from *Social Work* 8:2 (April 1963), pp. 48–56.

been inadequately examined. Thomas Szasz (1961), a provocative psychiatric theoretician, has made a beginning effort in this direction by examining the issue of lying, both conscious and unconscious, as it relates to communication of the patient to the worker. There has been no attention paid, however, to the problem of dishonesty in the other direction, namely, for the professional worker to the client or patient. Szasz touched on this issue when he discussed the need of persons in our society to maintain traditional cultural patterns by lying to their children. He postulates that much of adolescent rebellion may be related to the fact that it is during this time of life that adolescents first become intellectually mature enough to perceive that significant adults in their lives have lied to them repeatedly.

These concepts raise intriguing issues for those who are entrusted with the professional management of disturbed adolescents. Is it possible that they communicate information, values, and morals to adolescent clients that they themselves do not believe fully? Do professional workers contribute to the perpetuation of rebellious behavior or do they perhaps even precipitate it by a failure to present themselves and their world in an honest, straightforward manner? The answer to these questions may unfortunately be a qualified "yes."

Most adults, including child-care workers, do fail at times to communicate an honest picture of the adult and adolescent world to their patients. They are often less than straightforward in presenting themselves as helping persons. In subtle ways they communicate a wish for the adolescent to develop values and moral codes that many adults would themselves have difficulty in accepting. The dishonesty described in this paper is frequently perpetuated by parents and other adults who come into contact with adolescents. While such behavior is obviously deleterious when nonprofessionals are involved, it is especially harmful when employed by a professional youth worker.

In approaching an issue as emotion-laden as lying, the author is tempted to be provocative, cynical, or pessimistic. It is not his intention to communicate these attitudes. He contends, however, that adult workers in all the clinical behavioral sciences tend to lie to their adolescent patients. The lying

may at times be on a fully conscious basis; at other times it may be more or less beyond awareness. The net effect of this behavior is to confuse and at times infuriate the adolescent, which in itself may produce greater rebellion, more symptoms, and more pain—or exactly the opposite of the original goals. As is true for most dynamic situations, whether one is dealing with individuals or with groups, positive growth must often follow a painful appraisal of less acceptable behavior and motivations. A realistic examination of dishonest behavior on the part of professional workers can then be considered a painful but necessary procedure that may encourage freedom to develop new and more effective techniques.

This discussion is focused primarily on the interaction of professionals with adolescents who are either institutionalized or who are involved with community agencies. This group certainly constitutes a great majority of adolescents who come into contact with psychiatrists, psychologists, sociologists, and social workers. In some instances, particularly in private practice, when the worker may function only as the patient's— or at most the family's—agent, some of the aspects of dishonest behavior may not apply, and these exceptions will be noted. There are at least seven areas in which adolescent clients are deceived either through conscious fabrication or through subtle and unconscious communication of attitudes to which professional workers do not adhere.

The lie of adult morality

In confronting the chaotic sexuality and poorly controlled aggressiveness of the adolescent, most professional workers tend to communicate the possibility of a world in which such impulses are resolved easily. They imply that adults control their impulses and that success in the world is dependent upon such restraint. To a limited extent this is certainly true. Too often, however, they present a picture of the world that is far removed from reality and that does not take cognizance of the social usefulness of certain kinds of aggressive and sexual behavior. The adolescent boy knows that aggressiveness, and sometime unscrupulous aggressiveness, may be a prerequisite for success. He knows that the interviewer sitting behind the desk has probably struggled aggressively to gain the status of a professional position. The sexually promiscuous adolescent girl knows (even if she has not read the Kinsey report) that on a statistical basis the professional people with whom she interacts have probably at some time in their lives been guilty of the same behavior for which she is being punished.

It may be unrealistic to communicate readily the worker's own deficiencies and therefore provide the adolescent rationalizations for disturbed behavior. There is a frequent tendency, however, to err in the other direction. Professionals communicate a picture of themselves and their world as one in which only the highest type of values and moral standards prevail. Adolescents cannot understand this. Their personal experiences, their observational powers, and their intuitiveness tell them that something is wrong. They want to like and to identify with adults, but they are painfully aware of the inconsistency or basic dishonesty in the adult's approach. They may come to believe that adults are incapable of being anything but "phony" and react by rebellious behavior or isolation from the adult world.

This type of dishonesty is seen with considerably less frequency in private psychotherapeutic interactions, especially with adults. Here the worker tries to produce a climate in which the universality of antisocial impulses is accepted and usually discussed freely. An unwillingness to extend this same honesty to a large portion of adolescent patients is a serious error. Adolescents are struggling to understand the adult world. They will learn the truth about it whether they are told or not.

The lie of professional helpfulness

The professional worker who confronts adolescents in the courtroom, the commu-

nity clinic, or the state institution serves a dual role, as an agent of the community and as a helping person. The community wants the worker to control, attenuate, or in some way modify the behavior of an individual who is causing it some distress. Workers are also interested in their clients; they feel some wish to make the disturbed adolescent a more comfortable and effective person. It is important to understand, however, that in the majority of these situations (there are exceptions in private practice) the worker does not function as an agent of the adolescent patient. The worker's salary is paid by the community. When the community's needs conflict with the adolescent's needs, it is the community that will be obeyed, and decisions are not always made entirely in the patient's interest. It is still possible within the limitations of this role for the worker to maintain an honest identification as someone who wants to help the adolescent. If workers do not communicate, however, that one of their most basic roles is other than help oriented, they are being dishonest.

Most adolescents do not seek help; they are sent. For example, take the case of an adolescent boy who has been a behavior problem in school and has been referred to the school psychologist. The boy is told that he must see a professional person and that the psychologist will try to help him. He knows, however, that the school is somewhat provoked with him and that its officials are going to act to prevent him from being an annoyance. He does not know what will be done. He does know that the school psychologist, functioning as the agent of the community, may exert a tremendous amount of power over him. As a result of his interaction with this professional worker he may be removed from school, forced to attend special classes, or even removed from his home and sent to an institution. No matter how benign a person the school psychologist then turns out to be, it is very difficult for the adolescent to perceive the psychologist as a helping person.

As long as the worker and the adolescent

are aware of the fact that the professional may be participating in mutually antagonistic roles, effective communication is possible. The situation is complicated, however, when workers pretend that their only motivation in seeing the adolescent is to help. The adolescent realizes that this is obviously untrue. The adult worker is then perceived as dishonest, which only makes the adolescent want to be dishonest in return. Experienced workers have learned that the word "help" rarely evinces a positive response from adolescents. They experience it as a kind of "Kafka"-like double talk. In many settings, then, the word *help* is perceived by the adolescent as an unreliable and perhaps dangerous word.

The lie of confidentiality

The issue of confidentiality is closely related to the problem of helpfulness. Most caseworkers, psychologists, and psychiatrists have been taught that the model for a professional helping relationship is derived from the psychotherapeutic situation. In traditional forms of psychotherapy the communications of the patient or client to the worker are considered private material to be shared with no one outside the treatment situation. Many of the techniques professional workers use in interviewing, evaluating, diagnosing, or counseling the adolescent are derived from what they were taught about psychotherapy. Often the worker behaves as though the adolescent is entitled to expect confidentiality and as though it were going to be provided. It is extremely rare for the adolescent to be told directly who is going to see the report the worker writes, who is going to read it, and with whom the case is going to be discussed.

The issue here, as with helpfulness, is that workers cannot guarantee confidentiality to the patient since they are not agents of the patient. The worker has obligations to the child's family, the clinic, the agency, or the institution. Even if after submitting an initial diagnostic report the worker be-

gins to see the adolescent in a more traditional psychotherapeutic relationship, complete confidentiality can rarely be promised. While it is true that useful communication can take place between the worker and the adolescent without the guarantee of confidentiality, it is also true that to imply that this guarantee is extended, or to extend it with the full knowledge that it is not meant to be kept, can result in development of situations that inhibit communication. It does not take a very clever adolescent to understand that the worker has primary responsibilities to the agency and to the community. Adolescents may fully understand that whatever information they give will be shared with others and can be used in making important decisions about them. If professionals do not let adolescents know this, they will perceive their behavior as dishonest, and their communications to the adult world will be effectively diminished.

The lie of rewards for conformity

The necessity of conforming to adult standards is most often communicated to adolescents whose behavior deviates from the norms of the community. To this sizable proportion of disturbed adolescents, professional workers seem to be saying, "Your behavior is unacceptable, it produces more difficulty and leads you to experience more pain. It is to your own infinite advantage to be passive, to conform, to obey." There is ample evidence, however, that in attacking the behavioral defenses of the adolescent, workers remove character armor, leaving the adolescent more susceptible to anxiety. There is really little in the way of pleasure that can be promised to adolescents if they risk giving up characterological defenses. This has been discussed previously in terms of the problems imposed on criminals when they are viewed as "patients."

Society and the psychiatrist in particular may be imposing an almost intolerable burden on delinquents in asking them to exchange the "bad" role for the sick role. It is not surprising that the criminal looks upon the usual rehabilitation program with cynicism and distrust. Only when those in charge of treatment searchingly ask themselves what they are trying to do to delinquents when they try to make them into conforming citizens and are able to appreciate what they are giving up in accepting the sick role, can therapy be successful (Halleck, 1960).

It is always a moving, sometimes an overwhelming, experience to see an adolescent abandon behavioral expressions of conflict for a more introspective way of life. This is never accomplished without considerable pain and sometimes despair. If adolescents are told that the simple expedient of conforming to adult standards produces pleasure, they are told a lie. Conformity on the part of the adolescent certainly meets the immediate needs of the community; whether it meets the needs of the individual adolescent is questionable. When workers pretend to adolescents that it does, they encounter only confusion and anger, especially when they experience the inevitable anxieties that come when they attempt to control their behavior.

Denial of limitations

The majority of adolescents who come to the attention of community agencies are from troubled homes and lower socioeconomic groups. Many of them have been subjected to severe psychological and economic deprivations. Their educational experiences have been limited. Psychiatric studies have produced data which indicate that the effects of early emotional deprivation are to a certain extent unmodifiable (Bowlby, 1958; Engel, Reichsman, and Segal, 1956; Harlow, 1958). Deficiencies in early educational experiences may also seriously limit potentialities for achievement in the world.

The average professional worker comes from a middle-class background, which in our culture implies a far greater potentiality than that seen in most adolescent clients. (Here, of course, must be excluded selected disturbed adolescents of superior intelligence, of middle-class background, or from reasonably well-integrated homes.) Many workers fail to see that with a few exceptions they are dealing with people of limited potential who will never be like them. Failing to realize this fact, the worker may then encourage identifications, ambitions, and achievements that are not possible for the client and which leave the adolescent with a feeling of frustration.

Few workers are guilty of consciously pushing their clients to achieve beyond their limits. Many of them, however, repeatedly deny the impressive limitations of some of their patients and assure them that the development of certain identifications and goals is entirely possible. This is a type of unconscious dishonesty that may produce considerable harm. Adolescents may righteously say to themselves. Who are these people kidding? Are they trying to reassure us or reassure themselves? Maybe they are trying to humiliate us by throwing our inadequacies in our faces. They'll never understand us."

"Open up; trust me; all will go well"

A close relationship is a foundation of any successful therapeutic interaction. Experiencing closeness to another person leads to the possibility of examining one's behavior in such a way that unfavorable personality defenses can be modified or exchanged for more useful ones. Most professional workers leave school with the feeling that they will be successful with clients if they can persuade them to be open and close. Adolescents, however, especially disturbed adolescents, frequently are struggling with some of the negative aspects of closeness that they experience as stultifying or smothering. They have begun to find certain types of relationships among their peers that provide them with a feeling of considerably more safety. To abandon movement in this direction and again attempt to develop a close relationship with an adult involves grave risk-taking for them. They are well aware that the little freedom they have gained may have to be surrendered if too much closeness develops.

If workers realize this, they can gently, tactfully, and with some humility gradually allow a meaningful, nonsymbiotic relationship to develop between them and the child. In a healthy close relationship between adolescent and adult, adolescents are allowed certain kinds of independence, dignity, and, of course, distance when they want it. The social structure in which most professional workers function makes it extremely difficult to provide this kind of relationship. They usually begin in settings in which they have tremendous power over the adolescent, who is thrown into a forced dependency. Adolescents are often forced into a relationship that they, at least on a conscious level, have not sought. The possibility of prolonged relationships is often limited by the fact that both professionals and their clients are extremely mobile, frequently changing responsibilities, jobs, and geographical locations. A sustained, intensive relationship is not a common occurrence in most situations developed in community agencies.

Professional workers are guilty, nevertheless, of continuously exhorting the adolescent to "open up; trust me; if you rely on me and share things with me, all will go well." But disturbed adolescents know that this is not true! They know that the person who is pleading with them to expose themselves may be a person with whom they will have only limited future contacts and whom they can see few reasons for trusting. They are further aware of the possibility that they can lose much in such a relationship and that the worker may not really be offering a true intimacy between equals. To adolescents it seems like a poor bargain. They feel that the worker is dishonest in offering this type of bargain and they react with fear, distrust, and cynicism.

"We like you but not your behavior"

Anyone who has spent much time with adolescents knows that their behavior can be provocative, frustrating, and at times infuriating. It is distressing to see how few professional workers are willing to admit honestly how angry they get with their adolescent clients. This anger frequently is rationalized with statements to the effect that "I like you but not your behavior." Sometimes the worker's anger is totally denied but comes out only through the behavior toward the adolescent. In these types of situations workers sometimes tell adolescents that they are not really angry with them but they feel that they must be disciplined for their own good, and that by depriving them of privileges or changing their situation, workers are really trying to help them. Frequently this anger is displaced onto the parents or onto other professional workers. Anyone who works with adolescents in a community or institutional setting is painfully aware of the extreme rivalry and sometimes open animosity between individual professionals and their groups. The fact is that it is almost impossible to work with adolescents for any period of time without becoming periodically angered.

It is dishonest and unfair both to the worker and to the adolescent to deny, rationalize, or displace this anger. It belongs in the therapeutic situation and should be communicated with as much restraint, tact, and honesty as the worker is capable of providing. To do less than this establishes a basically dishonest pattern of interaction and precludes the possibility of the adolescent experiencing positive emotional growth. Adolescents know that adults at times find them intolerable and cannot be expected to cooperate or communicate with people who are unwilling to admit this fact.

Prerequisites to an honest approach

By the time professional workers come to their first meeting with adolescents, they are encountering children who have probably been lied to repeatedly by parents and relatives. If adolescents have also had experiences with welfare agencies, this situation may have been compounded through dishonest behavior on the part of professional workers. They may by this time have learned a variety of techniques of resistance to cope with what is perceived to be the "phoniness" of adults. This situation is one of the most important contributing factors to the sullen inertia and negativism so often found with adolescent clients. A good portion of the malignant effects of this factor can be ameliorated through a change in techniques and attitudes on the part of the worker directed toward a more honest interaction. When efforts are made toward more scrupulous honesty with adolescent patients it is almost invariably gratifying to discover a child who is more open, talkative, and willing to discuss areas of life that are not ordinarily communicated. The child seems almost delightfully surprised to discover that adults can be talked to in a free and easy manner.

The methods of developing an honest approach to an adolescent patient or client are uncomplicated and straightforward. They are based on a conviction on the part of workers that they are going to be scrupulously honest with themselves and the child when the seven areas considered earlier are discussed. It is only necessary for the worker to be aware of any tendency to convey untrue attitudes and ideas and to make a constant effort to avoid doing so. A useful illustration can be obtained through outlining the behavior and attitudes of a professional who is trying to avoid the pitfalls previously discussed. The techniques and attitudes employed by this hypothetical male worker in his interactions with adolescent patients will be described. These techniques, whether utilized by youth workers, teachers, or parents, can effectively increase communication between adults and adolescents.

With respect to the "lie of adult morality" no effort is ever made by the worker to criticize, disparage, or in any way condemn the adolescent's antisocial behavior. Rather, it is considered as something the community (rightly or wrongly) will not tolerate if done openly and, most important, as something that *has not served the social or personal needs* of the adolescent. A routine and essential part of an initial interaction with any adolescent consists of a careful assessment of the net gains and losses caused by this behavior. The social usefulness of certain kinds of aggressive behavior is never disparaged. No attempt is made to discuss behavior in terms of right or wrong, neurotic or normal, or good or bad. Workers will attempt at times to communicate their own moral standards, which may or may not be more stringent than those of the patient. These are always clearly labeled as the workers' personal beliefs and it is made clear that they may not be relevant for the patient.

The lies of professional helpfulness and confidentiality are handled directly by explaining the evaluator's own position as precisely as possible during the initial interview. The child is told who is employing the examiner, what the examiner's responsibilities to the employer are, what kind of report will be written, and exactly who will see and discuss it. Contrary to what might immediately be expected, most adolescents respond favorably to such an approach. When the rules of the "game" of interviewing are wholly apparent to them, there is little need for defensiveness or negativism. The sheer surprising impact of having an adult be so direct with them often in itself produces a favorable effect that encourages them to be more open.

To avoid taking the stand that conformity or adjustment to adult standards breeds comfort and contentment, workers must have deep and thorough understanding of the role of antisocial behavior in maintaining the adolescent's equilibrium. They must be thoroughly able to empathize with the "fun" and at times pleasure associated with behavior that flaunts rules. They must also realize that such behavior may be all that stands between feelings of hopelessness and despair. Adjustment to the adult world is not presented as something that necessarily brings pleasure but rather as a necessary and sometimes unpleasant requisite to survival. At times workers might even openly discuss conformity as a burden and warn the patient as to some of the dangers of such behavior. Such an approach provides leverage when the issue of the adolescent's rigid conformity to the peer group inevitably arises during a prolonged relationship.

Avoiding the communication that most adolescent clients have the same potential as the professional worker involves a careful attention to not confusing the worker's own needs with those of the child. Our hypothetical worker freely discusses with adolescents the problems of moving from one social class to another and makes no effort to pretend that class distinctions do not exist. The barriers to advancement which minority group adolescents profess are more often accepted as realities than interpreted as projections. The adolescent boy who has a long police record and who has missed out on many educational opportunities is not deluded into believing he can "be anything he wants." The girl who may have had one or more illegitimate children is not assured of her potential for making a favorable marriage. The worker's general attitude is that this can be a "tough world" in which only a determined few manage to overcome the deprivations of their early background.

While the worker may firmly believe that a relationship with an understanding and skilled adult promulgates favorable personality change, all efforts are made to let adolescents develop the relationship at their own pace and without extravagant, implied promise of its value. The patient is told exactly when and for how long the worker will be available. Full attention is paid to the risks the client takes in developing a relationship; sometimes these risks are actually spelled out. Strenuous efforts are made to deal with the adolescent fear of being swallowed up in one's dependency needs. "Openness" is encouraged as a necessary prerequisite to gaining understanding but it is not held out as a "cure-all" or as a goal in itself. Exhortations to trust the worker are avoided rigorously. Rather, adolescents are told that they will have to decide about the worker's trustworthiness on the basis of their own experiences.

Perhaps the most outrageous dishonesty perpetrated against adolescents by professionals involves their tendency to cover up their own angry feelings, which invariably develop toward the patient. It is surprisingly easy to tell adolescents when they are annoying and such communications, when presented in a restrained but straightforward manner, rarely have a negative effect upon the relationship. A communication such as "I find your behavior during this interview extremely difficult and I'm having trouble keeping from getting annoyed myself" may in many instances be preferable to "What's bothering you?" or "How can I help?" or even to passive acceptance of provocative behavior. Adolescents appreciate this kind of straightforwardness. It tells them where they stand and enables them to look at their behavior without having to deceive either themselves or the adult.

Conclusions

Anyone who has reared children knows that occasional dishonesty is essential if the child is to grow up with a reasonable degree of security. The truth to children, if understood, may be unbearable. If an orderly, sane, and relatively nonchaotic way of life is to be maintained, it is essential that children at times be deceived or at the very least kept in the dark as to issues they are not yet ready to master. In the treatment of adults there are clear landmarks for the worker to follow. Adults who enter psychotherapy are greeted with an atmosphere that not only condones but puts a premium on truthfulness on the part of all participants. Exceptions are made only when it is felt that the patient is too seriously ill to comprehend or tolerate the impact of truth. In these cases various deceptive practices may be used for the patient's benefit.

If one could argue convincingly that the great majority of disturbed adolescents were similar to children or to the severely disturbed adult, there would be considerable justification for withholding truth and practicing deception for the adolescent's own gain. Anyone who works with adolescents, even seriously disturbed ones, however, is quickly aware that such a comparison is invalid. Adolescents are extremely open to learning. They are in the process of discovering new aspects of the world around them, and are also increasingly preoccupied with their own inner world. Even the most disturbed adolescent has rarely developed a fixed pattern of rigid personality defenses that preclude being able to look at the truth in a reasonably open way.

The professional worker knows adolescents are capable of serious volatile impulsive behavior and do not have available to themselves the controls that most adults have learned. Perhaps much of the explanation for an unwillingness to be honest with adolescents is related to a fear that they will not be able to tolerate the truth and that

it will be used in a destructive, unhelpful way. One can also speculate that dishonest behavior might be related to the frightening impact of aggressive and sexually provocative adolescent behavior that touches upon areas of one's own problems which have not been completely understood or worked through. When workers present a dishonest picture of the world to their clients, they may really be trying to avoid the despair of facing the frightening world in which they live and thereby to reassure themselves.

To interact honestly with an adolescent, all interested adults must believe that the growth of useful personality traits is more likely to take place in an atmosphere of truth than of dishonesty. This involves a willingness to take the risk of presenting communications that temporarily disturb the adolescent and a tolerance of the possibility that many of these disturbances will be directed against the adult. Any adult who wishes to communicate effectively in this manner must of course come to terms with self-deceptions in one's own life so that they do not interfere with one's ability to face reality with others.

Reading

5–2 A framework for establishing social work relationships across racial/ethnic lines*

Joan Velasquez, Marilyn E. Vigil McClure, and Eustolio Benavides

It is well documented that disproportionately large numbers of social work clients, particularly in public agencies, are racial/ethnic minority group members. When we examine the use of social work services by

---

* An original article prepared especially for this volume by the authors, two of whom have been instructors, and one a student, in a student unit of the University of Minnesota School of Social Work serving Latino clients in Remsey County Mental Health Center, St. Paul, Minnesota.

these clients, we find a substantially higher rate of discontinuance than among majority group clients (Miranda, 1976). It is our assumption that many of these clients "drop out" of service because they do not perceive what they are offered as helpful and that the partnership which ideally evolves from engaging a client in a positive, purposeful relationship does not develop.

Our purpose here is to explore the development of the social work relationship across racial/ethnic lines based on a framework of biculturalism. Although this framework has evolved primarily from social work with Latinos, we believe it applies to work with any ethnic or racial minority group.

Defining culture as a relatively unified set of shared values, ideas, beliefs, and standards of action held by an identified people, numerous cultural groups can be identified within this country. The dominant culture integrated the values and norms of European immigrant groups as each was encouraged to drop its language and become assimilated by the majority. Minority groups with recognizable physical characteristics have also been pushed to accept the dominant culture as their own, yet have been responded to as separate and inferior groups and thus not allowed to participate fully in it. Due to this exclusion and to a desire on the part of some to retain their original culture, distinct groups continue to exist. We view the retention of one's culture of origin as desirable and see the perspective of biculturalism as one which encourages acceptance of difference and the capacity to work with it.

Let us diagram a cultural continuum to reflect this perspective.

Relationship

dominant Anglo/white culture	minority group culture
values, norms, role expectations	values, norms, role expectations

Each group's cultural system is based on a set of values manifested in norms and role expectations which are distinct from those of the majority cultural system. Though a wide range of individual differences exists within each group and parts of one group's system may be similar to that of others, recognizable boundaries exist and must be bridged if relationships are to be developed across them.

At either end of the continuum are lo-

cated those who function within the boundaries of that cultural system. They identify and interact primarily with other members of the same group, govern their behavior according to its values and norms, and often speak a common language. Movement across the continuum in either direction indicates exposure to another cultural system and generally occurs as one interacts with members of the other group. At least one participant in a relationship which crosses racial/ethnic lines must move toward the other in order to develop common ground for communication. If movement does not occur, interaction remains on a superficial level. As noted earlier, such movement in society has generally been from right to left on this continuum, with differences viewed as negative characteristics in need of alteration. Alfred White's *The Apperceptive Mass of Foreigners as Applied to Americanization* (1971) exemplifies the concerted, largely unquestioned, effort made throughout much of our history to resocialize minority group members to abandon their heritage and become as much like members of the dominant group as possible. Majority group members have traditionally expected others to move toward them to understand their cultural system and modify their behavior accordingly. We maintain that the preferred alternative is for the social worker to develop the capacity to move across the continuum to wherever the client is located on it.

Let us consider the implications of this perspective for social work practice. Movement across the continuum essentially requires that one understand the values and norms of another cultural system, of one's own system, be aware of where differences lie, and accept both as legitimate. The Anglo/white worker, then, must acquire a substantial knowledge base including the values, expected role behaviors, historical experiences, and language of the group to which the client belongs as a basis for their work together. It is essential that the worker accept both self and other before this knowledge can be integrated and applied effectively. Workers, as they offer service to the client, then draw from this understanding and acceptance to assess where the particular individuals involved are located on the continuum.

Social workers who are members of a racial/ethnic minority group have, when working with other members of the same group, the advantage of having learned through life experience what is expected and appropriate within its boundaries. They also have the advantage of being identified by physical characteristics as people with common experiences, more likely to be trusted than Anglo/white workers who must overcome this immediate barrier if service is to be used. Minority workers in addition to understanding their own system, however, must develop the capacity to interact effectively within the Anglo/white system as well since its members predominantly control needed services and resources. When working with members of the other minority groups, the minority worker moves across two continua, developing his/her capacity to interact within both the dominant and other minority cultures.

Worker movement across the bicultural continuum is diagrammed in the examples below. The arrows indicate that workers move from wherever they are located both to where the client is and toward compe-

Minority (black) worker/client of other minority/Anglo service system

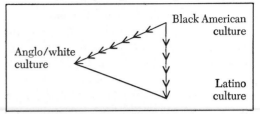

tence in interacting with the Anglo/white system.

In order to establish helpful, purposeful relationships across racial/ethnic lines, workers of all groups must be able to move along each continuum to interact within the cultural context which has meaning for the client.

The purpose of the social work relationship is to assist clients to become the kind of people they want to become, or to do something they have chosen to do in terms of overcoming barriers in dealing more effectively with the stresses of life. The magnitude of this task for the client will not be understood by the worker if the worker lacks empathy—"the capacity to enter into the feelings and experiences of another—knowing what one feels and experiences—without losing oneself in the process" (Compton and Galaway, 1979, see p. 175).

Unless workers have some knowledge of the values, norms, and expectations of the culture of the client and of this particular client, they will not be able to understand either the client's goals or the barriers impeding progress toward these goals. The worker will thus be unable to fulfill the purpose of the social work relationship. It is easier for each of us as workers to work with clients who share the same cultural values, norms, expectations and world view since it is easier to be appropriately empathic with such clients. A more conscious effort is required of workers to work effectively with clients of another culture who have a different frame of reference, particularly in regard to perceptions of the importance of

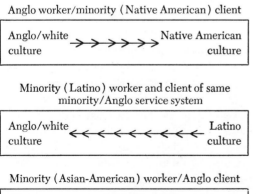

Anglo worker/minority (Native American) client

Anglo/white culture →>→>→>→> Native American culture

Minority (Latino) worker and client of same minority/Anglo service system

Anglo/white culture <←<←<←<←< Latino culture

Minority (Asian-American) worker/Anglo client

Anglo/white culture <←<←<← Asian-American culture

activity, the nature of relationships, and human nature.

Empathy, which requires openness to the reality of another person's feelings, experiences, and perceptions, facilitates the conscious efforts of workers in establishing relationships with clients of a different culture. Work with clients of a culture different from that of the workers requires, in addition, an openness on the part of workers to values, norms, and world views that their own culture may not share. This requires of the workers the capacity to understand and respect their own culture and the role it has played in their development, and to feel free to respect the culture of the other. It demands from workers a belief that no culture is inherently better than or superior to another, but that each is merely different. Such an attitude will allow workers to attempt to perceive situations from the point of view of the minority client.

We have chosen three dimensions of the Latino culture in order to illustrate factors that must be taken into account in the development of the social work relationship across racial/ethnic lines. The Latino culture is selected for illustration because it is the one with which we are most familiar. The dimensions of language, locus of control, and world view are not the only, or perhaps even the most important, dimensions of the Latino culture. However, they provide examples of how the bicultural framework can be applied in client-worker situations and illustrate points of possible incongruities between the perceptions of the worker and those of a Latino client.

Although these incongruities may not exist if either the Latino client or the worker has ease of movement on a bicultural continuum, nevertheless the onus of movement on the bicultural continuum is on the worker if he/she is to meet the client wherever the client is and if there is going to be any possibility of establishing a working relationship. This fact again emphasizes the necessity for empathy on the part of the worker.

Verbal and nonverbal communications express a person's feelings, ideas, and world view developed in a particular cultural context. The meanings assigned to verbal and nonverbal communication can result in incongruities between worker and client.

A nonverbal gesture, such as lowering of the eyes or not looking at someone directly, is interpreted by some persons as a sign of respect and deference to authorities and elders, while it is interpreted by other groups as a sign of the lack of veracity in a person. Nonverbal communication is much more open to misinterpretation than is verbal communication. However, verbal communication can also be misinterpreted when one language does not allow for the full expression of the nuances and concepts behind another language. This is especially true in regard to Spanish and English.

In Spanish there are two means of addressing another person depending on their status in terms of both age and social role. *Tu* is the personal pronoun used for addressing peers or persons who are younger, whereas *Usted* is used to address elders and persons in positions of authority. To address an authority or an elder by using *tu,* the familiar form, is not seen as a misuse of language but rather as a lack of respect due to that individual. This is not a cause for embarrassment, for there is no such term in Spanish. Rather it is a cause for shame, since disrespect is never seen as a matter to be taken lightly.

The use of *you,* the familiar pronoun in English, is appropriate at all times, since English usage does not distinguish its salutation either according to function or age. The general trend in the usage of English in this country is to do away with distinctions and to become acquainted with another on a first-name basis. To do the opposite in English is sometimes viewed as an attempt to create an artificial distance between the two parties.

In dealing with persons who are of Spanish heritage, the emphasis is not on creating an artificial distance but rather in acknowledging that which is already so, namely that some people have more power by virtue of position and some have more experience by virtue of age. To address another who is older or in authority on a first name basis is not viewed as an attempt to get closer to the other but rather as an attempt to challenge authority or to discount experience. A person who would do this would be viewed as being ill-bred or, at a minimum, ill-mannered and disrespectful.

Respect, then, becomes the key for dealing with authority. Respect, however, is not the same as *respeto*. In English one can respect another while violently opposing the opinions that that person holds. In English *respect* does not contain the element of acceptance of another's view as one's own. *Respeto*, on the other hand, means that one must not challenge the opinions of others. It means that if one chooses not to adopt the opinions of another as one's own, one must at least pay deference to the other person's views by not saying anything. Thus, the locus of control for Hispanic people tends to be much more external than internal, whether the locus is God, fate, nature, authority, or age, and this condition is constantly reinforced by means of language.

Because the respect for authority is essential to the highly structured and hierarchical world view of Hispanic people, relationships do not occur as often between equals as they do in the dominant culture. Relationships are perceived as occurring between one who is in authority and one who is not. A social worker is seen as a person who is an authority. The purpose of the social work relationship—the conscious and deliberate use of self for the benefit of the client—remains the same. The way that the purpose is viewed by Hispanic clients may be different from the way it is viewed by the majority clients.

As the Latino client enters into a social work relationship, he/she views the relationship as unequal. The worker is assigned a sense of authority and *respecto*. The client may disagree with the worker but remain silent rather than appear disrespectful. A worker, unaware of this culturally determined approach, may view the silence as resistance. Errors in assessment resulting from culture-based misinterpretations lead to antagonistic relationships and selection of inappropriate methods of intervention. Consider the discordant perceptions which may result from differences on the dimensions of locus of control and world view. Latinos tend to see many aspects of their lives in which the control is external. Anglos consider more aspects of their lives to be under internal control. The fostering of independence and self-reliance, if taken at face value, can be viewed by the Latinos as a lack of concern for others and as a pompous and unrealistic attitude on the part of the proponent. This logically follows from a Latino world view in which there is a balance of pain and pleasure and where the natural order is controlled by God. The white/Anglo world view is one in which the individual is the powerful force. Individuals are in charge of themselves and can change what they want to change about themselves or their world. Latinos view themselves as much more interdependent and not as solely in charge of themselves. What they as individuals can do is more dependent on others and the exernal environment.

Such contrasting views impede working toward common goals if not recognized and addressed. In working with adolescents, for example, the worker may decide to deal with that adolescent on a one-to-one basis. However, the Latino mother may view this as inappropriate since she sees herself as in control of her child. Failure to recognize and acknowledge the mother's position is likely to result in discontinuance from service. The reason might never be shared with the worker because of the authority element in the relationship.

In empathizing with a Latino client, a worker may want to move too quickly from recognizing the difficulty the client is experiencing to what could be done to help. For

202

the client, it may be more helpful to dwell on the difficulty longer to the point where the worker might interpret this as resistance or that the client does not have the capacity to use the service. From the Latino client's point of view, the dwelling on the difficulty could be viewed as helpful since he/she knows that pain is balanced by pleasure. The worker could acknowledge that cultural element and use it with the client to prepare for the more pleasant phase of life, thus resulting in a more useful service for the client.

We have presented a framework for viewing transracial/ethnic social work relationships as developing across a bicultural continuum. The dimensions of language, locus of control, and world view illustrate points of possible incongruities between the perceptions of an Anglo worker and a Latino client which, in turn, create difficulties in establishing effective working (social work) relationships. Empathy is required if workers of one culture are to move on a bicultural continuum toward clients of a different culture. We believe that recognizing the necessity of, and developing the capacity for, such movement will increase the likelihood of engaging clients of a different culture in positive, purposeful, and effective relationships. From this perspective the worker's capacity to both move across the continuum and to assess where the client is located on it are considered essential elements in the delivery of social services to minority clients.

Selected annotated bibliography

Bennis, Warren G.; Benne, Kenneth D.; and Chin, Robert. *The Planning of Change.* New York: Holt, Rinehart and Winston, 1961.
This is an excellent collection of readings on the dynamics of change. See especially Strauss's article "Transformations of Identity" and the editors' analysis of "Dynamics of Influence."

Biestek, Felix. *The Casework Relationship.* Chicago: Loyola University Press, 1957.
Biestek attempts to explain, define, and analyze the casework relationship. The attempt, however, gathers a great many things under the umbrella of the relationship.

Carkhuff, Robert B. *The Art of Helping: An Introduction to Life Skills.* Amherst, Mass.: Human Resource Development Press, 1973.
This is an interesting, brief presentation of the effective ingredients of all helping relationships from Carkhuff's experience and research.

Chaiklin, Harris. "Honesty in Casework Treatment," *Social Welfare Forum, 1973.* New York: Columbia University Press, 1973, pp. 266–274.
Honesty in treatment means that worker and client share themselves and a mutual understanding of treatment and the details of this practice. Examples include the sharing of self, professional information, test information, and notes, and sharing in the creation of the record. Honesty in practice relates to competence.

Gitterman, Alex, and Schaeffer, Alice. "The White Professional and the Black Client," *Social Casework* 53:5 (May 1972), pp. 280–291.
Gitterman and Schaeffer attempt to define some of the specific obstacles within the white professional–black client relationship and to make some suggestions for dealing with them. A specific case illustration demonstrates how one worker and one client struggled against the obstacles keeping them apart as separate, distrusting individuals.

Hardman, Dale. "The Constructive Use of Authority," *Crime and Delinquency* 6:3 (July 1960), pp. 245–254.
Hardman notes the constructive potential for authority relationships and identifies specific steps the worker in an authority position may take to maximize that potential.

Hardman, Dale. "The Matter of Trust," *Crime and Delinquency* 15:2 (April 1969), pp. 203–218.
This article analyzes the counseling use of trust in relation to a variety of theoretical positions. Published literature is the basic source of data.

Keith-Lucas, Alan. *The Giving and Taking of Help.* Chapel Hill: University of North Carolina Press, 1971.
This very helpful little book sets forth in simple, warm language the complex elements of the giving and taking of help. It contains chapters on the helping relationship, the helping factors, and the helping person.

Mahoney, Stanley C. *The Art of Helping People Effectively.* New York: Association Press, 1967.

This slim book will be useful to anyone who is in a helping relationship to another. Mahony sees helping as involving acceptance, presence, listening, and information giving.

Overton, Alice. "Establishing the Relationship," *Crime and Delinquency* 11:3 (July 1965), pp. 229–238.

Overton discusses the ingredients necessary to establishing a relationship in settings where the client is not voluntarily seeking help. These ingredients include clarity of purpose, clearly conveying that one has respect for the client, and dealing with resistances on the part of both worker and client.

Reid, Kenneth R. "Nonrational Dynamics of the Client-Worker Interaction," *Social Casework* 58:10 (December 1977), pp. 600–607.

This article further develops the significance of noncognitive elements—feelings, attitudes, and established patterns of behavior—which are unconscious but still affect the relationship.

Rogers, Carl. "Characteristics of a Helping Relationship," *Canada's Mental Health*, Supplement No. 27 (March 1962).

Rogers reviews research on the nature of relationship and suggests ten approaches which will facilitate the worker's establishing a relationship.

Rogers, Carl. "The Therapeutic Relationship: Recent Theory and Research," in Floyd Matson and Ashley Montague, (Eds.), *The Human Dialogue.* New York: Free Press, 1967, pp. 246–259.

The three essential conditions in the therapist's relationship to client growth are congruence of feelings, thoughts, and communications; unconditional positive regard for the client; and an accurate empathetic understanding of the client.

Sinsheimer, Robert. "The Existential Casework Relationship," *Social Casework* 50:2 (February 1969), pp. 67–73.

Writing from a philosophic base in existential philosophy, Sinsheimer discusses the casework relationship as an attitudinal framework within which the practitioner functions and is characterized by love, active caring, acceptance, and concern for the other person.

Vontress, Clemmont E. "Racial Differences: Impediments to Rapport," *Journal of Consulting Psychology* 18 (1971), pp. 7–13.

This article discusses the difficulties of establishing and maintaining productive helping relationships across racial lines in our society. Vontress makes suggestions for the training of helpers that may be productive in creating interracial understanding.

Oxle, Genevieve B. "The Caseworker's Expectations in Client Motivation," *Social Casework* 47:7 (July 1966), pp. 432–437.

The importance of expectation and stimulation in client progress is discussed, with particular emphasis on the responsibility of the worker to maintain the expectations of the client somewhat beyond where the client is.

CHAPTER **6**

Communication and interviewing

Interviewing is a basic social work skill. The interview is the major tool utilized by the social worker to collect data from which to make intervention decisions. While other data collection tools are available to the worker (these will be discussed further in Chapter 9, the interview remains the primary tool and the client the primary source of data. Many social work interventive strategies are also dependent on interviewing, with the interview used as the modality through which strategies directed toward change are applied. Because of the ubiquitousness of interviewing in social work practice, some brief consideration of interviewing and communication is essential in any book purporting to develop a practice model. A number of excellent books have appeared on the social work interview (de Schweinitz and de Schweinitz, 1962; Garrett, 1972; Kadushin, 1972; Rich, 1968; Schubert, 1971), and social work educational programs usually devote considerable time to the development of interviewing skills. We do not intend either to provide a comprehensive treatment of interviewing or to give the student a bag of tricks. Rather, this chapter will introduce the use of social work interviewing as a central tool of social work practice, identify some of the barriers to communication, offer some ideas concerning the role of the social work interviewer, and, present briefly some techniques they have found useful in the data collection interview. Interviewing skills will continue to be refined and developed throughout a social work career.

COMMUNICATION AND INTERVIEWING

Communication can be defined as an interactional process which gives, receives, and checks out meaning (Satir, 1964, chaps. 8 and 9), and occurs when people interact with each other in an effort to transmit messages, receive transmitted messages, and check out meanings. The checkout phase of the communication process is essential and is discussed as an interviewing technique by Robert Brown (1973). *A*, for example, sends a message to *B*, which *B* receives. But how does *B* know that *B* has received the message *A* intended to send? Perhaps *B's* receptors were faulty, perhaps *A's* transmitter was faulty, or perhaps there was noise or interference between *A* and *B* which distorted the message. *B* checks out the message with *A* by indicating what has been received in order to confirm that the message *B* received was the message *A* in-

FIGURE 6–1
The communication process

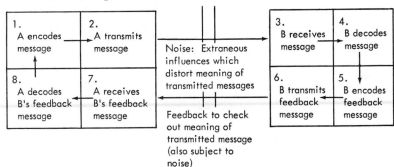

tended to send (see Figure 6–1). Communication difficulties result when this checkout process is omitted.

The communication theory concepts of encoding, transmitting, receiving, decoding, and noise provide a useful framework for understanding problems which may arise in the social work interview. Encoding refers to the process of putting the message to be sent into symbol form in preparation for transmission. Transmitting refers to the process of sending the encoded message; receiving to the process of interpreting the stimuli received; noise to extraneous influences that may have distorted the message when it was on its way from the transmitter to the receiver. Checkout or feedback provides a way of overcoming problems created by noise as well as by inadequate encoding or decoding or faulty transmission or reception.

Communications occur simultaneously on many levels. We can speak of verbal and nonverbal communications or overt and covert communications. Virginia Satir (1964, p. 76) speaks of denotative and metacommunication levels of messages. By the denotative level, she means the literal content of the symbols (usually words). She defines metacommunications as messages about the message; a metacommunication refers to such things as a voice inflection, gestures, manner of speaking, and so on, all of which provide additional clues about the meaning of the denotative level of communication. The ability to communicate several messages simultaneously provides opportunity for the famous double bind—the simultaneous transmission of contradictory messages leaving the receiver in a "be damned if I do, be damned if I don't" position (Bateson et al., 1963).

But what is the meaning of all of this to interviewing in social work? Interviewing can be looked upon as a particular kind of communication. Robert Kahn and Charles Connell (1957, p. 16) define an interview as a

> specialized pattern of verbal interaction—initiated for a specific purpose, focused on some specific content area, with consequent elimination of extraneous material. Moreover, the interview is a pattern of interaction in which the role relationship of interviewer and respondent is highly specialized, its specific characteristics depending somewhat on the purpose and character of the interview.

The social work interview is a set of communications with four special characteristics: (1) it has a context or setting; (2) it is purposeful and directed; (3)

it is limited and contractual; and (4) it involves specialized role relationships. The context or setting for the interview will usually be that of a particular agency offering defined services to clients bringing specified problems to the agency. The context, of course, provides a limit to the communications and becomes a basis for the "elimination of extraneous material"—that is, material not related to the particular context. Social work interviews are purposeful and directed in the sense that they are conducted to accomplish specific goals (a legitimate purpose may certainly be the definition of the goals or furthering worker-client communications). Conversely, interviews are not casual exchanges of information or informal conversations. The purposes of interviews provide a basis for limiting communications and eliminating extraneous material. Interviews are limited and contractual in the sense that the interviewer and the interviewee come together in a specific context for defined purposes; their communications are limited to meeting those purposes. And, finally, interviewer and interviewee occupy specialized roles and interact with each other on the basis of those roles. This, again, is a limiting factor inasmuch as client-worker interactions will usually be confined to the expected behaviors of the specialized roles.

To summarize, communication can be viewed as an interactional process involving the giving, receiving, and checking out of meaning; communication occurs on many levels and may not always be congruent. Interviewing is a specialized form of communication which is contextual, purposeful, limited and which involves specialized role relationships. This chapter focuses on interviewing to secure information which client and worker will use jointly in decision-making about the nature of the problem and of intervention. The primary source of data is the client; interviewing techniques are used to encourage the client to share data for joint client-worker use.

Since the data is to be used in decision-making about intervention, the social worker must be concerned about the reliability and validity of data collection procedures. The concepts of reliability and validity are defined for an interviewer in social work as they are defined in other scientific and research activity. Reliability refers to the extent to which data collection tools (in this case, the interview) produce consistent information. If different messages are received from the client at different times, the social worker wants to be reasonably certain that the differences reflect actual changes in the client and are not a consequence of the worker's interviewing style; otherwise a reliability problem exists. Validity refers to the extent to which the information being obtained reflects the actual perceptions, thoughts, feelings, and behaviors of the client. If the client is not sharing the client's actual perceptions, thoughts, feelings, and behaviors, a validity problem exists; the worker will need to adjust the interviewing techniques in order to secure more accurate information. One responsibility of the social worker is to create a climate in which the client is comfortable in sharing valid and reliable information.

The next section considers some potential barriers to communication—barriers which will affect the validity and reliability of data. In subsequent sections the role of the interviewer will be analyzed and suggestions will be offered which will assist the social work interviewer to increase the probability of securing valid and reliable data.

BARRIERS TO COMMUNICATION

Barriers to communication may occur at any phase in the communication process—encoding, transmitting, receiving, decoding, and checkout. Many of these barriers are obvious—inability to conceptualize and use symbols (encoding problems), speech impediments, hearing or receptor impediments, failure to understand the concepts received (decoding problems), and environmental influences (noise which interferes with the messages or prevents them from traveling clearly from the transmitter to the receiver). While these barriers are real and are of continual concern to the worker desirous of reliable and valid data on which to base decisions, they are also reasonably obvious sources of error in communications. In this section we will consider a series of subtler, less obvious, but equally serious barriers to communication which will affect the validity and reliability of the data on which intervention decisions are based. A total of six worker barriers in addition to the barrier of client resistance will be considered. Approaches on the part of the worker which may serve as barriers to the collection of valid and reliable data include anticipation of the other, the assumption of meaning, stereotyping, confusion of purpose, the urge to change, and inattentiveness.

The first worker barrier to communication—anticipation of the other—is alluded to by Carl Rogers (n.d.) as follows:

> But what I really dislike in myself is when I can't hear the other person because I'm so sure in advance what the other is going to say that I don't listen because it is afterwards that I realize I have only heard what I have already decided the other is saying. I have failed really to listen at those times when I can't hear because what the other is saying is too threatening, because it might make me change my ideas and my behavior.

The assumption of meaning, a second worker barrier to communication, occurs when a worker receives an ambiguous message, fails to check out its meaning with the client, and proceeds on the basis of a meaning which the worker has read into the client's message. The words themselves may be ambiguous, the way in which they are uttered may convey unclear feelings or thoughts, or the client's behavior may be communicating messages inconsistent with the words. In all of these situations the checkout of meaning with the client may prevent erroneous assumptions and proceeding on the basis of invalid and unreliable data. An example of assumption of meaning occurs in this brief excerpt from an interview with a 16-year-old boy on parole:

> I asked how things had gone this past week. He looked at me with a grin and said, "Fine." He added that he had not done anything. During this time he kept leafing through the magazine and pointed out someone's picture to me. At this point I told him that we were here to talk and that he should put the magazine away. It is very obvious that this boy knows very little or at least practices few of the common courtesies of everyday living.

This worker assumed from the boy's grin and his leafing through the magazine that he was trying to avoid entering into conversation. The worker, however, erroneously acted on the basis of this assumption without first checking it out with the youngster. A few minutes taken to ask the boy what it was about the magazine that interested him or to make a more direct checkout—"I get the message that you are not too interested in talking with me now"—might have clarified the situation and produced a more reliable and valid basis on which to act.

Worker stereotypes of clients are a third barrier to communication. This barrier relates directly to the problems of classification and categorization discussed in Chapter 4. It exists when clients are seen as members of groups—low income, delinquent, schizophrenic, black, and so on—and action is taken without permitting the client's individuality to transcend the stereotype of the client's group. Stereotyping leads to the two previous problems—anticipating the other and assumptions of meaning occur because of stereotypes held by workers. Stereotyping can be very subtle; after experience with several similar clients, workers may note similarities on the basis of which they begin to develop a stereotype of that particular kind of client. The stereotype then interferes with the worker's perception of new clients and may well serve to block out communications inconsistent with it.

Failure on the part of the worker to make explicit the purpose of an interview may lead to a condition in which the worker and client hold differing, perhaps contradictory, purposes. Given such confusion of purpose, both client and worker will then interpret their own and each other's communications in light of their particular understanding of the objective of the interview. As these subtle distortions continue, the client and the worker will be going in two entirely different directions.

One of the more serious barriers to communication arises from prematurely urging clients to change. This is a very easy pitfall for the social worker. *Change* is a common word in the profession; by and large, social workers are committed to being change agents, both to improve the conditions of the community and to assist individuals to utilize the resources of the community more effectively. Difficulties occur, however, when change efforts are attempted without sufficient data on which to base an assessment of the problem. Although change may occur through any human interaction, effecting change is not the primary purpose of the data collection interview—change efforts should be based on valid and reliable data and on a considered decision of the client and worker to engage in such efforts. The purpose of the data collection interview is to gather the information on which decisions about intervention can be based. To urge change at this early stage may create a barrier to communication—a barrier which limits the availability of important information that could influence decision-making. A secondary problem is that change efforts in these early contacts frequently take the form of directive approaches—such as persuasion and advising—which are seldom effective until a high degree of trust has been developed and which, used prematurely, create barriers to continuing communication. And it is the process of continuing communication which provides opportunities for the development of increased trust.

A very potent worker barrier to communication is inattentiveness. A worker whose mind wanders during an interview, who is thinking about other clients or planning future activities, creates barriers for continued client-worker communication. Clients can reasonably expect the workers to give undivided attention to their present communications, and workers have the responsibility for establishing a time frame that will enable them to attend to other matters that require attention without diverting attention from the interview of the moment.

As workers learn to avoid anticipating what the client will say, to check out the meanings of the communications received, to avoid stereotyping, to clarify purposes, to avoid attempts at change until the necessary data is available and change decisions can be made jointly, and to give all clients opportunities for undivided attention, the likelihood of securing resonably valid and reliable information will be considerably enhanced. But clients may also create barriers to communication. These barriers may be thought of as forms of resistance on their part against entering into a problem-solving process. Resistance may be considered as a specialized kind of defense utilized by the client to ward off the worker and to protect the client from any discomfort involved in participating in a problem-solving process.

Three sources of resistance can be distinguished. (1) Resistance may stem from the usual discomfort of dealing with a strange person and situation. Essentially this is a "normal" anxiety and discomfort with which many of us approach new situations. (2) Resistance may stem from cultural and subcultural norms regarding involvement with service agencies and asking for help. Norman Johnston (1956), for example, identifies a number of variables in the prison milieu which contribute to distortion and deception in the communications between inmates and prison counselors. Because of cultural norms, some persons may find it particularly difficult, to admit the existence of a problem and to seek a solution. Agencies may exacerbate such cultural differences by establishing procedures which intensify the discomfort of persons of certain cultural backgrounds. An agency emphasis on scheduled appointments and office visits, for example, may aggravate the resistance of clients from lower socioeconomic groups and hamper their ability to utilize more traditional social service agencies. (3) Some clients may be securing a degree of gratification from their problems. This type of pathological involvement with a problem is a serious source of resistance, which interferes with the client's ability to communicate and makes seeking a solution more dfficult.

What is the worker's responsibility in relation to client resistance? To facilitate communication, the worker may need to help the client identify and deal with any of these obstacles to communication. Dealing with obstacles to communication will become a necessary preliminary goal before the client and worker can move into any other problem-solving work. Dealing with resistances is one manifestation of the worker's second task as conceptualized by Schwartz—"the task of detecting and challenging the obstacles which obscure the common ground" (see Reading 1–1).

RESPONSIBILITIES OF THE WORKER

What are the social worker's responsibilities in the data collection interview? They can be conceptualized in three interrelated areas. First, social workers are responsible for creating a productive climate in which the client can comfortably participate and in which the client—the primary source of data—will share the thoughts, feelings, and perceptions necessary for intervention decisions. The climate should help secure valid and reliable data. To a large extent, the creation of such a climate involves the worker's skill in avoiding the worker barriers to communication noted earlier and in helping clients to deal with the obstacles to communication presented by their own resistances. The creation of a productive climate for participation might be construed as the development of a helping relationship. In Chapter 5 we referred to relationship as a climate or an atmosphere and suggested strongly that relationship is not the end of service but a stepping-stone toward the provision of problem-solving service for the client. One way to operationalize the concept of relationship is to define it as a climate or milieu which is characterized by open and verbal communications. Thus the presence of relationship might be inferred from the extent to which communications are open and verbal. Creating this kind of climate is a basic responsibility of the worker, a responsibility which is met primarily by the nature of communications and interactions with clients.

A second major responsibility of the worker is to provide a focus for the interview. This occurs by establishing a purpose for the interview very early and focusing the interactions in relation to the purpose. Tangents should be avoided; questions that lead into extraneous areas are not helpful; and the worker, when pursuing what the client has said, should pick up on areas related to the interview's central focus. Focusing the interview does not mean dictating the purpose, nor does it mean cutting off the client; it does mean, however, jointly establishing with the client a particular purpose for an interview and fulfilling the responsibility of maintaining that focus. Material brought out in a particular interview may suggest a purpose and focus for subsequent interviews; the worker may deliberately not respond to this material initially but may bring it up later. Aaron Rosen and Dina Lieberman (1972, p. 398) report on an experimental study of the extent to which workers' responses are content relevant—"the extent to which the content of an interactive response is perceived by a participant to be relevant to, and in agreement with, the participant's own definition and expectations of the content to be dealt with in the treatment relationship." With compliant clients, workers with more training did significantly better at maintaining content relevance. Workers with less training had more content-relevant response with aggressive clients; however, many of the responses were harsh and retaliatory and thus perhaps ineffective in helping. Rosen and Lieberman (pp. 410–411) suggest that their findings point to the need for clear worker and client orientation as to the purpose of the interview. A clear purpose may assist the worker in keeping the interview focused, although this is apparently difficult with an aggressive client.

A third major responsibility of the worker is to separate and identify the client's levels of response. Responses are typically on one of four levels—perceptual, cognitive, affective, and behavioral. The perceptual level of response refers to interactions and communications around what the client perceives or has perceived—what was seen and heard. The cognitive level refers to interactions and communications around what the client thinks—what meaning the client ascribed to what was seen and heard. The feeling, or affective, level refers to interactions and communications around the feelings that were generated in clients by either their perceptions or their cognitions—how the client feels about what was thought or about what was seen and heard. And the behavioral level refers to interactions and communications around either the client's past or anticipated behavior—how the client behaved and how the client might behave in relation to what was and will be seen and heard.

It is possible to interact with clients at all these levels. For data collection, however, a thorough exploration of the perceptual and cognitive levels is necessary before moving into the feeling and behavioral levels.

Perhaps an example will clarify this responsibility. Put yourself in the position of the worker whose client is a 16-year-old boy who has frequent arguments with his father and who angrily left the house one afternoon and drove off in a neighbor's car following an argument. In discussing the situation, the youth will probably initiate the conversation on the cognitive level—with some comment to the effect that he and his dad do not get along, that his dad does not understand him, or that his dad is unfair. These are all cognitive statements: they reflect a meaning or interpretation which the youngster has placed on perceived events. A frequent interviewing error is to simply accept the meaning which the client has reported and to move immediately into the areas of feelings and behavior. However, a careful prior exploration with the client of his perceptions of the events which led to this interpretation that his father and he do not get along will be very useful. What took place? What did the boy see and hear? What did his father say? What did the boy say? What happened then? After exploring the incidents in detail, the client and worker are both prepared to consider alternative interpretations of the events. After moving back to the perceptual level (What did you see and hear?) and reconsidering the cognitive level (What meanings do you ascribe to what you saw and heard?), the client and worker may then move legitimately to the question of feelings together (What did you feel when this was occurring? Do I still detect a note of anger in your voice? As you look back on it now, what kinds of reactions are you having?). And from the feeling level the next logical step is to behavior (What did you do when this happened? As you look back, what might have been other ways of handling yourself? In view of such experiences, if you and your father have future arguments, what are ways in which you think you might behave?). Before moving into a consideration of the client's feelings and behavior, considerable effort is expended to collect an account of the incidents that occurred and the interpretation of those incidents. Failure to explore the perceptual and cognitive levels in detail may lead to very incomplete data with which to engage the client in problem-solving plans.

To sum up, the worker has three primary responsibilities in the interview— creating a productive climate, focusing the interview, and separating and clarifying levels of response.

While the purpose of this chapter is not to offer a bag of tricks or to deal at any length with interviewing techniques, a few suggestions may help the reader to make a start in building a repertoire of interviewing methods for creating a productive climate, focusing the interview, and separating levels of response.

SOME IDEAS ABOUT TECHNIQUE

Open-ended questions are useful, especially in early phases of an interview or a subpart of an interview (Payne, 1951, chap. 3). An open-ended question is one that cannot be answered yes or no—rather it is one that requires an essay-type answer. Questions such as "Tell me a little about yourself" or "What would you like us to do?" are extremely open-ended. Open-ended questions are good questions to start with because they allow clients considerable leeway in beginning where they wish. If clients fumble, the worker can come back with a much more focused question. Figure 6–2 illustrates several open-ended responses that permit the interviewer to focus the interview and invite additional participation from clients. An interview can be thought of as a funnel—starting with very broad, open-ended questions that become much more specific and focused as worker and client narrow in on specific areas of concern.

FIGURE 6–2
Interviewing responses

The hypothetical situation I will use is one you will meet many times as a counselor. A client will say, "I don't get along with my parents." Here are numerous responses which can be used to fulfill the two important requirements of interviewing: (1) allowing the client to express feelings, and (2) helping you to direct the interview.
—You don't get along with your parents.
—Your parents?
—What do you mean when you say. . . .
—I don't understand what you mean when you say. . . .
—Help me understand what you mean. . . .
—Give me an example of how you. . . .
—Tell me more about this.
—Uh-huh.   —and   —For instance?   —Go on.
—Oh?   —but   —I see.
—When did you first notice that. . . .
—How do you feel about this? (Perhaps the most important question one could ask.)
—What are some of the things you and your parents disagree about?
—What are some problems kids like you have—not just you but all kids in general?
—What are your parents like? What is your dad like? What is your mom like? (General questions.)
—You seem to be very upset about this.
—You look worried (or you look unhappy).
—(Avoid asking a question which calls for a yes or no answer.)
—(Just be silent. A word about silence. In patients and particularly in adolescents, silence tends to provoke anxiety. Silence generally loses its effect if too prolonged.)
—You say you have trouble getting along with your parents. What are some of your troubles?
—Perhaps you could share some of your ideas about what has caused these problems.
—(It probably never helps to ask the question why. If they knew why they were having trouble with their parents, they wouldn't be seeing you.)
—Maybe it would help to talk about this.
—Compared to you, what type of people are your parents?
—If your parents were here, what would they say about this problem?

Source: Dr. Richard J. Bealka, psychiatrist, Mental Health Institute, Independence, Iowa.

The interviewer attempting to secure data on which to base interventive decisions must become adept at probing for additional information. *Probing* may be an unfortunate word—the intent is not to indicate an abrasiveness or harshness but rather an invitation to pursue a particular area. Questions such as "Can you tell me more about that?" or "I'd like to hear a little more in this area" are both open-ended and probing inasmuch as they are related to something the client has said and are asking for more information. Figure 6–2 illustrates a wide number of probing questions which are nonabrasive and which both invite clients to continue to express themselves and enable the worker to provide direction to the interview.

The data collection interview requires that the worker maintain neutrality and carefully avoid biasing questions. While people may joke about the "You do love your wife, don't you?" kind of question, biases creep in in subtler ways. The requirement of neutrality does not negate earlier remarks about worker input. The purpose of the data collection interview is to secure reliable and valid information about the client's perceptions and interpretations of experiences; worker input at this stage would have a biasing effect and should be avoided. First the worker learns the client's position and thinking and then may consider offering the worker's own experience to the client. The sharing of worker input comes when various intervention strategies are under consideration.

Throughout this chapter frequent references have been made to checkout. Checkout requires the use of feedback in which the worker consciously and deliberately reflects back to the client what the worker is perceiving in order to determine whether the communication is correct. This is what I hear you saying. Or, I seem to be hearing this. Or, I see you're doing this. Or, am I understanding what you are saying in this? These are all feedback probes and are an effort to refer back to the client what the worker is hearing in order to allow the client to correct any errors in meaning. Feedback is a very useful and necessary technique for clarifying communications. While it may sometimes seem awkward, because this technique is seldom used in everyday activity, reflecting back to the client what is seen and heard can avoid both pitfalls and misunderstandings and also serves the function of encouraging the client to pursue conversation in a particular area. Rosen and Lieberman (1972, p. 398) examined the use of feedback among workers of different levels of training. They used the concept of stimulus-response-congruence—"the extent to which a response by one participant in the relationship provides feedback to the other participant that the message sent was actually received"—and found that trained workers maintained a lower rate of incongruent responses than untrained workers (p. 409). This finding suggests that the use of feedback is a skill acquired by training and helps explain an initial awkwardness with its use.

One final suggestion for enhancing communications is to avoid asking why. *Why* is a frequently used word in our language. But the *why* question is basically defense producing—it is a question that asks a person to explain one's own behavior. Social workers, by and large, are not interested in asking clients to explain their behavior but are interested in asking them to describe the situation in which they are behaving and to explore alternative ways of interpreting and reacting to that situation. Such questions as What was happening then? What seemed to be going on? Can you tell me what you were doing? and What seemed to be the nature of the situation? are much more likely to elicit material which can be used constructively with the client in problem-solving.

WRITTEN COMMUNICATIONS

This chapter has been focused largely around the use of oral communications in an interview setting for data collection purposes. Social workers make extensive use of this type of communication. This is not, however, in anyway to negate the importance of written communication skills. Social workers are called upon to write reports, letters, and other written documents both to secure and to give information on the behalf of their clients. Ability to prepare written materials may be a necessary part of the data collection phase of service or may be required later as a part of an intervention plan. The ability to express ideas clearly and accurately in written form is just as essential to social work practice as interviewing.

RECAPITULATION

In this chapter we have tried to establish a number of points. Interviewing for data collection purposes can be regarded as a set of communications which the social worker uses to secure valid and reliable data from the client concerning the client's perceptions, and, perhaps, the feelings the client attaches to both perceptions and meanings. The process involves giving, receiving, and checking out meanings. The client is the primary source of the data on which decisions concerning problem-solving are based; thus social work interviewing techniques must be considered in terms of whether or not they contribute to the climate in which the client can share reliable and valid data. The reliability and validity of data may be impaired by six worker barriers to communication —anticipation of what the other is going to say, assumptions of meaning about communications from the other, stereotyping, inexplicit purposes for the interview, premature efforts to produce change, and inattentiveness. The quality of the data may also be affected by resistances stemming from the client's hesitancy to enter into strange situations, cultural norms affecting the client's ability to enter into problem-solving, and the client's pathological involvement with the problem. The social worker collecting data has the primary responsibility for creating a climate in which the client can participate productively, for providing a focus, and for securing data on the perceptual and cognitive levels as well as on the affective and behavioral levels. Open-ended questions, probing, neutrality, extensive use of feedback, and avoiding *why* questions are all useful interviewing approaches to data collection.

One final note. We regard interviewing as a disciplined art. But does discipline interfere with spontaneity? Does learning interviewing techniques make the interviewer mechanical and nonhuman? We think not. Learning interviewing techniques may increase the social worker's spontaneity for two reasons. First, in the process of learning about interviewing, social workers become aware of and able to deal with barriers to communication in their usual responses to people. Second, interviewing techniques expand the repertoire of responses available to the worker. The increased repertoire permits increased spontaneity because the worker is not locked into an earlier, limited set of responses. Alfred Kadushin (1972, p. 2) expresses this last point eloquently:

> The interviewer should, of course, be the master of the techniques rather than the obedient servant bound by rules. Technical skill is not antithetical to spontaneity. In fact, it permits a higher form of spontaneity; the skilled interviewer can deliberately violate the techniques as the occasion demands. Technical skill frees the interviewer in responding as a human being to the interviewee. Errors in relation to technique lie with rigid, and therefore inappropriate, application. A good knowledge of techniques makes the interviewer aware of a greater variety of alternatives. Awareness and command of technical knowledge also has another advantage. To know is to be prepared; to be prepared is to experience reduced anxiety; to reduce anxiety is to increase the interviewer's freedom to be fully responsive to the interviewee.

In Chapter 5 it was noted that the graceful figure skater could not become spontaneous and "free" without many hours of disciplined practice. So it is with interviewing. Spontaneity and freedom do not come naturally but with discipline, with practice, and with learning.

A LOOK FORWARD

In this chapter, there has been no explicit mention of problems encountered with communication across cultural or racial barriers. Interrracial and intercultural communication places even greater responsibility on the part of the worker to insure that messages are being clearly received and transmitted, to be sensitive to cultural differences both in communication patterns and in perceptions of the role of the worker, and to become disciplined enough to avoid the worker barriers to communication which have been identified. The two articles reproduced in this chapter further elaborate upon this material. John Cormican analyzes linguistic problem areas that may develop in interviewing including language differences, problems associated with the use of labels, and inability to articulate problems. Alfred Kadushin draws on several research projects to analyze the racial factor in the interview. He notes that the question is not Can a white worker communicate with a black client? but How can such contact be established? The communication principles discussed in this chapter assume increased importance as the social, racial, and ethnic gulfs between worker and client increase.

In the next chapter the problem-solving model is outlined. Later chapters will elaborate phases of the model. Material covered up to this point on knowledge, values, relationships, and communication are all necessary prerequisites to problem-solving.

Reading
6-1 *Linguistic issues in interviewing**

John D. Cormican

Unlike the medical helping profession which has at its disposal biological and chemical tests to help identify a client's problems and thus suggest an appropriate physiological treatment, social work practice relies almost exclusively on language for both diagnosis and treatment.

The social worker depends on the client's speech in obtaining a history of the problem, in

making a differential and social diagnosis, and in assessing levels of development and indications of social dysfunction. Social work treatment of all kinds is conducted primarily by oral means, both on the part of the worker and the client (Portner, 1977, p. 56).

Berta Fantl (1961, p. 430) observes that *"Communication—verbal and nonverbal— with an adequate understanding for the subtle aspects of the situation under which communication takes place is the vehicle for all treatment."* It is in the intake interview, however, that appropriate language is most

─────────
* Reprinted by permission from Family Service Association of America, publisher, from *Social Casework* 59:3 (March 1978), pp. 145–152.

crucial in social work, because this interview provides the information on which the agency's determination of the case lies and the client, if given the choice, chooses to engage himself or herself with the agency.

Linguistic problem areas

Linguistic problem areas which may develop in interviewing center on three major aspects of language use in social work practice. The first area concerns language differences between the worker and the client. The second is the use of labels, diagnostic and otherwise, which may lead the worker to lack of individualization of clients, or the clients to lack of individualization of the worker. The last linguistic problem area in interviewing is the client's lack of ability to articulate certain kinds of problems clearly.

Language differences

Two kinds of language problems may interfere with communication between the worker and the client. The first occurs between people who do not speak the same languages (for example, the worker speaks English, the client Spanish), and the second involves the use of different dialects of the same language by the interacting people.

Non-English-speaking client

In the United States, an obvious language difference occurs when the client does not speak English. Alejandro Garcia (1971, p. 276) charges that "Most agencies . . . continue their punitive practice of helping only those clients who can communicate in English." He cites a Chicano client whose dealings with social workers who did not speak Spanish had made her "feel guilty and inferior because she knew no English," and who "feared that she and the worker were not really communicating with each other" through an interpreter (p. 275). Ignacia Aguilar (1972, pp. 66–70) identifies another language difference between social workers and Mexican-American clients. Most social workers do not have the time for lengthy conversations preceding the identification of the client's problem. Aguilar has shown, however, that interviews with Chicano clients that can begin with a leisurely conversation—lasting an hour or more—that is not even related to the problem are most effective, because it is customary in the Mexican-American culture to have a preliminary informal and personal interchange before approaching any serious business to be handled. Inez M. Tyler and Sophie D. Thompson (1965, pp. 215–220) have shown clearly the effectiveness of having a caseworker who speaks the language and understands the culture in dealing with Navajo clients. Clearly then, any interview with non-English-speaking clients will be more effective if the worker is familiar with the particular client's language.

Varying dialects

The more common kind of language difference between worker and client, however, is that they speak different dialects of English. These dialect differences may be the result of the worker's use of professional jargon when speaking to clients, the difference in social classes of the worker and the client, the difference in geographic areas of origin of the worker and the client, the different ethnic backgrounds of the worker and the client, or the age difference between the worker and the client.

Professional dialects. Alfred Kadushin (1972, p. 29) observes that " 'Eligibility' sounds one way and has one meaning to the worker; it sounds quite different to and evokes a different set of responses in the client. [Workers] say 'home study' and 'court record' and 'therapy' without knowing how these unfamiliar words sound to the client." Florence Hollis (1965, p. 469) notes, "intellectualization and the use of technical language is helpful with neither lower-class nor middle-class [clients]. Social workers who "use simple, everyday English" are the most effective in conducting interviews.

Social dialects. When social workers who are middle class and whose previous work has been with middle-class clients are employed in lower-class neighborhoods, they sometimes feel that they and their lower-class clients are "conversing in different languages" (Fantl, 1961, p. 429). It is in this circumstance that the difference in social dialects may be most detrimental in an interview. Lower-class clients often "feel self-conscious about their speech . . . and uncertain how to act in initial contacts" with social service agencies (p. 427). A client who speaks a low-class dialect when talking to a middle-class worker may feel uncomfortable because of the social distance betrayed by their different dialects, and particularly so if the worker appears to be condescending toward the client either by emphasizing the differences in their speech or by attempting to speak the lower-class dialect when he or she is clearly uncomfortable doing so (Cormican and Cormican, 1977, p. 19). Hollis (1965, p. 470) points out, however, that lower-class clients are able to communicate effectively with a worker if the worker "uses words that are simple and expressive."

Regional dialects. There may be situations in which the worker and the client speak different regional dialects, because the worker has accepted a position distant from one's native geographic area, or because the client has migrated to another geographic area. In the first case, it is encumbent upon the worker to familiarize him or herself with the vocabulary differences between his or her native geographic area and the new area—for example, Northern "sweet corn" or "corn-on-the-cob" versus Midland and Southern "roasting ears" (Falk, 1973, p. 214), Northern and Midland "take" or "escort" versus Southern "carry" (Francis, 1958, p. 522). "Turnpikes" in Pennsylvania, Ohio, Indiana, New Hampshire, Massachusetts, and Maine, versus "parkways" in Rhode Island and Connecticut, versus "thruways" in New York, versus "expressways" in Michigan, versus "freeways" in California (Marckwardt, 1969, p. 151). The worker must also be aware of his or her own stereotypical attitudes toward the speakers of the regional dialect where the worker is and the attitudes of the people in that particular region toward persons who speak the worker's regional dialect, for example, the attitudes that Northerners and Southerners may have about each other. In some cases, the worker might be expected to become familiar with the regional vocabulary of any large section of the client population in the area that has immigrated from another section of the country and to be aware of the attitudes both he or she and the clients are likely to have about speakers of the different regional dialects in the area.

Ethnic dialects. If the worker and the client come from different ethnic backgrounds, the varieties of English they speak may also differ and interfere with communication in an interview. Kadushin (1972, p. 34) indicates that, "The word 'ghetto' evokes different images in the mind of a black militant in Chicago, a white matron in Greenwich, and a Hasidic Jew in Brooklyn." Thus, individual words may mean different things to the worker and the client when the words are used in an interview. Probably more important, however, are the attitudes held by the worker and the client about the dialects of English spoken by various ethnic groups. Much has been written about how black English differs from white English (Falk, 1973, pp. 224–225) and about "foreignized" English spoken by other ethnic groups (Francis, 1958, p. 517). What is important in interviewing, however, is not the particular ethnic dialect features that the worker or client uses, but the attitude the other person has about such features (sometimes labeled "nonstandard") and toward persons who use them. There is usually no problem understanding what a person speaking an ethnic social dialect is saying; what the worker needs to be aware of is his or her own and the client's prejudices toward people who speak or do not speak a particular ethnic social dialect. Of course, the worker who speaks a particular ethnic dialect of English would do well to avoid using it whenever possible while interviewing a client who does not speak it, but the worker who is interviewing a client who does speak a different ethnic social dialect must not indicate (or, it is hoped, even feel) any rejection of the client because of his or her speech.

Age difference dialects. The final way that language differences between the worker and the client may cause communication problems in an interview centers on language differences based on age differences. The vocabulary of older persons may differ from that of the professionals dealing with them (Cormican, 1975, pp. 104–105), and the vocabulary level of a child client may be lower than that of the worker (Cormican, 1976, p. 591). In the first case, the interviewing worker would do well to avoid using contemporary slang or new words with the client. In the second case, the worker might consciously choose Germanic, that is native English, words over Latinate synonyms during the interview. What is really required in both cases is that the worker must have a broad enough and flexible enough vocabulary to communicate clearly with a wide range of clients.

Use of labels

The second major area in which language may present problems within an interview is in the use of labels. Although it is a normal human process to categorize people, a situation in which a social worker mentally categorizes a client during an interview may result in the worker's failure to individualize the client's problem and to hear what the client is actually saying. Much of the social work literature deals with casework with lower-class or low-income clients. Hollis (1965, pp. 470–471) warns that "We must . . . guard against depriving [low-income] clients of the opportunity of receiving adequate casework help by our holding stereotyped and erroneous preconceptions about their limitations." Nevertheless, Carol H. Meyer (1976a, p. 598) concludes that "One may wonder whether a poor person any longer has an individual identity" to many social workers.

Diagnostic labels

Carolyn Dillon (1969, p. 337) writes of "the hapless client whose fate is sealed by the terms *anal character* or *pseudoneurotic schizophrenic, borderline state* or *depressive case,* flesh melted from bone and reduced to a record-fattening conundrum on syndrome and synthesis." Dillon argues that diagnostic labels can erect barriers between workers and clients by setting up two distinct classes of people, with the result "that the clients have subtly become simply 'them.'" One cause of the social worker's desire to label may be the traditional medical model for social work practice. Peggy C. Giordano (1977, p. 34) reports that there has been a "deliberate attempt on the part of medical professionals to mystify the client and, by creating language barriers, to keep the client in place." Dillon (1969, p. 337) suggests that diagnostic labels which have "blurred [the worker's] ability to see clients as human beings" may actually be attractive to the worker, because of the "painful similarity" between the worker's problems and the clients' problems.

Another problem with the diagnostic labels placed by social workers on their clients is that the labels are arbitrary and often not defined. For example, "a variety of terms—*personality disorder, neurotic character, character neurosis, behavior disorder, actor-outer*—are used synonymously with *character disorder*" (Jackel, 1976, pp. 200–201). As another example, "the term *depression* has been used to describe reactions as varied as mild emotional malaise to severe forms of psychotic melancholia" (Deykin, Klerman, and Weissman, 1966, p. 288). Because "mental health and psychosis represent the two extremes on a continuum" (Jackel, 1976, p. 204), the diagnostic terms applied to clients between the two poles of the continuum could logically divide that continuum into 30 or 300 parts or into only 2 parts, such as character disorder or neurosis. Because of the problems inherent in these diagnostic labels and because no label sums up the essence of a person, Fantl (1961, p. 430) states, "We have become cautious about the terms we are using to diagnose and describe clients' difficulties." Such caution is always appropriate, but particularly so in the intake interview setting.

Category labels

The more general use of category labels by social workers and their clients is another way that linguistc labels present barriers to communication in interviews. The Sapir-Whorf hypothesis shows that the language one learns as a child contains the language categories that make up one's reality (Chase, 1969, p. 100). Of course, an English-speaking person then learns racial labels such as black and white as part of his reality. Clearly, a person who was actually black or white would be a real novelty because people's skin colors are actually all shades of brown, but that is beside the point. If workers and clients think people are black or white, they are. It is true that other cultures such as the Union of South Africa and Guyana use three categories—*black, white,* and *colored*—to categorize people who would be either black or white in the United States, but that only confirms the arbitrariness of the labels. Nevertheless, category labels may determine the perceptions by the worker of the client and vice versa in an interview situation.

Andrew E. Curry (1964, pp. 163–164) has pointed out that "Difficulties arise when the worker's and the client's subtle responses to *Negro* and *white* begin to spill over into the contractual relationship between them. . . . In the social context, the designations *Negro* and *white* are emotionally laden signs and

symbols that have important sociopsychological stimulus value." This is so because ethnic labels as well as labels such as blind man or cripple, which indicate some major incapacity, are what Gordon Allport (1974, pp. 108–109) calls "labels of primary potency," that is, they overshadow all other labels an individual might properly have, such as teacher, father, bald, Democrat, and so on, and carry with them a great many features which the individual so labeled might not actually possess. Shirley Cooper (1973, p. 78) concludes that:

In clinical work with minority patients, an overbalanced stress on difference, on ethnicity, and on its concomitant psychological meaning can distort the helping process. It may lead a therapist to focus so centrally on ethnic factors that individual problems and individual solutions become obscured.

According to Cooper, "There is a danger of no longer treating people—only culture carriers." Similarly, Amy Iwasaki Mass (1976, p. 164) writes that "The social worker who acts on the stereotype of the model Japanese [successful and not in need of help] and expects Japanese clients to live up to this ideal will be doing the clients a great disservice."

Specific examples of how this use of linguistic category symbols may interfere with interviewing include a recent study of white job interviewers interviewing black applicants which showed "that although the whites felt they had done a credible job with black applicants, the blacks felt there had been scarcely any communication at all" (DeLo and Green, 1977, p. 295). Similarly, caseworkers working with black and white clients in interracial situations conclude "that each case had its unique configuration of factors from both [sociological and psychological] sources, and that the caseworker's interpretation might in itself be a stereotype of psychoanalytical, sociological, or personal derivation" (Fibush and Turnquest, 1970, pp. 459–460). Perhaps Aguilar was right when he wrote, "prejudice in its purest and ugliest manifestations becomes one of the most common problems the minorities face in their encounters with helping professionals" (1972, p. 69).

Inability to articulate problems

The third broad area of language problems in interviewing is the client's real or alleged inability to articulate certain kinds of problems clearly. The phrase "real or alleged" was used in the previous sentence because the author is not convinced that clients who fall within the normal range of intelligence are ever incapable of communication because of a language deficit; they may, however, be incapable of communicating because of the circumstances of the interview. One reads that the poor family "cannot even articulate its concerns well enough to communicate with a social agency" (Meyer, 1976, p. 515), that lower-class mothers are "so inarticulate that they literally did not have the words for their emotions" (Hollis, 1965, p. 463), and that workers interviewing lower-class clients have learned not to "expect verbalization of 'inner conflict.'" (Fantl, 1961, p. 431) Hollis (1965, p. 469) reports, however, that most workers have little difficulty getting clients to discuss feelings if they themselves use appropriate language in the interview. She cautions that "simplicity of language and slowness of thought should not be mistaken for incapacity" and that "once the low-income client's confidence has been established, he is likely to speak freely, particularly of feelings of anger and frustration (p. 469).

There are clients who, because of the particular nature of their problem, may verbalize one thing and mean something entirely different. "The attitude and expression of 'Who cares?' often actually are a cover for 'I care very much but I don't dare show it'" (Leader, 1976, p. 639). Because of "the ambivalence associated with suicide," the worker talking with a potential suicide "may hear: 'Leave me alone; I don't want your help,' from a person crying out loudly

for help" (Klugman, Litman and Wold, 1965, p. 45). Similarly, the alibi system used by an alcoholic may include:

Minimizing retrospectively the harmful consequences of drinking . . . attributing alcoholism to factors no longer present, thus implying that the illness may have waned . . . suggesting that a beverage with a lower alcoholic content will be safe . . . showing self-pity . . . clinging to resentments or blaming others . . . disparaging or avoiding the AA group (Weinberg, 1973, p. 87).

Even the drug addicts who come voluntarily to drug treatment centers and say they want to get off drugs for good "invariably . . . have a mental reservation that they would use drugs if they felt the need, but with 'proper management'" (St. Pierre, 1971, pp. 84–89). Bok-Lim C. Kim (1972, p. 278) points out that Japanese and Korean wives and their American husbands will often cite "difficulty in communication . . . [as] . . . an excuse for avoiding the inadequacies of both wives and husbands."

Subcultural differences

One real reason a client may not articulate his or her problem in an interview with a worker is subcultural difference. Herbert H. Locklear (1972, p. 77) notes that American Indians "tend to be reticent about speaking up and demanding their rights" when talking with a worker, and that workers are likely to interpret this reticence as indicating an unwillingness to cooperate. Jimm G. Good Tracks (1973, pp. 30–34) has suggested that the worker who adopts "a coercive tone and intervenes in an American Indian client's personal problems without being asked may very well fail completely in the interview because "any kind of intervention is contrary to the Indian's strict adherence to the principle of self-determination." Kim (1972, p. 279) cautions that "the reluctance of Oriental women to express their needs, feelings, opinions, and thoughts should not be equated with an absence of such emotions."

Worker attitudes

Of course, another reason that the client may not articulate a particular problem in an interview is the attitude of the worker. If the client fails to feel a rapport with the worker because of any of the language differences between worker and client identified earlier, or because he or she feels that the worker has treated him or her as a category rather than a person, one can hardly expect the client to be willing to discuss personal problems openly in the interview. Also, Alfred Benjamin (1974, p. 93) demonstrates clearly that a worker can tell clients either directly or indirectly that the worker does not want to hear about certain problems because of a personal value system.

Conclusion

There are actions, then, which the worker may take to minimize linguistic problems in interviewing. Problems based upon language differences between the worker and client can be ameliorated if the worker becomes familiar enough with the language or dialect of clients to allow clients to use their regular speech patterns in the interview and if the worker uses language that the clients can understand and accept. Problems because of the language labels used can be lessened if the worker can avoid thinking in terms of those categories and certainly if the worker can convey to a client that he or she is being considered as an individual rather than as one of "them." Finally, interviewing problems due to the real or alleged inability of the client to articulate problems can be minimized by creating an atmosphere conducive to the client's willingness to express him or herself, listening to what the client means rather than what is said, and, above all, being patient and tolerant of individual differences.

Reading
6-2 *The racial factor in the interview**

Alfred Kadushin

Ethnicity, broadly speaking, means membership in a group that is differentiated on the basis of some distinctive characteristic which may be cultural, religious, linguistic, or racial. The nonwhite experience in America is sufficiently differentiated so that race can be regarded as a specific kind of ethnicity. Although the term *nonwhite* includes Mexican-Americans, American Indians, orientals, and blacks, this article on the racial factor in the interview is almost exclusively concerned with black-white differences, not only because blacks are the largest single nonwhite minority, but because most of the descriptive, clinical, and experimental literature concerned with this problem focuses on blacks.

The black client often presents the interviewer with the problem of socioeconomic background as well as differences in racial experience. Although the largest number of poor people are white, a disproportionate percentage of the black population is poor. Hence the racial barrier between the white worker and black client is frequently complicated further by the class barrier—white middle-class worker and black lower-class client. However, the exclusive concern here is with the racial factor, that is, the differences that stem from the experiences in living white and living black.

The problem

Racial difference between worker and client is an ethnic factor that creates problems in the relationship and the interview. Understanding and empathy are crucial ingredients for an effective interview. But how can the white worker imagine what it is like for black clients to live day after day in a society that grudgingly, half-heartedly, and belatedly accord them the self-respect, dignity, and acceptance that are their rights as people or, more often, refuse outright to grant them. How can the worker know what it is like to live on intimate terms with early rejection, discrimination, harassment, and exploitaton?

A relaxed atmosphere and comfortable interaction are required for a good interview. But how can this be achieved when the black client feels accusatory and hostile as the oppressed and the white worker feels anxious and guilty about personal complicity with the oppressor? In such a situation the black client would tend to resort to concealment and disguise and respond with discretion or "accommodation" behavior (Duvinage, 1939, p. 264). Concealment and "putting the white person on" have been institutionalized as a way of life—they are necessary weapons for survival, but antithetical to the requirements of an effective interview. Often the black client openly refuses to share, as expressed in the following poem, "Impasse," by Langston Hughes:

> I could tell you,
> If I wanted to,
> What makes me
> What I am
>
> But I don't
> Really want to—
> And you don't
> Give a damn[1]

The attitude toward permeability of the racial barrier for the social work interview

[1] Copyright © 1967 by Arna Bontemps and George Huston Bass from *The Panther and the Lash*. Reprinted by permission of Alfred A. Knopf, Inc.

has changed over the last 20 years. In 1950 [Luna B.] Brown attempted to assess the importance of the racial factor in the casework relationship by distributing questionnaires to social agencies in Seattle, Washington. Eighty percent of the practitioners responded that the racial factor did intrude in the relationship, but it was not much of a problem for the experienced worker with some self-awareness.

By 1970 blacks' disillusionment with the integrationist stance and a great accentuation on their specal separate identity from the white culture and the unique effects of their historical experience resulted in frequently repeated assertions that no white could understand what is meant to be black. Consequently, it is said, an effective interview with a black client requires a black interviewer. Many who have studied this problem, although not ready to go this far, generally concede that currently the racial barrier in the interview makes rapport and understanding much more difficult than was previously imagined (Banks, 1971; Bowles, 1969; Gochros, 1966; Kincaid, 1969; Vontross, 1969, 1970, 1971).

Obviously people who share similar backgrounds, values, experiences, and problems are more likely to feel comfortable with and understand each other. In sociology the principles of homophyly (people who are alike like each other) and homogamy (like marries like) express these feelings. Synanon, Alcoholics Anonymous, and denominational agencies are organizational expressions of this idea.

Social workers tend to follow the same principles by selecting for continuing service those clients who are most like themselves and subtly discouraging or overtly rejecting those "who cannot effectively use the service." The rich research literature about differential access to mental health services by different class groups tends to confirm that this is a euphemism for people who are different from "us."

There is similar research with regard to agency selectivity relating to race. For example, a study of patients seen for ten or more individual psychotherapy interviews at a metropolitan psychiatric outpatient clinic found that "Caucasian women were seen proportionately longest, followed by Caucasian men (Yamamoto et al., 1967, pp. 630–636). Racial minority group patients had proportionately fewer contacts—black males had the lowest number of interviews. Nonwhites not only had fewer contacts, but their attrition rate was higher. All therapists, including psychiatric social workers, were Caucasian. Therapist ethnocentricity was measured with the Bogardus Social Distance Scale. Those who scored low in ethnocentrism were more likely to see black patients for six or more interviews; those who scored high treated black patients for this length of time much less often (differences were statistically significant). Worker ethnocentrism may help account for the higher attrition rate of black clients who apply for social servces. It is certainly true for black clients in family service agencies and black applicants for adoption (Bradley, 1966; *Family Service Highlights,* 1964).

But the following statement by a black mental health worker, retrospectively analyzing her own personal experience, indicates that a therapeutic relationship with a white person, although difficult, is possible:

In answering the question of whether a white middle-class psychiatrist can treat a black family, I cannot help but think back over my own experiences. When I first came to New York and decided to go into psychotherapy I had two main thoughts: (1) that my problems were culturally determined, and (2) that they were related to my Catholic upbringing. I had grown up in an environment in which the Catholic Church had tremendous influence. With these factors in mind, I began to think in terms of the kind of therapist I could best relate to. In addition to being warm and sensitive, he had to be black and Catholic. Needless to say, that was like looking for a needle in a haystack. But after inquiring around, I was finally referred to a black Catholic psychiatrist.

. . . he turned out to be not so sensitive and not so warm. I terminated my treatment with him and began to see another therapist who was warm, friendly, sensitive, understanding, and

very much involved with me. Interestingly enough, he was neither black nor Catholic. As a result of that personal experience, I have come to believe that it is not so much a question of whether the therapist is black or white but whether he is competent, warm, and understanding. Feelings, after all, are neither black nor white (as quoted in Sager, Brayboy, and Waxenberg, 1970, pp. 210–211).

Thus the question of whether a white worker can establish contact with a black client is more correctly stated as "How can such contact be established?"

White worker–black client

What can be done to ease the real difficulties inherent in white worker–black client cross-racial integration? Because white workers are initially regarded as a potential enemy, they should carefully observe all the formalities that are overt indications of respect—for example, start the interview promptly, use Mr. and Mrs. rather than the client's surname or first name, shake hands and introduce themselves, listen seriously and sincerely. Rituals and forms are not empty gestures to people who have consistently been denied the elementary symbols of civility and courtesy.

Discussions about racism have left every white with the uneasy suspicion that as a child of this culture one has imbibed prejudices in a thousand different subtle ways in repeated small doses and that the symptoms of one's racism, although masked to oneself, are readily apparent to a black person. These suspicions may be true. Thus a worker must frankly acknowledge to oneself that one may have racist attitudes and make the effort to change. To paraphrase a Chinese maxim: The prospective white interviewer who says, "Other white interviewers are fools for being prejudiced, and when I am an interviewer I will not be such a fool," is already a fool.

To conduct a good interview, workers must be relatively confident that they know their subject matter. But how can they feel confident if they are aware that there is much about the black experience they do not and cannot know? Certainly they can dispel some of their ignorance by reading about and becoming familiar with black history, black culture, and black thinking and feeling. This is their professional responsibility. When workers lack knowledge about the client's situation, they appear "innocent." Thus they are less respected, more likely to be "conned," and less likely to be a source of influence.

White workers may find it helpful to be explicitly aware of their reactions to racial differences. In making restitution for their felt or suspected racism, they may be overindulgent. They may oversimplify the client's problems and attribute certain behavior to racial differences that should be ascribed to personal malfunctioning. When color is exploited as a defensive rationalization, race is a weapon. Burns (1971, p. 93) points out that black children "have learned how to manipulate the guilt feelings of their white workers for their own ends. They have also learned to exploit the conceptions most white workers have about the anger of black people.

In interracial casework interviews, the participants are keenly aware of the difference between them. Yet, they rarely discuss the racial factor openly (Miller, 1970; Seligman, 1968, pp. 1–84). It is not clear whether this is because race is considered irrelevant to the work that needs to be done or because both participants agree to a conspiracy of silence about a potentially touchy issue. Nevertheless, race—like any other significant factor that contaminates interaction—must be at least tentatively discussed because to be "color-blind" is to deny real differences (Bloch, 1968).

The presumption of ignorance, necessary in all interviews, is more necessary when interviewng a black client because the worker is more likely to be ignorant of the client's situation. Therefore, one must listen more carefully, be less ready to come to conclusions, and be more open to having one's presuppositions corrected by the cli-

ent, that is, one must want to know what the situation is and be receptive to being taught.

It is frequently asserted that lower-class black clients lack the fluency and facility with language that are required for a good interview. Yet, studies of speech behavior in the ghetto suggest that blacks show great imaginativeness and skill with language (Kochman, 1969). Thus the worker has the obligation to learn the special language of the ghetto. The agency can help by hiring black clerical and professional staff. If black clients see members of their own group working at the agency, they have a greater sense of assurance that they will be accepted and understood.

Black worker–black client

If both worker and client are black, different problems may arise. The pervasiveness of the cultural definition of blackness does affect black clients. Thus they may feel that being assigned to a block worker is less desirable than being assigned to a white worker because the latter may have more influence and thus be in a better position to help them.

The fact that black social workers have achieved middle-class professional status suggests that they have accepted some of the principal mores of the dominant culture —for example, motivation to achieve, denial of gratification, the work ethic, punctuality. To get where they are, probably they were educated in white schools, read the white literature, and associated with white classmates—as they now associate with white colleagues.

Black middle-class workers may feel estranged not only from whites but from their own blackness. The problem of establishing a clearly defined identification is more difficult for "oreos"—those who are black on the outside, but white on the inside because of their experiences while achieving middle-class status.

The black worker who returns to the ghetto after professional training may be viewed with suspicion (Townsend, 1970). Aliens returning from the outside world, where they have been "worked over" by the educational enterprise to accept white assumptions, values, and language, they have supposedly lost contact with the fast-changing ghetto subculture in the interim.

If black clients see white workers as representing the enemy, they may see black social workers as traitors to their race, collaborators with the establishment. Therefore, barriers to self-disclosure and openness may be as great between the black worker and black client as between the white worker and black client.

The black client is also a source of anxiety to the black worker in other ways. A black psychiatrist stated it as follows: "For the therapist who has fought the way out of the ghetto [the black patient] may awaken memories and fears the therapist would prefer to leave undisturbed" (Sager, Brayboy, Waxenberg, 1970, p. 228). Thus Brown's findings (1950, pp. 91–97) that black workers were less sympathetic to black clients than to white clients is not surprising. They were made anxious by black clients' failure to live up to the standards of the dominant culture and felt that such deviations reflected on the race as a whole—thus decreasing the acceptability of all blacks, including themselves.

Calnek (1970, pp. 1–42) aptly defines overidentification in this context as a "felt bond with another black person who is seen as an extension of oneself because of a common racial experience." A black AFDC client described it as follows: "Sometimes the ones that have had hard times don't make you feel good. They're always telling you how hard *they* had to work making you feel low and bad because you haven't done what they done" (McIssac and Wilkinson, 1965, p. 753). The black worker also may be the target of displacement, that is, the black client's hostility toward whites is expressed toward the black workers because they are less dangerous.

One clear advantage in the black worker–black client situation, however, is that the black professional provides the client with a positive image that can be identified with. Kincaid (1969, p. 888) states that "a Black counselor who has not rejected one's own personal history may be most able to inspire a feeling of confidence and a sense of hope in the Black client."

When the worker is black and the client is white, other problems may arise. The client may be reluctant to concede that the black worker is competent and may feel assigned to the second best. Clients from the South may be especially sensitive to the reversal in usual status positions (Curry, 1964).

If the clients see themselves as lacking prejudice, they may welcome being assigned to black workers because it gives them a chance to parade their atypical feelings. They may be gratified to have a black worker since only an unusually accomplished black could, in their view, achieve professional standing. On the other hand, because the white who turns to a social agency for help often feels inadequate and inferior, the white may more easily establish a positive identification with the "exploited" and "oppressed" black worker (Grier, 1967, pp. 1587–1592).

Matching

Any discussion of the problems inherent in cross-cultural interviewing inevitably leads to the question of matching. On the whole, would it not be desirable to select a worker of the same race as the client? Would this not reduce social distance and the constraints in interactions that derive from differences in group affiliation, experiences, and lifestyle? If empathic understanding is a necessary prerequisite for establishing a good relationship, would this not be enhanced by matching people who are culturally at home with each other?

Obviously, empathic understanding is most easily achieved if the worker shares the client's world. However, the difficulties of empathic understanding across subcultural barriers can be exaggerated and the disadvantages of matching worker and client can be underestimated.

The world's literature is a testimonial to the fact that people can understand and empathize with those whose backgrounds and living situation are different from their own. For example, an American Christian, John Hersey (1950), demonstrated empathic understanding of a Polish Jew in *The Wall;* an American Jew, Elliott Liebow (1967), demonstrated his ability to understand ghetto blacks in *Tally's Corner;* and a white South African psychiatrist, Wulf Sachs (1947), showed his sensitive understanding of a Zulu in *Black Hamlet.*

If the worker's professional training enhances the ability to empathize with and understand different groups and provides the knowledge base for such understanding, the social and psychological distance between worker and client can be reduced. If the gap is sufficiently reduced, clients perceive workers as being capable of understanding them, even though they are products of a different life experience.

Some of the relative merits and disadvantages of close matching and distant matching are succinctly summarized in the following statement by Carson and Hein (1962, p. 68): "With very high similarity the therapist may be unable to maintain suitable distance and objectivity, whereas in the case of great dissimilarity the worker would not be able to empathize with, or understand, the patient's problems." Thus it is not surprising that relevant research suggests effective interviewing is not linearly related to rapport, that is, it is not true that the more rapport the better. The relationship appears to be curvilinear, that is, little rapport is undesirable, but so is maximum rapport. The best combination is moderate closeness or moderate distance between participants. Weiss (1968), in a study of the validity of responses of a group of welfare mothers, found that socially desirable rather than valid responses were more likely to result under conditions of high similarity and high rapport.[2]

Clinical evidence also suggests that racial matching is not always a crucial variable in the interview. A study that tested the degree of distortion in responses to black and white psychiatrists by patients in a county psychiatric ward concluded that "the factor of race did not significantly affect the behavior of the subjects in the interview situation" (Womack, 1967, 690). The patients perceived and responded to black psychiatrists as psychiatrists rather than as members of a different race. In a California study AFDC recipients were asked to assess the help they received from their caseworkers. The study group was large enough so that black and white caseworkers were able to contact both black and white recipients. The general conclusion was that the "race of the worker, per se, did not make a significant contribution to the amount of 'help' recipients received from the social service" (California Legislature, 1969, p. 10).

Paraprofessionals

The shortcomings of matching have become more apparent as a result of experience with indigenous paraprofessionals in the human services. In efforts to find new careers for the poor during the last few years, many social agencies have hired case aides from the area they serve. These indigenous case aides live in the same neighborhood as the client group, generally have the same racial background, and often struggle with the same kinds of problems. Therefore, they are in an excellent position to empathize with and understand the problems of the poor, blacks, and poor blacks— and in fact they often do.

In a study of agency executives' and supervisors' evaluations of paraprofessional

---

[2] See also Hyman (1954); Dohrenwend, Williams, and Weiss (1969); and Dohrenwend, Colombotos, and Dohrenwend (1968).

performance, it was found that these workers were rated high on their ability to establish rapport with clients. One agency administrator described this ability as follows:

In intake interviewing, paraprofessionals are very good at picking up clues and cues from the clients. They have a good ear for false leads and "put-ons." Their maturity and accumulated life experience, combined with firsthand knowledge of the client population, assists the agency in establishing communication with clients rapidly. . . . The new client is more comfortable with a paraprofessional because he or she is someone like the client (Gould, 1969, pp. 5–6).

Riessman (1969, p. 154), however, notes the following difficulties:

Frequently professionals assume that NPs [nonprofessionals] identify with the poor and possess great warmth and feeling for the neighborhood of their origin. While many NPs exhibit some of these characteristics, they simultaneously possess a number of other characteristics. Often, they see themselves as quite different from the other members of the poor community, whom they may view with pity, annoyance, or anger. Moreover, there are many different "types" of nonprofessionals; some are earthy, some are tough, some are angry, some are surprisingly articulate, some are sick, clever wheeler-dealers, and nearly all are greatly concerned about their new roles and their relationship to professionals.

Much of the research on nonprofessionals confirms the fact that with close matching, the problems of overidentification and activation or reactivation of problems faced by the worker are similar to those that concern the client. Clients, feeling a deep rapport with workers and anxious to maintain their friendship, may give responses that they think will make them more acceptable. They have an investment in the relationship and do not want to risk it by saying or doing anything that would alienate the worker (Grosser, 1969: Riessman, 1969, p. 154; Sobey, 1970).

If the effects of matching are not invariably advantageous, the effects of difference in cultural background between worker and client are not always disadvantageous. The problem that is created when a worker is identified with one subculture (for example, sex, race, age, color, or class) and the client is affiliated with another is one specific aspect of in-group—out-group relations generally. The worker, because of higher status, may encourage communication from the client. In addition, because of being an outsider, the worker does not reflect in-group judgments. If the client has violated or disagrees with in-group values, this is an advantage. Currently, for instance, a middle-class white-oriented accommodative black client might find it more difficult to talk to a black worker than a white worker.

If clients with upwardly mobile aspirations are looking for sources of identification outside their own groups, contact with a nonmatched worker is desirable. Thus lower-class clients anxious to learn middle-class ways, would seek such workers. The fact that workers do not initially understand them may be helpful. In trying to make their situation clear, clients may be forced to look at it more explicitly than before—that is, in explaining it to an outsider, they may explain it better to themselves. Further, clients may feel that white workers have more influence in the community. Thus they may feel more hopeful.

In contrast, however, numerous studies indicate that in most instances some disadvantages derive from racial difference between interviewer and interviewee (Sattler, 1970, pp. 157–60). With white interviewers blacks are more likely to make acceptable public responses; with black interviewers they give more private answers. For example blacks are less ready to share their feelings about discrimination with white interviewers. Carkhuff in a study in which black and white therapists from middle- and lower-class backgrounds interviewed white and black patients from various class backgrounds, found that both class background and race affected the readiness with which patients shared intimate material. They were most open to therapists of similar race and class (Bryant, Gardner, and Goldman, 1966; Carkhuff and Pierce, 1967).

Client preference

Research on client preference does not uniformly support the contention that clients invariably select professionals from their own group. Dubey (1970), for example, offers empirical support for the contention that blacks do not overwhelmingly prefer black workers. Using black interviewers, he asked some 500 ghetto residents questions such as "Would you rather talk with a Negro social worker or with a white social worker?" and "Would you rather go to an agency where the director is Negro or to one where the director is white?" About 78 percent of the respondents said they had no preference. Only 10–11 percent said they strongly preferred a black worker or agency director.

Backner (1970) encountered this problem over a three-year period as a counselor in the City College of New York's SEEK program, established to help high school graduates from poverty areas with problems encountered in college. Eighty percent of the students in the program were black and 15 percent were Puerto Rican. Backner was constantly admonished by students that "A white counselor can never really understand the black experience" and that "No black brother or black sister is really going to talk to whitey." However, the results of a questionnaire completed by about half of the 325 students in the program tended to substantiate the staff's impression that although the students responded negatively to white counselors in general, they reacted differently to their own white counselors. One item asked, "What quality in your counselor would make you feel most comfortable?" Only 12.7 percent of the respondents said that a counselor of the same racial background was the most important consideration. In response to the question, "Which SEEK teachers, counselors, and tutors are most effective and helpful to you?" 4.9 percent of the students checked "teacher, counselor, or student with the same ethnic and racial background," whereas 42 percent checked "those whose ability as teachers, counselors, tutors seems good."

In a subsequent survey all SEEK students, using a mail questionnaire that was completed anonymously and returned by 45 percent of the students, the relevant question was "Your own counselor's ethnic background (a) should be the same as yours, (b) doesn't matter." Although 25.3 percent of the respondents answered that their counselors should have the same background, 68.4 percent said it did not matter. Subsequent studies indicated that when students felt ethnicity was important, they were often expressing their feelings about the counselor as a person rather than a white person. However, in another study in which respondents had the opportunity to view racially different counselors via video tapes in a standard interview based on a script, blacks selected black counselors and whites selected whites (Stranges and Riccio, 1970).

Brieland (1969) showed that client preference was dependent on certain conditions. Black and white social work students asked black ghetto residents the following question: "If both were equally good, would you prefer that the (doctor, caseworker, teacher, lawyer, parents' group leader) be Negro (black, colored) or white?" One interesting result demonstrated the important effects of similarity or dissimilarity between interviewer-interviewee pairs. The white interviewers had a significantly larger percentage of respondents who said they had no preference as compared with black interviewers to whom respondents confessed they preferred a black doctor, caseworker, teacher, and so forth. However, only 55 percent of the respondents interviewed by black interviewers said they preferred a black caseworker, and 45 percent had no preference or preferred a white caseworker. The basis for respondents' preference for a black caseworker, other factors being equal, was that a black interviewer was more likely to be interested in their problems, less likely to talk down to them or make them feel worthless, more likely to give them a feeling of hope, and more likely to know the meaning of poverty.

A second question, which introduced the factor of competence, asked respondents to state their preference for a black or white worker if the white worker was better qualified. A large percentage of those who preferred "equally good" black caseworkers preferred white caseworkers if their qualifications were better. Competence, then, proved to be more important than race in determining black respondents' caseworker preferences.

Barrett's and Perlmutter's study (1972) of black clients' responses to black and white counselors at the Philadelphia Opportunities Industrialization Center—which offers training, placement, and vocational guidance services—supports Brieland's findings. Although black clients preferred black counselors in the abstract (the interviewers in the study were black), actual ongoing client-counselor contact indicated that competence was a more crucial and significant variable than race. However, Barrett and Perlmutter suggest that the importance of matching may be greater when the problems discussed focus on personal concerns rather than on concrete services and when the client initially contacts the agency.

Conclusion

After making the usual cautious provisos about the contradictory nature of the findings, the tentativeness of conclusions, the deficiencies in methodology, the dangers of extrapolation, and so forth, what do all these findings seem to say? They seem to say that although nonwhite workers may be necessary for nonwhite clients in some instances and therapeutically desirable in others, white workers can work and have worked effectively with nonwhite clients. They seem to say that although race is important, the nature of the interpersonal relationship established between two people is more important than skin color and that although there are disadvantages to racially mixed worker-client contacts, there are special advantages. Conversely, there are special advantages to racial similarity and there are countervailing disadvantages. In other words, the problem is not as clear-cut as might be supposed.

Not only is the situation equivocal, it is complex. To talk in terms of white and non-white is to simplify dichotomously a variegated situation that includes many kinds of whites and nonwhites. For example, interview interaction with a lower-class black male militant is quite different from interview interaction with a middle-class female black integrationist.

Findings like the ones reviewed here are understandably resisted, resented, and likely to be rejected because of the political implications that can be drawn from them. Nonwhite community leaders, in fighting for control of social service institutions in their communities, point to the special advantages to community residents of nonwhite staff and administration. Some studies tend to suggest that the need for nonwhite staff and administration is not that urgent. However, this ignores the current underrepresentation in social agencies of nonwhite workers and administrators, the clear preference of some nonwhite clients for a worker of similar racial background, the fact that many clients need workers of similar racial background as sources of identification for change, and the fact that although white workers may be able to understand and empathize with the nonwhite experience, nonwhite workers achieve this sooner, more thoroughly, and at less cost to the relationship.

Selected annotated bibliography

Arcaya, Jose. "The Multiple Realities Inherent in Probation Counseling," *Federal Probation* 37:4 (December 1973), pp. 58–63.

Arcaya analyzes the multiple realities of the probation officer–probationer relationship in four areas—relevant features in the situation, conflicts, ways the conflicts are handled, and suggested approaches to mitigate the conflicts. The mitigating approaches include active listening, responsive talking, and contextualization of language.

Benjamin, Alfred. *The Helping Interview.* New York: Houghton, Mifflin, 1969.

This small paperback is a profoundly simple treatment of the helping interview that social workers use everyday. It treats the interview as a serious and purposeful conversation between two people. Our students tell us that they find this one of the most helpful books as they begin fieldwork.

Brown, Robert A. "Feedback in Family Interviewing," *Social Work* 18:5 (September 1973), pp. 52–59.

Descriptive study of the use of feedback; feedback as sanctioned by theories of practice is widely used by social workers but frequently in an undisciplined manner. More conscious use of feedback as a technique can bring the worker and client closer together.

Duncan, Starkey, Jr. "Nonverbal Communication," *Psychological Bulletin* 72:2 (1969), pp. 118–37.

Duncan reviews research concerning the role of nonlanguage behaviors in communication.

Garrett, Annette. *Interviewing: Its Principles and Methods,* 2d ed., revised by Elinor P. Zaki and Margaret M. Mangold, New York: Family Service Association of America, 1972.

This is a revision of a classic in social work literature. Much of the revision lies in the updating of the case examples. The book has two sections, the first dealing with the art of interviewing and the second consisting of case examples.

Hartman, Henry L. "Interviewing Techniques in Probation and Parole," *Federal Probation* 27:1–4 (March, June, September, and December 1968).

This series of four articles analyzes steps a probation worker might take to establish a relationship and maximize communication with clients in an authority setting.

Ittelson, William, and Cantril, Hadley. "Perception: A Transactional Approach," in Floyd Matson and Ashley Montagu (Eds.), *The Hu-* *man Dialogue,* New York: Free Press, 1967, pp. 207–213.

The three major characteristics of perception are that it occurs as a total transaction, that it is unique, and that it is as much an externalization as an internalization.

Johnston, Norman. "Sources of Distortion and Deception in Prison Interviewing," *Federal Probation* 20:1 (January 1956), pp. 43–48.

The general attitudes of the prison community, the dehumanizing process of reporting for an interview, the frequent officiousness of the interviewers, the emotionally unrewarding nature of the prison environment, and the cultural gap between the professionals and the inmates are identified as variables which may create distortion and deception in information secured by professionals from inmates in a prison setting.

Kadushin, Alfred. *The Social Work Interview.* New York: Columbia University Press, 1972.

This book describes the general art of interviewing as it is practiced by social workers in agencies. It deals with the general definition and purpose of the social work interview, analyzes the interview in terms of its elements, and introduces the special factors of class, race, sex, and age for consideration.

Mullen, Edward. "Casework Communication," *Social Casework* 49:9 (December 1968), pp. 546–551.

Mullen reports the results of a research study using a typology of casework responses developed by Hollis and summarizes other research.

Payne, Stanley. *The Art of Asking Questions.* Princeton, N.J.: Princeton University Press, 1951.

Payne describes the formulation of various kinds of questions in reference to the development of questionnaires. Chapter 3, which deals with the open-ended question, offers useful suggestions for the interviewer.

Pfouts, Jane H., and Rader, Gordon H. "Influence of Interviewer Characteristics on the Interview," *Social Casework* 43:10 (December 1962), pp. 548–552.

This is a study of diagnostic interviews conducted with 71 patients by 31 fourth-year medical students as part of their rotating psychiatric clerkship at the University of North Carolina Medical School. The most significant finding was that regardless of the social class or the age of patients, they tended to equate warmth of the doctor with self-assurance, sensitivity, and competence. Patients tended to rate highest the students whose judgment and understanding they felt they could trust and whose actions suggested that they could help them do something about their problems.

Rich, John. *Interviewing Children and Adolescents.* New York: St. Martin's Press, 1968.

This is a practical guide to interviewing skills which are helpful in working with children and youth.

Rosen, Aaron and Lieberman, Dina. "The Experimental Evaluation of Interview Performance of Social Workers," *Social Service Review* 46:3 (September 1972), pp. 395–412.

This is an experimental study of trained (MSW) and untrained (non-MSW) social workers in two public welfare agencies. The interviewer was simulated by an actress. Interview performance was evaluated in relation to stimulus-response congruence and content relevance, both aggressive and compliant clients were represented.

Schubert, Margaret. *Interviewing in Social Work Practice.* New York: Council on Social Work Education, 1971.

Schubert's brief monograph, written for beginning students, covers various aspects of interviewing pertinent to the social work interview and gives insights into the techniques used in applying the interview method.

Stewart, John (Ed.). *Bridges Not Walls: A Book about Interpersonal Communication.* Reading, Mass.: Addison-Wesley, 1973.

This collection of articles on communication is based primarily on dialogical philosophy and humanistic psychology. It contains articles by Rogers, Kelly, Reusch, and Scheflen, among others and deals, among other things, with empathetic listening, self-perception, perception of others, and verbal codes.

Truax, Charles B., and Carkhall, Robert. "Concreteness: A Neglected Variable in Research in Psychotherapy," *Journal of Clinical Psychology* 20:2 (April 1964), pp. 264–267.

Truax and Carkhall's research report suggests that concreteness defined as specificity of expression correlates highly with three measures of the therapeutic process. The concreteness of the therapist's expressions seems to ensure emotional proximity between client and therapist, increases the accuracy of the therapist's responses, and encourages specificity on the part of the client.

Tessler, Richard C., and Polansky, Norman A. "Perceived Similarity: A Paradox in Interviewing," *Social Work* 20:5 (September 1975), pp. 359–362.

Simulation as used with a group of college students to experimentally test interviewees' perceived similarity with interviewer and verbal accessibility is the focus of this article. The commonsense view that the interviewees will be more verbal with interviewers they perceive as similar to them was not supported. Rather, the condition of dissimilarity lead to greater verbal accessibility. A possible explanation for this finding is that persons may be threatened by too much closeness and may prefer to reveal themselves from a distance.

CHAPTER 7

Problem solving: A model for social work practice

The last two chapters discussed the need for social workers to have well-developed capacities in relating to and communicating with others. Such capacities are ways of bridging distances between ourselves and others. They are ways of achieving understanding between the client system and the practitioner, and of communicating that understanding. However, as we stated in the earlier chapters, relationship and understanding do not develop just because two bodies, one called the worker and the other, the client, find themselves in a common enclosed space. Relationship, understanding, and a freedom of communication develop as practitioner and client system work together toward some purpose. Thus, considered in relation to the practitioner's interaction with the client system, social work process can be considered in terms of cooperation—resting on the ability of each to relate and communicate with the other—between the clients (or client system) who has available information about what (1) brings them in contact with the social work practitioner and (2) what they expect of this contact, and the social worker who has at hand (*a*) a body of information about a variety of problems, (*b*) available resources that may be available to bring to bear on the problem, (*c*) certain methods and skills of helping and (*d*) an orderly way of proceeding (a pattern of thinking if you will) that move client and worker toward a problem solution. This orderly way of proceeding increases the probability of appropriate selection and utilization of (1) what the client brings to the situation and (2) the practitioner's knowledge and information toward the end of improving the client's ability to realize aspirations and values.

These comments relate to a framework called the "problem-solving model." This model rests on the belief that for anyone or for any social system effective movement toward purposive change, or altering something that one wishes to alter, rests on the ability of the system, or of the professional helper, to engage in rational goal-directed thinking and to divide this cognitive activity into sequential stages. Each stage involves a particular kind of work aimed at the particular goal of that stage. The way the work on this phase is done will determine the effectiveness with which work on the next stage can go forward. Since this is the process by which each person's ego solves the inevitable problems of life or reaches the necessary decisions as to alternatives to be selected, the worker who follows this model is following a life model of human growth and development. This means that the worker is not involved in treating an illness, or in bringing about a cure for client troubles, but rather is joining the forward motion of the client system and is, along with helping the client, strengthening the client's capacity to cope more effectively with life.

DEWEY AND PROBLEM SOLVING

The ancestor to problem solving is typically identified to be *How We Think,* a volume written by John Dewey in 1933, in which he attempted to describe the thought processes of a human being when confronted with a problem. In doing so, Dewey was interested in clarifying reflective or rational thinking, goal-directed thinking, or problem solving. According to Dewey, problem-solving behavior is based on reflective thought that begins with a feeling of perplexity, doubt, or confusion. The person wants to eliminate the difficulty or solve the puzzle, but in order to do this effectively one must follow a rational procedure. If one fails to do so, one can act uncritically or impulsively, leaping to inappropriate conclusions, mistaking the nature of the problem, becoming involved in searching for the answer to the wrong problem, or making a number of other errors. Any one of these behaviors may very well compromise the capacity to cope with the situation and undoubtedly makes it likely that the problem will remain unsolved.

Dewey held that effective problem solving demands the active pursuit of a set of procedural steps in a well-defined and orderly sequence. Dewey referred to these steps as the "five phases of reflective thinking,'" and they include recognizing the difficulty; defining or specifying the difficulty; raising suggestions for possible solutions and rationally exploring the suggestions, which includes data collection; selecting an optimal solution from among many proposals; and carrying out the solution. Since Dewey, many persons, working in various areas of endeavor, have come to recognize that when one engages in investigation and problem solving, there is a preferred model for orderly thought and action that can be laid out in progressive steps and pointed toward the reaching of a solution, and that the conscientious implementation of such a model materially increases the likelihood that one's objectives can be achieved.

It has been recognized that Dewey's list of five successive phases can be broken down into finer incremental steps and that orderly precision follows when this is done. Further, it has been recognized that Dewey's list failed to include the terminal aspects of problem solving—the evaluation of the effectiveness of the attempted solution, and the use of feedback loops (see Chapter 2) into the process, by which modifications can be made in the procedures employed even as one is engaged in employing them. In social work literature one will find a number of models which divide the activities of a social worker into sequential phases, each phase characterized by some broad goal of its own which must be accomplished before the worker moves on to complete the next phase.

In the early 1940s a mathematics professor, George Polya (1957), developed a model to help mathematics instructors to teach mathematical problem solving, but his aim really went beyond that. He intended that the book should be used as a guide by all problem solvers. He presented a four phase model: (1) understanding the problem including understanding the problem situation, the goal of the problem solver, and the conditions for solving the problem; (2) devising a plan by which the goal could be attained; (3) carrying out the plan; and (4) evaluation of the plan, its implementation, and the results.

The scientific method itself may also be considered a model of problem solving, and other frameworks have been developed by other authors in the behavioral sciences. Notable among these efforts is the work of Bennis, Benne, and Chin (1969) in their development of strategies of effecting change in human systems. These authors, however, see the problem-solving process as a normative reeducative approach to change. It is the authors' position that the formulation is broader than that.

PROBLEM SOLVING IN SOCIAL WORK

We are neither the first nor only people in social work to have conceptualized social work practice within this type of framework. In social work Helen Harris Perlman must be considered the originator of the "problem-solving framework." Her principal work, *Social Casework: A Problem-Solving Process,* was published in 1957 and has had tremendous impact on social work thinking. She has written extensively, and readers will remember our use of some of her formulations on role in earlier chapters. Both Perlman and the present authors have based their formulations on constructs from ego psychology and on Dewey's work on principles of problem solving. One of the principal differences in the knowledge base utilized by Perlman from that used by the present authors is the use of systems theory as a foundation in the present text. This results in our extending of problem-solving methods to groups, organizations, and communities and in our broadening our model to include more emphasis than one finds in Perlman's work on transactions with and change in other social systems. Further Perlman puts particular emphasis on the worker's primary responsibility for thinking about the facts and for the other activities of diagnosis and planning. While we believe with Perlman that the worker carries responsibility to do this hard responsible "head work," we also believe that the worker must test out such thinking with the client and that there is a shared responsibility between worker and client for every phase of problem-solving work, including especially the assessment/decision-making phase. We see the worker engaging in broader array of helper roles than does Perlman. She primarily emphasizes the enabler role of the worker and does not distinguish as sharply as we do between the various stages of the process. She says that treatment begins with the first glance between worker and client, although she puts considerable emphasis on the fact that the work between worker and client cannot proceed until the client has moved from role of the applicant to that of client and thus our notions coincide with hers.

In social work literature one will find a number of other authors writing about problem solving who divide the activities of a social worker into sequential phases, each phase characterized by some broad goal of its own and requiring specific social work skills, which must be accomplished before moving on to complete the next phase. In general such models demand that the worker be successively involved with (1) recognition or definition of the problem and engagement with the client system, (2) goal setting, (3) data collection,

(4) assessment of the situation and the planning of action, (5) intervention, or the carrying out of action, (6) evaluation, and (7) termination. Included in this chapter is an article by Spitz and Welsch that discusses a model of problem solving in school social work (see Reading 7–1). They differ somewhat from the authors' model in many of the same dimensions as Perlman does. Their primary difference is in the responsibility they place with the worker to control the process.

PROBLEM SOLVING AND THE PRACTITIONER'S RESPONSIBILITY

Our own outline of such a model will be presented at the end of the discussion and will be discussed in the following chapters. But first, we wish to speak to another important matter in this business of problem solving in social work. While we believe that such a process is orderly, that it is sequential, and that any one phase depends on the successful completion of the preceding phase, we also feel that any linear sequencing of tasks is an oversimplification of the process. In any given situation the worker may be operating in more than one phase at a time. In spite of the fact that the phases follow each other in some rough order, one phase does not wait upon the completion of another before it begins. Problem solving in social work probably proceeds, not linearly, but by a kind of spiral process in which action does not always wait upon the completion of assessment, and assessment often begins before data collection is complete. In fact, one often becomes aware that one has not collected enough facts, or the proper facts, only after one begins the process of trying to put all one knows together in some sort of summing-up process. Also, when the worker and the client system begin to take action toward some solution of the problem, it might well be discovered that the worker is proceeding on the wrong problem and must start all over again. However, in this case, one begins again with the distinct advantage of having some knowledge and some observations and some working relationships that one did not have before.

We can well understand Perlman's statement about treatment beginning with the first glance between client and worker. However, it might be phrased somewhat differently. We would say that the beginning of the relationship comes with that first glance. And, as the problem-solving work progresses through the various phases, this beginning relationship will also change, perhaps, in a progressive developmental way and perhaps radically and abruptly. The beginning of work together on an identified problem still is to come, but it will be inevitably affected by that first glance. Thus it is important as we move through the sequence of the phases of the model to remember that it is not a simple linear process.

The fact that the problem-solving process is a squirming, wriggling, alive business which may be grasped as an intellectual concept that concerns what goes on in the worker's head but also vitally concerns the social reality between the worker, the client, and all the interrelated systems of which the worker and the client are a part, makes it a difficult model to carry out in practice. All parts of the model may be present at any one time in a way that may obscure for the ordinary viewer, and often for the worker as well, the fact that there is "rhyme and reason" in what is being done. But it is the worker's business to know, in general, what phase is the primary focus of coming together with the client, and it is the worker's business to check out constantly to see that all phases are dealt with. Failures in helping stem as often from the worker's impulsive leap to some action from what is seen at the moment as the problem, with no pause for thought and consultation in between as from the worker's inability to engage in a helping relationship. In fact, these two parts of the helping process (the capacity to relate to and communicate with others and problem-solving efforts) are so firmly interwoven that we often do not pause to see them as separate things.

The problem-solving process itself, in and of itself, is the process by which worker and client decide (1) what the problem or question is that they wish to work on; (2) what the desired outcome of this work is; (3) how to conceptualize what it is that results in the persistence of the problem in spite of the fact that the client wants something changed or altered; (4) what procedures should be undertaken to change the situation; (5) what specific actions are to be undertaken to implement the procedures; and (6) how the actions have worked out.

For the worker, the use of the process involves considerable skill and the cultivated capacity to keep a clear head as well as an understanding heart. However, the problem-solving framework gives the worker no specific guides to specific procedures. It does not promise that if one does this type of thinking and exploring one will come out with *the* (or with *this*) answer. It promises rather that one must do this type of thinking and exploring, consciously and knowingly, in about this order if one wants to increase the probability of coming out with *an effective answer* that is in the direction of the client's goals. What the answer is, specifically, will depend on (1) what the question is, specifically, (2) what the client wants, specifically, and (3) what the worker and the client can bring to the process in terms of knowledge, understanding, resources, and capacity for joint action.

Thus there are some very significant requirements that relate to workers' use of the model and of workers' approach to clients. There may be a tendency to think that since the model requires a lot of rational headwork on the part of the worker that it is appropriate only for clients who come with a well-developed ability to weigh and measure alternative courses of action. Nothing could be further from the truth. This burden for rational headwork lies with the worker, not the client. In fact, this way of working has been used successfully by the authors with families who had been judged by other community helping facilities—schools, mental health clinics, and social agencies to be totally unreachable and beyond help by any professional.

The key to the use of this treatment model with clients who appear to have no coping skills, or no ability to trust others, is to begin, just as the model indicates, with the problem *as seen by the client* at whatever level the client may present it. Workers run into great difficulty when they are so focused on their own definition of the problem, or their concern with client capacity, or with the real problem or cause of the problem, that they cannot hear the client. Also, workers often appear totally unaware as they begin on how they differ with the client as to the understanding of the problem. Not only can there be no use of this model at all, there can be no helpful use of any model, without the active engagement of the client, and that engagement must be around concerns congruent with clients' expectations and problem definition (see the discussion on basic role theory in Chapter 3). Also workers often find it difficult to accept the pace of the clients' early movement and the problems that often are involved in human change.

People who have little ability to weigh and measure alternative courses of action, and who have no reason to trust the help that the worker offers, will neither express their problems in the worker's terms nor will they express their goals in terms of learning to live a more productive life. Rather they express their problems in terms of basic survival needs. What is more important? The worker who understands the problem-solving process in terms of the model will see such expression of concrete needs as the place to begin. Such workers can then join with the client in setting the goals at this level—to secure necessary repairs on the refrigerator or to find a way to get a new stove. These are worthy goals in that *they do help to make the client's life more satisfying, or at least less hard,* and they are the clients' goals. Such problems and goals are the stuff of the beginning engagement. But for the worker there may also be the concern of using this problem and its solution as a way of building some trust and sense of success that can be used to move on to other problems and other goals, if there are others. The problem many people have in using the model is that they assume that the problem has to be a *basic problem in living from their perspective* rather than something that the client identifies as an important need.

Wendell Johnson's article (1951, pp. 176–177) discusses these symptoms and basic causes. Perhaps if the reader could substitute "presenting problem" meaning "the problem the client brings" for Johnson's word "symptom," it would be possible to understand why workers often have difficulty with the problem-solving model that says in essence that they *must start* with where the client is—which is usually not with "cause" but with relief of the symptom.

> Let us make this very absurd. What I am trying to say is that one of the things we do which tends to keep us from understanding handicapped children and adults better is that we do not spend enough time trying to appreciate the symptoms, as we call them. To them, they are not symptoms so much as they are causes of frustration and misery. They want to have everything possible done to alleviate or remove the symptoms. They want to work on the so-called causes, too, of course. But in the meantime, they are in pain or distress.
>
> Now, as I suggested, let us make the situation very absurd. Suppose that we were out in the woods and we came upon a man who had accidentally got his foot caught in a bear trap. There he is, howling and carrying on frightfully, weeping and straining in a most profane fashion. Then two psychologists come by and one of them wants to give the man the Rorschach test and an intelligence test and take a case history. The other psychologist, however, has undergone a different kind of training; and he says, "No let's start intensive psychoanalysis right now." So, they talk it over. They have their differences, of course, but they agree eventually that what this man in the bear trap needs is obviously psychotherapy. If he would just be trained to be a more mature individual; if he could have the release therapy he needs; if he would undergo the needed catharsis, achieve the necessary insight, and work through the essential abreaction, he would develop more maturity, he would understand the difficulty he is having, and he would then be able to solve his problem himself. Obviously, the psychologists agree, that is the only sound way to deal with the poor fellow.

Suddenly, however, a farmer comes by and lets the man out of the bear trap. To the utter amazement of the psychologists, the man's behavior changes greatly and quickly. Besides, he seems to take a great liking to the farmer, and goes off with him, evidently to have a cup of coffee.

The basic principle illustrated by this absurd example is that psychotherapy is more beneficial when it is carried on under optimal conditions. And one way to prepare optimal conditions for psychotherapy, or for classroom teaching, for that matter, or for any kind of special instruction, is to do everything possible first—or as you go along—to relieve any distressing symptoms that may be distracting the individual you are trying to help. If the symptoms make a difference to the individual, if they are producing impaired social relationships, impaired self-evaluations, impaired parent-child relationships, or tantrums, or anxiety—then clearly anything that can be done directly, by means of literal or figurative aspirin, to relieve the symptoms will be all to the good in helping to bring about favorable conditions for therapy.

We would like the reader to look at an actual situation of a woman who was seen as unable to use any type of social work help and at her reactions to the problem-solving approach.

Mr. and Mrs. S. had been known extensively to have visited at least 20 social service agencies over a 15-year period. Mrs. S. had three marriages, the first forced by her becoming pregnant while she was in high school. She never lived with her first husband. Her second husband was a feeble-minded ward of the state. She had four children by him, three of whom were placed in an institution for the retarded. She became involved with Mr. S. while still married to her second husband, her first child by Mr. S. arriving four months after their marriage. Mrs. S. has shown other signs of instability, having attempted suicide twice. She was reported as sexually promiscuous between marriages.

Mr. S. had been known to DVA since his army discharge as a psychoneurotic. Mr. S. was reportedly alcoholic. There had been numerous agency contracts around reports of a number of episodes of physical abuse of Mrs. S. and the children by Mr. S.

Also there had been a number of complaints of neglect of the children. These appear to have originated from Mrs. S.'s relatives, her former husband and his relatives, the school nurse, the minister, and neighbors. Workers found it difficult to work with Mrs. S. since when cornered by the worker, she was superficially cooperative. She also avoided workers whenever possible. If an appointment was made in advance, she was never home. There was great reluctance on part of agencies to open the case as all indications were that this woman could not use help. However, the county welfare board stated that there was no way they could work with the woman and the only alternatives were for us to try, or for them to attempt to get a court order to remove the children. We accepted the case.

After the case was accepted, the assigned worker attempted to reach Mrs. S. Whenever she found Mrs. S. home, she was denied admittance to the house for many reasons such as her husband was asleep, and so on. The worker did not press to come in as she did not believe in entering a home for an interview without an appointment. The worker had gone to the house to try to make an appointment because the family did not have a telephone and had not answered letters. Repeated appointments for either office or home visits were broken by Mrs. S. not appearing or not being home. Finally, in July, Mrs. S. came to the office asking for help with an immediate crisis, which is so often the only time the Mrs. Ss of the world are seen. Her AFDC grant had been cut off because she had broken so many appointments with the worker and had refused to tell the agency where she was living. She was eight months pregnant and worried about the pain she was having. She had had no medical attention, her husband had left her, and she had returned to live with her mother after having been evicted from the apartment. Her mother was threatening to make her get out if she did not contribute some money to the household. In recounting her problems she threw in the fact that the school had raised questions about accepting her oldest daughter back at the opening of the school year without some kind of psychiatric help which had been refused earlier.

The worker began with Mrs. S.'s most pressing problems: the need of the reestablishment of AFDC and the securing of medical care. The goals were to get economic support reestablished and secure medical care. Whether it would have been possible for the worker to have maintained contact with Mrs. S. long enough to have established some agreement to work together on problems she had identified in her first approach to the worker, such as a place to live, the children's behavior, and her problems with the welfare board, if childbirth and complications had not kept her in the hospital for a considerable period of time, it is not known. The worker used this time to consider with Mrs. S. her problems, what she wanted from life (initially Mrs. S. said nothing but to be left alone), and how she thought the worker could help. The worker also acted as an advocate for Mrs. S. with the welfare board and helped to find her a rather small, cramped apartment. There is not enough space here to detail the methods used by the worker except to say that they followed the model presented in this text, the worker acting as enabler, broker, advocate, and teacher for Mrs. S. in relation to problems identified by Mrs. S. However, two brief recordings are reproduced in which Mrs. S. attempted, for her own and the worker's learning, to evaluate what had been achieved on her problems.

12–8 Visit to Mrs. S. by appointment. (10 months after case opening)

I had neglected to state in recording of 12–7 that in this telephone conversation I suggested to Mrs. S. that we review "where we had got to" to date, and Mrs. S. had accepted this.

On my arrival for the interview, Mrs. S. started right in on pointing out her new apartment which has a large living room, kitchen, and two bedrooms, and will permit George to have his own room where he can be and later on joined by Peter. Mrs. S. had made the move to the new apartment on her own and had deliberately made the decision without advance consultation with her mother, which she used to always do, or with myself. She felt this was something of a gain in itself since she used to have so much trouble making decisions.

Mrs. S. also mentioned that the children are getting more attention than they used to. In fact, she feels they may be getting too much attention, particularly Peter whom she probably spoils. I didn't at this point pick up on this, but inquired in what other ways did Mrs. S. feel that changes had occurred.

Mrs. S. said that she feels more secure within herself. This is the first time she has ever had her own place. When her marriages failed in the past, she always went back to mother.

I raised the question with Mrs. S. of how *she felt she had been able to change this*. Mrs. S. mentioned first the fact that she has nice neighbors. They are friendly, cooperate with her, and she gets a real feeling of support from them. For example, the family across the hall, who have a car, take her shopping in order to permit her to buy her things at a supermarket, since there is no supermarket in the immediate area.

Along this same line Mrs. S. brought up the fact that she has had some activity with the school. Mrs. S. laughingly commented "I'm all tangled up with the school around planning parties." The school had asked the assistance of some parents to act as "party room mothers" to help look after the children. Mrs. S. and a neighbor Mrs. K. had gone to the school to act in this capacity and have been asked by the school to recruit more mothers to act in this capacity and Mrs. S. has been on the phone a lot about this. While it is a chore and a nuisance, she enjoys it, and she has a lot of respect for the school principal. It makes her feel good to know the school trusts her with such a job.

In response to my further questions as to why Mrs. S. feels she is functioning differently, Mrs. S. mentioned her increased self-confidence. She related this to her contact with us and our work with welfare, since the two agencies have demonstrated a lot of confidence in her. She said, "You must have this confidence in me or you wouldn't have spent as much time helping me as you did." This, Mrs. S. states, has raised her own self-confidence and her feeling of being able to do things. She also used to lie awake at night worrying about whether her ADC check was going to come. Now she doesn't do this, as she understands much more about the rules of welfare. She described also, the relation with me as having a feeling of having someone available to her if things did go wrong or get difficult.

Mrs. S. also brought up some negatives. She said for one thing thinking about herself makes her feel like "she is peeking inside other people." At times it makes her edgy and nervous. She sees other people making the same mistakes and having the same problems she did. This sometimes makes her uncomfortable. Then she either wants to leave such people or doesn't feel relaxed with them.

Last visit 2–15: (1 year and 11 months after opening)

In this termination interview, Mrs. S. summed up her feelings as follows:

"We've changed in the fact that we are more settled, more of a family instead of five people. Each is different, that is to be expected, but we are more united, kind of. That's the biggest change, more secure in ourselves as a family. Mary and George and I each worried about ourselves instead of all of us. Now it isn't so much a personal worry as how is this family going to get along. We think of the good of the family rather than for each one. It's not so much what you've said and done as what you've listened to. I could talk things over and sort 'em out, kind of. I could bring up things that I wouldn't ordinarily be able to tell people. If I told these things to others, they would get all mixed up in my problem, but you didn't.

I think, too, I've found out there is always a reason for the way welfare acts. And if I try I can usually find out what it is. And the school is so much help to me with Josie. They trust me."

Entry for record: (2 years and 3 months after opening)

5–17. Call from school staff social worker to report on the family. The school has been asking "What kind of social work did Mrs. S. receive?" There has been remarkable change in the children. Physical care greatly improved. Mary is described as "top girl in her class." Josie has made a great deal of progress in relating to other children. School wondering what has happened to account for the change.

The school social worker and I agreed that it is a cumulation of things over two years rather than anything recent and dramatic.

Later telephoned Mrs. S. and relayed the school's message. She was very pleased and said that she herself notices a big change in Josie. Application is pending for Josie's admission to a school for retarded children.

Entry for record (last entry—two years and five months after opening)

9–11. Mrs. S. called to say Josie enrolled at the school for retarded and enjoying the experience. She is very tired when she gets home. She leaves the home readily, however, in the mornings, much to the surprise of Mrs. S. Things are going well for the whole family.

Two articles that relate to problem solving with larger social systems have been reproduced in this chapter—one dealing with neighborhood and community groups and one with a whole social system. Certainly the reader would not have seen either the "C" street network or the Nobleteens as composed of what might be called well "integrated" and "rationally oriented" people. Yet, these groups responded with growth and strength to the offer of help from social workers who saw themselves as advisors to a neighborhood and a group on self-help projects—in other words, on *problems defined by the members of the systems* that the workers approached. The other article on identity and change puts the same emphasis on helping a society define its problems and its goals as a way of preventing dependency and as a way of assuring the integrity of the culture of the people one wants to help. These two articles are good examples of the considerations that go into the use of the problem-solving model with social systems larger than the individual or the family.

Generally, in carrying out the action plan with client systems, the worker will be involved in four primary activities: (1) provision of needed resources which may involve roles of broker and advocate (among others) and will undoubtedly require work with a target system that is different from the client system and a broad action system; (2) change in transactions between client system and other systems, which, in addition to the roles and systems mentioned earlier, may involve the worker in the role of enabler and teacher with the client system; (3) the problem-solving work which will involve the worker primarily in teaching and enabling a client system to work in this way; and (4) the use of the therapeutic relationship for change in the internal interaction of the client system which calls for roles of enabler, teacher, and therapist.

Although there are other frameworks for social work practice, the authors like the problem-solving framework for a number of reasons:

1. No assumptions as to the cause, nature, or location of the problem are built into the model itself. Thus the framework allows the problem to be defined as lying within the client system, as lying within the other systems with which the client system has transactions, as lying in some lack in social resources that should be supplied by the environment, or as lying in transactions among these factors.

2. The framework is based on a belief in the growth potential for all human systems and thus fits both social work's belief in human struggles toward growth and rests on the knowledge borrowed from systems theory and ego pyschology.

3   At the level of foundation knowledge, the framework is based on selected

constructs from ego psychology, systems theory, role theory, communication theory, and group dynamics—all of which depart from the personal deficit theory and put emphasis on social transaction. At the level of practice theory, the model is not based on any one theoretical orientation and thus allows the worker and client to agree on any method of help appropriate to the problem, the problem location, the goals, the client system, and the worker's competence and resources.

4. The framework gives a prominent spot to consideration of client goals, or goals of other social systems, with which one is working. This is congruent with social work values of the importance of the individual, of individuals' differences, and of self-determination and with systems theory, role theory, and ego psychology.

5. The way the problem is defined and the goal is established determines which data are relevant and where the emphasis and direction of inquiry will lie. This allows for data collection that is relevant, salient, and individualized. It further requires that intervention in the client's life be kept at a minimum.

6. The framework is congruent with the function and purpose of the social work profession in that it supports the client's right to personal definition of the problem and, in case the worker has a different view, demands that some negotiation be undertaken in defining the problem-to-be-worked (which simply means that worker and client must agree on what they are going to undertake together). The framework also recognizes the importance of the purposes of the client system.

7. In addition to supplying a method applicable to a wide variety of situations and settings in which social work is practiced, and to different sizes and types of systems, the problem-solving framework demands that the tasks and activities of the social worker be stated at a very specific level and related to client goals. This seems to the authors to be a distinct advantage over frameworks that allow for a more abstract treatment plan.

THE CLIENT SYSTEM AND PROBLEM SOLVING

It is difficult to speak of what is required of the client apart from the workers' activities. As in any system, including the helping system of worker and client, the behavior of one element has tremendous impact on the actions of other elements. Thus we must start our discussion of what is required of the client by pointing out that we begin with what is required of the worker. To speak of the clients' requirements without recognizing that these requirements rest on the assumption that the worker is concerned and caring, able to communicate a desire to understand, and willing to start with the clients' presenting the problem has little meaning.

In our experience, individuals, families, or groups who were often held by earlier helping systems to be unreachable and beyond help could participate as partners in the problem-solving process once they understood that we (once we learned to listen) really wanted to know them as people and were willing to help them pursue their own goals. They could tell us something about goals they had for themselves that were impossible to achieve because changes were needed that they alone could not effect. And it was here that the problem-solving process began. In other words, this process demands the following of clients (1) that they be able to share with the worker information about something that they would like to have changed (2) in order to achieve something that is of value to them, and that (3) as the worker is able to demonstrate concern and competence to help with the exploration of this problem, clients are able to trust this concern enough (4) to allow the worker to continue to meet with them around this purpose. That is all that is demanded of the client system.

BASIC ASSUMPTIONS OF THE MODEL

This model does not in any way deny people's irrational and instinctive characteristics, but it accepts the findings of social scientists who have studied the social milieu of the mental hospital that even the most regressed psychotic patients are at least as responsive to changes in external reality as to their internal fantasies, that altering their external reality alters their ways of coping, and that "given a chance to participate in making decisions that affected their lives, inmates generally did so in a responsible manner and with constructive results for all concerned—professionals as well as themselves" (Lerner, 1972, p. 161). This model further accepts the view that social work processes are not a set of techniques by which experts who understand what "is really wrong," seek in their wisdom to improve, enlighten, plan for, or manipulate the client system. Rather, it sees social work processes as an attempt "by one human being with specialized knowledge, training, and a way of working to establish a genuinely meaningful, democratic, and collaborative relationship with another person or persons in order to put one's special knowledge and skills at the second person's (or group's) disposal for such use as can be made of it" (Lerner, 1972, p. 11). It recognizes that decisions about what individuals and groups of individuals should be, have, want, and do are cognitive decisions that involve rational and nonrational processes, perceptions of the describer, and the possible, and values, an area in which "every person is a legitimate expert for oneself and no person is a legitimate expert for others" (Lerner, 1972, p. 161). The model rests on the assumption that the given in each human being is a desire to be active in one's life—to exercise meaningful control of oneself for one's own purposes. Systems theory states that living systems are purposive, and we believe that practitioners are more effective when they start with the client's purposes and the obstacles to their achievement. This does not mean that one is naive about unconscious and irrational factors. It simply means that one starts with the rational with consciously expressed problems and goals.

PRESENTATION OF THE PROBLEM-SOLVING OUTLINE

At the end of this chapter you will find two outlines of the problem-solving model. The first outline is a short outline—just the bare bones of the model. It is included here so that the reader can grasp the essentials of the model before being confronted with all the details. The second is a longer outline, but in use it is a good deal simpler and a good deal more complex than it appears to be on these pages. It appears more complex than it is because one section, IV C, contains a suggested outline for data collection on five separate systems: the individual, family, group, organization, and community. No practitioner is likely to collect information about all five systems in any one situation. In fact, the practitioner is not expected to become fully and completely knowledgeable about all the factors listed under IV C for any one system. The factors are listed for consideration and selection and not for unthinking adoption.

This notion of selectivity is what makes for the complexity in the effective use of the model. Every part of it is designed to be used differentially by the worker—given the problem, the goal, and the client system. Effective use depends on the worker's capacity for deciding and selecting. The type of client system (individual, family, group, organization, or community) that is involved, the type of need, the lack or felt difficulty that has been identified, and the goals and expectations of the client system in interaction with the worker's knowledge of what is usually involved in such instances and the sensitivity to the individual differences in this instance, will determine the range of the data to be secured and how and when it is collected.

The phases of the problem-solving process and the skills demanded of the worker will be developed further in the next five chapters. However, the process and skills may be briefly outlined as follows:

I. Contact (or engagement) phase
    A. Activities
        1. Engagement and problem definition
        2. Definition of the problem for work
        3. Goal identification
        4. Negotiation of preliminary contract
        5. Exploration, investigation, data collection
    B. Skills needed
        1. Ability to use self in the interests of the client system or potential client system based on self-awareness and understanding of change agent system, resources, and possible target and action systems
        2. Listening, which includes not only listening with ears to words and with eyes to body language, but a total kind of perceptiveness which is best described as "listening with the third ear," attending carefully both physically and psychologically to client
        3. Communication of empathy, genuineness, trustworthiness, respect, and support
        4. Use of such techniques as paraphrasing, clarifying, perception checking, focusing, questioning, reflecting, informing, summarizing, confronting, interpreting, assuring, and reassuring
        5. Skill in use of a range of data collection methods, including not only interviewing skills listed earlier but also the use of records, test data, other written materials, and interviews or conferences with other than the client, observations, and documentary evidence
        6. Skill in using a theoretical knowledge base to guide the collection of salient and relevant information
II. Contract phase
    A. Activities
        1. Assessment and evaluation

       2. Formulation of an action plan
       3. Prognosis
  B. Skills needed
       1. All of skills listed in contact phase
       2. Ability to use a basic theory of the growth, development, functioning, malfunctioning, interactions, and transactions of human systems to assign meaning and to analyze the data collected
       3. Ability based on above, plus knowledge of problems, goals, and resources available, to prioritize and organize data in such a way as to suggest useful action
       4. Ability to generate a range of alternative plans with associated predictions as to probable success and cost
       5. Ability to use own judgment and client participation to select among alternatives
       6. Ability to put all the above together in a statement of actions to be taken, when and by, or with, what systems, within what time frame

III. Action phase
  A. Activities
       1. Carrying out plan
       2. Termination
       3. Evaluation
  B. Skills needed
       1. All skills listed in contact and contract phrases
       2. Skills in use of a range of social work methods as appropriate to roles necessary to carrying out the plan (see Chapters 11 to 16)
       3. Skills in a range of evaluative skills (see Chapter 13)
       4. Skills in ending and disengagement (see Chapter 14)

RECAPITULATION

In this chapter we have introduced the problem-solving model of social work practice as we have developed it. This model is based on five selected theories of human development, growth, and transactions between and among human systems: systems theory, communications theory, role theory, ego psychology, and notions of human diversity and difference. From these theories we have developed the following basic assumptions that are the base of our approach to problem solving: (1) people want to control their own lives and to feel competent to master the tasks they see as important; (2) motivation for change rests on some integration between a system's goals and its hope-discomfort balance; (3) the social worker is always engaged in attempting to change some interactions or transactions within or among systems; (4) systems are open and the input across their boundaries is critical for their growth and change; (5) while a system must have a steady state for its functioning, it is constantly in flux; and (6) all human systems are purposive and goal seeking.

This model is constructed on the notion that the change process has three basic phases, each of which has its own stages and own list of activities. Each stage demands some different skills as well as requiring some similar ones.

These phases are so wound together that they are hard to disentangle for study, but it is important that the worker is aware of the primary phase of the work in which they are engaged. We take the position that this model demands two primary things of the worker—a rational, orderly approach to the process, and the ability to meet the clients where they are. It further requires that the worker be aware of the six systems with which they may be involved and to have the skills necessary to use any system or attempt to change any system. The initial demand on the clients is that they be able to share their view of their trouble with the worker and that they allow the worker to maintain some contact with them long enough to demonstrate the worker's intentions toward them.

One final caution! The following problem-solving outline has been developed to be used selectively by the worker.

A LOOK FORWARD

We would suggest that if the readers have not already read the three articles included with this chapter that they do so now, and that they keep in mind during the reading that the articles are about work within different sizes and types of client systems. Also it should be noted that all articles speak of the worker's activity with other social systems that may be either target systems (need to be changed if the client system is to achieve its goal) or are part of the action system (worker uses them to supply resources needed by client system).

We are not, at this time, going to deal further with the details of the use of the problem-solving model. These details will be presented in later chapters. To conclude this chapter an outline for use of the problem-solving model is presented below.

OUTLINE OF PROBLEM-SOLVING MODEL—SHORT FORM

Contact phase

   I. Problem identification and definition
      A. Problem as client system sees it
      B. Problem as defined by significant systems with which client system is in interaction (family, school, community, others)
      C. Problem as worker sees it
      D. Problem-for-work (place of beginning together)
  II. Goal identification
      A. How does client see (or want) the problem to be worked out?
         1. Short-term goals
         2. Long-term goals
      B. What does client system think is needed for a solution of the problem?
      C. What does client system seek and/or expect from the agency as a means to a solution?
      D. What are worker's goals as to problem outcome?
      E. What does worker believe the service system can or should offer the client to reach these goals?

III. Preliminary contract
  A. Clarification of the realities and boundaries of service
  B. Disclosure of the nature of further work together
  C. Emergence of commitment or contract to proceed further in exploration and assessment in a manner that confirms the rights, expectations, and autonomy of the client system and grants the practitioner the right to intervene
IV. Exploration and investigation
  A. Motivation
    1. Discomfort
    2. Hope
  B. Opportunity
  C. Capacity of the client system

Contract phase

V. Assessment and evaluation
  A. If and how identified problems are related to needs of client system
  B. Analysis of the situation to identify the major factors operating in it
  C. Consideration of significant factors that contribute to the continuity of the need, lack, or difficulty
  D. Identification of the factors that appear most critical, definition of their interrelationships, and selection of those that can be worked with
  E. Identification of available resources, strengths, and motivations
  F. Selection and use of appropriate generalizations, principles, and concepts from the social work profession's body of knowledge
  G. Facts organized by ideas—ideas springing from knowledge and experience and subject to the governing aim of resolving the problem—professional judgment
VI. Formulation of a plan of action—a mutual guide to intervention
  A. Consideration and setting of a feasible goal
  B. Determination of appropriate *service* modality
  C. Focus of change efforts
  D. Role of the worker
  E. Consideration of forces either within or outside the client system that may impede the plan
  F. Consideration of the worker's knowledge and skill and of the time needed to implement the plan
VII. Prognosis—what confidence does the worker have in the success of the plan?

Action phase

VIII. Carrying out of the plan—specific as to point of intervention and assignment of tasks; resources and services to be utilized; methods by which they are to be used; who is to do what and when
IX. Termination
  A. Evaluation with client system of task accomplishment and meaning of process

B. Coping with ending and disengagement
C. Maintenance of gains
X. Evaluation
    A. Continuous process
    B. Was purpose accomplished?
    C. Were methods used appropriate?

OUTLINE OF PROBLEM-SOLVING MODEL—LONG FORM

Contact phase

I. Problem identification and definition
    A. Problem as the client system sees it
        1. Nature and location of need, lack, or difficulty
        2. Significance and meaning assigned by the client system to the need, lack, or difficulty
        3. Length of existence, previous occurrences, precipitating factors identified
        4. Conditions that bring client system and worker into interaction at this time
        5. Significance and meaning assigned by the client system to this interaction
    B. Problem as defined by significant systems with which the client system is in interaction (family, school, community, others)
        1. Nature and location of need, lack, or difficulty as seen by these systems
        2. Significance and meaning assigned by these systems to this need, lack, or difficulty
        3. Significance and meaning assigned by these systems to client's interaction with interventive agent
    C. Problem as the worker sees it
        1. Nature and location of need, lack, or difficulty
        2. Precipitating factors that the client system knows about and believes to be related and that the worker knows about and believes to be related
        3. Significance of conditions that bring client system and worker into interaction
        4. Nature and degree of effort that client system has put into coping with problem and client system's feeling about such efforts
    D. Problem-for-work (place of beginning together)
        1. Problem or part of problem that the client system feels is most important or a good beginning place
        2. Problem or part of problem that in the worker's judgment is most critical
        3. Problem or part of problem that in the worker's judgment can most readily yield to help
        4. Problem or part of problem that falls within the action parameters of the helping system

II. Goal identification
  A. How does the client system see (or want) the problem to be worked out?
    1. Short-term goals
    2. Long-term goals
  B. What does the client system think is needed for a solution of the problem?
    1. Concrete resources
    2. Specific assistance
    3. Advice, guidance, or counseling
  C. What does the client system seek and/or expect from the agency as a means to a solution?
    1. Specific assistance (concrete service to enable the client system to do something)
    2. Specific resources (concrete things)
    3. Change in the environment or other social systems
    4. Change in specific individuals
    5. Advice or instruction
    6. Support or reassurance
    7. Change in self
    8. Change in interaction between client system and others
  D. What are the worker's goals as to problem outcome?
    1. Long-term goals—are they different from client system's goals?
    2. Short-term goals—are they different from client system's goals?
    3. Does worker believe client system's goals to be realistic and acceptable?
    4. What facilitating and intermediate goals can be identified?
    5. Level of agreement between workers and client system on goals
  E. What does the worker believe the service system can or should offer the client to reach these goals?
    1. Specific assistance
    2. Specific resources
    3. Change in the environment or other social systems
    4. Advice or instruction
    5. Support or reassurance
    6. Change in self
    7. Change in interaction between client system and others
III. Preliminary contract
  A. Clarification of the realities and boundaries of service
  B. Disclosure of the nature of further work together
  C. Emergence of commitment or contract to proceed further in exploration and assessment in a manner that confirms the rights, expectations, and autonomy of the client system and grants the practitioner the right to intervene
IV. Exploration and investigation
  A. Motivation
    1. Discomfort
      a. Quantity and quality of discomfort

      b. Is discomfort generalized to total life situation?

      c. Is it attached to present situation?

      d. Is it focused on presenting problem?

      e. How much discomfort is attached to help-seeking or help-taking role?

  2. Hope

      a. Quality and quantity hope

      b. Is there a generalized quality of optimism based on evaluation of past successes in coping?

      c. Are past experiences separated from present situation with realistic perception of the differences involved?

      d. Does client system perceive means of dealing with problems that are acceptable and does client system perceive ways of access to such means?

      e. Gratifications from efforts toward solution including relationship to worker, other critical systems, and resources.

B. Opportunity

  1. What opportunities have their been for client system to experience success in coping?

  2. What feedback has been available to client system as to value of these successes?

  3. What opportunities have there been for client system to acquire knowledges and skills needed for coping with present problem?

  4. What part of present problem is a result of departure from average level of opportunity made available to individuals, families, and groups in present society?

  5. What opportunities for solution of problem does the worker see in the present situation?

      a. Socioeconomic

      b. Within individual, family, or group as primary system

      c. Within family, group, or community as secondary sources

      d. In worker's skill, service system, and community or outside resources

      e. Other

C. Capacity of the client system

  1. Factors in the study and evaluation of the individual in any system—dyad, family, small group, organization, or community

      a. Physical and intellectual

        (1) Presence of physical illness and/or disability

        (2) Appearance and energy level

        (3) Current and potential levels of intellectual functioning

        (4) How one sees one's world—translates surrounding events—perceptual abilities

        (5) Cause and effect reasoning—ability to focus

      b. Socioeconomic factors

        (1) Economic factors—income level, adequacy of subsistence, and way this effects lifestyle, sense of adequacy, and self-worth

        (2) Employment and attitudes about it

      (3) Racial, cultural, and ethnic identification—sense of identity and belonging

      (4) Religious identification and linkages to significant value systems, norms, and practices

  c. Personal values and goals

      (1) Presence or absence of congruence between values and their expression in action—meaning to individual

      (2) Congruence between individual's values and goals and the immediate systems with which the individual interacts

      (3) Congruence between individual's values and practitioners—meaning of this for interventive process

  d. Adaptive functioning and the response to present involvement

      (1) Manner in which individual presents self to others —grooming—appearance—posture

      (2) Emotional tone and changing levels

      (3) Communication style—verbal and nonverbal—level of ability to express appropriate emotion—to follow train of thought—factors of dissonance, confusion, and uncertainty

      (4) Symptoms or symptomatic behavior

      (5) Quality of relationship individual seeks to establish— direction—purposes and uses of such relationships for individual

      (6) Perception of self

      (7) Social roles that are assumed for ascribed—competence with which these roles are fulfilled

      (8) Relational behavior

         (*a*) Capacity for intimacy

         (*b*) Dependency-independency balance

         (*c*) Power and control conflicts

         (*d*) Exploitative

         (*e*) Openness

  e. Developmental factors

      (1) Role performance equated with life stage

      (2) How developmental experiences have been interpreted and used

      (3) How individual has dealt with past conflicts, tasks, and problems

      (4) Uniqueness of present problem in life experience

2. Factors in the study and evaluation of the family

  a. Family as a social system

      (1) The family as a responsive and contributing unit within the social network of other units

         (*a*) Family boundaries—permeability of rigidity

         (*b*) Nature of input from other social units

         (*c*) Extent to which family fits into cultural mold and expectations of larger system

         (*d*) Degree to which family is considered deviant

  (2) Roles of family members
    (*a*) Formal roles and role performance (father, child, and so on)
    (*b*) Informal roles and role performance (scapegoat, controller, follower, decision-maker)
    (*c*) Degree of family agreement on assignment of roles and their performance
    (*d*) Interrelationship of various roles—degree of "fit" within total family
  (3) Family rules
    (*a*) Family rules that foster stability and maintenance
    (*b*) Family rules that foster maladaptation
    (*c*) Conformation of rules to family's lifestyle
    (*d*) How rules are modified—respect for difference
  (4) Communication network
    (*a*) Way family communicates and provides information to members
    (*b*) Channels of communication—who speaks to whom
    (*c*) Quality of messages—clarity or ambiguity
 b. Developmental stage of the family
  (1) Chronological stage of family
  (2) Problems and adaptations of transition
  (3) Shifts in role responsibility over time
  (4) Ways and means of problem-solving at earlier stages
 c. Subsystems operating within the family
  (1) Function of family alliances in family stability
  (2) Conflict or support of other family subsystems and family as a whole
 d. Physical and emotional needs
  (1) At what level does family meet essential physical needs?
  (2) At what level does family meet social and emotional needs?
  (3) Resources within family to meet physical and emotional needs.
  (4) Disparities between individual needs and family's willingness or ability to meet them
 e. Goals, values, and aspirations
  (1) Extent to which family values are articulated and understood by all members
  (2) Do family values reflect resignation or compromise?
  (3) Extent to which family will permit pursuit of individual goals and values
 f. Socioeconomic factors (see list under IV C 1 b)
3. Factors in the study and evaluation of small groups
 a. Functional characteristics

(1) How group came to be
    (*a*) Natural group
    (*b*) Group formed by outside intervention

(2) Group's objectives
    (*a*) Affiliative, friendship, and social groups—mutuality and satisfaction derived from positive social interaction—tendency to avoid conflict and to stress identification
    (*b*) Task-oriented groups—created to achieve specific ends or resolve specific problems—emphasis on substantive rather than affective content
    (*c*) Personal change groups—emphasis on psychological and social content—dynamics of interpersonal behavior
    (*d*) Role enhancement and developmental groups—recreational, educational, and interest clusters—emphasis on rewards and on gratifications of participation, observation, learning, and improved performance

(3) How group relates to contiguous groups—how it perceives itself and is perceived as conforming to or departing from outside values

b. Structural factors

(1) How the members were selected and how new members gain entry

(2) Personality of individual members
    (*a*) Needs, motivations, personality patterns
    (*b*) Homogeneity-heterogeneity
    (*c*) Age of members
    (*d*) Factors of sex, social status, and culture (see appropriate entries under IV C 1 and IV C 2) that relate to functions and purposes
    (*e*) Subgroups, their reasons for being, and the purposes they serve
    (*f*) Nature and locus of authority and control
        (1) How leadership roles develop
        (2) How decisions are made

c. Interactional factors

(1) Norms, values, beliefs, and guiding values

(2) Quality, depth, and nature of relationships
    (*a*) Formal or informal
    (*b*) Cooperative or competitive
    (*c*) Freedom or constraint

(3) Degree to which members experience a sense of interdependence as expressed in individual commitments to the group's purposes, norms, and goals

4. Factors in the study and evaluation of organizations

a. Organization as a system with a mandate

    (1)   Organization's task—its mission within the social structure
- (*a*)   Clarity with which task is stated
- (*b*)   How task is perceived by organization's members

    (2)   Individual and group roles relevant to the task
- (*a*)   Which persons have the responsibility for carrying out the mandate of the organization?
- (*b*)   Elements and parameters of their roles
- (*c*)   Congruence between expected role behaviors and how these roles are seen by role bearers and others
- (*d*)   Are roles assumed, delegated, earned, or appointed?

    (3)   Location of organization within system of organizations
- (*a*)   Population group organization is designed to serve
- (*b*)   Kind of problem for which it is accountable
- (*c*)   Organization's isolation from or cohesion with other organizations
- (*d*)   Quality of interorganizational communication
- (*e*)   Way organization manages input from other systems

b. Culture of the organization

    (1)   Style with which organization operates
- (*a*)   Governing beliefs of members
- (*b*)   Expectations and attitudes of members
- (*c*)   Theories that govern and guide organizational action

    (2)   Modes of interaction with external groups or within organization itself
- (*a*)   Formal or informal
- (*b*)   Deference to authority—hierarchical
- (*c*)   Ritual
- (*d*)   Channels of communication

    (3)   Organization's technologies—resources, methods, and procedures in implementation of organization's task
- (*a*)   Jargon
- (*b*)   Routine and protocol
- (*c*)   Accepted and approved modes of communication

c. Competence of the organization

    (1)   Availability and adequacy of funds, physical plant, equipment

    (2)   Scope of authority vis-à-vis the community

    (3)   Special status, force, and control in relation to larger community

      (4) Merit of guiding policies, flexibility, and responsiveness

      (5) Efficiency of internal decision-making process

      (6) Level of morale, spirit of commitment of members

      (7) Degree to which above factors combine to make the organization more than the sum of its parts

  5. Factors in the study and evaluation of a community

    a. Community as a social system

      (1) Organizations, institutions, and groups of the community which effect existing condition and how they are linked with one another

      (2) Location of the problem and community units related to it

      (3) Units that can be engaged to deal with the problem—their stake in change—their accessibility

      (4) How will change in any one unit affect other units?

    b. Community as an organic entity

      (1) Attitudes toward social control and conformity

      (2) Opportunities for social mobility

      (3) How the community defines success or failure

      (4) Beginning appraisal of the community power structure and how it exercises controls

      (5) How power is achieved in the community

      (6) How prevailing problems are identified and by whom

      (7) Beliefs held about causes of social problems

      (8) How the community labels the victims of social problems

      (9) Problem-solving capacity and resources

    c. Intercommunity structures and processes

      (1) Relationships and regulations within governmental and nongovernmental sectors

Contract phase

  V. Assessment and evaluation

    A. If and how identified problems are related to needs of client system

    B. Analysis of the situation to identify the major factors operating in it

    C. Consideration of significant factors that contribute to the continuity of the need, lack, or difficulty

    D. Identification of the factors that appear most critical, definition of their interrelationships, and selection of those that can be worked with

    E. Identification of available resources, strengths, and motivations

    F. Selection and use of appropriate generalizations, principles, and concepts from the social work profession's body of knowledge

    G. Facts organized by ideas—ideas springing from knowledge and experience and subject to the governing aim of resolving the problem—professional judgment

VI. Formulation of a plan of action—a mutual guide to intervention
    A. Consideration and setting of a feasible goal
        1. Goal is set as the direct result of, and during the process of, problem definition and analysis
        2. Goal should be mutually agreed upon and within a set time limit
        3. Goal should be within the commitment and the capacity of client system and worker to achieve, given the opportunities the environment can offer, the worker's resources and skills, and what the client system can bring to bear.
    B. Determination of appropriate modality of service
    C. Focus of change efforts
        1. Client system (what particular aspect of functioning?)
        2. Family system (what aspect?)
        3. Significant others in the client system network
        4. Agencies and other institutions in the community
        5. Worker's own service system
    D. Role of the worker
        1. Advocate: when legitimate resources are resistive or resources must be created
        2. Broker or mediator: locates resources for client system, interprets client system's needs to others, attempts to modify others' behavior toward client system, mediates between client system and others
        3. Teacher: provides information, explanations, and expressions of opinions and attitudes, models effective behavior
        4. Enabler: attempts to help the client system to find within the system itself and the system's situation the necessary answers and resources by communication of interest, sympathy, understanding, and the desire to help; encourages exploration or ventilation of content concerning the nature and interactions of the client system and the client system's situation; encourages the reflective consideration, awareness, and understanding of the present person-situation-problem gestalt; plans with the client system and encourages the client system to act independently
        5. Therapist: makes communications that contribute to or encourage reflective consideration, awareness, and understanding of the psychological patterns and dynamics of the client system's behavior; or aspects of the client system's earlier experiences that are thought to be relevant to such present behavior; or aspects of the person-situation gestalt that lie in the past
    E. Consideration of forces in or outside of the client system that may impede the plan
    F. Consideration of the worker's knowledge and skill and of the time needed to implement the plan
VII. Prognosis—what confidence does the worker have in the success of the plan?

Action phase

VIII. Carrying out of the plan—specific as to point of intervention and assignment of tasks; resources and services to be utilized; methods by
which they are to be used; who is to do what and when

IX. Termination

    A. Evaluation with client system of task accomplishment and mean-
ing of process

    B. Coping with ending and disengagement

    C. Maintenance of gains

X. Evaluation

    A. Continuous process

    B. Was purpose accomplished?

    C. Were methods used appropriate?

Reading
7-1   A problem focused model of practice*†

Kurt Spitzer and Betty Welsh

Social work is in serious danger of losing its sense of direction, its purpose, and its relevance to today's fast moving and ever-changing world. Much of the literature reflects the frustrations experienced when one attempts to bring traditional approaches to bear on a society that operates within a value system and political frame of reference totally different from the one that existed even ten years ago.

Concern is frequently expressed in regard to the need for the social work profession and the individual social worker to become meaningfully involved in political and social action and the need for social work to develop a position of greater influence in or-

der to bring about more constructive social change (Ginsberg, 1968, pp. 23–26). By contrast, many other groups that are far less knowledgeable about social problems are perched in positions of influence in relation to social legislation and the provision of resources and programs.

Scott Briar (1968, p. 6) identifies other frequently mentioned areas of concern. He points to the need to develop more effective ways of reaching "clients from the more deprived segments of our population . . . who are not disposed to see a prolonged and often indefinite series of interviews as a solution to their problems" and expresses concern about caseworkers' putting "commitment to a method before human need." Doubtless the implied criticism is equally applicable to workers trained in other methods.

Other factors frequently identified as limiting social workers' functioning are "the infusion of the disease model of psychiatry into the central stream of casework" and the "bureaucratization of practice" (pp. 7–8).

* Reprinted by permission Family Service Association of America, publisher, from *Social Casework,* 50:6 (June 1969), pp. 323–329.

† The authors wish to dedicate this article to Ella Zwerdling, professor, School of Social Work, Wayne State University, whose memory will serve as a constant inspiration to all who are committed to the cause of human betterment, just as her presence served to inspire those whom she taught and those who were fortunate enough to work closely with her.

Another area of concern is the matter of staying in touch with the realities of today's rapidly changing society and modifying social work functions in line with the changes. In an address to social work educators, Mitchell I. Ginsberg (1968, pp. 23–26) made reference to the changing nature of clients, many of whom do not currently present themselves as helpless, passive requesters or recipients of service. Rather, they are frequently verbal and outspoken and demonstrate considerable capacity to form themselves into viable action groups. Social workers should be aware of the fundamental change in the client stance and should welcome and support it as a sign of the increased participation and social consciousness of the deprived segments of society.

The rapid, dynamic changes in social problems occurring in our complex society require that the social worker also adopt a new stance. It should be a problem focused stance that will provide workers with (1) the means for evaluating a given problem and its impact at various levels of society, all the way from the individual to the community level; (2) guidelines to determine the level at which it is feasible to intervene; (3) a wide range of intervention procedures that will be needed for problem prevention, resolution, or amelioration; and (4) the ability to evaluate objectively the effectiveness of their interventions in order to determine the direction of the next steps in the process and the new tasks they may need to undertake.

This article represents a beginning attempt to conceptualize a problem focused practice model that embraces these basic elements. It identifies the prerequisites needed for the problem focused approach, describes the essential nature of the problem-solving process involved in the application of such an approach, presents an illustration of the practice model in action, and highlights some of the implications for the development of social work theory and for social work education.

Prerequisites for practice

The attempt to address a social problem comprehensively obviously cannot be the task of one social worker alone. It is the task of work groups within an entire program, an agency, or a network of services, which are identified in this article as the social welfare response system.[1]

A work group may be made up of a variety of professional services. It may include members of several human service professions, social workers of various degrees of competence, and ancillary personnel.[2] Its structure has to be flexible, so that it may be constantly responsive to the everchanging nature of the problem. All staff efforts must be geared toward problem prevention, resolution, or amelioration. False loyalties to parts of the social welfare response system or perpetuation of subsystems that are no longer helpful must be considered dysfunctional. The entire system should thus develop a group sense of self-awareness that keeps it in tune with the needs of the client system or systems—a concept that general systems theoreticians refer to as *feedback*. Feedback is an important process operating to keep a system viable, and moving toward the achievement of the objectives for which it was originally established or to change the original objectives in line with newly emerging needs or changed conditions. The social workers involved in such an effort have to take leadership to provide the conditions that are conducive to such a stance. They must guide the building of meaningful working relationships and constructive group processes,

[1] We are indebted to Howard Buchbinder and Virginia Ebbinghaus for the concept of the social welfare response system, which they include in their conceptual model related to the development of the integrated curriculum at the St. Louis University School of Social Work.

[2] A meaningful description of such work groups (seen as "people working together on client tasks") was presented by Elliot Studt (1968) in a paper at the 16th Annual Program Meeting of the Council on Social Work Education, Minneapolis, Minnesota, January 23–26, 1968.

the development of staff, and the provision of support to staff in times of difficulty in order to ensure consistent effort on everyone's part. Clarity of the specific role that each member of the work group carries in relation to specific tasks also should enhance constructive and effective working relationships.

The problem focused stance requires of the social worker the ability to be creative, innovative, purposeful, and fully identified with the basic value system of the social work profession and its emphasis on the inherent worth of every individual. Workers need to have knowledge of the various client systems with which they will be interacting. They need the skills that will allow them to become effectively involved in relationships with individual persons and families, with small groups and neighborhood groups, and within large and small systems and institutions.

The problem-solving process

The first step to be taken by social workers addressing themselves to a problem area is the identification and definition of the problem. They make an attempt to gain some understanding of the implications of a given problem and its impact on the individual, the family, the neighborhood, and the systems and institutions in the community. Fuller understanding is gained through detailed exploration and identification of relevant causal factors. Using the concept of "priorities and feasibility" suggested by Franklin Zweig and Robert Morris (1966), social workers next decide on short-range and long-range objectives and the strategy of intervention; they identify specific tasks to be carried out and decide when and where to take action and what resources should be used.

Problem focused practice requires an ongoing and continuing process, since problems are rarely totally resolved. As a result of intrapsychic or environmental events, the impact of the social welfare response sys-

tem, or the responses to the problem by other segments of society, new elements are introduced and the nature of the problem constantly changes. The changes require ever-changing forms of response by the social welfare response system and ever-changing emphases—from the individual to the family to the neighborhood level, back and forth, depending on what seems feasible or possible or seems to require priority consideration. Thus, continuous feedback based on evaluation of the impact of interventions by the worker or the social welfare response system is an indispensable part of the process. The essential steps of the problem-solving process may be outlined as follows:

1. Statement of the problem
2. Identification of causal factors
3. Development of a plan of action (service design)
   a. Identification of needs
   b. Determination of objectives
   c. Selection of intervention procedures and tasks
4. Evaluation and feedback.[3]

In carrying out the tasks identified as necessary and appropriate, social workers apply their knowledge of human behavior and the social environment, as well as their relationship skills, within the framework of professional ethics and values, in the context of one-to-one, group, and organizational interaction. In the process they may be carrying out a wide variety of tasks, including prevention, treatment, innovation, advocacy, consultation, supervision, research, and administration.[4] The essential point,

---

[3] This conceptualization is based, to a large extent, on the five classes of design tools that make up the Social Planning Design Guide developed by Zweig and Morris (1966).

[4] It is our belief that most social workers now engage in many such tasks almost daily, though frequently without recognition on their part of the nature of the task(s) they are engaged in or the tools (in terms of knowledge and skills) that they should possess for most effective carrying out of these tasks. Schools of social work will need to build into their curriculum designs adequate procedures for the preparation of their students of the effective performance of these tasks.

however, is the way in which workers utilize themselves, and that depends primarily on the kinds of tasks they set for themselves. Direction, form, and focus, therefore, are determined by the nature of the worker's tasks. Effective implementation of the tasks requires of social workers a clear understanding of their objectives and of the nature of the relationships in which they are involving themselves in working toward their objectives; a considerable amount of flexibility; and an ability to modify focus, objectives, and response as dictated by the ever-changing picture of the problems on which they are working.

It is necessary for social workers to have no special commitment to a particular method. They are thereby in a position to see the possible use of a variety of interventive methods, procedures, or tasks as they seem most applicable in the light of their assessment of the problem.

Clearly, the problem focused stance leads the social worker in many directions in practice, including social action activity and social policy development whenever feasible and appropriate. At the same time the worker does not ignore the needs of the individuals and the groups struggling with the immediate impact of social problems on their current lives. Again, help is not perceived as being available only on a one-to-one basis or through group process alone. Rather, help may be viewed as being available through various combinations of processes.

Illustration. The following illustration is drawn from the practice experience of a fieldwork unit of four graduate students of the Wayne State University School of Social Work, located in one of the largest inner city junior high schools with a student population of 2,100.

Statement of the problem. At a meeting with the student unit the female counselors of the school, with whom the social work unit had close working relationships, presented their concerns about the large number of girls requesting return to school fol-

lowing pregnancy. Almost all of the girls had not given up their infants. They lived in their own homes or parents' homes and had child-caring responsibilities. The study patterns of the girls had been disrupted by their long absence from school, since school policy required the immediate suspension of any student upon evidence of her pregnancy.

The counselors reported that the girls had difficulty maintaining regular attendance, were chronically late for classes, or had to be home early in the afternoon. Although class schedules had been adjusted, the counselors thought the girls needed many more additional services and much more concerted help.

Identification of causal factors. In order to gain a fuller and more dynamic picture of the problem, it was necessary to identify some of the pertinent factors and implications in relation to the problem as it pertained to the school's tasks and to the girls' tasks and their situations. They were identified as follows:

1. The girl's current life situation—being needed at home—resulted in disrupted attendance patterns and tardiness. In addition, the role of mother, with its attendant implication of maturity and independence, frequently was in conflict with the implications of the student role. The girls' poor attendance prevented the school personnel from having the opportunity to teach and, by policy, being able to maintain the girls on the rolls.
2. The demands and the structure of the educational system were in conflict with the girls' child-caring responsibilities.
3. The curriculum had nothing to offer that the girls could directly put to use in their roles of mother and homemaker.
4. Carrying out those roles tended to isolate the girls from their peers.

All the information about the girls was in the realm of inference and speculation, based on the material presented by the counselors. What was needed, however, was firsthand information about the impact of the problem on the girls and their families. The task of gathering it was assigned to one of the social work students. Five girls were referred to the student by the counselors, with the twofold purpose of providing social work services to them based on their needs and, at the same time, gaining some understanding about the nature of the problem, which would enable the unit to decide on future intervention objectives and strategy formulations.

It was apparent from the initial interviews that each girl wished to attend school and ultimately to be graduated from high school. Also apparent were several stumbling blocks, such as the following:

1. A lack of money for books and supplies
2. A need for arrangements for child care
3. Established patterns of nonattendance at school prior to pregnancy
4. The difficulty of returning to a rigorous school schedule
5. Little time for study at home
6. The complication of being new in a school and class and being a year older than classmates.

Each of the girls' situations was further complicated by individual factors similar to those of Joanne and Sally:

Joanne was 16 years old and married. She had had difficulties with her husband and had returned to her parents' home. Although she wanted to attend school, her immediate need was to work out her marriage situation and find a source of financial support, since she was no longer an AFDC dependent. Because her husband was not the father of the child, he was not required to support him. She was struggling with being rejected by her husband.

Sally, 15 years old, lived with her mother, who was a deaf mute. The mother had recently lost her job because of illness, and Sally's sister and her child had moved into the home to help financially. The sister worked, and Sally's mother was frequently out of the home seeking employment or public welfare support while Sally took care of the home. An eviction notice

had been served, and electricity had been cut off.

Development of a plan of action (service design). The next step consisted of an examination of what had been learned. This involved an identification of the needs of the pregnant school-age girl, an examination of the social welfare response system, and determination of feasible objectives and appropriate intervention procedures.

The problem was identified as relating each year to about 2,000 school-age girls in the city of Detroit.[5]

As a more complete view of the problem was obtained, needed interventive tasks became clearer, including tasks related to prevention of the situation the girls found themselves facing. The following needs were identified:

1. Comprehensive sex education programs in the schools during the latency and adolescent years
2. Services during pregnancy: health care; continuing education; individual and group counseling for the school-age pregnant girl and her family, such as counseling in child care, adoption procedures, and future planning, and guidance for the mother of the girl; classes in child care and motherhood; and social work services for the father
3. Increased research activity in relation to the problems of the pregnant school-age girl to establish a broad and accurate basis for more comprehensive community services for unmarried mothers.
4. Development of constructive policies by the school system relative to the school-age pregnant girl.

---

[5] According to data compiled by the Program Development and Research Department of United Community Services of Detroit, obtained from the Michigan Department of Public Health, there were 1,847 recorded illegitimate births to mothers 18 years of age and younger in 1965, 2,102 such births in 1966, and 2,387 in 1967. We do not have data on "nonillegitimate births" by age groups. The total number of births annually by school-age girls is obviously larger than these figures indicate.

The selection of specific intervention procedures is often greatly influenced by such considerations as feasibility—in terms of community readiness and support. And at the time at which this development occurred, there was a heightened sense of awareness of the problem of the pregnant school-age girl in many sectors of the community. As a result, the students took the initiative to call together a number of people from the human service professions who were particularly interested in doing something about the problem. In view of an assessment that it was not possible to change existing policies and procedures, a proposal was drafted for the creation of a Continuing Education for Girls program, consisting of neighborhood education centers for pregnant school-age girls. The proposal called for qualified teachers and official credit for the course work completed in the program. The program was to be essentially interdisciplinary in nature. Public health nurses were to conduct courses on physical health, sex education, and child care and child development. Social work agencies were to provide counseling for the girls, their families, and the fathers.[6]

It should be noted that the active moral support of community resources and agencies made it possible for the proposal to be developed and ultimately to receive favorable consideration. Much support also came from the Detroit public school system. The final draft of the proposal as formulated by a staff member of the Detroit Board of Education represented a synthesis of several ideas developed by concerned organizations and individuals. Few school systems in the country have taken such an enlightened step.

Evaluation and feedback. The implementation of the program also brought the magnitude of the problem into full view. Although the proposal was adopted, necessary funding was obtained, and the program is currently in operation, the problem-solving

process has not ended. Indeed, it goes on *ad infinitum,* since the needs are continuous and the problem extremely complex. No one single intervention procedure can ever provide total resolution. Continuous evaluation is necessary to determine future needs and tasks. Further steps in the selection of objectives, tasks, and implementation procedures will depend on the nature of the findings of continuing evaluation of the effectiveness of the program, as well as identification of unmet needs. For example, consideration now must be given to the role and responsibilities of schools in providing sex education and meaningful social services as an integral part of the public school program and in revising policies in relation to pregnancy. The community, however, will have to support such efforts by means of programs providing effective maternal and infant health care, community mental health services, family life education, family planning, and above all more adequate provision of resources for basic survival needs.

Review of essential aspects. First, it was recognized that the provision of traditional social work services, such as casework or group work, was inadequate, since one of the major factors in relation to the problem was the interruption of the educational process. Whatever casework or group work services could be offered could only be labeled "picking up the pieces after the damage was done." In view of the negative overall environmental situations of the majority of the girls, this was clearly a totally impossible task. Even granting that casework or group work services might have been helpful, they could have reached only a small number of the girls. In addition, social work services were less significantly related to pregnancy and more related to the effects of policies adopted by the educational system (which is part of the social welfare response system) in regard to pregnancy. In other words, the situation was illustrative of a not uncommon situation in our society: namely, a large number of our social problems are frequently more significantly the re-

---

[6] The writers of the original draft of the proposal were Ella Zwerdling and Betty Welsh.

sults of the nature of the response—the stance—of the social welfare response system than of the causative factors outside the social welfare response system.

An assessment led to the conclusion that the policies and procedures regarding the pregnant school-age girl could not be readily changed within the existing public school structure. At that time, however, there was considerable broad community concern about the needs of unmarried mothers and the fate of their babies, as evidenced by the many conferences held in relation to the problem, newspaper publicity, and concern expressed by large segments of the public school community. All were attempting to find new and more effective approaches to the problem and demonstrated a general readiness for *innovation*. The readiness of the community is a very important factor in the selection of intervention procedures.

Moreover, when large segments of the community can be meaningfully engaged in the development of a program, continued significant community involvement can be relied upon after the inception of the program, in the ongoing problem-solving process, as new needs are identified and require action by the social welfare response system.

Another important aspect of the Continuing Education for Girls program is its *preventive* feature, not only in terms of the problems that plague students attempting to return to school after pregnancy, which is a form of secondary prevention, but also a much more fundamental one. When a girl is able to complete her high school education and thereby acquire the basic tools for meaningful employment or higher education, is provided with basic knowledge about childcare and child-rearing, and is benefiting from social services, she is able to rear her infant under much more advantageous circumstances than those under which she herself was reared. She can be expected to provide better care for her child, thus breaking the multigenerational cycle of poverty, dependency, and family pathology.

Many other important programs that can further enhance preventive efforts must be developed and made available on a wider scale in order for social work services to be effective in the area of prevention.

Summary

This article has presented a formulation of a new social work practice model. The model was devised on the basis of the contention that such a new model is needed if social workers are to begin making a more viable impact on the social problems of our era. The approach suggested by the model is problem focused, in that the identification and definition of the problem leads to a determination of objectives, tasks, and priorities; the levels at which intervention should take place; and the methods of intervention to be used. To be most effective, the entire social welfare response system should be related to the prevention, resolution, and amelioration of a specific problem entity and the impacts it makes on the client systems at the individual, family, small group, or neighborhood level or in societal and institutional systems.

The social work profession will have to exert considerably more effort in developing useful guidelines for the application of appropriate theories of human behavior and the social environment. A basic need is the development of a unifying theoretical system,[7] providing for the integration of many theoretical systems into a meaningful whole, that is useful to social work and, possibly, other helping professions.

A group of faculty members at the Wayne State University School of Social Work developed an experimental curriculum for the preparation of students for problem focused social work practice as outlined in this article. After a year of planning, the program was begun in September 1968 with an initial enrollment of 16 first-year students. Al-

---

[7] We believe that general systems theory, which addresses itself to a study of living systems at various levels of organization, holds excellent promise for providing such a unified theory base.

though the period of time that has elapsed since its inception is too short to provide any definitive findings, the impressions of the learning outcomes are encouraging in terms of the students' ability to relate to the needs of a variety of client systems at various levels of organization and to address themselves to social problems intelligently.

Education for *social work practice* is unquestionably one of the soundest ways of educating students. As Herbert Aptekar (1967, p. 105) points out:

Learning the role of social worker and learning social work practice are comparable to learning to draw the human body. One can break either into parts, if one wants to. The question

that must now be faced, and the scientific obligation that the profession must carry out, is to see if there is a better way of introducing students to the integrated role of *social worker* (not caseworker, groupworker, or community organization worker) and if there is a better way of introducing students to *social work practice* (not casework, groupwork, or community organization practice). If a better way can be found, it will certainly be in keeping with the present developments in agencies and programs, and social work education will take a giant step forward.

It is hoped that this article will give impetus to further innovation in social work practice and education geared to meeting the ever-changing demands of society.

Reading

7-2 Identity and change: Does development imply dependency?*

William M. Dyal, Jr. and John B. Donovan

From the "new Soviet man" to psychologist David McClelland's man with "high need achievement" the bias of many modern thinkers in social and economic development has been toward changing traditional mentalities into modern ones. The theory assumes, dubiously, that the victory of progress will be a foregone conclusion if subsistence farmers and villagers can be transformed into technocrats, or at least develop the same attitudes as technocrats.

The obverse of this coin has been the approach to development that fails to take cultural traditions and attitudes into account at all. Advanced technology has been perceived as a multiplier of production whose benefits will eventually "trickle down" to those without the capital to take advantage

of it immediately. A more advanced version of this notion is the idea that the secret of development is for governments to make massive infusions of technology in some manner whereby the rural poor can get their hands on it.

The notion that traditional small farmers should be modernized, and the notion of revolutionaries that they should be "radicalized," insults their intelligence and value systems while disregarding their creativity and pride. Also, the imposition of labor-saving, energy-eating machinery has imparted many of the superficial values that accompany a devotion to gadgetry, and in some cases has tragically distorted entire investment systems in favor of consumer luxuries. A contemporary advocate of simpler technology, Edward Schumacher, has expressed it this way:

If the nature of change is such that nothing is left for the fathers to teach their sons, or for the

* Reprinted from *Américas*, monthly magazine published by the General Secretariat of the Organization of American States in English, Spanish, and Portuguese; *Americas* 29:4 (April 1977), pp. 13–18.

sons to accept from their fathers, family life collapses. The life, work, and happiness of all societies depend on certain "psychological structures" which are infinitely precious and highly vulnerable. Social cohesion, cooperation, mutual respect, and above all, self-respect, courage in the face of adversity, and the ability to bear hardship—all this and much else disintegrates and disappears when these "psychological structures" are greatly damaged.

An important difference exists, in other words, between the kind of change that bears an organic relationship to a person's way of life and attitudes, and one that touches things irresponsibly. If initiatives from elites, for example, intrude on what psychologist William James called the "core" of the personality—"the truest, strongest, deepest self"—out of which role learning and identification emerges, the unfortunate results to economic structures may eventually equal the results of psychological structures.

The point we are making here relates directly to the key notion in the entire North-South dialogue—dependency (and its opposite, self-reliance). As Indian economist Samuel L. Parmar has pointed out, the term "self-reliance" can be seen in the shallow sense—"a mere balancing of accounts in the foreign trade sector of the economy"—or in the deeper sense, in which it refers to the process of structural change *within* the economy. He says, "Thus where growth fails to promote social justice, to utilize the economy's most abundant resources, to engender public participation in the development process, to reduce the concentration of economic power, or to assist in the establishment of more egalitarian patterns of international economic relationships, there may be self-reliance in the narrow sense, but not in the deeper, structural sense."

Thus the solutions to underdevelopment and dependency must relate, as Mahatma Gandhi suggested, directly to the impoverished rural majorities, but without their being capitulated into the modern world by technology.

Traditional development assistance policies have been slow and largely inept in grappling with the two horns of this dilemma. Only very recently has there been any serious recognition of the necessity of relating directly to the rural majorities (and to the slum-dwellers who have recently escaped from the farms). And a full awareness is still lacking that machinery and new seed varieties can accomplish very little without thoroughgoing social change. Foreign investment has often served merely to widen the gap between rich and poor by installing the kind of industry that redounds greatly to the prosperity of the capital-owning class but little to the well-being of the unemployed. The illusion still prevails that this strengthening of the capital-owning class increases stability and discourages radical solutions, but the potentially explosive frustration of those unable to participate in the economy has rarely been calculated.

Only quite recently have those in charge of forming development assistance policy begun to realize that the situation will worsen unless mechanisms are found by which low-income farmers and slum-dwellers can control the direction of their own lives. The poor do not basically need an alteration of their cultural values, and the insistence that they do has chiefly had the effect of diverting attention from the necessity of altering social structures. They *have* the ideas and initiative that can move them forward, and if there is anything that elites and foreigners can do for them it is to collaborate with these initiatives on a small scale and in a nonmanipulated manner. Solutions consistent with local values can be defined and carried out best by those who have grown up struggling with the problems.

Strong evidence for this is seen in the five-year experience of the Inter-American Foundation, a U.S. Government corporation founded to support independent social change groups in Latin America and the Caribbean. Groups under local control are springing up in every part of the Hemisphere. When they seek assistance, it is on their own terms, and almost never on a scale that permits such assistance to become a prevailing factor. Many of their projects have demonstrated for us beyond doubt that when social change proceeds on a locally managed basis it can release a natural creativity and adaptiveness that is little short of astonishing.

The self-reliant psychology engendered by social change is overwhelmingly evident in many projects, and its possibilities for releasing individual potential frequently seem limitless. On one worker-managed farm in the Caribbean, for example, cane pickers devised a way of building a bamboo pipeline to irrigate one of their fields. Furnishing them a metal pipe would have solved the short-run problem equally well. But the finest pipe in the world could never have equalled the long-range impact of the creativity released and the self-concept bolstered. These gains are a direct result of workers assuming responsibility for their own farm, rather than leaving all important decisions to owners. No program of deliberately changing attitudes is involved. The kind of collaboration that can be helpful is usually along the lines of enabling workers to seek technical assistance in the principles of accounting and cooperative management.

A similar project involves sugar workers in Jamaica, where small farmers have 6 percent of the sugar production, with the rest going to large plantation owners. In 1973, with the encouragement of a church-related group, 350 workers came together to form a Sugar Workers Cooperative Council, which petitioned the Government for recently acquired lands. These cooperatives are now surviving successfully with the aid of small worker-education programs.

A different, and innovative, kind of project focuses on the imperatives of self-affirmation without immediate economic objectives. The goal is not merely to affirm the participants' traditions and values, but to enhance their legitimacy in the minds of members of the dominant society.

In one Colombian project, for example, participants have been gathering material for theater presentations from the rich body of traditional folklore to be found throughout the country while recruiting local people to serve as actors. The leaders of the project, called the Theater of Identity, have tried to reconcile two points of view about development. The first point of view is that traditional cultures modernize only when the modern sector penetrates them with material and cultural advances. The second is that forceful confrontation of the dominant society must be encouraged. They feel that the paternalistic model ignores the energy of indigenous values and practices, and that the class struggle model calls for needless polarization.

What the theater has tried to do is provide an alternative to the gallery-and-concert-hall mode of culture forced on the country by the elite as the only legitimate one. The Theater of Identity now stages outdoor performances throughout the country using actors recruited in the areas represented by the particular style of folk life being shown. The directors are also in the process of studying the impact of these performances on both the modern and the traditional sector. Meanwhile, their performances are richly colorful proof of their own first principle, namely, that all men are creators.

The National Dance Theatre in Jamaica was founded along similar principles. According to its artistic director, Rex Nettleford, the meaning of the company's performances relates directly to what he calls the "syndrome of dependency." The relationship between master and servant throughout colonialism, he says, persists now with "our dependence on foreign markets, foreign price mechanism, foreign technology. It's time we worked in the interest of ourselves rather than in the interest of somebody else. . . . We don't have to borrow sound, or dance, or movement; we don't have to borrow anyone else's.

The company is composed mainly of low-income Jamaicans, most of whom are working simultaneously at other jobs. The widely acclaimed originality and power of their performances reveal their dedication. It is difficult to assign an exact socioeconomic meaning to these rhythms, which range from the ethereal and choirlike to the exuberant and explosive. Jamaican arts critic Edna Manley says: "The load of responsibility that he (the artist) carries to society, whether a growing or a dying one, is the validity of his own being." To which Rex Nettleford adds: "Isn't the validity of one's own being the measure of one's own liberation?"

Ethnic obstacles also exist in many areas of Latin America to block productive access to society. The unique fusion of Indian and non-Indian traits in the Paraguayan elite, for example, has determined the social values of the nation. The mestizo elite systematically relegates the pure Indians to a subhuman position, which is well reflected in the Indians' own self-esteem.

Recognizing the paradox of a situation in which Indian culture is officially idealized but in which Indians are neglected, some distinguished anthropologists embarked on an information and communication project to encourage Indians to express themselves to the dominant society in a practical, nonidealized manner. The conferences begun by the project provided the first significant forum for some groups that have been brutally abused by members of the dominant society.

Most local groups, however, have been involved with the kind of cooperative community development and organization that could, town by town and region by region, rise into a force of enormous impact throughout the Third World. Networks and service institutions are already broadening the horizons of many a subsistence farmer, and a few are finding any lack of ideas at the local level.

This is not to say that the traditional mentality of the farmer is compatible with social change in every respect. Some psychological attitudes and social customs do seem to stand in the way of the modernity that many sincerely desire.

One pattern that prevails throughout much of the developing world has been called "familism," or the tendency to narrow one's spirit of cooperation to the immediate family, thus blocking larger enterprises. Edward Banfield of the Massachusetts Institute of Technology, for example, has furnished persuasive evidence that familism is the overwhelming tendency among impoverished peasants in Southern Italy. One cannot conclude from this, however, that the answer would somehow lie in engineering a new set of attitudes among these peasants. In fact, it would seem fairly plausible that the cohesion of the peasant family contributes enormously to psychic stability compared to their modern counterparts struggling with problems of crime and drug abuse. Even if this kind of imposition could be justified ethnically, "progress" might not be a satisfactory label for the results.

Another such pattern is fatalism—the tendency to feel powerless in the face of one's future. No one who has spent much time with villagers and small farmers in the Third World is likely to doubt the prevalence of deep-seated leanings toward submission and resignation. But even this very often has a realistic foundation in an area like the Northeast of Brazil, where people entirely dependent on the whims of nature are often greeted by floods during one part of the year and a scorching drought during another part of the year. Nor should one discount the value of a stoic resignation in dealing with such circumstances. Nevertheless, some modification of these attitudes invariably accompanies any alteration of social structures.

If outsiders are to relate to these attitudes at all, we submit that it should be on a basis of response to local promotion rather than on a basis of imposition. It has been shown that social workers, reformers, and revolutionaries can display the same paternalism as large landlords, enabling identical attitudes of dependency to reappear in another form. In contrast to this, many social promoters throughout the Hemisphere are discovering methodologies whereby, through dialogue, they can help instill in farmers and slum-dwellers an appreciation of themselves, an openness to others, and an understanding of the potential inherent in group action. Such participatory forms of problem-solving are rapidly becoming recognized as the most suitable type of collaboration by local development professionals. The formation of local groups also tends to keep control of the change process in the hands of the poor, and not allow it to pass into the portentially lethal control of elites. As stated by Thomas George, a community promoter in Trinidad: "I blame the governments— and the so-called radicals—for imposing their own ideas on the people, often without consulting them and usually without reference to their feelings. . . . We must light fires of confidence in people's ability to run things for themselves."

Individuals grow in self-concept during the community building process, probably because of the way people tend to mirror each other, so to speak. We develop what U.S. social psychologist C. H. Cooley (1902) called a "looking-glass self" or a later colleague D. R. Miller (1963) called our "subjective public identity"—our perception of how others feel about us, a perception that determines much of our self-concept out of which role learning and identification emerges. Just as children in their self-concept tend to mirror the attitudes of their parents, self-concepts of the poor often seem to mirror the attitudes of those who make the important decisions regarding their lives.

Thus when the poor acquire roles as producers and entrepreneurs during the cooperative process, they often seem to experience a gain in self-concept that cannot be matched by a mere windfall profit. Their familism is broadened to include the notion that the welfare of the community in general relates directly to their own; their fatalism is reduced when they realize that their fortunes need not rise and fall with vicissitudes of the upper class.

If this autonomy, this freedom from manipulation, is recognized as the most important end result, it is obvious that aid which creates dependency is a direct contradiction. A commonsense strategy for collaborating with the social change process in the Third World would aim to enter the process *after* solutions have been defined and set in motion. Successful assistance, in our view, relies on bolstering existing community mechanisms and community spirit. Recipients should not be made to feel inferior in some way by virtue of their acceptance of assistance.

Noninterference should be studiously preserved. At the Inter-American Foundation, for example, personnel reviewing prospective projects do not reside in the receiving countries for fear of fostering an "advisor" or "evaluator" relationship with grantees.

In an era when energy-eating technology is losing its luster, these Third-World experiments in cooperative effort should prove valuable to us all. If human development is actually the achievement of a *convivencia,* or art of living together, as Mexican thinker Agustín Basave-Fernández says it is, the growing pains of the poor may yet result in the social enrichment of all mankind.

Reading

7-3   A systems approach to the delivery of mental health services in black ghettos*

Richard H. Taber

In our attempt to develop new and more effective models for the delivery of mental health services to children in a black lower socioeconomic community, we have found the concept of the ecological systems approach extremely useful. Using this model, we have explored the ecology of our community in order to define naturally occurring systems of support within the community—systems which, when utilized as a target for special types of intervention, could maximize the impact of our work.

This paper will focus on the rationale for our selection of two small natural groups: a partial social network composed primarily of mothers of highly disorganized families with young children, and a peer subsystem of 14–17-year-old boys. The ecological framework provided significant direction to our attempts to approach and work with these indigenous systems in such a way that members of the natural groups were given mental health services without being required to perceive themselves as patients.

The Rebound Children and Youth Project is jointly sponsored by the Children's Hospital of Philadelphia and the Philadelphia Child Guidance Clinic. It is charged with providing comprehensive health, dental, mental health, and social services to children in the area adjacent to these two institutions.

The community is a black ghetto in which 47 percent of the families have incomes below $3,000 and "only 38 percent of the 1,131 children covered in our survey are growing up within an intact family unit" (Leopold, 1968). The project enjoys a posi-

tive image in the neighborhood because of the involvement of the community in ongoing planning and the sensitive work of indigenous community workers as well as the provision of much needed pediatric services on a family basis.

We began this project with the view that many children in the black ghetto live with several pervasive mental health problems, primarily poor self-image and the concomitant sense of powerlessness. There are three ways of conceptualizing this problem. One is the individual psychological approach, which would identify early maternal deprivation as a primary cause. This factor can be identified in numerous cases we see clinically. Many children in this population have experienced early separation, abandonment, or maternal depression.

A second is the sociopolitical point of view, which directs attention to the systematic oppression and exploitation of this population by a predominantly white power structure. It also identifies historical and current influences which have undermined the family structure in the black ghetto and points to white racism as the source of black feelings of inferiority.

The ecological systems approach, the third way, directs our attention to the transactions and communications which take place between individual members of the poor black population and the systems within and outside of their neighborhood—that is, what actually goes on between the individual and the family, the individual and the extended family, the individual and the school, the individual and work, the individual and the welfare agency, and so on. Our exploration of these transactions, or "interfaces between systems," shows that most

* Copyright © 1971, the American Orthopsychiatric Association, Inc. Reproduced by permission of author and publisher from *American Journal of Orthopsychiatry* 49:4 (July 1970), pp. 702–709.

of the transactions which take place are degrading and demoralizing and are experienced by the ghetto resident as "put downs."

When the problems of poor self-image and sense of powerlessness are approached from the concept of ecological systems, pathology is seen as the outcome of transactions between the individual and surrounding social systems. Because no one element of these systems can be moved or amplified without affecting other elements, the ecological approach to the delivery of services requires exploration of the ways in which "the symptom, the person, family and community interlock"(Auerswald, 1968).

As an example, to plan effective services for a 15-year-old boy we must explore not only the boy as an individual but also what takes place at the interfaces between the boy, his family, the school, and other formal institutions and at the interface with peers, adults, and other representatives of the larger society. Chances are that his family expects little of him that is positive except that he stay out of trouble. He may often hear that he is expected to turn out to be a no-good bum like his father. At the interface with adults in the neighborhood he meets with open distrust and hostility. If he should wander out of the ghetto into a white area, his blackness, speech, and dress quickly cause him to be labeled as a hoodlum and treated with suspicion. He sees the police or "man" as a source of harassment and abuse rather than protection. If he is still in school, he has become used to not being expected to learn (Clark, 1965). He may not know that the curriculum was designed with someone else in mind, but he is certainly aware that his style of life and the style of learning and behavior expected in school do not mesh (Minuchin, 1969). If he is in contact with a social or recreational agency, chances are that its program is designed to "keep him off the streets" and control his behavior. Competence is not expected from him and cannot be demonstrated by him. However, his peer system, usually a gang, does give him an opportunity to demonstrate competence. He is needed by the gang in its struggle to maintain "rep" and fighting strength. Gang membership offers him structure, a clear set of behavioral norms, a role and opportunity for status—all essential elements in the struggle toward identity. He is, however, then caught up in a system of gang wars and alliances which he has little or no control over, and which limits the availability of role models.

Adults in the ghetto neighborhood have similarly limited opportunities for self-definition as persons of worth and competence. For reasons which have been dealt with elsewhere (Malone, 1966), a mother may not perceive herself as able to control her children's behavior outside of her immediate presence; yet she is expected to do so by a whole series of people representing systems within her neighborhood—her neighbors and relatives, the school, and so on—and outside her neighborhood—the attendance officer, the police, and so on. Her transactions with people representing formal social agencies and other social systems are usually experienced as destructive. In the interface with welfare, legal, medical, and other services, she receives attitudinal messages which are critical or punitive or, at best, patronizing. If she goes for therapy or counseling in a traditional psychiatric setting, she must accept another dependency role—that of patient. One of the conditions of receiving such help is usually that she admit to a problem within herself. She may also perceive the therapist's interpretations of her behavior as robbing her of any expertise about herself. What may hurt her most are the verbal and nonverbal attacks she receives from moralistic neighbors.

One source to which she can turn for acceptance and support in dealing with personal and interfamilial crises is her social network of friends, relatives, and neighbors. An important function of the network is to offer her guidance in her contacts with external systems. A friend or relative may accompany her to an appointment. Often after an unsuccessful encounter at an interface, the group will offer sympathy from collective experience and suggestions for avoiding or coping with the system the next time the need arises.

Having identified the existence of these two social groups in our community (the social network and the gang), we began to wonder how to utilize our knowledge so as to intervene in these systems in a way that would maximize their natural mental health functions. Unlike members of an artificial group, members of a natural group have day-to-day contacts and ongoing significance in each others' lives. The effects of therapeutic intervention in them should be able to transcend a one-hour-a-week interview and reverberate through the ongoing system. Also, intervention with natural community groups fits with our point of view that the answer to the problems of ghetto residents must come from the emergence of self-help groups within the community. Sources outside the community will never be willing or able to pour enough resources into the ghetto to solve the problems there. And our recognition of the value of local self-help organization brings us to a point of substantial agreement at the interface between our project and emerging black awareness and black nationalism.

We sought to work with natural systems without requiring that the people perceive themselves as patients. The intervenors sought to define their roles as that of advisors rather than leaders or therapists. We felt that this model would prove most effective for the promotion of indigenous leadership and help establish the self-help system on a permanent basis. Through successful task completion, people would have concrete reason to see themselves as worthwhile and competent.

In order to avoid making people patients, we chose to focus attention on transaction and communications at strategic interfaces rather than on individual problems. We find that this focus is more syntonic with the point of view of our target population, because members of the disorganized lower

socioeconomic population tend to see behavior as predominantly influenced by external events and circumstances rather than intrapsychic phenomena (Leopold, 1968; Minuchin, 1969).

One advantage of an approach which does not require that people perceive themselves as patients is that the natural group and the intervenor's involvement are visible. This increases the potential of the group for having an impact on other individuals and systems in the community. And individuals far from being shamed because they are patients, feel the pride of being publicly identified as members of a group which enjoys a positive image in and outside the community.

The "C" Street network

The social network we chose to work with was one of highly disorganized family units which had been observed in the course of an anthropological study of families in the neighborhood (Leopold, 1969). The families which formed the core of this network lived on "C" Street, a street which has a reputation in the neighborhood as a center of wild drinking, promiscuous sexual and homosexual behavior, the numbers racket, and gambling.

The approach to the "C" Street network was planned by a project team which included a pediatrician and two indigenous community workers. Our plan was to seek to improve child-rearing practices and parent-child communication by raising the self-esteem and effectiveness of the parents. The indigenous community workers played a key role in introducing the mental health intervenor to members of the network and have played important ongoing roles as linking persons in the interface between network members and the white middle-class social worker.

Our approach to the system was through one couple in the network who in response to a survey question had indicated interest in participating in a discussion group on neighborhood problems. The worker introduced himself as a person interested in working with neighborhood discussion groups. It was agreed that such a group might be most effective if it were limited to people who knew each other well or who were related. Despite the expressions of interest by the network members, it was several weeks before the group began meeting formally. Before the members could trust the intervenor and before they could feel that meeting together might really accomplish something, it was necessary for the social worker to have many contacts with the members in their homes or on the street. In addition to discussions of members' ideas of what could be accomplished by meeting together, these contacts were social in nature, since it was necessary for the members to see the intervenor as a person who was sincerely interested and was not turned off by clutter, roaches, and so on.

Initially we wanted to let the network define itself, but we were also committed to including the men of the community in our intervention program. Because of the sex role separation in this group, however, we had limited success in including men in formal group meetings, although the intervenor did have other contacts with the men in the network.

One critical step in the development of this program was that the network members, assisted by the community workers, needed to help the intervenor unlearn some of the antiorganizational principles of group therapy and to recognize the importance of ordered, structured communications. In other words, the group itself had to push "to stop running our mouths and get down to business." Once officers had been elected and rules had been developed for conducting meetings and a dues structure set up, the group became task-oriented. The format was that of an evening meeting in the home of one of the members, the formal business meeting followed by a social time during which refreshments including punch and beer are served. The first main areas of concern were more adequate and safer recreation for the children and improvements in housing. Through group and individual activity, houses were fixed up and the street beautified. Recreation for the children included children's parties and bus trips, planned and executed by the mothers, and the sponsorship of a play-street program.

One of the community workers is now working more closely with the group as the social worker begins to step back. The group plans to run its own play-street program this summer, as they are convinced that they can do a better job than the community house that ran it last year.

The Nobleteens

The other natural group which we began to intervene with was a subsystem of the local gang. The boys initially contacted were still in school although far behind; they did not have major police records. The intervenor discussed with them the idea of getting together with other boys to discuss what it's like to grow up black in a ghetto community. They were asked to bring their friends.

Letters and personal reminders were used for the first several weeks. The intervenor was frequently out on the street, available for informal encounters. Unlike the adult network, where almost all our contacts have continued to be in the group's neighborhood, the boys have had their meetings in the clinic from the outset. They still stop by almost daily to see their advisor.

The initial ten-meeting program was focused on current relationships with school, police, and community, on vocation and the development of black pride and awareness, on sex and parenthood. Use was made of movies such as the "Lonely One" and "Nothing But a Man" and dramatizations of written material such as *Manchild in the Promised Land.*

At an early meeting of the group one of

the more articulate members referred to the tape recorder and asked if this was to be like a study of ghetto youth. The intervenor said that that was not the purpose but that one project that the boys might be interested in would be to make tape recordings about life in the ghetto to educate "dumb white people." The group picked this up enthusiastically as an opportunity of showing people outside the neighborhood some of the positive things about themselves, since they thought that the papers usually talked about the bad things. The passive process of having discussions that were tape recorded turned into the active process of making tape recordings. From his position as a learner from a white middle-class background, the intervenor could ask questions and promote reflections. It became possible to highlight and underline examples of positive coping. The group became for the boys a place in which they could express the most positive aspects of themselves.

After the initial period, the group decided to become a club, and the intervenor's role was then defined as that of advisor. (One of the club president's functions is to be a "go-between" between members and advisor.) The group structured itself and took a more active task focus—throwing dances, starting a basketball team, starting an odd-job service (which has since involved contracts to move furniture), writing articles for the Rebound Newsletters. Carrying on their "thing" about educating people outside their system, the boys made presentations to the staff and agency board of directors, spoke on a "soul" radio station, and wrote articles about themselves. Maximum use of these experiences was made by the intervenor in promoting recognition and development of individual assets and skills.

As a result, new opportunities for role experimentation and contact with role models have been made available to the boys. Through successful completion of tasks the group has won a "rep" in the neighborhood and gets positive reinforcement from adults.

One development is that the Nobleteens have "quit the corner." As they became involved in the Nobleteens and began to see themselves as valuable people with futures, the boys spent less time hanging out with the gang and reduced their delinquent activities. This affected the fighting strength of the gang in the balance of power with other gangs and so it challenged the Nobleteens' existence, beating up several members. The next day, a member of the gang happened to be stabbed, but when a runner came to enlist the Nobleteens for revenge, they refused to fight.

A black male community worker is now co-advisor to the Nobleteens. His focus with the group will be to further promote positive black identity through involvement in activities such as a Black Holiday marking the date of the assassination of Malcolm X. He will also be helping the boys take on a business venture of benefit to the community. The present intervenor hopes to develop a program in which a subgroup of the club will be hired as big brothers to younger boys who have been clinically identified as needing a relationship with an older black male.

The role of the intervenor

Because the intervenor or advisor is in frequent contact with group members, often on a social basis, he enters into and can influence the social context on their behalf. He also stands in a unique position in the group in that he is conversant with external systems. He can therefore provide a linking function by bringing the systems together, promoting what is hopefully a growth-producing transaction for the group member and an educational one for the representative of the external systems. In terms of communication he can act as a translator for both sides. Because accommodation has taken place between him and the group members, he is better able to use their language, and they, his.

Several examples here may illuminate the

therapeutic possibilities of the intervenor's role in the interface between the natural group and the external system.

Example 1. In the first several months of the Nobleteens, Rick, a 14-year-old boy, visited as a guest, a cousin of a member. He was known by the nickname "Crazy" because of his impulsivity and lack of judgment. He impressed the worker as a depressed, nonverbal youngster. He then stopped coming.

During the summer the advisor was approached by Rick's mother to act as a character witness. Rick had been arrested for breaking into a parking meter and she was panicky because he had already been sent away once. The advisor talked with Rick while they cleaned paint brushes. Rick convinced the advisor that he really didn't want to be sent away again, and the advisor convinced Rick that it wasn't going to be as easy to stay out of trouble as Rick pretended it would be. They finally agreed that the advisor would recommend Rick's inclusion in the club and would report his impressions to the court.

Rick was known to the boys in the Nobleteens but usually hung out with a more delinquent subgroup. When the advisor recommended his inclusion in the club, one of the members (who happened to be retarded) questioned why Rick should have preference over the boys who were waiting to get in. He then recalled seeing the advisor coming down in the elevator with Rick's mother, realized that it was about the trouble Rick was in, and quickly withdrew his objection.

Beyond this there was no discussion of Rick's problem, but the message was clear. The club members included him in their leisure activities and protected him when trouble was brewing. Eventually the charge was dropped, and he has not been picked up for delinquent behavior since that time. He has responded positively to the feeling of group inclusion, appears noticeably less depressed, and is more verbal. The payoff came for Rick when he was unanimously elected captain of the basketball team.

Example 2. A well-known child psychiatrist was brought to a Nobleteen meeting to consult with the boys in writing a speech for influential people in the health and welfare field. His goal was to argue for more flexibility on the part of youth-serving agencies. The intervenor's only role was to bring the two together. The psychiatrist was familiar with the boys' language, and they were experienced in discussing topics which focused on their relationships with external systems. Tape-recorded material from the meeting was included in the speech, and the boys gained a great sense of competence in verbalizing their concerns and points of view.

Example 3. At one meeting of the "C" Street network club, two members informed the advisor that Mrs. White, the club president, was having an extremely severe asthma attack. The group discussed this informally and came to the conclusion that it was really her "nerves" and that she should go into the hospital. Mrs. White had been hospitalized several times previously and was diagnosed as a borderline schizophrenic. Mrs. White's main supports, her sister and her closest friend, were extremely anxious, their own fear of death and separation coming to the surface. This placed them in a real approach-avoidance bind. The advisor agreed to visit Mrs. White after the meeting.

Mrs. White was lying on the couch coughing in uncontrollable bursts. The advisor soon labeled the coughing (which was panicking her and the other two women) as a "good thing" and encouraged it. He sympathetically listened to Mrs. White recount her dramatic collapse on the hospital's emergency room floor and her subsequent hallucinations. While she talked, the two network members busied themselves cleaning up the house and attending to the children. Once the advisor had listened, he began exploring areas of stress with her. The most recent crisis was that she was being threatened with eviction for nonpayment of rent. She had contacted her relief worker, who had promised to contact the landlord. The advisor promised to talk to the relief worker. He also learned that in desperation she had gone to a different hospital. She had confidence in the treatment she received there, but did not see how she could go back for an early morning clinic. The advisor agreed that Rebound could provide her with a cab voucher.

Then the three women and the advisor sat and discussed the events of the club meeting. Mrs. White's coughing subsided, and she became calmer as she related to outside reality. The friend's and the sister's anxiety was also reduced. They could then respond in ways which reduced rather than heightened Mrs. White's anxiety.

The significance of this intervention lies not so much in the availability of the professional to meet the immediate dependency needs and to manipulate external systems on the woman's behalf as in his being in a position to repair her system of significant supports. A member of her own system would thenceforth be able to remind her that her rent was due when she got her check and remind her about the attendance officer if she became lax in getting her children off to school. The program continued to meet her dependency needs and support her medical care through the cab vouchers. Initially the vouchers were obtained for her by the professional; later she took responsibility for reminding him about getting them; eventually she went to the clinic's business office to get them herself. She has not suffered a severe attack or psychotic episode since the intervention.

Our commitment was to develop models for the delivery of services which multiply our therapeutic impact by bringing about change in existing systems. By focusing on competence and mutual support rather than on pathology, we have experimented with a model for the delivery of services to people who do not wish to perceive themselves as patients.

Selected annotated bibliography

Bales, Robert F., and Strodtbeck, Fred L. "Phases in Group Problem-Solving," *Journal of Abnormal and Social Psychology* 46 (October 1951), pp. 485–495.

The authors discuss the various phases of problem-solving by a group.

Benne, Kenneth D.; Bennis, Warren G.; and Chin, Robert. "General Strategies for Effecting Changes in Human Systems," in Warren G. Bennis, Kenneth D. Benne, and Robert Chin (Eds.), *The Planning of Change.* New York: Holt, Rinehart and Winston, 1969.

This excellent article discusses three models for planned change: rational-empirical, normative-reeducative, and power-coercive. The problem-solving model is discussed under the normative reeducative approach to change. This is different from our approach.

Betz, Barbara J. "The Problem-Solving Approach and Therapeutic Effectiveness," *American Journal of Psychotherapy* 20:1 (January 1966), pp. 45–56.

Betz presents psychotherapy as essentially a problem-solving process. She maintains that good results are based on accurately defining the problem right from the start. The article deals primarily with work with psychotics.

Davis, Sheldon A. "An Organic Problem-Solving Method of Organizational Change," in Warren G. Bennis, Kenneth D. Benne, and Robert Chin (Eds.), *The Planning of Change.* New York: Holt, Rinehart and Winston, 1969.

This paper features laboratory training and problem-solving as the strategy of change. The author places emphasis on man as an active growth-seeking person and on a value influence process that is transactional, rather than one-way. There is an interesting discussion of problem-solving.

Hallowitz, David. "The Problem-Solving Component in Family Therapy," *Social Casework* 51:2 (February 1970), pp. 67–75.

This article deals with the problem-solving component in family therapy.

Perlman, Helen Harris. *Social Casework: A Problem-Solving Process.* Chicago: University of Chicago Press, 1957.

Perlman conceives of casework as a problem-solving process. She discusses the knowledge that the worker needs to possess about the nature of the person, the place, and the process and makes a clear distinction between relationship and the work the client and worker may engage in.

CHAPTER 8

The contact phase: Problem identification, initial goal setting, and data collection

As discussed in Chapter 7, the problem-solving process may be divided into three major phases, each with its own tasks. This chapter will deal with the contact phase in which the client and the worker come together and begin the initial exploration that will result in a decision as to whether they will go on together and, if so, how.

The social worker and the client may come together in several different ways; the individual, family, or group may reach out for help with a problem they have identified as being beyond their means of solution, or an individual or group may identify another individual or group as having a problem and request that the social work agency or the social worker become involved. In this situation we could well consider the system that identifies the problem and asks the social worker to intervene as the client system, in that it is this system that has requested the services of the social worker as change agent to alter the situation. Earlier, the person or the group who makes this initial contact with the change agent was labeled "the problem identification system."

In social work we have not given enough thought to the impact of this problem identification system upon the implicit goals with which we approach the potential client system. One of the most common problems occurs when we accept the problem definition or the outcome goals of the problem-identification system as our own without examining them for ourselves. It is always the responsibility of social workers, if asked to contact a potential client system, to determine through their own experience with the potential client what is involved in the situation. To accept someone else's view without making a personal assessment is to court disaster. On the other hand, we must always be very aware of the meaning that the problem identification system has for us and our activity and for the potential client system and its activity.

Two very important principles stem from these concepts. The first one is that the potential client system be approached as just that, a potential client system that has been identified by someone else as needing help, and that we keep an open mind as to whether this is an accurate assessment. Second, recognizing that, at this point the problem identification system is really the client system, we need to go through a brief problem-solving process with this system. We identify what such systems see as the problem, how they identify it as a problem, what are the facts that bear on the problem, how they see it being changed, and what outcome is sought from the referral. Above all, we need to complete this process by evaluation and termination by reporting back to the problem identification system whether or not the identified problem-bearer and we have agreed to work together. Further, we need to exercise caution as to giving the problem identification system any assurance that we will work toward any goals that they may have in mind when clients ask for intervention.

If we feel that we cannot help, or that there is no problem, or the potential client is unwilling to become a client, we need to consider with the problem identification system how this will be dealt with. It may be that in this process the client identification system will become the client system in the full sense of the term. As an example of this: there are parents who come to the agency to report a child's problem. Quite often they become the clients and the child may, or may not, be seen. Or another example: a neighborhood group may be incensed and upset over the behavior of a new family in the neighborhood. A visit by the social worker reveals that the new family is functioning quite well, but very differently from the neighborhood. Perhaps the neighborhood needs to become the client for purposes of examining the meaning of their problem in being unable to accept this different behavior. Or a further example: upon contacting the potential client system it is found that it really does need and want some help with some difficulties, but the help to be given does not fall within the defined parameters of sanctioned service. We may then want to suggest to the problem identification system that they seek help elsewhere. Above all else, we should never ignore the client identification system's position in the situation. We must engage in a problem-solving process with it and we must bring our contact with it to an orderly termination. This is critical, even though this whole process just described may take place in one telephone call. These notions will be discussed in more detail in Chapter 13 on referral.

GIVING AND TAKING HELP

What is meant by the term *giving help* to someone? Help needs to be understood as far more than something that one person gives to another. What someone else does on our behalf only becomes help when we can make use of it. Keith-Lucas (1972, p. 15) defines help as something tangible or intangible offered by one person or group to another person or group *in such a way that the helped person or group can use it* to achieve some solution of the issue at hand. Help thus has two important elements: (1) *what* is given and (2) *how* it is given and used. To be helpful, what is given must be something of value and of use to the recipients, and it must be given in such a way as to leave the recipients free to use it in their own way without paying the penalty of loss of self-esteem or a loss of control of their own lives. Potential clients, whether self-initiated applicants or other identified clients, move from being a potential client to being an actual client when they decide that it is possible to accept the help offered.

In our culture, asking for or taking help (at least from others beyond one's intimate circle of associates) is often a severe blow to one's sense of adequacy.

The person who accepts help has to face the fact that (1) there is something in one's situation that one wants changed but that one cannot change by oneself; (2) one must be willing to discuss the problem with another person; (3) one must accord to that other person at least a limited right to tell one what to do or to do things for one; and (4) one must be willing to change oneself or one's situation or, at the very least, to go along with changes that others make in one's situation (Keith-Lucas, 1972, p. 20). How difficult these steps are depends on several things. The difficulty in asking for help is greatly increased if the problem is one that is generally seen in our culture as being a fault in the person who has it. If people have usually been taken advantage of or if their confidence has been abused when, in the past, they revealed their situation to another, or if their previous attempts to live in a supposedly better way have always resulted in defeat, the business of asking for help may be excruciatingly difficult. On the other hand, for parents who support a group work agency financially so that their children can have positive developmental group associations, the enrollment of their children in various helping programs, while it is a recognition that they as parents need help in offering their children growth experiences, is usually seen as a positive and normal thing to do. Or the neighborhood group which seeks the worker's help as an advocate to change another system, such as the school or the housing project, may also see this quest for help as a positive step to control its own situation. However, since the social problems of poverty and unemployment are often viewed as the result of individual pathology, the family faced with them may feel inadequate.

Anyone who has driven through miles of confused streets before stopping to ask someone for directions might well ask why one had to waste time, gas, and energy before admitting that one did not know where one was going. And how many persons have said to themselves that there was little point in asking because very few "natives" are ever able to give adequate directions? This attitude is a way of preserving a sense of adequacy, if not superiority, while asking for help.

In the beginning phase of their work together worker and client have to clarify what the difficulty is that they are going to work on. (Such clarification is the end product of the considerations outlined in Section I of the problem-solving model in Chapter 7). They have to determine the expectations and goals that the client holds for the outcome of the work together. They have to jointly understand the realities and boundaries of the practitioner's abilities and the service system's resources (see Section III A of the model). The client has to have some realistic understanding of what the work together is going to personally require. As a result of the execution of these tasks, a preliminary contract to proceed with the necessary exploration and data collection is formulated. The mutual decision as to problem, goals, and expectations will determine the focus of the data collection. It is not necessary to know all there is to know about a client, but rather to understand what knowledge is necessary in order to solve the problem and achieve the outcomes sought.

GETTING STARTED

Regardless of the size or type of client system, in the accomplishment of these tasks the practitioner will be involved in two major forms of human association that are typical of social work practice: the interview and the group meeting. The following discussion relates to principles that are important in either instance. (In that discussion the reference will be to the clients rather than to the client system simply because this allows the use of the pronoun they—a human term—rather than the mechanistic *it* which seems to be called for in references to the client system.) The first task the practitioner faces is that of preparation for the initial contact. Because one cannot divide individuals, or groups, or human interactions into discrete and entirely orderly parts, this first meeting will undoubtedly involve some elements that bear on all the tasks outlined in the preceding paragraph. However, the primary focus of the beginning will concern Section 1 A through Section 1 C in the model—the problem as it is seen by the client system, by systems with which the client system is in interaction, and by the worker. Certainly these aspects will need to be clarified before the problem-for-work (Section I D) can be settled, and focused work on data collection (as apart from incidental data collection) cannot begin until this point has been established.

In preparation for the initial contact, workers will want to collect and review any pertinent data they have about the client system and the purposes of the coming encounter. In addition, they may want to discuss with others in the setting the kinds of help that the service system can offer. Because beginnings are important in establishing the pattern of ongoing relationships, and because they wish to demonstrate respect and concern for the client system, the worker will want to do everything possible to reduce unnecessary obstacles to complete and free communication. An understanding about the time and place is essential, as are arrangements to ensure that the meeting will be comfortable, private, and as free from interruptions as possible. The worker may also want to give some thought to contact with other elements of the client system or other systems whose interest and/or participation may impinge on the change endeavor, such as the family of a referred adolescent or the school which suggested that a certain neighborhood group might find a home in a nearby community center. Thought should be given to contact with referral sources— very serious thought, because this action will have many implications for both the practitioner and the client system as they begin work together.

There are no universally applicable rules for information collection which can be set forth before the worker meets with the client system, but some principles of data collection for the practitioner's consideration can be discussed. The key principles of data collection in social work are (1) the client system should be the primary source of information; (2) data is collected for use so that the data collected should be related to the problem at issue; and (3) the practitioner should not acquire information that the worker would be unwilling to share with the client system. In addition the worker should be willing to share the process by which the information was secured with the client system and to explain why it was secured in the way it was. Further, it is our conviction that if a worker has information about a particular aspect of the problem, this information should be shared with the client before asking how the client feels and thinks about that particular point. In this way, the worker scrupulously avoids trapping the client and gives the client the opportunity, before taking a position, to reconcile what the worker knows with what the client thinks and feels. If the worker must seek information in advance of the initial contact with the client system, the worker should limit that data to the situation that brings client and worker together—nothing more. It is possible that amassing large amounts of information unrelated to the problem at hand may well get in the way of the worker's really hearing what the client is saying about the here and now. In general, it is our position that, if information should be sought from other sources than the client system and the files of the worker's agency, this can be done *after* the first meeting when the practitioner and the client have established the need for such information and the purposes it serves. Thus, most data collection will take place after worker and client have agreed to work together and have defined the problem on which they will work and the ends that will be sought.

Perhaps it is time to clarify the earlier discussion in its relationship to two types of clients: (1) the voluntary client who comes to the worker of free will with a problem that has been identified, and (2) the involuntary client who comes to the worker either because someone in a power position has demanded this or because the worker has been asked to see the client and has initiated the transaction. At the first meeting the involuntary client may or may not be willing to share with the practitioner what the client sees as the problem, but usually advance information about the client has been supplied by the individual or agency that took the initiative in forcing client and worker to come together. It is our position that the principles of data collection outlined earlier apply to the worker's contacts with both the voluntary and the involuntary client.

The involuntary client may not (and usually will not) have given permission for information to be shared with the worker or have knowledge of what information was shared. This makes it very important that the worker, at the very beginning, share the advance information and, if possible, the source of that information with the client. Sometimes the worker cannot share the source of information, for example, in cases involving the neglect and abuse of children in which the informant asks not to be identified. In the interest of protecting the children, such requests are granted. With the involuntary client it may also be necessary, in order to protect the rights of others or in the client's own interest, for the worker to collect certain information without the client's permission. This does not relieve the worker of the responsibility to inform the client of the intention to take such action and to report to the client the content of the information collected. In fact, in order to give the client as much control of the involuntary relationship as possible, the sharing of the worker's intent is essential. If one cannot decide the action taken, having knowledge of the action and the reasons for it gives one some sense of being in at least partial control.

As previously mentioned, there are two types of beginnings: in the first, clients have decided that they need to explore what can be done about some felt need, lack, or difficulty and have asked for help; in the second, someone other than the client has been concerned about this matter, and the worker has initiated the contact with the client at that other person's request. When someone has asked to see the social worker, the most sensible thing to do is to let one state in one's own terms why the person has come. But the first contact starts on a different note when workers initiate it. Then workers must be prepared to explain why they have taken this action, being careful to allow the client time to respond to the statement of purpose and concern.

When the practitioner initiates contact with the client around a problem identified by someone other than the client, the worker often feels like an intruder. In such instances it is easy to become more worried about oneself than about the client's problem. Following the natural human course of wanting to be liked and accepted by people, we often hope to somehow slip into a pleasant relationship and then to get down to business. This seldom results in a helpful beginning. When a social worker reaches into other people's lives uninvited the worker must be able to define one's reasons so directly, so simply, and so clearly (not with "weaselly" double-talk or words that do not quite portray the situation) that they do not need to worry about what the worker knows or what will be found out—clients do not need to ask themselves why the worker is *really* here. The worker needs to be concerned about the client system and for the stress that one's presence may add to it.

THE CROSSING OF SYSTEM BOUNDARIES

The giving and taking of help requires the crossing of the boundaries of the potential client system. The client system cannot request help without having a member of the system (or if an individual client, the whole system) cross the system boundary to interact with another system, the change agent system and the change agent. Also, the potential client system cannot become a client system without allowing the change agent (or if you prefer, the actions of the change agent) to cross their boundaries and become a part of their life.

This requires that workers always be sensitive to the meaning of boundaries for the client system, and for the meaning to the client system of the interactions within its boundaries of the system members. This becomes *critically important* when workers are involved with systems that may have different notions about boundaries (where they are located, how one crosses them, and the pattern of transactions necessary to show respect for the boundaries) and different patterns of interaction within the boundaries, as in working with minority groups and families. An article on working with the family behavior of urban American Indians has been reproduced in order to serve as an example of the importance to the worker's actions of an understanding of the system (see Reading 8–2). It does not exactly address the issue of boundary crossing, but workers who have successfully negotiated this with families different from themselves are those who are sensitively aware that there are different culturally determined patterns of appropriate boundary crossing and of the necessity to scrupulously respect the boundaries and the ways of crossing them.

DEFINING THE PROBLEM

So workers begin with a consideration of the problem that is seen by the client as the beginning place. For many individuals and groups, needs and wants come in bulk size. But one cannot do everything at once, so the first job the practitioner has is to engage with the client in the business of deciding where to start. The client's selection of a starting point is where one would ordinarily hope to begin. But if the client's choice is dangerous to self or others, or if it promises more trouble and failure, the worker has the responsibility of pointing out the risks. A social worker cannot be a part to planning that is destructive, but one needs to be very sure of one's ground before rejecting out of hand the client's chosen starting place.

This indicates that the practitioner must utilize the skills of interviewing, communication, and use of relationship discussed in the preceding chapters to help in arriving at some understanding of the client's perception of the problem. This does not mean that any worker needs to be, or can be, an instant expert on problems. The primary job at this point is to seek to understand, to take the time and ask the questions necessary to help one gain understanding. Not understanding immediately is not necessarily an indication of inadequacy. The worker can simply ask the client to help the worker see what is in the situation. In working with a problem beyond one's understanding or a system very different from one's own it is important that the practitioner not burden either oneself or the client with the unrealistic expectations of immediate mutual understanding. This is particularly true when practitioners are talking with someone whose life experiences are very different from their own. On the basis of some perception of what the client is telling the worker, on the basis of some understanding of personal reaction to the client's problem, and on the basis of information that one may already have about the problem, the worker will need to formulate a notion of the problem and its meaning. This view is then shared with the client. Arriving at a notion of the problem is no more an instant process than is arriving at an understanding. It may well take several meetings. The client's perception of the problem and the worker's perception of the problem may not be the same. Frequently, they are not. Then it becomes necessary for the worker and the client to enter into a series of negotiations and discussions directed toward arriving at a definition of the problem on which they are to begin work. An example of this is found in a paper by Purcell and Specht (1965) that discusses a case called "The House on Sixth Street."

> "The House on Sixth Street" became a case when Mrs. Smith came to an MFY Neighborhood Service Center to complain that there had been no gas, electricity, heat, or hot water in her apartment house for more than four weeks. She asked the agency for help. Mrs. Smith was 23-years old, Negro, and the mother of four children, three of whom had been born out of wedlock. At the time she was unmarried and receiving Aid to Families with Dependent Children. She came to the center in desperation because she was unable to run her household without utilities. Her financial resources were exhausted—but not her courage. The Neighborhood Service Center worker decided that in this case the building —the tenants, the landlord, and circumstances affecting their relationships— was of central concern.

Thus the worker who listened to Mrs. Smith's troubles saw the problem as broader than one person. The worker visited the tenament and found conditions were as described and that all families were suffering from the lack of adequate facilities in their apartments. The worker then defined the problem as one belonging to all the tenants of the house and secured the tenants' agreement to this definition. The client system became all the tenants of the house, and the problem became to help them to organize their demands for services and utilities in their housing to which they were legally entitled. The target system became the landlord, and an attempt was made to form an action system of the seven different public agencies responsible for housing code enforcement and other agencies responsible for supplying benefits and services to tenants.

One of the greatest difficulties in identifying the problem occurs when workers are so focused on their definition of the problem that they do not hear what their clients are communicating about how they see and feel the difficulty. The workers then continue on their course without being aware of the incongruity between what they are about and what the client requested.

As an example of such a situation the work with Mr. K over a 14-month period is summarized below. Mr. K had been referred to a private family agency by the court following the hospitalization of his wife for mental illness because the court believed that Mr. K would need help in caring for the three children, ages four, two and one. In this situation both the worker and the court seemed to have defined the problem as securing care for the children, without hearing the pain, guilt, and confusion of Mr. K. As a result at the end of the recording the worker is again asking Mr. K how he wants to solve the problem she had identified. However, it would appear to us that Mr. K probably sees the problem first as the absence of his wife and, second as his lack of comprehension of mental illness and third the guilt he carries about what has happened. It could be expected that there will continue to be problems with child care as long as the worker does not recognize Mr. K's problems and does not begin there. This case is a good example of how, if we want to be of help, we must start with where the client hurts. If we cannot start there, as in emergency situations involving child care, we can at least recognize with the client what the situation is about and how the views differ. We can at least recognize with clients that we heard them and that their view of the problem is understood.

> Mr. K had need of and sought a great deal of help in financial management. He looked to the worker as to a parent to decide on specific expenditures. For several months in weekly contacts the worker had helped him manage through putting money for monthly budget items in envelopes each payday. Gradually he had become able to figure expenditures himself and to regulate some of his erratic spending. His major problems in financial management were an uncontrollable impulse to overspend on useless gifts to his wife and an inability to deny the children toys, sweets, and recreation jaunts. He would agree with the worker when she carefully figured out with him what would be reasonable and appropriate spending on these items, but he would persistently overspend. At times he would laugh at himself for taking his wife something she was not permitted to have and then would justify it by saying someday she could use it. In 12 months, however, he was able to assume the expense of the housekeeper.
>
> His relationship to the children was characterized by anxious fretting over them, indulging them, and demanding the utmost in care of them from the housekeepers. Momentary sternness with them would be quickly replaced by petting and indulgence. Any illness or behavior deviations caused extreme worry. Though alarmed at Patrick's temper tantrums he would give in to them. The restlessness, hyteractivity, and food fads of Mary, age two and one half, worried him. Certain comments indicated that he connected the children's symptoms with their mother's behavior. He persisted in taking the children to visit their mother even though the worker advised against this and he himself would agree that the visits meant little to his wife and were exhausting and disturbing to the children. The worker's efforts to help him had been largely that of giving recognition to his desire to be a good parent and using his concern for their welfare to argue for con-

sideration of their health and emotional comfort. Mr. K always presented problems to the worker with an earnest request for advice and the worker gave sound child guidance advice freely. However, Mr. K had been able to use the advice only fragmentarily.

The worker observed repeatedly in the record that Mr. K was very devoted to his wife. He visited regularly and excessively, taking gifts, and writing letters. He talked repeatedly of her eventual return. He would react to slight improvement in her condition with great optimism and with urgent demands for her discharge. Recently he had brought her home against medical advice. She had become disturbed and after she had disrupted a smooth running home, he had been forced to return her to the hospital. He was recorded that he often referred to his wife's competence prior to her illness, adding "And I didn't know she was ill." This statement was not explored.

Mr. K's relationship to the housekeepers had been problematic. The first housekeeper probably was incompetent, but this was not clear because of Mr. K's nagging and his constant comparisons of her activities to those of his wife. He fired this woman because she was unkind to the children.

The second housekeeper, a competent person who got along fairly well with the children, quit because she could not endure his demands, or his competitive undermining of her efforts with them. Mr. K was remorseful about this recognizing too late that she was a good housekeeper and mother substitute. This woman complained to the worker that she was expected to do the man's chores and to coax Mr. K to get up every morning. The worker's efforts in helping Mr. K with his housekeeper problems had been to try to get him to see their side of the situation and to face the errors of his ways. He readily would admit his wrong doing and declare his intention to do better next time.

The third housekeeper was a competent motherly woman who got along smoothly with Mr. K through joking with him, mothering him, and bossing him. She mended his clothes and packed his lunches. She allowed the children to play without restraint and they became more quiet and contented. Mr. K assumed more responsibility with chores and reported enthusiastically to worker that now his problems were solved and he would not be needing help much longer. Impulsively, without consulting worker or the housekeeper, he brought his wife home from the hospital with grudging medical consent but on the basis of his reports of favorable conditions for her care at home. Later he justified his action through saying that he had been unhappy that his wife was not at home to enjoy everything with them. The housekeeper could not put up with the wife's very disturbed behavior and threatened to leave. Mr. K turned to the worker who helped him face the fact that his wife was not ready to live outside a hospital. In returning her, Mr. K had to call plain clothes police and win her cooperation through deception. Subsequently, he was very disturbed about this and about his wife's reproachful remarks to him for betraying her.

The present situation

Now, following this episode, Mr. K is anxious and undecided as to future plans. He thinks he probably can mend matters with the housekeeper, but she is still angry and fearful and on the verge of leaving. How will he ever bring his wife home if no one will give her a trial? Will she ever get well? He cannot always be changing housekeepers. It is bad for the children. This is a good housekeeper, and perhaps he should urge her to stay. He might never find her equal. Certain comments show some anger with her for not putting up with his wife, even though she was irrational and clearly unable to assume responsibility or to permit anyone else to do so in her home. He cannot endure the thought of separation from the children. Foster home care was discussed but he thought he could not face not seeing his children everyday. The pros and cons of the two plans— foster care and a continuation of the present plan—were reviewed. Mr. K left the interview undecided but leaning toward another trial of the housekeeper service.

One of the other problems with a situation such as the one discussed is that the client gradually begins to develop a sense of failure. Mr. K must feel that he is not being a "good client." The worker is doing so much for him, but he can not seem to carry through as she expects him to. In our view, he cannot and will not be able to carry through until the worker understands what is the central issue in the situation for him. Just one further comment on the situation. This is not a chapter on interventive roles, but it would seem to us that the worker should well have involved the hospital and its staff in the action system for Mr. K and have utilized roles of broker and advocate for Mr. K with the hospital around his understanding of his wife's illness.

We cannot possibly overemphasize the point that *everything else depends upon appropriate problem identification.* The way we define the problem will define what data is collected and will dictate what is seen as appropriate answers. *This step must be right or all else fails.* There can be no engagement between client and worker without a common understanding of what they are about together from the clients' frame of reference. This does not me in that the worker should set aside her definition of the problem. It means that she and Mr. K need to spell out both definitions and agree on ordering the problems-for-work.

Another important difficulty often found in problem definition is that workers get the problem and the cause all mixed up. Thus, when presented with a case of a 13-year-old boy, James C., who (1) has just stolen a car; (2) comes from a home in which the father has just died in an automobile accident and (3) has a mother who says that she may overprotect her son, most students, acting as probation officers and just introduced to the notion of problem definition, will write that the problem is the mother's overprotection and the lack of a father. The *central problem at the moment is that the boy has just been apprehended by the police driving a stolen car.* There may be some relationship between his and his mother's interaction or their situation and the problem. However, consideration of the meaning of the home situation falls under assessment and follows considerable more data collection. The mother recognizes this difference in that she does not say that the problem is her overprotection, but *that the cause of the behavior* stems from this type of relationship with her son.

We need to recognize that if we see the problem as the mother's overprotection, we have shifted the problem from that of the son's behavior to the mother. In addition we may be terribly wrong even in settling on this explanation as cause. For example, if the boy is asked to tell what happened, he may contribute the information that he was a candidate for gang membership and initiation rites required that he steal a car. If this type of explanation is received, assessment would require that these two possible explanations (those of mother and son) be put together in an attempt to plan what can be of help in *preventing a recurrence of the delinquency.* It may be, in the course of the exploration and assessment, that the client system and the worker will redefine the problem-for-work as the mother's overprotection. However, that awaits the problem definition, the goal-setting, the data collection, and the assessment of what this all means and what is to be done about it.

Let us return to Mr. K. In that case, as in this, the worker has a goal identified by a problem identification system: Mr. K's children have to have care. Obviously that will have to be one problem-for-work between worker and client, but there must be recognition of Mr. K's definition of the problem. In the boy's case, there must be recognition of the mother's definition of *cause*, and that may well become the primary problem-for-work. But it is important to recognize that everyone involved saw stealing the car as the primary problem.

Sometimes the development of a common ground for work can be established quickly, sometimes a series of interviews may be necessary, and sometimes a common ground cannot be found. However, without a common place to begin, the worker and the client cannot proceed further. When a common ground cannot be reached, the worker and the client may find it necessary to simply acknowledge this fact and, for the present at least, discontinue their efforts. In an authority-related setting, where the worker has a legal mandate to provide supervision and the client has a legal mandate to report the client's activities, there are two possibilities. Workers may return to the court and acknowledge that there is nothing that can meaningfully be accomplished between the client and the worker and ask that the court decide the next steps. This might be a wise course of action if the situation involves, for example, the court's charge that the practitioner work with a mother who has been abusing her child, and the worker is concerned about the danger of such behavior to the physical well-being of the child. Or the worker might agree with the client that the worker will only attempt to meet the responsibilities mandated by law. In either of these situations, however, the possibility of reaching a common ground at a future date should be kept alive by leaving the door open for future negotiations.

Partialization is an important aspect of problem definition. Partialization refers to the process of separating out from the universe of problems brought by the client and/or identified by the worker the specific problem or problems which are to become the focus of worker-client attention. No one can deal with a whole range of problems at one time, even when they are closely related, and an attempt to do so may lead to floundering, lack of focus, and an overwhelming sense of despair as worker and client recognize the multiplicity of the client's stress experience. These difficulties can be avoided by partializing out from the universe of problems a specifically defined problem (the problem-to-be-worked[1]) as the beginning point. Later other problems may be tackled. Partialization also provides greater opportunities for finding a common ground—client and worker do not have to agree on all problems in order to find a beginning place.

Another word of caution—at this stage in the exploration of the problem, one must be careful not to assume that it lies with the person who first approaches the agency. Although the problem may be very troublesome for this person, it may lie in another system. The target of change may not be the client.

---

[1] One of the authors first heard this phrase used by Helen Harris Perlman in a lecture. It seemed so expressive of the concept discussed here that we adopted it. It carries for us at least, the connotation of worker activity with the client toward solution of the problem.

If the client does not have any suggestions as to where to start (as was true for the mother who said to the worker that she did not know which problem was the largest one: "All I know is that we are in a mess for sure"), the worker may introduce suggestions as to a starting place. Sometimes the worker and the client may find that where to begin can very well turn into the immediate problem-to-be-worked. In other words, it is perfectly possible that the problem-for-work is the definition of the problem. And even if this sounds like double-talk, it is not. In order to work on something, one has to decide where one should begin and where one is going. The inability of various interests involved in a situation to perceive the problem in the same way—to define it in a congruent way that allows work to be done on it—may well be a central problem. Consider the following example:

> Miss B, a 29-year-old schoolteacher, was admitted to a rehabilitation service following a massive stroke. She had been diabetic since she was five-years old and, despite constant medical attention and rigid personal self-discipline in diet and medication, the disease was becoming progressively worse. During the last five years she had been losing her sight, and now she is considered legally blind. The stroke, which was also related to the diabetic condition, had resulted in a paralysis of her right side. Miss B had always been a very goal-directed person and, in spite of an ever more handicapping illness, has an advanced degree in the education of handicapped children. She sees her problem as one of getting well quickly so she can return to her classroom; and she has a somewhat unrealistic notion of what is involved in such an accomplishment, denying the hard and difficult work of learning to walk with a cane and of learning to read by the use of braille. She is angry with the nurses and often refuses to cooperate with them because she feels that they are trying to keep her dependent. The diagnosis of her doctors (which has been shared over and over again with her) is that she is in the last stages of an irreversible terminal condition and that she can never return to teaching. From their view, the problem is that Miss B is unwilling to accept the diagnosis and behave properly. The staff feel that the problem is that the patient won't accept the massive damage that she has and will not participate with them in the small, painful, and difficult tasks necessary to achieving minimal self-care. A social worker sees the problem as getting Miss B to apply for welfare because her own funds are almost exhausted and to engage Miss B in planning for a move to a nursing home, as the rehabilitation facility cannot keep her much longer.

In this situation, the problem-for-work probably has to be that of attempting to resolve the incongruence among the various views of the problem and of finding a beginning that can permit the client and the various other necessary systems to interact to some productive purpose for the client.

GOAL SETTING

This case situation leads us to another consideration that interacts closely and constantly with the definition of the problem-to-be-worked. That is the question of how the client system or other systems see the problem as working out. Not only did each of the significant participants in this situation have a personal view of the problem, but each view of the problem encompassed an objective or an answer to it. Professional people involved with Miss B wanted her to accept both the inevitability of her physical deterioration and a "realistic" plan for future care—although they differed on the plan. Miss B wanted to return to teaching.

We often find that persons involved in a problem situation present us with the solution rather than with the problem. The client comes to request help in implementing an already decided solution rather than in examining alternatives to action. This makes eminently good sense, in that the search for some desired end is a constant thrust of all of us. Goal seeking is what gives the problem-solving process its thrust and purpose, and the consideration of client goals is an important part of each phase of the problem-solving model. The way workers recognize goals and the way they work with goals will differ in each phase, but client goals must never be ignored. In the beginning contact it is important that the practitioner separate the problem from the goal so that each may be considered separately. Thus when a mother comes to a child-welfare agency saying that she needs to place her child, she may well be presenting the worker with her goal in the shape of a problem. This may be her answer to any one of a whole range of problems; but while it is the only answer she can see, it may be an answer that will cause her great pain and despair. The worker will need to become involved in the question to which placing the child is the client's answer. Worker and client may or may not find a better answer, but in any case the worker should not confuse question and answer. However, in the process of defining and exploring the client's problem, the worker must never lose sight of the fact that the client's original goal was placement, and it is essential for the worker to understand the meaning that this goal had for her. We do not dismiss client goals lightly—we simply seek to separate goal and problem for more effective work.

Let us return to Miss B, a real person whom one of the authors knew. How does one reconcile the disparate views of the goals in this situation? Miss B, desperately needing to deny the diagnosis, is determined that she will get well and return to teaching. All she wants is recognition of this goal and help in achieving it. The medical staff are certain that she can never return to teaching, that the illness is progressing rapidly, that her only hope is to stay its progress somewhat by certain attempts at self-care, and they want her to accept these conclusions. A social worker, concerned over the limits of hospital care and Miss B's finances, wants Miss B to plan soon for other care.

There are different types and dimensions of goals that need to be recognized and discussed at this point. One may be concerned with an optimal goal—or an ultimate goal—which is the final desired outcome to which the effort is directed. Or one may be concerned with interim goals—objectives that are significant steps on the journey toward the optimal goal. Before the ultimate objective can be realized, a series of intermediate objectives usually need to be met. Often these intermediate objectives can be a way of testing whether the ultimate goal is sound. There are usually several layers, or levels, of interim goals. The first goal achieved becomes an aid to the achieving of more complex or more advanced interim goals. Just as one needs to determine a problem-for-work with which to begin, one often finds that the initial steps have to do with facilitative or interim goals as a way of collecting data and making decisions on the feasibility of the ultimate goal.

If one examines the different levels of goals stated at the time the social worker entered Miss B's case, one finds that the interim goals are not different for the various systems involved. The struggle is over ultimate goals. All the professional people involved in the situation want Miss B to participate in re-habilitative efforts that will keep her functioning as well as possible for as long as possible. These same efforts are necessary if Miss B is to be able to carry through her ultimate goal of returning to teaching.

The worker's efforts may very appropriately be directed to sharing with Miss B (1) that the medical staff and Miss B see the problem differently, (2) that they are in strong disagreement over the ultimate goals, (3) that the worker questions whether Miss B can return to full-time teaching, but (4) that perhaps the place to start is with the problem of her ability to work on certain interim goals that are necessary to *either* ultimate goal. So they can begin with what is involved for her in trying to walk again, to read braille, to care for herself in certain physical matters, while collecting data about her progress and planning for the future. Eventually there will come a time (and there did) when the worker and Miss B will have to put the results of their efforts together and make an ultimate plan—either she returns to the community as an independently functioning person or she accepts some alternate plan for at least partially sheltered care. The time of assessment and renegotiation of goals and of planning for the longer future will have to come. But for now they can explore the problem and the feasibility of certain long-term goals by starting with interim goals that become the facilitative goals in that all can agree on them and that they allow further data collection before assessment and final decision making.

We believe that both ultimate goals and the means of change are obtained from objective study, evaluation, and planning. These procedures are essential to the effective use of the problem-solving model. But all too often we see cause, truth, and knowledge as absolutes. Sure of ourselves and our under-standing, we manipulate our data into firm conclusions, or we use the informa-tion to arrive at a psychosocial explanation that seems reasonable to us and set off on a course of action toward our immediate goals—goals that may not be shared with clients or take account of their expectations. Instead, the con-tact phase of the problem-solving process demands that the practitioner begin with an exploration of the common definition of a problem-to-be-worked and a common understanding of and acceptance of goals which at this stage may only be (and probably should only be) facilitative goals that serve to engage the client systems and the worker in jointly unearthing the ongoing knowledge that will eventually establish (in the contract phase) firmer means and ends around the central issues such assessment will identify. The problem-solving model, as we use it, demands that the client's purposes and expectations in joining the worker in interaction be explored, understood, and kept in the center of concern. It is our firm conviction that lack of initial exploration of expecta-tions and goals and lack of careful selection of the starting place in the contact phase of the worker-client interaction account for a large percentage of the failures of the helping process (Mayer and Timms, 1970).

PRELIMINARY CONTRACT

In arriving at the preliminary contract, which is in essence an agreement between the worker and the client on the problem-to-be-worked and the facili-tative goals, there are some other absolutes that must be clarified with the client. The worker must clarify the realities and boundaries of what can be offered and must behave in such a way as to help the client understand the nature of further work together. To make a brief comment on the first point: this requires that the worker be able to convey to the client the limits of the service that can be offered while at the same time conveying to the client the worker's belief in the ability to help within those limits, and interest in helping the client find another resource should the service that can be offered be too limited. In other words, the workers do not want to promise more than they can deliver and so trap the client by false hopes, but neither do they want to operate in such a way as to imply hopelessness to the client. The client may come to the worker out of pain, or despair, or anger but will only become involved in action with the worker when this feeling of discomfort is joined to a hope that something can be done.

One usually finds clients confused about how the helping process will work. As was pointed out in Chapter 1, people find it difficult to grasp the nature of the social work job. There are seldom visible technologies or artifacts that will give others some notion of what the process is all about. The practitioner's actions in the beginning phase can give the client a sample of the social work method. That is one reason the beginning is so important. Another reason is the pattern-setting nature of communication between elements of a system or among systems.

At the end of the beginning phase of problem identification and goal determination, client and worker decide whether they wish to continue together. If they do, the worker is then free to begin to collect the information that will be the data on which assessment and planning will be based. The problem-solving model in Chapter 7 includes a long list of the kinds of information that may need to be collected, given certain problems and certain client systems. We would caution again that nothing is more sterile than information collecting for the purpose of information collecting. Information is collected for the purpose of taking effective action, and all efforts must be directed to that end. The kind and amount of information collected will be dictated by the defined problem-for-work and the preliminary goal that is established.

AREAS OF DATA COLLECTION

It is difficult to deal with areas of data collection concretely because the specific areas to be explored depend upon the situation. However, there are some principles that should be considered:

1. It is a joint process, and the client should be involved in helping to determine the areas to be explored.
2. The client should be aware of the sources being used for data collection (note: clients are not always asked for their permission).
3. There should be a connection between the problems identified and the data collected. The client should be aware of this connection.
4. It is critical to explore all areas that the clients see as connected as well as helping them to understand the areas the worker seeks to explore.
5. Data collection goes on all the time, but it is critical to the problem identification, goal setting, and assessment stages of work.
6. The primary areas of data collection are all points listed under the contact phase of the model presented in Chapter 7.
7. It is important to note that, under exploration and investigation, the type

of client system will determine the areas of data collection to some extent. Please give some attention to these differences.

8. It is crucial that the worker understand the clients' view of all areas of data collection—their thinking about the meaning of the items, their feelings in those areas, and any actions they may have taken.

It is important for the readers to note that there are three areas of data collection that are the same for all systems and all problems. They are the areas of hope, discomfort, and opportunity. Readers may want to go back and read the discussion as to the importance of these areas in human growth, development, and functioning, found in Chapter 3 on foundation knowledge. In our thinking these are the most critical areas in this stage of work—both in terms of the worker's collection of data and in terms of the worker's actions with the client.

What causes people to act? As was stated earlier, for action to take place, discomfort with things as they are must be felt, but this is not enough. If a worker is to act, to discomfort, mild or severe, must be added the hope of being able to reach a goal that is seen as the answer to wants, and in addition there must be some ability to consider what has gone wrong and some opportunity for change in the situation. Productive engagement in the social work process is dependent on the client's "hope-discomfort balance" and on the extent to which the practitioner is able to engage that pressure by the hope and clearly defined opportunity offered. The study states that before work can begin on a problem the client must be uncomfortable about the present state of affairs and hope that something can be done about it, and the worker must be able to communicate understanding (empathy, if you will) of the client's discomfort and, even more important, the worker must engage oneself with the client's hope. As was once said, when hope is weak the practitioners must find a way of "hitching the motor to the client's wagon." For this reason, we would urge that workers always be concerned, with all client systems and in all problem situations, with the level of the client's hope-discomfort balance and with early activity with the client in this area and the way they engage themselves and the client with the opportunities for reaching objectives.

SOURCES AND METHODS OF DATA COLLECTION

Before closing this chapter, we would like to make some general observations about the sources from which worker and client will collect the information that is needed to make an assessment. The first, and most important principle, is that the client system must be aware of the resources the worker is using and why they are being used. If at all possible (as was noted earlier in the chapter), the client's permission should be secured before any particular source of information is used. However, whether or not permission is secured, the client *must know* about the sources used, the information sought, and why the information is believed to be appropriate to the task at hand. If commitment is to the clients' participation in decision making that will lead to action toward their goals, then we must share with them all the information on which decisions may be based. Otherwise, we deprive them of an opportunity for representative participation in the discussion about themselves.

In general, modes of data collection can be divided into three groups: (1) questions, either verbal or written; (2) observation; and (3) other professional or institutional systems. Perhaps the most widely used tool for data collection is the interview or group meeting with the client system in which questioning and observation are used to gain information. The interview or the meeting requires a knowledge of the principles of relationship and communication that have been discussed in previous chapters. In addition to the material in these chapters, there is a selected bibliography that give guidance for further reading in this area. In the use of the face-to-face meeting, the practitioner will need to decide its purpose, the information needed to be obtained from it, and how the worker wants to structure it. At one extreme is the nondirective interview or meeting in which the worker follows the feeling and thinking of the interviewee or allows the group to reveal itself as it will. At the other extreme is the completely structured interview or meeting, in which the worker has a scheduled set of questions from which there will be no departure. However, workers are also giving some structure to the interview and determining what data may be collected when they decide where and when it will be held, when they establish ground rules and norms for content and participation, and even when they arrange the chairs of the persons involved. Careful thought should be given to the place of the first meeting: Is it to be on the "client's turf or the worker's?"

Obviously, the interview may be used to collect information from sources other than the client system. In using these other systems, workers will want to consider carefully the kinds of information they think they can provide and the need they have for this information. They will need to give thought to the fact that certain information sources may expect the interview to involve a sharing of information. If workers are to share information, they will need to discuss this with the client system. If they are unwilling to share information, they must make this known to their source when the interview is requested.

Many kinds of written questioning techniques are in use. Clients are often asked to fill out application or information forms when they first approach an agency. There are various questionnaires that may be used with various client systems for various purposes. If a group is trying to decide a focus for future meetings, and members seem reluctant to share their views openly with other members, an anonymous written questionnaire may be helpful. It allows members to express an opinion without penalty. Written exercises are sometimes used in work with families to allow members to express themselves without feeling that they have directly attacked other members of the family. In certain community organization projects, the use of a survey based on a written questionnaire is a very valuable technique. Obviously, one would not want to use a written questionnaire with clients who do not express themselves well in writing, or clients who might see it as a dehumanizing device, or clients to whom it might imply that they were being classified into just one of a similar group of persons.

In speaking of both verbal and written questioning as data collection tools, it should be mentioned the use of other persons to collect information for the worker. In certain situations, someone close to the client system and knowledgeable about the situation may conduct an interview for the worker. An indigenous Spanish-speaking community worker might be asked to talk to a Chicano woman who has just suffered the loss of her husband and who should not be asked to take on the additional burden of speaking in English to a stranger at such a time. Also the worker may have other professionals, such as psychologists, administer tests to gain certain knowledge. These tests may be oral or written. Psychologists often use projective techniques, which allow the respondents to impose their own frame of reference upon some stimulus, such as a picture. Or, in order to have two sources of information, workers may ask a psychiatrist, or perhaps their supervisor, to interview the same client that they are dealing with.

Along with questioning, the worker usually utilizes observation as a way of gathering data. Though we all use observation of others in daily interactions, much will be lost unless we learn to make deliberate, planned use of the technique. As with verbal questions, observation can be structured or unstructured, and the worker can be a totally uninvolved observer, a participant observer, or a leader-and-initiator observer. For example, workers might give a group of children a game to play and then observe and record their actions without being in any way involved in the game. Or they might be a committee member, both involved and observing. Or they might serve as a committee head while trying to observe the interactions of the members. This last possibility will probably cause many to ask how effectively a chairperson can observe the interactions of other committee members. This is an example of questions that are often raised about the use of observations. What about the bias and the selectivity of the observer? No one can possibly observe all the interactions of a group, or even all the facial expressions and changes in posture of one person, in an interview. Observation requires a sensitivity to others and the capacity to see small changes. In addition it requires that workers know themselves and their biases. It requires them to have given thought to what they want to learn through this process and to how they do it. Since they cannot collect all the data on any one transaction, they must recognize that they collect only certain information and are, therefore, selective. Workers must know what framework guides this selectivity.

The last general way one collects information is from the use of existing written material—material not gathered specifically for the present situation. Often workers may find that their agency, or some other place has records of previous contacts with the client system. Usually, it is wise for the worker to know the contents of such records and to discuss them with the client. Otherwise the client may waste valuable time and trouble in worrying over what you may know. If previous written materials are available, they can be a very efficient means of data collection. Their use places little demand on the client system and is within the worker's control. But therein lies a seductive danger— such records can be used so easily without the client's knowledge. There is another danger—when something is read, there is a tendency to feel that it is really known. For these reasons, we would like to especially caution practitioners against the indiscriminate use of such material. They must question written material as they do a human informant. Does it give the facts? Are the facts documented? Or does the material merely reflect another person's judgments? The practitioner must also recognize that such material deals with the past; that it may not bear on the present problem and may even confuse the issue in that it was written or gathered for a purpose unconnected with it; and (to repeat) that it may reflect the biases and selective perceptions and evaluations of the persons who collected it. Often there is a tendency to see written material as holding more of the truth than the practitioner's present experiences. This tendency should be strongly resisted. On the other hand, appropriate written material can be an effective source of data.

One of the problems in data collection is the organizing of the material. An excellent original article by Ann Hartman is reproduced in this chapter that should help workers both to be aware of what data they may need to collect and to organize this data for assessment. The readers may want to compare the model developed by Hartman to Figures 3–4 through 3–7 Chapter 3 which deals with basic knowledge.

SKILLS IN THE CONTACT PHASE

Most of this chapter has been devoted to answering the *what* question of the activities in the contact phase. We shall now try to answer the *how* question. Once again we must say that it is difficult to be specific and concrete. It is difficult to be sure that our words can communicate to the readers what we think we are saying. This difficulty stems from two factors: words are the symbols of human interaction and they carry meaning only within some context, and the same words often mean different things to different people and a common meaning can be established only by the sender accurately hearing the feedback from the system receiving the communication. Written communication can be put together in such a way that the writer believes that it establishes a context and a meaning, but one can be sure about that only through feedback. Thus we are dreadfully handicapped in communicating with our readers, particularly about some matters such as "self-awareness."

If workers are to carry through effectively on the tasks of the contact phase, they must engage the feelings and the thinking of the client in the process. This is not saying that "a relationship needs to be developed," and especially it is not saying that "a good relationship needs to be developed." What it is saying is that both client and worker must engage with each other (interact with each other in a way *that has meaning to the client system*) as a beginning of what will later become a working relationship. The first step in this engagement is that the worker needs certain types of knowledge and that the greatest of these is knowledge of self—of the way one feels and thinks about the type of problem and the client, and cognitive knowledge of the resources available in both the change agent system and other usable community systems.

Let us go back for a moment to the Mrs. C's case. There are a constellation of factors that trap people immediately into defining the problem as Mrs. C's overprotection of her son. They are

1. An immediate identification with the son as the "victim" of what has happened.
2. An emotional readiness to blame parents for their childrens' pain and trouble.
3. A belief in the personal-deficit concept of deviant behavior.
4. A belief that childrens' behavior is usually caused by parents' treatment of them.
5. An emotional and intellectual commitment to wanting to find "the real problem" which leads to the mistake of defining "cause" as "problem." (Readers may want to go back and read the quotes from Johnson in Chapter 7 on problem solving.)

6. The fact that the worker is presented with an upper-middle class client who has internalized points 1 through 4 in her own thinking and who is so upset over this crisis situation (following upon another crisis that she may still not have mastered) that she is very ready to fix blame on herself and spare her son. So we define the problem as hers rather than her son's and help her beat herself into a further sense of inadequacy while we give the son a nice way of beginning to blame others for his actions.

Please note that this is not to say that there is no relationship between the mother's treatment of her son and his actions; nor is it to say that that connection and the mother's spontaneously suggesting it is ignored in setting the problem-for-work. One further comment, if we are seeking the "real problem," maybe it lies in the father's death, which is responsible for the mother's feelings and actions, which in turn is responsible for the son's behavior. Should those feelings be the problem-for-work? What would happen to the mother's sense of adequacy and her ability to develop different ways of treating her son if the problem-for-work was defined as her reaction to her husband's death, and that reaction was assessed as being a "normal" response to such an overwhelming stress and crisis situation? And what about her son's reaction to his father's death? These questions need to be thought about by the worker and considered thoughtfully with the client system (mother and son). Data will be collected on all these possible life stresses that may have led to the problem behavior. The work of considering their impact and integrating them into some meaningful assessment of the situation and planning the work together is a part of the next several chapters. What we are trying to make very clear here is the importance of not mixing the presenting problem with the cause.

If the readers will go back to the factors listed earlier, they will note that some of these factors are cognitive, some are emotional, and some are both. Perhaps the most critical handicap in problem-solving is our tendency to need a consistent frame of reference both intellectually and emotionally. This results in a tendency to define problems within our usual, working notion of the human condition—to view clients' problems, as it were, from within our frame of reference. Even to explain our clients' insistence that we look at it from their point of view as their resistance to seeing things correctly, and thus in itself proof of the correctness of our formulations.

In order to make this clear, we would like for you to try to solve the following problem.

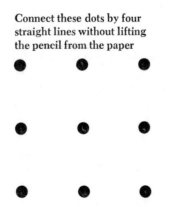

Connect these dots by four straight lines without lifting the pencil from the paper

After you have tried to solve the problem we would like for you to turn to the end of the chapter for the solution. Are you surprised? The thing that leads to failure in solving this problem is the fact that the first time people try it, they almost inevitably make an assumption that the dots compose a square and that the problem must be defined as falling within the boundaries of that system. Thus, the failure to solve the problem does not lie within the difficulty of the problem, or the worker's capacity to do the necessary tasks—it lies within the worker's self-imposed assumptions that nowhere are given as a part of the problem. Workers must be aware of their assumptions and make initial contact within the potential client's frame of reference.

Some further cautions before we move on to some specifics in the use of "self" in the contact phase. (1) The questions asked determine the answers given, and it is the worker's responsibility to determine the questions. (2) Any behavior in the presence of another communicates a view of the nature of one's relationship with that person, and this principle applies to the worker as well as to the client. (3) An important part of human communication takes place through silence or lack of communication as well as through what is said and how it is said. Therefore, the worker needs to be aware of what is not being dealt with by the client as well as what is and must recognize that the client will interpret the helper's silence in their own way. (4) Dependency and lack of responsibility for our actions are caused by someone else taking responsibility for our own thinking, feeling and planning and *is not caused by people giving one too much or doing things for us.* The greatest causes of emotional dependency (as distinguished from the "normal" dependency of not being able to deal with concrete tasks because of handicaps of knowledge, skill, or other capacity) is the taking over of feelings, thinking, and decision-making responsibility by an authority. In fact, not doing *appropriate things* for clients may further break down their coping skills and result in further apathy. Readers will want to refer again to the Dyal and Donovan article (see Reading 7–2).

The skills required in this phase require those described in Chapters 5 and 6 on relationship and communication, especially those of the ability to communicate empathy, genuineness, concern, trustworthiness, respect, and the conditions of service. Listening and attending skills are very important, as it is important to attend both physically (in posture and body language) and psychologically to what the client is trying to communicate. It is important to listen both "with ears to the words and with eyes to the body language" and with "the third ear" to some total messages such as how clients feel and think about themselves, the world, significant others, and people in general; how clients perceive others related to them; and what clients' ambitions, goals, and aspirations are.

To be sure that one is interpreting the client's words and feelings accurately, the worker will need from time to time to check this out with the clients. This may be done by restating the basic messages that one thinks one hears in similar but fewer words, in submitting a tentative summary of what one made of the client's discussion, by connecting things that the client leaves unconnected but that one thinks may be connected. One will, of course, need skill in questioning which is discussed in Chapter 6 on communication. There are times when one may use some tentative interpretation ". . . is it possible that what you are telling me means . . .?" And, often one will be tempted to use reassurance, "I understand . . . ," "that is hard . . . ," "most people would be upset . . ."

One should be careful in the use of such phrases. They often serve to cut off the client's further exploration of the difficulty.

Many workers who feel the client's pain and have the impulse to help are greatly tempted to overuse reassurance. They want to remove the pain from the clients. But the purpose for which the clients come to them is not for the removal of the pain but for doing something about it. In order to help others, we must understand what the problem is that brings the client to us, and often this includes great pain for the client. However, help requires empathy, not pity or sympathy, which too early and too often communicates reassurance. Pain is a signal that there is trouble, and understanding the pain will help us to understand and define the problem as the client perceives it.

Emanuel Tropp (1976, p. 223) has developed an important set of statements related to the worker's presentation of self to the group. We see this as not limited to the group but as summing up in a very impressive way the necessary elements of the worker's presentation of self to the potential client system both at the initial contact and during the work together:

1. Compassion—I deeply care about you.
2. Mutuality—We are here on a common human level; let's agree on a plan and then let's walk the path together.
3. Humility—Please help me to understand.
4. Respect—I consider you as having worth. I treat your ideas and feelings with consideration. I do not intrude upon your person.
5. Openness—I offer myself to you as you see me; real, genuine and authentic.
6. Empathy—I am trying to feel what you are feeling.
7. Involvement—I am trying to share and help in your efforts.
8. Support—I will lend my conviction and back up your progress.
9. Expectation—I have confidence that you can achieve your goals.
10. Limitation—I must remind you of your agreed-upon obligations.
11. Confrontation—I must ask you to look at yourself.
12. Planning—I will always bring proposals, but I would rather have yours.
13. Enabling—I am here to help you become more able, more powerful.
14. Spontaneity and control—I will be as open as possible, yet, I must recognize that, in your behalf, I need to exercise some self control.
15. Role and person—I am both a human being like you and a representation of an agency, with a special function to perform.
16. Science and art—I hope to bring you a professional skill which must be based on organized knowledge, but I am dealing with people, and my humanity must lend art to grace the science.

RECAPITULATION

In this chapter we have discussed the contact phase of the problem-solving process. We have pointed out that this phase involves eight essential tasks that can be summarized as (1) the initial contact, (2) the determination of the problem-for-work, (3) goal clarification, (4) the clarification of service limits, (5) the clarification of what will be asked of the client system, (6) the development of appropriate relationships, (7) the emergence of a commitment to work together, and (8) data collection. It will be noted that these tasks demand the activity of the worker as well as the client.

This beginning part of the problem-solving process is extremely important because it sets the pattern for the phases of work that follow. We have suggested that, given the limits of any specific situation, we collect information about at least three elements of the client system: the hope-discomfort balance that the client brings to the first encounter; the opportunities that the client sees and that the worker can bring to bear; and factors within the client system and in its relationships to the world around it.

One further caution—it is perhaps a misunderstanding of the level and magnitude of problem definition and goal setting that leads some professionals to view the problem-solving model as only of value to the client capable of highly rational functioning. It is our view that every human being has wants (if only to get rid of the worker) and that these wants can be translated into wishes and wishes into goals. The meaning and value of the goals has nothing to do with the worker's evaluation of their value, rather it relates to the client's wishes. Practitioners often see the only goals worth setting as those that seem to the practitioner to involve a generally better life. However, for many clients the securing of essential survival needs and life supports are the only goals worth setting, at least when they have no reason to trust either the practitioner or life itself. If the problem that the client sees is the lack of certain concrete essentials of life, this can become the problem-to-be-worked, client and worker can agree that the securing of these essentials is the first and most important goal at the moment, and the plan can well be that the worker will find a way to supply this resource. In this situation the worker may have done a good deal of the initial work in defining the problem and the achievement of the goal may have come from the worker's concrete giving. The essential factor here is not the level of goal or who works toward the goal but that the client was involved in the thinking and planning that was done, and that what was given was related to the client's wishes and not something that the worker unilaterally thought was needed. The inability to see small concrete goals as important objectives for work and the assumption that the worker's supplying of concrete needs to apathetic, withdrawn, depressed, or angry people need not involve mutual problem definition and goal setting (no matter how primitive the level) are built upon certain unconscious, or not so unconscious, practitioner assumptions about what is meaningful professional interaction that need to be seriously examined.

A LOOK FORWARD

In the last part of the chapter we discussed some of the modes of information gathering that are available to the practitioner. Thus ends our discussion of the contact phase of the problem-solving process. Articles of two other authors are reproduced in this chapter to extend the development of the points made in it. In the next chapter the contract phase of the transaction will be considered. The contract phase is the core of the work together.

Solution to puzzle

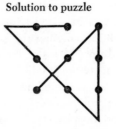

Reading
8-1 Diagrammatic assessment of family relationships*

Ann Hartman

Integrating new knowledge and conceptual frameworks from the many sources that inform and support social work practice is a long and arduous process. General systems theory, which was introduced to social workers over 20 years ago (Lutz, 1956), has been particularly difficult to assimilate because it is so abstract. The distance is great between the lofty principles enunciated by systems theorists and the practical knowledge and skill that guide the practitioner's work with people, day by day. The field has made some progress in utilizing systems concepts in developing middle-range theory, in organizing practice models (Hearn, 1969), in extending and clarifying the boundaries of the unit of attention (Germain, 1968), and in prescribing general directions for action (Hartman, 1974). Professionals in the field are now at the point of attempting to translate concepts from this middle-range theory into specific and testable prescriptions for practice.

Particularly interesting is the potential a systems orientation has for altering cognitive styles and enabling practitioners to organize and process increasingly complex systems of variables (Hartman, 1970). The attempt here is to derive from systems framework new conceptual models that can enhance the practitioner's and the client's perceptions of reality, thereby contributing to competence and creative adaptation in therapy.

Social workers, in attempting to understand their traditional unit of attention— the person in the total life space over time —are faced with an overwhelming amount of data. These data must be ordered, se-

lected, and arranged to reduce confusion and overload. Edward Tolman has likened this mediating process to a map room where intervening cognitive charts shape data, lending meaning and manageability to the influx of information (Bruner, Goodnow, and Austin, 1962). These cognitive patterns have tremendous influence on how reality is perceived but are not readily observed or easily changed. They are an ongoing and familiar part of the self, and, as Frederick Duhl (1969) has pointed out, "that which is constantly experienced is neutral to awareness, being so immersed in the identity, so 'egosyntonic,' that it is rarely open to observation or challenge." As social workers interact with their environment, these mediating cognitive processes so strongly imprint a particular view of reality that they may well be just as crucial as knowledge and values in determining professional decision-making.

In dealing with almost continual information overload, cognitive processes tend to operate analytically: to partialize, to abstract parts from wholes, to reduce, and to simplify. Although this makes data more manageable, it does damage to the complexity inherent in reality. Ways of conceptualizing causation have tended to be particularly reductionist as reality is arranged in chains of simple cause and effect reactions. Such linear views reflect the limitations of thought and language rather than the nature of the real world, where human events are the result of transactions among multiple variables.

An emphasis on identifying the roots of problematic conditions in tremendously complex situations has frequently pushed social workers into supporting simplistic explanations and into arguments over what is the cause and hence the cure. Since 19th century scientism found expression in Mary

---

* From *Social Casework,* October 1978 (New York: Family Service Association of America).

E. Richmond's *Social Diagnosis* (1917), the profession has struggled with the temptation to deal with this "radically untidy universe" through reductionist solutions growing out of reductionist assessments.[1]

If social workers are to avoid reductionism and scientism, if they are to translate a systems orientation into practice, they must learn to "think systems," or to develop within their own cognitive map rooms new and more complex ways of imprinting reality. They must then devise ways of using this view in specific interventive techniques and strategies.

As one learns to "think systems," one tends to move to the use of metaphor and to the use of visual models in order to get beyond the constraints of linear thought and language. Social workers have always been frustrated in writing psychosocial summaries—they find it not unlike the attempt to describe the action in a football game over the radio. In attempting to describe the complex system of transacting variables, the meaning and the nature of the integration of the variables, and the totality of the events and action is lost. The use of metaphor in poetry and of two- and three-dimensional simulations in painting and sculpture demonstrate the integrative power of such approaches. Similar artistry can be used to expand the social worker's understanding of the nature of reality. Of many possibilities, two simple paper-and-pencil simulations have proved to be particularly useful, not only as assessment tools, but in interviewing, planning, and intervention.

One simulation is the ecological map of "eco-map," which was originally developed three years ago as an assessment tool to help workers in public child welfare practice examine the needs of families.[2] This tool pictures the family or the individual in the life space and has since been tested in a variety of settings with a wide range of clients. The second simulation is the genogram, which has been used by systems-oriented family therapists to chart intergenerational family history.[3] This tool has also been found to be highly adaptable for use with individuals or families in many different settings where it is important to understand the development of the family system through time.

The ecological metaphor

The task of making general systems concepts operational and humane, of giving them flesh and blood meaning, presents a difficult challenge. Although "input," "throughput," "moving steady state," and "deviation amplifying feedback loops" are precise and useful concepts, they mean little to social workers if they are unrelated to a human context. Recently, there has been a growing effort to utilize the science of ecology as a metaphorical way of humanizing and integrating system concepts (Germain, 1973). The science of ecology studies the delicate balance that exists between living things and their environments and the ways in which this mutuality may be enhanced and maintained.

In utilizing the ecological metaphor, it is clear that the salient human environment includes far more than air, water, food, spatial arrangements, and other aspects of the physical environment. Human environments also include networks of intimate human relationships. Further, over the centuries, human beings have erected elaborate social, economic, and political structures that they

---

[1] For a discussion of casework's relationship with science ad scientism, see Germain (1971).

[2] The eco-map was developed in 1975 by the author as a part of the Child Welfare Learning Laboratory, a project of the University of Michigan School of Social Work Program for Continuing Education in the Human Services. The project was supported in part by a grant from Region V, Social and Rehabilitation Service, U.S. Department of Health, Education, and Welfare, Section 426, Title IV, part B of the Social Security Act. The author is grateful to Lynn Nybell, Coordinator of the Family Assessment Module, for her ideas, criticisms, and encouragement.

[3] The genogram has been used extensively by systems-oriented family therapists. For example, see Guerin and Pendagast (1976).

must sustain and through which their needs are met. People must maintain an adaptive mutuality with these intricate systems which are required for growth and self-realization.

An ecological metaphor can lead social workers to see the client not as an isolated entity for study but as a part of a complex ecological system. Such a view helps them to focus on the sources of nurturance, stimulation, and support that must be available in the intimate and extended environment to make possible growth and survival. It also leads to a consideration of the social, relational, and instrumental skills individuals must have to use possibilities in their environment and to cope with its demands.

The eco-map

The eco-map is a simple paper-and-pencil simulation that has been developed as an assessment, planning, and interventive tool. It maps in a dynamic way the ecological system, the boundaries of which encompass the person or family in the life space. Included in the map are the major systems that are a part of the family's life and the nature of the family's relationship with the various systems. The eco-map portrays an overview of the family in their situation; it pictures the important nurturant or conflict-laden connections between the family and the world. It demonstrates the flow of resources, or the lacks and deprivations. This mapping procedure highlights the nature of the interfaces and points to conflicts to be mediated, bridges to be built, and resources to be sought and mobilized. Although all one needs is a piece of paper and a pencil, it saves time to have "empty" maps available. These maps can be worked on by an individual or a family (see Figure 2).

Instructions for drawing an eco-map. First the nuclear family system or household is drawn in a large circle at the map's center. It has been common practice in mapping families to use squares to depict males and circles to depict females. Relationships are indicated as in the traditional family tree

or genetic chart. It is useful to put the person's age in the center of the circle or square. Thus, a circle with "80" in the center would represent an elderly woman.

FIGURE 1

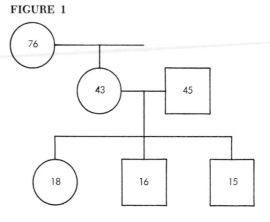

Figure 1 represents a household consisting of a father, a mother, three children, and the wife's mother. The usefulness of this is demonstrated when one considers the number of words it would take to portray the facts thus represented. (The mapping of more complex nuclear family systems will be demonstrated in the discussion of genograms.)

After drawing the household in the large circle in the middle, add the connections between the family and the different parts of the environment. In the empty map (see Figure 2), some of the most common systems in the lives of most families have been labeled, such as work, extended family, recreation, health care, school, and so on. Other circles have been left undesignated so that the map can be individualized for different families.

Connections between the family and the various systems are indicated by drawing lines between the family and those systems (see Figure 3). The nature of the connection can be expressed in the type of line drawn: A solid or thick line represents an important or strong connection and a dotted line a tenuous connection; jagged marks across the line represent a stressful or con-

302

FIGURE 2

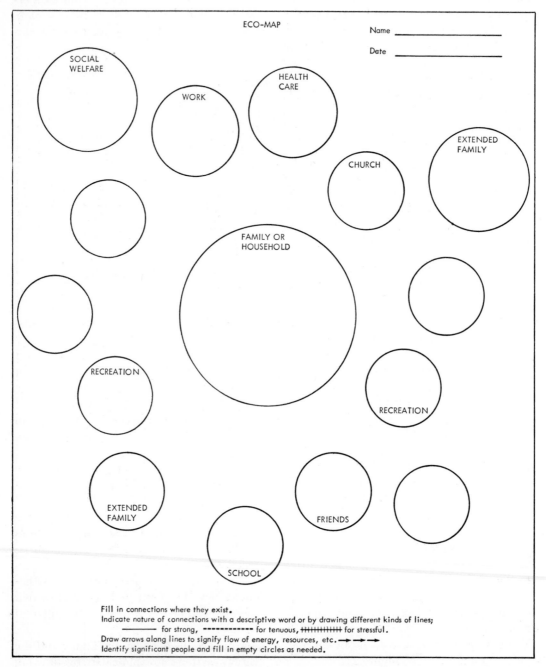

ECO-MAP

Name _____

Date _____

SOCIAL
WELFARE

WORK

HEALTH
CARE

EXTENDED
FAMILY

CHURCH

FAMILY OR
HOUSEHOLD

RECREATION

RECREATION

EXTENDED
FAMILY

FRIENDS

SCHOOL

Fill in connections where they exist.
Indicate nature of connections with a descriptive word or by drawing different kinds of lines;
———— for strong, ------------ for tenuous, ┼┼┼┼┼┼┼┼┼┼ for stressful.
Draw arrows along lines to signify flow of energy, resources, etc. ─►─►─►
Identify significant people and fill in empty circles as needed.

flicted relationship. It is useful to indicate the direction of the flow of resources, energy, or interest by drawing arrows along the connecting lines:

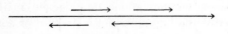

In testing the eco-map, it has been found that the use of the three kinds of lines for conflicted, strong, and tenuous relationships is an efficient shorthand when the worker uses the eco-mapping procedure, without the family, as an analytic tool. However,

FIGURE 3

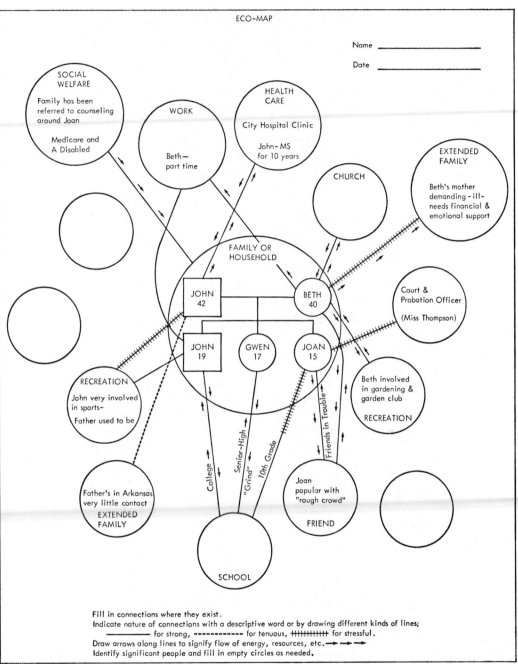

when using the map as an interviewing tool, this code has often been felt to be too constraining. Workers have preferred to ask clients to describe the nature of the connection and will then qualify that connec-

tion by writing a brief description along the connecting line.

Connections can be drawn to the family as a whole if they are intended to portray the total family systems relationship with some system in the environment. Other connections can be drawn between a particular individual in the family and an outside system when that person is the only one involved or different family members are involved with an outside system in different ways. This enables the map to highlight the contrasts in the way various family members are connected to the world.

It is easy to learn to plot the eco-map, and it is important to become comfortable with the tool before using it with clients. A simple way to learn is to sketch one's own eco-map. It is also useful to practice with friends. By then, one is generally ready to use it with clients.

Uses of the eco-map. No matter how the eco-map is used, its primary value is in its visual impact and its ability to organize and present concurrently not only a great deal of factual information but also the relationships between variables in a situation. Visual examination of the map has considerable impact on the way the worker and the client perceive the situation. The connections, the themes, and the quality of the family's life seem to jump off the page, and this leads to a more holistic and integrative perception. The integrative value of visual experience was aptly expressed by one 12-year-old client when he said, "Gee, I never saw myself like that before!"

Initially, the eco-map was developed as a thinking tool for the worker. It was helpful in organizing material and in making an assessment. Sketching out an eco-map in the early stages of contact brought out salient areas of the family's life space that had not as yet been explored and suggested hypotheses for treatment. Before long, it became apparent that the eco-map would make a useful interviewing tool. Client and worker cooperated in picturing the client's life space. This led to much more active participation on the part of the client in the information-gathering and assessment process. The growing collaborative relationship between worker and client was often expressed in a change in seating arrangements as the two tended to sit shoulder-to-shoulder, working together on the joint project.

Sharing the eco-mapping process also led to increased understanding and acceptance of the self on the part of the client. For example, an almost empty eco-map helps the client objectify and share loneliness and isolation. An eco-map full of stressful relationships showing all of the arrows pointing away from the family may lead a father to say, "No wonder I feel drained, everything is going out and nothing is coming in!" The eco-map has been extensively tested with natural parents working toward the return of their placed children through the Temporary Foster Care Project of the Michigan Department of Social Services (Thomas, 1978). Foster care workers noted that parents who were generally angry and self-protective following placement of their children because of abuse or neglect were almost without exception engaged through the use of the map. Workers were aware of a dramatic decrease in defensiveness. The ecological perspective made it clear to parents that the worker was not searching for their inner defects but rather was interested in finding out what it was like to be in the clients' space, to walk in their shoes.

In working with the eco-map, clients have responded in some unanticipated ways. Although it was expected that they would gain a new perception by being able to step outside and look at themselves and their world, the emotional importance of the maps to the clients was a surprise. One mother demonstrated this early in the project by putting the eco-map up on her kitchen wall. In responding to clients' attachments to the maps, workers have regularly arranged to have them photocopied or have used pencil carbon so that clients may have a copy.

Contracting and intervention. The eco-map has also been a useful tool in planning and has had considerable impact on intervention. Because it focuses attention on the client's relationship with the life space, interventions tend to be targeted on the interface, with both worker and client becoming active in initiating changes in the life space. Problematic conditions tend to be characterized as transactional and as a function of the many variables that combine to affect the quality of the individual's or the family's life.

In the Temporary Foster Care Project mentioned earlier, the worker and client moved quite naturally from the eco-map to a task-oriented contract.[4] They talked together about the changes that would be needed in the eco-map before the family could be reunited. They identified problem areas, resources needed, and potential strengths and planned what actions were needed to bring about change. Further, they established priorities and developed a contract describing the tasks to be undertaken by the worker and by the client.

The uses of the eco-map have multiplied in the hands of creative practitioners. For example, it has been used to portray the past and the future: In a rehabilitation program in a medical setting a social worker used eco-maps with clients to picture their world before their accident or illness; this helped clients to objectify what changes would be made in their lives following hospitalization. It helped them to mourn interests and activities that would have to be relinquished and also to recognize sources of support and gratification that would continue to be available. The mapping encouraged anticipatory planning and preparation for a new life, consideration of appropriate replacements for lost activities, and possible new resources to be tapped, all of which could expand the client's horizons. This technique was not only useful with the patient alone but was very helpful in conjoint work with disabled persons and their families.

Retrospective use of the map tends to highlight changes in a client's life space that could have precipitated current difficulties. When families and individuals seek help, a major question is always "Why has the client sought help now?" A review of the changes that have taken place in the previous months may well bring to light shifts of which the client was quite unaware.

Recordkeeping and measurements of change. A complete eco-map deposited in a case record is a useful tool to present and record a case situation. Not only does it tend to keep the total situation clear for the worker, it can also serve as a means of communication to others should a staff member have to respond to a client in the absence of the regular worker. A crisis walk-in center where case responsibility is shared by a team to provide extended coverage uses the eco-map this way.

Finally, eco-maps can be used to evaluate outcomes and measure change. For example, a ten-year-old boy on a return visit to a school social worker asked for the map. He had made a new friend and wanted to put him on the map. The mother who had hung the map in the kitchen called her worker after two months of considerable activity on both their parts. She wanted to come into the office to plot another map so that she and the worker could look together at the changes. A comparison of eco-maps done at outset and at termination can help clients and workers measure the changes that have taken place. As such the maps can become an important device in maintaining accountability.

The genogram

Families not only exist in space but also through time, and thus a second kind of simulation is needed to picture the development of this powerful relationship system. Not only is each individual immersed in the complex here-and-now life space, but each individual is also a part of a family saga, in an infinitely complicated human system which has developed over many generations and has transmitted powerful commands, role assignments, events, and patterns of living and relating down through the years.

---

[4] The work of William Reid and Laura Epstein (1977) and their collaborators has been useful in this area.

Each individual and each family is deeply implicated in this intergenerational family history.

Just as the eco-map can begin to portray and objectify the family in space, so can the genogram picture the family system through time, enabling an individual to step out of the system, examine it, and begin to gain a greater understanding of complex family dynamics as they have developed and as they affect the current situation.

Instructions for drawing a genogram. A genogram is simply a family tree that includes more social data. It is a map of three, four, or more generations of a family which records genealogical relationships, major family events, occupations, losses, family migrations and dispersal, identifications and role assignments, and information about alignments and communication patterns. Again, all that is needed is paper and pencil. For most genograms, a rather large piece of paper is usually required. It is important for the genogram to be uncrowded and clear to make visual examination possible.

The skeleton of the genogram tends to follow the conventions of genetic and genealogical charts. As in the eco-map, a male is indicated by a square, a female by a circle, and if the sex of a person is unknown by a triangle. The latter symbol tends to be used, for example, when the client says, "I think there were seven children in my grandfather's family but I have no idea whether they were males or females." Or, "My mother lost a full-term baby five years before I was born, but I don't know what sex it was."

A marital pair is indicated by a line drawn from a square to a circle; it is useful to add the marital date, on the line. A married couple with offspring is shown as illustrated in Figure 4. Offspring are generally entered according to age, starting with the oldest on the left. The family diagramed in Figure 4 has an older son followed by a

FIGURE 4

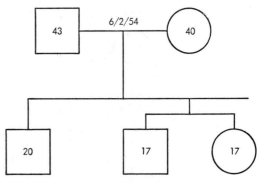

set of twins. A divorce is generally portrayed by a dotted line, and again, it is useful to include dates (see Figure 5). A family member no longer living is generally indicated by drawing an "X" through the figure and giving the year of death. Thus, a complex, but not untypical, reconstituted family may be drawn as shown in Figure 5.

FIGURE 5

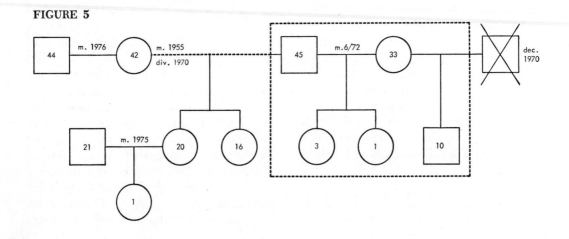

It is useful to draw a dotted line around the family members who compose the household. Incidentally, such a family chart enables the worker to grasp who is who quickly in complicated reconstituted families.

With these basic building blocks, expanded horizontally to depict the contemporary generation of siblings and cousins and vertically to chart the generations through time, it is possible to chart any family, given sufficient paper, patience, and information (see Figure 6). As one charts the skeletal structure of the family, it is also important to fill this out with the rich and varied data which portray the saga of the particular family being studied.

Many different kinds of information may be gathered. First and middle given names identify family members, indicate naming patterns, and bring identifications to the

surface. In understanding where a client may fit into the family and what expectations and displacements may have affected the sense of self, a first step is to discover who, if anyone, the client was named after. Once this person is identified, it is important to discover what he or she was like, what roles he or she carried, and, perhaps most salient, what the nature of the relationship was between the client's parents and this relative.

Sometimes meanings and connections are not obvious and emerge only through careful exploration. For example, in charting a genogram with a young man who was struggling with identity issues and a complex tie with his mother, naming patterns were being discussed. The client's name was Tony; his American soldier father had met his mother abroad and, immediately after

FIGURE 6
Sample genogram

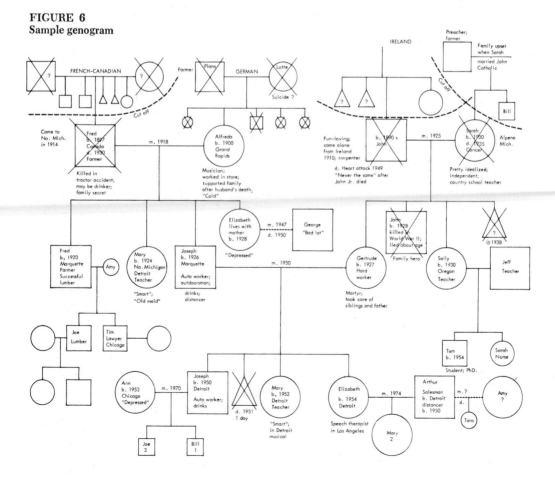

their marriage, the couple had moved to the United States. The move and subsequent political events resulted in the wife's being completely cut off from her family. The client, their firstborn child, was born a year after the marriage. When asked whom he was named after, he replied, "I wasn't named after anyone in the family—I was named after St. Anthony—the patron of lost objects." The symbolic meaning of Anthony's name to his mother became dramatically apparent: Tony was named after everyone in his mother's family!

Dates of birth and dates of death record when members joined the family, their longevity, and family losses. Birth dates indicate the age of family members when important events occurred. They indicate how early or late in a marriage a child came and the age of the parents at the birth. In a sense, birth, marriage, and death dates mark the movement of the family through time. In working with a client's genogram, it is helpful to discover all of the events that took place around the birth. Major losses experienced in the family around that time can be of particular significance. The tendency to use newborn family members as replacements for lost members seems almost universal and has even been institutionalized in some culturally proscribed naming patterns.

Birth dates also identify each individual's place in the sibship. This brings to the surface such potential roles as "older responsible," "firstborn son," or "baby." It is also relevant to discover who else in the family has occupied the same sibling position. Sibling position can be a powerful source of intergenerational identifications.

Place of birth and current place of residence mark the movement of the family through space. Such information charts the family's patterns of dispersal, bringing into focus major immigrations or migrations and periods of loss, change, and upheaval. Such information may also point to the fact that generations of a family have stayed within a fairly small radius except, perhaps, for a particular individual in each generation who moves away. If a client happens to be this generation's "wanderer," that could be a valuable piece of information.

Picturing the family's movement through space may communicate a good deal about family boundaries and norms concerning mobility. Is this a family that holds on or lets go? Further, the impact of world history on families often becomes evident as responses to war, persecution, westward migration, depression, industrialization, and even climatic or ecological changes are often seen in relocations.

Occupations of family members acquaint one with the interests and talents, the successes and failures, and the varied socioeconomic statuses that are found in most families. Occupational patterns may also point to identifications and can often portray family proscriptions and expectations.

Finally, facts about members' health and causes of death provide overall family health history and also may say something about the way clients see their own future. These predictions may well have some power of self-fulfillment.

This demographic data can take a worker a long way toward understanding the family system. However, gathering associations about family members can add to the richness of the portrayal. One can ask, "What word or two or what picture comes to mind when you think about this person?" These associations tend to tap another level of information about the family as the myths, role assignments, characterizations, or caricatures of family members come into the client's mind. Characterizations such as lazy, bossy, martyr, beautiful, caretaker, are likely to be offered, bringing forth reminiscences or stories that have become a part of the family biography and mythology.

Finally, certain aspects of the family's communication structure can be indicated. Parts of the family that have been cut off become quite obvious because the client generally has very little information about them. Cutoffs can be portrayed by drawing a fence where the cutoff exists whereas tight communication bonds can be demonstrated by drawing a line around portions of the family that form close linkages. It helps to keep things clear if a colored pencil is used to indicate communication linkages and cutoffs so as not to confuse these with the basic genealogical structure. Cutoffs are of particular significance as they are usually indicative of conflict, loss, and family secrets. Cutoffs generally develop to protect family members from pain and conflict, but they are usually indicators of unfinished business and may leave the person out of touch with important aspects of family and perhaps of self.

It is often found that a client doing a genogram will have considerable information about one section of the family, for example, the maternal grandmother's family, and almost none about other relatives. This uneven distribution of knowledge is significant in assessing communication and relationship patterns.

Uses of the genogram. The genogram is a classic tool for gathering and utilizing family data in any family oriented practice. No matter what the setting, if the individual is to be understood in the context of the total family system, the genogram can portray that system and move worker and client toward an understanding of the impact of that system and its relevance to the issues at hand. In counseling regarding marital and parent-child conflict, the routes or prototypes of these conflicts may well emerge. The use of the genogram in conjoint marital counseling can increase empathy between the marital pair and help each to identify the old family issues that have been displaced in the marriage.

In working with the aging, the genogram is an invaluable tool in life review. Elderly people can reminisce and organize memories but also, in working with the genogram, can experience themselves as a central link between the past and the future. This process expresses continuity and the generative process and illustrates that, although

the individual's life span may be brief, the family's life reaches back into the past and on into the future. One residence for the aging encourages staff to meet with family members to teach them how to build genograms and help their aged relatives reconnect with their family saga. This sharing of the genogram has been an important experience for both the aged person and the younger family members.

Genograms have also been used in child welfare agencies. As part of an adoptive home study, for example, the genogram may clarify why a couple experiences their family as incomplete and also brings to the surface considerations and plans concerning who an adopted child is intended to be. Charting a genogram with natural parents insures that, should family ties be legally severed, there will be a full family history available to the child in the future. One child-care agency that regularly makes use of the genogram in adoption practice has found that often the experience of doing the genogram has been very meaningful to natural parents who see the process as giving something of themselves to the child. The issue of open adoption has yet to be settled but, in the interim, the genogram can gather and keep available the kind of information adopted children often want.

In a hospital setting, a genogram can be used to gather an expanded health history. Such a history provides information about patterns of illness and health in a family: for instance, a paternal grandmother may have died of heart disease at 38 while the maternal grandmother lived an active life to age 94. Further, patterns of illness as well as attitudes toward illness and ill people may appear.

Summary

The eco-map and the genogram are paper and pencil simulations that can organize and objectify a tremendous amount of data about the family system in space and through time.

Such objectivity and visual portrayal can lead to new insights and to altered perceptions, of the complexity of human systems.

Such altered perceptions may point to new ways of bringing about change, ways that relate to the complexity of human existence.

Reading
8-2 Family behavior of urban American Indians*

John G. Red Horse, Ronald Lewis, Marvin Feit, and James Decker

Ecological formulus are becoming increasingly popular as protocols for human service models. This trend represents a certain irony in the context of service provision to minority families. The function of American Indian families, for example, has long been disabled by social service personnel who appear insensitive to unique Indian family cultural and structural needs. Removal of children from American Indian families following a variety of social diagnoses is approaching epidemic proportion. William Byler (1977, p. 1) cites that 25 to 35 percent of American Indian children are raised outside their natural family network. If ecological standards are applied, American Indian families appear qualified for endangered species status.

This article examines characteristics unique to American Indian families and attempts to relate these to developing human ecology models in casework.[1] Attention is directed toward extended family networks which represent the interactive field in which caseworkers should conduct transactions.

* Reprinted by permission of Family Service Association of America, publisher, from *Social Casework* 59:2 (February 1978), pp. 67–72.

[1] This article was made possible by grant no. 90–C624 from the National Center on Child Abuse and Neglect, Children's Bureau, Office of Child Development, Office for Human Development, U.S. Department of Health, Education, and Welfare. Its contents should not be construed as official policy of the National Center on Child Abuse and Neglect or of any agency of the federal government.

Irving M. Levine's social conservation model (1976) serves as a theoretical orientation. This model assumes that individual mental health is linked to a sense of selfhood which is accomplished through adherence to an historical culture and is transmitted principally through family socialization. Family structure and process, therefore, represent the cornerstone for individual behavior, cultural acquisition, and mental health.

Family structure and cultural behavior

American Indian family networks assume a structure which is radically different from other extended family units in Western society. The accepted structural boundary of the European model, for example, is the household. Thus, an extended family is defined as three generations within a single household. American Indian family networks, however, are structurally open and assume a village-type characteristic. Their extension is inclusive of several households representing significant relatives along both vertical and horizontal lines.

Network structure influences individual behavior patterns because family transactions occur within a community milieu. This is important for professionals to understand so that mislabeling may be avoided. Normal behavioral transactions within the network relational field, for example, may appear bizarre to an outside observer.

Case illustration. The following case

illustration provides a typical example of this point.[2]

A young probationer was under court supervision and had strict orders to remain with responsible adults. His counselor became concerned because the youth appeared to ignore this order. The client moved around frequently and, according to the counselor, stayed overnight with several different young women. The counselor presented this case at a formal staff meeting, and fellow professionals stated their suspicion that the client was either a pusher or a pimp. The frustrating element to the counselor was that the young women knew each other and appeared to enjoy each other's company. Moreover, they were not ashamed to be seen together in public with the client. This behavior prompted the counselor to initiate violation proceedings.

A Minneapolis American Indian male professional came upon the case quite by accident. He knew the boy's family well and requested a delay in court proceedings to allow time for a more thorough investigation. It was discovered that the young women were all first cousins to the client. He had not been frivolously "staying overnight with them"; he had been staying with different units of his family. Each female was as a sister. Moreover, each family unit had a responsible and obligated adult available to supervise and to care for the client.

A revocation order in this case would have caused irreparable alienation between the family and human service professionals. The casework decision would have inappropriately punished the youth as well as several members of his family for simply conducting normal family behavior. Moreover, its impact would affect people far beyond the presenting client and those members of his family who were directly responsible

for his care. The young man had a characteristically large Indian family network consisting of over 200 people and spanning three generations.

Structural characteristics of American Indian family networks confront human service professionals with judgmental issues beyond that of labeling. Extended family often serves as a major instrument of accountability. Standards and expectations are established which maintain group solidarity through enforcement of values.

Single-parent and single-adult households do appear in American Indian communities. Professionals bound by nuclear family parameters point to this fact in planning service resources. Consequently, they are reluctant either to use or legitimate aunts, uncles, cousins, and grandparents as alternate or supportive service care givers.

Other case illustrations. Nancy, for example, was an 18-year-old mother identified as mentally retarded and epileptic by the department of welfare officials. Although retardation was subsequently disproved, the department assumed control and custody of Nancy's infant child.

Nancy's parents insisted that the family network was available for assistance, if necessary. The welfare staff, however, considered this offer untenable. The grandparents were deemed senile and unable to care for an infant. They were in their early 50s.

The staff ignored the fact that the grandparents had just finished caring for three other young and active grandchildren without dependence on institutional social intervention. Moreover, these children appeared to be well-adjusted. The officials simply insisted in this case that standard placement procedures be followed; a foster home was obtained for Nancy's child.

The placement orders were eventually overruled in Nancy's case, but not without heroic legal intervention. It is unfortunate that such adversary strategies are necessary to prove competencies of natural family networks. Often, as the following case illustrates, family competency and responsi-

---

[2] This case illustration and all subsequent cases are drawn from the files of Ah-be-no-gee, an innovative demonstration program in child abuse and neglect. Ah-be-no-gee is located in Minneapolis, Minnesota, and funded by the National Center for Child Abuse and Neglect, Office of Child Development, U.S. Department of Health, Education, and Welfare.

bility evolve as a normal process of network accountability.

Anita was the elder within the family. She was a direct descendent of the most renowned chief of her band and enjoyed high status. She lived alone in a trailer. Shortly after her seventieth birthday, she became ill and unable to care either for herself or to perform routine household chores. A social worker arranged for Anita's admission to a rest home.

The family accepted this interventive plan without comment. Subsequently, however, the situation changed. Anita received regular visits, but these did not satisfy family needs. Anita became lonely for home, and the family became lonely for her. A ritual feast was held which Anita attended. Family concerns regarding her absence were expressed, and a decision was made that she should remain at home.

The family developed its own helping plan. Each member was given a scheduled time period to provide homemaker services for Anita. Through this shift system, the family network assumed service responsibility. In this case the family in the immediate vicinity consisted of ten households. Service providers ranged from 13-year-old grandchildren to 50-year-old children.

Family network hierarchy

American Indian family network behavior also contributes to a very conservative cultural pattern. A vigorous network is both retained and developed for transmission of cultural attributes. Continually reinforced and enduring relational roles serve to illustrate this behavior.

Grandparents retain official and symbolic leadership in family communities. Both are active processes sanctioned by the children and their parents. Official leadership is characterized by a close proximity of grandparents to family. It is witnessed through the behavior of children who actively seek daily contact with grandparents and by grandparents who monitor parental behavior. In this milieu, grandparents have an official voice in child-rearing methods, and parents seldom overrule corrective measures from their elders. Symbolic leadership is characterized by an incorporation of unrelated elders into the family. This prevails during an absence of a natural grandparent, but it is not necessarily limited to, or dependent on, such an absence. It is witnessed through the behavior of children and parents who select and virtually adopt a grandparent. In this milieu, younger people are seeking social acceptance from an older member of the community. Symbolic grandparents will not invoke strong child-rearing sanctions. Because their acceptance is sought, their norm-setting standards are seldom ignored.

Three distinct family patterns

Extended family networks represent a universal pattern among American Indian nations. Data from one American Indian family service program, however, point to significant variability among the networks. Specific family characteristics, therefore, serve as critical information in the development of methodological guidelines for casework practice.

Three distinct family lifestyle patterns serve for initial identification: (1) a traditional group which overtly adheres to culturally defined styles of living, (2) a nontraditional, bicultural group which appears to have adopted many aspects of non-American Indian styles of living, and (3) a pantraditional group which overtly struggles to redefine and reconfirm previously lost cultural styles of living.[3] Selected behavior variables for each pattern appear in Figure 1.

Many observers of American Indian life tend to hold biases concerning which pattern is most legitimate or functional in contemporary American society. This judgmental behavior represents a luxury that caseworkers must avoid, because each pat-

---

[3] Data on family patterns were drawn from Ah-be-no-gee.

FIGURE 1
Some selected variables of behavior according to family lifestyle—patterns among Minneapolis Urban Chippewas

Variable of behavior	Family lifestyle pattern		
	Traditional	*Bicultural*	*Pantraditional*
Language	Ojibway constitutes conversational language of parents and grandparents Children are bilingual and able to transact family affairs following Indian language.	English constitutes conversational language by parents, grandparents, and children. Grandparents are usually bilingual. Some Indian language is recaptured through formal classes	Either English or Ojibway constitutes conversational language of parents, grandparents, and children. Indian language is recaptured through formal academic classes.
Religion	Midewiwin remains as the belief system. It retains the characteristics of a very closed system, following family networks.	Anglo belief system prevails; is generally, but not exclusively, Catholicism. Some all-Indian congregations exist with culturally adapted canons.	A modified Indian belief system mixing several traditional forms; that is Midewi-win, Native American Church, and so on. Unlike closed structure of traditionalists, proselytizing strategies are employed.
Family relations field	Extended network	Extended network	Extended network
Social engagement	Some acceptance of dominant society's activities; that is, bowling, and so on. Cultural activities such as feasts, religion, and pow wows prevail and take precedence over all others.	Dominant society's activities prevail, that is, bowling, baseball, golf. Relate to non-Indians well. Cultural activities remain of interest but not necessarily enacted through behavior, for example, will sit and watch at pow wows and read about religion. Very active in Indian meetings and politics.	Openly eschew activities of dominant society. Cultural activities prevail. Those who are not expert try to recapture singing and dancing skills.

tern is legitimate within its own relational field and contributes to a family sense of selfhood.

Many observers assume that different family lifestyle patterns point to an ongoing erosion of cultural values. Studies suggest, however, that American Indian core values are retained and remain as a constant, regardless of family lifestyle patterns (Hallowell, 1967; Krush et al., 1969; Native American Research Group, 1975). Pattern variables, therefore, do not represent valid criteria for measuring "Indianness."

The importance of family lifestyle patterns to human service professionals is that each pattern represents a different interac-

tive field, that is, a different environmental context for social casework. As would be expected, family responses to intervention vary. Traditional families, for example, cannot relate to professionals and prefer to ignore mainstream social methodologies. Generally, these families are very courteous to strangers. They will politely listen to professionals, but seldom respond to any social prescriptions which depart from customary practice.

Conversely, bicultural families are able to relate to professional care givers. They are able to accept and cope with contemporary social prescriptions. Pantraditional families denounce professionals and mainstream social methodologies. They are engaged in attempting to recapture and redefine cultural methodologies.[4]

Family network dynamics

Diverse family network interlockings have emerged over time as a result of geographic movements and intertribal marriages, and these complexities warrant scholarly investigation. Of critical significance to this discussion, however, is the fact that American Indian relational values have remained intact through the years: Extended family network remain as a constant regardless of family lifestyle patterns.

Network behavior patterns clearly point to the emergence of a distinct, closed American Indian community. Outsiders, including representatives of agencies providing mandated services, do not gain entrance easily. This attitude has influenced the development of health and welfare services. Ninety percent of the American Indians in Minneapolis responding to questions relating to health needs behavior, for example, indicated a preference for receiving services from American Indian workers (DeGeyndt, 1973). This preference is clearly demonstrated by American Indian clients in the St. Paul-Minneapolis "Twin Cities" metropolitan area of Minnesota who rely upon American Indian service agencies. This contrasts with non-Indian health programs located in the same community, which are continuously involved in strategies to recruit American Indian clients and are unable to serve a representative number (Red Horse and Feit, 1976, pp. 18–22).

Outside observers often cite this network behavior as fraught with dangers, because many American Indian service providers are not professionally trained. American In-

dians, however, have a commendable history in medicine and in community mental health. American Indian families, for example, traditionally organize supportive networks for children through a naming ceremony (Densmore, 1970). This ceremony actually reconfirms the responsibilities of a natural network, that is, aunts, uncles, and cousins. The family emerges as a protective social fabric to provide for the health and welfare of the children. Namesakes provide what professionals define as "substitute services" if parents become incapacitated. Unlike similar religions and cultural rituals, namesakes become the same as parents in the network structure.

American Indian programs in the "Twin Cities" metropolitan area formally incorporate aspects of ethnoscience, such as naming ceremonies, into care-giving strategies. Traditional feasts represent a common activity. Ritual feasts are held according to customary standards, for example, at the seasons' changes or at naming ceremonies. Preventive feasts are conducted to bring a family together whenever danger is imminent. Celebrative feasts are held during special occasions, such as Mother's Day observances. American Indian people, of course, feel comfortable in these surroundings. Moreover, they are secure in developing relationships with American Indian service providers who attend the feasts.

Ronald Lewis (1977, p. 9) developed an interesting schematic through a tracking of Indian health behavior in Milwaukee, Wisconsin. Figure 2 identifies various resource levels and a sequence of behavior that emerged from his investigation. It confirms network behavior. Its prevailing characteristic is that the mainstream health care system is used only after network resources are exhausted.

Conclusion

The objective of this article has been to identify important attributes of American Indian family network structure and cultural behavior and to inform professionals

---

[4] Caution must be exercised in appraising the issues of "coping ability" and "openness to mainstream social methodologies." Staff at Ah-be-no-gee, for example, have witnessed an overwhelming preference by American Indians for self-determination and self-governed programs, regardless of differences in family lifestyle patterns.

FIGURE 2
Individual seeking aid—numbered according to order of significance and sequential path followed by urban Indians seeking help

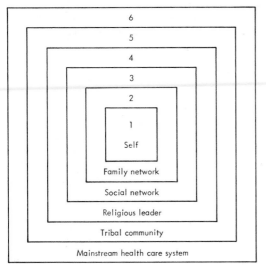

1. Individual
2. Goes to immediate family first
3. Goes to extended family (cousins, aunts, uncles)—social network
4. Goes to religious leader
5. Goes to tribal council
6. Finally goes to formalized health care system

about the importance of culture as a variable in human services, especially as it affects understanding within an interactive field.

Because any health care is dependent upon client utilization, an understanding of American Indian network behavior appears critical to policy development and service planning efforts.

Using Levine's social conservation model, two critical human ecology imperatives emerge: (1) to identify traditional, long-standing cultural attributes, which have contributed to family cohesiveness and individual mental health, and (2) to develop human service systems which reaffirm a sense of family purpose.

An exigency specific to American Indians is that the cultural and structural integrity of extended family networks be revitalized and be supported. The authors believe that the adoption of a social conservation model by the human services would greatly improve service efficiency and, at the same time, vigorously enrich the quality of life of a currently alienated and underserved client population.

Selected annotated bibliography

Lewis, Harold. "Morality and the Politics of Practice," *Social Casework* 53:7 (July 1972), pp. 404–417.
This excellent article presents two primary problems, for social workers in their efforts to engage clients in beginning work on their problems: the problem of establishing trust between worker and client, and the problem of the distribution of justice in our society. Lewis develops some guides for the worker's consideration. The authors would recommend his article to all readers of this text.

Perlman, Helen Harris. "Intake and Some Role Considerations," *Social Casework* 41:4 (April 1960), pp. 171–176.
This article considers the bearing of role expectations and role performance on the ability of worker and client to engage in problem definition. Perlman sees the concept of role as important in determining the quality of client engagement.

Perlman, Helen Harris. *Social Casework: A*

Problem-Solving Process. Chicago: University of Chicago Press, 1957.
See chapters 8, 9, and 10 for an excellent discussion of process, content, and method in the beginning phase of work with clients.

Phillips, Doris Campbell. "Of Plums and Thistles: The Search for Diagnosis," *Social Work* 5:1 (January 1960), pp. 84–90.
This is an excellent discussion of the sources of data collection for purposes of assessment. Phillips says that one must look for important data in the spontaneous reaction to the client, in the clients spontaneous reaction to the worker, in the client's statement of the problem, and in the plans the client has for problem solution. This article is highly recommended for reading with this chapter.

Purcell, Francis P., and Specht, Harry. "The House on Sixth Street," *Social Work* 10:4 (October 1965), pp. 69–76.
This article presents a case example of how the

problem presented by one client was redefined as a problem-for-work. In the redefinition, the problem became the problem for the whole neighborhood and the social worker's role became that of advocate.

Rhodes, Sonya L. "Contract Negotiation in the Initial Stages of Casework Service," *Social Service Review* 51:1 (March 1977), pp. 125–140.

This article is a report of a study that examines the negotiation of the beginning contract and its relationship to the expectations client and worker bring to the process. This is an important examination of some of the principles developed in this chapter.

CHAPTER 9

The contract phase:
Joint assessment, goal setting,
and planning

This chapter is about decisions—decisions concerning the nature of the client's problem, desired outcomes (goals), and how the outcomes will be achieved. The chapter will define the contract phase of the problem-solving model, present an outline of the process by which worker and client jointly arrive at the contract, and enumerate a set of principles to guide the worker's participation in this process.

DEFINITION OF THE SERVICE CONTRACT

In discussing the problem-solving process, identification of the problem, and data collection, we have maintained a consistent emphasis on the partnership nature of the interaction between client and worker. The partnership is working together to define and explore a common task. Mutuality between client and worker needs to be established at the very outset and to continue through all their associations. In the service contract, however, the partnership concept is fully developed and made explicit. Anthony Maluccio and Wilma Marlow, in an article produced in this chapter (see Reading 9–2), say:

> Webster's *Third New International Dictionary* defines contract as a "covenant," a "compact," or "an agreement between two or more persons to do or forbear something." These words suggest mutuality, participation, and action.
>
> For the purposes of social work, the contract may be defined as *the explicit agreement between the worker and the client concerning the target problems, the goals, and the strategies of social work intervention, and the roles and tasks of the participants.* Its major features are mutual agreement, differential participation in the intervention process, reciprocal accountability, and explicitness. In practice these features are closely interrelated.

Increased research into "outcome" in social work practice is accumulating evidence that social work is often not helpful because the worker and the client are not working toward the same purposes (Lerner, 1972; Mayer and Timms, 1970: Polansky, Borgman, and de Saix, 1972). When clients approach an agency expecting a certain kind of help toward a certain kind of goal, they will be confused and perhaps will feel even more inadequate if the worker offers something that clients do not understand and were not aware they wanted. In such situations clients often leave the agency in frustration and disappointment.

When considering the importance of mutuality in the partnership and in the joint understandings and operating principles that are involved in the concept of contract, one should not lose sight of an equally important notion— that of difference. The concept of partnership does not mean that client and worker bring the same knowledge, understanding, feeling, and doing to the business of working together. Partnership and contract also highlight the differences that worker and client can contribute to the process. "The contract is a tool for such delineation, and for both client and worker it is an ongoing reminder of their collaborative relationship and different responsibilities" (Maluccio and Morlow, 1974, p. 30).

The service contract involves input, decision-making, planning, and commitment from both the client and the social worker. The process of arriving at a service contract protects the client's individuality and maximizes opportunities for exercise of self-determination. In discussions, negotiations, and choosing among available alternatives, or in making commitments to engage in developing new alternatives, the client's opportunities for meaningful decisions about self and situation are greatly increased.

The next section describes what goes into the process of arriving at a service contract, and a final section will make explicit a number of principles which are implicit in the process. In many respects the process may appear similar to that described in Chapter 8 on the beginning phase of working together. The similarity exists partly because of the "spiral" nature of work with clients (a process which will be made more explicit in Chapter 12 on evaluation) and partly because the concept of contract also appears in the initial contact phase. A preliminary contract is developed to facilitate the process of collecting data— a prerequisite for joint worker and client decision-making concerning the problem-to-be-worked, the desired outcomes, and the means or interventive efforts to be utilized in achieving those outcomes.

Arriving at a service contract involves a series of client-worker negotiations directed to answering these questions: Is the problem we want to work on the one that was identified when we began work together? Why has the problem persisted despite earlier client attempts to solve it? What is the desired solution (that is, what outcomes or objectives should the interventive effort be directed toward achieving in relation to the problem)? How will this solution be achieved? (Remember that the client may be an individual, a family, a group, or representatives of a community and that the worker may be interacting with the client in a variety of settings.)

JOINT ASSESSMENT AND DECISION MAKING

Joint assessment and decision making is at the very heart of the development of the service contract. In the contact phase, worker and client have arrived at an initial definition of the problem-to-be-worked. They have set initial goals, collected some data, and done some exploration together related to the identified problem and goals. Now they must put this data together to determine what the problem is, what the client wants done about it (a re-working of the goal), and how they are going to do it. This process involves the ordering and organizing of the information, intuitions, and knowledge that client and worker bring so that the pieces come together into some pattern that makes sense, at least in the here and now, in explaining the problem and in relating this explanation to alternative solutions. There is movement from what is observed, inferred, or deduced, based on knowledge and experience, to some conclusive explanation of what we make of it, and thence to a determination of goals and how they can be implemented. Such assessments evolve not from one person's head, or from the simple addition of one item to another, but rather from a combination of data in relevant ways. They evolve from viewing the relationships of all elements to one another as client and worker appraise the client-in-situation, and from the assessment of their total significance to the client in light of what the client wants to accomplish. Harriett Barlett (1970, p. 144) refers to these processes as "analysis of a situation to identify the major factors operating with it" and "identification of those factors which appear most critical, definition of their interrelationships, and selection of those to be dealt with." At its best the processes involve both client and worker in assembling and ordering all information and in making judgments as to their meaning for their work together.

Social workers often mistakenly assume that only the worker engages in these tasks. We do not deny that both the worker and the client must do hard and independent thinking (for the worker this is a professional obligation), but the test of the soundness of such thinking is how well their thinking fits together. Sometimes the culmination of this process is erroneously seen as putting the client in a category or affixing a label. That is emphatically not the purpose of the process! The process is not focused on the client alone; it is focused on the client, the problem, and the situation in a systematic interaction. In work with human beings, thinking and action cannot move in a straight line from cause to effect. Systems theory teaches us that problems are the result of complicated interactions among all system variables, and that to seek a single ultimate cause or reason is to doom oneself and, more important, one's client to frustration and failure. So our aim is not to come up with an answer in terms of labels or categories, but to order the understanding of the client-situation-problem for purposes of decision making concerning goals and actions.

Sometimes this process is called *diagnosis*. We dislike this term for several reasons. First, the preferred definition of the term in Webster's is "The art or act of identifying a disease from its signs and symptoms." Thus the term carries the implication that there is something wrong with the client. Second, the term implies that the decision about what is wrong is made by the professional person through an examination. There is no inkling of dynamic interaction and joint responsibility in the term. Finally, diagnosis is often seen as a process by which a professional arrives at a label for something. After all, that is what happens when doctors diagnose. They assign labels signifying what is wrong. This is their assessment as the knowing authority, and, at even greater variance with the notions of the contract, doctors usually tell their patients what they have determined to be the most satisfactory form of treatment. We hope that the process of assessment and decision making in social work is understood to be quite different from diagnosis. The phrase *process of assessment* is used because we think that this is the way assessment must be regarded—as an ongoing, joint process, a shared endeavor.

Consistent with the approach outlined in Chapter 1, the problem may be defined as residing with clients, as outside clients but experienced by them, or as the result of the client-situation interaction. The target of change may or may not be the client. After client and worker have jointly defined the problem-for-work (this may or may not be the same as the presenting problem), the next decision is to define goals—what is to be done?

SETTING GOALS

What are the desired outcomes of the client and worker's joint work? What is perceived as the appropriate solution for the problem? What are the goals of our actions? Essentially the same process is utilized in arriving at an answer to these questions as in developing a definition of the problem-for-work. The worker's first responsibility is to use interviewing skills to elicit from clients their view of the desired outcome. The worker may also have developed a view of the desired outcome which is shared with the client. If the two views are not congruent, then this difference must be negotiated, just as incongruent perceptions of the problem were negotiated. Unless the worker and client can arrive at mutually agreeable goals, there is no sense in proceeding further because they will be working in opposed directions.

Specifying goals is a crucial element of the service contract. Particular attention must be paid to two characteristics of the goals. First, goals should be sufficiently specific and concrete to be measurable. Only in this way can the client and worker know whether the goals have been accomplished, and only in this way can the profession of social work establish its accountability. Broadly stated goals, such as helping the client feel better, or increasing the client's opportunities for socializing experiences, or improving the parent-child relationship, are meaningless. This topic will be discussed further in Chapter 12 on evaluation. A set of procedures—Goal Attainment Scaling—which requires the setting of specific, measurable goals that will enable the client and worker to determine the extent of goal attainment will be introduced there.

Second, there should be a reasonable chance of attaining the goals set. In establishing goals, worker and client will, of course, consider such variables as the client's degree of interest in attaining them, the client's abilities, and the resources available to the client. Lilian Ripple (1956, pp. 38–54) and others have referred to these variables as motivation, capacity, and opportunity, and, of course, goals may be established in any of these areas—that is, legitimate objectives of client-worker activity might be to increase the client's motivation, abilities, or opportunities in defined areas. Regardless of the areas in which goals are established, consideration is given to the variables of motivation, capacity, and opportunity with a view toward establishing goals with a reasonable chance of attainment.

In recapitulation, goal setting in social work is a joint client-worker process in which mutually agreeable solutions to the problems are developed. These solutions or goals should be specific enough to be measurable and proximate enough to be attainable.

PLANNING FOR INTERVENTION

Given a mutually determined definition of the problem and its solution, the task of planning a way to move from problem to solution remains. The development of an intervention plan consists of decisions, again jointly made by the client and the worker, as to the steps which will be taken to solve the problem, that is, reach the goals. The steps taken in making these decisions parallel those taken in defining the problem and arriving at goals. The worker will first discover from the client what steps the client would like to take to reach the solution and what steps the client expects the worker to take. The worker must establish what is expected of the client as well as what the worker expects to do to accomplish the goals, and, again, any differences in these expectations must be negotiated and resolved.

Social workers, while negotiating interventive means, are responsible for considering four important limitations on worker activity. These limitations are time, skill, ethics, and agency function. First, no worker can make unlimited time available to a specific client. Time constraints on the worker must always be considered in entering into a service contract. Workers cannot responsibly commit themselves to activities which extend beyond the time they have available; conversely, a client can reasonably expect workers to do what they say they will do. Consider this incident, for example. A skilled, generally capable worker recently placed a 14-year-old boy in a foster home. The worker was cognizant of the fact that the youth might have some initial adjustment problems and indicated that they would be visiting together on a weekly basis to talk about any placement problems. This worker, however, was employed in a large agency with a heavy case load and, because of the pressure of time, was unable to visit with the boy until four weeks after the placement was made. By this time, the boy had justifiably become disillusioned and angry with the worker and rejected efforts by the worker to become jointly involved in problems that were occurring in the placement. The youth ran away and eventually became institutionalized. Had this worker made a realistic contract—to see the boy once a month instead of once a week—the client and worker might have been able to maintain their communication and to engage in more effective problem-solving. A common misconception held by many new workers is to confuse the intensity of service with the quality of service. Poor quality service is provided when workers make commitments that they cannot meet, and, conversely, frequent contacts between worker and client do not necessarily imply high quality service. What is required is the ability of workers to plan their time so that they will not make commitments beyond the time available.

Second, workers will not enter into service contracts that call for activity on their part which exceeds their skills. It is a professional's responsibility to be aware of strengths and weaknesses and not to enter into agreements that exceed one's ability. When a client requires a specialized skill which a particular worker does not possess, such as marriage counseling or bargaining with a large bureaucracy, then the negotiated intervention plan will include involvement of another resource to assist with this aspect of the intervention.

Third, workers will avoid involvement in intervention plans that commit them to unethical behavior. An obvious example would be the securing of economic resources through illegal means. An economic crisis might be alleviated by a burglary, but it would not be appropriate for a worker to participate in planning or executing such an action.

Fourth, as Schwartz noted in Reading 1–1, worker-client contracts are always limited by the functions of the agency in which the worker participates. This unfortunate limitation derives from the tendency to organize social services in this country around functional specializations rather than to provide generic services (Wilensky and Lebeaux, 1965, 233–282). Workers can seek to define agency functions broadly and, when necessary, will consider the possibility of requesting exceptions to agency limitations or attempting to work within their agency to secure a broader definition of its functions. Some ways to accomplish such changes are discussed further in Chapter 15. But as long as agencies have community sanctioned functions workers must be cognizant of this source of limitation on the commitments they make to clients.

In the next chapter, worker activity in moving from problem to solution will be discussed as interventive roles. Before these roles are utilized, however, a service contract must be developed to specify the nature of both worker and client activity. As in the definition of the problem and of goals, any differences between worker and client in these areas are to be resolved prior to implementing any intervention plan.

RECAPITULATION

The service contract is a plan jointly negotiated by the worker and the client which defines the problem-for-work, specifies the objectives, and provides an intervention plan designed to move from the problem to the objectives. The process of negotiating the service contract culminates in a commitment on the part of both worker and client to implement the plan. Once negotiated, the service contract is binding on both the worker and the client and is not subject to unilateral changes—changes can, of course, be jointly negotiated.

Four principles have been implied in this chapter which can be stated explicitly.

1. Joint negotiation of the service contract connotes precisely what the words imply. The contract involves input from both worker and client. We indicated disagreement with the concept of diagnosis because of a lack of client input in the decision-making that leads to a diagnosis. But frequently workers also err in the other direction—in failing to provide their own input for fear that it might hamper the client's right to self-determination. A worker's professional judgment, experience, and background are all sources of knowledge and information that should be available to the client in joint decision-making. The key is to arrive at a service contract which is truly joint—one representing the best merged collective judgment of both worker and client.

2. The worker is expected to bring a broad knowledge base to the process of arriving at a service contract. This base will include knowledge of human functioning, of the social environment, and of the interaction of the two. The worker will be expected to draw on the sources of knowledge identified in Chapters 2 and 3 and to apply those sources to the specific client situation under consideration.

3. The focus of the service contract and the intervention plan will be consistent with the concept of social functioning. This means that the worker and the client must be alert to the widest possible range of goals and interventive

approaches. The target of change may be the client, forces in the environment, or the interaction of the two. Although no worker can be expected to master all change strategies, the worker can be expected to be aware of the broad repertoire of change strategies available to the profession and to be able to select jointly with the client the strategy most appropriate for the client and, if the worker cannot provide that service, to be able to locate it elsewhere in the community. Methodological specialties may be necessary, but they cannot be justified as blinders.

4. The development of a service contract is a cognitive process involving thinking, reasoning, and decision making. Feelings are important, but planning should be done on a rational basis. The planning may, of course, involve plans to deal with feelings. Further, rational planning precedes interventive activities. This does not deny the spiral concept of practice which has been identified in earlier chapters and which will be made more explicit in Chapter 12 on evaluation. But whenever the worker is consciously engaged in interventive efforts, those efforts should be based on a deliberate, rational service contract negotiated with the client.

A LOOK FORWARD

This chapter has described a crucial component of social work processes. The joint client-worker development of a rational plan that defines the problem-to-be-worked, establishes objectives, and specifies an interventive plan is a prerequisite to intervention. In Chapters 10 and 11 the discussion centers on worker intervention activities. Evaluation is discussed in Chapter 12. This essential part of work with clients shows social work processes to be more dynamic and continuous than has been implied in the linear description of the problem-solving process.

The two articles reproduced in this chapter offer additional ideas concerning contracting. Burt Galaway illustrates the use of contracting in a more specific setting—the placement of children and youth in foster family care. The article by Anthony Maluccio and Wilma Marlow offers a very useful discussion of contracting which provides for explicit client involvement and is applicable with client systems of various sizes.

Reading

9-1 Contracting: A means of clarifying roles in foster family services*

Burt Galaway

One of the recurring problems in foster family services, and certainly one of the major concerns of foster parents, is a lack of defini-

* Reprinted from *Children Today* 5 (July–August 1976), pp. 20–23.

tion of the foster parent role. What does a social worker expect foster parents to do? What do foster parents expect to do? What do natural parents expect of foster parents? What does the foster child expect of foster parents? The failure to answer, or even to discuss, these questions can result in confusion over the foster parents' role and create conflicts and tension that interfere with the foster parents' ability to provide good services and a stable living arrangement for the child in their care.

When the obligations or responsibilities which foster parents are expected to meet are not clarified—when foster parents say, for example, "I didn't know I was supposed to make that appointment" or "It wasn't clear who was going to go to the school conference"—they are experiencing what can be called role ambiguity. Many times, however, some areas of responsibility may deliberately be left ambiguous to avoid another problem—that of role conflict.

A foster parent experiences role conflict, for example, when he or she may expect to be able to deny the child opportunities to have telephone conversations with the child's biological mother, while the social worker may expect him or her to permit these contacts. Or the foster parent may believe that he or she is expected to take the child to church or to arrange for baptism, whereas the social worker may expect this prerogative to remain with the biological parent. The division of responsibilities—shared by foster parents, biological parents, and social worker—is not always clear.

One of the major challenges confronting foster parents and others involved in foster family services is to find some effective mechanism to reduce role ambiguity and to achieve a workable solution to role conflict. One such mechanism, a placement contracting process as developed by the Professional Association of Treatment Homes (PATH) in the Minneapolis-St. Paul area of Minnesota, has been successful in both preserving flexibility in planning to meet the needs of individual children and foster parents, and in reducing the problems of role conflict and ambiguity.

Placement contracting by PATH

PATH is a small agency, created and controlled by foster parents, which provides specialized foster family services. Children are referred to PATH by other agencies, usually a county welfare department. The children are generally those who cannot be placed in an agency's own foster home resources and who would be placed in a residential facility if a specialized foster family home were not available. PATH parents, who are considered agency staff and participate regularly in staff meetings held two evenings each month, receive preplacement training and a fee for their services over and above the cost of providing foster care.

Before any child is placed in a PATH home, a series of steps is taken by PATH staff (that is, foster parents and social worker) to develop a placement contract which clarifies the role of the foster parent for this particular placement and outlines the responsibility of everyone who is to be involved with the child.

After a referral is made to PATH, the PATH social worker requests from the referring agency the child's social history, recent progress reports and copies of any recent psychological, psychiatric or other evaluations. The PATH social worker then presents the referral at the next regularly scheduled staff meeting and if a PATH family is interested in considering the child, all the available information is shared with the parents. (Additional information, if necessary, will be requested from the referring agency.) If a PATH family wishes to begin placement planning, this is reported to the referring agency, which then has the responsibility of discussing the potential placement with the child and family.

If both the referring agency and PATH are interested in proceeding further, the PATH social worker sets up a placement planning team consisting of the child (if appropriate), the biological parents (when possible), the PATH parents, the PATH social worker, the social worker from the referring agency, and any others (a probation officer, a special education teacher or a therapist, for example) who will have ongoing involvement with the child or family.

The placement planning team meets as a group and, through negotiations and discussion, develops a service contract which, minimally, covers the following points:

• The goals for this particular placement. The placement planning team members are expected to be able to arrive at a mutual understanding as to why foster family care is necessary and what should be accomplished as a result of this placement.

• Plans for maintaining involvement between the biological parents and the child in placement. Even when the placement is anticipated for an extended period of time (or indefinitely), the interests of children are best served if they can maintain some continuing knowledge and communication with their biological parents. This may take many forms—telephone contacts, home visits by the child, visits by the biological parents to the child in the foster home, and so on. To avoid confusion, the service contract spells out the nature and frequency of these contacts. The plan will also arrange for regular communication among the biological parents, foster parents, and social worker.

• Plans for meeting the child's medical and dental needs. Is the child to continue seeing the child's previous doctor, or is a change indicated? If the child has chronic medical problems requiring regular supervision, explicit plans must be formulated to secure necessary services, including an agreement as to who will be responsible for transporting the child to clinics.

• Arrangements for specialized counseling services if team members feel these are necessary for either the child or biological parents, and a plan for financing the counseling. (PATH does not provide counseling directly to the child or biological parents as part of its program; all of the social work and psychological services of PATH are used to provide consultation and training to the foster parents, who provide the primary service to the child.)

• Determination of the educational needs of the child and how these will be met. This might include assigning responsibility for the transfer of school records, or arranging for special educational programs.

• Plans for the child's religious experience. Will the child participate with the foster parents in religious services, or will he or she attend services with the biological parents? Will the biological parents provide transportation? Since this area is frequently a point of contention, it is important that an agreed upon plan be developed.

• The responsibilities of social workers from the referring agency or other agencies that may be involved with the child or the family. Will the child be seen regularly? Will there be work with the biological parents? What will be the responsibility of the foster parents to these workers, and how will they coordinate their work with that of the PATH social worker?

• The financial plan for the placement. Who will be paying the PATH fees? How will the cost of medical services be covered? If the child has special needs, what arrangements are made to cover the cost of these special services?

• Review of the placement. The placement planning team is expected to continue to monitor the progress of the placement by meeting periodically to reevaluate the service contract, make any changes that are needed, and try to secure compliance from participants who may not be fulfilling their agreements. Thus, an important part of any service plan is the setting of a review date on which the placement planning team will again meet together. Generally, reviews are conducted at three-month intervals, but they may be more or less frequent. The date and place of the first review, however, is a part of the contract.

While the team is working to develop a service contract, arrangements are also being made for preplacement visits. It is hoped that both the child and biological parents will be able to visit in the home with the foster parents and, sometimes, the foster parents will have an opportunity to visit in the biological parents' home. Meetings of the placement planning team may take place in the home of either the biological parents or foster parents, as well as the agency's office.

When an agreement is reached on the details of the placement contract, the PATH social worker writes a memorandum of agreement outlining the provisions. This document is signed by all participants on the placement planning team, and a copy is provided to each team member. After the memorandum of agreement is signed, the child can be placed in the PATH home.

Through placement contracting, 19 children have been placed in PATH foster homes since the program began in early 1974. One discharge has occurred as planned when the child returned home, while another discharge was the result of a placement failure. Of the 17 children now in placement, 10 are over age 12, 6 are between the ages of 6 and 11, and 1 is under age 6.

Thirteen children were themselves involved in the contracting sessions. Of the four who were not, two are mentally retarded (one also has limited speech and mobility resulting from multiple sclerosis); another, a 9-year-old, is extremely handicapped and withdrawn, and the other, a 4-year-old, was considered too young to be involved.

All present referrals have come through county welfare departments, which have responsibility for financing the placement. Although in some cases the department may be receiving a portion of the cost of care directly from parents, all present placements have been made under agreements in which the welfare department pays a per diem cost of care for PATH services (presently $19 per day). The per diem is paid directly to PATH, and PATH makes a payment of $12 per day to the foster parents to cover both maintenance costs for the child and a service fee. The balance is used to provide social and psychological services and to cover administrative costs.

While many of the contracts for these placements were worked out in one session, others may require three or more sessions.

The team members—and there were as many as ten persons involved in one PATH placement planning—must have the opportunity to get to know each other, to discuss their differences, and to work out necessary compromises in order to arrive at an agreeable plan and placement contract.

The time between a child's referral to PATH and his or her placement in a PATH home has ranged from 10 to 120 days, with the mean being 49 days.

Advantages of a placement contract

Although the placement contracting process may involve considerable expense, time, and travel, it does offer three distinct advantages which more than offset these expenses. First, since the service contract clearly defines the roles and responsibilities of all parties to the agreement, role ambiguity on the part of the foster parents (and on the part of all other parties to the placement, as well) should be reduced. Any existing conflicts should also become evident in the planning process and ways to either resolve the conflict or to work around it can be found. As role ambiguity is reduced and methods are found to cope with role conflict, the plan for the child will become more stable, placement goals are more likely to be accomplished, and the foster placement experience for the child is more likely to be a beneficial, growth-producing experience.

Second, the contracting approach allows for a highly individual plan to be designed to meet the needs of each child. A model or ideal role is not imposed on any of the participants and, although roles are clearly defined and explicit, responsibilities may vary considerably from contract to contract.

Finally, the placement contracting process, by involving all of the adults who are most important to the child in a communication process prior to placement, permits the working out of at least tentative solutions to some problem areas—before the child is placed. And, since the placement is continually monitored and reevaluated, other changes can be made as necessary. As the adults resolve their differences and find ways of cooperating and working together, the likelihood of the foster family experience being a positive one for the child will increase.

Suggestions for contracting

Although the placement contract process described here was developed by a small, very specialized foster family program, contracting need not be limited to this type of a setting. The notion of careful preplacement planning and the idea of an explicit contract governing the conditions of placement should be easily transferable to any foster family service. Indeed, foster parents might, on a case-by-case basis, provide leadership in the development of sound placement plans. There are at least three ways in which foster parents might accomplish this.

• Foster parents can refuse to accept unplanned, alleged emergency placements unless their home is designated as an emergency foster family home and they are being paid a special rate to provide emergency services. Foster parents may appropriately require that a plan be developed before a youngster is placed in their home and can indicate to social workers that while they are prepared to consider a particular child, they are not prepared to permit the placement without adequate information, discussion and preplacement planning. An alternative would be for the foster parents to permit emergency placement but to insist upon a substantially higher rate until an explicit plan is developed. This latter course of action is entirely justifiable since without adequate plans, foster parents are likely to encounter considerable crises in the placement and will be dealing with an ambiguous, unknown situation.

• Foster families might develop clear policies concerning the use of their homes. How often have foster parents been told that they cannot do something because it is "against agency policy?" Foster parents may develop their own policies for foster family homes and notify agencies that they cannot do something because it is against *their* policy. Specifically, foster parents may develop policies governing opportunities to meet and visit with biological parents before accepting a placement, information to be shared prior to accepting a placement, and a written plan prior to the placement of a child.

• Foster parents should not hesitate to discuss fees and services. Questions about rates to be paid, special needs to be provided, services that can be expected from the social worker, and so on can all most successfully be bargained for prior to placement. Once a child has entered the home, and significant attachments are developing, foster parents lose most of their bargaining leverage. Prior to the placement, however, when the agency needs the service, it is most vulnerable; this is when the hard bargaining should take place and explicit agreements be developed.

Will these actions result in a refusal on the part of the agencies to use the home? Probably not. Foster parents who are able to provide a quality service and are able to deal comfortably with the difficult youngsters now requiring foster family care, are providing a service which is in short supply and high demand. Foster parents have a position of strength and should use the strength comfortably and aggressively on behalf of the children who require their services.

Reading
9-2 *The case for the contract**

Anthony N. Maluccio and Wilma D. Marlow

The contract is among the basic concepts utilized in social work that are inadequately formulated and incompletely incorporated into practice. There has been little effort to clarify its theoretical foundations, delineate its uses, and test its validity. It has been mentioned frequently in the literature as a pact, working agreement, or therapeutic alliance. Referring to clients' and workers' hidden or double agendas, writers have spoken of covert, implicit, and "corrupt" contracts. However, a review of the literature reveals no comprehensive discussion or formulation of a conceptual framework.

Lack of clarity about the contract, its limited development, and its restricted application to social work practice may be factors that contribute to the clash of worker-client perspectives, client discontinuance, and the frustrations that clients and practitioners encounter when they try to work together meaningfully and productively.

This article attempts to stimulate interest in examining, conceptualizing, and using the contract. To do so seems timely in light of the current critical reassessment of roles and methods of social work, changing attitudes toward consumers of services, and new ideas about the helping process.

A pertinent aspect of changing theory and practice is the growing conviction that the client or consumer has an important role in formulating policy and planning program. One model of service delivery proposes that the consumer have a choice in what services are provided, some control over how and by whom services are delivered, and a real opportunity to participate (Meenghan and

Mascari, 1971). It is logical to extend the concept of "maximum feasible participation" in policy-making and planning to direct and personal interaction between social workers and clients, whether the latter are individuals, families, groups, or communities. Clearly conceived and properly used, the contract can serve as an important tool in helping consumers achieve such participation. It might also become an integral feature of the emerging "life model" of practice, which stresses optimum utilization of the client's own life processes and resources.

The contract in theory

The origins of the term *contract* as applied to social work are not clear. Writings on group work in the 1940s and 1950s include implicit references to the contract, as seen in Coyle's discussion (1948, pp. 88–90) of the "grouping process" in group formation and Trecker's formulation (1955, pp. 23–35) of the group worker's role as "agent of the agency." In 1951, Hamilton (pp. 148–180) alluded to the contract, without naming it, in discussing the application process. She saw as fundamental the worker's responsibility to make explicit the conditions and the terms of help available from the agency. In 1957, Perlman (p. 149) made one of the earliest references to the contract as a pact.

Major social work scholars gave the contract some attention at a 1969 symposium on comparative theoretical approaches to casework. In formulating the problem-solving model, Perlman (1970, p. 155) indicated that people establish a contract when they decide to use the agency and the worker for help in coping with their problem, thus moving from the role of applicant to that of client. Rapoport (1970, p. 291) identified the contract as a significant step in crisis intervention, noting that by the end of the initial interview goals should be agreed upon and mutual expectations spelled out between client and worker (1970, p. 291). Scherz (1970, p. 237) defined the contract in family therapy as a "conscious agreement between family and worker to work in certain ways toward certain goals." In the behavior modification approach to casework, Thomas (1970, p. 196), saw validity in an explicit contract and spoke of written as well as verbal agreements. In Smalley's discussion (1970, pp. 98–121) of the functional orientation, the concept of the contract is implicit in her use of time phases related to beginnings and endings of treatment; according to her, a time-limited contract may be fulfilled, renewed, or renegotiated. In the psychosocial approach, Hollis (1970, p. 45) acknowledged that the term was widely used and that practitioners increasingly preferred to state explicitly the end results of the initial phase of casework before engaging in treatment.

Although these scholars represent differing philosophical and theoretical orientations to casework, the concept of the contract appears compatible to practice within the separate frameworks. In particular, they convey a sense that clients are emerging from their traditional roles as passive recipients of service to active self-determining people who cooperate with the worker more and more consciously and deliberately in the helping process.

The literature on community organization has given limited consideration to using the contract for reaching a working agreement between the worker and the client. On the contrary, goals and roles have usually been analyzed from the perspective of the worker (Rothman, 1964).

In group work, Schwartz has stressed that the establishment of a "working agreement" is a fundamental task of the worker. According to his formulation, the rules and boundaries within which worker and group members operate determine their working contract and influence their functions (see Reading 1–1). The contract essentially corroborates the convergence of the worker's and the client's tasks and "provides the framework for the work that follows, and for understanding when the work is in process, when it is being evaded, and when it is finished" (Schwartz, 1971, p. 8). Other writers on group work concur with Klein (1970, p. 51) that the contract is "an agreement about expectations of the reciprocal roles of the worker, the members, and the sanctioning agency."

Thus the contract has received some attention in social work, but its elaboration has remained at a limited and simplistic level. In general, theorists have tended to equate it with the working agreement that concludes the initial, exploratory phase of social work intervention. Similarly, writing from a psychoanalytic perspective, Menninger (1964, pp. 15–42) has argued that the contract can be used to clarify the mutual expectations of patient and therapist, reach agreement about appropriate expectations, and spell out the conditions of their cooperation.

The underlying thesis of this article is that the contract has potential value as an ongoing, integral part of the total process of intervention. Further elaborated in theory and deliberately applied to practice, the contract can crystallize and exploit to the maximum degree the process and substance of the work in which practitioner and client engage. The use of a contract can help facilitate worker-client interaction, establish mutual concerns, clarify the purposes and conditions of giving and receiving service, delineate roles and tasks, order priorities, allocate time and constructively for attaining goals, and assess progress on an ongoing basis.

The contract defined

Although it is a much talked about term among practitioners, the contract has not been clearly defined in social work. The legal profession has attempted to define it since the contract constitutes the basic framework for a substantial portion of legal practice. Although the diversity of elements and perspectives inherent in the concept has prevented the devising of an entirely satisfactory or universally accepted legal definition, one that is widely quoted is the following: "A contract is a promise, or set of promises, for breach of which the law gives a remedy, or the performance of which the law in some way recognizes as a duty (Williston 1957, sect. 1). Except for the idea that the contract is a legally enforceable agreement, the elements in this definition are pertinent to social work, especially the notions of mutual promise and duty between the contracting parties.

Webster's *Third New International Dictionary* defines contract as a "covenant," a "compact," or "an agreement between two or more persons to do or forbear something." These words suggest mutuality, participation, and action.

For the purposes of social work, the contract may be defined as *the explicit agreement between the worker and the client concerning the target problems, the goals, and the strategies of social work intervention, and the roles and tasks of the participants.* Its major features are mutual agreement, differential participation in the intervention process, reciprocal accountability, and explicitness. In practice these features are closely interrelated.

Mutual agreement

Mutual agreement between worker and client concerning the nature and course of interaction is an essential component of practice. Many writers agree that mutuality must be established at the outset and maintained throughout contact (Gottlieb and Stanley 1967). Agreed upon goals, roles, and tasks are fundamental in determining the direction, quality, and content of intervention.

Research studies and clinical reports substantiate the fact that difficulties and frustrations result from a lack of agreement between client and worker or from a clash in their perspectives (Mayer and Timms, 1969; Silverman, 1970). Worker and client may be operating under different assumptions—especially if varying expectations were not adequately discussed—and thus may not always have the same perceptions of what constitutes help or treatment.

Practitioners often find it difficult to establish mutuality in the crucial areas of goals and methods. Some resort to a double agenda, in which workers formulate for themselves a set of goals that are different from the ones they share with the client. Greenhill (1972, p. 509) reports that he used to set up therapeutic contracts with families that included agreement to work together in relation to a child's problems. Covertly, however, he would intend to work with the entire family's problems, a plan he divulged to family members only after they became involved in treatment. Greenhill was referring to experiences of his early years in family therapy, but seasoned practitioners sometimes superimpose their own goals on those of clients. Beall (1972) warns of the dangers of a "corrupt contract," when the client's stated goals conceal implicit and opposing ones. Operating with such a contract in a clinical setting can reinforce neurotic aims rather than promote therapeutic change.

Deliberately considering the contract in each situation can help reduce clashes in perspectives, clarify vague or confusing expectations, and enhance the possibility of meaningful cooperation in working toward realistic, mutually agreed upon goals. Client and worker must share their understanding of assistance sought and to be given. Without this, the concept of mutuality is hollow. Furthermore, exploring and spelling out mutual expectations can help client and worker stay attuned to the reality of the current situation and can reduce the tendency toward regressive transference and countertransference (Rapoport, 1970, p. 291).

As Schubert (1971, p. 7) notes, the contract is useful at an early stage for formulating certain basic understandings in order to determine whether the client has come to the appropriate agency, whether the service needed can be offered, who is going to give it, what if any are the conditions for providing the service, whether any eligibility requirements are to be met, what fees if any will be charged, and what other persons may be involved. Client-worker agreement about these important aspects can be a powerful force in mobilizing energies for a common cause.

In group work, Garvin (1969) describes research showing that agreement between the worker and the group member on their expectations of each other is positively correlated with the worker's performance and with progress in group problem-solving. Similarly, Brown's intensive investigation (1971, pp. 99–115) of early group sessions reveals that developing mutual expectations as early as possible is significantly related to later group functioning and member satisfaction. The findings of studies of small groups support these results. They indicate that members' agreement about a group's goals and means of achieving goals leads to improved motivation and functioning (Rietsema and Raven, 1960).

In community organization, the contract might be applied, for example, when worker and clients are preparing to negotiate and bargain with their change target. It is essential that group and worker agree on proposed demands, lines of attack and defense, potential concessions, allocation of roles, and choice of strategies. Discussing and adopting an explicit contract that establishes consensus on these points could clarify planning and give the participants a sense of solidarity.

Differential participation

Practice theory has focused primarily on the worker's functions and responsibilities, devoting limited attention to the client's role and tasks. The respective contributions of client and worker to social work intervention have not been clear, especially with regard to the client's perception of the worker's role.

The concept of the contract not only emphasizes the importance of *joint* participation in the common enterprise of intervention but also highlights the *differential* participation of client and worker. As Grosser (1969, p. 19) points out: "A view of worker and client as having different but equal roles is not simply a theoretical concept; it is a practical prerequisite to operationalizing such innovations as worker partisanship and client participation."

The worker has a major responsibility to delineate with the clients the unique aspects of their participation at each phase of the process. The contract is a tool for such delineation, and for both client and worker it is an ongoing reminder of their collaborative relationship and different responsibilities.

Efforts have been made recently to differentiate between tasks and roles of clients and workers. Reid (1972, p. 67) formulates the worker's primary roles as follows: to define with the client the most effective course of action in resolving the problem and to direct intervention toward helping the client achieve the necessary tasks.

Vattano (1972) speaks of the "power-to-the-people movement" as a challenge to traditional practice through its emphasis on self-help groups. Members of the groups provide direct services to each other, while social workers function as peers, catalysts, researchers, or theory builders.

Zweig (1969, pp. 26–27) depicts the role of the legislative ombudsman, in which the worker is a bridge between the client and the elected representative. The worker may motivate applicants initially seeking help with their own needs to deal with policies affecting them. The client then becomes an activist rather than a target for intervention. As an administrative ombudsman, the worker expedites the bureaucratic processes involved in service delivery and guides the client or consumer through them.

Studt (1968, pp. 42–46) proposes a basic

framework for social work practice that incorporates the following features: (1) The client is the "primary worker in task accomplishment" and carries the major responsibility. (2) The social worker has a secondary responsibility "to provide the conditions necessary for the client's work on a task." (3) No one but clients can perform the tasks that their own life-stage and specific situation require.

Implementation of the contract is founded on the belief that clients ultimately must exercise their rights to self-determination. When clients assume the responsibility for choosing among alternatives and use their own skills and resources to deal with their agreed-upon tasks, this enhances their motivation, investment, and self-esteem. The client's meaningful participation in making decisions and formulating the contract is based on the recognition that people are spontaneously active, seeking, and striving beings. The insights of ego psychology highlight the fact that the active, seeking person who carries out personal commitments and who takes responsibility for one's actions experiences a sense of achievement and competence in performing this role. In the process of developing the contract, the worker can discover ways to enhance the client's sense of identity and independence by offering opportunities for choice, self-determination, and self-mastery.

The possibilities inherent in this approach are increasingly evident as social workers move away from the traditional view of service planned for and provided to the client by a worker who is more knowledgeable, objective, or expert. For example, involuntary clients in a correctional setting were able to engage in meaningful decision-making once the opportunity was offered and stimulated (Studt, 1968, pp. 42–46). In a child-care agency an innovative focus on decision-making was constructive, time saving, and advantageous to adoptive applicants and children awaiting placement. Applicants were given the responsibility for deciding, on the basis of photographs shown them early in the adoption process, which child they wished to adopt—a decision traditionally made by the worker at the end of the evaluation process (Shireman and Watson, 1972).

Reciprocal accountability

The client and the worker are accountable to each other in various ways, each having an ongoing responsibility to fulfill agreed upon tasks and work toward agreed upon goals. The contract can help make both parties as aware as possible of their reciprocal obligations.

The client's responsibility must be emphasized. Insufficient attention to it may partially account for the limited involvement of some clients in the helping process or their withdrawal from it. In child welfare settings, this lack may help explain parents' psychological abandonment of placed children. A contractual alliance with parents of emotionally disturbed children in residential treatment would clarify their accountability, bring into sharp focus their role in treatment, and make the concept of a family-centered program more dynamic.

Beck (1969) points out that "professionals tend to be accountable to other professionals rather than to the consumers of their services." In social work, accountability has typically been related to the worker's role as agency representative and to the agency's mandate from the community. It has been stressed that being within an agency complicates the worker's efforts to be accountable to the client. But this view is changing. Patti and Resnick (1972, p. 57) argue that, although organizational expectations realistically constrain workers, "professionals can work within an agency and retain their primary commitment to client welfare.

The increased responsiveness to clients that is inherent in the use of a contract helps shift the worker's sanction away from the community toward the client. This is especially evident in situations of advocacy, in which a worker's engagement by the client system is established through a contractual alliance featuring mutual accountability.

Explicitness

Explicitness is the quality of being specific, clear, and open. Although its importance is obvious, the degree to which it is implemented in practice is debatable. Frequent double agendas, implicit or covert contracts, and discrepant client-worker expectations have been mentioned. Often in casework practice the client sees one problem or target of intervention, while the worker sees another—usually related to a subtle or underlying difficulty. The client is interested in obtaining tangible help with an immediate need but "the caseworker doggedly pursues a different agenda, namely one of trying to get the client to see the 'real' problem underneath it all" (Reid, 1972, p. 61).

The contract offers an opportunity to spell out as openly as possible the conditions, expectations, and responsibilities inherent in the planned interaction. Therefore a fundamental task of the worker is to clarify contractual expectations and obligations. Research on brief treatment has corroborated the value of formulating explicit and specific goals (Reid and Shyne, 1969). To the traditional exhortation to "start where the client is" might be added: "and let the client know where you are, and where you are going." An explicit contract can help give the client more ethical protection than is possible through unspoken or covert contracts.

The client must be explicit as well as the worker. Emphasis on explicitness in contract formulation would actively engage the client's cognitive functions and resources—and such engagement has proved valuable in crisis intervention. In addition, the worker would be more likely to be continually "tuned in" to the needs that the client feels. In his formulation of task-centered casework, Reid (1969, p. 61) suggests requiring "that clients themselves explicitly acknowledge the problem and express a willingness to

work on it." The rationale is derived from evidence that in social work practice the client's perception of the situation is more important than the worker's view of the problem.

Application to practice

Little experimentation with the contract has been reported in social work practice. At present, its formal use appears to be atypical or innovative rather than regularly incorporated in practice.

Child welfare workers have used a written contract to delineate mutual responsibilities between agency and foster or adoptive parents. However, no published account of their experiences is available.

In a mental health setting oriented toward transactional analysis, the concept has been used with patients briefly hospitalized following a crisis. The initial interview was focused on establishing "a clear verbal contract" that outlined specific problem areas, appropriate goals, and methods of treatment. The contract alleviated "many of the fears of the patient concerning "strange" things that might happen on a mental health unit. The patient knows exactly the nature of the therapeutic contract and realizes that the patient will have an important role to play in determining the course of treatment" (Brechenser, 1972).

A family agency serving an upper-middle-class community reports successful experiences with the written contract as an integral tool in treatment. Goals and tasks of participants, schedules for contacts, fees and methods of payment, options for renegotiation, and other pertinent factors are spelled out. The agency has noted a clearer understanding of treatment goals by client and worker, wiser use of time, and greater awareness of time limits. There was also a growing realization that the contract could be used in setting boundaries for the treatment relationship (Lessor and Lutkus, 1971).

The written contract has considerable merit with clients requesting help with interpersonal problems. Whether it can be validly adapted to others needs further testing.

Flexibility

To be a truly dynamic tool, the contract should be used flexibly. If either the worker or the client rigidly adheres to its condittions —which they may tend to do with a written contract—this limits its usefulness, especially when the client's or the worker's perception of the situation changes. The binding restrictions and penalties of legal contracts would be inapplicable to social work and would constrain the creativity and spontaneity of both client and worker.

To guard against rigidity, there should be provisions for reformulation or renegotiation by mutual consent as circumstances change, problems are resolved, or the focus of intervention alters. Changes in the contract should be based on open discussion by all parties and should not be subverted by client, worker or agency. Emphasis should remain on the client's perceived need rather than on the worker's interpretation. When a short-term contract expires, a client wishing further help over a protracted period could ask to negotiate a new one.

Questions may be raised in connection with flexibility. How meaningful is a contract if its breach does not incur some form of punishment, loss, or suffering? Will contract modifications be discussed so frequently that the real issue of working on the problem is delayed or avoided? Will the contract become the goal of client-worker interaction rather than the means of attaining the client's goals? These are potential problems to explore.

As social workers formulate contracts more actively and deliberately, they should also consider the legal ramifications. In our society a contractual agreement may be legally binding even when it is not written. Will partial or total failure to fulfill its terms therefore render the practitioner or agency subject to law suits or malpractice claims?

It is evident that much more must be done in exploring the use of the contract, putting it into operation, and developing principles of action applicable to different client populations in diverse settings. Implementation must take into account the client's characteristics, capacities, and motivation. For example, using the contract with children or with involuntary clients may require special modifications of techniques and procedures.

In effect, the contract can be more or less complex, depending on how ready and able the client is to engage in formulating and utilizing it. In many situations, the client's social, physical, or psychological characteristics limit the ability to formulate an explicit contractual agreement. It is important to experiment with use of the contract to test its validity, identify its limitations, and derive specific operational guidelines.

Potential of the contract

The contract can contribute significantly to the positive outcome of social work services. In particular, it can bring focus and meaning to inherent values and principles implicit in social work practice and make the contracting parties more aware of them. If workers have a conviction about the contract and implement it fully, they can help the client participate more actively in dealing with the client's own situation. In so doing, they can affirm the client's preeminent role in social work intervention.

The contract has the potential to serve as an active instrument for engaging worker and client in meaningful and productive interaction for the following reasons:

It is derived from their shared experience in exploring a situation and reaching agreement on goals and tasks.

It gives both practitioner and client a sense of immediate involvement and meaningful participation and signifies their mutual commitment and readiness to assume responsibility.

It provides a base line for periodically reviewing accomplishments, assessing progress, and examining the conditions of agreement.

At its present stage, the contract does not offer specific propositions and principles of action for use with different types of consumers of social services. But there is sufficient evidence from clinical practice and from research on crisis intervention, brief treatment, and client discontinuance to suggest that the use of some form of contract in social work merits systematic experiment and research in various settings, with varying periods of service, and with clients having different characteristics and problems.

This article aims to contribute to developing cumulative theory for practice in this important area. Analysis of practice experiences and research findings could refine the concept further, formulate its specific components and operational guidelines, validate its incorporation into the helping process, and explore its efficacy in enhancing the client's perception and use of social services.

Selected annotated bibliography

Croxton, Tom A. "The Therapeutic Contract in Social Treatment," in Paul Glasser, Rosemary Sarri, and Robert Vinter (Eds.), *Individual Change through Small Groups.* New York: Free Press, 1974, pp. 169–183.
Croxton summarizes legal/historical perspectives on contracts as well as the use of contracts in social work and social practice. He conceptualizes the contracting process into six phases—exploration, negotiation, the preliminary contract, the working agreement, secondary contracts, and termination and evaluation.

Estes, Richard J., and Henry, Sue. "The Therapeutic Contract in Work with Groups: A Formal Analysis," *Social Service Review* 50:4 (December 1976), pp. 611–622.
This article provides the framework for understanding the complexity of use of contracts with groups (both group as a whole and individual members). The contract evolving and changing over time is a central dynamic in therapeutic process and furthers individual and group conflict resolution.

Gottlieb, Werner, and Stanley, Joe H. "Mutual Goals and Goal-Setting in Casework," *Social Casework* 48:8 (October 1967), pp. 471–477.
The development of mutually acceptable goals is essential if casework with families is to be effective. Casework consists of worker and client goal-directed activities to bring about constructive change.

Leifer, Ronald. "The Medical Model as Ideology," *International Journal of Psychiatry*, vol. 9. New York: Science House, 1970–71, pp. 13–21.
The acceptance of the medical model in psychiatry obscures important differences between psychiatry and medicine which in turn obscures the social functions of psychiatry.

Lessor, Richard, and Lutkus, Anita. "Two Techniques for the Social Work Practitioner," *Social Work* 16:1 (January 1971), pp. 5–6, 96.
Lessor and Lutkus report the use of chart pads and contracts in a private family service agency.

Rhodes, Sonya L. "Contract Negotiation in the Initial Stage of Casework Service," *Social Service Review* (March 1977), pp. 125–140.
This is a descriptive study of client-social worker contracting by 15 client-social worker dyads in an outpatient VA clinic. The understanding of worker role seems pivotal to successful contract negotiation; greater emphasis is needed on increasing participation of client, clarifying focus of work, and developing contracting as an ongoing process.

Schapler, James H., and Galinsky, Maida J. "Goals in Social Group Work Practice: Formulation, Implementation and Evaluation," in Paul Glasser, Rosemary Sarri, and Robert Vinter (Eds.), *Individual Change through Small Groups.* New York: Free Press, 1974, pp. 126–148.
This article discusses who sets goals and how they are set, implemented, and evaluated in group work. It is an interesting article to compare and contrast with our statement on goal setting.

Shevrin, Howard, and Shectman, Frederik. "The Diagnostic Process in Psychiatric Evaluations," *Bulletin of the Menninger Clinic* 37:5 (September 1973), pp. 451–495.
This article on the process of clinical diagnosis was

written to help the psychiatric practitioner to develop a concept of the diagnostic method. It is not an easy article to read but would be of value to students who want to pursue the concept further.

Stein, Theodore J.; Gambrill, Eileen D.; and Wiltse, Kermit. "Contracts and Outcome in Foster Care," *Social Work* 22:2 (March 1977), pp. 148–150.

This article reports on the study of use of "restoration contracts" with parents of children going into foster care. Statistics show a significantly greater number of children returned to the homes of parents with restoration contracts than parents who did not have a contract.

Stein, Theodore J.; Gambrill, Eileen D., and Wiltse, Kermit T. "Foster Care: The Use of Contracts," *Public Welfare* (Fall 1974), pp. 20–25.

The use of contracts with parents of children coming into foster care will clarify the goals which the parents are expected to accomplish, will become a basis for decisions regarding planning for the children, and may reduce unnecessary time in temporary living arrangements.

Sundel, Martin; Radin, Norma; and Churchill, Sallie R. "Diagnosis in Group Work," in Paul Glasser, Rosemary Sarri, and Robert Vinter (Eds.), *Individual Change through Small Groups.* New York: Free Press, 1974, pp. 105–126.

This article discusses the content of diagnosis, the information required in a diagnostic assessment, and the diagnostic procedures in a particular model of group work.

CHAPTER 10

Interventive roles: Implementation of the plan

The service contract has been negotiated and agreement achieved, and client and worker are now prepared for the hard business of intervention. The worker is confronted with the challenge of actually using abilities, skills, knowledge, and contacts to assist the client in reaching their mutually defined goals. The worker's activity in this area will be discussed in terms of interventive roles. The concept of interventive roles will be defined, and five such roles—broker, enabler, teacher, mediator, and advocate—will be discussed. Some general considerations about conceptualizing intervention in terms of roles will be noted, and finally a configuration of interventive roles which is very appropriate for the generalist worker will be set forth.

THE CONCEPT OF INTERVENTIVE ROLES

A more explicit statement of the concept of interventive roles can be developed by examining meanings for the terms *intervention* and *roles*. Throughout this book we have been using the term *intervention* in a more restricted and narrower sense than do many of our social work colleagues. This usage of the term refers to activities undertaken subsequent to the development of a service contract and directed toward the achievement of goals specified in the service contract. Some social work scholars and practitioners use the term in a more global way to refer to all social work activities, including data collection and contracting (or assessment) functions as well as actual change efforts. This concept is often expressed by the statement that "treatment begins at the opening of the first contract between worker and client."

We do agree with the notion that patterns of relationship and communication begin to develop when the client and the practitioner first meet, but we wish to differentiate the exploration of problem and goals and data collection on the part of both worker and client from goal-directed, jointly planned change efforts. We prefer a more limited use of the concept of intervention: (1) to maintain the focus on activities directed toward goal attainment and (2) to minimize the danger of making the concept of contracting secondary, or perhaps losing it, in efforts to produce change. We see danger in the desire of workers, and sometimes clients, to produce change quickly and move ahead with change activities without first developing a contract which clearly specifies the problem, objectives, and interventive activities to be utilized in accomplishing the objectives. Maintaining a narrower definition of intervention and also stressing the functions of data collection and contracting will tend to keep these three aspects of social work processes in a more balanced perspective. Intervention in our usage therefore refers to social work processes which occur after a service contract has been developed and are directed specifically to the achievement of goals specified in that contract.

Role is a global concept with wide usage in the sociological, social-psychological, and psychological literature; but the term is not always used consistently (Biddle and Thomas, 1966, pp. 1–50; Gross, Masson, and McEachern, 1958, pp. 21–47; Neiman and Hughes, 1959). For our purposes, role refers to the behaviors expected of a person. Role enactment will refer to the actual translation of these expectations into behavior. In a global sense people's roles, can be conceived as comprising the total universe of expectations which they hold for their own behaviors as well as the expectations of their behaviors which are held by others. But our focus is much narrower; interventive roles will refer to the behavior by means of which both client—an individual, a family, a group, or a community—and the worker expect the worker to accomplish goals specified in the service contract. One of the central points stressed in Chapter 9 was that intervention, along with all other social work processes, is undertaken jointly by the worker and the client. This chapter, however, focuses specifically on the worker's interventive activity.

In this chapter discussion will center on five interventive roles—those of social broker, enabler, teacher, mediator, and advocate. This is not an exhaustive listing. Some authors conceptualize the social worker's roles differently or add other roles. Charles Grosser's article discusses four roles in relation to community development programs (see Reading 10–1). The literature also includes references to such additional roles as therapist (Briar, 1967, pp. 19–33), encourager (Biddle and Biddle, 1965, p. 82), ombudsman (Payne, 1972), bargainer (Brager and Jorcin, 1969), and lobbyist (Maheffey, 1972). Bisno's conceptualization (1969) of nine social work methods appears very similar to our concept of role (see Chapter 1). The interventive roles of broker, enabler, teacher, mediator, and advocate, however, provide a useful framework for the beginning social work practitioner to utilize in conceptualizing interventive activity. The value of the framework is further enhanced because, as is true of the concept of contract, it is not limited by the size of the relational system; workers can use it to conceptualize their interventive roles whether they are working with individuals, small groups, or larger systems.

Our limiting of the definition of intervention and our organization of this chapter around the concept of interventive roles is not meant to deny or ignore the importance of specific change modalities.[1] Rather than attempt to catalog change modalities (many of which wax and wane as the culture and the profession emphasize different approaches), we chose to conceptualize interven-

---

[1] For one such list of modalities with additional references, see Whittaker (1974, pp. 200–248). Other works which may be of use include Roberts and Nee (1970); Rothman (1968, pp. 16–47); Tropp, (1968); and Whittaker (1970), pp. 308–322). See also articles under "Social Casework," "Social Group Work," and Social Planning and Community Organization" in the *Encyclopedia of Social Work* (National Association of Social Workers, 1977).

tion in a way which transcends specific modalities. The concept of interventive roles provides a framework for the analysis of interventive activity that is independent of the change modalities currently in vogue. Chapter 11 will discuss some change methods and processes which are generic to social work, useful for the beginning practitioner, and have withstood the test of time for social work.

THE ROLE OF SOCIAL BROKER

How does a worker enact the role of social broker? Analogies from other fields may be useful. How is the role of stockbroker enacted? Presumably a stockbroker assists clients in defining their resources and developing investment objectives; once this has been accomplished, brokers utilize their contacts and knowledge of the market to select stocks that will assist clients in reaching the defined investment objectives. How about the real estate broker? Again, realtors assist clients in analyzing their resources and needs to define objectives in terms of the type of home the client wishes to buy. Then, using their knowledge of the available resources, realtors will assist in matching the client's needs to the available housing. And so it is in the enactment of the social broker role. The worker serves as a linkage between the client and other community resources. Harold McPheeters and Robert Ryan (1971, p. 18), writing for the Southern Regional Education Board, note that the primary function of the broker is linkage, which they describe as follows:

> The primary objective is to steer people toward the existing services that can be of benefit to them. Its focus is on enabling or helping people to use the system and to negotiate its pathways. A further objective is to link elements of the service system with one another. The essential benefit of this objective is the physical hook-up of the person with the source of help and the physical connection of elements of the service system with one another.

The activities of the worker are directed toward making connections between the client and the community in order to accomplish the objectives specified in the service contract. Serving as a social broker requires a broad knowledge of community resources as well as a knowledge of the operating procedures of agencies so that effective connections can be made.

What are some examples of social brokering? The worker who arranges for a client to receive marital counseling, for job placement of an unemployed person, or for improved housing functions as a social broker if these activities involve connecting the client to other resources. The worker who brings specialized resources to groups—outside experts who may provide valuable information to the groups—is functioning as a social broker in that the worker provides linkages between the client and additional community resources. Or, when working with a community group, the worker can assist the group by identifying sources of funding for programs or additional outside expertise that can assist the organization in moving toward defined goals. A common element in all these examples is making a referral in order to connect the client to another resource. Referral is a basic part of the enactment of the social broker role; and assisting a client to find and use a needed resource is frequently the most important service a worker can provide. The process of making a referral will be reintroduced in the concluding portions of this section as we discuss the integration of the roles of brokers, enabler, teacher, mediator, and advocate and will be further developed in Chapter 13.

THE ROLE OF ENABLER

Workers take the enabler role when their intervention activities are directed toward assisting clients to find the coping strengths and resources within themselves to produce changes necessary for accomplishing objectives of the service contract. The major distinguishing element of the enabler role is that change occurs because of client efforts; the responsibility of the worker is to facilitate or enable the client's accomplishment of a defined change. A common misconception in discussing the enabler role is to see it only as a change that occurs within the client or in the client's pattern of relating to others or the environment. However, the enabler role can also be used to help the client find ways of altering the environment. The distinguishing feature of the enabler role is that the client effects the change with the worker performing a supporting or enabling function for the client.

The worker who assists a group of neighborhood residents in thinking through the need for a new day-care center, in identifying factors that must be considered in establishing the center, and in planning the steps that might be taken to provide day care will be serving as an enabler to a community group. The worker who helps a group to identify sources of internal conflict as well as influences that are blocking the group from moving towards its defined goals and then to discover ways of dealing with these difficulties is serving as an enabler in relation to the group. Likewise, the worker who assists a mother in identifying problems in her relationship with her child and in identifying and selecting alternative courses of action to improve that relationship is also serving as an enabler.

Encouraging verbalization, providing for ventilation of feelings, examining the pattern of relationships, offering encouragement and reassurance, and engaging in logical discussion and rational decision-making are also avenues by which the enabler role might be enacted. In an article included in this chapter, Nicholas Hobbs discusses enabler approaches which assist clients to make progress in one-to-one relational systems (see Reading 10–2). Utilizing enabling as the interventive role will, of course, involve the worker primarily in contacts with the client system rather than with external systems. But, as noted, the client system can be an individual, a group, or a community.

THE ROLE OF TEACHER

Teaching is another interventive role available to the social worker and client. The social worker may provide the client with new information necessary for coping with the problem situation, assist clients in practicing new behaviors or skills, and may teach through modeling alternative behavior patterns. The worker who supplies low-income parents with shopping and nutritional information or who provides parents with information regarding child development for coping with difficult problems of children is performing a teacher role. The worker who uses role playing to transmit different ways of responding to the authority of teachers and principals to an adolescent may be performing a teaching role. Or a neighborhood group desiring to influence a city council to secure more frequent refuse services may need to be taught through role playing or other approaches how to make the request to the city council. And the worker who carefully checks out the meaning of words and phrases may, through modeling, teach clients how to communicate. The teaching role has many similarities to the enabling role inasmuch as it is directed primarily to strengthening clients abilities to cope and change the problems in the situation they are experiencing. The role is sufficiently important and useful in social work, however, that it warrants separation from enabling. Although the two roles may tend to overlap we perceive the enabling role as involving the worker's effort to help clients mobilize existing resources within the client systems whereas the teaching role involves introducing additional resources into client systems.

Teaching is an important aspect of social work practice. Frequently workers will provide clients with information necessary for decision-making; in some situations information may be all that a client needs to accomplish the defined goals. Giving information must be clearly distinguished, however, from giving advice. "Giving information" implies supplying clients with data, input, or knowledge which clients are free to use or not to use on their own behalf; "giving advice" implies that the worker knows what is best for the client. Workers rarely give advice, but providing information is an important service they render to clients.

One of the five tasks of the social work function as identified by Schwartz is the contribution of data which may help the client cope with social reality and the problem which is being worked. Schwartz also, however, offers three important warnings: (1) workers must recognize that the information they offer is only a small part of the available social experience; (2) the information should be related to the problem that brings the client and worker together; and (3) opinions should be clearly labeled as opinions and not represented as facts (see Reading 1–1). Virginia Satir (1964, pp. 97–100), a noted family counselor, clearly identifies workers' responsibilities to contribute from their own experiences in working with troubled families. She also notes a second major function of the educational component of counseling—modeling communication. In their approach to clients and to problem-solving, workers provide a model of behavior which clients may emulate. Albert Bandura (1967), a behavioral psychotherapist, further describes the use of modeling as a device for teaching clients new behavior patterns. In the sense of providing information and of providing modeling behavior, teaching is an important interventive role.

THE ROLE OF MEDIATOR

Mediation involves efforts to resolve disputes that may exist between the client system and other persons or organizations. When resolving disputes is an important step in accomplishing the service goals, social workers will use the role of mediator. If a young person has been expelled from school and the service contract has the goal of getting the student back into school, then the social worker may need to serve as a mediator between the young person and the school authorities. Or, perhaps a neighborhood group wishes to secure a playground but is unable to mount sufficient political clout to do so because of rivalries with another neighborhood organization; such a situation may call for the social worker to serve as a mediator between the two organizations. A worker serving in a battered women's shelter will undoubtedly find themselves needing to mediate disputes between clients and the husbands. Likewise, in many child welfare settings, workers will find themselves mediating conflicts for the child between the parents regarding custody in child-care decisions.

The mediator role will involve the social worker in efforts to assist their client and the other party to the dispute to find a common ground on which they might reach a resolution to the conflict. The worker will be called upon to engage in a series of actions directed towards constructive conflict resolution. There is a burgeoning literature regarding conflict resolution (Deutsch, 1973; Jandt, 1973; Miller and Simons, 1974; Smith, 1971; Tedeschi et al., 1973; Walton, 1969).

The social worker in the role of mediator will use techniques to try to bring about a convergence of the perceived values of both parties to the conflict, help each party recognize the legitimacy of the others' interests, assist the parties in identifying their common interests in a successful outcome, avoid a situation in which issues of winning and losing are paramount, attempt to localize the conflict to specific issues, times, and places, break the conflict down to separate issues, and help parties identify that they have more at stake in continuing a relationship than the issue of the specific conflict. Persuasion and conciliation procedures will be used by the social work mediator.

We have identified the use of the mediator role in resolving disputes between the client system and external systems. Some of the same procedures may also be used to resolve disputes within the client system as may occur when a social worker is working with groups or families. While in one sense this is mediation, intra-client system dispute settlement can also be considered use of the enabling role inasmuch as resolving these intra-system disputes is essential in enabling the client system to mobilize resources to move towards the accomplishment of the goals in the service contract. A debate as to when is mediation mediation and when is it enabling is not particularly useful although this issue illustrates that the boundaries separating the various interventive roles may not be fixed.

THE ROLE OF ADVOCATE

Advocacy is a concept which social work has borrowed from the legal profession. As advocate, the social worker becomes the speaker for the client by presenting and arguing the client's cause when this is necessary to accomplish the objectives of the contract. As Charles Grosser notes, the advocate in social work is not neutral but, like the advocate in law, is a partisan representative for the client (see Reading 10–1). The advocate will argue, debate, bargain, negotiate, and manipulate the environment on behalf of the client. A report of the Ad Hoc Committee on Advocacy of the National Association of Social Workers, reproduced in this chapter, notes the techniques and issues involved in the use of advocacy (see Reading 10–3). Advocacy differs from mediation; in mediation the effort is to secure resolution to a dispute through give and take on both sides. In advocacy the effort is to win for the client; advocacy efforts are frequently directed towards securing benefits to which the client is legally entitled. Advocacy, like the other roles, can be used with client systems of various sizes.

Advocacy is becoming an increasingly popular role of social workers. Unlike the broker, enabler, teacher, and mediator roles, however, advocacy can be used without the direct involvement of the client. This creates a danger of falling to the temptation of serving as a client's representative without having a clear contract with the client to do so. Lawyers do not become the representatives for clients until clients have retained them and authorized them to extend this service; likewise, social workers should be sure they have an explicit contract with the client prior to engaging in advocacy activities.

ROLES ARE NOT FUNCTIONAL SPECIALIZATIONS

The discussion of social work intervention roles as discrete entities can lead to misconceptions. We do not recommend this conceptualization of interventive roles as a basis for functional specializations, but we think it would be inappropriate for workers to consider themselves as specializing as brokers, enablers, teachers, mediators, or advocates. Any such specialization would limit a worker's ability to be of service to a client. Rather than specializations, all workers will require abilities in all roles so that they can select the most appropriate interventive role for each client situation. Each of the roles may be used in some client situations; this provides the worker and the client with alternative approaches to use in achieving goals. Consider, for example, the following excerpt from a report made by a social worker in a Head Start program. At the request of Mrs. B, the worker had come to her home to take an application to enroll the child in the program; the discussion described here occurred right after the application was completed.

> The last question was "Why do you want your child in Head Start?" Mrs. B answered by saying that he had to learn to behave better and he needed to be around other children more than he was. Putting the form aside, I asked her what sort of problems she was having with Jimmy. He had been sitting at her side, surprisingly quiet for a three-year-old. In response to my question Mrs. B told me about taking Jimmy to the child guidance center and what the doctor had told her. Apparently the doctor had tested Jimmy and then talked to Mrs. B. She had complained of his bad behavior and that she didn't know how to discipline him. Apparently the doctor told her that the problem might be hers and not Jimmy's. He said that she was lonely and insecure and maybe needed some guidance in handling her children. She discussed this freely and admitted that this might be true. I asked her whether she would like to have me come over to talk to her about ways to handle Jimmy. She said definitely yes, that she couldn't do a thing with him.

In this excerpt we note the development of a preliminary service contract. There appears to be agreement that Mrs. B is having difficulty in the way she is handling Jimmy, and the goal is for her to learn new ways of handling him. The interventive role by means of which the worker proposes to accomplish this is to talk with Mrs. B about her parenting of Jimmy. The worker is proposing the enabler and possibly the teacher role, but this is a situation where the roles of broker, mediator, and perhaps advocate might have been used. Had this worker explored the situation more completely with Mrs. B, the intervention plan might have been different. For example, further exploration with Mrs. B about what happened at the child guidance center, about her perceptions of what the doctor said, about her thinking and feelings concerning the experience, and about her willingness to return to the clinic might have led to an intervention plan involving the worker's serving as the linkage between Mrs. B and the clinic. Or, possibly, if there appeared to be a problem with the manner in which the clinic related to Mrs. B, the worker might have used a mediator role to solve these disputes or advocate role to serve as Mrs. B's representative at the clinic. Note that the objective remains the same—to help alter Mrs. B's way of relating to her son—but that the intervention plan to accomplish it may involve counseling with Mrs. B, serving as the linkage between Mrs. B and the clinic, or acting as Mrs. B's representative at the clinic. Consideration of all three alternatives is not likely to occur, however, unless the worker is both willing and able to use all three roles and is prepared to explore the client situation adequately before arriving at an intervention plan.

A second misconception that can grow out of a discussion of roles is that a worker will use only one role with each client. To the contrary, an intervention plan may combine elements of various roles. This can be illustrated by discussing the referral process—a major part of the social broker role. If a contract has been negotiated which calls for referral in order to achieve its objectives, three distinct subsequent steps are involved. These are preparation of the client, preparation of the referral organization, and follow-up. Preparation of the client includes discussion of what the referral will involve, what the referral agency expects, and so on and requires enabling and teaching roles. At this stage the worker is attempting to enable the client to make effective use of the referral agency. Ethel Panter (1966) offers a useful discussion of client preparation in terms of its ego-building impact on clients. Referral also generates feelings and reactions to loss on the part of both client and worker; this aspect of referral will be discussed further in Chapter 13. Enabling skills are used to help clients deal with their reactions to new agencies or workers and are necessary to successful completion of a referral.

Preparation of the referral agency involves the sharing of information about the client (with the client's full knowledge and usually with the client's consent). In some situations an agency may be reluctant to accept a referral and to provide a service which it is mandated to provide. When this happens, the worker may need to use either mediation or advocacy. After the actual referral has been made (that is after the client makes initial contact with the referral organization), the worker will follow up with both the client and the organization. Ideally, follow-up should be a part of the initial planning. As a result of follow-up, the worker may learn about client resistances to continuing the service or the referral organization's resistance to continuing with the client which may require use of enabling, teaching, mediation, and/or advocacy.

This model of social brokerage supplemented by the other roles to help a client secure services required is one which will frequently be used by the generalist social worker. A worker skilled at involving the client in developing a service contract and skilled at helping the client to find and utilize the resources necessary to meet the objectives of the contract will provide an extremely useful, largely unavailable, service to clients. Such an approach, however, requires the ability to use skills to humanize the ways in which services are delivered and to assist agencies in meeting their responsibilities to clients.

RECAPITULATION

Intervention has been defined as the social worker's activity directed toward achieving the objectives of a service contract. Five major interventive roles have been discussed—social broker, enabler, teacher, mediator, and advocate. Any of these roles may be used to reach the same contract objectives: this provides client and worker with alternative approaches to intervention. In addition, the roles may be used in conjunction with one another to reach the same objectives. A focus on social brokerage in which enabling and teaching are used to assist the client in utilizing community resources, and mediation and advocacy are used to influence the way the resources are delivered to the client may be a major part of the services provided by the generalist social worker.

A LOOK FORWARD

The readings in this chapter elaborate further on interventive roles. The article by Charles Grosser discusses the application of roles in a community development program. The paper by Nicholas Hobbs offers a statement on enabling approaches which can be used effectively in supporting clients, and the statement of the National Association of Social Workers Ad Hoc Committee on Advocacy notes approaches and issues that can be used in implementing advocacy roles.

The next chapter discusses evaluation, an essential part of the problem-solving model which will lend a more systematic dynamic quality to social work processes. Evaluation provides feedback loops through which worker and client negotiate changes in their plans; through the continuous use of evaluation and feedback social work becomes less linear and more systemic.

Reading

10-1 *Community development programs serving the urban poor**

Charles F. Grosser

A discontinuity exists between the theory and the methodology of community organization. Recognition of this is evidenced in the recent literature. Kahn (1964, pp. 9 and 19) notes:

---

* Copyright 1965, National Association of Social Workers, Inc. Reprinted by permission of the author and publisher from *Social Work* 10:3 (July 1965), pp. 15–21.

One cannot plan for the education, job training, placement, or counseling of deprived inner-city youth without new concentration on the public sector generally. What was often tokenism in welfare council participation would not do for these endeavors. . . . One must learn to deal with, involve, plan with, bring pressure upon, or even to cause changes in, local and state governmental bodies. . . .

. . . until recently, the community organization method was conceptualized entirely in relation to the enabling role. . . . The enabling took the form of facilitating leadership development of consensus about direction to be taken or winning local assent to leadership-sanctioned direction and plans—not of shaping planning out of true communitywide involvement in goal setting.

Morris and Rein (1963) similarly indicate that

the requirements of the new community demand skill in invocating special points of view and in living with other professionals who advocate competing points of view.

One major factor impelling new developments in community organization practice is the increased attention by the field to the client group with which it is engaged: specifically, beginning to work directly with the recipients—rather than exclusively with the providers—of social welfare service. As the term is used in this paper, *neighborhood community development* means community organization efforts being made with lower-class, minority group, urban slum residents. The goals of these efforts are to engage the poor in the decision-making process of the community, both to overcome apathy and estrangement and to realign the power resources of the community by creating channels through which the consumers of social welfare services can define their problems and goals and negotiate on their own behalf. Much of the experience gained from these efforts can be generalized for application to most groups of deprived persons.

The purpose of this paper is to explore some of the consequences emerging from community organization's growing engagement with the poor person. Briefly discussed are (1) the substantive areas and issues with which community organization practice will have to deal, (2) a consideration of the role of the community worker, and (3) a brief review of the issue of the organizational forms that practice will take.

Substantive areas and issues

Community organization in neighborhood development programs signifies direct engagement with the problems of the poor person. More than any other group in our society, the poor expend a major portion of their efforts to achieve the "good life" through interaction with agencies of city government. It is with the local branches of the department of welfare, the police, the housing authority, the board of education, and similar agencies that the poor person negotiates for a share of the community's resources. Striving toward the equitable distribution of these resources is the programmatic strategy that must accompany any bona fide effort to encourage the residents of the inner-city slum to help themselves. If neighborhood development denies or ignores this fact, in the eyes of the local residents it is at best sham and window-dressing, at worst, deceit. Lower-class, minority group individuals cannot be expected to feel that they have a part in the determination of their own destinies in the face of such grievances as denial of welfare to nonresidents, forcing parents to take legal action against their child under the relatives' responsibility laws, categorization as an "undesirable tenant" with no right to face one's accusers and no recourse to appeal, arrest and interrogation characterized by prejudice and brutality, and an inferior, segregated school system. To attempt to facilitate clients' adjustment to such a social system is to betray their interests. Therefore, if local community development programs are to be successful, it must be recognized that local efforts at self-expression will be directed at the agents of government in an attempt to bring about solutions to such injustices as these.

Further, in order to arouse people who have been systematically socialized into apathy and inaction—in some cases, over several generations—it may be necessary to teach them that the solutions to their problems lie in the hands of certain governmental agencies, and that these agencies are sensitive to well-publicized mass efforts, particularly in election years. Lower-class, alienated, non-participating people will not be induced to organize by appeals to their sense of civic duty, patriotism, or morality, or other exhortations to exercise their obligations of citizenship. Such individuals will organize only if they perceive organization as a means to an immediate end. It should be pointed out —without becoming involved in a means-ends, process-content discussion—that these programs require a great deal more attention to material objectives than has been true in the past. Community development in slum neighborhoods is, after all, essentially a process for the redress of grievances that are the cumulative result of the differential distribution of community resources. To avoid partisanship in the name of objectivity and service to the "total community" is, in effect, to take a position justifying the pittance that has been allotted from the health, educational, and social welfare coffers to the residents of the inner-city slum.

An applied example of the foregoing was a voter-registration campaign conducted in New York City by Mobilization for Youth last summer and fall (Bailey and Pinsky, 1965). Geared to the registration of eligible minority group nonvoters, the campaign was not run on the model of the League of Women Voters, which presses voters to fulfill their civic duty. Instead, it was focused on the ballot's Proposition 1, which provided for additional low-income housing, and on the recently enacted "stop-and-frisk" and "no-knock" laws. Because these issues have great pertinence for the Lower East Side slum community, they were used to encourage voter registration. MFY was careful to avoid creating unrealistic expectations of immediate success regarding these issues; rather, it argued that Proposition 1 was sure to be defeated unless the people of New York City carried it by a large enough plurality to overcome the upstate opposition, and that the "stop-and-frisk" and "no-knock" laws violate the rights and dignity of the

suspect and are a reflection of a general lack of political accountability and of abstinence from voting by the poor person, who is more often arrested and interrogated than any other citizen.

The enabler role

The traditional stance of the community organizer as enabler is based on two assumptions, one valid, the other invalid. The valid assumption is that self-imposed actions growing out of a community's assessment of its own needs have a value and permanence that do not inhere in actions imposed from the outside. The invalid assumption is that the enabling role is the only one by which this desirable end may be brought about. In this section several alternatives are suggested that are believed to be viable.

It should be noted, first, that the role of enabler, geared to process, may itself be limited as a strategy for facilitating community self-help. For example, one text on community organization method draws on the experience of a special governor's committee set up in Colorado to deal with pervasive problems in the state's mental institutions as illustrative of proper work by a community organizer. Conditions within the institutions were unsatisfactory, and individuals were being improperly and illegally committed:

the legislation [directed at the problems] recommended by the governor's committee did not get very far in the ensuing session of the state assembly, although a more substantial program might have resulted if the committee, or even a considerable bloc within the committee, had been willing to manipulate or use undemocratic methods. It was rightly felt, however, that this might jeopardize future working relationships— in short, that process or means was as important as the immediate goal (Murphy, 1954, p. 22).

Although such judgments may be possible in statewide interdisciplinary committees, direct contact with those immediately affected by such decisions in a neighborhood community development program precludes any such cavalier determination of the client's fate.

The "broker" role

Familiar in such nonsocial work contexts as real estate and the stock market, the role of "broker" was instituted in the Mobilization for Youth program in 1962. It appears to have been first suggested for social work practice by Wilensky and Lebeaux (1958, p. 286). These writers postulated a need for "guides, so to speak, through a new kind of civilized jungle" and spoke of social work as "an example par excellence of the liaison function, a large part of its total activity being devoted to putting people in touch with community resources they need but can hardly name, let alone locate."

The community organization worker brings the component of collective action to the broker role, adding a potent factor to the process. Through collective "brokerage activity," the notion of collective solutions is introduced; that is, administrative and policy changes are undertaken to affect whole classes of persons rather than a single individual. The following comment, taken from a report of a Mobilization for Youth community organizer, illustrates the point:

Residents of the Lower East Side have brought their welfare problems . . . such as late checks, insufficient funds to pay large utility bills, no winter clothing, dispossess notices, and a host of others . . . to Casa de la Communidad, since it first opened in February 1963. These problems were handled by the caseworkers . . . who shared the facilities with the C.O. worker. . . . All too often, no real change seemed to result either in the lives of the clients or in the procedures of welfare. The same clients tended to come over and over again from emergency to emergency (Kronenfeld, 1965).

It was as a result of this experience that two community organization efforts in the welfare area were launched: a welfare information center and an organization of welfare clients holding court support orders. The latter group sought a collective resolution to the problems created by the determination of budgets on the basis of income ordered by a court but rarely received by the family.

The advocate role

It has been the experience of workers in neighborhood community development programs that the broker role is frequently insufficiently directive. Therefore, the role of advocate has been co-opted from the field of law. Often the institutions with which local residents must deal are not even neutral, much less positively motivated, toward handling the issues brought to them by community groups. In fact, they are frequently overtly negative and hostile, often concealing or distorting information about rules, procedures, and office hours. By their own partisanship on behalf of instrumental organizational goals, they create an atmosphere that demands advocacy on behalf of the poor person. If the community worker is to facilitate productive interaction between residents and institutions, it is necessary to provide leadership and resources directed toward eliciting information, arguing the correctness of a position, and challenging the stance of the institution.

In short, the worker's posture, both to the community residents and to the institutional representatives with whom the worker is engaged, is that of advocate for the client group's point of view. While employing these techniques, the worker is not enabler, broker, expert, consultant, guide, or social therapist (Ross, 1955, pp. 220–228). The worker is, in fact, a partisan in a social conflict, and the worker's expertise is available exclusively to serve client interests. The impartiality of the enabler and the functionalism of the broker are absent here. Other actors in this social conflict may be using their expertise and resources against the client. Thus the community organizer may need to argue the appropriateness of issuing a permit while the police argue its inappropriateness, or the worker and tenant may take the position that building-code violations warrant the withholding of rent while the landlord argues their nonexistence. There may even be differences among social workers. For example, a community organization worker may claim certain welfare benefits for a group of clients over the opposition of a social investigator, or a community worker and a city housing authority worker may take opposite sides over the criteria the housing authority uses to evict tenants in city projects as undesirable.

In jurisdictional disputes or if organizational prerogatives are at issue, it is not uncommon to find social workers at odds with each other. When issues of professional ideology or politics are involved, vigorous advocacy is the rule rather than the exception, as a casual glance through the professional journals shows. Why is it not possible for such advocates to be recruited for the poor from the ranks of social workers? This is one of the orders of today's business.

Outside the courtroom, attorneys for defendants and plaintiffs often mingle in an atmosphere of congeniality. . . . Social workers do not enjoy this kind of professional relationship. It is likely that the partisan advocacy postulated will evoke virulence from the public agency that is directed against the worker. The following charges were made by school principals of a local district ("Report of Twenty-Six Principals of Districts 1–4," 1964) as a result of the actions of a group of parents who were part of the MFY community organization program:

We find that a group of its staff is fomenting suspicion and enmity toward the schools . . . this group is largely in the CO program. . . .

Mobilization workers have been engaged in a war on the schools. . . .

Parents and children are encouraged to make such complaints. This means the MFY is accumulating a secret dossier on the teachers in the area. . . .

The social worker from MFY began to assume the mantle of "guardian." . . .

It should be noted . . . how a controversy between MFY and the principals is transformed into a conflict between the community and the schools.

Such a response is not surprising since advocacy, if effective, will cause public agencies to spend more money, create more work for their already harassed staff, and focus the community's attention on the agencies' shortcomings.

The activist role

Once the fact is recognized that community development efforts on behalf of the poor will produce partisan situations, it must be conceded further that the community organizer—or, for that matter, any other service worker in the urban slum—must choose which side to be on. The same logic that legitimates the roles of broker and advocate leads inevitably to another role, that of activist. Morris and Rein (1963, p. 174) have pointed out:

Political knowledge and skill to achieve one's ends have often been considered by social workers to be unprofessional. We have somehow believed that strong advocacy of a particular point of view and the development of techniques to achieve those ends violate our professional commitment to the democratic process. The question for us is whether our commitment to professional neutrality and noninvolvement is to continue to sustain our professional practice.

The traditional neutrality of the social work profession has much to recommend it, but it has been exercised to the detriment of certain client groups. Morris and Rein suggest that if this policy of noninvolvement persists, the function of community organization practice will be limited to coordination. If community organization is to find a role in community development, it cannot be exclusively neutral, hence the role of activist must also be embraced.

Except for the heroes of the American Revolution, this nation has had a culturally estranged view of the political and social activist. Despite their ultimate vindication, the abolitionist, suffragette, and labor organizer are still viewed as historical mutants by the community at large. Activists are characterized as "outsiders" and "agitators" to this very day, whether they play their roles in Selma, Alabama, or between Houston and Delancey Streets in New York City.

However, the activist role is and has been a legitimate stance for the social worker, especially the community organizer, and it must be available to be chosen from among other strategies when community needs require such activity. The passivity and objectivity of the service professions is after all something of a myth: people are urged to action of all sorts—to visit a dentist, sit up straight, curb their dogs, contribute to the Red Cross, and, in some communities, to register and vote and to support the PTA. In neighborhood community development, students are urged to stay in school, tenants to keep off project lawns, dropouts to join the Job Corps, and mothers to use well-baby clinics. Why should not tenants who are without heat also be urged to withhold rents, parents with grievances to boycott the schools, or citizens without franchise to take to the streets in legal public demonstration as a means to redress their grievances?

The answer to this point has been a matter of contingency, not reason. Some members of the profession have expressed concern that recourse to roles other than that of enabler—particularly that of activist—entails manipulation of the client group or community. The writer is convinced that the choice of role bears no relevance whatsoever to the issue of manipulation. As an attempt to achieve goals determined by the worker rather than the clients, manipulation can be accomplished by many techniques. Activists and advocates, no less than enablers and brokers, must make judgments on the basis of their professional appraisal of the client's needs, without regard to political expedience, personal ideology, or the vested interests of the agency.

Who is doing significant neighborhood community development with the impoverished today, and where? It is being done in the Negro ghettos of the North and South by nonprofessional activists in such organizations as the Congress of Racial Equality, Council of Federated Organizations, Student Nonviolent Coordinating Committee, and Southern Christian Leadership Conference. With few exceptions, neighborhood community development is taking place outside the field of social work, reflecting a narrowness of concept, not a paucity of resources in social work. Law students already have participated systematically in organizing drives for such organizations as SNCC and CORE. For a number of years, community organization practice and training of community organization students has taken place within such groups as the NAACP and the National Urban League. Therefore, it would seem appropriate for social work to place students in more activist areas within the civil rights movement.

Although techniques of activism are being sought, they are, in the main, unformulated. A body of literature is beginning to evolve, however, based on the philosophy and tactics of nonviolent direct action. For example, Oppenheimer and Lakey (1965) describe such techniques as haunting, renouncing honors, hartal,[1] boycott, demonstrations, leafleting, picketing, vigils, and role playing. They also suggest forms for record-keeping any typical budgets for votor registration projects, provide notes on security in the Deep South and offer advice on how to conduct oneself if arrested (including such specific suggestions as wearing two sets of underwear to absorb the shock of being dragged and using a bucket of water to remove traces of tear gas). Social workers should not be intimidated by the notion of incorporating some of these suggestions into their method: their strangeness stems largely

---

[1] "Hartal" is defined by *Webster's Third New International Dictionary* as "concerted cessation of work and business especially as a protest against a political situation. . . ."

from unfamiliarity. It might be noted that the many civil rights workers who have sought counsel and technique from social workers have frequently found social work methods somewhat strange also and have wondered how they might be incorporated into the methodology of nonviolence.

ORGANIZATIONAL FORMS OF NEIGHBORHOOD DEVELOPMENT

Those in community organization practice who have wrestled with the problems of neighborhood development in urban slums have found the issue of the organizational forms that their efforts should take a troublesome one. In what form should slum residents organize to mount efforts toward self-help? When the forms that voluntary associations take in the middle-class community are examined, a proliferation of styles, purposes, and patterns of participation, as varied as the personalities and social circumstances of those who participate in them, is discovered. Social workers do not have the temerity to suggest that there is a single optimal form that middle-class voluntarism should take. The assumption that such a form exists for collective action in the slum community is equally untenable.

Rather than debate on the relative merits of various alternatives, what is needed is to determine the strategies that will be most effective.

Forms of organization, their structure, and their affiliations if any will depend on the job decided on and the personnel available. The worker may want to join an existing group in order to influence it; the worker may want to set up an ad hoc or temporary group composed either of individuals or of representatives of other groups; or the worker may want to create a new group (Oppenheimer, Lakey 1965, p. 43).

Neighborhood work has been conducted with groups on the basis of common cultural patterns (hometown clubs), common social problems (welfare or housing organizations), physical proximity (building or block organizations), social movements (civil rights groups), specific task orientation (voter-registration campaigns), and the operation of a resource center (storefronts). If it has not yet created the technology or method of neighborhood community development work, social work efforts at community organization in urban slums have at least established the legitimacy of such efforts.

Commenting editorially on this issue as reflected in the MFY experience, the *New York Times* (1964) stated:

If Mobilization for Youth is to do more than merely ameliorate the lot of the poorest elements of the community, it must teach them to help themselves by concerted efforts. . . . Any form of social protest is bound to generate controversy, and some forms clearly raise serious questions of propriety for an agency that draws so much of its support from government funds. . . . But the poor must be encouraged to believe that there are ways to express their views on the need for social betterment. . . . The right to fight City Hall is as much a prerogative of the poor as of any other group of citizens; it is only when those who dwell in the slums and have too little to keep themselves and their families in dignity surrender to a supine sense of total futility and helplessness that the community has real cause to worry.

Reading

10–2 *Sources of gain in psychotherapy**

Nicholas Hobbs

This paper needs a subtitle. Let it be: "Five Hypotheses in Search of a Theory." One of the firmly rooted assumptions in psychotherapeutic practice is that the development of insight on the part of the client is both a major goal of the therapeutic endeavor, intrinsically worth promoting, and a primary means of achieving, step by step in the therapeutic process, the overall objective of more effective functioning. If clients can be helped to understand why they behave as they do or to recognize and understand the origin of the neurotic tactics that continually defeat them, they will gradually abandon the inappropriate behavior and substitute therefor more rational tactics in the management of their lives. Increased self-understanding is regarded as inherently good and as a means to the end of good psychological health.

The promotion of insight is thus the tactic most heavily relied upon by most therapists who write about their work. Other strategies—the encouragement of catharsis, of abreaction, of transference—are valued to the extent that they lay the groundwork for the achievement of insight. The interpretation of behavior, perhaps the most widely used tactic of all, is aimed directly at the promotion of self-understanding. Furthermore, the achievement of insight by clients is a welcomed signal to therapists that their efforts are paying off, and that their clients armed with new understanding, will gain a new measure of control over their lives. All of this is a part of the folklore, both amateur and professional, of helping people by talking with them. But I have come seriously to doubt the presumed relationship between the achievement of insight and the achievement of more effective functioning.

My doubts about the efficacy of insight as a change agent were first aroused a number of years ago while working in a clinic with a staff with diverse theoretical persuasions. In staff discussions of therapy cases, the occurrence of a significant insight on the part of a client was greeted with approval and satisfaction and with the expectation that there should follow some change for the better in the client's behavior. When anticipated changes did not occur, there was general discomfort. If the client persisted in behaving contrary to theory, as some obstinate clients did, we countered with a very useful, theory-preserving gambit. We said, "Well, it is obvious that the client did not have real insight. The client may have had 'intelligent insight,'" we said, "but the client did not have 'emotional insight'." This was always an after-the-fact adjustment. We were not attracted to the obvious alternate interpretation, namely, that insight need not lead to changes in behavior. We were too much a part of our culture, both general and professional, to question the time-honored relationship between self-understanding and effective functioning.

I began to wonder why we never examined the alternate explanation of the failure of insight to produce changes in behavior. Once jarred from the point of usual perspective on this issue, I began to see a number of arguments for an alternate explanation, namely, that insight may have nothing to do with behavior change at all, or is, at best, an event that may or may not occur as a result of more fundamental personality reorganizations. Here are some of the arguments:

Item 1.   In interpretive therapies, great

* Reprinted from *American Psychologist* 17 (November 1962), pp. 721–724. Copyright 1962 by the American Psychological Association. Reprinted by permission.

stress is placed on the exquisite timing of interpretations. The thought occurs that an interpretation may be acceptable to clients only after they have achieved sufficient self-reorganization for the interpretation no longer to be relevant. They can accept but no longer "need" the interpretation.

Item 2. In play therapy with young children, most therapists do not bother to try to develop insight. Rational formulations are adult fare, a consequence of the adult's addiction to words. Instead, therapists provide children concrete experiences in relationship with a particular kind of adult and get good results.

Item 3. The equipotentiality of diverse interpretations is a bothersome thing. It is quite apparent that therapists of different theoretical persuasions seem to promote different but equally effective insights. An Adlerian interpretation based on assumed relationships between organ inferiority and lifestyle seems just as effective as a Freudian interpretation based on disjunctions among id, ego, and superego requirements. A Jungian interpretation based on the relationship between the individual and the cosmos seems as effective as an existential interpretation of the estrangement of people resulting from the subject-object dichotomy, currently described as an invention of Descartes. Or the therapist can get equally good results by making no interpretations at all, as Rogers has shown. All this suggests that the occurrence of an insight merely means that the client is catching on to the therapist's personal system for interpreting the world of behavior. The therapist does not have to be right, mainly convincing.

There are other arguments but these will suffice. They do not, of course, disprove the accepted relationship between insight and change in behavior, but they do suggest that one should give serious consideration to an alternate hypothesis. It seems to me that the traditional formulation of the relationship between self-understanding and effective behavior may be backwards. I suggest that insight is not a cause of change but a possible result of change. It is not a source of therapeutic gain but one among a number of possible consequences of gain. It may or may not occur in therapy; whether it does or not is inconsequential, since it reflects only the preferred modes of expression of the therapist or the client. It is not a change agent, it is a by-product of change. In a word, insight is an epiphenomenon.

The role of insight in therapeutic progress has probably escaped detailed analysis because we have no good definitions of what is meant by the term. Particularly are we lacking in criteria for differentiating between intellectual insight and emotional insight, if there are, indeed, two such entities, which I doubt.

The best definition that I have been able to come up with is this: Insight is manifested when clients make statements about themselves that agree with the therapist's notions of what is the matter. This is not a particularly useful formulation.

The acceptance of insight as the sovereign remedy for all neuroses represents both an unwarranted extrapolation from Freud's position and a failure to take into account the kinds of neuroses generated by Viennese life at the turn of the century and by American or European life today. Freud could not have been more explicit in insisting that his method worked best, if not solely, in cases of massive repression with accompanying conversion symptomatology. Contemporary culture often produces a kind of neurosis different from that described by Freud. Contemporary neuroses are frequently characterized not so much by repression and conversion as by an awful awareness and a merciless raw anxiety. The problem of the contemporary neurotic is not lack of insight but lack of a sense of identity, of purpose, of meaning in life. Because of a dehumanization of existence, as Kierkegaard pointed out, humans have a sickness unto death. Indeed, in many of the people I work with there seems to be a substantial component of realism in their neurotic condition. Nothing can make a person more anxious, or more guilty, than an unrelenting clear appreciation of the absurd and desperate condition of people today.

Let us suppose for the moment that insight plays no significant role in the therapeutic process. How then does change come about? What are the sources of gain in psychotherapy? My effort will be to identify sources of change that are common to all approaches to therapy, with the hope that the analysis will provide a theoretical matrix for more adequate quantitative and comparative studies of the therapeutic process. At present it seems to me that there are five major sources of gain, five kinds of experiences that are the well-springs of personality reorganization. I might add that these experiences often occur in daily life quite apart from psychotherapy and are the sources of healthy integrations and reintegrations that develop throughout the life span. Psychotherapy is a unique life situation deliberately designed to make these five sources of gain available in an intense and usable form in a compressed time span, especially for those people who are unable, because of their neurotic tendencies, to avail themselves of the normal healing and nurturing experiences of life. Psychotherapy may thus be practiced, as indeed it is, by anyone who comes into intimate contact with a client on a professional basis.

The first source of gain is in the therapeutic relationship itself. This is a widely accepted notion, and I only wish to specify, which is seldom done, what it is about the relationship that has therapeutic impact. It is this: Clients have a sustained experience of intimacy with another human being without getting hurt. They have an experience of contact, of engagement, of commitment. They learn directly and immediately, by concrete experience, that it is possible to risk being close to another, to be open and honest, to let things happen to their feelings in the presence of another, and indeed, even to go so far as to dare to include the therapist as an object of these feelings. Neurotics, on the basis of earlier attempts at intimate rela-

tionships with important life persons, primarily their mothers and fathers, have come to the deep-seated conviction that other people cannot be trusted, that it is terribly dangerous to open oneself up to them. This conviction may well have a very realistic basis: When they reached out to their parents they were rebuffed. When they made tentative, affective overtures to other important life persons, they got clobbered. On the basis of these hurtful experiences, they have adopted the tactic of alienation that is so characteristic of the neurotic. They may simply withdraw from significant human contacts. They may live and work in proximity with others, but let it be known that the relationship stops where the self begins. Or they may get engaged with others in intense relationships that should lead to intimacy but always with reservations, always on terms that guarantee that they are not really exposed. These are the counterfeit friendships and marriages of neurotics. And in all this, of course, they will not even be intimate with themselves; they cannot let themselves feel how they actually feel about themselves and others. Now I argue that human intimacy is necessary for human survival. Intimacy may be an instinctual, a biological requirement. But even if it is not a built-in requirement, the prolonged period of dependency of the human infant with its all but inevitable experience of some sustaining intimacy provides ample time to require, to leran a need to be close to others. The risking and handling of intimacy are learned by immediate experiencing; talking about intimacy, acquiring insight about intimacy, do not help much.

Now psychotherapy is a situation carefully designed to make it possible for a client to learn to be close to another person without getting hurt. For example, therapists do not, or should not, punish the client's tentative and fearful efforts at being open and honest about feelings. On the contrary, the worker is alert to and reinforces any reaching-out behavior. Therapists permit clients to use them to learn how to be intimate but do not make reciprocal demands of a personal character, such as those inevitably involved in friendship or marriage, for these would be too threatening to the client. The therapist may make formal demands but not personal ones. In this special accepting situation, where the ground rules are clear, the client dares to establish a fully honest relationship with another person, and finds it a tremendously reinforcing experience. The client is encouraged on the basis of this concrete learning experience to risk more open relationships outside of therapy. Of course, the client takes the chance of getting hurt again, as in childhood, but more likely than not finds that others are responsive and that one is after all capable of richer, of more giving and more sustaining relationships with other people. This first source of gain lends itself readily to analysis in learning theory terms.

Now, source number two. Much of the time in psychotherapy is spent, or should be spent, in helping the client divest verbal and other symbols of their anxiety-producing potential. Shaffer is the author of the rich declarative sentence that states that people are forever signaling to themselves. It is their ability to acquire, store, and manipulate symbols, and signal to themselves in symbolic form, that makes them so distinctive, and so interesting. It also makes them uniquely susceptible to neurosis. Each individual has a tremendous store of symbols that are the residuals of experiences with which they were originally associated. In the domain of interpersonal relationships, some people have a collection of symbols that, for the most part, set off in them at the deepest and most pervasive somatic level feelings of well-being, of comfort, of safety, of assurance. Other people, the ones we call neurotic, have a collection of symbols that set off in them, for the most part, feelings of anxiety and guilt or of somatic distress of specific or pervasive character. Actually, most of us have a mixed collection of distressing and sustaining symbols, and we call ourselves psychologically healthy if we have a clearly favorable algebraic balance of the positive

and the negative. The negative symbols, associated with earlier life experiences of a hurtful nature, tend to stick tenaciously with us. In ordinary life circumstances we do not have an opportunity to learn new and more appropriate responses to them. Here is what seems to happen. A child suffers more than can be tolerated at the hands of the father. The concrete experiences get associated with specific symbols that are a product of this unique relationship and its attending circumstances. As an adult, even after the father has long been dead, experiences with authority figures evoke the symbols which evoke anxiety, guilt, hostility, or perhaps headaches, nausea, or other somatic reactions. Because of the distress that has been aroused, the person retreats either literally or psychologically from the situation. Distress diminishes, thus reinforcing the avoidance of the authority relationship, and leaving the symbols as strong as ever. But authority cannot be avoided, and the cycle gets repeated over and over again. The crucial thing to note is that the person never has an opportunity to learn new and more appropriate responses to the symbols that are evoking what we call neurotic behavior. The conditioned response cannot get extinguished.

The task of the therapist is not to help clients gain insight into the fact that they have trouble with authority figures because of their unfortunate experiences with their own fathers. This is far too abstract a formulation to be of help. They have got to be helped to identify and use comfortably the specific symbols that are elicited in them by authority figures. The symbols must be divested of their anxiety-producing potential.

At this point my communication problem becomes exceedingly difficult because there is no general way to identify or categorize these symbols. They are all highly personal, highly concrete, highly specific to the particular individual. And they have got to be talked about by the client in highly specific, hot, personal, intimate terms. The terms used must get as close as possible to the client's own idiosyncratic symbol system. A bright girl who had frequent attacks of nausea explained early in therapy that she feared she was homosexual and that she recognized the unsatisfactory character of her relationship with her mother, a fine insightful statement. Much later, after she was sure that it was safe to talk to the therapist using the same symbols that she used when talking to her most private self, she described in specific detail the experiences she felt had warped her relationship with her mother. At the end of the very difficult hour, she said, "This is the blackness that I have been trying to vomit."

The transference relationship is a third source of gain in psychotherapy. It also provides the clearest illustration of the differences between therapies which stress, respectively, the rational, abstract, and verbal, or the nonrational, concrete, and experiential components of the therapeutic process. Freud's discovery of the transference situation was a brilliant achievement. It made available to the therapist a most valuable instrument, comparable to the microscope or telescope in its clarifying powers. The essence of the situation is this: Clients do not talk about their neurosis, they act it out. Their neurotic stratagems are no longer filtered through semantic screens; they are tried out in concrete, specific acts of hostility, overdependency, seduction, dissimulation, and so on. The therapist and the client are both immediately involved in the client's desperate and always self-defeating and yet so very human ploys and gambits.

In the Freudian prescription for the handling of transference one finds the great psychoanalytic paradox: The cure for unreason is reason. Freud gave us a 20th-century discovery that unreasonable (that is, neurotic) behavior is determined by specific life experiences, thousands of them probably, and that neurotic behavior is unconscious and preeminently nonrational in origin. He could have said that neurosis is a summary term describing an extensive matrix of conditioned responses built up in a lifetime of hurtful relationships with important life persons, hardened around an armature of assumed guilt. He might further have observed that no person by taking thought becomes neurotic. But for his 20th-century diagnosis, Freud had a 19th-century prescription. Be rational. Transference represents the neurosis in microcosm; when transference appears it should be interpreted. As Fenichel so clearly instructs us, clients should be shown that they are behaving in an irrational manner.

Now I think it likely that this tactic will result in the client's learning that certain neurotic stratagems are not approved of, and they may well be abandoned in favor of other protective mechanisms. In the face of repeated interpretations, clients may learn to repress particular transference symptoms. But nothing has been done about their need for these symptoms; their underlying distrust of themselves and of other people remains untouched by the therapist's efforts to promote insight by interpreting the transference.

Transference develops when clients feel that the relationship with the therapist is becoming too dangerous, that they are losing control of the situation. They do not know how to handle the growing intimacy of the relationship without resorting to well-established neurotic defenses. They do not need to be told that their tactics are inappropriate, that their tactics are characteristic of a way of life, but they need to learn through an immediate experience with another human being that the tactics are not necessary. Transference is best handled by providing clients with the kind of understanding and unqualified acceptance that have been so notably absent in their lives. Transference stratagems disappear when the client has an opportunity to learn through concrete experience that it is possible to establish a simple, honest, open relationship with another person.

A fourth source of gain is available in those therapies which place the locus of control of the situation in the client rather than in the therapist. The client has hundreds of opportunities to practice decision-making, to learn to take responsibility to develop a self-concept as a person capable of managing one's own life. Here again, you will note the emphasis not on insight but on specific opportunities for the acquisition of new ways of behaving.

Before proceeding to examine a fifth source of gain which seems to be different in character from the four already mentioned, I should like to discuss briefly two possible explanations for our confident advocacy of insight as a primary change agent in psychotherapy.

Insight and understanding appeal to us as central mechanisms in therapy because of our strong general commitment to rationality in problem-solving. As F. S. C. Northrup has pointed out, Western culture (in spite of its immense irrationalities) has a deeply ingrained rational component. For us, reason is a faith. From earliest childhood we are taught to apply rational principles to the solution of many kinds of problems. If our automobile breaks down, we do not ordinarily kick it, pray over it, or assume that its spirit has departed, as a person from a primitive culture might do. We first try to discover what is wrong and then make appropriate interventions to correct the difficulty. It is perhaps the very strength of our faith that has led to a curious short circuiting in the domain of psychotherapy. Faced with a breakdown of personal functioning, we seem to assume that the development of understanding itself is a sufficient intervention to correct the difficulty. If a person can be helped to understand the origins and current manifestations of the neurotic behavior, particularly if the person feels deeply while gaining this insight, the neurotic behavior should disappear. A good rational question is Why should it disappear unless appropriate learning experiences follow?

Even if we do have a cultural bias regarding the importance of insight and understanding, our convictions would gradually be extinguished in the therapy situation if they were not occasionally reinforced. And they are. Insight sometimes does lead to changes in behavior—but not for the reasons commonly assumed. Insight is usually thought of as a freeing or releasing mechanism. I think it may actually operate through the facilitation of repression and the elimination of a particular symptom. A good example is provided by Dollard and Miller. A girl had a habit of thumbing rides with truck drivers at night and then being surprised when men "took advantage of her." The therapist pointed out to her what she was doing and she stopped doing it, thus seeming to validate the assumption of insight as a releasing influence. But Miller's conflict theory provides a better explanation of her behavior, I think. She could either give up hitchhiking or run the risk, as she would see it, of incurring the disappointment of her valued therapist. She might be expected to repress her hitchhiking symptom. But nothing would have been done about her neurotic need for affection.

The same insight-related mechanism may operate outside of therapy to change behavior through repression. A person who expresses hostility through malicious gossiping reads in a newspaper column that if one gossips one will inevitably alienate all one's friends. If this prospect arouses enough anxiety, the person will feel much in conflict and may repress the tendency to gossip. But since the person is as hostile as ever, it may emerge in sarcasm or learning to excel at bridge. Again nothing would have been done about the neurotic need to be hostile. It should be pointed out that the repression of some symptoms may have subsequent therapeutic benefits if the person is thereby brought into more intimate human relationships that are intrinsically healing in accordance with the four sources of gain already described. Some symptoms are better than others. The worst symptoms are those that engender most alienation from significant others, for this cuts the person off from the normal sources of therapeutic gain in daily living.

There is a fifth source of gain common to

all psychotherapies that is qualitatively quite different from the four sources that have already been described. You may have noted in the preceding arguments not only a disavowal of the efficacy of insight as a change agent but also the strong emphasis on specific and concrete opportunities for learning new ways of responding, new ways of relating to other people, and new ways of perceiving oneself. The stress is on immediate experience and specific behaviors. Throughout the discussion there is an implicit invitation to recast the analysis in terms of learning theory of a general reinforcement type. Now the fifth source of gain involves a different level of abstraction and can best be talked about in terms of cognitive processes. I, of course, imply no disjunction between learning and cognition, but simply accept the fact that, at its current stage of development, psychology tends to use different constructs to describe these two aspects of human behavior.

All approaches to psychotherapy seem to have a more or less elaborated conception of the nature of humans which they, in essence, teach to the client. In doing so, they tie in with an ongoing process which is a unique and most exciting and engaging characteristic of people. People constantly engage in building and repairing and extending and modifying cognitive structures that help them make personal sense of the world. Individuals have got to have a cognitive house to live in to protect themselves from the incomprehensibilities of existence as well as to provide some architecture for daily experiencing. They have to build defenses against the absurd in the human condition and at the same time find a scheme that will make possible reasonably accurate predictions of their own behavior and of the behavior of their wives, their bosses, their professors, their physicians, their neighbors, and of the police officers on the corner. They must adopt or invent a personal cosmology. When they invest this cosmology with passion, we may call it their personal mystique.

There are many available cosmologies for ordering the universe and increasing predictive efficiency in daily life. One of the first of these was provided by Pythagoras, some 3,000 years ago. Contemporary religious systems seem useful in reducing uncertainty in at least some realms of experience, and for some people. Religions with established dogmas, elaborated rituals, and extensive use of personification appear to have widest appeal, as one would expect. Those with almost no formal doctrine probably appeal most to people who have at hand alternate systems for construing the world. Psychoanalysis provides a cognitive structure of remarkable cogency. Its range of applicability is not cosmic but mundane, which is one source of its appeal among pragmatic people. Its metaphor is engaging; its extensive use of reification simplifies matters, but not too much; its formulation of behavior dynamics is occasionally useful in preditcing one's own behavior and the behavior of others. On the other hand, existential therapies would seem to be most acceptable to people who have come to suspect all institutionalized solutions (such as psychoanalysis) to the problem of meaning. Albert Ellis' rational therapy seems eminently suited to his clientele. I would guess that he works largely with bright, articulate, nonreligious, and reasonably well-educated but not too disenchanted people who find the process and the model of rational analysis appealing and convincing. Client-centered therapy probably works best with clients who already have well-developed but conflicting cognitive structures; they do not need to be taught a system for bringing order into their lives, but rather need to be helped to discover which system makes sense and feels right to them. George Kelley's fixed role therapy is, of course, the most forthright and charming method for providing a client with a cognitive structure for construing his world.

I think it possible to identify some criteria for assessing the adequacy of a personal cosmology and thus provide a therapist with some guidelines for dealing with the cognitive structures of the individual. Above all a person's cosmology must be personally convincing; when doubt occurs, anxiety mounts. Second, it should overlap reasonably well with the cosmologies of the people with whom one associates. If a person adopts a too divergent cosmology, the person runs the risk of being declared psychotic and incarcerated. Then it should be perceived by the individual as internally consistent—or relatively so. When there is too great a discrepancy between self and self-ideal, for example, discontent ensues. It should contain, on the other hand, some dissonances of either internal or external origin. With a bit of dissonance, the individual will work to strengthen major propositions about oneself and one's world. In addition, it should bring one into more intimate relationships with other people, for without such sustenance the spirit withers. Finally, it should have built-in requirements for revision, for to live is to change, and to remain static is to die.

People seek psychotherapy (or some other source of cognitive control) when their cosmology, their personal system for imposing order on the world, breaks down to an alarming degree. With increasing anxiety, order must be restored.

There are two summary points that I would make about this fifth source of gain in psychotherapy: (*a*) Human beings by their nature are going to erect cognitive structures to increase their feeling of control over their destiny, and (*b*) there is no way of establishing the validity of a particular order-giving structure independently of the individual who is going to use it. The concept of insight can have meaning only as a part of the process of elaborating on some particular system for interpreting events. There are no true insights, only more or less useful ones.

All systems of psychotherapy involve in varying measures the five kinds of experiences that I have described. Their effectiveness will depend on the extent to which they provide an opportunity for clients to experience closeness to another human being without getting hurt, to divest symbols associated with traumatic experiences of their anxiety-producing potential, to use the transference situation to learn not to need neurotic distortions, to practice being responsible for themselves, and to clarify an old or learn a new cognitive system for ordering their worlds. I am not prepared at the moment to assign beta weights to these several functions.

Reading

10–3   *The social worker as advocate: Champion of social victims**

**The Ad Hoc Committee on Advocacy,
National Association of Social Workers**

The new interest in advocacy among social workers can be traced directly to the grow-

ing social and political ferment in our cities in the past decade. Social workers connected with Mobilization for Youth[1] (which took its form in the context of this ferment) first

[1] Mobilization for Youth, Inc., started as an action-research program in juvenile delinquency control on New York City's Lower East Side.

brought the advocacy role to the attention of the profession (Brager, 1968; Grosser, 1965). But the notion that the social worker needs to become the champion of social victims who cannot defend themselves was voiced long ago by others and has recently been revived. (Cohen, 1964, p. 374).

Present events are forcing the issue with new urgency. Externally, the urban crisis and the social revolution of which it is the most jarring aspect are placing new demands on social work; internally, the profession is reexamining itself with an intensity that has few precedents. The profession's faith in its own essential viability is being severely tested. It is especially timely that social work turn its attention to the role of advocate at this time, both because of its clear relevance to the urban crisis and because it has been an integral part of the philisophy and practice of the profession since its earliest days.

What is advocacy?

Webster's defines advocate in two ways. On one hand, he is "one that pleads the cause of another." This is the meaning given to the legal advocate—the lawyer—who zealously guards the interests of his client over all others. Another definition describes the advocate as "one who argues for, defends, maintains, or recommends a cause or a proposal." This definition incorporates the political meaning ascribed to the word in which the interests of a class of people are represented; implicitly, the issues are universalistic rather than particularistic.

Both meanings of advocacy have been espoused in the social work literature. Briar (1967a, p. 28; 1968, pp. 5–11) describes the historical concept of the caseworker-advocate who is "his client's supporter, his advisor, his champion, and, if need be, his representative in his dealings with the court, the police, the social agency, and other organizations that [affect] his well-being." For Briar (1967b, p. 90), the social worker's commitment to the civil rights of *his own client* "takes precedence over all other commitments." This is, in essence, the orientation of the lawyer-advocate.

Brager (1968, p. 6) takes another view. He posits the "advocate-reformer" who "identifies with the plight of the disadvantaged. He sees as his primary responsibility the tough-minded and partisan representation of their interests, and this supersedes his fealty to others. This role inevitably requires that the practitioner function as a political tactician."

Brager does not rule out of his definition the direct-service practitioner who takes on the individual grievances of his client, but his emphasis is on the advocacy of the interests of an aggrieved *class* of people through policy change. The two conceptions do overlap at many points, as for instance when the worker must engage in action to change basic policies and institutions in order to deal effectively with his client's grievances.

Social work's commitment to advocacy

Advocacy has been an important thread running throughout social work's history. Some individuals have been elevated to heroic status because they have fulfilled this role—Dorothea Dix and Jane Addams come most readily to mind. However, it would be safe to say that most social workers have honored advocacy more in rhetoric than in practice, and for this there are at least two reasons.

To begin with, professional education and practice have tended to legitimate a consensus orientation and oppose an adversary one, and this has been perpetuated in the literature. A combative stance, often an essential ingredient in the kind of partisan alignment implied by the concept of advocacy, is not a natural one for many social workers. As a result, most social workers lack both the orientation and the technical skills necessary to engage in effective advocacy. Finally, the employee status of social workers has often restricted their ability to act as advocates.[2]

At the same time that the current upheaval in society adds a note of urgency to the issue of social work's commitment to advocacy, it also adds complications to the task of fulfilling that commitment because of the emotion surrounding many of the issues. For example, some members of the profession feel strongly that fighting racism and deepening the social conscience are the only means to combat these social evils; others—equally adamant—feel that social workers are not equipped to solve these ills, which are a problem of the whole society. There is still another group of social workers who tend to avoid involvement with controversial issues at any cost. What is needed is a consistent approach on the basis of which each social worker can feel confident in fulfilling his professional commitment, an approach that can be responsive to the current crisis but must outlive it.

Obligations of the individual social worker

The obligation of social workers to become advocates flows directly from the social worker's Code of Ethics.[3] Therefore, why should it be difficult for a profession that is "based on humanitarian, democratic ideals" and "dedicated to service for the welfare of mankind" to act on behalf of those whose human rights are in jeopardy? According to Wickenden (1964); "In the relationship of individuals to the society in which they live, dignity, freedom and security rest upon a maximum range of objectively defined rights and entitlements."

---

[2] It is not the intent to blame the agencies entirely for lack of advocacy in the discharge of a worker's daily duties. It is recognized that progressive agencies have already inculcated advocacy in their workers, often in the face of adverse community reactions and resistance by staff.

[3] This code was adopted by the Delegate Assembly of the National Association of Social Workers, October 13, 1960, and amended April 11, 1967.

As a profession that "requires of its practitioners . . . belief in the dignity and worth of human beings" (see Reading 4–1), social work must commit itself to defending the rights of those who are treated unjustly, for, as Briar (1967b, p. 90) asserts: "The sense of individual dignity and of capacity to be self-determining . . . can exist only if the person sees himself and is regarded as a rights bearing citizen with legitimate, enforceable claims on, as well as obligations to, society."

Each member of the professional association, in subscribing to the Code of Ethics, declares, "I regard as my primary obligation the welfare of the individual or group served, which includes action to improve social conditions." It is implicit, but clear, in this prescript that the obligation to the client takes primacy over the obligation to the employer when the two interests compete with one another.

The code singles out for special attention the obligation to "the individual or group served." The meaning seems clearest with respect to the caseworker or group worker who is delivering services to identified individuals and groups. It would appear to be entirely consistent with this interpretation to extend the obligation to the line supervisor or the social agency administrator who then is bound to act as an advocate on behalf of clients under his jurisdiction. A collateral obligation would be the responsibility of the supervisor or administrator to create the climate in which direct-service workers can discharge their advocacy obligations. As one moves to consider other social work roles, such as the consultant, the community planner, and the social work educator, the principle becomes more difficult to apply. But how can an obligation be imposed on one segment of the profession and not on another?

The inherent obligation is with respect to the work role and to those persons on whose lives the practitioner impinges by dint of his work role. It is in this role that the individual social worker is most clearly accountable for behaving in accordance with professional social work norms. Through this role he is implicated in the lives of certain groups of people; thus his actions affect their lives directly, for good or ill. Similarly, his work role gives him authority and influence over the lives of his clients; thus he has special ethical obligations regarding them. Finally, there are expected behaviors inherent in the work role on the basis of which it is possible to judge professional performance.

At this point it is important to remind ourselves of the distinction between the obligation of the social worker to be an advocate within and outside of his work role, both of which constitute an obligation of equal weight. However, the obligation to be an advocate outside the work role is general, not specific, and does not have the same force as the obligation to the client. In a sense, this obligation is gratuitous, or, as some might say, "above and beyond the call of duty." An additional problem is that there are no external criteria for judging whether a person is fulfilling this broad responsibility adequately. To use an extreme example: voting might be considered a way of carrying out the role of the advocate-reformer, yet would one say that failure to vote was failure to fulfill a professional obligation? To lump together the two obligations, that is, to be an advocate in one's work role and outside of it, might appear to reinforce the latter. In reality, it only weakens the former.

Yet the profession as a whole has consistently treated the broad social responsibilities of social workers as important to fulfillment of their responsibilities. Schools of social work make an effort to provide their students with both the orientation and skills to become involved in social issues well outside their future assigned responsibilities. The difference between the two obligations is a moral, not a formal, one. In other words, enforcement of the obligation to be an advocate outside the work role would have to be self-enforcement.

Competing claims

Until now, most discussions of the advocacy role in social work have limited their consideration of competing claims to those of the employing agency (Brager, 1968) or society as a whole (Briar, 1967a, p. 91). These have overlooked the possibility that in promoting his clients' interest the social worker may be injuring other aggrieved persons with an equally just claim. Suppose, for instance, that a child welfare worker has as a client a child who is in need of care that can only be provided by a treatment institution with limited intake. Does he then become a complete partisan in order to gain admission of his client at the expense of other children in need? What of the public assistance worker seeking emergency clothing allowances for his clients when the demand is greater than the supply? Quite clearly, in either case the worker should be seeking to increase the total availability of the scarce resource. But while working toward this end, he faces the dilemma of competing individual claims. In such a situation, professional norms would appear to dictate that the relative urgency of the respective claims be weighed.

A second dilemma involves conflict between the two types of advocacy—on behalf of client or class. Such conflicts are quite possible in an era of confrontation politics. To what extent does one risk injury to his client's interests in the short run on behalf of institutional changes in the long run? It seems clear that there can be no hard and fast rules governing such situations. One cannot arbitrarily write off any action that may temporarily cause his clients hardship if he believes the ultimate benefits of his action will outweigh any initial harm. Both ethical commitment and judgment appear to be involved here. (Is it, perhaps, unnecessary to add that institutional change does not always involve confrontation?)

A third dilemma is the choice between direct intercession by the worker and mobilization of clients in their own behalf. This is less an ethical than a technical matter. One can err in two directions: it is possible to emasculate clients by being overly protective or to abdicate one's responsibility and leave them to fend for themselves against powerful adversaries.

Technical competence

Questions of competence can compound these dilemmas, for good intentions are not enough for the fulfillment of the advocacy role. Workers must not only be competent, they must also be sophisticated in understanding the appropriate machinery for redressing grievances and skilled in using it. If social workers are required by the profession to carry the obligation to be advocates, they must be equipped to fulfill the role.

While any responsible profession constantly strives to improve its technology, the dissatisfaction of social workers with their skills at advocacy seems to go beyond this. For a variety of reasons, most social workers seem wholly deficient in this area. On the direct practice level, the traditional techniques of environmental manipulation have tended to become peripheral to the practice of social workers, as they have become more sophisticated in the dynamics of inter- and intrapersonal functioning. Second, knowledge of the law, which is vitally tied up with client entitlements, has had less emphasis in the social work curriculum in recent years. Even though increased attention has been given to the client in deprived circumstances—the one who is most likely to need an advocate—this emphasis in the curriculum must be further strengthened.

Regardless of the type of advocacy in which the practitioner engages, knowledge of service delivery systems, institutional dynamics, and institutional change strategies are crucial. Although great advances in this technology have taken place in certain sectors of practice and education, they must be disseminated to the field.

Among the basic content areas that need development and expansion both in school curricula and in continuing education of social workers are the following:

1. Sensitization to the need for and appropriateness of advocacy.
2. Techniques of environmental manipulation and allied practice components.
3. Knowledge of the law, particularly as it bears on individual rights and entitlements.
4. Knowledge of service delivery systems and other institutions that impinge on people's lives and from which they must obtain resources.
5. Knowledge and skill in effecting institutional change.
6. Knowledge and skill in reaching and using the influence and power systems in a community.

The relative emphasis on these different components would vary, depending on the specific work role, although all are necessary in some degree for all social workers.

Professional autonomy and the role of NASW

But lack of technical skills is not the greatest deterrent to advocacy by social workers; actually, it is their status as employees of organizations—organizations that are frequently the object of clients' grievances. Unless social workers can be protected against retaliation by their agencies or by other special interest groups in the community, few of them will venture into the advocacy role, ethical prescripts notwithstanding. It would seem to be a *sine qua non* of a profession that it must create the conditions in which its members can act professionally. For the profession to make demands on the individual and then not back them up with tangible support would betray a lack of serious intent.

This does not mean that all risks for the worker can or should be eliminated. A worker's job may be protected—but there is no insurance that he will advance within his organization as far or as fast as he would have if he had not been an advocate. Rather, the object is to increase the social worker's willingness to take risks to his self-interest in behalf of his professional commitment.

This brings us to the role and obligation of the professional association—NASW— and once again back to the context of social unrest, social change, and militancy in which this discussion is taking place. In view of the need for the profession to act quickly and decisively to focus on advocacy as being germane to the effective practice of social work, a program is needed—one that should be undertaken by NASW as soon as possible.[4] This program would do the following:

1. Urge social workers to exercise actively and diligently, in the conduct of their practice, their professional responsibility to give first priority to the rights and needs of their clients.
2. Assist social workers—by providing information and other resources—in their effort to exercise this responsibility.
3. Protect social workers against the reprisals, some of them inevitable, that they will incur in the course of acting as advocates for the rights of their clients.[5]

Certain assumptions are implicit in these three program objectives, namely:

That the social worker has an obligation under the Code of Ethics to be an advocate.

That this obligation requires more than mere "urging."

That under certain circumstances, as discussed later, the obligation is enforceable under the Code of Ethics.

That the *moral* obligation to be an advocate is not limited to one's own clients, although this cannot be enforced in the same way.

That encouragement of advocacy and provision of certain kinds of assistance to advocates need not be limited to members of the professional association.

To return to the relationship of NASW to the social work advocate who gets into trouble with his agency because of his attemps to fulfill a professional obligation: *NASW has an obligation to the worker that takes priority over its obligation to the agency.* In effect, the worker is acting in behalf of the professional community. While the conditions of such responsibility of NASW must be spelled out precisely (to avoid misleading members or jeopardizing the interests of the profession), there can be no question about the member's prior claim on NASW support. Without this principle, the association's claim on the member is meaningless.

The Committee on Advocacy considered two extensions of NASW's obligation. One was in relation to the social work employee who is not a member of NASW. Should the same aids and protections be offered to nonmembers of NASW as to members? It was recognized that a majority of social work positions are held by nonmembers and that they are concentrated particularly in public agencies, which are often the object of client grievances. Furthermore, many indigenous workers in poverty and other neighborhood programs are especially likely to be performing an advocacy function. Obviously, the profession cannot impose a professional obligation on such persons, yet it is consistent with professional concerns that such efforts be supported even when NASW members are not involved. The committee recommends that certain types of help be provided

---

[4] As the first step in implementing the program, the Commission on Ethics reviewed these findings of the Ad Hoc Committee on Advocacy and recommended that they be widely disseminated. The commission interprets the Code of Ethics as giving full support to advocacy as a professional obligation.

[5] This is the wording of the charge given to the Ad Hoc Committee on Advocacy by the NASW urban crisis task force.

but states that NASW is not in a position to offer the same range of support to nonmembers as to members.

The other extension of NASW's obligation is the possible assumption by NASW of the role of advocate when a client has no alternative channel for his grievances. The committee agreed that NASW could not become, in effect, a service agency, offering an advocacy service to all who request it, although it was felt that the association should work toward the development of such alternative channels. The association should be encouraged to engage in selected advocacy actions when the outcome has potential implications for policy formulation and implementation in general. An example of this would be participation in litigation against a state welfare agency for alleged violation of clients' constitutional rights; in this instance NASW would be using the

courts to help bring about social policy change instead of interceding in behalf of the specific plaintiffs in the case.

Broadly stated, then, the proposed program for NASW calls for concentrated and aggressive activities coordinated at local, regional, and national levels, to achieve the needed involvement by individual social workers, backstopped by members in policy-making and administrative positions and community leaders, through education, demonstration, and consultation in program planning; adaptation of NASW complaint machinery to facilitate the adjudication of complaints against agencies with stringent sanctions when indicated; and assistance to individuals who may experience retaliatory action by agencies or communities, ranging from intervention with employers to aid in obtaining legal counsel or finding suitable new employment.

Selected annotated bibliography

Brager, George A. "Advocacy and Political Behavior," *Social Work* 13:2 (April 1968), pp. 5–15.

Five considerations should be evaluated before engaging in class advocacy via political action—who benefits and who is hurt by this behavior, who is the target of this behavior, what values are behind the behavior, and what action is being taken.

Brager, George A., and Jorcin, Valerie. "Bargaining: A Method in Community Change," *Social Work* 14:4 (October 1969), pp. 73–83.

Brager and Jorcin analyze a bargaining role for practitioners in relation to the variables of the bargainers' power resources, how the issues are formulated, and the strategies used.

Briar, Scott. "The Current Crisis in Social Casework," in *Social Work Practice, 1967.* New York: Columbia University Press, 1967, pp. 19–33.

Briar notes the overemphasis on the therapeutic role in social casework and suggests the need for greater use of the broker and advocacy roles.

Davidoff, Paul. "Advocacy and Pluralism in Planning," *Journal of the American Institute of Planners* 31:4 (November 1965), pp. 331–338; also in Ralph M. Kramer and Harry Specht (Eds.), *Readings in Community Organization Practice.* Englewood Cliffs, N.J.: Prentice-Hall, 1969, pp. 438–450.

Davidoff suggests moving away from unitary planning in cities and instead of having planners attached to special interests groups and serving as their advocates, decisions concerning which plan to implement would be made through a political process.

Hallowitz, David; Bierman, Ralph; Harrison, Grace P.; and Stulberg, Burton. "The Assertive Counseling Component of Therapy," *Social Casework* 48:9 (November 1967), pp. 543–548.

This article develops the concept of assertive counseling within the context of a positive therapeutic relationship. Six elements are essential to this component—crisis intervention, the confrontation of disparities between perception and reality, the confrontation of discrepancies between behavior and goals, acceptance of responsibility, active direction finding, and direction implementation.

McCormick, Mary J. "Social Advocacy: A

New Dimension in Social Work," *Social Casework* 51:1 (January 1970), pp. 3–11.

McCormick discusses the concept and history of advocacy and explores its advantages and disadvantages as an instrument of social action within the context of democratic and treatment processes.

Rothman, Jack. "The Models of Community Organization Practice," in *Social Work Practice, 1968*. New York: Columbia University Press, 1968, pp. 16–47.

Rothman conceptualizes and contrasts three types of community organization—locality development, social planning, and social action.

Sander, Irwin. "Professional Roles in Planned Change," in Robert Morris, (Ed.) *Centrally Planned Change: Prospects and Concepts*. New York: National Association of Social Workers, 1964, pp. 102–116.

Sander conceptualizes and discusses the roles of analyst-planner, organizer for change, and program administrator.

Sharttuck, Gerald, and Marrin, John M. "New Professional Work Roles and Their Integration into a Social Agency Structure," *Social Work* 14:3 (July 1969), pp. 13–20.

This article analyzes the integration of new roles in a project to prevent school dropouts. The new roles are conceptualized as convener, mediator, interpreter, advocate, and collective bargainer. The problems of integrating these roles into a traditional agency are noted, and suggestions for future planning are offered.

Specht, Harry. "Social Policy Foundation: The Role of the Social Caseworker," in *Social Work Practice, 1967*. New York: Columbia University Press, 1967, pp. 72–94.

Specht presents an eight-step model of social policy formulation—identification of the problem, analysis and fact gathering, bringing the problem to the attention of the public, the development of policy goals, building public support, formulating a legislative program, implementation and administration of the program, and evaluation. Understanding this process will enable caseworkers to make a contribution to social policy.

Thursz, Daniel. "The Arsenal of Social Action Strategies: Options for Social Workers," *Social Work* 16:1 (January 1971), pp. 27–34.

Thursz calls for a disciplined, planned approach to social action which is not necessarily in opposition to militancy. Violence is not acceptable as a social work strategy, although disruption to symbolize wrongs may be used. Thursz warns against faddism and suggests that in addition to action in the political arena a watchdog role in relation to existing programs is needed.

Vinter, Robert D. "The Essential Components of Social Group Work Practice," in Robert D. Vinter, (Ed.), *Readings in Group Work Practice*. Ann Arbor, Michigan: Cowpers Publishers, 1967, pp. 1–7.

In this article Vinter presents a statement of the essential elements of a problem—focused group work practice. This is an excellent article for student study in that it addresses very succinctly the core competencies needed to utilize the multi-person group session as a medium of problem solving in which worker's role is that of enabler.

Wade, Alan. "The Social Worker in the Political Process," in *Social Welfare Forum, 1966*. New York: Columbia University Press, 1966, pp. 52–67.

Involvement of the social worker in the political arena necessitates overcoming the barriers associated with the notion that politics is dirty, the preoccupation with mi ro intervention, and the employment of most social workers in bureaucratic agencies. Social workers are a source of data for political policy decisions and must involve themselves in the hurly-burly world of politics to use their interpersonal relationship skills effectively in the political world.

Warren, Roland. "Types of Purposive Social Change at the Community Level," in Ralph M. Kramer and Harry Specht (Eds.), *Readings in Community Organization Practice*. Englewood Cliffs, N.J.: Prentice-Hall, 1969, pp. 205–222.

Warren conceptualizes three types of change strategies in relation to the extent of issue consensus. He labels them collaborative strategies, campaigning strategies, and contest strategies.

Zweig, Franklin. "The Social Worker as Legislative Ombudsman," *Social Work* 14:1 (January 1969), pp. 25–33.

Zweig reports favorably on the experience of students placed in legislative offices. The experience included the use of political power to achieve professional ends; study, assessment, goal setting, implementation, and evaluation were found to be indispensable; a wide range of assessment tools and skills was necessary; and no magic formula for producing positive legislative change was found.

CHAPTER **11**

Process and method:
Implementation of roles

This chapter continues the discussion of the action phase of the problem-solving process and focuses on the carrying out of the varying roles that the social worker may find useful. To carry out a plan requires the same knowledge and skills discussed previously: (1) use of communication; (2) development and use of the relationship; (3) use of resources; and (4) the social worker's use of self. However, the action phase often requires that these skills be differently organized and utilized in that the purpose of their use has changed. Rather than trying to define the problem, or set the goals, or analyze and integrate as in the assessment stage, the worker and client are now involved in a focused effort to bring about some action toward the goals that have been set by the methods agreed upon and guided by the plan.

In all social work activities with all sizes of systems and types of systems (client, target, action, change agent, professional and problem-identification system), the practitioner uses these skills, although their organization and focus will be different depending upon purpose, plan, and type of action. For example, in carrying through on acting as an advocate for the client system, the worker may be engaging in the negotiation of conflict. This will require the use of self in setting a particular climate (relationship), great self-awareness and self-discipline, and excellent skills in use of certain types of communication. In attempting to carry out the role of helper for an individual client, workers will also be interested in setting and maintaining a particular climate, will use certain types of communication, will need to be aware of their own needs and impulses, and will discipline their use of self. However, the *particular* type of relationship, the *particular* things communicated, the *particular* use of self will be different because the purpose, role, and type of system are different. Thus all social work activities require the four primary abilities in some combination.

There are four tests that all change processes need to meet if they are to be helpful to others. First is the rule of *parsimony*—all actions taken should be as simple and economic as possible in the ways they intervene in the life space of any living system. Work with the client systems is very seldom focused on total change of a total system. Actually, the social work process becomes more individualized and differentiated the more it is shaped by the goal, the problem, and the individual plan. All action should follow the salient features of the plan. By this we mean that careful consideration should be taken of the major thrust of the plan. Above all both action and plan should be relevant to the goals. We need to view ourselves as agents of the clients in attempting the changes. We need to be guided by the climate goals and we need to have considerable humility as to our ability to contribute effectively.

Another important principle of working toward change is that efforts to bring about change in either the client system, or other systems, may be addressed to the feeling, the thinking, or the acting of the individuals that compose the target system or toward their transactions as guided by them. These three capacities of the human ego are, as we have said before, so interrelated that change in any one characteristic may result in change in all, and change in any one capacity of one person in a group may change all aspects of the system. It is important to address the element or elements that seem most salient to resolving the problem.

For example: a mother, with a seriously retarded child, is having great difficulty developing skills to care for it properly. She does not understand retardation and feels that it must all be her fault. She has overwhelming feelings about what has happened and about the responses of others to her and her child. It is best to start with her feelings and hope that as one helps her through acceptance and reassurance, she will feel better and thus act better in the ways she approaches her child? Or is it better to see that she has some help with the child and is taught some needed skills and hope that by acting better she can feel better? Or do you rely on knowledge and hope that if she understands mental illness better, her feelings will change and her actions improve? In this situation, the best action will undoubtedly combine some judicious use of all three.

This principle is equally true (as a further example) in an advocacy situation in which the worker has demanded and received the opportunity to meet with the board of directors of an agency about certain policies that exclude many clients who need the service. One may approach the board by trying to assess whether it is the board members' feeling about these clients and such service, or their belief about the problems that might lie in such an expansion or their lack of the resources needed for expansion that keeps them from offering service and to attempt to focus change efforts on that element. Or is it one board member's feeling, thinking, and so on that is causing the problem; or is it a battle for control between two groups on the board that is holding up action?

In considering the selection of approaches to the client or target system, the worker will also need to consider the focus of the work. In other words is the primary focus to produce some effect on an individual or is it to change the interaction of individuals within a family system, or is it to change the community target system?

A simple scheme for categorizing the focus of the work follows:

1. *Primarily focused on some change in the individual client as target system either through one-to-one work with the individual or through work with the individuals' experience as a member of their family or a group.*
2. *Primarily focused on change in the interactions of the members of a client group or family as a social system.* Here the interaction between and among members is the target system.

3. *Primarily focused on helping the client system to carry through on plans to change a target system.* One of the primary examples of this is the task-oriented group called a committee. There are also tenants' groups, welfare rights' groups, and so on. Although many times this may be the focus of one-to-one work, as well.
4. *Primarily focused on helping the client system to change the transactions between itself and another system.* In this instance the target system is the transactions between the two systems. Often this may be transactions between a family and another social system, but it may also be between an individual and another social system such as the school, or even the extended family.

In working with human systems for whatever purpose and toward whatever change, there are two factors to take into consideration in everything one does. One factor is the climate that the worker offers the system (relationship) within which the work is done, and the other is the work itself. In other words, the how and the what is a part of every action. We are going to develop some suggested classifications of the what and how in the following discussion. These suggestions are not related to size of system but rather to the purpose of the process and may be used with any size system. We are going to discuss these techniques as they apply to the target system as they are aimed at bringing change. In many instances the target system will be the client system, but it may be other systems with which the practitioner is involved. These techniques are not exhaustive, as they do not cover everything a social worker does, however, they do represent the approaches most commonly used by social work practitioners. They are grouped in clusters because that is the way they are usually used. However, one may borrow from different clusters in order to more effectively carry out purpose.

ENCOURAGEMENT

Encouragement, by itself, is used as a cluster with a system that has the capacity, ability, and knowledge to work at the problem on its own, provided it has a little support. It will often be used with other types of client systems in combination with other techniques. In fact, it is one of the most used clusters of techniques. The techniques used for this purpose are listening, reflection back to the system of what it has been communicating, giving an opportunity for ventilation, occasionally giving reassurance, or expressing confidence in the system's work. In using these techniques, the worker is responding to the actions and communication of the system but is not adding new things so what is already being produced by the system.

The climate that the worker offers to accompany these techniques involves freedom and independence for the client system to pursue its own course and acceptance and expectance that the system can and will pursue the work. The worker is emotionally responsive to the system's feeling, thinking, and doing but always in such a way as to convey respect for the system's own ability to act.

ENHANCING AWARENESS OF OWN BEHAVIOR

Enhancing awareness of the system's own behavior is used primarily with a system that needs to understand just what it may be contributing to the problem.

Behavior as used here includes both feelings and thinking. The useful techniques are outlined in the following discussion. The system may be helped to see itself more clearly if the worker paraphrases what the system has said.

Paraphrasing. This means that the worker restates the basic message in similar, but usually fewer, words—both as a test of the worker's understanding but also in order that the system might hear its own productions. In order to do this, the worker must listen very carefully for the basic message. Then, the worker, in what is communicated to the client, must remain very close to what is being expressed, simplifying to make clear, and synthesizing what the content, feelings, thinkings, or behavior mean to the worker. Workers are always tentative in their synthesis submitting it for the system's approval, amendment, or rejection. While sharing how they heard the system's message, the worker watches carefully for clues that either confirm or deny the accuracy and helpfulness of the rephrasing.

Clarifying and reflecting. Clarifying and reflecting are other techniques that are helpful in improving awareness of behavior. These go beyond paraphrasing, which expresses only what is implied by the system. Clarifying and reflecting both connect islands of feelings, experiences, and thinking that the system left unconnected or may not see as connected. Thus, the workers' communication will be seen by the client system as something very different from paraphrasing. Reflecting carries the feeling of trying to understand the world as the target system does. It is a sharing of the way the worker reads the total message. The worker selects and pulls together the best mix of context, feelings, and action from the productions of the target system in order to advance the understanding of the system and thus bring change from new understanding. Clarifying summarizes core material and brings vague material into sharper focus. It identifies themes that seem to run throughout the behavior of the client system, drawing conclusions from the material presented. In clarifying, the worker makes a guess regarding the system's basic meaning and offers it, along with an admission of the worker's confusion, for consideration, or the worker may admit confusion as to meaning and try to restate what the client has said. The worker may also ask for clarification, repetition, or illustration from the client system if it appears that the clients might understand the situation better if they tried to clarify it for the worker.

Checking perception and focusing. Perception checking is a way of helping the system realize what it has just produced. The worker paraphrases what the worker believes was said and asks for confirmation or further clarification. Focusing is helpful in that it can be used to emphasize a feeling or idea from a vast array of verbalization and to reduce confusions, diffusion, and vagueness. Thus the worker assists the system in focusing on assumptions, ways of thinking, notions, or feelings which may be hidden in the discussion. Workers should use their own feelings of confusion and sense of the system's direction as a guide to decide when to focus. *Appropriate questioning* is also helpful in clarifying for a system the effect of its behavior. Questions can be used to lead the system to further clarify information, feelings, experiences, and can serve to encourage the system to explore feelings and thinking or to elaborate on those already discussed.

Summarizing and interpreting. As with questioning, summarizing can be used for many purposes, but in this cluster, it is used to check the worker's understanding and to encourage the clients to explore the material more completely. Interpreting is an active process of explaining the meaning of events to clients so that they are able to see their problems in a new way. The worker may interpret events presented from three perspectives: the client's own frame of reference, the worker's frame of reference, and from the frame of reference of another system. This latter is often done in the brokering or mediating role when the worker may present the target system with the frame of reference of the client system for the target systems' consideration, and hopefully for its understanding. Or the process may be reversed, and the client system may be presented with the target system's frame of reference. The worker also may offer alternative frames of reference by relabeling the material presented. An example of relabeling is found in the old story of the pessimist as one who sees the glass of water as half empty in which case the worker then pointed out that it was half full. Another example is found in the behavior of Tom Sawyer who labeled the work of whitewashing the fence for his Aunt Becky as a privilege rather than drudgery. As a result, he was promoted from worker to supervisor and collected considerable treasure as his friends bid for the privilege of becoming his workers.

In interpreting, practitioners introduce their understanding of *what they think the message or behavior means* from their theory of human growth and behavior. This requires considerable skill and the following rules must be observed. Keep the language simple and close to the system's message. Offer notions in a very, very tentative way as a possible contribution. Always solicit the client system's evaluation of just what the contribution is. In face of the client's denial that the contribution is pertinent, do not hold to it as correct, but also do not negate it entirely, for example, "It may not be a helpful idea, but I would like to do some more thinking about it . . ."

Informing. Another technique useful in increasing one's awareness of one's own behavior is informing which involves giving information, suggestions, or advice. Informing is probably underused by many workers in that they assume that the system has certain knowledge and skills that they may not possess. If, in informing, the system indicates that it already has such information, the worker can apologize for the repetition. Generally workers give information, suggestions, or advice about four aspects of the situation. The worker may use informing and checking to establish a common understanding about the situation between worker and other system. Informing is also used to share with the system the worker's view of the situation—how the worker adds it up. Informing may involve the sharing by the worker of some suggestions as to actions the system might want to try or it may involve the straight communication of new knowledge about the situation.

Confrontation. This technique is discussed last because it is probably the most difficult to use correctly. Confrontation is always hard for the system to accept or consider because it always involves some unmasking of distortions in the system's feelings, experiences, or behavior. The worker identifies certain patterns that lie buried, hidden, or beyond the immediate knowledge of the system. It is something the system never either thought about and/or was willing to accept before. Acceptance of confrontation is also difficult because it carries some challenge to do something about these things that have not yet even been acknowledged by the system. It must be used as a mode of caring and involvement and not as punishment or discipline. Possibly no other technique offers such a tempting avenue for the worker to act out unacknowledged feelings about either self or the other system than the use of this technique. It is so easy to say that the system needs to face honestly what it is doing, that it needs to be shocked out of an unwillingness to work, and so on. These comments may cover the worker's anger or frustration with the client system, may cover the worker's punitiveness toward the client, or may reveal the worker's own hidden need to appear powerful or all knowing in interaction with the client.

To be used effectively, the confrontation must be based on a deep understanding of the implication for the system in being presented with this material by the worker. The worker needs always to keep in mind the question of how this action helps the client to move toward desired change or cope with the situation's demands. Confrontation is always given tentatively with a motivation to help and as a part of the involvement with the client. Done poorly with a vulnerable system, it can result in a quick accommodation to the worker's views or in the system's withdrawal from contact with perhaps considerable anger, either of which are ineffective ways of trying to solve problems. A problem of using confrontation with a system, other than the client system, is that the target system may take out its anger and hurt at the worker's activity on the client system and punish that system since the worker is not so vulnerable. Finally, confrontation should be used only after a careful evaluation of the relationship and what such information will mean to the system within the already established climate of working together.

Relationship. In using this group of techniques to enhance the system's awareness of its own behavior, the primary stance of the worker is that of a concerned collateral resource. The worker uses such techniques when there is considerable expectation that the system is capable of taking the lead in problem solving with a little help. The relationship while warm and supporting is also strongly task oriented and leaves the control for the action in the hands of the client involved. The worker stands beside, supports, and comments on the action toward problem-solution but does not become actively involved in the "doing." This stance on the part of the worker is also important for the next group of techniques. The worker may be more active in contributing information and perspective in the type of work discussed in the next section.

ENHANCING THE CLIENT'S AWARENESS OF OTHERS' BEHAVIOR

In working to enhance the system's awareness of the meaning of other ways of behaving, the worker may use all the techniques described earlier but will be much more active in informing the client about the perspective of other systems. The worker may be much more active in simply giving knowledge about the expected norms of behavior. As an example of this, it is often found that parents who are experiencing trouble in their interaction with their children may have no notions of what kind of behavior to expect from their children. Or the school system may be very punitive toward a child for certain behavior that is a part of the culture from which the child comes. Or a group of male professors may be totally unaware of why the group's climate changed after they referred to the middle-aged woman professor, who was chairing the group, and two other women members as "the girls." In these situations when client systems are ignorant of the values or needs of the other systems, new information alone may be extremely helpful.

Allowing the client to ventilate feelings and to think about expectations and norms of others is helpful and may prepare the way for some reframing of what is expressed. If a client can express anger or frustration with the other system, it will then be better able to either listen to new information or engage in logical discussions, which may be helpful. Perhaps two of the most helpful techniques in this area are the prediction of events and the discussion as to how they may be handled differently than the client's usual way of responding. Another helpful way is to rehearse certain actions with the worker (see Reading 11–1).

SOCIALIZATION INTO EFFECTIVE ROLE PERFORMANCE

These techniques are usually used with a client system (individual, family, or group), although they could be adapted to any other system that is having significant difficulty fulfilling its role. Usually the client systems, for which this is a problem, are identified by another system, and the worker enters the potential client system uninvited. There will be a range of clients within this group—many of which may respond to techniques discussed earlier—but here the worker is central to the process.

Relationship. In discussing this type of intervention, we are going to begin with a discussion on the stance of the worker because, in no other situation are the worker's feelings about the client and the worker's ability to trust and to give without expecting back more important.

In this type of situation, workers must exercise exceeding care as to how they cross the boundaries of the potential client system as uninvited intruders. They must demonstrate complete respect and complete concern for the system, but paradoxically, they also may need to take a firm, positive stance within most of these situations. They need to be strong and active in their involvement with the system. They are not standing by as a collateral resource, but rather they must be part of the action. In such situations the worker usually needs to come across as a knowing authority with considerable power, but this must be connected with the communication of a commitment to using it in behalf of the client and the communication of the belief that the client is someone special. Needless to say—the worker must deeply feel this as the client will quickly sense a fraud. Initially these clients usually do not trust, and there is no reason why they should. The workers must understand and accept that they do not have the right to demand liking or trust from either the client or target system if they are to work in these types of situations. They must not only deeply respect this stance on the part of the client, but they must prove their trustworthiness by pointing out to the client that there are realistic limits to their trustworthiness. Since they initially entered the system as the agent of a community problem-identifier, there are usually requirements that the worker must report certain things back to the community or take certain actions on behalf of the community. Thus there are realistic limits to workers' ability to act totally as agents of the client system. This must be acknowledged from the beginning of contract. The worker needs to allow and encourage such clients to be as dependent as necessary in the interests of protecting them from further damage and in the interests of building the kind of relationship necessary for the problem solving that has to go on. This is critical. Workers who are fearful of dependency are seldom helpful in these situations. Workers must have frequent contacts with the client. One can never socialize certain client systems into a role with once a month visits. These types of situations call for a very special kind of person. The worker who would do this kind of work needs to be a strong, courageous person willing to risk a great deal without expecting a return and yet able to accept the dependency of others freely. It requires the greatest of caring, because it requires unconditioned giving while leaving the system free to fail without recriminations.

The worker needs to start work in these situations by attempting to establish some mutual goals. But again we would caution that these goals are something the client wants—often involving the worker in some concrete giving of agency resources or of finding other resources to give aid. In order to help clarify what is meant, we wish to quote the following:

> The idea of setting goals by mutual agreement may be a good, professional one in most instances. But [with this type of client] it is an empty exercise. Any objectives involving a generally better life must be the worker's . . . [the clients] will believe them only after they have been demonstrated. More to the point are the basic survival needs . . . which [the clients] may expect the worker to supply (Polansky, 1972, p. 26).

This quote is an excellent demonstration of a misunderstanding of goal setting, at least in the problem-solving model. The author of this quote makes the automatic assumption that the only meaningful goals are those the workers might wish for. It highlights the importance of the position of differentiating between the worker's view and the client's view. The client's wish for some basic survival needs is the clients' goal, a very important goal, and the very best goal to start with. The exercise of setting such a goal should not only give the worker a place to start, but it should remind all workers of the differences between their perspective and that of the client. There can be no more important goals than those that involve the worker in securing concrete needs for decent living on the part of the client.

Active supplying of resources.   Since in many of these situations, the goals that are important to the client involve concrete survival needs, the activities of the worker in supplying such concrete resources are extremely important in solving some very critical problems of the client system. In the securing of such resources, the worker is usually actively involved in the work of physically getting the things. The worker does not act as broker or mediator for the client, expecting the client to carry through on most of the action alone. In attempting to help an individual to cope with role demands that have not been met previously, the worker also will need to be skilled in the use of advice, guidance, and encouragement. In addition they will need to use the skills of helping the client in gradually being able to understand the others' position.

How active and firm the worker is in the use of these techniques will be based on the clients' motivation, ability, resources within their own control, and how they see the problem and goal. One of the important techniques is that of the worker's active securing of resources for the client. The worker does the work of securing the material things rather than acting as a broker or mediator for the clients' activities.

Direct intervention. The worker also intervenes directly into the living situation of the client and acts for the client in the transactions with many systems. The worker usually imposes minimal demands on the client. However, in all of this, the goal is to help the client toward better role performance. Therefore, the worker needs to be scrupulous about reporting back what is being done and using this as teaching-learning material. The worker also uses modeling and identification, sets appropriate limits for client behavior, and requires clients to be as active in their own behalf as they can be with success. The worker uses all the minute particular details of life as material for teaching appropriate role behavior.

DEALING WITH ROLE TRANSITIONS OR ROLE LOSSES

In this situation, the client system usually has functioned satisfactorily within a certain role but now faces the certain transitions within that role (switching from being the mother of a teenager to the mother of a married woman) or certain losses of that role function (the loss of the role of wife with the death of the husband and all that means in both feeling and finding new behavior patterns or similarly the loss of the role of worker with retirement).

Given this purpose, the worker needs to use a good many of the techniques described earlier, with special emphasis on ventilation, informing about the resources and pitfalls in the new role, reassurance, listening, and conveying acceptance. In addition, temporarily the worker may need to act for clients and may need to intervene in the in-life situation.

Relationship. The relationship that the worker offers is one of warmth and caring. The worker must appear strong and yet compassionate. The worker must allow the client to be dependent for a period of time and must have frequent contacts. The worker is active and central in the process of working together.

SUPPORTING ROLE PERFORMANCE

Both institutional systems and client systems often have trouble with adequately fulfilling their role performance. This classification overlaps with other classifications. However, it is very important and in many ways represents the heart of social work practice: for many people the purpose of requesting help is to find a concrete resource that is needed to support them in adequately fulfilling their notion of their accepted performance. Many of these clients need little but information as to the appropriate resources, how to find them, and how to gain access to them.

In such situations the work with the client is usually reality oriented, and the stance of the worker is such as to leave the client in full control of feeling, thinking, and acting. The only change effort is to supply information about resources, or perhaps to act as broker. To engage in this type of work, the worker needs to have a good, sound knowledge of the community and its resources. The worker needs to be as skilled as possible in the requirements of eligibility and routes of access to such services. The worker also needs to know who to approach in the other system if some brokering is needed.

Although with many clients the worker may be involved only with supplying necessary information about resources, there are other clients that fall into this classification that need much more help. They need much encouragement and support. They may need help in understanding their own behavior and that of others. As an example: Mr. K (the client whom we met earlier, whose wife had been hospitalized and whose children needed care) is a good example of a client that needed tremendous help and support in performing an effective role as a father once he had lost the support of his wife for his role performance. However, he was also suffering from problems in role transition in that he was having to take over some of the activities that, in his culture, are ordinarily found within the mother's role. In addition, his role as a husband was suddenly significantly altered, and the transactions between the husband and wife in the family system were shattered. Thus, he needed help both with certain aspects of role transition and with most aspects of role support. The worker's efforts to supply resources to shore up the parent role were not enough. He needed help with self awareness and with understanding others' behavior. He needed to understand ways to relate to and to utilize the new systems in his life, such as the doctors and the hospital personnel. He needed to understand how alteration in the capacity of his wife to perform both the role of wife and of mother affected his role performance of husband and father. And, remember, effective role performance involves feeling, thinking, and acting. Mr. K needed to be approached on all three levels.

USE OF NETWORKS AS RESOURCES

Included in this chapter are some articles that emphasize particular types of worker action. One very important paper is a description of the use of the clients systems' social networks as resources for help (see Reading 11–3). While this article discusses working with Indian tribes as social networks, the principles of the article are true for any social network.

The author identifies five distinctive functions of social networks that need to be considered. (1) Social networks provide an identity for their members and meet other religious, social, or financial needs (this is particularly true with oppressed groups in which the social network offers much social and financial protection). (2) Networks usually include the extended family as a central part and may use kinship terms. (3) There is an organized hierarchy present in each network, and it is important for the worker to know and respect this organization. (4) Rapid informal communication is a characteristic of social networks, and workers need to understand, respect, and know how to use this to the advantage of the client system. (5) The network has much unconscious meaning to the members. Networks, as a social system, have boundaries and accepted ways of being admitted to the system. The worker needs to know something of the accepted pattern for crossing these boundaries as well as how one shows respect for these. Once across the boundaries, and accepted as a helper, the worker will often find that techniques listed under the two increasing awareness categories will be of help in working with network systems. In this type of work, the worker's stance is that of a collateral resource to the network in its effort to deal with its members.

SUPPORT AND ACTION

There are two other papers reproduced in this chapter. One is a paper that one of the authors wrote as a way of questioning the notion that certain techniques do not result in personality change and growth (see Reading 11–1). This paper has somewhat more elaborate discussions of some of the techniques mentioned in the earlier material, and it looks at what techniques are supportive of ego-growth and functioning of the individual. The paper is not developed to apply to other than the client system—group or individual. The same is true of the paper on action (see Reading 11–2). Both papers are significant in considering the change process of client systems.

THE RELATIONSHIP OF ROLES AND TECHNIQUES

Depending upon the fit between the purpose for which the clusters of techniques may be used and the purpose of the use of the role, the various clusters of techniques fit within certain roles. We have attempted to organize them as follows:

1. In the enabler role the worker operates to help clients find resources within themselves and will find the techniques listed under *encouragement, awareness of self,* and perhaps *awareness of others* to be useful.

2. In the roles of broker, mediator, or teacher, the worker will find the techniques listed under *awareness of others* and *awareness of self* useful with the client system, the action system, and the target system. The techniques under supporting role functioning, or working with role transitions will be useful with client systems. And certainly the use of social resources and use of social networks are basic to these roles.

3. This brings us to the role of advocate and to the fact that in attempting to socialize a client system into certain role expectations, one is acting as an advocate of either society or other systems. For example, in an abuse situation, one is acting as the advocate of the child although one may see the parents as both the target system and the client system. In addition, many of the suggestions about relationship, use of power and authority, and active intervention are applicable to advocacy work with action or target systems as well as with client systems.

RECAPITULATION

In this chapter, we have discussed certain techniques that may be used in carrying out the action plan that has been made. These techniques fit within the roles discussed in Chapter 10. We would urge that all readers read the selections that follow this chapter for a richer development of certain critical aspects of action techniques.

A LOOK FORWARD

In the next chapter, we focus on evaluation, or just how does one know one's actions were effective or helpful. This is an important chapter. However, we should also point out to readers that there are two others chapters, Chapters 14 and 15, that have suggestions for worker action in relation to transactions with action systems and target systems. These chapters should be viewed as contributing some knowledge about techniques that, combined with the techniques listed here, are effective in work with other than the client system in brokering or advocate roles.

Reading

11-1 An attempt to examine the use of support in social work practice*

Beulah Roberts Compton

The concept of support in human interaction is much older than social work practice. Social work as a profession grew out of the concern of individuals in an urban society of ever-growing complexity to find a way of assisting their fellow men and women in distress. Early social workers were "friendly visitors" attempting to sustain and encourage those who had fallen on evil days by environmental manipulation, direct advice and guidance, and expressions of concern and encouragement. These early visitors became the forerunners of a profession, and the techniques they used became, along with other techniques, a part of the methods of support and environmental manipulation.

Practice with the individual

In the early 1940s with the appearance in casework of attempts to define and describe the major treatment methods and to organize and structure these methods into a system of practice theory, supportive treatment was first given recognition as a major helping approach, although it was still considered a simple one (Selby, 1956, pp. 400–415). All attempts to develop concepts of differential treatment methods that have appeared in the literature of the profession from 1940 until the present have represented casework

_____
* An original article prepared for this edition.

practice and have included a group of techniques that have been called "supportive" or "sustaining." Just as the method has constantly appeared in the classification system, the techniques grouped together to make up the method have also been consistent. The commonly mentioned techniques are (1) direct guidance and advice in practical matters, (2) environmental modification with the provision of specific and tangible services as needed, (3) the provision of opportunity for clients to discuss freely their troubling problems and their feelings about them, (4) expressions of understanding by the helper, along with assurance of interest in and concern for the client, (5) encouragement and praise implying confidence in the client's worth and abilities, and (6) protective action and exercise of professional authority when needed. The commonly listed supportive techniques suggest that the worker provide a therapeutic environment, based on understanding, concern, and acceptance in which clients can feel free to talk about their worries and concerns. The helper must take an active rather than a passive role in helping the individual to focus on the problem, in giving pertinent advice and suggestion, in reassuring, encouraging, and helping with specific practical planning. The worker should also be willing and able to enter into planning for everyday problems.

With the exception of Hollis's work (1964, pp. 52–63), the classification systems in casework have tried to label the therapeutic methods according to "level" or "depth" of help given. Support has been considered a "simple" method on the lower end of the scale of casework treatment; the aim or goal of this method was seen as helping the clients to feel more comfortable and to assist them in calling on existing strengths and resources. Support was thought to bring about relief of symptoms and better adaptive functioning through making the client feel more secure, reassured, accepted, protected, safe, and less anxious and less alone. This method was considered appropriate for (1) the person who was too weak to tolerate work toward change and (2) the well-integrated person who was temporarily threatened by an overwhelming external crisis (Selby, 1956, pp. 400–415). It was assumed that the help offered by this method would not lead to personality change. Through environmental change and increased internal comfort, the individual might be enabled to maintain present functioning or to function at a somewhat improved level, but this was not assumed to represent basic change.

It might be well to consider that the early attempts to identify treatment methods and goals in casework practice came only a few years after the theory of the unconscious and the theory of psychic determinism as developed by Freud and other psychoanalytic writers and teachers had become widely available to social workers. These insights into human motivation and the increased understanding of human behavior that they offered were eagerly sought by caseworkers as such knowledge offered a new understanding of and seemed to hold the answers to questions that previously seemed unanswerable. In the light of the impact of this new knowledge on social casework practice and of the limits of the knowledge available (at this time only Freud's early writings about the ego were available in America), it is perhaps understandable that caseworkers tended to see internal structural conflict as the primary factor that brought people to grief in the business of living. In the excitement at the promise of this new understanding, it is perhaps also understandable that early caseworkers did not differentiate between using psychoanalytic theory to advance the aims and understanding of their own professional practice and the taking over of aims of psychoanalytic practice for themselves. Thus there grew within the profession a tendency to allot the highest status and value to those activities that seemed aimed at the resolution of internal conflict by helping the clients to develop "insight" into their conflicts whose genesis was to be found in early life experience (Simon, 1964).

In recent years social work has perhaps become more sophisticated about the use of borrowed concepts and certainly psychoanalytic researches into the development and functioning of the ego have extended knowledge about personality structure and its interrelationship with social reality. However, these developments do not seem to have had the same impact upon social casework practice theory as did the earlier materials. Casework has used the knowledge of defense mechanisms provided by ego psychology, but it has not been as active in attempting to extend other concepts from ego psychology (except in certain fragmented instances, such as the development of crisis theory or in certain family counseling practices) to the reciprocal relationships between individuals and their situation.

Practice with the group

Group work practice grew from different roots and at a different time. At the time when social caseworkers were struggling with the new knowledge of intrapersonal structure and functioning, group work was only beginning to be conscious of itself as a movement. Group work did not begin as a method of helping people in trouble to solve their problems but as a way of organizing individuals into groups for purposes of self-help toward a better way of life. The insights and concepts used by the early group workers did not come from the psychoanalytic theory with which caseworkers were struggling. Rather they came from education, especially from John Dewey, and from sociologists who were active in the self-help movements. As the years passed and group work became a part of the social work profession, its practitioners still were primarily engaged in helping groups of essentially normal individuals toward an increased self-development.

At the present time, however, the utilization of group work as a way of dealing with the individual's problems of social functioning is growing at a fast pace, and group work practitioners are becoming increasingly involved in attempts to use the insights from psychoanalysis and from group dynamics in developing practice theory for use with "treatment groups." There is also evidence of borrowing from casework practice theory; for example, Louise Frey (1962, pp. 35–42) took the list of treatment techniques considered "supportive" in casework literature and attempted to apply them to group work practice. She accepted the casework theory that support is "generally regarded as beneficial to people with weak egos and to the usually well-functioning person who is in a crisis that has impaired integrative capacity to some extent." This makes support seem safe enough, yet it does leave a question about the people served in groups who do not belong in these categories and who may actually be harmed in such a group and kept from treatment (more intensive?) sorely needed.

Frey's effort is the only example I could find in group work literature of a consideration of the interrelationship of certain group work techniques and the concept of support. In her consideration she seems to have borrowed the concept whole from casework including the dictum regarding the limits of its usefulness. Yet, the group worker's experience in work with developmental groups should be able to make a very large contribution to the concept of the ways in which the client system is supported in its efforts toward growth. At the other end of the continuum, Fritz Redl's efforts (1957) with the aggressive and disturbed child in a group or life-space situation offers much material that workers need to consider in building a common theory of supportive practice with client systems for the totality of social work practice.

It would be hoped that in borrowing personality theory as a basis for a further development of work with groups, group work would not attempt to apply the older theory that casework borrowed at a particular point in time in its development of practice theory to group work practice in the present. Rather the two methods should join in attempting to see what both the older and the more recent theories of the nature of human beings mean for the totality of social work practice theory with any size of client system and for the specifics of method and technique.

There is a growing literature of ego psychology and of the nature of human learning that challenges the earlier Freudian psychoanalytic view of human beings as primarily seeking homeostasis as the most desirable state of human life. Rather the human need for goal-directed growth is seen as being a basic need. The ego analysts give increased importance to situational events and to the learning of adaptive behaviors for reasons other than to discharge or control instinctual psychological energies. They emphasize that people select and control their own behaviors to achieve particular consequences which have meaning to them quite apart from innate psychological energies. People give evidence of response patterns learned independently from the reduction of instinctive drives. There is a growing push to integrate knowledge of the cognitive and affective aspects of the individual; a growing recognition that one cannot separate the need to learn and grow from the need to understand and control feelings so that an individual can grow. Social rules and individual behavior are seen as reciprocal influences, with society making possible the existence of the person and the full expression of innate characteristics other than the instinctive psychological energies (Erickson, 1959, 1950; White, 1963).

The implicit model, at least for many psychiatrists, if not for social workers, is psychoanalysis. The ideal model, I believe, is life itself, the natural processes of growth and development and the rich trajectory of the life span. . . .

The more we learn about the optimal conditions for human growth—the psychophysiology of health, the normal methods of satisfying needs, ways of learning to achieve sublimations and problems—and conflict solving—the more we shall be able to utilize the knowledge as a model for our psychotherapy. . . .

There are two assumptions underlining my argument which should be made explicitly. The first is that there are two major tendencies in all people from birth to death which are ceaselessly in opposition. These might be termed the progressive trends . . . in human nature. Our lives are circumscribed by these polarities. The second assumption is that, other things being equal, progressive forces are the stronger. Growing up, all education and that special form of education known as psychotherapy are based on such forces. Viewed in this framework, mental illness would then be an expression of blocks, obstructions, interferences, arrests and fixations of the progressive forces, which leads to and results in a strengthening and reinforcement of the regressive trends. Our therapeutic task, then, is twofold. First we must identify and help remove the blocks and obstacles; with our typical orientation to pathology this is often the major focus of many psychotherapists. Second, we must identify the progressive forces with which we can ally ourselves and which at the appropriate time, we can help mobilize. This aspect of our therapeutic task tends to be relatively neglected. Yet it may be the most effective instrument for the removal of obstacles. Of all these forces, love is the most effective antidote to anxiety.[1]

---

[1] From "The Concept of Ego-Supportive Psychotherapy" by Bernard Bandler, in *Ego-Oriented Casework: Problems and Perspectives,* ed. Howard J. Parad and Roger R. Miller. Family Service Association of America, publisher, 1963.

Supportive practice with different size client systems

If we as social workers may borrow Dr. Bandler's suggestion that we model our helping processes on life itself and the natural processes of growth and development, we essentially have two tasks in helping people: (1) to identify obstacles and blocks to the system's growth and to become a partner with the strength of the client to remove or ameliorate them and (2) to identify the progressive forces of the client system with which we can ally ourselves at the appropriate time. Given this position, all our efforts with client systems in social work practice are supportive as the focus is on development and is aimed in increasing ability to cope with life pressures.

Given this way of regarding social work practice, we have moved beyond the earlier concept of support as a way of maintaining the status quo to the concept of support as growth-producing. We could perhaps borrow further from the Bandler article and identify two large classifications of direct treatment methods: (1) those methods aimed at sustaining or restoring previous capacities now buried under crisis and stress and (2) those aimed at progressive growth, at developing new and different capacities and strengths.

Louis Towley (1957, p. 422) once wrote, "Social work's secret tool is the infinite untapped, unused, unsuspected capacity for growth in the sovereign individual personality . . . of all types and breeds of social worker, the group worker most consciously accepts this democratic premise in his work." We do not want to do violence to Towley, but in the light of the greater understanding of the ego that is available to us today, it seems that it might be possible to rephrase the statement somewhat, for example, in the attempt to help people with problems of social functioning, social work must be primarily concerned with the infinite untapped, unused, unsuspected capacity for growth in the sovereign individual personality . . . all social workers should be most concerned with this principle of ego psychology.

If one is to operationalize the concept of ego-support, it is perhaps necessary that one state the functions of the ego, the techniques that support each function, and the way that such techniques are held to be useful. This task needs to be done but is beyond the scope of this paper. However, perhaps we can examine it in light of how we might move from the broad idea that all social work techniques may be considered to have this broad purpose to the examination of the specifics of treatment.

The provision of needed concrete resources, the therapeutic relationship, and the problem-solving process (in other words, the work on the task) are the elements of social work and must be worked within any size client system. Perhaps these elements might be examined in relation to the concept of the two classifications of social practice. The provision of resources to clients in need is as old as social work itself. Early social workers often felt that they could help people solve their problems by doing things to them—by rearranging their life situations for them. This often proved totally ineffective and, with the advance of the Freudian view that people come to grief because of internal conflict, often came to be viewed as a lesser part of the social work process. There were times when it appeared as though environmental manipulation was something done for the client quite apart from the rest of the "treatment" effort, and the client could be made to feel as though the need of concrete aid was an obstacle in the path of more elegant treatment.

Use of resources

In supportive practice the worker is active in securing necessary concrete aids for the clients so that their energies may be saved for the problem-solving work and life made more comfortable—a human value of some worth in itself. It is recognized that the workers' willingness to involve themselves freely in the active seeking out and utilizing of concrete aids may not only help the client deal with obstacles and so preserve or restore system functioning, but it may also serve to build a sense of worth that is important in system growth. It is recognized that doing things for the clients even when they could possibly do them for themselves is not necessarily dependency producing but rather may be strengthening when the client is fully engaged in the decision-making process and allocation of problem-solving tasks that should precede any action of a professional person on behalf of the client system. The considerations of concrete resources and their selection for use, the considerations of how one uses such resources and to what end, the growth of a feeling of responsibility as one participates in decisions about one's life—all serve to support the progressive forces of the client system. If clients are able then to actively seek out and utilize resources on their own, so much the better, but to require them to do this at the expense of greatly heightened anxiety or possible failure feeds the regressive forces of the personality.

Use of relationship

In supportive social work, the quality of the relationship that the worker seeks to create, regardless of system size, is that of a partnership for work. It is based in current reality as a good working relationship needs to be. The relationship has both a nurturing quality and an expectation that the client or group will participate appropriately in the problem-solving process. However, the expectation is paced to the client's capacity, and the acceptance will continue even if clients find it difficult to work on their part(s) of the task. Within the relationship, there is a lending of the worker's strength to supplement areas where the client is weak. To be effective this must be a loan freely given, but it is a loan, not a gift, for while the loan need not be repaid and carries no interest payments, there is the implication that this loan is made for the purposes of the system's development of its own strength. Elements of concern and respect have a major place in such a relationship. There is a recognition that both the client and the worker bring something of value to the working together. We believe that there is a common quality in the development and use of the relationship in supportive work whatever the size of client system that lies in the climate for work and in the attitude of the worker toward the clients—attitudes of attentiveness, receptivity, acceptance, and expectation.

Use of supportive methods

The problem-solving methods themselves do not lend themselves as well to the global approach as does the discussion of the relationship and the provision of resources. Whatever may be said about the commonness of methods of offering service to different-sized client systems, when things get to the point of the worker across the desk from an individual or a worker in a circle with a group we see that they are doing different things, and workers need to develop somewhat different skills for different-sized client systems. However, it would seem possible to consider some common techniques of support and examine what these mean for what one does with any system. In the first place, we suspect that no one technique of problem-solving can be considered supportive in and of itself. It is supportive within the context of the relationship and within a pattern of techniques. In other words, we do not use any one technique in grand isolation but rather techniques are used in patterns and within a relationship. Let us attempt to examine some common techniques to see how these are used differentially in the one-to-one and in the one-to-group situation.

Reassurance. Reassurance, the expression of recognition and approval of the client's capacities, achievements, feelings, and needs, is a common procedure of supportive treatment. It is usually seen as a passive technique in which the worker approves an expression of the client. It could well be broadened into an active search for the strengths of the client—for the areas in which the system is able to cope successfully. When these areas are identified, the worker needs to take an active part in identifying them with the client. It might be well to keep reassurance as it is now understood and add "active recognition of the coping strengths of the client" to the list. The active component of the search for strengths seems to convey the worker's active concern and partnership to the client. Reassurance is primarily used as a technique of sustaining or restoring system capacity, but when used in conjunction with other techniques, it can be a part of help aimed at growth. In the one-to-one situation workers carry the burden of doing the reassuring. However, this depends upon a positive, warm relationship and the client's acceptance of the worker's authority to make the technique a helpful one. In the group situation group members may carry the burden of this with any particular member. The group members' discussion of their common problems and the client's growing awareness that feelings and needs are shared by others is reassuring.

Educational methods. It is important in this consideration of the techniques of support that thought be given to the position of the worker as a teacher. One of the contributions of ego-psychology has been the recognition that the ego operates by means of its cognitive processes as well as its affective energies. Problem-solving in our complicated society requires not only that feelings and impulses be controlled but that the ego have at its disposal the knowledges and skills necessary to problem-solving. We often made the tragic mistake of confusing lack of cognitive and/or social skills for resistance or low motivation. We must remember that the client without cognitive or social skills in our society is as vulnerable as the emotionally ill. This technique demands that the worker give careful, painstaking consideration to the small details of daily living. It requires a careful examination of reality with the worker actively supplying the knowledge the client does not possess. In work with groups, the group members may supply much of this direct teaching. The use of program media to provide opportunities for mastery and achievement and the development of structure and democratic organizational procedures are important ways that the group work may implement this technique. Workers may also use the members' involvement in decision-making and conflict resolution as education in social skills as well as finding this technique useful for developing the ability to control feelings and to express oneself in a disciplined way that is an important part of personality growth. In the one-to-one situation the worker teaches decision making by carefully helping the client to collect the facts, to weigh them, to make considered judgments, to consider consequences of choices made, and to plan to implement the choice. The technique of education in cognitive and social skills is primarily one directed at growth rather than ego-sustaining. It is time-consuming and demands patience on the part of the worker. It has been used more extensively in work with client groups rather than in one-to-one work and has been used most extensively in work with groups of children, but it needs to become a better-understood part of practice with any size client system.

Rehearsal. In working with groups the worker may use the group interaction so that the individual has a specifically structured experience in a protected social environment in which social learning may take place and within which the client may practice carrying out a task. There is a somewhat similar technique called "rehearsal" that may be used in work with individuals. This is a detailed consideration in the interview situation of the exact details of how the client will carry out a specific task. In either situation the clients may be encouraged to "role play" the way they intend to carry out the

action later in the real situation. They can be encouraged to think of any obstacles that may appear in actually attempting the task and to consider why they may come up and how they can meet them. This technique is used as either a sustaining or a growth technique. Its purpose is determined by whether it is used to help the clients accomplish tasks that they have previously been able to handle but are now unable to cope with or whether it is used to help clients carry out new methods of coping with problems.

Advice and guidance. Advice and guidance are appropriate parts of the supportive treatment method. Here the worker uses professional knowledge and authority to express to the client, individual group member, or group an opinion about a course of action. As a rule this procedure is only used at a time when the clients are unable to find their own solution or when they need permissive authority to pursue a course of action. In the group the members often offer each other this type of support or they may become auxiliary helpers of the worker in this regard. This technique is usually considered a sustaining technique—a way of rescuing a faltering system in an emergency —with the hope of helping the client through a crisis situation. However, one of the most remarkable facts of the helping process is that a gain in one area of functioning can release the progressive forces of the system and effect a redistribution of energies which is reflected in an improvement of functioning in many areas not directly touched on. Thus advice and guidance, if it helps a client deal successfully with an overwhelming situation, may be a growth-producing technique.

Modeling and identification. Closely related to advice and guidance is the worker's presentation of self as an ego-ideal for the client's consideration. In using this procedure the workers do not, as in advice and guidance, present themselves as authorities. Rather they present themselves as active partners who might act this particular way if confronted with this problem. They attempt to leave the client free to adopt or reject this particular pattern, but they present it as a possible model that might be examined if the client were interested. In work with the group, one or several, group members may assume this role with any other member. This fact allows greater use of this technique in work with groups, where other members may support or reject any model offered, than in individual work where, unless the client recognizes the need of help, is ready to use it, and is secure in the worker's concern, it may be impossible to resist the inherent authority of the worker and reject the model that does not fit. This technique is used primarily in situations where one is hoping for ego-growth through identification with the strength of another.

Logical discussion. The system's capacity for rational behavior is used in the technique of logical discussion. If the client or the group has certain strengths in the methods of problem-solving, if there are skills and knowledge to make appraisals of reality, if there is the ability to see alternatives and consequences, then logical discussion can serve to both sustain the system and to support its growth as it appeals to the capacity for rational behavior. However, if the client system had no opportunity in the life situation to approach the problem-solving process in this manner, this technique may be totally beyond it and may lead to further frustration and the destruction of motivation. Again, this is a technique that can be used with a client group with less concern as the group members can support each other in expressing openly the group frustration with such expectations. In the individual situation the client, alone with the worker, often does not have this strength and so must internalize frustration as a discouragement with self and functioning that cannot meet the expectations of the worker.

Ventilation. The worker often needs to elicit the client systems' expression of feelings about what may be happening to them. This technique releases energy that was bound up in the management and repression of the feeling and so acts to increase the capacity of the client system. It also serves to increase the client's sense of worth and thus the sense of hope. In the group the program activities may be used to increase the individual's acting out of feelings in an appropriate way and may thus increase the individual's capacity to handle emotions appropriately without excessive denial or repression.

Use of limits. The use of limits appropriately is often another neglected technique of the supportive method. Workers so often think of treatment in terms of the liberation of the ego of the client from maladaptive restrictions that we do not consider carefully enough that limits set within a nurturing relationship may also be a need and may contribute to the support and growth of the client system. The appropriate use of limits may serve to help the client gain control of the impulses, but in addition it may build a sense of worth within the client system in that we care enough to risk hostility by such action, and that we believe the client is strong enough to accept the limits set. In work with groups the worker does not have to carry the entire burden of this technique. Group members will often set limits for each other either by a direct limit-setting in relationship to the behavior of one or a number of members, or by setting rules for the entire group. In fact, the preoccupation of certain groups with rules is indicative of the importance of such limits for the growth of the system.

Confrontation. Confrontation may be used two ways in supportive help. It is used to identify stereotyped or patterned behavior or ways of feeling and thinking in order that the clients' or system members' capacity to see themselves more accurately is increased. It may also be used with certain clients in order that they may better see and understand the way they are seen by others. This is the first step in helping the clients or members consider whether in light of new awareness they want to change their behavior or learn ways of accepting the judgment of others if they do not change. In working with a group the worker may do this with the entire group or in relation to a particular member. However, members often engage in this kind of activity in relation to each other. As the member's relationship to other members does not carry the authority aspects of the worker's relationship, this can be used with a greater freedom and less precaution in the group than in the worker-to-client relationship. This technique is used primarily when the goal is the growth of the client system.

Summary

There are other techniques that need examination in light of their use to support the functioning of the client system. It is hoped that this brief list will serve as only a beginning. Certainly the use of ego-supportive techniques differentially with proper attention to the diagnosis of the clients or members with their problems in their situations is a challenge worthy of the highest knowledge and skill of the worker. It demands a unique combination of mind and heart and hand from the worker who would practice it in the interest of the client.

Reading

11-2 Action as a tool in casework practice*

Anthony N. Maluccio

In casework practice there is extensive use of action—active doing, performing, or experiencing. Yet, action as a concept has received very little attention in the literature. There are various reasons for this omission. An important one is the emphasis on the person as a sentient being and on the primacy of clinical dialogue. Perhaps a more crucial reason is the lack of a theoretical framework capable of providing an adequate rationale for the use of action and stimulating the emergence of pertinent practice principles.

Theorists have long recognized the significance of action and have alluded to its theoretical underpinnings,[1] but the conceptual development of action has been so limited and fragmented that it appears to be a tool in search of a theory. An appropriate framework is necessary to give meaning and substance to action as a tool and to further its integration into the processes of casework.

This article examines the use of action in casework largely within the context of ego psychology. The central aim here is to clarify the purposes of action, its rationale, and the conditions necessary for its effective use in practice. The reason for choosing the context of ego psychology is that it offers a promising approach, especially through its recent emphasis on the autonomous development and functioning of the ego, the dynamic transaction between the person and the environment, and the crucial role played by a person's activities in adapting and coping efforts and in the ongoing struggle to achieve autonomy, competence, and identity. The formulations of such theorists as Erik H. Erikson (1959), Heinz Hartmann (1958), and Robert W. White (1963) counteract the classical Freudian emphasis on instinctual

---

* Reprinted by permission of Family Service Association of America, publisher, from *Social Casework* 55:1 (January 1974), pp. 30–35.

[1] See Austin (1948); Hamilton (1951, pp. 246–249; and Oxley (1971). Austin and Hamilton point to the use of action in restructuring the environment and providing the client with positive reality experiences and opportunities for growth. Oxley highlights action as a major feature of a proposed life-model approach to casework treatment and suggests its significance in varied social work contexts.

forces and tension reduction as the determinants of behavior. At the same time, they underline the notion of the human organism as an active rather than merely reactive participant in life.

Positive purposes of action

Action has been viewed as appropriate in social work primarily with such clients as hard-to-reach or nonverbal persons, severely deprived or disorganized families, and psychiatric patients in resocialization programs. Increasingly, however, empirical evidence supports the validity of the use of action as an integral feature of casework with a wider range of clients. Crisis intervention, behavior modification, Gestalt therapy, family treatment, and milieu therapy emphasize experiential learning and the use of activities in the here-and-now situation of the person.

In family therapy, practitioners introduce role-playing and other activities in order to develop the client's capacity to cope with life challenges through involvement in concrete experiences. In residential treatment of disturbed children, workers arrange for children and parents to participate in social and cultural activities as a means of enhancing their competence and promoting a positive sense of self. In crisis intervention, quick involvement in life activities by the client is viewed as an essential step in resolution of the problem. In play therapy with children, activities constitute a basic medium of communication and interaction.

Ego psychology highlights the value of using action for such broad purposes as enhancement of the client's self-image, development of autonomy and competence, flowering of latent potentialities and innate creativity, and provision of opportunities for growth and mastery. Action can also serve as a means of facilitating and making alive in practice the expression of such basic elusive professional tenets as client participation and self-determination.

The utilization of action for these purposes is especially pertinent within the context of an expanded conception of casework, one encompassing not only clinical treatment but help through a variety of resources, services, and practice modalities. Such a conception underscores the worker's responsibility to identify, mobilize, and ally with the client's potentialities, natural life processes, and adaptive patterns. The purposes of action thus are consonant with a revitalized casework method patterned after life itself. In her formulation of a life model of practice, Carel B. Germain (1973) stresses the use of purposive activity as a major means of stimulating the client's growth, adaptation, and progressive forces.

Many case situations typically encountered by social workers may be imaginatively redefined to generate opportunities for the productive use of coping, striving, and goal-directed action. For example, activities may help a young unmarried mother to gain competence as a new parent, when her situation is defined as one involving a problem in role transition rather than an underlying personality conflict. A crisis such as the death of a father in a young family may be approached as a challenge to the mother, suggesting multiple action strategies for helping her to call on her own resources and to enhance her skills in bringing up the children. A disorganized, multiproblem family may be helped to engage in an active struggle toward fulfillment, as well as survival, through involvement in meaningful activities and growth-producing experiences.

Action may be employed differentially in casework practice: as a diagnostic tool, to assess a person's special areas of aptitude and competence, quality of interaction with others, and so on; as an instrument of treatment, to provide a client with an opportunity to test him or herself or to develop social skills; as the culmination of treatment, by facilitating a course of action, such as obtaining a job; as a measurement of the outcome of casework, by evaluating the results of particular client and worker activities; and as a means of mobilizing other people, instrumentalities, and resources in the client's ecological context.

Artificial and natural activities

A distinction should be made between artificial activities that are provided for a client and natural activity or action that arises out of the life situation.

Artificial activities include role-playing, play therapy, and participation in activity groups. These activities are appropriately used as vehicles for learning, as media of communication, or as opportunities to practice desired behaviors. Often, the client's participation in one or more of them is necessary as preparation for engagement in life itself. Thus, there can be a complementary use of artificial and natural activities. For example, a school social worker found that, following participation in a discussion group of mothers with similar needs, an inner-city mother was able to go successfully through the experience of conferring with school personnel on behalf of her underachieving child. She then felt a real sense of satisfaction as she shared her experience with other mothers in the group.

In contrast to activities that are artificially introduced into the helping situation, action involves real experiences (such as work, or play, or social interaction) emerging from life. Natural activities can be more meaningful and potentially more effective, since they are more closely related to the person's natural life processes of growth and adaptation.

A family service agency worker had tried to involve Mr. A, an isolated elderly man, in social activities at a neighborhood center. These efforts were unsuccessful, as Mr. A seemed disinterested in contact with his peers or in leaving his home. Eventually, he was faced with the need to relocate owing to redevelopment. As the worker accompanied him on various apartment-hunting trips in different parts of the city, Mr. A began to reminisce about his life experiences, showed much interest in the ways the city had changed, and expressed his desire to move into a setting with opportunity for companionship.

Rationale for the use of action

In an earlier era of casework, insight or self-understanding was idealized as the preferred goal of treatment. More recently has come the realization that insight is not enough and may not even be necessary. It has been recognized that, with or without self-understanding, a person's activities play a critical role in personality growth, adaptation, and social functioning.

An individual's active participation in successful transactions with the environment appears to be a prerequisite for growth, mastery, and identity. White (1963, p. 150) postulates that human behavior is motivated by an innate, autonomous drive to deal with the environment, which he terms *effectance* or *competence motivation*. He also stresses that the ego is strengthened through the person's successful action upon the environment, resulting feelings of efficacy, and the cumulative development of a sense of competence. The individual changes and grows through involvement in activities providing opportunities for need satisfaction, task fulfillment, crisis resolution, and learning of social skills (Cumming and Cumming, 1962, pp. 213–218).

Engagement in purposive, goal-directed activities can stimulate the person's coping efforts and strengthen the adaptive capacities. The experience of success in meaningful life activities can serve to improve coping skills, enhance personal well-being, and encourage new attempts. In his discussion of extratherapeutic experiences in psychoanalysis, Franz Alexander (1946, p. 40) notes that

successful attempts at productive work, love, self-assertion, or competition will change the vicious cycle to a benign one; as they are repeated, they become habitual and thus eventually bring about complete change in the personality.[2]

In her extensive research on child development, Lois B. Murphy (1962, pp. 354–355) observes that there is a significant correlation between a child's activity and the capacity to cope with the environment; although excessive degrees of activity can lead to destructive consequences, in general it seems that active children are more successful in achieving mastery partly because they come in contact with more aspects of the environment, are confronted with more choices, and have more opportunities to practice and develop different skills. A child's successful completion of activities is closely related to the sense of adequacy and self-worth and the capacity to gain respect from others.

With adults as with children, doing can lead to feelings of worth and satisfaction, to fuller awareness of one's self and one's impact upon the world, and to greater understanding of one's environment. In many important ways, action constitutes an essential instrument for learning, for development of one's reality-testing, and for self-actualization.

Many of the people who come to the attention of social workers reveal a limited capacity for reality-testing, a seemingly inability to learn, a sense of helplessness and frustration in their efforts to act upon their environment, and a low degree of self-esteem. Often, their life situations and environmental pressures have launched them onto a path of despair and frustration leading to cumulative failures and the dulling of their innate potentialities and creative strivings. In Bruno Bettelheim's terms (1971, pp. 68–78), they are human beings whose autonomy or ability to govern themselves has withered away through excessive external management of their affairs in a mass age.

---

[2] For an extensive analysis of the role of action from a psychoanalytic perspective, see Wheelis (1950).

In casework practice, it is with these persons in particular that action can be utilized as a means of providing opportunities for developing their identity, for exercising their often atrophied drive toward competence, and for turning the trajectory of their ego development toward a positive direction. In an increasingly mass-oriented society, human beings increasingly need to be meaningfully involved in purposeful activities in their own behalf.

Every social worker encounters cases in which opportunities for constructive action evolve naturally out of the client's situation.

An institutionalized man in a psychiatric hospital finds that he can perform well in a work experience. An adolescent in a correctional setting is given the opportunity to channel leadership qualities into organizing leisure activities with peers. A troubled child in a public school experiences delight in completing a difficult assignment. An unwed pregnant woman plans temporary living and working experiences which keep her in the mainstream of active life rather than passively awaiting confinement.

Conditions necessary for effective action

Action does not necessarily lead to constructive change; there is no simple, linear connection between engagement in action and achievement of desired results. The eventual outcome is dependent upon a variety of interacting variables or conditions.

Client's readiness to change. The worker needs to consider the client's readiness to undertake certain activities. Beyond the capacity to perform a given action, there must be some tension needing release and some motivation toward an objective of importance to the person. The tension and motivation can be expressed in different forms, such as anxiety, dissatisfaction with life, guilt, or even a hopeless dream or a fanciful ambition.

The quantity and quality of the client's tension influence the timing of the activity.

In some situations, an impulse-ridden person may need help in delaying action. In general, however, the timing of the activity should be geared to the person's spontaneity. Henry A. Murray and Clyde Kluckhohn (1953, p. 19) point out that human beings in our society are typically required by social commitments and role responsibilities to act, even when they are not truly ready, in order to integrate their actions with those of others. Although this pattern is functional in terms of survival and role relationships, it results in a loss or reduction of spontaneity.

Choice of alternatives. Another necessary condition in the effective use of action is the opportunity for client consideration of alternative courses. This opportunity can help people to evaluate various possibilities, to test their readiness, and to choose the most appropriate alternative. Furthermore, the deliberative process can stimulate people's cognitive growth and mastery, mobilize their decision-making functions, and reinforce the sense of autonomy that comes from involvement in purposive activities consonant with their needs as well as societal requirements. The worker plays an important role through provision of information concerning the potential effects of the action, of feedback heightening the client's awareness of reality, and of support in taking a risk. Client-worker interaction becomes more meaningful and productive as both parties go through the process of reaching agreement on specific goals, tasks, and procedures.[3]

In considering alternative courses of action, it is useful to keep in mind the principle of equifinality derived from systems theory or the notion that the same result can be achieved through following diverse pathways. The provision of diverse opportunities for action may tap the individuals' potential to look at the world in novel ways and facilitate the selection of the activity most suited to their personal method of coping and their particular drive for competence. People cope differently with similar life crises, and if workers understand the person's unique ways of coping and adapting, they will be better able to perceive prospective opportunities for action that may maximize the effective outcome of the client's struggle toward mastery.

A child welfare practitioner described a pertinent experience with Jean, a blind 12-year-old girl placed in foster care following the death of her parents. When Jean was confronted with the impending demolition of her natural family's home owing to urban renewal, she urged the worker to take her on a final tour of the house. During this visit, Jean methodically touched everything in each room, climbed into the attic, played the piano, and ran repeatedly around the backyard. While alternately crying, laughing, talking, and pausing in silence, Jean recalled innumerable family experiences and vividly traced her family's history and her own development. In reliving the past in a spontaneous and active manner at a crucial point in her life, Jean was courageously bracing herself for the future.

Relevance. The relevance of the proposed activity to the client's life situation is a further determinant of its effectiveness. The action should be meaningfully related to the person's goal or problem as defined. In addition, it should be consonant with natural growth processes, lifestyle, significant life events, and developmental stage in the life cycle. Good opportunities for action are often missed because of excessive reliance on artificial or formal procedures such as the office interview. Practice could become more meaningful and rewarding if social workers would function more spontaneously in the natural surroundings of clients and thus discover and encourage their often dormant potentialities.

In this regard, Esther E. Twente (1965) poignantly describes the strengths and cre-

---

[3] The client-worker contract can serve as a dynamic tool in the process of considering and selecting appropriate courses of action. See Maluccio Marlow (1974).

ativity shown by older clients in their own home or group activities: the retired farmer who gains pride and pleasure in seeing others enjoy his singing; the elderly woman who takes music lessons by correspondence and derives satisfaction from entertaining her fellow residents of a nursing home; the 90-year-old widow who seeks fulfillment in her embroidery, gardening, and vase collection; and the many others in whom the creative urge finds rich expression as life draws to a close.

In a life-oriented model of practice, the worker need not carry the entire or even major responsibility in direct work with the client. A fundamental function of the worker is to identify and mobilize the energies of people and systems that are more directly and significantly involved in the client's own life space, such as resources in the immediate family, in the social network, or in the school or work settings. In some situations, the client-worker relationship will appropriately be the primary vehicle of help. In others, however, the effective use of action will occur through other people, with the worker playing indirect roles. The emphasis will be on utilizing the environment itself as a basic means of helping (Germain 1973, p. 326).

Client's participation. Another important condition for effective use of action is maximum participation by the client in the activity. Through its focus on the role of one's own action in personality development, ego psychology underscores the primacy of client tasks and reinforces the hierarchy of interventive strategies, which has served as a guiding principle in casework practice: Doing *for* the client ⟶ Doing *with* the client ⟶ Doing *by* the client.

Availability of support systems. Finally, a prerequisite for action is the availability of appropriate social systems and supports, of an environmental climate with varied opportunities for success and achievement. Following an extensive review of clinical and experimental findings in situations of social isolation and extreme stress, Stuart C. Miller (1962, p. 8) concluded that the maintenance of ego autonomy is strongly dependent on appropriate inputs or "stimulus nutriments" from the environment. In social work there is an increasing awareness of the validity of this conclusion and of the urgent need to develop social institutions and systems more conducive to human growth. There is emphasis on the importance of the worker's (and the profession's) participation in action designed to "socialize" services, to restructure inadequate or detrimental societal systems, and to contribute to the development of environmental conditions providing maximum opportunity for each person to grow, to establish identity, and to achieve an increasingly satisfying level of competence (Meyer, 1970). Action is one of the basic tools through which the client and worker can seek to modify and humanize the environment.

Conclusion

Action, informed by the insights of ego psychology, can become one of the more promising and fundamental features of a life-oriented casework practice. However, to exploit the potential inherent in its use, social workers need to devote more deliberate attention to action. Their rich experiences should be gathered and examined, so that more specific guidelines and principles can be derived and action can be moved closer to becoming an explicit component of practice theory.

Action should not be viewed as an exclusive or separate mode of treatment. In life there is normally no rigid dichotomy between action and thought or feeling and talking. Action is an integral part of the complex whole representing human behavior and social interaction. To be effectively used in casework practice, it must be creatively integrated with the emotional, cognitive, and perceptual components in each client's experiences.

Reading
11-3 *Therapy in tribal settings and urban network intervention**

Carolyn L. Attneave

Most professionals in therapy are aware of the importance of extended family and friends in the lives of their patients. In a growing wave of experimentation and innovation, the walls of the one-to-one therapeutic model have been breached or rebuilt around new groupings. A variety of group process models, ranging from group therapy sessions, through sensitivity training and marathon weekends, attempt to supply social settings artificially created. Family therapy has become established as one mode of incorporating an intimate social context into the consulting room. One of the newest groupings to be presented to the professional mental health community is *network therapy.*

Network therapy seems to be based upon the concept of mobilizing the family, relatives, and friends into a social force that counteracts the depersonalizing trend in contemporary life patterns. The concept appears particularly attractive to those attempting to counteract the isolation experienced by urban residents. Ross Speck (1967a) refers to the networks as creating a "clan" or "tribal unit" which can then support, oppose, expose, and protect its members in effective ways (Speck 1967b; 1967c; 1967d; 1967e). Such networks have been potent forces in breaking through the isolation of schizophrenic patients, and network therapy in various forms could also be used in community psychiatry with other types of patients.

In reading or listening to presentations of this type of therapy, one notices that the professional therapeutic role is often obscured

by the novel elements associated with conducting therapy in homes, sometimes with groups of 40 to 70 people. The dramatic results from the mobilized resources of the simulated clan seem to follow without the processes involved being seen clearly. Because the facets of network therapy activity most frequently given attention by the reader or listener are those new to psychotherapists, the network therapist is often seen as a catalyst—or perhaps deprecated as a social director. In actuality, the network therapist's role is probably more nearly analogous to that of the orchestral conductor. Good conductors do more than beat out the time and set limits for individual solos or subgroup harmonies, but specifying what they do in objective terms is difficult. Comparing therapy as it is applied to an already existing clan structure with what is done in a created network may clarify some of the essential elements of the network therapist's role.

It is tempting to assume that if there were enough networks to replace lost ties with clans and tribes, therapists would become unnecessary or perhaps would automatically be able to increase effectiveness many fold. However, this halo hung over from the dream of the noble savage can be partially challenged by the presentation of two cases from a natural tribal setting where the professional role can be seen from a slightly different perspective. Natural clans and networks, like other human institutions, can focus energies in healthy or pathological directions.

The interventions to be described took place during a period when several American Indian tribes composed 30 to 40 percent of the population being served by a com-

---

* Reprinted by permission of the publisher from *Family Processes* 8 (1979) pp. 192–210.

munity guidance service. A real effort to develop methods of providing services to this population, previously nonconsumers of psychiatric assistance, was enhanced by the fact that the therapist was of American Indian descent, belonging to a closely related tribe. This is mentioned in passing since some of the opportunities for participatory intervention might not have been accessible to other therapists. The aim of the current discussion is not to write a prescription for how to do therapy with Indian families. Rather it is hoped that by describing and reflecting on this experience, basic understandings of the processes of network therapy will be clarified.

Characteristics of the tribal network-clan

Before presenting case material, a description of the social organization as it has evolved in these tribes may be helpful. While close-knit extended family ties are not unique to American Indians, or even universal among them, extended families are often seen as viable social units. Predictable meetings of the extended family and a focus of concern for its members can be found in many tribes. In spite of the kinship of members, its composition is not technically an exact replica of the "clans" described by anthropologists. The term *network clan* seems to describe its combination of contemporary social organization and its links with a more classically described past.

There are five distinctive features characterizing a social unit that combines the traditions of an older clan structure and the features of urban networks as described by Speck and by Bott (1957).

1. Each network-clan has a constellation of reasons for existence. Various foci provide not only an identity but also activities that satisfy religious, social, or financial needs in varying combinations. Religious elements are broadly defined to include the use of ritual related to, and derived from, older tribal customs and ceremonies. Social elements include family reunions, festival elements, vacations, and status recognition of individuals and groups in a formal manner. Financial factors include charging tourists and non-Indians admission to public pow wow's, barter sale of crafts and costume materials, and the yearlong money raising projects that support group activities. Many of these are familiar activities of any similar group, such as box suppers and bingo games. Other events such as wild onion dinners and hand games have an Indian flavor, as do the organizing work of a pow wow club and its committees, the practicing of dancing and singing, and the making of costumes.

2. Although the network-clan may or may not use kinship and adopted kinship terms among all members of the network, an extended family always seems to be a nuclear part of a network-clan unit. Originally anthropologists derived the idea of clans from inherited and automatically assigned family roles. These strictly hereditary clan structures are often no longer viable units of contemporary Indian life, although aspects remain observable in some tribes. (All cultures have such remnants, although we often do not recognize our own—for example, the survival of the social register as a vestige of the feudal aristocratic system.)

At this point in social evolution, each individual, upon reaching maturity or thereafter, has the choice of continuing in the family's network of Indian relationships, changing networks, or disengaging from all close-knit tribal participation.

Where a role is passed from father to son, this process is not automatic but done by group consensus. The son or daughter can also decline, a modern option not free of stress but sometimes exercised consciously as well as by default. Much of the confusion about inherited clan membership may be due to the Indian use of kinship titles "in the Indian way." "Uncle," "grandfather" and the like are not easily translatable, falling between functional realities and geneological abstractions.

3. Some organizational hierarchy is present in each network-clan. The power struc-

ture is usually organized as simply as possible while still permitting the attainment of goals. This hierarchical characteristic permits rapid mobilization and provides elements of continuity and stability over time, which therapist created urban networks often lack. The persistence of newsletters and meetings of urban networks beyond termination by the participating therapist points toward a feeling of need for continuity by the substitute clan. However, the urban therapeutic network is mobilized out of a crisis of social and individual pathology and focuses on a self-limiting purpose, while the Indian network-clans have a life pattern independent of a single personal crisis.

4. Informal rapid communication among members is characteristic of network-clans. The "Mocassin Grapevine" is often astounding in the efficiency with which information is transmitted within and between networks. One dramatic historical example is the arrival of an Indian leader in El Paso, Texas to pay respects at the time of President Harding's death before most of the white community had received the news. In the urban network setting, the therapist tends to encourage or organize telephone committees and newsletters in an attempt to supply this characteristic formally. Within the observed tribal networks no addition of formal authority and structure seems to be necessary, although occasionally the white man's techniques of assigned responsibility are used by the tribal business committee or in activities involving non-Indians.

5. An important characteristic of network relationships, either clan or created, is the presence of significant unconscious components. Many observations provide evidence of this, such as the speed of informal communication and the tremendous amount of energy that can be mobilized to accomplish a common goal. Often therapeutic gains from participation which remain otherwise unexplained can be understood by analyzing the unconscious transactions.

However, in a created network therapists are much freer to interpret to the assembled group. While it may seem that therapists often call attention to those unconscious elements as part of their role, they also must at times resist pressures by parts of the network to bring out material ahead of another segment's readiness.

In a clan or tribal setting one is somewhat protected by the need to fill a role and to use the language understood by the people in a literal and symbolic sense as well as a verbal one. Its members would be unable to discuss their own activities in language other than their own. For example: Even if the identity of the tribes in these examples were divulged, no would-be researcher could go there and ask to be taken to a meeting of the network or the "clan." The demands of courtesy would forbid the Indian to lose all ability to speak English. Since the researcher wanted something, (goodness knows what), he/she would be sent or taken to someone. The results might well resemble Coronado's search for the Seven Cities of Cibola—with less serendipity of discovery.

This therapist became a participant in the network-class, and while retaining a professional role, used the Indian modes of relationship and communication rather than clinical techniques alone. Although this was facilitated by a heritage of Indian descent, these skills can be acquired by non-Indians who are genuinely interested and concerned. In urban networks the same factors operate but are often masked by the assumption of a common culture.

The existence of viable network-clans with these characteristics is probably to be found in many American Indian tribes which have survived with identity and integrity. In these healthy tribal cultures some variety of network-clans permits individuals to deal with the tensions of living in two worlds: a non-Indian world of occupational, technological, and educational elements and a social-religious-cultural world organized around "the Indian way." In socially deteriorating and disorganized tribes, a few very rigid structures may exist, and their hierarchical control of social relationships may operate to perpetuate the pathology.

A more descriptive analysis of the Indian way of life belongs elsewhere. To examine the processes of therapy involving the network-clan, two examples are appropriate. In the first case discussed, the chronology will be detailed to show the evolution of therapeutic modes of intervention from a referral for individual therapy to the involvement of a network-clan of about 40 or 50 persons.

Traditional approaches prior to network-clan therapy

The case of Maria was a direct referral after the Court's Child Protective Agencies had intervened. An Indian mother was charged with child abuse and a six-year-old girl had been placed in a foster home before the therapist was peremptorily summoned to the task of making clinical evaluations and "doing therapy."

Several options were open in fulfilling this role of therapist. A traditionally oriented therapist could have found grist for years of 50 minute hours by focusing on the life history of the mother and daughter: The mother, who was from a deprived non-nurturing family of another tribe in another state, had borne this girl before her present marriage and had left her at age three months to be raised by the maternal grandmother. After acquiring sufficient education to become both socially and geographically mobile, this woman had entered into a marriage with a man from a different tribe and was raising four more children successfully. Into this household was thrust a previously rejected child symbolizing a repressed and rejected past. This situation could have been seen as a classic case for prescribing classic therapy.

A social reformer could have attacked the white man's officialdom for demanding parental acceptance of responsibility without an investigation, planning or providing social service support. Added steam could accrue from observing that when the girl ap-

parently acted out her mother's frustrations, one could have easily established that the local officials reacted punitively toward the family. Careful investigation revealed a superficial scalp cut which bled profusely as the only evidence of a "battered child." The need for reform and improvement was obvious, and making a test case of this situation could have been justified by a good many professionals and politicians. However, it did not appear that "justice" was desired by the Indian family. Nor could this clinician see any therapeutic gain for the child and mother in the court hearings that would have been involved.

A family therapist might have worked with the household around the problems of introducing an older sibling into a home with four younger children and would have recognized the presence of the husband's 80-year-old father in the home. These several subsystems within the household would be included.

In fact, this was the initial level of interventive contact. During a series of home visits to the parental household, the brief history sketched earlier was amplified. The stepfather related his willingness to assume parental responsibility but expressed his confusion about the realities involved. Maria was very different from the couple's own children, for her early childhood had little in common with theirs.

During the intervening six years, the maternal grandmother had become an alcoholic and Maria had survived by wandering about the village snatching or begging food, lucky to get an occasional bath, sleeping, playing, watching as the life of the streets ebbed and flowed about her. The authorities were forced to take notice as she reached school age and, as is often the case, summarily notified the mother that she should assume her forgotten responsibilities.

A drive of over 1,000 miles each way during a single weekend left little time for orientation and preparation of either family or child, even if anyone had tried to do so. A confused child and willing but exhausted family had trouble understanding one another from the start. Induction into household and school patterns hit many snags. Some routines were explicitly explained or easily absorbed. Others were not, often because no one realized the need for it.

For instance, Maria was said to be unwilling to share with the other children. It was a family custom that about once a week one of the adults brought home a bag of candy. One of the children was selected to have the privilege of passing it around the family circle. The child then could have those few pieces of candy left over as a special treat. When it was Maria's turn to do this, she grabbed the sack of candy, ran off, and ate it all herself. The hue and cry of righteous indignation left the parents exhausted, all of the younger ones in tears, and the paternal grandfather silent, brooding, and withdrawn.

There had been many such incidents, which became explicable only in terms of Maria's past. She had never lived with an intact family. How could she know that there would be a bag of candy *every* week? She didn't know from experience that if you had a morning meal, you were going to have a second meal during the day. She didn't know how to set a table, she didn't know how to wash a dish. She didn't know much about washing clothes, or even that somebody would wash them for you if you put them in the right places. She had the idea that you wore clothes until they were worn out, and then if you threw them away, somebody might give you something new. She didn't know anything about the domestic organization of the home, and she didn't know the local Indian language.

Another factor emerged in these family sessions, Mrs. T., the mother, was probably not reacting solely in terms of classical theories of her own childhood neglect and of repression. This child was also playing out some of the mother's own present frustration in relating to her husband's family and tribe. Mrs. T. hadn't been fully inducted into it, and she felt isolated socially.

She particularly didn't know how to get along with her sisters-in-law. In the course of a family session, this feeling was clarified together with the therapist's query about how they might become better understood.

Up to this point therapy had proceeded along familiar family therapy dimensions. The case could be abstracted to fit almost any intercultural family pattern. However, Maria's mother had married into a network-clan organized around her husband's parents, his sisters' families, and their close friends.

This network clan had been concerned about the problem of Maria and was scheduled to convene that weekend to consider it. A non-Indian therapist might not have been invited to attend, or might even have attempted to convene a similar meeting elsewhere. In this instance, a recognition of intertribal kinship as well as professional concern about Maria and her family brought about the invitation for the therapist to attend the meeting, and the therapeutic arena shifted.

Induction into the network-clan

The first meeting was almost like moving into a marathon session since it lasted from sundown to sundown and involved, all told, about 50 people. After a hearty and fortifying supper, the key family members, about 20 adults, sat in a ceremonial meeting all night. Others cared for children, visited, and prepared a regular and a ritual breakfast as well as the midday feast.

During this first meeting there were three types of change accomplished. (1) The therapist was inducted into the network-clan. It was now possible to define the professional role as that of helping them solve problems in their own context, not of imposing outside solutions. Being a participant gave the therapist maneuvering power as a part of the network as well as providing a link to the outside world. (2) There was a better definition of the problem as details were shared. (3) The helplessness which everyone in the network felt was nondestructively expressed.

At this stage, it was possible to shift the attitudinal balance from one that piled on shame and guilt, with ostracizing behavior, to one of shared problem-solving. But goodwill alone is not enough, and much work continued in the related areas.

Maria herself was permitted by the court to revisit her home only in the therapist's company for the 24 hours of the "meeting." Meanwhile in the foster home, she was being taught how to live in an organized household—washing, dressing, daily chores, routines of meals, and weekly shopping from a secure income. These lessons, in addition to individual therapy sessions, over a period of three months, were undoubtedly preparing her for reentry into her own mother's home as a more competent part of a family.

Network intervention—"Indian style" therapy

Another absent ghost haunted the parental household, that of the grandmother who raised Maria and her mother. Following the generally expected principle that talking about her might lead to insight and reintegration, the topic was introduced during the continued family sessions.

It is tempting to describe the frustrations experienced by a traditionally trained psychotherapist interacting with the Indian culture. When one's whole learning is oriented around discursive discussion, insight development, and verbal tools, it is disconcerting, to say the least, to seek for toe holds in a situation where they are not the modal avenues of communication. Perhaps this exchange about the grandmother will give a sample:

Therapist: "It might help us understand if we knew more about your mother—." Mrs. T. reacts with a startled glance, immediately her eyes lowered to her lap, and a faint blush . . . Grandfather directs a piercing look at therapist and then stares out the window—. Mr. T. sugars his coffee and shifts in his chair, checking visu-

ally the group around the table. . . . Therapist sits like a bump on a log . . . as do all the others. Mr. T. picks up his cup, sighs and says, "Well it might—." More silence, but it feels less tense.

At this point, a 4- and 3-year-old tumble into the room excited and everyone's attention is shifted to their immediate needs.

As this confusion simmers down, the family turns their attention to practical immediate problems. School is to begin shortly, and they feel Maria should be at home to begin locally. A weekend before school opens is also time for another meeting and they wish to use it to celebrate Maria's birthday along with that of one of the younger siblings, according to their custom. Permission for the visit as well as the therapist's participation is arranged. An hour or so later, as time to leave arrived, one of the older men asked the therapist abruptly, "You think it might help if we knew more about the grandmother?" The only possible response is to count silently to 10, echo aloud the father's earlier, "Yes, I think it might," and finish putting on one's coat while listening to the familiar "um-gh" in response.

Maria and the therapist arrived on a sunny afternoon a couple of weeks later, carefully prepared for Maria's reentry into the network. She had purchased a bag of candy and gum with the pennies she had "earned" in the foster home, and during the 40-mile drive she counted over and over one piece of candy and one piece of gum for each half sib and adult she knew, and a reassuring surplus for any others who might come. This time Maria was bringing the bag of sweets, and her anxiety was as high as if someone had explained that by doing so she could make amends for her past behavior and henceforth participate in the family ritual of sharing. Symbolically it was her bid for induction into the family.

This was indeed accomplished, but in even more dramatic and comprehensive fashion than the therapist had foreseen. As the car pulled up under a tree and the family came out to greet Maria, she suddenly gave a cry of recognition and thrust one of her offerings into the hands of a strange woman standing on the porch. The network, mulling over the therapist's remark, had stretched its links across two states and brought the absent grandmother to spend two weeks!

During the next 24 hours the bestowing of a tribal name at dawn and the eating of a very American birthday cake at the noon feast completed Maria's restoration to the family and network. During the ceremonial meeting of adults, the grandmother and her new husband sat as honored guests and had many things explained to them. Included were elements that had not been explicitly comprehended by Maria's mother, but which she now learned without embarrassment or loss of status. She was also able to fulfill an important ceremonial role, with her mother present, and thus symbolize the new integration of self and identity she had acquired without having to deny or bury her past. The husband also gained some sense of unsuspected dimensions of her as a person. Mr. T. was able to express his appreciation of his wife publicly as well as to secure the network's expressions of supportive interest and pleasure in her and in Maria.

The next afternoon sitting on the hillside the therapist observed Maria and her half siblings and cousins playing around a tire swing. Around an outdoor fire, Mrs. T. and some of the other women were showing the grandmother how to make "fry bread" and over further under the trees a group of men, including step-grandfather, were drumming softly, practicing songs, and shaving kindling.

Grandfather T., the eldest member of the network-clan, stopped beside the therapist and watched the same scene. After a few minutes he observed "Hum—a good idea to know that grandmother. . . ." Then with a piercing glance and the suspicion of a twinkle he gathered himself up to walk off. Turning, he raised an arm that embraced the group below in a majestic sweeping gesture—"*That* is much better than a lot of noisy talk."

Follow-up implementation

The network had delegated to the therapist the role of negotiating with the court and child welfare system for Maria's return. There was ample clinical evidence that the emotional climate in the household had changed, and that both parents and daughter had experienced growth that foreshadowed good prognosis. This professional opinion enabled the court to return custody, providing the therapist maintained contact and assumed responsibility for "supervising" the family during a probationary period.

During subsequent network meetings, the therapist shifted the arena of interaction from the ceremonial fire to the women's and children's activities behind the scenes. It was possible then to handle in context a series of minor misunderstandings by helping the sisters-in-law make explicit many things which neither they nor Mrs. T. realized were not being communicated.

Hatty's tea is an example. Hatty, 60 years old plus, arrived at each meeting for the final midday outdoor feast in a clattering wheel chair with several devoted assistants. She was old, cranky, and imperious—a chronic diabetic who had lost a leg and most of her eyesight. To an outsider it appeared that her every whim brought scurrying subservient people to bring her what she wanted. But, whenever Mrs. T. tried to follow suit, she was brushed aside, often abruptly. The ice tea she prepared especially was poured out. If she passed the bowl of canned peaches, it was devoured by someone else, while another woman or teenager ran up to the house to open a new can for Hatty.

The therapist could ask the "dumb questions" Mrs. T. had not and uncovered the fact that Hatty's tea must be made with dietetic sweetner, so the whole group drank that type rather than risk a mix-up. Mrs. T.'s pitcherful had been dumped quickly so that this secret would not be divulged to Hatty. However, only Hatty was given nonsugar packed peaches, or other special foods. Everyone else had lived with the collusion to protect Hatty from her own appetites so long that no one realized they needed to explain it ahead of time. Then when Mrs. T. had tried to fit into what she understood only partially as deference to the matriarch, she had kept creating minor emergencies. No space or time was left at the moment of crisis for explanations, and her hurt pride and withdrawal had not helped find them later.

It was also possible to utilize the informal group situations to deal with the toilet training lapses of the oldest sibling who had been displaced by Maria, and with a number of other situations which could have erupted again into a cycle of frustration and anger. The dual roles of supporting appropriate role behavior and catalyzing and clarifying interactions in the various subsystems were interspersed with periods that permitted ventilation of feelings and instruction in child care and normal development. Holding all this together in context was the sharing with the network-clan joys, sorrows, tasks and satisfactions. In this setting, network therapy becomes a variant of participant observation that might be termed "participant intervention."

At the end of 15 months, this family had survived several other crises without disintegration. Both mother and daughter were functioning well socially and intrapsychically. The network-clan remained intact and consisted chiefly of the grandfather, wife, husband of this family, 5 paternal aunts and their families, together with about 8 or 10 other families of men designated as uncles or nephews in the Indian way.

At the latest word, this network-clan had coped with arrangements for the guardianship and protection of another patient—a handicapped youth whose parents had died. Their plan and efficiency have saved the white community the cost of institutional care, and the youth from developing a full blown psychosis. In between such meetings for therapeutic purposes, the network-clan has celebrated birthdays, coped with the disruptions of death, the drafting of young men, and welcomed home Viet Nam veterans. Continuity into the future seems assured for a healthy social unit which already has a history of more than 50 years.

Death and despair in a sick network-clan

The second example also involves a network-clan with a single extended family at its core. At the time the therapist entered the picture, it was composed of a grandmother, several adult sons' and daughters' families, and their close or significant friends. This network was deteriorating rapidly. There had been two murders, a suicide, a crippling assault, and the death from a heart attack of the grandfather who had headed the group.

The man upon whom the network then depended for survival was acutely and suicidally depressed. He was ambivalent about assuming the leadership role. He was not only concerned about his ability to cope with the task, but he was overwhelmed with a feeling of guilt and loss of face about a dishonorable Army discharge, after 15 years of honorable military service. This element assumed real importance because of the cultural importance of honor in battle as an Indian tradition, which might not have parallel importance in another culture. In addition to suicidal ruminations, his symptoms included an inflammation of shrapnel induced arthritis sufficient to render him unemployable, at a time when many of his kin were also facing financial crisis.

Clinical judgment indicated that this man required inpatient hospitalization. Rather than arrange a quick admission to the United States Public Health Service Indian Hospital, the network-clan and the patient were invited to participate in finding a solution. This seemed imperative since it had appeared to the therapist even before this man presented himself as a patient, that the network-clan itself was sick.

The first stage was a rapid gathering of the network-clan at the grandmother's home. This permitted introducing two elements that had been lost: First, an element of hope in getting treatment for the potential leader and second, some success experiences in reaching short-term reachable goals. These quick success experiences actually consisted of raising $20.00 via a bingo game and finding temporary employment for one son. It was also possible for the clan to offer support and help for the therapist in treating the depressed patient, which could be received gratefully.

The network-clan, reeling from a series of disasters, had been unable to exchange positive experiences in this fashion between its members for some time and consequently had been resonating and amplifying pathology. Once this pathology was dampened, it was possible to discover that admission to a VA Hospital would symbolically expunge the dishonorable discharge. This was arranged through the therapist's liaison with the professional agencies and was ceremonially validated in a formal meeting.

As a result of the opportunities for interaction with individual network members during these activities, the therapist was able to share the grief with the grandmother and other individuals in such a way that they found a release in tears and could get about the work of mourning, which eliminated another source of pathology within the network.

Supportive contacts between the network-clan and the depressed man began within hours of his brief hospitalization. Although the VA psychiatry department found him "unsuitable" for psychotherapy, his somatic and suicidal symptoms disappeared and his arthritis was brought under medical control. The network worked through the patient's practical problems by helping him find a job, transportation, and so on, as well as providing the therapeutic relationships needed. He was able to show his own resilience three months later when he handled the details of a terminal illness and funeral of another of the network members. That event would probably have triggered another wave of suicide-murder catastrophies had not pathology been halted within the group.

Within 12 months the destructive processes had been reversed and the reciprocal healing strengths of network and ex-patient

network-clan leader were such that he and one or two others were visibly assuming interlocking leadership roles as tribal representatives at pow wows and in the elected tribal business organization.

Evidence that real changes in network pathology had occurred is deduced from the fate of one family unit which for a variety of reasons (mainly job opportunities) moved several hundred miles away at the height of pathological period. This family was not present during the period of therapeutic intervention and was out of touch with the network in an unusual fashion. Before contact was reestablished, the state newspapers headlined that this family had another "unexplained" murder and suicide incident which left only one surviving child. In an institution for delinquents at the time of the parents' deaths, the child continues to be both "incorrigible" and "isolated."

This continued antisocial experience of that one surviving delinquent is in contrast to the other children of the network-clan who survived similar family destruction during the pathological period. They have now faded into public anonymity. Local authorities ignore them since they are in school, not delinquent, and not in need of "public assistance" as they have been scattered among network-clan families. While clinicians might predict some psychic scar tissue, they probably could not write a better therapeutic prescription than the network's cooperative distribution of nurturing responsibilities. It is probable that a professional clinic or agency could not deliver these services as efficiently as the restored network-clan.

Essential elements of the therapeutic role in network intervention

The purposes of these brief descriptions of therapeutic intervention within existing rather than newly constituted networks has not been to write a prescription for delivery of psychotherapy to American Indians, although it was proven to be one effective way to provide clinical service to a previously unreachable population. One hopes that by examining the experience one may be better able, in various settings, to isolate the essential features of network therapy as a process of intervention.

That a clan type of social organization can be either healthy or pathological is one concept that needs overstatement because it may get lost in a discussion of urban network therapy where emphasis is on creating a new social institution. Where therapists can utilize an existing clan-network, they may have to spend as much time on repair as innovators do in creating a healthy social system for urbanites who have become isolated.

A requisite then for network therapy is to have leverage to promote social health and to limit, control, or reverse the sickness of the network itself, as well as that of some of its individual members. Simply to assemble or create a network unleashes a great deal of psychic energy and the odds are generally in favor of this having a positive balance. However, the therapist needs the same skills and insights obscurely understood as operative in group processes in order to reinforce positive vectors and permit network organization to align itself in such a way as to heal rather than hurt its members.

An advantage of working with existing clan-networks is that they already have established channels of communication, mechanics of assembly, and a simple power structure. The urban network therapist often uses up a good deal of time creating the minimal social organization. This makes it difficult at times for therapists to disengage themselves from responsibility for administrative tasks in order to retain a set of therapeutic roles. They also need some disengagement in order to retain some efficiency, because they serve a total client population of which any single network is only preconsciously aware.

The energy required to organize a network and be clinically effective as well may dampen the ardor of many therapists initially attracted by the powerful tool of network therapy. It also probably accounts for the comparatively short life of most urban therapy networks. The novelty of the organizing role and the sense of power derived from successful network intervention are both certainly attractive to therapists. However, one must be wary lest one become preoccupied with being a "chief" when one wants and needs to be a "medicine man."

The "medicine man" role of offering therapy cannot be lost if network intervention of any type is to be successful. Networks and clans are made up of individuals, some of whom from time to time need to be seen and treated as individuals. These may require only on the spot, in context, opportunities to ventilate, express grief, or grasp an insight firmly. Such brief interventions are often handled peripherally in a clan network, but they may and sometimes should be accompanied by interpretations to part or all the group. There is no substitute for clinical judgment about this and there is a real need for freedom of action to follow up insights and play out subliminal clinical hunches.

In addition, other individuals within networks may need one of the more traditional therapies, either medical or psychiatric. These services may be supplied by therapists in their own practice or by the referral and follow-up route depending on the combination of particular circumstances, therapists' ability and time, and the availability of other resources. There seems to be no evidence to substantiate a preference for either referral or do-it-yourself individual therapy as part of network activity. There does seem to be evidence that if network intervention is to be effective the members should validate and support the referral. The therapist must also have the type of clinical judgment that can recognize the need for intensive individual therapy and the sense of responsibility that will see that it is provided.

The question of referral brings up a third

probable role of a network therapist: that of linking or coordinating between the network and the institutionalized resources of the external community at large. This really is not a new concept of a therapeutic role. Community mental health professionals have become aware of the need to provide support to clients in order to utilize a host of already established institutions and services. In fact, such coordination is one of the basic services required for federal funding and for professional interest in the techniques of "consultation" and "coordination" of ecological systems in relation to treatment.

This linking role is very clear-cut when a therapist enters the network-clan of a tribal minority culture. As was indicated in these two examples, effective liaison with the Veteran's Administration, courts, child protective agencies, and so on, were essential facets of the solution of referred problems. In the Indian network-clan setting, it becomes obvious that the therapist is often the only person present who can translate clan needs into terms acceptable to majority culture's institutions. However in urban middle-class situations, a therapist should be wary of assuming that the network members have knowledge and skills to communicate with the existing resources and to handle problems in the supra-network power structure. When a lack of these techniques is recognized, therapists must thread their way between the Scylla of doing the coordination themselves and the Charybdis of teaching the network members social-political skills.

Probably the only safe guideline to offer therapists is a warning not to choose either route at the expense of their other therapeutic roles. Separating this role from that of treating social and individual pathology may make such decisions easier and may elicit some additional impetus to develop techniques that will accomplish several tasks at once.

A final comment may be made in comparing the processes of network therapy in urban settings and in clan-oriented social settings. Where network clans do not exist, they can be created effectively for critical cases. However, it often is difficult to justify the effort and expense of this activity for situations in which the supportive interaction might be seen as optimal therapy, but the symptoms are not dramatic enough to assemble family, friends, and neighbors. A network-clan such as the one described here exists independently of the crisis of a member and can be mobilized to deal with many situations before they require drastic last ditch measures.

It is probable that even in the socially isolating environment of our present megalopolitan centers the vestiges of old networks and the seedlings of new ones can be found. Some pioneers in preventive mental health practice are already turning attention to nurturing these potentials (Taber, 1969). Others have less consciously developed a "sense of community" or of "family" in their research interventions. Mental health consultants may find that time invested in creating new social institutions or in "revitalizing" old ones may be an excellent investment of resources. Creative social engineering may seem far afield from therapy, yet the processes of pathology and health in any personality cannot be separated from the network of social relationships in which the individual is enmeshed.

In comparing network therapy as intervention in a setting where a clan-like social structure already exists and in settings where it must be created, it has been possible to focus on several facets of the therapeutic role: first, the need to treat social pathology by an application of skills and insights derived from family and group therapy; second, the need for individual therapeutic skills, both in crisis interaction and on a long term basis; and, third, the need for providing linkages with the institutions and external community as is seen in community psychiatry.

Areas for further study are sketched in relation to the functioning of healthy and pathological networks in other contexts, both urban and tribal. In passing, questions are raised of theoretical and practical importance concerning the extent to which the network therapist can or should become a "social engineer."

Selected annotated bibliography

Ewalt, Patricia, and Katz, Janice. "An Examination of Advice Giving as a Therapeutic Intervention," *Smith College Studies in Social Work* 47:1 (November 1976), pp. 3–20.

This is an excellent discussion of a study of the use of the technique of advice giving which generally has been held in low regard in social work.

Garrett, Annette. *Interviewing: Its Principles and Methods.* New York: Family Service Association, 1972.

This is the second edition of a splendid classic statement about the use of interviewing in social work practice. The authors would highly recommend it to anyone reading their text.

Kadushin, Alfred. *The Social Work Interview.* New York: Columbia University Press, 1972.

This is an excellent text on the use of the interview. It is recommended if one wants to explore beyond the material in the chapter.

Reid, William J., and Epstein, Laura. *Task-Centered Casework.* New York: Columbia University Press, 1972.

If the reader wants to pursue some of the material in the chapter and to develop further knowledge of serving the individual client, this book describes a particular, task-centered method of working which is important.

Roberts, Robert W., and Northen, Helen. *Theories of Social Work with Groups.* New York: Columbia University Press, 1976.

This book and the companion text following are important contributions to the literature of social work. They pull together much of what is known in social work methods, however, they may be somewhat beyond beginning students' understanding. The authors would especially recommend the articles by Hartford; Garvin, Reid, and Epstein; and McBroom.

Roberts, Robert W., and Nee, Robert H. *Theories of Social Casework.* Chicago: University of Chicago Press, 1970.

This book is a very good summary of the major treatment approaches in social casework. The authors would recommend the articles by Perlman, Smalley, Hollis, and McBroom.

Schulman, Lawrence. "A Study of Practice Skills," *Social Work* 23:4 (July 1978), pp. 274–280.

This is a research study that attempts to investigate 27 specific social work skills and their effects on social workers' helpfulness to clients. It may be somewhat technical for students, but the list of skills found in the article should lead to an interesting discussion.

CHAPTER 12

Evaluation

Social workers, along with other human service professionals, are increasingly being called upon to justify the effectiveness of their services. The 1970s might be considered the age of accountability for human services—a decade in which evaluation has taken on serious proportions with both clients and other persons in the communities being served requiring evidence of the worthwhileness of social service programs. With growing indications of taxpayer reluctance to fund unproven programs and the effects of California's Proposition 13, the demand for hardheaded evaluation will continue into the decade of the 80s.

We consider evaluation to be the application of scientifically sound research methodology to measure both change processes and the results or outcomes of change efforts. As in any good research, the evaluation is directed toward measuring the outcomes of interventions (the dependent variables), to measure the change processes or the nature of the interventions themselves (the independent variables), and to do so with a research design which permits workers to attribute the outcome to the change processes. The terms *sumative* and *formative* are frequently used to refer to the two types of evaluations. Sumative refers to the study of program outcomes or effectiveness; while formative evaluations refer to the study of program processes.

Both types of evaluation will also occur on two levels. At the program level, social workers are asked to measure the impact of and the nature of programs such as child protection, family counseling, head start, and so on. This might be referred to as program evaluation research. But evaluation research will also occur at the level of individual worker and client relationships. Just as we can ask what is the nature of human service programs, what are their outcomes, and what leads us to believe that the programs lead to the outcomes so too can we ask what is the nature of individual intervention made by social workers and clients, what are their presumed outcomes, and what leads us to believe that the interventions led to the outcomes. As part of the services provided to each client, each individual social worker is called upon to be a researcher, to apply sound scientific methodology to an understanding of the nature of interventions and a measurement of impacts. Each worker and client might ask what are our activities (independent variables)? What are our goals (dependent variables)? And how can we relate activities to the goals? In Chapter 2 we talked about testing our assumptive knowledge and the commitment to the scientific method as a response to the discomfort which occurs in the light of incomplete knowledge. As we carry out this commitment in our cooperation with program evaluation efforts and our own obligations to be competent researchers with our clients, we test our assumptive knowledge and contribute to knowledge development in the profession.

BALANCING SUMATIVE AND FORMATIVE EVALUATIONS

For many of us the term *program evaluation* carries the connotation of a sumative program evaluation, that is, an attempt to assess the extent to which a program is reaching its objectives. While sumative evaluations are useful in making judgements about the worth of a program, they have very little usefulness unless the program or interventions used are well conceptualized and understood. Knowing that goals are being accomplished is of little use unless we also know how they are being accomplished; likewise, knowing that goals are not being accomplished is not useful unless we are clear as to what interventions were used and failed to accomplish the desired goals. For example, if one finds a reduction in child abuse after a parent skills training program, a laudable goal might well have been accomplished. But unless we understand clearly the nature of the parent training program that presumably led to the reduction in child abuse, the finding is of little practical value because, not knowing the nature of the program, we would not be in a position to replicate it in the future. Or, assume that a social worker is working with a senior citizens group toward a goal of securing more adequate police protection in their neighborhood. Even if the goal is accomplished, say more foot patrols are assigned to the neighborhood at hours when senior citizens would like to be on the streets, unless the worker can document how this goal was accomplished, the finding is of limited value and will not contribute to the developing knowledge base of the profession.

Unfortunately, in much of social work, as well as other human service professions, our independent variables (the program or intervention methods used) are poorly conceptualized. Thus efforts to measure outcomes may be very premature unless workers are also simultaneously engaging in formative evaluations directed toward conceptualizing and measuring the nature of the intervention used. Studies of program and interventive processes are essential to the development of the knowledge base of the profession and, as Rutman and Hudson suggest, are an essential prerequisite to sumative evaluations (see Reading 12–2). Before talking about program or intervention effectiveness (that is, sumative evaluations) we first need to be able to answer a series of questions about the program itself:

1. What am I attempting to accomplish? What are the goals which have been set for the program or the service contract for the individual worker and client? Clarity about goals is essential for either type of evaluation.

2. What is the population for which these goals are to be accomplished? In some cases this may be an individual, a group of clients, a neighborhood, or an even larger population.

3. What are the components or parts of the program or intervention plan which are necessary to accomplish the goals for the defined population or client? One should be able to specify all of the program components or interventions which will be occurring in an effort to accomplish the goals.

4. How do these components or parts fit together? Do some need to precede others? Do some occur concurrently? How do the parts of the program fit together into an integrated intervention plan to accomplish the desired goals? At this point flowcharts might be drawn to illustrate relationships among the various intervention strategies and how they relate to accomplishing the final goals.

5. What are the reasons for believing that, if the intervention strategies are carried out, the goals will be accomplished? This, of course, moves into the area of intervention theory; workers must have some ideas, some hypotheses that will lead them to predict that goals will be accomplished if they accomplish the prescribed intervention plan. Part of evaluation is to test these hypotheses—to test their assumptive knowledge and expand the knowledge base of the profession.

Perhaps an illustration of this process would be helpful. Let's go back to the senior citizens group who are working with a social worker to increase public safety in their neighborhood. These seniors like to be out visiting during the late afternoon and early evening hours; however, they feel very insecure in their immediate neighborhood because of concern about muggings, purse snatchings, and so on. If it is assumed that they have decided on an immediate goal of attempting to have a pair of police officers assigned to patrol the neighborhood on foot during the 3:00 to 11:00 P.M. shift to supplement the regular squad car patrols. The goal is rather clear, the immediate plan is to develop an intervention plan which will presumably lead to that goal. In thinking through ways of accomplishing the goal, the seniors and their social worker decided that they first needed to influence the chief of police to secure the chief's support for the notion of a foot patrol for their neighborhood and then second to influence the city council to secure some additional resources for the neighborhood. They decide that in the process of implementing this plan, they will need to bring two kinds of pressure to bear—knowledge and political. They will need to assemble facts concerning the number of crimes against the elderly that are occurring in the neighborhood as well as the extent to which activities of the seniors may be limited by fear of being out at night. Second, even with the knowledge, they will need to in some way mobilize a show of political support to convince the city council members that this is an important issue for their attention. After considerable brainstorming and planning, the social worker and clients may well have developed an intervention plan similar to that represented in Figure 12–1.

Figure 12–1 is a flowchart of an intervention plan which indicates the various components to the effort to produce change and shows their relationship. Formative evaluation would then be directed at monitoring the extent to which each of these activities occurs. If the persons responsible for gathering the evidence failed to do so and failed to have an impact on the police chief, then the worker and clients have a clearer understanding of what went wrong in accomplishing their goals. Or, conceivably, the plan may be perfectly implemented but still the goals are not accomplished; if this should happen we may well have done a sumative evaluation and are able to make a judgment that the plan itself was not appropriate. Client and worker in this situation would then consider alternative plans and strategies for accomplishing their goals—perhaps they are going to need to work to unseat some city council members or perhaps form coalitions with other organizations in order to bring additional political pressure to bear to secure the desired goal.

FIGURE 12–1
Flowchart of intervention plan

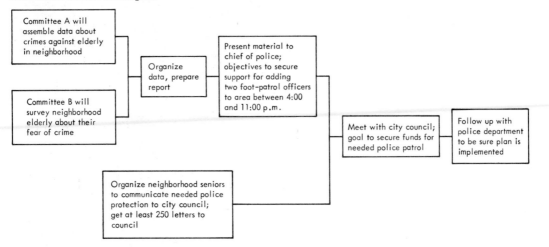

This illustration also points out another distinction which is sometimes useful in regard to sumative evaluation—the distinction between outputs and outcomes. We have generally been referring globally to outcomes as the program results. But one might note from this illustration that the output of the intervention was the assignment of a team of foot patrol officers to the neighborhood whereas the desired outcome was the reduction in crime against senior citizens. The question of whether the output, that is, the two patrol officers, will actually lead to the outcome is, of course, a separate research question which will be of critical interest to this social worker and the group of clients. Thus one can ask, do the program activities lead to the outputs and do the outputs lead to the outcomes? In this connection outputs are referred to as the immediate desired accomplishments of the program and the outcomes as the more long-term gains which the outputs are presumed to accomplish.

All social workers have a responsibility to be researchers with their clients. An appropriate beginning place for our research efforts will be in conceptualizing and measuring the nature and extent of our intervention activities. Before we do this, we need to have a clear picture of how we are going to go about intervening and why we believe that the interventions, if accomplished, lead to the immediate goals we and our client(s) have established. If this is done, we can then begin thinking about sumative evaluation or measuring the extent of goal attainment. Research, and evaluation in the sense that we are using it, is frequently a continuous process providing a flow of data in which we can continually reassess goals, intervention plan, and even the problem definition.

CONTINUOUS CLIENT EVALUATION

Figure 12–2 offers a schematic representation of the problem-solving process showing evaluation as providing feedback loops permitting client and worker to assess continuously the problem they have defined for work, the objectives they have selected, and the interventive plan they have formulated. Client and worker are continuously involved in an ongoing evaluation of their experiences in trying to produce change. Their evaluation may indicate a need to redefine

FIGURE 12-2
The problem-solving model

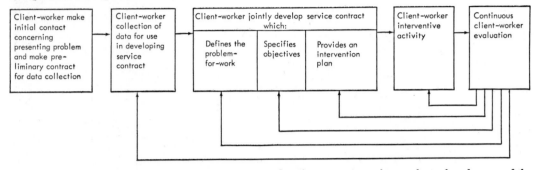

Evaluation provides feedback loops enabling client and worker to continuously reevaluate the adequacy of the data base and/or renegotiate the service contract by changing the problem definition, the objectives, or the intervention plan.

the problem (or define an entirely new problem), to reassess objectives (or develop new objectives), or to alter the intervention plan. The impact of evaluation and feedback loops is to reduce the linearity of the problem-solving model and to permit the model to take on a dynamic, systematic, constantly changing quality. The opportunity to change problem definition, goals, and intervention plan does not, however, remove from the worker the responsibilities of being sure that any changes are negotiated with the client and that any intervention activities are undertaken on the basis of a clearly specified service contract. Experience with interventive activities may indicate a need for a change in the contract, but changes in contracts cannot be made unilaterally.

In Chapter 9 the stress was on the importance of clearly specifying goals. This is an essential prerequisite to evaluation. Without client and worker clarity as to goals, the evaluation of progress toward the accomplishment of goals is impossible. Likewise, a clear specification of the intervention plan is necessary to assess whether client-worker activities are appropriate for reaching the desired goals. Without a clear specification of the intervention plan, client and worker cannot evaluate whether what is happening leads or fails to lead to goal accomplishment.

The specification of measurable, concrete goals is one of the more difficult tasks of the social work practitioner. The article by Thomas Kiresuk and Geoffrey Garwick provides a useful evaluation tool (see Reading 12-1). Kiresuk and Garwick describe Goal Attainment Scaling procedures which were developed to evaluate patient progress in mental health programs but which can be utilized in any program where goal-setting is a part of the process. Goal Attainment Scaling procedures have been used to measure client progress toward service goals, student social workers' progress toward the accomplishment of learning goals, and agency progress toward the accomplishment of organizational goals. Goal Attainment Scaling is particularly useful to the social work practitioner, because it permits the individualization of goals; there is no effort to impose predetermined, standardized goals. Rather, client and worker work toward the accomplishment of goals individually tailored to a particular situation. The procedures, however, only measure the extent of goal attainment; they do not in anyway measure the importance or significance of the goals themselves, nor do they determine the intervention methods. How goals are achieved is not a part of Goal Attainment Scaling.

The grid used in Goal Attainment Scaling is reproduced in Figure 12–3. It provides for the development of scales—one for each goal—with five levels of predicted attainment; the levels range from the most unfavorable to the most favorable outcome thought likely, with the expected level of outcome at the midpoint on each scale. At least one scale should be developed for each problem area, and a heading should be provided for each scale. As many scales as are necessary may be developed. Once the scale headings have been provided, a follow-up date should be set, and the predicted level of outcome for each scale as of the follow-up date should be indicated.

FIGURE 12–3
Goal Attainment Follow-Up Grid

Program using GAS_____		Date of scale construction _____ Follow-up date _____		

LEVELS OF PREDICTED ATTAINMENTS	SCALE HEADINGS AND SCALE WEIGHTS			
	SCALE: 1 ($w_1 =$)	SCALE 2: ($w_2 =$)	SCALE 3: ($w_3 =$)	SCALE 4: ($w_4 =$)
Most unfavorable outcome thought likely				
Less than expected success				
Expected level of success				
More than expected success				
Most favorable outcome thought likely				

Where do client and worker expect to be at the specified follow-up date? The entire goal may not be attained by that time; the task, therefore, is to indicate the expected level of accomplishment by the follow-up date. The next steps are to indicate the most unfavorable outcome and the most favorable outcome thought likely by the follow-up date; then the intermediate levels—less than expected success, expected level of success, and more than expected success—can be completed. The levels of predicted attainment should be specified objectively enough to be reliably scored on the follow-up date. Whenever possible, quantification is desirable, but it is not absolutely essential in establishing the scale levels.

A second concern is to be sure that each scale is both exhaustive and mutually exclusive. None of the five levels of success should overlap (each should be mutually exclusive), and the scale levels should account for all outcome possibilities thought likely (be exhaustive). After the scales have been developed, they can be set aside for scoring until the designated follow-up date. Scoring consists of checking what has been accomplished on each scale at the designated follow-up date. Kiresuk and Garwick present a formula for calculating an overall Goal Attainment Scale and also discuss the procedures for weighting scales if some are thought to be more important than others.

Figure 12–4 illustrates a completed set of Goal Attainment Scales which might have been developed with Mrs. B in the situation described in Chapter 10. After study of this example as well as careful study of the Kiresuk and Garwick article, the student might begin experimenting with Goal Attainment Scaling. The procedures can be used in any situation where goals are set, so Goal Attainment Scaling can be learned without actually working with clients. Personal learning goals can be set. How many books will be read next month? How many articles? What are the student's goals in terms of grades this term? What percent of written assignments will be completed on time? The student's

FIGURE 12–4
Goal Attainment Follow-Up Grid (examples of scales which might have been developed with Mrs. B)

Program using GAS: Intercity Head Start				
Client: Mrs. B		Date of scale construction: 8-1-73 Follow-up date: 9-1-73		

LEVELS OF PREDICTED ATTAINMENTS	SCALE HEADINGS AND SCALE WEIGHTS			
	SCALE 1: ($w_1 =$)	SCALE 2: ($w_2 =$)	SCALE 3: ($w_3 =$)	SCALE 4: ($w_4 =$)
Most unfavorable outcome thought likely	Mrs. B reports angrily yelling at Jimmy daily or oftener during last week in August.	No action on or discussion of Mrs. B's loneliness.	No discussion or action about returning to clinic.	
Less than expected success	Mrs. B reports angrily yelling at Jimmy more than 3 times but less than daily during last week in August.	Mrs B discusses her loneliness but can not make plans to deal with it.	Mrs. B is discussing her reaction to the clinic but has not formulated plans to return.	
Expected level of success	Mrs. B reports angrily yelling at Jimmy no more than three times during last week in August.	Mrs. B is discussing her loneliness and making plans to join a group.	Mrs. B has discussed her reaction to the clinic and plans to secure a return appointment.	
More than expected success	Mrs. B has discontinued angrily yelling at Jimmy but has not discovered another way to discipline him.	Mrs. B has initiated contacts with a group.	Mrs. B has telephoned the clinic for a return appointment.	
Most favorable outcome thought likely	Above, and Mrs. B is using another form of discipline before becoming angry with Jimmy.	Mrs. B has attended one group meeting.	Mrs. B has been into the clinic for a return appointment.	

learning plans will provide ample opportunity to begin work with Goal Attainment Scaling.

ASSISTING WITH PROGRAM EVALUATION

Increasingly social agencies are being called upon to establish the effectiveness of their services. Accountability extends beyond the evaluation by worker and client of the extent to which they are achieving service contract goals. It also utilizes the principles of scientific research to measure the extent to which agency program goals are being attained and at what cost. The article by Leonard Rutman and Joe Hudson identifies phases in program evaluation and discusses issues and problems of each phase (see Reading 12–2). Studies can be made of outcomes (the extent to which programs are achieving defined goals) or of efforts (the processes agencies utilize to reach goals). Process studies are particularly necessary to enable social agencies to more adequately conceptualize and identify the program inputs they utilize to reach goals. Just as interventive means must be conceptualized and related to objectives defined in the service contract, so at the level of program evaluation, inputs must be conceptualized and related to program goals or outputs. The need to adequately conceptualize inputs and goals is the same whether the effort is to evaluate a client's progress or a program's accomplishment.

A recurring theme noted by Rutman and Hudson is the conflict between practitioner and researcher. They think both must make compromises if program evaluation is to be conducted, and they regard program evaluation as essential to the establishment of accountability. Practitioners may be asked to more completely conceptualize their activity and goals. However, practitioners utilizing the service contract as described should find this a comparatively easy process. In addition, the practitioner may be asked to fill out forms and maintain records which are essential for the evaluation function. Just as the evaluation of client progress provides feedback from which the worker and client can renegotiate their service contract, so formal program evaluation should provide feedback to the worker concerning the effectiveness of particular interventive means. While cooperating with researchers may involve additional effort on the part of the practitioner, ultimately the payoff in knowledge and better service should justify the effort.

RECAPITULATION

The practitioner's involvement with evaluative effort occurs at two levels. Worker and client will be involved in a continuous process of evaluating the extent to which the goals of the service contract are being accomplished. This evaluation provides feedback loops and an opportunity for client and worker to continuously renegotiate their contract for work, objectives, and interventive means in relation to the problem. Workers may also be called upon to cooperate and assist with broader agency program evaluation. Such efforts should also provide feedback concerning the interventive approaches which appear to be most effective in given circumstances. Evaluation at both levels requires an explicit statement of goals and conceptualization of interventive means or program inputs. One model for measuring goal attainment—Goal Attainment Scaling—was discussed in relation to the measurement of client progress.

A LOOK FORWARD

The articles reproduced in this chapter relate directly to the material discussed previously. Kiresuk and Garwick provide a further discussion of Goal Attainment Scaling procedures which should be very useful to practitioners. Rutman and Hudson discuss the program evaluation process, conceptualize different phases in the process, and note issues and problems of each phase.

Chapter 13 will confront the student with the difficulty of bringing a working relationship to a conclusion. Earlier the discussion was on the process of establishing a relationship—a process which is given considerable attention in the social work literature. Frequently, however, writers fail to deal with the difficulties of constructively terminating a relationship. This process will be discussed as it occurs when a client is referred to another agency, transferred to another worker, or the service is brought to a planned termination.

Reading
12-1 *Basic Goal Attainment Scaling procedures**

Thomas J. Kiresuk and Geoffrey Garwick

Background on Goal Attainment Scaling

Goal Attainment Scaling is a methodology for developing personalized, multivariable, scaled descriptions which can be used for either therapy objective-setting or outcome measurement purposes. Originally developed as an assessment approach for individual clients in a community mental health milieu, Goal Attainment Scaling has since been applied to goal-setting for both individuals and organizations across the whole spectrum of human services.

The Goal Attainment Scaling concept was first proposed in a 1968 article by Drs. Kiresuk and Sherman (Kiresuk and Sherman,

* Reprinted by permission of the authors and the National Institute of Mental Health, United States Department of Health, Education and Welfare, from *Project Evaluation Report, 1969–1973*, chap. 1, of the Program Evaluation Project, Minneapolis, Minnesota. This project was supported by Grant #5 R01 1678904 from the National Institute of Mental Health.

1968). The methodology was then implemented by the staff of the Program Evaluation Project which was directed by Dr. Kiresuk and funded by the National Institute of Mental Health. The Program Evaluation Project staff has undertaken a variety of efforts to examine the feasibility, reliability, and validity of the basic Goal Attainment Scaling approach. The investigation of new possibilities and variations of Goal Attainment Scaling has continued through the efforts of both the Program Evaluation Project staff and persons in other agencies.

This chapter begins with an overview of the core of the Goal Attainment Scaling methodology. The second section discusses the characteristitcs of utilizing the Goal Attainment Follow-Up Guide for assessment purposes. The final section briefly outlines some of the major possibilities which have been implemented or suggested for varying the basic Goal Attainment Scaling format while retaining the basic Goal Attainment Scaling approach.

I. Basic Goal Attainment Scaling procedures

Designed for great flexibility, Goal Attainment Scaling is neither a specific set of instructions, nor a particular collection of prespecified scales. Instead, it is a combination of an ideology, a type of record-keeping, and a series of techniques. The basic future-oriented, reality-testing approach on which Goal Attainment Scaling is based, duplicates in part the informal goal setting so often used by effective therapists and educators. In brief, Goal Attainment Scaling involves four steps:

a. Collection of information about the person or organization for which goals will be scaled;
b. Specification of the major areas where change would be feasible and helpful;
c. Development of specific predictions for a series of outcome levels for each major area; and
d. Scoring of the outcomes as they have been achieved by the time of a later follow-up interview.

(Even this fourth step is not essential to all uses of Goal Attainment Scaling. In some settings Goal Attainment Scaling has been used only to plan therapy and help the client set goals, so that the follow-up interview is not held and scoring is not carried out.) Roughly the same procedures are utilized when using Goal Attainment Scaling with organizations.[1] These four basic points will be discussed in greater detail below.

A. The collection of information

From the client's statements, reports from the spouse, from other agencies, from rela-

___
[1] See chapter on using Goal Attainment Scaling with organizations in *Program Evaluation Project Report 1969–1973* for more specialized suggestions for goal-setting for groups or organizations.

tives, from friends, and from any other available information source, a pool of information is accumulated. In the original Program Evaluation Project staff research at the Hennepin County Mental Health Service Adult Outpatient unit one or two 50-minute interviews plus examination of the client's information forms were the most common sources of knowledge for the clinician. In other settings, however, different schedules have been used for information collection. For an inpatient setting, information may be collected through records and contacts with the client over a period of several days.

B. Designation of problem areas

The information collected about the client will often be a relatively amorphous mass of facts. This pool of information could be analyzed in a variety of ways, but Goal Attainment Scaling is based on separating the mass of facts into a series of "problem areas." These problems indicate areas where an undesirable set of behaviors should be minimized, or where a favorable set of behaviors should be increased. The most significant, relevant problem areas should be selected for inclusion.

The Goal Attainment Scaling selection of problem areas may be carried out by a professional working alone, by the client, by both client and professional working together, by the family of the client and the professional, or through other possibilities. The procedures should be varied to meet the needs and capabilities of the agency. For example, if client participation is highly valued by the agency, then the client should be involved in the development of the problem areas.

The specified person(s) will select the problem areas most relevant to the client or organization involved. Each of these problem areas will be used to develop a continuum or scale of behaviors individually tailored to the client. In Figure 1, a completed form for the recording of the problem areas appears. This form is called the Goal Attain-

FIGURE 1

	SCALE 1: Employment (interest in work) self-report $(w_1 = 10)$	SCALE 2: Self-concept (physical appearance) patient interview $(w_2 - 15)$	SCALE 3: Interpersonal relation-ships (in training program as judged by receptionist—do not score if he does not go to train-ing program) $(w_3 \cdot 5)$	SCALE 4: Interpersonal relationships (report of client's spouse) $(w_4 \cdot 8)$	SCALE 5: (w_5)
SCALE ATTAINMENT LEVELS					
a. Most unfavorable treatment outcome thought likely	Client states he does not want to ever work or train for work.	Client (1) has buttons missing from clothes, (2) unshaven (but says he is growing beard), (3) dirty fingernails, (4) shoes unshined (if wearing shoes needing shine), (5) socks don't match.	Never spontaneously talks to anyone. May answer if spoken to.	No friends and no close friends (i.e., "close" equals friends with whom he can talk about serious, intimate topics and who he feels like his company).	
b. Less than expected success with treatment	Client states that he may want to work "some-day" (a year or more later) but not now, and wants no training.	4 of the above 5 conditions.	Spontaneously talks to his own therapists or caseworkers, but to no other clients.	One person who is a friend or acquaintance but not a close friend.	
c. Expected level of treatment success	Client states that he might be interested in working within the next 12 months, but only if no training is required.	3 of the above 5 conditions.	Spontaneously talks to therapists, caseworkers, and one other client.	Two or more persons who are friends, but not close friends.	
d. More than expected success with treatment	Client states that he might be interested in working within the next 12 months and training for no more than 30 work days.	2 of the above 5 conditions.	Spontaneously talks to therapists, caseworkers, and 2 to 4 other clients.	One close friend, but no other friends.	
e. Most favorable treatment outcome thought likely	Client states that he might be interested in working within the next 12 months. Will train for as many days as are necessary.	One of the above 5 conditions.	Spontaneously talks to therapists, caseworkers, and 5 or more other clients.	One or more close friends, plus one or more other friends or acquain-tances.	

ment Follow-Up Guide, and each vertical scale represents a scale of outcomes related to a problem area for a client.

In Goal Attainment Scaling as used in the Program Evaluation Project research, there is no upper limit on the number of scales to be prepared for each client. The follow-up guide in Figure 1 has only four completed scales, but others could have been added. If necessary, a second or even a third form could also be used if more than five scales were desired. The highest number of scales known to have been constructed for one individual is 10. For organizations, from 10 to 60 scales have been utilized on the Goal Attainment Follow-Up Guide. It is recommended that at least three or four problem areas be chosen, although a few clients may have only one or two scales.

Once the problem areas have been picked,

each should be given a title. This title is designed to focus the attention on the problem areas of someone inspecting the follow-up guide. Each title should summarize a problem area in a few words and should be placed in the blanks across the top of the follow-up guide. The title may be abstract, theoretical, or vague. This possibility is mentioned to emphasize that though the titles may be abstract or generalized, the remainder of the descriptions on the follow-up guide should be relatively specific and objective. In Figure 1, the titles selected are Employment, Self-concept, and Interpersonal relationships.

When titles have been selected for the client's follow-up guide, a numerical weight can be added to each scale, beside the title. The weighting system utilized by the Program Evaluation Project staff to indicate the relative importance of the scales does not incorporate any prespecified weights, but allows any one- or two-digit number to be used. The higher the number used in the weight, the more significant the scale is, relative to the other scales. In Figure 1, the weights selected are 10, 15, 5, 8, so that Scale 2 for the problem area "self-concept" with the weight of "15" is seen as the most important.

The title box can also be used to indicate any special sources of information for the scale. Special information sources might include "speak to spouse," "contact police department," "employer should help score this scale," and so on.

C.   Predictions for each problem area

Goal Attainment Scaling operates within a time frame or time limit, and all outcomes should be linked to this time frame. Thus, all Goal Attainment predictions should refer to specific outcomes at a specific target date in the future. In the original research at the Hennepin County Mental Health Service, clinicians constructed the follow-up guides and were allowed to set their own time frame for the follow-up guide. The most common option was the Program Evaluation Project suggested schedule of a follow-up interview six months after the time the Goal Attainment Follow-Up Guide was constructed. In the Hennepin County Crisis Intervention Center, where clinicians and clients worked together on most scales on the follow-up guides, the follow-up interview was usually scheduled for from one to three weeks after the construction of the follow-up guide. Currently, under the new evaluation system being developed for the Hennepin County Mental Health Service Outpatient Unit, follow-ups on therapy effectiveness are held three months after the follow-up is constructed. In a special study at the Hennepin County Mental Health Service Day Treatment Center, clients are constructing follow-up guides to be followed up four months later. In short, the Goal Attainment scales

should be constructed to be applicable to a future follow-up interview, and the length of time between follow-up guide construction and the follow-up interview should be adjusted to suit the needs of the individual agency.[2]

With the problem areas selected and the date of the follow-up interview established, a series of predictions about the client's outcomes should be made. For each problem area, a number of variables are probably applicable as sources of measurement of outcome. The person (or group) constructing the Goal Attainment Follow-Up Guide should select a variable for each problem area—a variable which is maximally useful for indicating treatment outcome and which can be efficiently, cheaply, and reliably measured at the time of follow-up (see Figure 2).

For each variable, a range of outcomes is possible at the time of follow-up. These outcomes should be presented in accord with the descriptions along the left edge of the Goal Attainment Follow-Up Guide (see Figure 1). These five descriptions range from the "most favorable outcome thought likely" to "more than expected level of outcome" to "expected level of outcome" to "less than expected level of outcome" to the "most unfavorable outcome thought likely." Judgment of the persons constructing a follow-up guide is used to assign a part of the range of a variable to each of these five levels. These five levels with behaviors assigned to them comprise an individually developed continuum or scale for each variable relevant to the client.

The key level for predictive purposes is the middle or "expected" level on each variable's five-point scale. The expected level presents the best and most realistic prediction possible of the outcome which will have been reached by the client by the date of the follow-up interview. The expectations ought

---

[2] See chapter on follow-up Goal Attainment Scaling in *Program Evaluation Project Report 1969–1973*.

FIGURE 2
Hypothetical field of information collected about the client on the follow-up guide in Figure 1

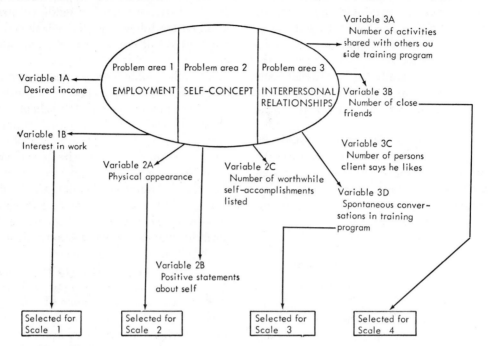

to be pragmatic, so that the expected level of each scale reflects what outcome actually "could" be attained by the follow-up date, not necessarily what "should" be attained.

The estimate of the "expected" outcome ought to be independent of the client's current level of functioning. As a matter of fact, for some very regressed or chronic clients, the most accurate and realistic expectation might be that they would have deteriorated

FIGURE 3
Outcome probabilities

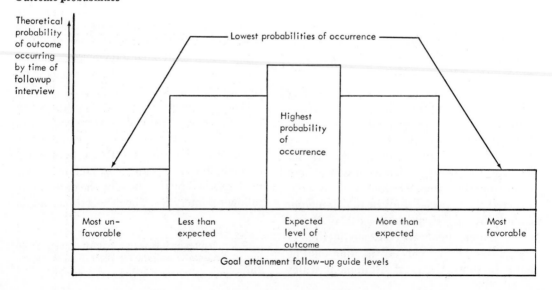

by the time of follow-up, so that their level of functioning when the follow-up guide is constructed might be better than the expected level of outcome. Of course, it is hoped that such cases are rare, but Goal Attainment Scaling is based on obtaining the best prediction possible so that the clinician is not penalized by being forced to set over optimistic goals for very difficult clients.

The expected level is usually developed first. The expected level of outcome should be the *most likely* outcome. The other outcome levels, which should be constructed after the expected level, should be less likely to occur.

The client's level of functioning at the time the follow-up guide is developed can be noted on a separate, standard form (see Figure 4). This form, called the "Client's Status at Intake," is intended to show the level on each scale on the Goal Attainment Follow-Up Guide which is equivalent to the client's current functioning. When the initial level of functioning is known, the *Goal Attainment Change score* can be calculated after the level of functioning at the time of the follow-up interview is scored.[3] Thus, at least two different kinds of effectiveness measures can be collected from the Goal Attainment Scaling system:

a. Whether or not the "expected" levels of outcome are reached.

b. Whether or not change occurred.

Experience with Goal Attainment Scaling suggests that an experienced follow-up guide constructor is able to complete the Goal At-

_____

[3] See chapter on goal attainment change score in the *Program Evaluation Project Report 1969–1973*.

FIGURE 4
For the client in the Goal Attainment Follow-Up Guide in Figure 1

Client Status at Intake

To facilitate the retention of the "level at intake" date, please complete this form for each Goal Attainment Follow-up Guide, using the following format.

Indicate the "level at the time of intake" with an asterisk in the appropriate cell for each scale completed. If the client's "level at intake" does not appear on a scale, put an asterisk in the cell marked "D.N.A." Any additional comments concerning the client's "level at intake" should be indicated on the reverse side of this form.

Scale 1	Scale 2	Scale 3	Scale 4	Scale 5
Much less than expected	Much less than expected	Much less than expected	Much less than expected	Much less than expected
Less than expected	Less than expected	Less than expected	Less than expected	Less than expected
Expected	Expected	Expected	Expected	Expected
More than expected	More than expected	More than expected	More than expected	More than expected
Much more than expected	Much more than expected	Much more than expected	Much more than expected	Much more than expected
D.N.A.	D.N.A.	D.N.A.	D.N.A.	D.N.A.

tainment Follow-Up Guide in 15 to 30 minutes. If the follow-up guide is constructed jointly with the client, the process will require more time but there is greater opportunity for therapeutic interaction. At the Hennepin County General Hospital Mental Health Service, clinicians of all disciplines have constructed follow-up guides and have predicted outcomes fairly accurately. More than one third of the scales scored at follow-up were scored at the "expected" level, with another one third of the scales scored above that level. The types of problems and clients which are particularly difficult to predict are being studied by content analysis methods of the Project staff.[4]

D. The follow-up interview

At the Hennepin County General Hospital Mental Health Service study, the follow-up guides are prepared by one clinician, while a different clinician undertakes therapy. The follow-up interviews are carried out by still other persons, who are not part of either the Mental Health Service staff or the regular Program Evaluation Project staff. The bulk of the interviews have been carried out by master's degree social workers, but bachelor's degree social workers, registered nurses, and under graduates majoring in the social sciences have also participated as follow-up interviews.

The Program Evaluation Project follow-up interview begins with a standardized series of questions about the client's satisfaction with the services received.[5] Then the follow-up interviewer, without actually showing the follow-up guide to the client, will ask questions designed to lead to enough information to score the scales on the Goal Attainment Follow-Up Guides. Other agencies using Goal Attainment Scaling have used different procedures and follow-up workers, with a variety of backgrounds, including therapy teams, psychiatric aides, and secretaries. The interviewer should score the most appropriate level of each scale on the follow-up guide, and the follow-up results are then collected by the Program Evaluation Project staff. These procedures are described in "Interviewer Procedures for Scoring the Goal Attainment Follow-Up Guide" (Audette and Garwick, 1973).

II. The Goal Attainment score

The most commonly used Goal Attainment score is based on the Kiresuk-Sherman formula, and is calculated based on the weights assigned to each scale and the level of outcome attained for each scale as is shown in Figure 5. This formula is used to

FIGURE 5

$$\text{GAS} = 50 + \frac{10 \sum_{i=1}^{n} w_i x_i}{\sqrt{(1-\rho) \sum_{i=1}^{n} w_i^2 + \rho \left(\sum_{i=1}^{n} w_i \right)^2}}$$

where

x_i is the outcome score on the ith scale of the Goal Attainment Follow-Up Guide,

w_i is the relative weight attached to the ith scale,

ρ is a weighted average intercorrelation of the scales, and

n is the number of scales on the Goal Attainment Follow-Up Guide.

produce a single summary score for each Goal Attainment Follow-Up Guide with a mean of 50 and a standard deviation of 10 plus a correction for the possibility of differing variances among the variables on the scales. Two manuals giving the Goal Attainment scores without calculation are available (Baxter, 1973; Garwick and Brintnall, 1973).

The basic Goal Attainment score converts the −2 to +2 values presented in Figure 6 to a score with a theoretical range from 15 to 85. A simplified "Scale-by-Scale" score can also

[4] See chapter on clinicians' ability to predict outcomes in the *Program Evaluation Project Report 1969–1973*.

[5] See chapter on consumer satisfaction in the *Program Evaluation Project Report, 1969–1973*.

FIGURE 6
The values of the level of a single Goal
Attainment Scale

Much less likely than thought	-2
Less than expected	-1
Expected	0
More than expected	+1
Much more than thought likely	+2

be calculated by directly using these −2 to +2 outcome values.

If a summary score with a −2 range is desired, the mean value can be determined, or a specialized formula, developed by Sherman and shown in Figure 7, can be used.

FIGURE 7

$$GAS = 50 + C \cdot \sum_{i=1}^{n} x_i$$

where C is a constant dependent only upon n:
Table of computational constants, $\rho = .3$
Number of scales

$n =$	1	2	3	4	5
Computational constant $C =$	10.00	6.20	4.56	3.63	3.01

The scores based on the follow-up Goal Attainment Follow-Up Guide can be used for feedback to administrators, supervisors, clinicians, or clients.[6] The basic Goal Attainment score reflects "whether or not the treatment accomplished what it was expected to accomplish." Thus, the Goal Attainment score is probably most valuable as a comparative measure, not an absolute measure. In the next section, a few new possibilities for producing or scoring the Goal Attainment Follow-Up Guide are presented. Both procedures and type of score used should fit the agency.

III. Varieties of Goal Attainment Scaling

The Goal Attainment Scaling methodology has been continually expanded ever since it was initiated. Part of this expansion is based on new and better knowledge of the way in which the Goal Attainment methodology operates. Another portion of this expansion is possible because of the development of new ideas and forms, such as the *Guide to Goals, One* format or the idea of collaborative client-therapist follow-up guide construction.

Actually, the title of this section is somewhat misleading, for there are no clear-cut "varieties" or specific variations of Goal Attainment Scaling. Instead, there are several points within the Goal Attainment Scaling process where procedures can be varied and options can be added. Thus, there is a whole spectrum of applications and "variations" of Goal Attainment Scaling and the scores produced which can be used to meet the specific needs of agency clients, administrators, and clinicians.

The four major steps within the Goal Attainment Scaling process were listed in Section I. Some recent possibilities for varying Goal Attainment Scaling within each of these steps will be discussed in the following sections.[7]

A. The collection of information

Many clinicians express interest in changing the Goal Attainment Follow-Up Guide as new information about the client is accumulated. Some persons have suggested that the follow-up guide be altered when new problems appear or when earlier problems disappear. It is recommended that such alterations of the Goal Attainment Follow-Up Guide be undertaken only on a systematic basis, if at all. For example, if an agency staff decides to permit the alteration

---

[6] See chapter on feedback in the *Program Evaluation Project Report, 1969–1973.*

[7] See chapter on the varieties of Goal Attainment Scaling in the *Program Evaluation Project Report 1969–1973* for a more exhaustive list of possibilities.

of the follow-up guide, it should only be altered within a given time after the original construction.

Short-term goals could, however, be represented on special forms. One possibility is shown in Figure 8. With this form, the clinician may indicate short-term goals changes without destroying the predictive value of the original long-term Goal Attainment Follow-Up Guide.

FIGURE 8
Linking long-term to short-term objectives

Program_____ Date_____
Scorer_____ Short-term follow-up number_____

Current status of_____
(Client's name)

A. Long-term goals (to be scored ___ in months)	Much less than expected	Much less than expected	Much less than expected	Much less than expected	Much less than expected
	Less than expected	Less than expected	Less than expected	Less than expected	Less than expected
	Expected	Expected	Expected	Expected	Expected
	More than expected	More than expected	More than expected	More than expected	More than expected
	Much more than expected	Much more than expected	Much more than expected	Much more than expected	Much more than expected
	D.N.A.	D.N.A.	D.N.A.	D.N.A.	D.N.A.

	OBJECTIVE 1A:	OBJECTIVE 2A:	OBJECTIVE 3A:	OBJECTIVE 4A:	OBJECTIVE 5A:
	Method to be Used _____	Method _____	Method _____	Method _____	Method _____
	Date _____ Objective Should be Reached	Date _____ Objective Should be Reached	Date _____ Objective Should be Reached	Date _____ Objective Should be Reached	Date _____ Objective Should be Reached
B. Short-term objectives (to be scored ___ per week)	Is Objective Reached ? _____ (Yes, No, Un-sure)	Is Objective Reached ? _____ (Yes, No, Un-sure)	Is Objective Reached ? _____ (Yes, No, Un-sure)	Is Objective Reached ? _____ (Yes, No, Un-sure)	Is Objective Reached ? _____ (Yes, No, Un-sure)
	OBJECTIVE 1B:	OBJECTIVE 2B:	OBJECTIVE 3B:	OBJECTIVE 4B:	OBJECTIVE 5B:
	Method _____	Method _____	Method _____	Method _____	Method _____
	Date _____ Objective Should be Reached	Date _____ Objective Should be Reached	Date _____ Objective Should be Reached	Date _____ Objective Should be Reached	Date _____ Objective Should be Reached
	Is Objective Reached ? _____ (Yes, No, Un-sure)	Is Objective Reached ? _____ (Yes, No, Un-sure)	Is Objective Reached ? _____ (Yes, No, Un-sure)	Is Objective Reached ? _____ (Yes, No, Un-sure)	Is Objective Reached ? _____ (Yes, No, Un-sure)

1. Indicate the "current status or outcome" with a mark in the appropriate level for each scale. If the client's "current status" does not appear on a long-term scale, put a mark in the cell marked "D.N.A."

2. Link at least one short-term objective to each long-term scale.

3. This form is derived from the Client Status at Intake form.

B. Designation of problem areas

Some agencies may wish to specify some types of problem areas which should be scaled for all clients. A criminal justice agency, for instance, may wish to have "Rearrest" used as the basis for a scale for all of its parolees.

It may be useful for record-keeping purposes to outline a number of general types of problems. Each type could be given a number. When a problem area is selected, its number could be inserted at the top of the scale. These numbers are easily data-processed and enable an agency to get a rapid survey on the general types of problems being confronted by its clients.

C. Predictions for each problem area

The *Guide to Goals, One* format is a programmed version of Goal Attainment Scaling designed to lead the user through step-by-step development of a useful Goal Attainment Follow-Up Guide (Garwick, 1972). This format has been applied to the Hennepin County Day Treatment Center, where clients appeared to be able to produce their own Goal Attainment Follow-Up Guides with a mean of about five minutes of assistance from the clinical staff. A group of these Goal Attainment Follow-Up Guides have been scored at follow-up, and the results indicate a fairly high degree of reliability. If the clients can set their own predictions, the possibilities for cost-saving in evaluation with Goal Attainment Scaling are considerable.

D. The follow-up interview

As commented earlier, one of the most striking developments in Goal Attainment Scaling utilization has been the popularity of clinical uses where the interactional aspects of the Goal Attainment Scaling process are emphasized more than evaluative uses. One survey suggested that of all the agencies considering Goal Attainment Scaling utilization, 52 percent were interested in the non-evaluative uses where the follow-up and scoring are not stressed.[8]

The dynamics of using Goal Attainment Scaling in this way have not been extensively studied by the Program Evaluation Project staff. However, the interactional, reality-testing features of developing the Goal Attainment Follow-Up Guide as part of therapy may be eventually as important as program evaluation with Goal Attainment Scaling.

Conclusion

Further instruction on Goal Attainment Scaling may be obtained from various chapters of the *Program Evaluation Project Report 1969–1973* and from manuals such as the Programmed Instruction Manual (Garwick, 1973). The Newsletter Compendium may also be helpful (Brintnall, 1973).[9]

---

[8] See chapter on dissemination, consultation, and utilization in the *Program Evaluation Project Report, 1969–1973.*

[9] For more information, please write to Ms. Joan Brintnall, Program Evaluation Resource Center, 501 Park Avenue South, Minneapolis, Minnesota 55415.

Reading

12–2 *Evaluation research in human services**

Leonard Rutman and Joe Hudson

In the past several years there has been a growing demand for the formal evaluation

---

* An original article prepared for this book.

of human service programs. This increased interest has been reflected most dramatically in the amount of funds being allocated for program evaluations and this work is becoming increasingly accepted as an integral part of program planning and policy-making in the human services. It is expected that evaluation research can meet two major goals: (1) identify the manner in which programs are carried out, particularly to determine whether they are actually implemented in the way intended; and (2) assess the impact of programs on the target group of consumers. In other words, the expectation is for evaluation research to provide a basis for both monitoring programs and holding them accountable. Ultimately, soundly conducted evaluative research aims at contributing to the more effective and efficient delivery of human service programs.

The increased demand for evaluation research stems from several sources. Funding organizations are exerting greater demands for rigorous research on the programs they support. In part due to the relative scarcity of funds available for human service programs, funding bodies are searching for relatively objective measures on program effectiveness as a condition for the provision of ongoing financial support. No longer are funding bodies satisfied with testimonials from program personnel about the value of their service. Assessments of program effectiveness provided by practitioners and administrators are likely to be viewed with some skepticism inasmuch as any criticism of the worth of these programs poses a threat to professional practice, status, and, ultimately, job security.

In addition to the increased skepticism of funding organizations to potentially self-serving statements by program managers regarding the worth of the services being provided, descriptive reports which provide little more than bookkeeping information on the numbers, characteristics, and per unit cost of clients served by the agency are being viewed as insufficient to warrant the allocation of scarce funds. Instead, human service programs are being asked to provide evidence derived from outcome studies to demonstrate the extent to which programs are meeting stated goals.

Concern about the effectiveness of human service programs has been accelerated with the appearance of research reports showing that many programs have not achieved significant positive effects for the clients served (Bailey, 1966; Eysenck, 1961; Fisher, 1973; Robison and Smith, 1971). In fact, it has become almost axiomatic that the more rigorous the research conducted, the less significant the demonstrated outcomes of a variety of programs. A consequence of such research findings is a growing disenchantment with human service programs by the public as well as by various funding organizations.

Aside from the general concern of determining the effectiveness of programs, human service professionals have become interested and involved in evaluative research for the purpose of testing theory and improving practice. This trend is particularly evident in the considerable amount of research conducted on various learning theories and the "behavior modification" approaches developed from them.

The increasing demand for rigorous evaluative research has also been influenced by the growing popularity of the demonstration project as a strategy for program development and policy-making. Many federal departments have taken the initiative in stimulating the growth of demonstration projects through legislation providing for the funding of "innovative" programs. The usual pattern in funding demonstrations has been to support the development of small-scale pilot programs which include an extensive research component. It is expected that information provided through rigorous study of pilot programs will have relevance for more general program development and policy formulations.

Despite the optimism about the possibilities of evaluation research in monitoring and measuring the impact of human service programs, there are formidable obstacles to pursuing these aims. Several factors contaminate efforts to implement adequate research procedures: (1) the existence of latent purposes for conducting the evaluation study, which can result in the distortion of research to justify decisions about the possible termination, continuation, or expansion of programs; (2) ethical issues, especially in regard to denying service to a control group; (3) administrative constraints; (4) legal requirements; and (5) professionals' prerogatives. The prevalence of these factors in evaluation research efforts underscores the need for an understanding of the sociopolitical process of planning and implementing evaluative research. Such an endeavor would place particular emphasis on adjustments in the stages of planning and conducting the research with particular attention paid to the potential consequences of choosing various alternatives in the development of the final research design and the way in which it is implemented. Also required is an understanding of the factors related to the use of research findings for program changes or policy-making. In this context, a sociology of evaluative research would help to explicate the numerous issues relevant to evaluative studies of human service programs.

Perspectives for evaluating human service programs

Judgments regarding the relative worth of human service programs are common. The general public have varying opinions regarding the success of programs such as Aid to Families with Dependent Children (AFDC) in meeting the problem of low income among these families, of health insurance programs in meeting the medical problems of the aged and/or indigent, and of such child welfare services as foster care in meeting the needs of children requiring substitute care. In the absence of a factual basis for making such decisions, judgments are largely based on values. Programs are viewed as being "good" or "bad" in relation to the characteristics of people availing themselves of the service, attitudes toward work and independence, and differing views about the appropriate role of the state in attempting to ameliorate social problems and personal difficulties.

In addition to the common process in which the public formulates opinions about various programs, assessments about the relative worth of human services are also continually made by practitioners and administrators who are responsible for implementing the services as well as by the funding organizations supporting these programs. Having a deep investment in the services being provided, practitioners and administrators quite naturally extoll the virtues of their program. And it is such subjective testimonials which all too commonly are presented to funding organizations in an effort to gain continued support. Not having access to more rigorous types of information for assessing the value of particular programs, funding organizations are frequently placed in the position of relying upon the subjective information provided by the program personnel.

While evaluation research also entails making judgments of worth about particular programs, it differs from the relatively simple and common process of informal evaluation based largely upon opinion. In evaluation research, emphasis is placed on the application of commonly accepted research procedures to collect data which provides the basis for judgments of worth. Evaluation research is, first and foremost, a process of applying scientific procedures to accumulate reliable and valid evidence on the manner and extent to which specified activities produce particular effects or outcomes. The focus is on the end product—the effects of programs and policies—as well as on the efficiency and effort involved in achieving these outcomes. In addition to providing a basis for determining the relative success or failure of human service programs, the evidence derived from evaluation research can be used to suggest needed modifications in the current operation of the target programs.

The evaluation research process

As indicated previously, a crucial feature of the planning and conduct of evaluation research is the sociopolitical process in which the researcher and the relevant program participants (clients, practitioners, and administrators) develop the focus of the evaluative task, engage in working through the design, specify the procedures for implementing the research, cooperate in the research undertaking, and consider the implications of the research findings for program planning. There are numerous reasons for engaging in such a collaborative process. Through this involvement, the researcher can become more familiar with the organizational context within which the program operates, the explicit purposes of the research, the goals which the service presumably attempts to accomplish, and the attributes of the program being evaluated. As a consequence there is a greater likelihood that the evaluation will deal with the concerns considered most important by those intimately involved with the program as opposed, for example, to those which are of interest only to the researcher. Involvement in this process is also likely to increase the probability of obtaining the cooperation of practitioners who are often anxious about having their work evaluated. Finally, the likelihood of implementing changes suggested by the study is increased when program personnel have been involved in the entire planning process.

The formal collaboration of program administrators and staff with the evaluation team should focus initially on completing what Wholey (1977) and his colleagues have called an "evaluability assessment." The aim of such an assessment is to help clarify the decision-making system to be served by the evaluation and the questions to be answered. A number of sequential tasks are involved. First, identifying the primary intended users of the evaluation and determining from their perspective what activities and objectives go to make up the program under study. A second task then becomes the collection of information on the program activities, goals, objectives, and underlying causal assumptions. Such information can usually be found in program documents or obtained by interviewing program staff. A third task is to synthesize the information that has been collected in a "rhetor-ical program model." This is a flow model or series of models that depict the program resource inputs, intended program activities, intended impacts, as well as the assumed causal links between the program inputs and the expected impacts. A fourth task is determining the extent to which such a program model is sufficiently clear so that evaluation is likely to be both feasible and potentially useful to the intended users. Two criteria are applied in arriving at such judgments: (1) The extent to which the intended users of the evaluation agree on a set of measures for program activities and program objectives and, (2) the extent to which the intended users of the evaluation agree on a set of plausible, testable assumptions that link program activities to program outcomes and impacts. An "evaluable program model" is the expected product of this task and will include only those program activities and objectives for which there exist agreed-upon measures of success and testable causal relationships. The fifth and final step in the evaluability assessment then involves presenting the results of the analysis to the program managers and intended users and reaching agreement on an evaluation plan.

The sociopolitical context in which the evaluation task is formulated and conducted having been mentioned, and the importance of assessing the evaluability of the program having been underscored, it is now possible to identify the various stages of the evaluation process. (1) The purposes or motives for undertaking the evaluation research must be made explicit. (2) The program must be clearly defined. (3) Program goals need to be stated in clear and relatively simple language which is free of jargon and ambiguous terminology. (4) Measures must be developed which can provide information on the relative progress that the program has made toward the attainment of the stated goals. (5) A research design must be developed which incorporates the purpose of the investigation as well as peculiarities of the program and its goals. (6) The implementation of the research requires continuous monitoring to facilitate reliable data collection as well as to determine whether the program is actually carried out in accordance with the originally agreed-upon procedures. (7) The findings are interpreted and the implications of the results for program changes and policy formulations are drawn.

It should not be assumed that an evaluation effort entails a linear progression from one discrete research stage to the next. Rather, the identified stages should most accurately be seen as dynamically interrelated. The resolution of critical issues at any one stage will often have implications for others. For example, an original purpose of conducting evaluative research may have been a desire to test program effects. This purpose is likely to be modified if there is no clearly defined program with specific goals to be evaluated. The revised purpose may then be one of conducting research aimed at "discovering" the specific nature of the program and eliciting the relevant goals. In turn, this revised purpose will have direct implications for the research design since the focus is on exploration and discovery as opposed to verification.

Unlike research conducted in laboratories, the stages of evaluation research are usually exposed to a variety of constraints in the "real world" and, as a consequence, are subject to a number of contaminating and confounding factors. These factors pose major problems to the evaluation effort. Such annoying realities dictate that the planning and conduct of evaluation research as well as the implementation of the research findings be viewed as a sociopolitical process involving the joint efforts of the researcher, administrator, and practitioners.

Aside from their service orientation which usually involves relatively little appreciation of the benefits and requirements of research, practitioners are generally anxious about having their practice scrutinized under the microscope of the researcher because of the possibility of having practice weaknesses revealed. In addition to fears about pointing out the shortcomings of their program, agency administrators are naturally concerned about the extent to which the introduction of research procedures will disrupt the provision of service to clients. The researcher, on the other hand, is mainly concerned with applying rigorous research procedures to the agency setting in spite of administrative or programmatic constraints. By being sensitive to these differing orientations and commitments, potential conflicts which often emerge in evaluative research dealt with to the benefit of the program studies can be anticipated and, hopefully, and the evaluative task. Consequently, there is a great need in the field of evaluation research to explicate such research/program conflicts and work toward providing alternative and mutually satisfying resolutions. This kind of perspective on the part of both the researcher and agency representatives can help develop potentially fruitful negotiations to the mutual benefit of the research and, ultimately, the program.

Purpose. Evaluation research efforts are generally justified on the basis that they contribute to the assessment and modification of human service programs through a rigorous investigation of the relationship of particular interventions to the outcomes produced. Viewed in this light, evaluation research is a feedback mechanism providing the necessary information for adapting programs to more effectively meet client needs. For the funding organization, evaluation research can provide the necessary justification to terminate, continue, or expand human service programs. In addition to these explicit or overt rationales for conducting evaluation research, there may be latent or covert reasons for conducting such studies that may be at variance with the explicit or overt purpose (that is, better understanding the nature of human service programs and the assessment of their impact). Suchman (1972) has termed studies guided by such covert purposes as "pseudo-evaluations." Included in this list of such misuses of evaluation are (1) *eye-wash*—a deliberate focus on the surface appearance of a program to make it look good, (2) *whitewash*—an attempt to cover up program failures during the investigation, (3) *submarine*—the political use of research to destroy a program, (4) *posture*—evaluation research as a ritual that has little substance, and (5) *postponement*—using evaluation to postpone needed action.

For the specification and clarification of research purposes, it is necessary to clearly identify the type of information which the research is expected to produce. This entails a process involving the researcher and the program representatives jointly clarifying the explicit purposes of the evaluation prior to the formal initiation of the project.

Three major purposes of an evaluative project can be identified—assessing program effort (inputs), program effects (outcomes), and program efficiency (economy). The evaluation of program effort is typically geared toward an assessment of the amount and kind of inputs used in pursuing program goals. These inputs may take the form of money, equipment, personnel, work activities, and so on. In the human services, program inputs typically constitute the experimental or treatment variable. That is, assessments of program effort involve descriptive accounts of the program "means" assumed to be causally linked to the program "ends" or goals. However, the mere assessment of program effort does not provide a test of such an assumption. While a necessary condition, effort is not in itself sufficient for the achievement of program goals. Suchman (1967), for example, has compared studies of effort to assessments of the number of times a bird flaps its wings without any attempt being made to determine the distance flown.

Evaluations of effort in human service programs are common. Most agencies are expected to provide yearly reports on the number of clients served by the program, the number of client contact hours, number of staff, and the allocation of staff to various duties. These "service bookkeeping" reports or output measures are roughly analogous to stockholder reports with the major difference that statements of profit and loss—the effects of the effort—are excluded.

Two assumptions about the program effort are crucial. First, it is assumed that there is a logical and empirical relationship between the goals which have been specified for the program and the procedures to be used in their achievement. Second, it is usually assumed that the program is implemented in the originally specified manner. Both assumptions point to the need for outcome studies to provide descriptive accounts of the effort expended. In short, evaluations designed to measure the effects of programs should also include a relatively clear specification of the amount and type of effort expended toward the accomplishment of the desired outcomes.

The evaluation of program effects or outcomes has to do with the extent to which the program achieves its stated goals. Questions of effect deal with the ends or goals of the program and in this way provide a yardstick to be used in assessing the central concern of an evaluation project: Does the program accomplish what it is designed to do? To use Suchman's analogy (1967) again, the assessment of program effectiveness attempts to determine how far the bird has flown and only secondarily, as in the case of effort studies, how many times it flapped its wings.

Efficiency in achieving specified program goals is another explicit purpose for conducting evaluative studies. Essentially, this means testing the relationship between the amount and type of effort expended and the effects accomplished. In other words, efficiency is a function of the relationship of inputs to outcomes. In assessing program efficiency, one is concerned with obtaining information on the extent to which alternative and less costly means could have been used to achieve comparable results.

All too often people involved in human service practice react to questions of program efficiency as somehow below their professional dignity. This reaction seems to be based on the assumption that where humans are involved in receiving service, questions relating to the efficiency of these services are callous or are irrelevant to professional practice. However, the concern with efficiency merely acknowledges an obligation to provide such services in the least costly form compatible with considerations of the dignity and respect which is due to program recipients.

Each of these three explicit purposes of evaluation research warrants serious consideration. Ideally, provision should be made in the research design to collect information pertinent to each purpose. The extent to which it is possible to include measures for each of these purposes, however, is related to the nature of the program being evaluated (that is, its stage of development, the specificity of the program and its goals, and so on) and the reasons established for undertaking the research.

Articulation of the program's components. As noted earlier in the discussion of the evaluability assessment, prior to the implementation of an evaluative study, a program's components must be identified, conceptualized, and standardized. This should result in a clear explication of the "experimental" or independent variable. Rather than referring to programs by such a vague term as *counseling* it becomes necessary to clearly conceptualize and operationalize this term into such varied activities as budgeting, job finding and placement, and particular typing treatment procedures. Unless program components are clearly specified, questions regarding which particular program ingredients have a major effect on the accomplishment of specific as well as on overall goals cannot be adequately answered.

The specification and measurement of the impact of a program's components are important since experts in the field of evaluative research generally agree that the evaluation of entire programs is often beyond the capabilities of existing methodology (Such-

man, 1967; Wholey, et al., 1971). Since evaluations of total programs are so complex and have such limited generalizability, a more common strategy is variable testing—singling out specific components of the program and testing their effectiveness in meeting limited goals. Despite the obstacles involved in conducting global program evaluations, they are commonly undertaken because such information is used as a basis for decision-making about continuation, expansion, or termination of programs. On the other hand, variable testing is commonly viewed as a means of improving specific interventions without, in the process, posing a threat to the entire program.

Specification of goals. Since evaluation research attempts to determine the manner and extent to which a program achieves particular effects, a basic precondition of conducting such research is the clear articulation of program goals. In many respects, clearly stating the goals of human service programs is one of the most difficult and vexing problems of the evaluative process. A major reason for this is that programs commonly set lofty and vague goals. Such goal statements as "the improvement of social functioning," "increasing mental health," "prevention of criminality," and "strengthening family ties" are so vague as to make it difficult, if not impossible, to develop empirical referents or measures.

The formulation of operationalized program goals requires a joint effort between agency personnel and the researcher (Mager, 1972). In this collaboration both the agency representatives and the researcher can make major contributions by bringing their respective expertise to the process. The agency representatives should have a clearer understanding of what the program entails in its day-to-day work and what they consider program priorities, particularly as these relate to possible indicators of "success" or "failure." On the other hand, the researcher—especially in the case of an external evaluator—presumably brings a more objective perception to the program and should therefore be able to view it in a relatively detached manner which can be of assistance to program personnel in ferreting out and articulating simply stated and relevant goals.

Besides helping to facilitate the articulation of specific and discrete program goals, the researcher must constantly emphasize the necessity of formulating goals which have direct relevance to the program being evaluated. Goals stated in specific and practical terms are useless as focal points for evaluating a program unless they clearly relate to the program services being provided. Otherwise, program failure can be attributed to the existence of irrelevant goals and not to the weakness of the program itself.

A problem to bear in mind constantly in the goal specification stage is the possible existence of conflicting goals. When viewed independently, each goal statement may appear to be appropriate, but when goals are appraised in conjunction with each other, potential conflicts may then become apparent. An example of conflicting program goals would be the case of increasing the number of police walking beats in a part of a city and, along with this, the goal of reducing "juvenile delinquency" as measured by police apprehensions. The very fact of increasing the number of police walking beats within the area may well have the effect of increasing the number of young people apprehended and brought to court.

Deciding whose goals should be used as the basis for evaluation is another thorny problem. The program may not be pursuing the goals which have been listed in organizational manuals or conveyed to the general public. On the other hand, a potential danger of having the researcher identify goals for the program is that program personnel can disclaim such goals as their priorities in the provision of services. A similar danger exists if the funding organization specifies the goals of the program to be evaluated. The funding body should, however, examine the goals which program personnel have identified and make decisions regarding the allocation of funds on that basis. This provides further justification for relying on a joint process in which researcher and program personnel articulate relevant goals.

A further task of the goal specification stage is the careful consideration of goal levels. For most human service programs a number of different goal levels can be specified—from the most ideal or ultimate level down through the intermediate level to more immediate and practical goals. An assumption is made that there is a logical connection between the most immediate through the ultimate goals. That is, the achievement of the immediate goals should have relevance for goal achievement at more remote levels.

In evaluation research, theory should be an important consideration in goal-setting and particularly in terms of the generalizability of results, the replication of the test in different situations and in suggesting further related studies. Goals can be specified on the basis of some *a priori* theoretical rationale underpinning the program. Conversely, it is possible to proceed in reverse order and generate theoretical propositions from the test of efforts in accomplishing program goals (Glasser and Strauss, 1967).

Specification of measures. Once the human services program and its goals are identified, a major task is the development of measures or indicators which provide a basis for determining whether or not the services were successfully implemented and whether or not they succeeded in achieving the stated goals. A number of considerations are crucial at this stage. First, in addition to developing measures on the overall goals of the program (for example, reducing poverty), there is also the need to specify measures aimed at the outcome of discrete program goals (for example, increased employment, improved education and health, and so on). Measures for the program's components (that is, its methods and procedures) must also be developed. In evaluating group treatment, for example, it would be possible to develop measures which would yield data on the frequency of meetings, attendance at meetings, the focus of group sessions, the nature of the members' participation, the particular approaches used by the group leader, and the quality of the worker's intervention.

A second consideration is the criteria used to reflect the accomplishment of program goals. On this question the use of "soft" versus "hard" data is relevant and basic to the question of the reliability and validity of the measures used. Such tangible measures as age, sex, time, grades in school, as well as relatively objective data on standardized personality and attitudinal tests can be assumed to have a known degree of reliability and validity. There are also relatively "soft" criteria which are commonly used in less rigorous evaluation studies—personal opinions, subjective estimates, ratings obtained from participant observations, case illustrations, and so on. While these types of information can be used to reflect the flavor of a program and to document typical or extreme situations which may occur in the life of a program, their use as indicators of program success are limited. Such measures are commonly biased both by the interests of the evaluator as well as by the unrepresentative character of the events or cases to which the evaluation is applied.

A third major issue centers on data collection procedures. Evaluation research studies vary in the extent to which practitioners are relied upon for the accumulation of data. Although relying on information collected by practitioners may be less expensive and threatening to these workers, the possibility of bias is great.

Developing the design. The design for evaluative studies must take into consideration the purpose of the investigation as well as the nature and goals of the program to be evaluated. Once these considerations have been taken into account in developing an "ideal" design, modifications are often

called for because of ethical issues and a host of administrative and political constraints pertinent to the implementation of the design.

In those situations where it is both administratively feasible and relevant to the type of information desired, the model of a controlled experiment represents the ideal design for evaluative studies. It is depicted in the accompanying diagram (Stouffer, 1950).

	Before	*After*	*After—before*
Experimental group	X_1	X_2	$d = X_2 - X_1$
Control group	X'_1	X'_2	$d' = X'_2 - X'_1$

To implement this design, two equivalent groups are developed. Equivalence is best obtained through random assignment to experimental and control groups. The "before" measure provides the base line from which change is determined. The experimental group is exposed to the program being evaluated while the control group is not. At a determined follow-up period, "after" measures are made. By comparing the "before" measures with the "after" measures, it is possible to indicate the changes logically assumed to have been produced by the experimental program.

This controlled experimental design can provide information on (1) effectiveness—by comparing the difference in outcome between the experimental and control groups; (2) the nature of the program—by monitoring the program and documenting how it is actually implemented in practice, particularly in regard to desired outcomes; and (3) efficiency—by purposefully manipulating program components to determine comparative expenditures in time, staff, money, and other resources.

Although the experimental design can yield various types of fruitful information, it is extremely demanding in regard to the preconditions which must be met for its proper implementation. The use of this design assumes that the experimental variable (that is, the program or treatment) is clearly articulated and operationalized, stable over time, accessible to manipulation, and amenable to being monitored. It also assumes the existence of clearly defined goals and/or effects with a rationale linking the program to the goals and/or effects. These preconditions should be met through program planning and management and involve a collaborative effort between researchers and program staff. Unless these preconditions have been met, the evaluation of program effectiveness and efficiency is not warranted.

Even if the purpose of the investigation and the preconditions for conducting an experimental design exist, there are formidable obstacles in implementing such an approach for the evaluation of human service programs. Ethical arguments concerning the denial of service have been advanced in opposition to the development of experimental and control groups. Such arguments assume that the service being evaluated is highly beneficial to potential clients and that to deny it to some people would be cruel. However, considering the evidence on the outcomes of human service programs, this argument is not terribly convincing. Rigorously conducted evaluation studies have revealed that many programs do not produce major changes. In this light, there would seem to be some merit in denying or delaying the provision to some people of a service which is of questionable value in order to ultimately improve the program. This issue can also be dealt with in another manner. Rather than to deny service entirely, the experimental program can be compared with an alternative approach administered to a control group.

In addition to difficulties posed by ethical arguments, administrative contraints may prevent the establishment of control groups, by the use of random assignment procedures. Such constraints include geographical considerations, the nature of the service, or the characteristics of the client. Instituting random assignment procedures often necessitates major changes in the delegation of cases to practitioners. Such changes can create havoc in implementing the program (for example, by having probation officers cover a very wide geographical area). Alternative methods of developing control groups are available. The most common alternative is to establish a control group through matching procedures as this involves the selection of cases which are comparable on variables which seem to have some relationship to the outcome.

Monitoring the program and the research. Once the research design has been developed and plans for implementing the research as part of the everyday routine of the agency have been arranged, the task of monitoring the project becomes a primary concern. It is not sufficient to initiate a research project and assume that the agreed upon program procedures and data collection arrangements will be closely followed throughout the life of the project. Rather, carefully conducted evaluation research demands that close attention be devoted to determining the extent to which the program as well as the research procedures are in fact carried out in accordance with the originally stated plans.

A major reason for monitoring the evaluation project is the common conflict which often develops between the service goals of the program, which requires relative freedom to operate, and the demands of research for control. The crucial question here is whether research can be done in settings where a prime concern is the care and treatment of people and where the control of all factors influencing the results may be impractical. In a controlled experimental design, for example, it is usually necessary for the researcher to act like a snarling watchdog ready to oppose any alteration in program and procedure for fear that it might contaminate the agreed upon procedures and render the evaluation useless. On the other hand, some writers view the relationship between research and program development as dynamic and reciprocal (Suchman, 1970). In this view, feeding back information from the evaluation to the program in order to affect both the objectives and procedures is held to be paramount. The extent to which there are controls on the program's operation and feedback of research findings are largely dependent on the purpose of the evaluative study. If information is needed on the ultimate worth of program ideas as a basis for continuation or termination of a particular program, then a controlled situation would be insisted upon. And there would only be deliberate manipulation of program variables which have been predetermined for their contribution to the overall experiment. On the other hand, if evaluative research is viewed primarily as an ongoing means for modifying programs, then feedback of information can be provided to change the program.

Utilization of findings. The ultimate payoff of conducting evaluation research is the extent to which the research findings are incorporated into program policies and procedures for the more effective and efficient delivery of services. The degree to which such an aim is accomplished will be largely a function of the extent to which relevant program staff are aware of, involved in, and committed to the research. This leads to the major thesis: Evaluation research should be viewed as a sociopolitical process which involves applying research methods to an organizational context. It re-

quires a partnership between research specialists and those directly involved in the delivery of program services. Such a partnership should, ideally, be initiated and formalized during the initial planning and negotiating stages and maintained through the conduct of the research to the assessment of the information obtained and the discussion of the implications of the findings for needed modifications in the program. This is not meant to underemphasize the political and social factors extraneous to the research which will exert a major influence on the manner and the extent to which the findings will be used. Nevertheless, a high degree of involvement by the administrative decision-makers in the evaluation process should at least minimally help to ensure the relevance and use of the information obtained for the central issues confronting the organization.

Conclusion

This paper has identified and discussed the major components of the evaluation research process. Particular emphasis has been placed on the linkages between each of the stages in the research and the sociopolitical aspects of planning and conducting evaluation research of human service programs. The manner and extent to which relevant parties—practitioners, administrators, and representatives of funding organizations—are actively involved in the research process will, in large part, determine the quality of the information obtained as well as its relevance and utility for improving the human services.

Selected annotated bibliography

Bloom, Martin, and Block, Stephen R. "Evaluating One's Own Effectiveness and Efficiency," *Social Work* 22 (March 1977), pp. 130–136.
This article illustrates the use of the single case design which might be used by individual social workers to evaluate work with each client.

Giordano, Peggy C. "The Clients' Perspective in Agency Evaluation," *Social Work* 22:1 (January 1977), pp. 34–41.
This article emphasizes the importance of the clients' perspective in gauging agency effectiveness and discusses the problems involved in obtaining such judgments.

Haselkorn, Florence. "Accountability in Clinical Practice," *Social Casework* 59:6 (June 1978), pp. 330–337.

This article is a very interesting one in that it attempts to distinguish between accountability and evaluation. It should provide for some interesting class discussion.

Kiresuk, Thomas J., and Sherman, R. E. "Goal Attainment Scaling: A General Method for Evaluating Comprehensive Community Mental Health Programs," *Community Mental Health Journal* 4:6 (1968), pp. 443–453.

Kiresuk and Sherman describe the development, use, and scoring of Goal Attainment Scaling.

Mager, Robert F. *Goal Analysis.* Belmont, Calif.: Fearon, 1972.

This is a practical step-by-step guide for reducing abstract statements of objectives to observable, measurable goals.

Patton, Michael Quinn. *Utilization-Focused Evaluation.* Beverly Hills: Sage Publications, 1978.

This is both a practical and theoretical text that introduces a process for conducting evaluations which will be useful to decision-makers.

Program Evaluation Project. "Four Ways to Goal Attainment," *Evaluation,* Special Monograph #1, 1973. Minneapolis: Program Evaluation Project, 1973.

This special issue of *Evaluation* presents and compares four methods of assessing goal attainment. The methods are Concrete Goal Setting (CGS) by Theodore Bonstedt, Goal-Oriented Automated Progress note (GAP) by Richard H. Ellis and Nancy Wilson, Goal Attainment Scaling (GAS) by Thomas J. Kiresuk, and Patient Progress Record (PPR) by Gilbert Honigfeld and Donald F. Klein.

Rutman, Leonard. *Evaluation Research Methods: A Basic Guide.* Beverly Hills: Sage Publications, 1977.

This text is an overview of evaluation research with attention to the sociopolitical context in which it occurs. Materials on planning evaluations, assessment of evaluability, formative research, measurement problems, research design and randomization, information systems, cost/benefit studies, and innovation and dissemination of experimentation are included.

Suchman, Edward A. *Evaluative Research.* New York: Russell Sage Foundation, 1967.

Suchman's book is an introduction to evaluative research. It discusses types of evaluation, the conduct of evaluation studies, evaluative design, measurements issues, and the relationship between evaluation and program administration.

CHAPTER 13

The ending phase:
Referral, transfer, and termination

This chapter will deal with three endings of the client-worker relationship: referral, transfer, and termination. So often, we are deeply concerned about clients only as long as we are involved in the interaction, but when we are no longer the primary professional(s) we may leave the clients to find their own way(s). It should be recognized that how a client-worker relationship ends may be crucial to what clients take with them in terms of gains. In situations involving nonvoluntary adolescent clients, one cannot help but be struck at the way, in which we make ourselves indispensable at the beginning of our contacts with clients; and when clients feel they need workers most, which is always at the time of termination or transfer, we are often so preoccupied with our own new beginnings either with other clients or with a new setting that we are unavailable to the client. Referral, transfer, and termination have three factors in common: (1) some kind of problem identification has brought the worker and the client together for a greater or a lesser period of time; (2) the client is being sent on to a new phase, a new experience, another source of help, leaving the worker behind or being left behind by the worker; and (3) more is involved than simply saying good-bye and wishing everyone well. However, as each of the three tasks is different, they will be discussed separately in this chapter. We will begin with referral.

REFERRAL

Referral is a process that comes into play whenever a client or a service instigator requests our involvement in a situation that falls outside the parameters of the agency's defined services or whenever workers define a problem as beyond their expertise or their agency's parameters of service. In its simplest terms, referral means that, rather than explore the situation themselves, they suggest that someone who has come to them for help should go to another source. Since the request for help has been defined as falling outside the agency's service responsibilities, it is often tempting to see their responsibility as ending when we state this fact to the person who requested our involvement. This is perhaps the end of their responsibility as an agent of a particular bureaucracy. But it is not the end of the professional responsibility. Professional commitment requires workers to assume responsibility not only for judgments and actions but for the results of judgments and actions. If workers hold themselves out as persons concerned with the struggles of others, with problems of coping, then they must be concerned not only with offering adequate service in connection with those problems that fall within the defined "turf," but also with offering the same skilled help to enable persons to reach the proper source of help. The first step in developing skills in referral is to know what it means to an individual to ask for help either for oneself or for others. (The subject of asking for help was discussed in Chapter 8.) That knowledge is crucial in considering referral.

As a way of considering referrals, let's examine the case example discussed in Chapter 8 of "The House on Sixth Street." The reader will remember that Mrs. Smith came to the neighborhood center to request help with her housing situation. Fortunately, she came to an agency which could offer help not only to her but to all the tenants who shared her problem. Thus, Mrs. Smith's original request came within the agency's parameters of service, and in the process of exploring her request the practitioner was able to redefine the problem so that it became a community organization problem. This resulted in more effective action than would have been taken if the worker had defined the problem as only Mrs. Smith's. But suppose that Mrs. Smith had turned to her Aid to Families with Dependent Children (AFDC) worker (as the only worker she knew) to talk about her problem, and suppose that the worker had pointed out to her that the welfare board already had knowledge of the situation and had reduced the rent it was paying the landlord and that that was all it could do. What would have happened? Or suppose that Mrs. Smith had felt that her AFDC worker really cared very little about her troubles and that she had then gone to a family agency she had heard about, and that the worker there had pointed out that the agency could not offer help in a situation that was primarily between her, the welfare board, and the landlord. Is it not conceivable that Mrs. Smith would decide that there was no help for a person in her situation and that all the tenants would have gone on living in the same situation?

Now suppose instead that the female worker at the private agency had told Mrs. Smith that she could not help with the problem but that she would help find someone who could. Three days later the private agency worker reaches the welfare worker who says she has done all she can and she does not know what else can be done. Two days later the worker at the private agency finds out about the service center. The first of the next week, she calls Mrs. Smith and tells her about the center, urging her to go there. By now Mrs. Smith and her children have endured another uncomfortable week, two social workers have said they cannot help, but she has been told that another worker might. How likely is it that Mrs. Smith will again bundle her four children up and trudge out to seek help at this new place?

But suppose that the female family worker tells Mrs. Smith that she cannot help directly, but that this does seem to be a very difficult situation for her and her children so she would like to find out who could help. The family worker calls the welfare worker while Mrs. Smith is in the office and learns that the welfare worker cannot help. She asks the welfare worker whether she knows where such help can be sought. She looks up the agencies listed in the agency directory that most communities publish. While Mrs. Smith is still in her office, she finds out about the service center and calls to see whether it can help and what Mrs. Smith needs to do to get its help. She asks Mrs. Smith whether and when she wants to go there and arranges an interview time with a worker whose name she gives Mrs. Smith. She shares this information with Mrs. Smith (often writing down names and addresses is helpful), being sure Mrs. Smith understands how to get in touch with the center worker and what the center worker will need to know about her situation. She expresses her interest in seeing that Mrs. Smith gets some help and her understanding that it is hard to be shuffled around from agency to agency before finding anyone who will really listen. She expresses concern that Mrs. Smith get help and urges Mrs. Smith to get in touch with her again if this particular plan does not work out. In this case Mrs. Smith will probably get to the service center. She will also approach the new worker and the demand that she repeat her story once again with some confidence in herself and her judgment in seeking help. Because of the experience she had with the family worker she will expect to be met by a center worker who is concerned. Her quest for help has been met in a way that has furthered her confidence in her capacity to manage her life in a manner more satisfying for her.

Driving in a strange city, thoroughly lost, but hoping to work the problem out rather than stop and ask someone is a common experience. What happens if you stop and ask someone who reels off complicated, generalized and vague directions? When you ask for an estimate on how far away the destination is, the person says "quite a ways" and looks "put off" by the question. How do you feel? Do you decide that you were better off trying it on your own? You have taken the trouble to ask, but are no further ahead now than before. In fact, you may be worse off because you have now wasted another half hour and feel more confused and less adequate than before.

This example illustrates the problems and principles in referrals. First, it is necessary to recognize that asking for help for yourself or others is not a simple process. Second, it is necessary to understand that when you decide to talk the situation over with someone else, the time of that decision and the move to implement it is a vulnerable period. It has taken something to get to this point. This short, vulnerable period, in which the client is open to consideration of the work to be done, is all too often followed by despair if something positive and forward moving is not offered.[1] Most people wait until long after they have become aware of a problem before they seek help. They try to solve the problem alone until they become convinced of their inability to do so, so that their sense of capacity to cope has already had enough blows without the worker's telling them that they have again made a mistake by approaching the wrong resource.

The more threatening a problem is to the people asking help, and the more disorganized and confused they are, the less able they are to follow through on complicated directions or to gather up the strength to retell their problem. Anyone who has experienced certain difficulties and been sent to several places before they reached the person who could help (even if the problem was only getting approval to drop one course and add another) can well understand the feeings of frustration or discouragement or anger that come with the demand

---

[1] This principle is the basis of crisis theory and other emergency services which the reader may want to explore but which cannot be developed here.

that one explain the situation over and over again only to be referred somewhere else each time. Maybe the problem was finally straightened out to one's satisfaction, but at the cost of considerable time and effort. What would it have meant to have had someone pick up the telephone and find out the right place to go and what to do?,

Social agencies and the help they offer are complex businesses. It is a testimony to most people's competence that they are able to approach the appropriate agency most of the time. Rather than expect all clients to be able to handle the original request appropriately, workers should be surprised that any do so. The worker should treat client confusion and uncertainty as a natural effect of the confusing pattern in which we seem to work.

A generalized goal for practice should be that, if workers cannot offer active help toward solving a problem, they at least leave clients as well prepared to deal with it as they were when workers met them. Workers should recognize that by holding themselves out as helping persons and by being in a position that invites or allows the client to approach the worker, they have engaged in an interaction with them that places a responsibility upon the worker that is not to be discharged by a simple statement that they have come to the wrong place.

TRANSFER

Transfer is the process by which the client is referred to another worker, usually in the same agency, after the initial worker has been working with the client on the problem. Although the transfer is sometimes made because workers find that they have difficulty in working with the problem or the client, usually it occurs because the initial worker is leaving the agency to take a job elsewhere.

In transfer three entities are involved: the present worker, the client, and the new worker. When clients learn that practitioners are soon to leave the agency, or that for any other reason the workers cannot continue with them, they may feel deserted and resent an ending that is imposed prematurely on them. They may feel that, in leaving, the worker is breaking the contract in which they were offered service and may resent what appears to be the worker's irresponsibility and lack of concern. Many factors may interact to determine the client's reaction. The most important will be the type of client system, the problem, and the type of relationship developed between the worker and the client. For the client whose problem involves internal system changes and who has had life experiences involving painful separations, the worker's departure may evoke all the accumulated pain of the other separations. A task-centered adult group working toward change in the community may also feel a sense of betrayal and desertion but may be more actively concerned about the competence of the new worker who will be involved with them in their work. Unexpected endings are a part of life, and workers who have made a decision that forces an ending to their association with clients must be aware of their own feelings, workers who will replace them, and the possible reactions of clients if the experience is to be as positive as possible for the clients.

Workers may have difficulty with their own feelings. They may feel that they are indeed betraying the client and violating the contract. They may feel that no other workers can really take their place with their clients and may subtly impart this judgment to the clients in ways that increase the clients' feelings of uncertainty. Leaving the agency can evoke painful feelings of separation in the worker. Workers may also be anxious about the demands of their new jobs, or so deeply absorbed in these new demands that they do not give the problems of transfer their full attention. Or all these feelings may churn within them in some complex, interrelated struggle.

The transfer may also pose some problems for new workers. They may wonder whether they can offer as effective help as did the first worker and may meet clients with a kind of defensiveness and a determination to prove themselves rather than continue the work together. They may, therefore, move out too rapidly with new ideas that clients are not ready for. Clients may be angry and hurt about the transfer and because of this, as well as their feelings of loyalty and trust for the first worker, it is often necessary for them to mark some time and do some testing before they are willing to move on. It is to be expected that certain clients will lose much of their trust in the worker and be afraid to risk establishing a new relationship with another person who may also leave. The new worker needs to recognize all these things, especially the right of the clients to have their feelings and take the time they need to deal with them.

A transfer is less hurtful and destructive to the work being done when there is time for both client and worker to deal with it, and for the new worker to get involved in an orderly manner. When a transfer is necessitated by the first worker's leaving the agency, clients often regard it as a desertion. They may feel that if they were important to the worker or, worse yet, if they were a good and satisfying client, the worker would stay with them. Clients need to be told as soon as possible about the worker's leaving, and they need to participate with the worker in the planning for transfer to another worker or, possibly, to terminate their contact with the agency. The clients' feelings about the change should be recognized by the worker. The worker can invite the client to discuss these feelings. At times, and particularly in group situations, clients can be encouraged to role play the transfer, from their concern about the first worker's departure through their beginning with a new worker. They can discuss or role play their fantasies about the new worker.

Clients need opportunities to meet with the new worker. The first time the new worker may just stop in for a minute to be introduced by the old worker and say hello. After the new worker leaves, the old worker may discuss with clients what their feelings and thoughts are about the new worker from just this introduction.

The second time, if the client system is a group, the new worker may attend a meeting as an observer, or, if the client system is an individual or a family, may sit in on an interview. The old worker remains "in charge," so to speak, and the new worker is just there to get acquainted. At the third encounter the two workers operate as a team, with the new worker gradually assuming the primary professional role. At this encounter the two workers can talk together, trying to assess where they are and how the new worker understands and evaluates the contract, with the client as observer. This helps the client to understand very clearly what the new worker is told and what the new worker's commitment is. There might be a fourth, formal session at which the new worker is in charge, but there should be a time at the end of the session for the client and the old worker to meet together (in the absence of the new worker) for good-byes and for assessment—both of what has been accomplished by the first worker and of the client's expectations of the second.

If the transfer is being brought about because the client feels that there is a problem between the client and the first worker, the situation is different in that it is the client that is leaving the worker. In this situation, the worker needs to carefully examine the worker's own feelings and to be sure that the client is left totally free to move on to another relationship.

TERMINATION

Social work intervention is always time-centered. At its best, it is directed toward the realization of goals that are specific enough for progress to be measured in relation to them. In *Social Work with Groups* Helen Northen (1969, p. 222) makes a statement about termination with groups that is applicable to all sizes and types of systems:

> The purposeful nature of social work implies that from time to time it is necessary to assess the desirability of continuing service to the members. The judgment may be that there has been progress toward the achievement of goals and there is potential for further improvement, in which case the service should be continued. Another decision may be that little, if any, progress has been made; if this is combined with little potential for changing the situation, the service should be discontinued. Still another evaluation may be that progress toward the achievement of goals has been sufficient, and the service should be terminated. Social workers have undoubtedly anticipated termination from the beginning of their work with the group and have clarified with the members its possible duration, so that the goals and means toward their achievement have been related to the plans for both individuals and the group. Nevertheless there comes a time when the worker and the members must face the fact of separation from each other and often, also, the end of the group itself.

Evaluation, the appraisal of the progress that worker and client system as a working partnership have achieved, is an ongoing process. The ultimate test of the effectiveness of social work practice is the extent to which positive movement toward the goals set has been accomplished. Thus the goals as initially developed between client and worker, as periodically evaluated, and as modified periodically by joint agreement become the criteria for evaluating progress. Whenever termination is being considered, a thorough review and evaluation of what has or has not been accomplished and of the processes by which these gains were made or failed to be made, is imperative. In their own, unilateral evaluation, workers may begin to wonder whether the goals are in sight, and they may be the ones to introduce the matter of termination. Or, clients may indicate that they are beginning to believe that they are ready to move on to a new experience and leave the worker behind. This is often communicated to the worker by the client's behavior rather than by verbal discussion. Clients begin to miss appointments or indicate with pride that they took some unilateral action toward the goal. These are ways of saying that they can "go it alone."

In talking about the indications for termination in the group, Helen Northen (1969, p. 225) says much the same thing:

As the group moves toward readiness for termination, there are clues to guide practitioners in their activities with the group. The goals that members have for themselves and each other have been partially achieved, at least, although movement in the group may have been faster for some than for others. Members come to talk about some of the changes that have taken place in them and in the group. Attendance becomes irregular unless the worker makes special efforts to motivate members to continue until the final meeting. . . . The structure tends to become more flexible; for example, by giving up official roles within the membership or by changes in time, place, and frequency of meetings. . . . Cohesiveness weakens as the members find satisfactions and new relationships outside the group.

The need for termination, whether introduced by the client or the worker, should be discussed well in advance of the termination date to allow sufficient time for this aspect of worker and client experience with each other to be as productive as other parts of work together. To quote Helen Northen (1969, p. 228) once again:

The time span between the initial information about termination and the final meeting of the group will vary with many factors, including the group's purpose, the length of time the group has been together, the problems and progress of the members, their anticipated reactions to termination, and the press of the environment on them.

These elements should be considered in working with individuals or families. In general the tasks of termination are (1) working out the conflict for both worker and client between the acknowledgment of improvement and goal achievement and the movement away from help; (2) working out the fear of loss of the relationship and of the support of a concerned person; (3) examining the experience and recognizing the progress made; (4) considering how this experience can be transferred to other problems as they come along; (5) examining what is involved in stabilizing the gains made; and (6) clarifying the worker's continuing position.

Termination of a relationship has great meaning, and a great investment of emotions and feelings of one person with another entails grief at such a loss. This grief may involve the following typical reactions: (1) the denial of termination (clients refuse to accept the notion of termination and behave as though it were not going to happen); (2) a return to patterns of earlier behavior or a reintroduction as problems of situations and tasks that have been taken care of long ago; (3) explosive behavior in which the client says that the worker was wrong when the worker thought that the client could go it alone; or (4) a precipitate break in the relationship by the client as though to say that the client will leave the worker before the worker leaves the client.

For social workers, termination stirs up emotions about both their professional activities and their feeling for their clients. They will undoubtedly feel pleased about the progress which has been made, but, like the client, will feel a sense of loss and grief in the parting. They may find that termination stirs up mixed feelings about the quality of their work: guilt about not having been able to do better; fear of the client's efforts to go ahead independently.

In the final disengagement, workers make it clear that the door is open, that they will be available for future problem-solving if this falls within their agency's services, and if it does not, that they will help find an agency that is appropriate. They assure their clients of their continued interest in them and of their belief in their ability to move on to other goals and other efforts. It is often well to mark the last contact by some symbol. With a family, group, or organization a party can be helpful. In some instances, a formal letter of accomplishment of goals may be very meaningful.

RECAPITULATION

This chapter's discussion has focused on three special tasks in social work—referral, transfer, and termination. These are situations in which workers terminate their relationship with clients. In referral the client's request is considered to be beyond the parameters of the agency's services and the client is referred to others before any significant work on the problem is done. In transfer and termination, the client and the worker have established a relationship over a period of time. The authors have urged that these three special tasks are important aspects of the social work process and that workers should see them as involving significant skills.

A LOOK FORWARD

In this chapter the concept of the limits of the agency's services has been introduced. In the next the agency structure itself will be discussed, with emphasis on its bearing on the worker's functioning. With the conclusion of this chapter we have begun to move toward a termination of the author-reader relationship.

Reading

Termination of psychotherapy: Some salient issues*

Hilliard L. Levinson

This article focuses on some salient issues and problems that arise within the patient, therapist, and treatment relationship during the ending period of psychotherapy. While the subject is not new to psychotherapists, it is surprising to find that it is sparsely covered in the professional literature, irrespective of the wide-ranging theoretical schools of psychotherapy and the various mental health disciplines.

Although much attention is given to the necessity for, and the methods of, structuring the opening phase of treatment, relatively little is devoted either to the process of the ending period or to the problems arising at this time. More surprising, minimal consideration is given in the literature to the nature of the patient-therapist relationship during termination; to the therapist's emotional reaction in ending the treatment; and to the therapist's experience of loss in separating from the patient with whom there was a prolonged and intimate experience

* Reprinted by permission of Family Service Association of America, publisher, from *Social Casework* 58:8 (October 1977), pp. 480–489.

(Firestein, 1974; Solnit, 1969; Robbins, 1975). Furthermore, the deficiency in the literature is paralleled by the lack of attention that termination issues receive in agency settings in case conferences, ongoing inservice training programs, and supervision. It is as if many mental health professionals have little exposure to, or awareness of, the importance of this phase of treatment either in their own professional training or in their own experience of it in a psychotherapeutic relationship (Fox, Nelson, and Bolman, 1969). Even among practitioners who have experience related to termination, it appears that they keep themselves from being affected by the emotional reactions of either the patient or themselves at the ending period of therapy. This distancing is, of course, in sharp contrast to a very genuine clinical need to attend closely to the issues aroused at this time.

While the initiation of psychotherapy presupposes its eventual dissolution, the termination period is most likely to stimulate substantial problems for therapist and patient alike, because it is at this time that the meaning, in affective terms, of the course of therapy and the nature of the therapist-patient relationship is most keenly experienced by both (Schiff, 1962).

The manner in which the therapeutic relationship is brought to a close is crucial to the outcome of the treatment: it has a major influence on the degree to which the gains that occurred are maintained and further growth promoted following treatment. Failure to adequately explore and work out these feelings during the ending period may result in a weakening or undoing of the completed therapeutic work, giving rise to a number of complications and difficulties, both during the terminating phase and after the patient has ended treatment.

It is the purpose of this article to review some of the crucial issues that arise during the ending period of psychotherapy so that they may be more clearly recognized, understood, and effectively managed.

Characteristics of the ending period of treatment

The terminating period of psychotherapy can be viewed as a final recapitulation of the beginning stage of treatment. It is analogous to a coda found in a musical form. As such, it should be a well-crafted independent passage introduced toward the end in order to bring the composition to a satisfactory close. It serves as a summation of the themes and motifs that preceded it. Thus, the ending period of treatment should usher in a discussion of termination that can serve as an evocator of the repetition of earlier topics and issues.

Like a musical form, treatment, with some exceptions, may be divided into three periods; a clearly demarcated beginning, a distinct middle, and an undeniable finale. In the beginning, a relationship is formed in which efforts are made to attach the patient to the person of the therapist; at this stage it resembles the early symbiotic and anaclitic union between a child and a parent. The ongoing relationship will be monitored, mutually influenced, and shaped by the nature of both participants' very early interactions. The middle stage brings ambivalence marked by an awareness of individual differences in styles and capacities, and the growth of human struggles as they occur both in transactions with other persons and in the intrapersonal relationship one has with oneself. At times, this middle stage of treatment may be quiet and playful while at other times strident and conflictual. Regardless, it is a time in which it is crucial that the patient and therapist steadfastly maintain themselves and their work together through the treatment alliance. The ending period ushers in an unavoidable awareness of the reality that the treatment and the treatment relationship must now be terminated. Themes of termination must now be worked out in a multitude of ways, sometimes in relation to the real loss of the therapist and the therapeutic relationship, and sometimes in connection with the memories of earlier losses of other relationships. Ultimately, termination must be considered in connection with the loss of one's old self. Certainly, themes of mourning and grief will play an important part in this section of treatment. How the finale will be crafted and in what manner the themes will be resolved will depend on a number of factors.

Variable factors in response to termination

There are a variety of important elements that can influence the reaction of the patient to termination, and among them are the following:

1. The greater the degree of involvement of the patient in the treatment and emotionally with the therapist, the more intense will be the nature of the reactions to termination (Dewald, 1971, p. 274). Conversely, the more patients have avoided or minimized their emotional investment in the therapy and therapist, the less aware of and intense will be their reactions to termination (p. 276).

2. Reactions to termination will vary with the degree of success and satisfaction with the treatment.

3. The greater the degree of transference involvement and wished-for gratification or fulfillment of childlike wishes, the more intense will be the nature of the patient's reaction to termination. Toward the ending period, these patients may have a peak in negative critical reactions to the therapist inasmuch as the approaching termination dashes their hopes for being considered the special one for whom real and fantasied favors will come from the therapist.

4. Patients who have sustained earlier losses of significant persons in their lives will reexperience, as termination approaches, the arousal of affects and conflicts from those earlier periods. The character of the patient's reaction to termination can be considered representative of those emotional reactions and behavior patterns that were developed earlier, in response to previous separations from significant others.

5. Whether patients have experienced key losses or not, their reactions to termination will be influenced by the level at which they have achieved mastery of the early separation-individuation crisis and the manner in which they have come to deal with the polarized conflicts of dependence and independence, passivity and activity, trust and mistrust, love and hate. The characterological style in which patients have coped throughout their lives with these conflicts and their attendant modes of defense will suggest their possible reactions to real loss and their capacity to tolerate and manage their responses to the loss of the therapist and the therapy. When, in the process of growing up, the patient has not mastered separation and loss from key people at appropriate developmental levels, this failure can serve as a foundation of significant concern and anxiety. Thus, terminations can become an especially difficult issue for such patients.

6. The patient's reaction to termination may be more intense and complicated by issues related to the termination of the treatment, because of the therapist's departure from private practice or from an agency setting. The latter is often seen in settings in which there are major changes in agency functioning, or a large portion of the therapists are trainees whose educational assignments and attendant treatment responsibilities frequently shift. In such instances, termination is more related to the needs of the therapist-trainee and the administrative structure of the agency than to the needs of the patient or the stage of progress in therapy. It is the therapist who leaves the patient, frequently before the natural course of treatment has been completed. In these occurrences, the issue of termination can be viewed as a clear rejection or narcissistic injury to the self-esteem of the patient. Thus, the timing and careful planning of the termination can be of great importance in allevi-

ating difficulties and allowing for effective working through.

7. Termination may occur at either difficult or propitious moments in the patient's life. Thus, the state of the patient's life and life situation can influence, for better or worse, the patient's reaction to termination.

8. Whether the termination is individually or institutionally determined, the nature of the patients' responses will be affected by the knowledge, skill, experience, and willingness of the therapist to remain sensitively observant, empathic, and skillfully responsive to patients and their security operations. Because a patient can respond both to the prospect and the eventuality of termination in a multitude of ways, it is important that the therapist respond to these manifestations and help the patient deal with issues related to the tasks of separation and growth. During the ending stage, it is essential that therapists not allow themselves to be manipulated or deceived into repetitive delays of the termination date. Therapists need to be aware that while the patient's responses may be indicative of internal stress, the patient is also carefully attempting to test out the therapist's judgment, as well as the quality and steadfastness of the working relationship.

In the long view, it remains useful for the therapist to respond to the patient's anxious security operations and oscillations between regression and progression as they are part of both the process of separation from treatment and the developmental process of self-fulfillment. In this manner, patients may be encouraged and comforted in knowing that they can face life as it is, take risks, deal with painful struggles, and come to mourn losses as they occur, in addition to enjoying their capacity to survive and to get on with their lives. Ultimately, it is important for patients to come to recognize that they are alone; that despite their wishes to the contrary, no one can do for them what they must do for themselves. In the words of an American spiritual [Lonesome Valley], "You got to walk that lonesome valley, you got to walk it by yourself, there ain't no one can do it for you, you got to walk it by yourself."

The experience of loss

The termination of treatment entails a separation, a loss of a real relationship that has developed over a period of time. Moreover, it is a relationship that has unique characteristics seldom experienced in one's social contacts.

Under ideal conditions, patients experience in the therapist a person who listens to them, who takes them seriously, who treats them with respect, who tries to understand them, who extends liking, and who sustains relatedness with the patient even when they express a variety of rebellious, resistive, suspicious, self-defeating, and despairing ways. Therapists convey their own individuality by being individuals who are strong, who have convictions of their own, who have sufficient strength and capacity to be firm, critical, and angry, as well as tender and empathic, but who, nonetheless, remain objective and uninvolved, while steadfastly remaining friendly allies.

The therapist serves as a teacher and a guide who stimulates the patients' curiosity and understanding, so that they may achieve some perspective about themselves and the reality in which they live. Within the therapeutic relationship patients have an opportunity to gain freedom and permission to experience themselves, their affects, sensations, thoughts and behaviors; to experiment and grow; to live up to their own best potential; and to have the courage to be.

For therapists, too, the process of termination can reawaken their own feelings of separation and loss. For them, the loss of the patient and the ending of the therapeutic relationship can reverberate conflicts and fears. It can also afford them ". . . a place and time in which some of life's truest and most significant and poignant moments occurred" (Yalom, 1970, p. 280). It can stimulate them to learn and to grow. Furthermore, during the treatment the therapist has an opportunity to participate in a creative process in which a new or modified self emerges. This process entails a parting with the old self of the patient and having insufficient time to know the new self. Saying good-bye to the patient by the therapist can be akin to saying good-bye to a part of "self." Thus, in many ways patients can come to serve as useful guides and teachers to therapists, and this parting may bring therapists to a reexamination of who they are and what they experience.

Crucial issues during the ending period

Clinging to the therapy and the therapist. For many patients, the wish to be treated far outweighs the wish to be cured. Such patients express in a variety of ways a wish to perpetuate therapy endlessly. Some fear that without the therapist they will be unable to deal with themselves or their life situation; they seem to wish to remain attached to the therapist, while simply refusing to grow. They repeatedly postpone engaging in activity or completing some work outside of therapy useful for their growth, thereby forestalling any movement in the direction of change. The basic issue is that these patients are unwilling to separate from any part of their past and avoid and fear doing so. They remain locked into situations and relationships that are unsatisfying and unworkable for them. In clinging to the therapist, patients protect themselves from anxious and angry feelings related to experiences of rejection, abandonment, and separation. Furthermore, maintaining the status quo while binding the patient's anxieties aroused in risking forward independent moves toward maturity prevents the patient from achieving changes within.

Sometimes the patient's resistance to termination is, overtly or covertly, supported by the therapist. In such instances, both participate in a parent and childlike relationship that is repetitively similar to relationships from their own past. Here the drama revolves around instances of the child fearing separation from the parent, and the parent fearing the child's separation. In such transactional maneuvers, the tentative moves toward separation, individuation, and independence become frightening to patient and therapist alike (Fleming and Benedek 1966, p. 174). If the therapist sees separation and termination not as a matter of growth but as a traumatic event for the patient, then the therapist will act in a variety of ways to postpone the eventual day of termination. Subsequently, this delay will retard the patient's progress toward finding new solutions to old problems. It will also block constructive growth processes in the patient, thereby depriving the client of the encouragement or expectation of a self-directed attitude. Simply put, patients cannot take steps away from therapists who hold them back from moving on. As Joan Fleming and Therese Benedek (1966, p. 175) succinctly state:

Mourning work and healthy growth are accomplished only when a relationship is given up which is realistically over and when giving it up can be differentiated from a sense of being deprived or rejected. The problem of termination is similar to mourning and psycho-social development in that a current experience should be "metabolized" into a memory and energy freed to be directed toward new objects and new levels of relationships.

One of the ways in which therapists can assist patients in dealing with, and finally dissolving their relationship with, the therapist is by being aware of their own attitudes toward the patient. It is important that they be aware that some of their own attitudes and behaviors can be inimical to the patient's growth and prolong the treatment. The following factors represent a partial list of such attitudes and behaviors.

1. Therapists are motivated by therapeutic ambition to produce a perfect case, or a case that is more perfect than colleagues, or a patient, who after the termination of

treatment will be able to withstand the "slings and arrows of outrageous fortune."

2. Therapists may expect and demand more from patients than either the patient's motivation, capacity, or situation warrants.

3. Therapists may derive gratification from patients and be unwilling to let go of them. This issue may be idiosyncratic and may relate to the life history of the patient, or the patient may have special meaning to therapists. Because of these factors therapists may allow patients to use the treatment as a sanctuary, or they may view the intimacy involved in the treatment process as a compensatory means of making up to patients and themselves for their previous childhood traumas, deprivations, and losses.

4. Therapists may prolong the treatment, because it reflects their own helplessness and sense of limitation as feelings of defeat and inadequacy are aroused within them as the therapy continues.

5. Therapists may prolong patients' treatment in order to shield and protect themselves against hurtful feelings of loss of people with whom they have experienced a great deal and for whom they have come to feel deeply.

6. Therapists may react compensatorily with patients for losses that the therapists are currently experiencing in their own lives.

The clinical problem involved in therapists' clinging to the patient is that in doing so they are holding back the patient. Consequently, patients may either remain forever gratefully dependent upon their therapists, or they may finally break away abruptly in an indignant and protesting mood. In addition, the therapist may finally become weary with the stagnating treatment and find some way to precipitate the termination. Either kind of extended ending can vitiate the beneficial gains made during the course of psychotherapy.

Particularly if the treatment had been meaningful and effective and the therapist's skills have had a positive impact, patients may believe that in terminating they are leaving behind not only an important source of satisfaction, but also a person without whose support they may risk the loss of all that they have gained. It is important, therefore, that the patients be encouraged in the belief that they can take care of themselves and direct their own lives and that they do not have to remain in difficulty in order to maintain contact with the therapist. Generally, such attitudes and comments to this effect are reassuring to patients and do not encourage or give them permission to act in ways that will stimulate problems in order to ensure their return to treatment.

Recurrence of old problems and the repetition of symptoms. As treatment approaches closure, it may be noted that there is, with some degree of regularity, a return of symptoms or difficulties which originally brought the patient into treatment, but which for some time have not been manifest. When prior difficulties do reappear in the terminating period, it is as if the whole difficulty is repeated in compressed and attenuated form in a short period of time (Buxbaum, 1950).

Some patients respond to the initiation of the terminating period (especially if the therapist is departing, or the patient has failed to improve or manage effectively) with serious self-defeating, suicidal, or homicidal behaviors. These borderline forms of behavior can become significantly frightening for both the therapist and the patient. Furthermore, such episodes can introduce further complications into the treatment process by involving other persons or precipitating incarceration in criminal or psychiatric settings.

It is important for therapists to assist patients in working through their feelings and ideas about terminating before therapists either change the termination plan or before they resort to emergency measures, which may both confuse patients and keep them in treatment. The resurrection of old difficulties can easily cause the therapist to believe that the patient has become worse and is in need of further treatment.

Either continued treatment or hospitalization at this time can instill fears in patients and in therapists regarding their professional judgment(s). Such fears may cause both of them (and even the supervisor) to wish that termination had never been considered. These issues are compounded by some patients who manipulate the therapist with critical persecutory remarks regarding the return of symptoms or the worsening of difficulties which they view as the therapist's fault. Sometimes it is simply necessary for the patient to be terminated. To postpone the termination in such a case is to fail to grasp the meaning of the patient's response and can be a serious tactical error in the treatment of the patient. It is certainly important, however, that therapists reevaluate patients and their difficulties at this critical time with a view toward assessing the very serious nature of the problem, and the possible need to continue the treatment.

Introducing new problems. Some patients initiate a discussion of new stresses and problems to work on during the closing sessions and even during the final treatment hour (Lipton, 1961). Patients who have been uncommunicative suddenly begin to talk, while others begin to open up new problems. Still others suddenly begin to entrust to the therapist vital confidential information that they had not previously revealed.

Several motivations may be involved in this behavior as it relates to termination and may include the following: (1) an endless pursuit of self-perfection, (2) a wish to insure the continued maintenance of the therapy relationship rather than face the forthcoming separation, (3) an attempt to appeal to, if not seduce, the therapist's concern and investment in order to persuade the therapist to continue the treatment and stay with the patient, and (4) an attempt to master the fear that if the "real truth" is known about the patient that the client will not be humiliated or abandoned by the therapist. When the patient brings up new problems and stresses, it is important that the therapist not simply dismiss them as seductive maneuvers or termination phenomenon. The

therapist should pay close attention to the reports of new problems and stresses, their frequency, and their seriousness as an indication that the patient is possibly engaging in increased acting out of provocative behavior.

Finding new substitutes and replacements. Some patients respond to the approaching end of treatment with a beginning search for substitute persons to take the place of the therapist. While this endeavor can be seen as growth promoting, it can also be viewed as a means by which the patient wards off the affects arising from the impact of the loss. In such instances patients find new friends and reestablish relationships with old friends in order to replace the therapeutic relationship, and to have someone with whom they can continue to talk over problems. This friendship-seeking activity is also an adaptive means by which patients inform themselves and the therapist that they are adult, mature, social beings. This process may eventuate in the patient falling in love, finding a new spouse, separating or divorcing. In three cases that the author recently supervised, each with a different therapist, each of the adolescents (two females and one male) began a desperate search to find someone to go steady with or to marry immediately after the issue of termination was initiated.

Defensive reactions

Some patients maintain defenses of denial, repression, reaction-formation, and intellectualization to ward off their inner affects, and these patients may react in a variety of ways to the approaching termination of their treatment.

There are patients who will respond with cool, calm composure and insist that they have no reaction. Such patients easily accept the announcement of termination or the forthcoming departure of the therapist and express that they "feel nothing." If anything, they may feel relieved that they no longer have to put up with a variety of expenses and inconveniences connected with coming to the sessions.

Other patients will steadfastly deny or openly devalue and depreciate the therapist and the therapy as having had any influence on their lives. In so denying they also devalue and disown themselves and what they have accomplished. It is in this manner that patients attempt to reassure themselves that they are losing nothing of value. Minimally, they may express disappointment that nothing of significance was accomplished.

There are patients who will exaggerate and exclusively dwell on their difficulties and deficiencies. Although they may have made significant progress, they either fail to see it or deny it. Despite the gratification they derived from the treatment relationship and from the changes that occurred during treatment, they will not openly acknowledge them, for to do so means giving credit to the therapist and to themselves for what was accomplished.

For other patients, it is simply too difficult for them to acknowledge that the therapist has been a useful or effective person with them. Such patients are generally very dependent people who are fearful that if their dependency cravings approached even subsistence levels of satisfaction that they would lose not only their sense of identity, but may also lose their own personal boundaries and become a putty-like substance to be molded by the therapist.

Because of the relatively slow progress of these patients and the continuous barrage of criticisms and devaluations of self and therapist by the patient, therapists may become weary and withdraw emotionally. They may also become rash and critical toward the patient and push interpretations in an attempt to induce curative results faster than is warranted. Or, the therapist may act out in sarcastic guilt-inducing and provocative ways. Under these conditions, the therapist will be unable to empathize with the patient and will be unable to see some of the positive changes that the patient has made. Therapists may then, however, attempt to convince themselves and others that they have done a very creditable job with the patients in order to salvage their own pride and subsequently use this conviction as a rationale for abruptly terminating with the patient. If therapists can master their own irritation with their patients, they will be in a position to observe and interpret both the meaning and value of the patients' maneuvers. Furthermore, they will be able to give credit to patients for the important changes that they themselves have made during the period that they worked together.

The issue of denial and devaluing may be highlighted for the therapist or trainee who is departing from an agency. The situation is especially compounded when the therapist leaves with a significantly negative attitude toward the agency. At termination time the therapists may deny their investment in the patient. They may rationalize the termination in terms of the agency's educational or administrative system, thereby making themselves out to be helpless pawns of the establishment. This rationalization reinforces the patients' denial, supports their sense of helplessness and worthlessness, and inhibits them from expressing hurt and anger. Therapists, because of their own sense of worthlessness and impotence, may deny that they could in any way have been important as professional people to the patient, for if they did so they would have to face their own feelings of worth and feelings of loss of the patient. Simply put, it is as if the therapist under these conditions is saying: "It is better that we should rid ourselves of each other and in a way that is as quick and painless as possible." In the haste to end, the therapist may be prone to ignore the patient's distress or fail to comprehend that what the patient is saying is in any way related to termination. Subsequently, the therapist will fail to deal adequately with the patient's attitudes and feelings during the termination period.

When the patient's overt reaction is one of denial or depreciation, it remains important for the therapist to continue to diagnostically assess the patient's responses. Some of the issues to be considered in such instances are (1) whether the patient is capable of becoming emotionally involved and engaged in a therapeutic alliance, and (2) whether the denial is part of the patient's desperate attempt to keep internal upheaval under control by maintaining protective bulwarks against strange and frightening feelings.

Once therapists have taken time to sensitively observe the patient's reaction, or its absence, then they are in much better positions to assist the patient. Therapists should not allow themselves to be misguided by the lack of overt signs. With patients who deny and devalue, it is important for the therapist to confront them not only with their genuine progress, but also with their depreciating lifestyle. The therapist must make this confrontation with patients if they are ever to develop any insight into their life-sustaining views of themselves and others (Singer, 1970, p. 340). It is only when therapists afford patients this opportunity that they may come to see ending as a time at which fear and pain over separations are recognized as legitimate and healthy reactions.

Acting out behaviors. While progress and change in ongoing therapy may bring to the patient an increased realization of growth, it also brings with it a growing sense of separation from the patients' habitual attitudes and behaviors, from their old selves, and from parental introjections and their associated injunctions. These changes, in addition to the approaching termination of treatment and the treatment relationship may arouse considerable tension, anxiety, depression, and other very intense affects which the patient may attempt to discharge by engaging in a variety of self-defeating behaviors.

Many patients attempt to handle the feelings and thoughts aroused in the ending period of treatment, not by talking about them and working them through to a satisfactory resolution, but by behaviorally displacing them through acting out, either within the treatment situation or by displacing them onto other situations with other persons. Someimes patients may become resistive or explosive. They may come late for their appointments or fail to come. They may suddenly begin reporting to the therapist that other assigned tasks or chores make it impossible for them to keep the closing appointments. Others may become involved in activities and relationships that are destructive for them. Some patients will abruptly run away from treatment or insist on terminating the treatment immediately, thereby rejecting the therapist before the therapist separates from them. This reaction may represent a characterological defense developed in earlier years of doing unto the therapist as was done unto them. In other instances, the patient's wish to terminate swiftly can be related to their correctly sensing the countertransference attitudes of therapists who themselves may not be able to deal with the emotional issues of termination. The author has observed many unfortunate instances in which therapists began to act out in the treatment in a manner not too unlike the patient, as the ending sessions approached.

If therapists primarily interpret patients' feelings, symptoms, and acting out behaviors at termination as their need for more therapy, or the need for more extensive working through, or of the possibility for achieving more perfect results, then therapists will reinforce patients' helplessness and dependency and thus can trap patients into a continuance of the relationship. Patients may then become convinced both of their inability to separate from the therapist and of their incompetence to deal with their own lives. Instead, when patients act out their feelings and impulses, it is particularly important for the therapist in the ending period not to react to this symptom as provocative behavior itself, but to keep a close watch on the dynamics of the behavior. It is useful to utilize the terminating process as a planned period in which the patient and therapist continue to learn about the meaning of the anxiety as it is aroused by the forthcoming separation. This stance will also allow patients to assume further responsibility for the changes they have already effected through both their own efforts and in their working relationship with the therapist.

During the ending period of treatment, it is important that therapists encourage patients' continued curiosity about how their behaviors relate both to the termination and to their characteristic ways of dealing with and ending relationships. Because terminations are part of all human relationships and because throughout one's life there are many occasions to say good-bye to people who have become important in one's life, it only seems germane to bring into being an opportunity for termination feelings to be expressed within the context of the treatment relationship. Such an opportunity should result in expressions from both the patient and the therapist.

Recapitualtion

It is of strategic importance that sufficient time be set aside prior to the impending date of termination so that the patient and therapist can experience their reactions, have an opportunity to work them through, and resolve them in a therapeutically useful way. How long a period of time needs to be set aside depends on the nature of the treatment, its length, and the problems of the patient.

It is usually more useful for the patient and therapist to mutually agree on a termination date. It is, of course, not always possible in clinic and agency settings where termination dates are set by administrative-supervisory groups removed from the actual treatment process. But even in instances in which a particular termination date is not an option, it can be propitious for the therapist and patient to remain cognizant of the time they have remaining and to determine how they can best use themselves within this time span for optimum benefit. Sometimes,

it may be in the best interest of patients even if they do not concur, for therapist to set and maintain a reasonable date for termination, especially when patients and therapists are mired in an endless stalemate, or there is little prospect for much further benefit despite the best intentions of both. In such cases it is best to face the issue that under these conditions it is simply useful to terminate. This decision can give patients an opportunity to see how they function alone. Then, if the patients do wish to return for further treatment, they may be motivated to do more than mark time or to prolong the stalemate indefinitely (Dewald, 1971, p. 274).

In the process of termination it is important that the therapist avoid getting entangled by the patient's attempts to engage in a variety of intimidations, seductive enticements, adorations, and dependent demands. The issue in such instances is not that therapists maintain an invincible defensive system against these encounters, but that they recognize that at times they can become hooked into responding to the patient's defensive maneuvers. It then behooves therapists to find options that allow them to disentangle themselves and to utilize these incidents to facilitate the patients looking at what they are doing with the therapist and other people in their lives.

In agency and clinic settings in which a significant portion of the patients are seen by trainees and relatively inexperienced staff, it is important that the supervisor, who has helped the therapist understand the patient and assisted the therapist in forming and maintaining a treatment alliance with the patient, also be available to assist the therapist in dealing with problems that arise in the ending period. The supervisor should not only encourage therapists to understand the particular nature of this aspect of treatment, but also facilitate therapists in becoming aware of and dealing with their own reactions to the termination with the patient. Additionally, it is important that the supervisor assist therapists in dealing with their own thoughts and feelings as they are aroused in the process of termination with the supervisor and the agency setting. It can be propitious for the supervisor to be available, both emotionally and with time, for frank discussions with therapists about these issues and to stimulate therapists to view their own emotional investment with the patient

and the problems involved. Simply and essentially viewed within an interpersonal model of psychotherapy, it is not surprising to find that at the termination the therapists also have feelings of anxiety, anger, and depression as well as relief, satisfaction, and joy and a longing for other experiences and new beginnings.

Selected annotated bibliography

Fox, Evelyn F., Nelson, Marian A., and Bolman, William M. "The Termination Process: A Neglected Dimension in Social Work, *Social Work* 14:4 (October 1969), pp. 53–63. This is an excellent discussion of the termination process, which the authors would recommend be read in conjunction with this chapter. It gives a detailed series of examples of the interaction between client and worker around the separation process and its meaning.

Gould, Robert Paul. "Students' Experience with the Termination Phase of Individual Treatment," *Smith College Studies in Social Work* 48:3 (June 1978), pp. 235–269. A study of the students' experiences with termination of their work with clients at the end of their field experience, this article focuses on forced termination in that the separation between student and client at the close of the students' placement is forced by circumstances and is not a result of either student or client choice.

Northen, Helen. *Social Work with Groups.* New York: Columbia University Press, 1969. This group work text is a good addition to the reading list of any social work student, but it is listed here because the chapter on termination is superb.

Panter, Ethel. "Ego Building Procedures That Foster Social Functioning," *Social Casework* 47:3 (March 1966), pp. 139–145. Preparation and accompaniment are useful techniques to help clients confront new situations constructively.

CHAPTER 14

The nature of teamwork

This chapter moves from a primary focus on the client system and the change agent system that has been the center of the discussion throughout most of this book to consider other systems that involve the social worker. The focus is now on the principles of constructing and working within a particular type of action system—the professional team. Social workers may, of course, be involved in other types of action systems, but teams are such an important part of their work that the authors feel that a chapter should be devoted to the principles of building and using them.

In working with the client system, a practitioner often becomes aware that members of that system are also being served by other helping institutions of the community. Or it may be that in the role of broker (see Chapter 10) workers become aware of the need to link clients with various services they may require but cannot supply. Or it may be that a service that workers are able to offer, such as the care of children away from their homes, require them to become part of a team in order to supply that service effectively. (In the care of children away from their homes, the social worker will of necessity be involved either with foster parents or with the child-care personnel of an institution.)

In any case, *one* important skill of social work practice is the capacity to operate as a productive member of a "service team." The following concepts and methods, which the authors believe are important to the notion of teamwork, will be discussed in this chapter: the problem of competition, the problem of professional and agency culture, and the problem-solving approach to teamwork and methods of planning and sharing.

In addition to the material in the chapter itself two other articles have been included that should be read as an integral part of this chapter. The two articles deal with two separate types of teamwork. The Hooyman article deals with teamwork within an agency, an institution, or some rather structured system in which certain assignments can be made to certain staff members on the part of an administrator or director and in which there are certain sanctions that can be applied by this same authority as to assigned task performance (see Reading 14–2). In this type of situation, it is possible for the team members to be selected for their expertise, for them to be bound by the common goals of the setting even if they come from different professions, and for them to develop working relationships over a period of time. This is a difficult assignment, and one about which little has been written in the literature.

However, there is another aspect of teamwork that may be even more diffi- cult to understand and about which equally little is written. This involves teams composed of individual social workers representing a wide variety of agencies, who are brought together on an ad hoc basis to operate cooperatively in the interests of a particular client system. The members of this type of team could be considered as making up the action system discussed in Chapter 3 of this text. This chapter and the Kramer article (Reading 12–1) focuses on the dy- namics of the interactions of such teams. These teams differ from those Hooyman discusses in that there is no one sanctioning authority to make assignments or evaluate performance. Instead each member represents and is responsible to a different authority. Time allocated for defining the problem, establishing work- ing relationships, and performing the tasks may be extremely brief and pressures to come up with a quick and simple answer are often great. It is the hope of the authors that the readers can draw an understanding of the team process from both the chapter and the two articles that will be useful as they attempt to construct, or participate in constructing, action systems.

THE PROBLEM OF COMPETITION

When helping persons, groups, or organizations attempt to work together on a common problem shared by a common client system, there are both co- operative and competitive elements in the relationship between the helpers. Cooperative work requires that we disclose our relationship with the client to other helping authorities who are valuable because they bring different knowledge, roles, and functions to the helping process. This means we must be willing to cross barriers of difference. This is not easy. One is constantly amazed at the subtle, and sometimes not so subtle, ways practitioners compete in professional interaction whose stated purpose is cooperation. In most agen- cies and professional associations, there are infinite possibilities of competitive behavior: "I understand the needs of those children better than the foster mother or the teacher"; "My work is more central to the client's welfare than yours"; "My supervisor knows more than your supervisor"; "My agency or my job is where the action really is."

The prevalence of competition in areas in which it is inappropriate, and even destructive to the rational interests of the competing individuals, has been highlighted by experiments in game theory. Game theory is a discipline that seeks to obtain understanding of the problems of human interaction and de- cision-making by studying human exchange from the perspective of strategic games. One game that game theorists use in many different forms is the "non- zero-sum game." Its purpose is to determine under what conditions players will cooperate. In contrast to win-lose games, where there is a winner and a loser, these games are so structured as to make it absurd to play uncooperatively. A player who fails to cooperate has no chance of winning and considerable chance of losing. Nevertheless, researchers in the area of human cooperation are always struck by the frequency with which uncooperative play predom- inates and, even more surprising, by the frequency with which the play be- comes even more competitive as the games go on, and players experience the full negative effects of competition. It is almost as though, once caught in a win-lose situation, the players cannot extricate themselves even though it is demonstrated that it is a destructive situation. And, in social work practice, the most unfortunate aspect of competitive interrelationships of practitioners is that it is the client who is damaged by them. Perhaps social workers are especially vulnerable to competitiveness because it is their status and authority that are involved and the client's welfare that is at stake.

Game theorists have sought to explain this behavior and to isolate variables that will determine how a player will behave. As a result of their efforts, players have been classified into these categories: (1) maximizers, who are interested only in their own payoffs; (2) the rivalists, who are interested only in defeating their partners and are not concerned with the result of the game itself; and (3) the cooperators who are interested in helping both themselves and their partners. There have been studies of non-zero-sum games under conditions in which communication between players was impossible and under conditions in which it was encouraged. Improved communication seemed to increase cooperation only in the case of the cooperators, who were aready interested in bettering the results for both sides. It failed to change the behavior of the maximizers or the rivalists (David, 1970).

It is possible for practitioners to work toward changing a "maximizer" (one interested only in one's own gain) or a "rivalist" (one only interested in "being one up" or in "putting others down") into a "cooperator" (one interested in helping both oneself and one's colleagues to aid the client) by the kind of climates they establish in their professional conferences and associations. For example, the practitioner can actively recognize the importance of each team member in the execution of a task. Child-care staff, who often carry the heaviest burden of the daily stress of living with and loving disturbed and deviant children, often find that their efforts go unrewarded by the professional staff, who may assume that they are the only ones who *really know* what the child is like or what the child needs. In a conference where helping people risk proposing a change in a particular way of working, it becomes critical whether they are rewarded for having attempted something worthwhile or whether their suggestions are seen as something for someone else to "top" or "negate." Rivalists often spend a great deal of time developing verbal ability and skill in the use of professional language. They aften use this ability and skill to make the point that anyone who risks a new suggestion really does not understand the underlying dynamics or the person would not be so naive as to make the proposal. This is a cheap way to be "one-up," if that is what is sought. It demonstrates superior knowledge and sophistication at absolutely no cost as the one who is "put down" seldom challenges the negative predictions for fear that they might prove true, thus further revealing ignorance. Such challenges are especially difficult to contend with when they are presented in elegant professional language and with a knowing air. In such a situation the cost is borne by the person who risks making a proposal and by the client system involved.

THE PROBLEM OF PROFESSIONAL AND AGENCY CULTURE

Effective collaboration requires that helping persons demonstrate respect and trust, expectation and acceptance, in their interactions. The discussion of how respect and trust are demonstrated in the helping relationships also has relevance to professional working relationships. We are all taught the importance of accepting and respecting clients, but we seldom examine what this means when applied to colleagues.

To work effectively together, to have meaningful exchange, one somehow has to respect the position from which the other acts. The worker who is involved in work across professional agency lines must be perceptive and understanding about the point of view of the other organizations and their professional staff. One mark of a profession is its value system. An important part of all professional education and staff development is the attempt to socialize workers to their agency and their profession (see Chapter 4). By this we generally mean working toward the internalization of the values and culture of the profession so that the professional person in whom this process has taken place is constrained to work in certain ways and to take certain positions. This is critically important as protection to the client system, since in the helping process workers must use themselves and their judgment. There is no way another can dictate to the worker exactly how to use oneself to carry out any specific action in any specific situation. Therefore, the only assurance we have that a professional person really can be trusted with professional tasks is that action is on the basis of deeply internalized feelings and judgments that stem from professional values and knowledge. This is the only meaningful protection we have in using a professional's services. However, internalization of professional values and culture as the "right" way is usually an unconscious process. Internalization can cause tremendous problems in interagency collaboration unless we become aware of our values and culture as our beliefs and our climate and learn to recognize that others have their values and their culture.

In addition to undergoing a process of professional socialization and identification, professional social workers (and members of other professions as well) as a rule work within established institutional settings. The machinery through which they do their work sets boundaries to the ways in which, for practical purposes, they define the problems with which they work. Also, within these institutional settings a professional subculture grows up which, like all cultures, has its own value system and accepted ways of operating. Workers who are engaged in collaborative work with persons outside their own agency need to care about their agency and be a part of it and yet to have the capacity to step out of this culture in order to be analytical about it. They need to be understanding of what is going on in their own agency and yet not be trapped within a particular way of approaching problems. They need to be able to recognize that other workers have an equal identification with their agencies and an equal need to protect the functioning of those agencies. The social and helping services in the community, their organization, and ways of working must be understood if we are to utilize their services effectively in the service of our clients. Specialized conceptions of how people in need act, or should act, and how they should be helped, guided, or treated can result in bitter rivalry and conflict.

In speaking of fragmentation in the helping professions, Lawrence Frank (1954, p. 89) writes:

> For example, a family may in its varied contacts receive professional care, advice, and services from a physician, a nurse, a social worker, a nutritionist, a home economist, a probation officer, a lawyer, or judge, a minister, a psychologist, a teacher, a guidance counselor, an industrial relations advisor, a banker, a

group worker, and so on, each of whom may give that family irreconcilable advice and treatment, guidance in how to live, keep health, maintain a home and family, care for and rear children, resolve family discord, and all other aspects of living, especially human relations. The family is expected to resolve these professional conflicts, to reconcile these incongruities, and often mutually contradictory advices into a coherent, consistent pattern of living, a reconciliation which the professionals will not or cannot attain.

In that same article Frank (p. 90) writes:

Thus students in medical school, nursing, social work, law, engineering, business, architecture, public administration and the graduate departments of the social sciences and humanities are being inculcated each with a different conception of human nature, of human conduct, with different beliefs, assumptions, expectations about people, what and how they act and carry on their human relations. All of these students are going out to practice in our communities, with what Veblen once called the "trained incapacity of specialists" unable to communicate or collaborate in their practice or even to recognize what other specialists see and do. Indeed, we often find bitter rivalry and open conflicts arising not entirely from professional competition but from these very different beliefs and expectations, these specialized conceptions of how people act, or should act and how they should be treated, guided and helped when in need.

THE PROBLEM-SOLVING APPROACH TO TEAMWORK

How does one define the concept of teamwork? The American Heritage Dictionary defines it as the "cooperative effort of an organized group to achieve a common goal." The definition seems to refer workers to some of the concepts of problem-solving. It seems to require that team members see the payoff in the honest attempt to identify the most appropriate actions and resources which they can supply to help the client. Thus the purpose of coming together as a team is not to "win" one's way or prove one's "rightness" but to utilize the different capacities brought by the different members of the team in order to expand our knowledge and our range of skills so that we can offer the client the best service in the direction that the client wishes to go. Teamwork requires that we keep this direction clearly before us as the reason we are together. In teamwork it is essential to recognize that we are trying to build interagency organizations and/or professional teams that function effectively in the interest of the client and the desired goals. We need to function in the interests of the job to be done. They need to keep a problem-solving focus so that we can communicate around a defined task. Our own problems of communication and relationship must be worked out so that they can offer the client the most effective help possible.

METHODS OF PLANNING AND SHARING

In working with the client system, workers have come to the conclusion that they cannot offer all the service clients need or that clients may need some help in thinking through what is seen as important factors in service. What do the workers do? The first thing they may want to do is to discuss this with their supervisors in order to check out their thinking, and their knowledge of where they might turn for help. The second important step is to talk with the client about how the client sees this notion. Workers may present this to the client as something that must be done in light of the nature of the problem, the goals sought, and the limits of service (for example, they may tell parents who need to place a child about foster home services and the necessary work with the foster mother), or they may present it as something on which they and the client can come to a decision (for example, workers may say that their understanding and assessment of the situation might be helped if they could discuss the problem with the psychiatrist on the agency staff).

In beginning a working relationship with other helping persons toward offering their clients better service, workers have the choice of asking clients whether they want to join workers in their conferences and planning or whether they assume that workers should carry this role alone. Practitioners working jointly with a client seem to have developed a pattern of meeting together privately in order to pool their observations and knowledge of the problem and to come to some understanding of how to proceed. Sometimes clients are told about this meeting, and sometimes they are not. Sometimes the possibility of such a meeting is used as a threat to clients. It is our position that clients should be actively involved in consideration of the way different professionals can be used to help with their problems and that clients must be told about all professional consultations involving them. We would much prefer to offer our clients the opportunity to come with us to meetings with other professionals and to participate in the deliberations so that they may understand what is involved and that they may speak for themselves.

In any case, before approaching another resource, the worker should talk with the client about that resource, about how it may be used, about what it can offer, about why it is suggested at this point, and about what is involved in getting in touch with it and utilizing it. The client should understand what will need to be shared with the other agency. The street gang that the practitioner has been working with as an unattached worker may be very anxious and concerned when the practitioner suggests that an organized agency could offer them a meeting place and opportunities for recreation. What is the worker going to have to tell the agency about them? Will the agency invite them in if it knows about their behavioral history? Is the agency going to try to run them? The parents of an angry, acting-out daughter will have similar questions if foster home placement is suggested as a temporary measure to help both child and parents think things out. Will the foster parents need to be told that the girl steals? What will the foster parents expect of them? Under what conditions will they be able to see their daughter? To take her home? How can foster parents help when they, her own parents, have failed?

The client and the worker will need to discuss how the new service will be contacted and involved in their affairs. The expectations and requirements of the new service vis-à-vis the client will need to be carefully gone into and understood. What will be shared about the client will need to be considered. It is usually helpful to ask clients what they think the agency will need to know or should be told about them?

What does one share with another agency about one's client? One shares with team members what they need to know in order to work with the client toward solution of the problem in the way the client and you have decided it will need to be worked out. The problem of sharing information with others is not a simple one. When we do this type of sharing, we are inevitably confronted with the question of how the other person will use the information in the interests of the client? Social workers who place children in foster homes often face conflicts about what to tell foster parents about the children placed with them. And what information about the natural parents do they share? We have a need to present our clients (parents and children) in a positive light— yet how much information can be kept secret when foster parents and children live intimately as a family? There is no ideal answer to this question. However, one principle that is essential in approaching it is to keep the client system aware of what is being shared and why.

When more than one worker is involved with the same client system, the best device we have for joint planning and joint monitoring of our work is the case conference. The client should be told about these conferences and their outcomes. As stated earlier, it is very productive to give some thought to the client's involvement in such conferences. The questions one must ask in deciding this are "Will attending the conference help clients in their analysis of the problem?" "Will it help give clients a sense of being in control of their own destiny?" "Or is the conference likely to make them feel overwhelmed by professionals and by the problems they see in the situation?" "Will the decisions being made demand specific behavior of the client, or are they primarily decisions related to agency policies and parameters of service?" "Is it possible for the client to provide meaningful input into the conference?"

In order to work together successfully with a client, the practitioners involved usually need to meet together at least once. There is no substitute for this meeting, and lack of time is not an adequate excuse. Having served as practitioners in large public agencies and carried large case loads, the authors must admit to violations of this principle. However, the fact that something is not done does not negate its importance. We hope that workers will adopt this as a desirable way of working even if they cannot follow through in all cases. Letters and telephone calls are an unsatisfactory substitute for at least one face-to-face planning session around a particular case. In each case conference someone must take the position of leader. The leader takes the responsibility for seeing that all agencies and persons involved in the case are included in the conference, for defining the purpose and focus of the conference, for seeing that everyone present is heard, for clarifying the plans of action and who is to do what and when, and for helping to resolve any conflicts. The conference should result in group acceptance of the part each agency is to play. This agreement is facilitated by recording the conclusions of the conference before its termination. Thus everyone has a chance to correct the common plan, and later everyone receives a copy of it. Each agency then carries the responsibility for following through on the plan (which can be seen as a design for coordination) or for pointing out the necessity of changing it. The leader should also have the responsibility of seeing that the plan is implemented by each agency involved. The leader, in effect, becomes the "captain of the treatment team." Who is to serve in this role and how one is to be selected should be decided before the team actually begins the action phase of the work with the client. The assignment of this responsibility is an allotment of power and authority. The problems involved in accepting such a position must be considered in this light. There should be a clear focus on the purpose of the conference, and drifting away from that focus should be limited. If there are problems of working relationships between the members of the team, these should be approached as problems-to-be-solved and worked through to some acceptable conclusion or they will distort the team's relationship to the client.

RECAPITULATION

In this chapter we have discussed the problems of teamwork in the interests of offering the client system more adequate help in their problem-solving. The aspects of competition that may be involved have been discussed as well as the problem of professional and agency culture. Some of the things that go into establishing a team have also been suggested.

A LOOK FORWARD

We want to emphasize once again the importance of using the two articles at the end of this chapter as a part of any consideration of teamwork. In the next chapter we will be considering the importance to the practitioners of two basic facts: (1) practitioners are usually employed within a bureaucratic system and (2) they are bound as professionals to work within the ethics, value system, and organization of the profession. The issues that stem from the interaction of bureaucracy and profession are critical to the functioning of all social workers.

Reading
14-1 *Dynamics of teamwork in the agency, community, and neighborhood**

Ralph M. Kramer

Perhaps it is because teamwork—whatever it may connote—is often regarded as "everyone's business" that it frequently becomes nobody's business. While continuous and specialized leadership in this task is indispensable, there seems to be a growing recognition that every direct service agency and its administrative components—executive, staff, and board—all have some responsibility in this sometimes nebulous process of achieving teamwork. This implies that no one group in the agency or community has a

monopoly on the responsibility for teamwork, and that no group can consistently evade its own responsibility (Johns and De Marche, 1951, pp. 6–7, 81–83).

Need for interagency teamwork

There are at least four major forces accounting for the greater need for and emphasis on teamwork: (1) the increasing number of public and private agencies; (2) the continuous development of a wide range of community services; (3) the growth of professional specializations; (4) the emerging awareness of the basic unity of all health, welfare, and recreational agencies. As a result, it has been estimated that a typical youth-serving agency would be involved in various cooperative relationships with at least 18 different community agencies as they affect more than a dozen different aspects of its program (Trecker, 1950). Nevertheless, it is not easy to overcome the compartmentalization of much of the services today, so often agency-centered instead of community-centered. For this reason, the argument for really effective teamwork must begin with recognition and acceptance of the following six principles which might constitute a creed:

1. We are all members of a single, inclusive profession of social work united by a common philosophy and objective—to help people attain satisfactory personal and social goals.
2. We are all concerned with the same human needs and problems.
3. We all share a common body of specialized knowledge which is applicable to these problems.
4. We all have a common core of basic professional methods, skills, and processes which are applicable in our dealings with individuals, groups, and communities.
5. We all share certain fundamental concepts such as the right of self-determination of individuals and groups; the importance of a nonjudgmental attitude; the recognition of causal factors in behavior, and the confidential nature of any material exchanged dealing with our work.
6. We are on common ground in that we serve the same community and the people in it, and therefore we can make a more significant contribution if we work together than if we work independently.

So far, we have been concerned with teamwork between social agencies. This is, however, only one half of the picture. If such cooperative relationships are to be fully effective, they must not be restricted to agency executives and staff members only but must involve citizens in the community served. There is, therefore, teamwork between agencies of all sorts, and teamwork between these same agencies and representatives of the community they serve. This is represented structurally, for example, in the differences between a council of social agencies, a community welfare council, and a community or neighborhood coordinating council.

A council of social agencies involves only representatives of the health, welfare, and recreation agencies and covers the area of an entire city. A community welfare council has a broader membership base and embraces all operating agencies, governmental and voluntary, and includes many community groups and citizens' organizations which are interested in adequate services. A community or neighborhood coordinating council is built upon the interest of citizens in a small locality and is concerned with any problem which arouses concern in the neighborhood.

The concept of teamwork

It may be helpful to conceive of teamwork in terms of a continuum with seven stages: (1) acquaintance, (2) exchange of information (communication), (3) consultation, (4) referrals, (5) planning and coordination, (6) concurrent cooperative service, (7) joint operating responsibility.

As can be seen, these cooperative relationships increase in intensity and complexity as we proceed from (1) to (7). Individually and in combination it is suggested these seven relationships are the referents of the term *teamwork* (Johns and De Marche, 1951, pp. 193, 214).

Before examining some of the barriers and blocks to teamwork, we should note some of the prerequisites for any one of these seven levels of cooperative relationships. Certainly it is expecting too much of agencies that do not have any teamwork within their own staff to participate meaningfully with other groups. Consequently, *intra-*

agency teamwork in the form of adequate communication and recognized channels of authority would seem to be a precondition. In addition, it would be necessary for the agency to have a clear conception of its function and relationship to other community groups, and for its staff to be familiar with this. Hopefully, the agency would also have developed a community strategy in writing, noting the groups with whom it needs to maintain cooperative relationships and the types of representation needed. To implement this, there should be a planned method for staff participation in community relations and an organized procedure for reporting back and involving the agency in a responsible manner (Trecker, 1950, pp. 144–149).

Six barriers to interagency teamwork

In view of these rather rigorous requirements, it is not surprising to learn that a recent study of cooperation among agencies found no less than 23 different blocks to effective teamwork (Johns and De Marche, 1951, p. 214). For our purposes, it is possible to reduce them to the following 6 major obstacles: (1) lack of knowledge of other agencies and the community organization process, (2) "agency-mindedness," (3) intra-agency barriers, such as lack of adequate communication between executive and staff, (4) stereotypes of other professionals and agencies, (5) ineffective machinery and structure for community coordination, (6) "too many meetings."

1. *Basic lack of knowledge of function of other agencies and of the principles of community organization.* Perhaps one reason why many staff members are unfamiliar with the precise nature of the services offered by other agencies which impinge on their work is that they are often unacquainted with many of their colleagues. Too often we wait for a crisis or some problem situation to develop before we arrange to meet with other agencies. In addition, some social

workers may be unaware of the role of information and referral services, usually under community chest or welfare council auspices, with the result that agency members fail to obtain needed services—either because the worker did not know about their existence, or because it is just assumed that the other agency is overloaded to the extent that there is no use in referring someone.

2. "*Agency-mindedness.*" Behind this characteristic are a host of rugged individualistic and isolationist survivals from an earlier period of social work. Agency needs are considered more important than community needs. Out of habit, inertia, or tradition, there is a lack of conviction regarding the need for cooperation with other agencies. Every community seems to have one or more such self-centered agencies. It is often expressed in an unwillingness to reach out and take the initiative in starting discussions regarding a commonly felt need or problem. Instead, such agencies fall back on their limitations and "function" rather than trying to see what can be done about a troublesome situation.

Other manifestations of an agency-centered orientation are the reluctance to share staff and board members for community participation for fear of losing them, jurisdictional disputes, aggressive competition for funds and status, and the belief that one's own program of services is the most important and necessary one for the community. Often behind these vested interests are personality conflicts and professional jealousies, which are frequently the subject of "shop-talk" and gossip.

3. *Intra-agency barriers.* Another block to teamwork on an intra-agency level is the gap between the participation of the executive in community planning and the teamwork responsibilities of the staff. Because of failure in communication, high-sounding expressions of cooperation between agencies made at a committee meeting are not always translated into workable arrangements between staffs. Thus it will happen that

group workers may not know what to do when they find that other agencies are providing services to various members of their group. Frequently there is no organized plan for the participation of the staff in working toward community teamwork, and no systematic passing on of information gained from such participation to all staff members.

4. *Stereotypes of other professionals and agencies.* These are among the most powerful obstacles to teamwork; they are truly barriers which are responsible for much of the lack of understanding and respect which is found in many communities. It is possible to note here only a few of the attitudes and feelings—one could almost call them prejudices—which are behind many of the failures to coordinate our community services effectively.

Because there are relatively few fully trained social workers practicing today, there tends to arise a certain snobbishness on the part of those who have completed their professional training, and an equivalent defensiveness by the untrained. Sometimes this is an almost unconscious feeling: that the other agency's workers are not "professional," that they cannot be trusted with "confidential" information, and that they are somehow inadequate for their jobs. All this is reinforced because our profession is so young, and there are still no common standards or even an acceptable terminology which cuts across all fields of service.

We are dealing here with a whole series of tensions and conflicts which spring from *differences* in setting, auspices, practice, and training. These include feelings which workers in public agencies may have about voluntary agency staffs and vice versa; group workers versus recreation workers; caseworkers versus group workers; those who work with "normal" youngsters versus those who work with "problem" children. There is certainly a real need for us to understand and accept differences among ourselves as professional persons to the same extent that

we try to do this with our clients or members.

5. *Ineffective machinery and structure for community coordination.* While all four of the preceding barriers to teamwork directly involve the agency and its staff, this fifth block to cooperative relationships is rooted in the community. There may not be a community chest, council of social agencies, or a community welfare council in the area—with the result that there is no one organization with a community point of view, one which is "neutral" and which can bring together the separate agencies on mutual problems. Thus, agencies shift for themselves and plan programs with little or no regard for the activities of other organizations. Or there may be a welfare council, but it provides no leadership—it is weak and not respected in the community. As a result, agencies start new programs or change existing ones without clearing with each other or the council. Why does this happen? Perhaps one explanation is that such a condition may reflect either an inadequate council staff, or more probably that the community itself is not yet convinced of the need for sound social planning since it tolerates this condition.

6. *"Too many meetings."* What is behind this perennial complaint? Going to endless committee meetings is not in itself community planning or teamwork. Evidently many people do not have a creative, satisfying, or meaningful experience at meetings; they are often bored, impatient, or frustrated. One cause of dissatisfaction may be a lack of clarity regarding one's role and function. Responsible participation in meetings is based on knowing why one is present, as well as a commitment to and understanding of the group and community organization process. It is necessary to realize that all groups go through periods of confusion, lack of direction, and resistance to change. Social change is inevitably and annoyingly slow. The fact that productivity may be low at a meeting needs to be analyzed and not be a source

of disgust. These and other principles derived from some of the recent findings of group dynamics should be better understood and accepted by all persons participating in committees involving teamwork.

Overcoming these obstacles

First, the individual worker should assume the responsibility of *getting acquainted with other workers in the neighborhood or community* on an informal basis before a crisis or troublesome situation develops. This means that we must make a conscious and planned effort to rise out of our own agencies and their limited programs to become more familiar with our colleagues and the work of their agencies. From this it is but a step to consulting with other agencies on common problems, perhaps arranging a conference and then striving together for a more coherent pattern of services. Such efforts cannot help but improve and sharpen our own effectiveness.

A second responsibility of the worker would be to alert the agency to the importance of *formulating a community relations policy* if the agency does not have one. The preparation of such a policy should involve the participation of both board and staff members if it is to have maximum utility. Among some of the major elements in a community relations policy as suggested by Harleigh Trecker (1950, p. 157), I would single out the following:

1. Identification with the community and its agencies, which is really a "state of mind" expressing positive and purposeful attitudes.
2. Assignment of representation of the agency to board and staff members to those community groups where there is a reason for participation.
3. Establishment of channels of communication between those who represent the agency and the rest of the board and staff with reporting back and clearance procedures carefully formulated.

4. Participation widely distributed and of a responsible kind, with agency representatives convinced of the worth of their participation and knowing how to take part in this process.

Third, workers should be concerned that their *agency's inservice training program includes a discussion of the work of other agencies, the community organization process, and how to participate in it effectively.* This needs to be done in a systematic, planned, and continuous way. This assumes that the agency has some responsibility for providing staff members with such information and orientation, and that it will be responsive to the requests of staff regarding the content of inservice training programs.

Probably the most effective, overall way of overcoming any one or all six obstacles to teamwork is for workers to bring to the attention of their agencies the need to *strengthen the effects of the central planning and coordinating body,* or to organize one if none is in existence. For a community welfare council, which is the primary organization of this type, is by its nature dedicated to fostering teamwork among agencies and between agencies and the community. It is the unique instrument which has evolved during the last 30 years to combat lack of knowledge of resources, "agency-mindedness," lack of communication, stereotypes, duplication, and outlived usefulness in the health, welfare, and recreation fields. If effective—and it is the responsibility of board, staff, and interested citizens to make it work—it can become a synonym for teamwork.

Community organization considerations

What should be done if there is no such council? The answer is to organize one. The existence of unmet needs is one of the most eloquent arguments for a planned and coordinated, communitywide approach through a welfare council structure. In a community without a council, an agency can either ignore unmet needs, complain about them, or do something about them. It can rarely meet the needs itself, nor does it often have the skill, time, and basis for broad support to mobilize the community for such an effort. Consequently, it is suggested that under these circumstances agencies should seek to get together for the purpose of organizing a community welfare council.

We are saying once more that in order to discharge their full professional responsibility, direct-service agencies must not only carry out their programs of service but must also undertake community organization responsibilities to a certain extent when they are confronted with unmet needs or lack of communication and coordination between agencies serving their area. Consequently, it is important for all staff members to know something about the community organization process, the necessary skills involved, and the role they should play. The whole matter of the provision of staff time for participation in community organization is actually an index to the agency's conviction of the relative importance of planning and coordinating its services in the community's interest.[1]

Rationale for neighborhood organization

In this concluding section we shall apply our analysis of teamwork and some of its implications for community organization on the level of a neighborhood. What kind of structure and machinery is needed to bring a variety of services to people in a geographic area? Before answering this question, it is important to observe that the philosophy of most youth-serving agencies underscores the importance of neighborhood organization—of being close to the people

served. Organizations such as the Scouts and other nonbuilding-centered agencies lay particular emphasis on the centrality of the home, the church, and the neighborhood. Building-centered agencies such as the "Y" are also concerned with the development of extension services so that programs can be brought closer to their constituency. Public recreation departments have been neighborhood-centered for many years.

Because the wide range of governmental and voluntary agency services are not always available in a neighborhood in a coordinated way, a variety of forms of neighborhood organization have been devised and used with varying degrees of success.[2] Based on this experience, at least four related efforts are needed today to (1) make more services available; (2) develop integrated patterns of services to meet the varying needs of neighborhoods; (3) coordinate services to prevent overlapping and overlooking; (4) provide opportunities at the neighborhood level for people to form groups through which they can act together. "In carrying out these functions, the keynote must be the participation in these processes of people in their neighborhoods—where families live, shop, go to school and church, and where they vote (Dillick, 1953).

In line with this, there has been a renewed interest in establishing community centers to make available a variety of services under many auspices in the neighborhood. There has been a parallel development as the council of social agencies evolved into a community welfare council with district community councils. These district or neighborhood councils have facilitated citizen participation and have helped make available in the neighborhood the services of citywide agencies. It is suggested here that the district or neighborhood community welfare council can provide certain values and principles which are necessary and valid

---

[1] There are some special problems of participation faced by agencies that are not decentralized, or where excessive work loads prevent release of staff for committee service. Under these conditions, such agencies may have to be very selective by setting priorities and participating in those projects where their services are directly affected.

[2] See Dillick (1953) for the best exposition of the background and principles of neighborhood organization for social welfare purposes.

not only in urban metropolitan centers, but also for "problem" areas in suburban and rural communities. It is in a key and unique position to meet today's needs for neighborhood organization by (1) coordinating health, welfare, and recreation services at the neighborhood level; (2) helping people become articulate about their needs and enlisting their participation in meeting them; (3) serving as a medium for interchange of ideas among rank and file professionals; (4) serving as a medium for joint planning and action by agencies and civic groups; (5) providing a means for communicating to the citywide level the neighborhood view or problems (Dillick, 1953, p. 161)

The district or neighborhood community council, as a coordinating, interorganizational body related functionally and staffwise to an overall community welfare council, is one of the principal means through which direct service agencies and citizen organizations can work together within the larger context of a city or metropolitan area.[3] Indeed, in these days of growing suburban and satellite communities, extensive subdivisions of tract housing, this type of approach to community organization is essential if programs are to get to the people who need them.

Some suggested patterns

For example, these new areas have some special problems involving identity and integration with the larger community, lack of adequate park and recreational space, including meeting places. They tend to contain a large concentration of families with growing children who can utilize and want a wide variety of health, welfare, and recreation services. How are we to get them? The

standard reply is in terms of "extension services," which implies a willingness and a capacity to take staff and services to the place where people live. Some agencies have been able to do this more effectively than others, particularly the national youth-serving organizations. There is a real need, though, for a pooling of resources among the agencies having a common interest in serving these subdivisions. Together they can more effectively promote adequate meeting facilities; through joint use of church, school, or home facilities more children can be served—if agencies are willing to share some of their resources. The problem of locating volunteer leadership is often a formidable one and it would seem to make sense for all agencies seeking volunteers to combine their efforts into one recruitment campaign. Similar campaigns for foster mothers or club leaders have been most successful when developed on a joint-agency basis. This approach eliminates competitiveness and, because more people can be reached, results in a better caliber of volunteer leadership.

The same argument would hold for joint training of such leaders. This would require agreement as to the common-core basis for leadership, apart from the special information and knowledge needed in working with specific organizations. But even more important is the awareness of the type of organizational structure which would facilitate this type of cooperative planning and also acquaint the area with the existence of other community services. It is suggested that the organization of a district community welfare council is probably the most appropriate way of meeting these needs of new neighborhoods.

Many agencies have already organized neighborhood councils or advisory committees for their own programs. What is required is a neighborhood council for *all* groups serving the area. Experience has shown that this can best be done under the auspices of a communitywide organization such as a welfare council, rather than by any direct service agency.

---

[3] See also *A Geographical Approach to Community Planning*, a symposium based on papers from the 1951 National Conference of Social Work, for a description of current thinking on the role of neighborhood councils (Community Chests and Councils of America, 1951).

Summary

While it has become fashionable to espouse the principles of "teamwork," practice and advocacy have not always been related. Cooperative relationships have become even more necessary as a result of the growing complexity of social work practices. In analyzing the concept of teamwork, certain prerequisites and barriers were noted. Four specific suggestions to overcome such obstacles have been offered; this has implications for community organization, particularly on a neighborhood level. Decentralization of the machinery for planning and coordination is proposed as one of the major means of meeting today's need for teamwork in agencies and within the community.

Reading
14-2 Team building in the human services*

Gene Hooyman

Everyone has a different definition of a team. Some think of teams in very general terms (for example, football team, family, or symphony orchestra), while others have a very specific image (for example, social work professionals working together 40 hours per week planning for their clients' needs). While football teams, families, and symphony orchestras all involve some critical aspects of team functioning, they are obviously not this paper's focus. Nor is the focus so narrow that it excludes paraprofessionals, clients, and/or professionals other than social workers or limits the purpose to planning for clients' needs.

A variety of views have been expressed regarding the nature of teams including teams as "action systems" (Pincus and Minahan, 1973, p. 194), "a group of people interacting together" to accomplish the work of the organization (Leuenberger, 1973, p. 26), "relatively permanent work groups" (Reilly and Jones, 1974, p. 227), "workers who are functionally interdependent" (Solomon, 1977, p. 181), and a "group of people who possess individual expertise," make individual decisions, and have a common purpose (Brill, 1976, p. xvi). Views expressed regarding the composition of teams include "the social workers and the people they work with" (Pincus and Minahan, 1973, p. 194), "any grouping of social welfare personnel" (Briggs, 1973, p. 4), and "peers and their immediate supervisor" (Reilly and Jones, 1974, p. 227). Regarding the purpose of team building, views include "improving the problem-solving ability" (Reilly and Jones, 1974, p. 227) and "improvement of interpersonal relationships among those workers who are functionally interdependent" (Solomon, 1977, p. 181).

Each of these views emphasizes a different aspect of teamwork or team building. Reilly and Jones (1974) and Solomon (1977) focus on the process of developing teams as a strategy in organizational development which is applied to business and industry as well as the human services. Brill (1976) defines a team as a group of human service professionals, that is, an interdis-

* An original article prepared for this book. The materials included in this article are based to a large extent on materials used in a two semester 12-credit course sequence entitled "Team Building in the Health Services" offered from 1976 to 1978 by the School of Public Health, University of Minnesota. The author acknowledges the contributions of the following faculty team members who helped team-teach this course: Robert Schwanke (public health interdisciplinary studies.), Miriam Cohn (social work), Eleanor Anderson (public health nursing), and Barbara Reynolds (public health nursing).

ciplinary or interprofessional team. Pincus and Minahan (1973) view the team from the perspective of social workers and who can best assist them in influencing some change. Leuenberger (1973) and Briggs (1973) perceive the team as composed of only social workers. All these views share the perception that the team is an ongoing, interdependent group with a common task. While the task focus distinguishes the team from other growth groups or social groups, effective interpersonal functioning is recognized as essential to teamwork.

In this article, teamwork or team building will be discussed as it relates to the human services, excluding business or industry but including the social worker and other human service professionals. In this discussion, teams may include paraprofessionals and clients as well as professionals, depending upon the team's purpose. Although the team's composition may include clients, the work of the team has a focus different than providing therapy.

Benefits underlying team building

What are the values implicit in team building? When is teamwork most appropriate? What are the strengths and limitations of the team approach? These questions are important considerations for anyone expecting to be a team member in the human services.

The team idea began to emerge as early as 1928 when the famous Hawthorne Experiment revealed that the most significant factor in increasing productivity among workers was the "building of a sense of group identity, a feeling of social support and cohesion that came from increased worker interaction" (Dyer, 1977, p. 8). Other studies revealed that trainees who developed into cohesive team units during training programs demonstrated the largest increase in community service activity after the workshop (Lippitt, 1949), and that the efficiency and effectiveness in services to clients improved more with the team ap-

proach than with the case method of service (Briggs, 1973).

The decision to assign a task to an individual or to a team is often a difficult one. There are five factors to consider: (1) nature of the task; (2) characteristics of individual team members (that is, expertise, commitment to the outcome, and dependence on each others' support of the outcome); (3) importance of producing a high quality product; (4) importance of a high degree of commitment to the solution—the importance of accepting the product or decision; and (5) operating effectiveness of the team. Individuals are generally better than teams with respect to creative tasks and independent tasks while teams are generally better than individuals with respect to convergent or integrative tasks and goal-setting tasks (Sherwood and Hoylman, 1978).

Figure 1 summarizes the strengths and limitations of the team approach (Brieland, Briggs, and Leuenberger, 1973; Brill, 1976; Dyer, 1977; and Sherwood and Hoylman, 1978). This summary clearly illustrates most teamwork values. Although the list of limitations is as long as the list of strengths, many limitations are examples of poorly functioning teams (for example, poor leadership, dominating individuals, unresolved conflict, poorly defined outcomes, and so on). Thus these limitations are not rooted in the nature of teamwork but rather in the inadequacies of skills in leadership, conflict resolution, good formulation, and so on.

Forming a new team

Four major factors need to be considered in forming a new team: (1) the size of the team; (2) the composition of the team; (3) the structure under which the team will begin functioning (for example, basic norms); (4) the procedures by which the team will begin functioning (for example, time and place of meetings). Although the structure and procedures develop primarily throughout the team's growth, it is highly desirable to identify beforehand or early in the team's

FIGURE 1
Strengths and limitations of the team approach

Strengths	Limitations
Pools more knowledge and information	Pressures members toward conformity
Facilitates communication between professionals, paraprofessionals, agencies, and clients	Primative discussion of solutions leads to hasty decisions
Breaks down sterotypes members might have of other professionals, paraprofessionals, agencies, and clients	Lack of members' commitment to the team approach and/or outcome blocks progress
Encourages the development of individual areas of expertise	Causes greater fragmentation of services
Provides opportunities for personal and professional development	May be less contact with clients
	Takes more time than consultation or referral
Provides for examination and evaluation of ideas and issues with differing perspectives represented	Communication processes become complex and difficult to control
Increases the variety of potential solutions to a problem	Complex processes make teams cumbersome and slow-moving
Focuses on total problems rather than segments	Poorly defined outcomes create confusion, tension, and conflict
Reduces overlapping functions	Lack of role definition and overlap in functions create confusion, tension and conflict
Provides a more comprehensive range of services	Status differences produce tension and conflict
Creates an opportunity for wider and more effective use of relevant experts/specialists and paraprofessionals	Poor leadership causes leadership struggles and wastes time
Provides for an effective way of introducing paraprofessionals into an agency	Unresolved conflicts block progress
	Hidden agendas detract from team purpose
Provides for support among members	Dominating individuals stiffle other potentially productive members
Generates enthusiasm and motivation among members	Difficulties in scheduling meetings
Produces work more meaningful and personally satisfying to members	Difficulties in including the right mix of people while maintaining a workable size
Increases the influence upon the target of change	Difficulties in justifying to administrators costs in time and money
Produces a higher quality product	
Increases the acceptance of the outcome	

life the basic structure and procedures by which the team can begin to function. The team's size and composition also may change as the team develops, but there must be some clear definition of these from the very beginning.

Size. A team's size depends primarily upon the desired outcomes and the best ways of achieving these. The team should be large enough to include all the skills and perspectives important to task achievement. The type and degree of interaction needed to achieve the desired outcome should also be a consideration in determining the size (Brill, 1976). Five to six members is a desirable size for teams in the human services (Kane, 1975).

Small teams may not provide sufficient opportunities for members to develop their individual areas of expertise, and team members may become overworked because

they do not have sufficient resources for achieving the purpose. Also small teams may provide too limited a range of learning opportunities, if that is a desired outcome of the team (for example, training of paraprofessionals) (Brieland, 1973). However, in teams of three, there is a tendency for two-one splits.

If the team is too large, on the other hand, communication can become unwieldy. Great demands are placed on the leader of large groups because the processes become more complex. Active members tend to dominate more as the team size increases, while passive members tend to withdraw more. Actions become more anonymous, and the feeling of closeness among members diminishes. Rules and procedures tend to become more formalized in larger teams (Kane, 1975). Formation of subgroups or subteams which would work on specific tasks is frequently used effectively to counteract some of the difficulties caused by teams being too large.

Composition. Determination of the team's composition refers to putting together the best mix of people who will contribute to and gain from the team's internal functioning as well as the achievement of the team's external purpose. There must be a workable balance of certain heterogeneous and homogeneous characteristics. The type of characteristics to be considered are (1) descriptive—the position an individual occupies—profession, age, race, sex, and so on; and (2) behavioral—the way in which a person functions in a position (Pincus and Minahan, 1973).

Descriptive characteristics may be either heterogeneous or homogeneous, depending upon the team's purpose. For example, if the team's purpose requires input from numerous disciplines, the team should be composed of members heterogeneous with respect to their profession (that is, an interdisciplinary or interprofessional team). If the purpose of the team is to provide services to a minority population, it may be essential for the team to be homogeneous with respect to race.

Behavioral characteristics refer to the following three functions that may be used by team members: task function, maintenance functions, and self-oriented functions. Task functions are those functions most directly related to performing the task of the team. Their purpose is to facilitate the team in the problem-solving process. Maintenance functions are related to team-centered activities and behavior. Their purpose is to maintain productive interpersonal working relationships and provide a cohesive team climate in which all members' resources are used effectively as the team is working on its task. Self-oriented functions are either irrelevant to the task or are disruptive to the team's problem-solving process and interpersonal working relationships (Morris and Sashkin, 1976).

Some of the task functions which are needed in the team are

- *Initiating* Giving ideas and directions; proposing objectives or tasks, defining a team problem; suggesting a problem-solving procedure.
- *Elaborating and clarifying.* Exploring and expanding ideas; interpreting ideas and suggestions; defining and proposing alternatives; clarifying confusions.
- *Coordinating.* Putting together and integrating ideas and concepts.
- *Summarizing.* Focusing the work flow on the task; drawing the work together; proposing to the team a decision or conclusion which they can accept or reject.
- *Technical and recording.* Arranging the physical setting, recording the work of the team.
- *Giving and seeking information.* Offering facts and asking for clarification; requesting more facts relating one's own experience to the problem.
- *Giving and receiving opinions.* Stating an opinion or belief; looking for expressions of feeling from members.

Some of the maintenance functions which are needed in the team are

- *Encouraging and supporting.* Praising members for their relevant contributions.
- *Harmonizing.* Mediating and working through differences; relieving tensions.
- *Gatekeeping.* Providing opportunities for others to share ideas and participate in discussions; keeping communication channels open.
- *Process observing.* Giving feedback to the team on how the team is working together.
- *Following.* Giving acceptance to the ideas of others; showing acceptance with nonverbal behavior.
- *Standard setting.* Helping to set standards or norms for the team.
- *Compromising.* Problem-solving one's own conflicts with others.

Some of the self-oriented functions which are visible in teams are

- *Aggression.* Attacking others.

- *Blocking.* Resisting without cause; opposing most of time.
- *Attention seeking.* Calling attention to oneself; boasting; pleading a special interest.
- *Dominating.* Taking over and leading the team in an inappropriate direction.
- *Diverting.* Joking inappropriately; indulging in horse play inappropriately.

An effective team must have an appropriate balance of task and maintenance functions and a minimum of self-oriented functions. Too many maintenance functions and too few task functions may result in more of a social club than a work group. Too many task functions and too few maintenance functions may result in a unproductive work group which is frustrated with its inability to resolve critical interpersonal barriers (for example, unresolved conflict). Although most team members with training in teamwork are able to perform several of these task and maintenance functions, it is rare for anyone to be skilled in all functions. Team members tend to be skillful in either the maintenance functions or the task functions, but not both. Thus it is extremely important for a team to be composed of members who collectively will fulfill all of the task and maintenance functions necessary for effective teamwork.

Although there are numerous other considerations for the composition of the team, such as personal compatibility and complementary needs, the most important considerations are the descriptive and behavioral characteristics mentioned earlier.

Structure. The basic structure of a team is oftentimes set up before the team first meets. Structure refers to the basic norms or standards of behavior and belief that are imposed on a team from the outside (that is, by the organization, group, and/or individual to which the team has some accountability) or within (that is, by other group members) (Kane, 1975).

Norms around leadership and decision-making, that is, how leadership is defined and how decisions are made, are two types of norms which determine to a large extent how the team will function. For example, the choice for an agency director to appoint an authoritarian leader to a team or allow a team to choose its own leadership will have far-reaching consequences in that team's life. The societal norm of democracy that the majority rules, often imposed implicitly on organizations and teams, limits the team in creatively considering other decision-making procedures which may be more effective for it.

Procedure. There are a number of administrative or operating procedures which need to be established before a team is able to begin functioning. Setting the time and the place for the first meeting is an obvious administrative procedure, but it is frequently done without adequate consideration. A meeting time must be found which is most convenient for everyone's schedule. Setting the time without consultation from all team members may result in major problems at a later stage. The length of time devoted to each meeting, the frequency of meeting, the length of time between meetings, and the time of the day when the team meets are also important considerations about the use of time (Pincus and Minihan, 1973).

The determination of the place to meet, and the physical or structural arrangement of chairs, tables, and so on can have a great impact on team functioning. For example, a carpeted room of an appropriate size for the team with pleasant colors, adequate lighting and ventilation, and appealing pictures significantly influences the creation of a supportive and trusting climate, whereas the absence of these physical qualities makes it difficult to achieve such a climate.

Dynamics and stages of team functioning

Earlier reference was made to the behavioral characteristics necessary in the composition of the team, that is, task functions and maintenance functions. Self-oriented functions, although present in teams, hinder overall effectiveness and should be eliminated to whatever extent possible. The appropriate mix and balance of task and maintenance functions are without a doubt the most critical determinants of effective team functioning. The lack of appropriate mix and balance of these functions are the most frequent cause of serious problems in team functioning.

The necessary mix and balance of task and maintenance functions will vary, depending upon the team's needs at any given point in its life. For example, at one point in time it may be necessary to spend a considerable amount of time focusing on the resolution of interpersonal conflict (that is, a maintenance function) and temporarily set aside working directly on the external task (that is, all task functions). By focusing all energies on the resolution of the conflict, the team is more likely to resolve the conflict and therefore be able to move on to accomplishing the team's purpose. By ignoring the conflict, or by suppressing it, the conflict is likely to become more explosive and more difficult or impossible to resolve. Consequently the team will neither resolve the conflict nor accomplish the team's purpose. The team members are likely to become frustrated and react to the critical internal issue (that is, the conflict) in counterproductive ways, such as not coming to meetings, nervous laughing which further suppresses the conflict, isolating the members involved in the conflict, expressing frustration through hurtful and indirect comments, and so on.

Considerable skill is needed by team members to first diagnose team needs in relation to the mix and balance of task and maintenance functions at any given point in time and then to perform the needed task and maintenance functions in an effective manner. These diagnostic and intervention skills need to be developed through skill building experiences and cannot be developed through reading alone. However, it is also necessary to have conceptual frameworks upon which diagnostic and intervention decisions are based.

At least two important dimensions need to be included in team skill building and knowledge acquisition: (1) dynamics in team functioning and (2) developmental stages of teams. Just as theorists have conceptualized stages of individual development (Erickson, 1950), they have also conceptualized stages of team development (Brill, 1976; Jones, 1973; Schutz, 1966). Within each stage of team development, as well as across stages, certain predominant team dynamics can also be identified.

Dynamics in team functioning. The dynamics in the team's life are innumerable and often-times interdependent and occur simultaneously. The task and maintenance functions already discussed are thought to be the primary influence on these dynamics.

Five important team processes or team dynamics are problem-solving, communication and feedback, leadership, decision-making, and conflict resolution. These areas are not mutually exclusive but overlap a great deal. Dynamics in team functioning have been identified in the literature on group dynamics (Cartwright and Zander, 1968; Johnson and Johnson, 1975; Pfeiffer and Jones, 1971, 1978).

Problem-solving. Problem-solving is a systematic approach the team may use to accomplish its task. It is a process that involves changing the present state of affairs to a desired state of affairs. The sequential steps are identifying the problem, diagnosing the problem, establishing goals, considering alternative ways of resolving the problem, choosing one of the alternatives, implementing the selected alternative, and evaluating its effectiveness.

It is essential for the team to proceed on the accomplishment of its task systematically. Therefore, it is helpful if all team members are aware of the general problem-solving process and the particular step which the team is focusing on at any point in time. Problems arise when steps are passed over, when some team members are focusing on one step and others are focusing on a different step, or when the team becomes "stuck" on one step. Four elements are considered basic to small group problem-solving: (1) agreement on the desired state of affairs; (2) structures and procedures for collecting, understanding, and utilizing relevant information about the present state of affairs; (3) structures and procedures for generating potential solutions, for deciding upon and implementing the best solution, and for evaluating its effectiveness; and (4) accomplishing the above three activities while at the same time increasing the effectiveness of the group's problem-solving capabilities. While the first three elements are critical to resolving the immediate problem or task in any team, the last element is especially critical to team building when the work group will continue functioning beyond the resolution of the immediate problem or accomplishment of the task (Johnson and Johnson, 1975).

Communication and feedback. Interpersonal communication is a process through which one person sends a message to a receiver with a conscious intent of affecting the receiver's behavior. Communication is basic to all small group functioning, and includes receiving, sending, interpreting, and inferring verbal messages (words) and nonverbal messages (expressions, gestures, and environmental arrangements) all at the same time. The communication process is strongly influenced by the sender "encoding" or putting part of "self" in the message being sent and the receiver "decoding" or putting part of "self" in the message being received (Johnson and Johnson, 1975).

Several skills are important to effective small group communication. Specific skills of sending messages involve the following:

1. Clearly "own" your messages by personal pronouns, such as *I* and *my.*
2. Make your messages complete and specific.
3. Make your verbal and nonverbal messages congruent with each other.
4. Be redundant.

5. Ask for feedback concerning the way your messages are being received.
6. Make the message appropriate to the receiver's frame of reference.
7. Describe your feelings by name, action, or figure of speech.
8. Describe other member's behavior without evaluating or interpreting.

Some specific skills of receiving messages involve the following:

1. Paraphrase the content of the message and the feelings of the sender accurately and in a nonevaluative way.
2. Describe what you perceive to be the sender's feelings.
3. State your interpretation of the sender's message and negotiate with the sender until there is agreement as to the message's meaning (Johnson and Johnson, 1975).

Feedback refers to verbal and nonverbal responses which express the effects one's behavior has upon others (Bormann and Bormann, 1976). Giving and receiving feedback is a use of the communication process which is most important to team building because it is the mechanism through which effective behavioral change does occur. Giving and receiving feedback may take on a number of dimensions: (1) verbal, such as "no"; or nonverbal, such as leaving the room; (2) conscious, such as nodding assent; or unconscious, such as falling asleep; (3) spontaneous, such as "thanks a lot" or solicited, such as "yes, it did help"; and (4) formal, such as completing a post meeting reaction form; or informal, such as a slap on the back or a hug for a job well done.

Feedback can be helpful or destructive depending on several variables. The rules or guidelines for giving and receiving effective and helpful feedback are similar to the skills needed for effective communications. They are

1. Helpful feedback is descriptive, not evaluative, and "owned" by the sender.
2. Helpful feedback is specific, not general.

3. Helpful feedback is relevant to the self-perceived needs of the receiver.
4. Helpful feedback is desired by the receiver, not imposed on him or her.
5. Helpful feedback is timely and in context.
6. Helpful feedback is useable, concerned with behavior over which the receiver has some control (Lippitt, Watson, and Westley, 1978).

While feedback can be considered the basis for any effective team skill building effort, communication can be considered the basis for all human interaction and for all group functioning.

Leadership. Leadership can be broadly defined as the process of influence occurring among mutually dependent team members. Leadership implies influence from one member upon other members and can be designated from an outside authority, chosen by other team members, or assumed by an individual exerting some type of influence on other members. Although there is oftentimes one recognized leader in a team, any member is involved in leadership behavior when that member influences others to help the team accomplish its purposes (Johnson and Johnson, 1975).

Leadership can be looked at in terms of the source of the power or influence being exerted on other members. There are six sources of power which a leader might possess: reward, coercive, legitimate, referent, expert, and informational. Reward power refers to the ability to deliver positive consequences or remove negative consequences as a response to other members' behaviors. Coercive power refers to the ability to inflict negative consequences or remove positive consequences in response to other members' behaviors. Legitimate power refers to that influence resulting from a person's position in the team or organization or larger group, and/or from special responsibilities a person has as a result of that position. Referent power is that influence a person has because of being respected and/or

well liked. Expert power is that influence a person has as a result of team members' perceptions that the member has some special knowledge or skill and is trustworthy. Informational power is that influence a person has as a result of resources or information which will be useful in accomplishing the team's purpose (French and Raven, 1959).

Leadership can also be defined in terms of behavioral functions. These task and maintenance functions—the primary leadership functions essential to a team—have already been identified and discussed earlier in relation to the team composition.

Leadership is situational with respect to the team's maturity level. The level of maturity refers to the team's ability to set high but attainable goals, the willingness and ability to take responsibility, and the education and/or experiences of the team. In a newly formed team, the effective leader is one who focuses primarily on task functions. As the team members' maturity increases in terms of accomplishing a specific task, the effective leader begins to diminish task functions and increase maintenance functions. Finally, when the group is fully matured, the effective leader becomes one of the members where task and maintenance functions are shared by all members. This final state of maturity is the ideal state most frequently desired by teams, but seldom achieved (Hersey and Blanchard, 1976).

Leadership can also be viewed in terms of the degree of direction given to a team. An autocratic leadership style refers to strong, directive behavior toward the team by the leader. While a democratic style encourages group decision-making and member choice, a laissezfaire style allows complete freedom to the team. Stronger work motivation and more cohesion develops with a democratic style; more dependence, discontent, and hostility develops with an autocratic style; and less work, poorer quality work, and more play occurs with a laissez-faire style (Lippitt and White, 1968).

How one chooses to provide leadership in a team depends primarily upon an analysis of what the team needs and the level and range of leadership skills. However, one's perception of need is strongly influenced by values about teamwork and about the nature of human interaction. One who perceives human beings as basically fallable and needing to be controlled will tend to choose a more directive or autocratic style, while one who perceives human beings as full of creative potential waiting to be released will tend to choose a less directive or democratic style.

Decision-making. Decision-making refers to one step in the problem-solving process whereby the team uses some method of agreeing on which alternative is the best solution for the problem or task facing the team. In a broader context, decision-making refers to any team situation which demands agreement by all members before it can move ahead. Because this step is so critical to the problem-solving process and to effective team functioning, it deserves special consideration.

An effective decision is one which maximizes the use of time and resources and is fully implemented by team members. An effective decision also enhances the problem-solving abilities of the team. There are several methods by which decisions can be made in teams: (1) agreement of the entire team whereby all members understand the decision and support it (consensus); (2) majority vote; (3) minority of team members imposing their agreement on the team; (4) averaging individual opinions of team members; (5) member with the most authority makes decision after group discussion of the issues; and (7) member with the most authority makes decision without a group discussion.

As mentioned earlier, the norm for decision-making frequently is imposed on the team explicitly by the person or organization to which the team is accountable or implicitly through the unspoken norms of organizations, the society, or other powerful groups to which team members are individually or collectively accountable. Ideally,

the team should set its own norm for decision-making before engaging in the problem-solving process. The team should choose the method that is best for (1) the type of decision that has to be made; (2) the time and resources available; (3) the history of the team; (4) the nature of the task; (5) the type of climate the team wants; and (6) the type of setting in which the group works.

Consensus is the decision-making procedure most preferred by teams when the decision is an important one and the consequences of the decision affect all team members. It is also the most time-consuming process because all members need to understand the issues and the decision, must have opportunities to tell how they feel about the decision, and must support the decision as an experimental effort even if they have reservations about it. This method tends to produce an innovative, creative, and high quality decision with high commitment from team members to implement the decision. It also enhances the team's decision-making and problem-solving capacities and builds cohesion. However, it would be a serious mistake to use this method inappropriately, that is, when these criteria do not warrant its use (Johnson and Johnson, 1975).

Conflict resolution. Conflict exists when incompatible activities occur. One activity is incompatible with another activity when it prevents, blocks, interferes with, or makes the other activity less effective or less likely (Deutsch, 1969). Several characteristics define a conflict situation: (1) at least two parties are involved in the interaction; (2) perceived or real mutually exclusive goals and/or mutually exclusive values exist; (3) interaction is characterized by behavior intended to defeat the opponent or to gain a mutual victory; (4) parties face each other using opposing actions and counteractions; and (5) each party attempts to gain a power advantage over the other party (Filley, 1975).

Several generalizations can be formulated relating to characteristics of social relationships which increase the likelihood of conflict. The likelihood or opportunity for conflict is greater when (1) the limits of each party's jurisdiction are ambiguous; (2) conflicts of interest exist between the parties; (3) communication barriers exist; (4) one party is dependent upon another; (5) there are a large number of organizational levels, specialties represented, and differentiated jobs in the organization; (6) there is informal interaction among the parties, and they all participate in decision-making; (7) consensus is necessary; (8) standardized procedures, rules, and regulations are imposed; and (9) unresolved prior conflicts exist (Filley, 1975).

Conflict can exist between a team and another individual or group external to the team or between team members within the same team. Conflict within a team is the most frequently suppressed type of conflict and the most difficult to manage. Team members with a strong value of cooperative involvement with one another often perceive conflict as a threat and inherently negative to effective team functioning. Furthermore, team workers frequently approach all conflict situations with one predominant style, and they lack the skill and adaptability to use the most appropriate approach for each conflict situation which arises.

Conflict, per se, is neutral. It is a reality that exists and must be recognized and managed. The individual, team, organization, and/or society involved in conflict situations give conflict its negative or positive value.

A practical model for dealing with conflict is one which takes the dimensions of personal goals and the concern for relationship into account. The degree of importance or concern for each of these dimensions then determines the conflict style. If one party in a conflict situation seeks to meet individual goals at all costs, without concern for a relationship with or the needs of the opponent, that party is using a "win-lose" conflict style. The party using this style defines the situation so that there will be a winner and a loser and will try to win at all costs. A second style is a "yield-lose" style where one party views the relationship with the second party as the most important consideration, much more important than the achievement of individual goals. The party using this style yields position in the conflict situation and loses, hoping that this will allow the relationship to survive. A third style is a "lose-leave" style where the party has low concern for both the goals and the relationship with the opponent. This party loses by default through withdrawing from the situation. A fourth style is a "compromise" style where the party has a moderate degree of concern for both the goals and the relationship with the opponent. The party using this style will attempt to reach compromises whereby everyone wins some and loses some. The fifth style is an "integrative" style where the party has a high concern for both the goals and the relationship with the opponent. The party using this style defines the conflict in terms of a problem situation to be worked out collaboratively by all concerned parties in order that everyone will end up a winner. This is the problem-solving style that is generally preferred. However, each style may be effectively used in different situations, depending upon the issue's nature and importance and how the opponent views and approaches the conflict situation.

The parties to a conflict situation must hold several beliefs if the problem-solving style of conflict resolution is to be used effectively. Parties must believe in the availability and desirability of a mutually acceptable solution. They must believe in cooperation rather than conflict and that everyone is of equal value. They must believe that others' views are legitimate statements of their positions and that differences of opinion are helpful. They must believe in the members' trustworthiness and that other members will choose to cooperate rather than compete (Hall, 1969). Teams must work towards developing a problem-solving approach to conflict resolution. Team members must openly explore their beliefs and orientations with respect to conflict. Conflicts within teams must be viewed as problem situations in which mutually acceptable solutions are not only possible, but desirable.

Stages of team functioning. Individuals, small groups, communities, organizations, and societies each have a life span, a beginning to an ending. Analysis of the life processes that occur within the life span indicates similarities in the way in which they develop. These similarities are frequently formulated into models depicting the phases or stages of development. The team also has a life span, with numerous life processes occurring at different times in its development.

A variety of views have been expressed regarding the phases or stages of team development. One view which focuses on the dimension of the team's interpersonal relations, is that there are three basic phases: *inclusion,* or finding one's place in the team; *control,* or determining one's influence in the team; and *affection,* or determining one's closeness with other team members (Schutz, 1966). Another view, which focuses on the two dimensions of the team's

primary maintenance functions and its primary task functions, is that there are four developmental stages related to each dimension: dependency, conflict, cohesion, and interdependency for the maintenance dimension; and work orientation, organization, information sharing, and problem-solving for the task function dimensions (Jones, 1973).

A third view, which also focuses on the two dimensions of the team's maintenance functions and its task functions, is that both of these dimensions are related to five developmental stages: orientation, accommodation, negotiation, operation, and dissolution (Brill, 1976). Figure 2 summarizes the relationship of the two dimensions to each of the five stages. The frequency of waves with respect to each of the task and maintenance functions represent the importance and intensity of a particular function to each of the five stages.

The first stage, orientation, refers to the determination of each member's position in

FIGURE 2
Task and maintenance skill development in the life stages of the team

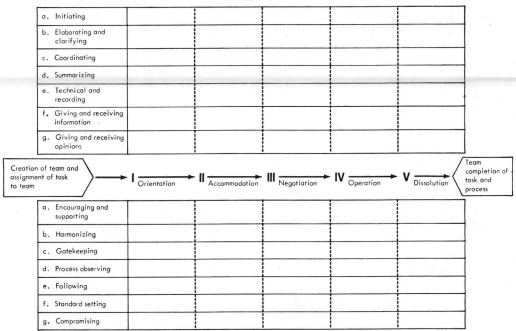

A. Task achievement skills: Task functions related to productivity

	I Orientation	II Accommodation	III Negotiation	IV Operation	V Dissolution
a. Initiating					
b. Elaborating and clarifying					
c. Coordinating					
d. Summarizing					
e. Technical and recording					
f. Giving and receiving information					
g. Giving and receiving opinions					

Creation of team and assignment of task to team → I Orientation → II Accommodation → III Negotiation → IV Operation → V Dissolution → Team completion of task and process

	I Orientation	II Accommodation	III Negotiation	IV Operation	V Dissolution
a. Encouraging and supporting					
b. Harmonizing					
c. Gatekeeping					
d. Process observing					
e. Following					
f. Standard setting					
g. Compromising					

B. Human relations skills: Maintenance functions related to building and maintaining effective interpersonal working relationships

the team. Members define boundaries and learn what is expected of them. They become acquainted with one another and provide support to each other in dealing with common anxieties about both the task and their relationships with one another. The primary task functions related to this stage are initiating and giving and receiving information. The primary maintenance functions are encouraging and supporting, gatekeeping, and standard setting.

The second stage, accommodation, refers to the adaption of team members to each other and to the team model. Members find their place in the team in terms of how their expertise relates to the task and how they relate to one another. Communication processes become developed, values and norms become set, and the structure and climate of the team become established. This stage is characterized by conflict. The primary task functions are giving and receiving information, giving and receiving opinions, and initiating. The primary maintenance functions are harmonizing, standard setting, and compromising.

The third stage, negotiation, refers to those transactions related to both positions and tasks carried out. Members bargain with one another about who is going to do what and who will be dependent upon whom. The primary task functions are elaborating, clarifying, technical, and recording. The primary maintenance functions are harmonizing, standard setting, and compromising.

The fourth stage, operation, refers to purposeful action resulting in change. Team members actually carry out the responsibilities agreed to in the previous stage. The primary task functions remain the same as above. The primary maintenance functions are encouraging, supporting, and following.

The final stage, dissolution, refers to the completion of the task and the separation of team members' from one another. The primary task function is summarizing, and the primary maintenance function is process observing.

While Figure 2 summarizes the necessary integration of task and maintenance func-

tions with the team's dynamic life stages, it is important to emphasize that neither the functions nor the stages are as distinct and separate as they may appear. For example, although summarizing and process observing are functions most predominant in the final stage of a team's life, these functions must also occur at other stages of development. The team is a complex and dynamic functioning system which integrates task and maintenance dimensions throughout its life.

Common problems and issues in team building

A list of ten of the most common problems and issues which someone working on a human services team is likely to confront is presented as follows, and some brief suggestions are made for dealing with each of the problem areas.

Bringing and keeping all team members on board. New members frequently join a team after it has been functioning effectively for some time, while other members leave the team before it has accomplished its task. Still other team members fail to be involved in all meetings, come late, and/or leave early. The process of integrating new members into the team, catching up members who have missed one or two meetings or come late, and adjusting to members who temporarily or permanently leave before the job is done is an important process frequently neglected in teamwork.

It is essential to take the necessary time to quickly bring the new or late members up to date with the team's accomplishments. The time spent doing this can also serve to summarize events for the rest of the team. If a new member joins a team, it is important to make introductions to the rest of the team and help that person feel welcome and needed. Clarifying role and responsibilities in relation to the task and in relation to other team members' roles and responsibilities also can be helpful in this respect. Team members who leave temporarily or permanently often create gaps with respect to both the task and the team process. It is quite appropriate, and important, to spend some time in team meetings to express group feelings of loss and to reintegrate their functioning.

Maintaining a clear focus and strong team commitment to purpose. Team members frequently lose sight of goals and/or lose their commitment to the goals, particularly when an unresolved team process (for example, unresolved conflict) misdirects or suppresses team energy and prevents the team from moving ahead. Periodically, it is necessary to restate for everyone what may seem to be explicit team goals and to test each member's commitment to accomplishing those goals. Doing this is especially important immediately after the team has struggled with a major process issue (for example, an unresolved conflict).

Dealing with appropriate interpersonal needs. As mentioned earlier in this article, work groups tend to ignore interpersonal processes important to task accomplishment. The skills of diagnosis and intervention with respect to maintenance functions in teams are basic to team building.

Struggles over leadership. The most frequent conflicts in teams arise around the issue of how much influence one member has in relation to other members. One effective way to deal with leadership struggles is recognize and legitimize that all members have valuable contributions and maximize each member's opportunities to make their contributions to the group. Clarifying and defining individual areas of expertise helps to create an atmosphere of mutual influence and shared leadership. In situations where a strong leadership style exists but is not accepted, it may be necessary for someone in the team to raise the issue of leadership with the team and openly discuss and decide upon what leadership style would be preferred.

Physical and time arrangements. Problems are often related to making arrangements for meetings which take into account everyone's time schedule and are reasonably convenient for all concerned. The physical setting for meetings is much more important to effective team functioning than most people realize. Taking time for making necessary arrangements can save time in the long run.

Communication. Communication processes become tremendously complex in teams, particularly as the team size increases. The failure to send clear messages and to listen actively can cause anger and resentment among members. Effective team communication skills are an absolute necessity to the smooth functioning of a team.

Conflict. Intense, unresolved conflicts, whatever their causes, are probably the most frequent reasons for team members losing commitment and leaving the team before the job is done. People who have experienced more negative than positive consequences from conflicts are understandably afraid of conflict and avoid it or withdraw from it whenever possible. Most people are without the necessary skills to deal with conflict resolution effectively.

Coping with self-oriented behavior. In most teams, at least one individual engages in destructive self-oriented behavior. If this behavior is allowed to continue unchecked, the team will undergo severe difficulties and may discontinue functioning altogether. Self-oriented behavior needs to be redirected in order that the needs expressed can be met outside the team situation.

Unrealistic work expectations. Teams are occasionally assigned unreasonable tasks or are requested to complete tasks by unreasonable deadlines. If the team accepts this responsibility without confronting the realities of the situation which make the task completion impossible, the team is setting itself up for a failure experience.

Acceptance and respect among team members. Team members frequently fail to recognize, accept, and respect other members' values and expertise. This occurs most frequently with respect to members' value orientations and expertise in performing task or maintenance functions in the team. Members with a strong value on the importance of task functions in team building tend not to see the value of maintenance functions, and vice versa. Thus members who have the real potential of complementing one another in two very important dimensions of team building perceive themselves in conflict.

Maintenance functions are especially important, not because they are more important considerations than task functions, but because they are so frequently overlooked or ignored in teams. Societal and organizational norms generally stress the importance of task accomplishment (for example, the Protestant work ethic) much more than the achievement of strong interpersonal relationships. A team that is influenced by the norms of the larger units to which it is accountable most frequently overemphasizes task accomplishment and underemphasizes interpersonal working relationships. Therefore, to achieve the best task-interpersonal balance in teams, it is especially important to emphasize maintenance functions.

Summary and conclusion

Team building is a dynamic process of developing effective interpersonal working relationships and problem-solving abilities among several individuals who are mutually dependent upon each other for achieving a task objective. An ideal team is one which is continually in the process of evaluating and improving its task and maintenance functions throughout every stage of its life.

The team approach is not appropriate for every situation. In choosing whether or not to use the team approach, strengths and limitations of teams must be carefully reviewed in light of the desired outcomes and the characteristics of potential team members. Size, composition, structure, and operating procedures are important considerations in forming a new team.

Achieving an appropriate balance of task and maintenance functions is the most critical aspect of effective team functioning. Considerable diagnostic and intervention knowledge and skills are needed with respect to achieving the most appropriate balance of these functions throughout all stages in the life of a team.

The need for team training in the human services often becomes most apparent after the human service professional has had a number of negative team experiences on the job. Unfortunately, a negative attitude toward the team approach is also frequently developed with avoidance becoming the response. Individuals who expect to work in the human services should recognize that a large part of their work will involve ongoing collaborative relationships with other professionals, paraprofessionals, and clients. The people who ultimately have the most to lose by a lack of professional expertise in teamwork are the poor, the disadvantaged, and the oppressed people whom workers are trying hardest to serve.

Selected annotated bibliography

Chaiklin, Harris. "A Social Service Team for Public Welfare," *Social Work Practice, 1970.* New York: Columbia University Press, 1970, pp. 103–113.
This is an interesting and enlightening article on an attempt to change and improve the staff service delivery pattern in working with public welfare families. Community organizers and case aides were added to the social casework staff to make a team.

Edson, Jean Brown. "How to Survive on a Committee," *Social Work* 22 (May 1977), pp. 224–226.
A brief, easily read article that presents some very interesting tips on how the average social worker can avoid being manipulated in committee meetings. The authors would recommend that all students read this article.

Whitehouse, Frederick A. "Professional Teamwork," *Social Welfare Forum, 1957.* New York: Columbia University Press, 1957, pp. 148–157.
This excellent article gives the background of the concept of teamwork and sets forth 18 elements that are found in good teams and teamwork.

CHAPTER 15

The social worker, the profession, and the bureaucratic structure

Up to this point in the text we have discussed social work primarily as a profession and the social work practitioner as a professional person with the responsibility of working within professional knowledge and values in the interests of the particular client with whom the worker is involved. We now need to examine other aspects of the social work profession. Most social workers practice their profession within some sort of bureaucratic structure, and this structure inevitably affects the work they do. We alluded to this structure in the last two chapters when we discussed the need for referral of a client because of the limits of an agency's services and when we discussed the fact that one kind of teamwork was teamwork across agency boundaries. As a professional person, the social worker is also a component within a professional system with its own purposes, culture, internal interactions, and external transactions. We now want to examine the meaning of these realities for the social work practitioner.

THE INTERSTITIAL PROFESSION

In the first chapter of this text we spoke of social workers as concerned with the interactions between the individual and society. We now need to return to a consideration of social work as an interstitial profession which serves both the client in need and society at large. This issue is complex in that the individual social worker's function is defined, and the worker's salary paid, by an agency (public or voluntary, traditional or nontraditional) which receives its sanction from and is accountable to the community or to some community group whose members differ from, although they may include, the members of the client system. This point is of fundamental importance since the parameters of the service any particular professional can offer are determined by the parameters of the agency's societal charge. Social workers utilize two types of tools in their work. The first type are the tools of internalized knowledge and skill, which, while they cannot be used up and, in fact, may be increased and sharpened by practice, are costly in that they are what social workers (or any other professional) sell in order to obtain the money they need to maintain their physical existence in society. Most professionals (lawyers, doctors, and so on) sell their services directly to their clients or patients. In the case of social work, however, services to the client are paid for by the community and may be, at least in theory, available to all members of the community, many of whom cannot afford to pay for them themselves. In addition to knowledge and skill, social workers frequently dispense external resources, such as money. Now, money, whether it is used to pay for the knowledge and skill of the worker or for concrete resources, or is given directly to the client, is usually scarce. And money to support social work efforts is not the social worker's property but belongs to some identified community. The community that allocates its scarce resources to the support of social work services wants to assure itself that these resources are used responsibly.

Clients who go to a lawyer for service, or patients who go to a doctor for treatment, may look elsewhere for help if they think the service they receive is not adequate. Thus they express their evaluation of that professional's competence by depriving the professional of income. If professionals want to support themselves and their dependents, they must practice in a way that satisfies the users of the services by which they support themselves. However, since most client systems do not pay the full cost for social work services, their withdrawal in disappointment and disgust from the inadequate social work practitioner seldom directly penalizes that practitioner. Social workers (and their agencies) are thus well protected from their client's evaluations. However, they are open to the evaluation of their supporting community. The supporting community, however, neither pays nor evaluates workers directly. Rather, it gives its money to an organization, usually called an agency, which hires the professional practitioners. It is usually the agency in interaction with its supporting community through certain representative groups which both sets the parameters of practice within which workers must operate and which evaluates their performance within the parameters.

THE BUREAUCRATIC ORGANIZATION

In the modern world most formal organizations are structured in a particular way. This particular type of administrative organization is known as a bureaucracy and has triumphed in modern society because it is thought to operate with an efficiency superior to that of any other form of secondary group social structure thus far devised. The classical criteria for a bureaucracy were originally set forth by Max Weber (1947, pp. 333–334) as follows:

1. [The employees] are personally free and subject to authority only with respect to their impersonal official [work] obligations.
2. [The employees] are organized in a clearly defined hierarchy of offices.
3. Each office has a clearly defined sphere of competence.
4. The office is filled by a free contractual relationship. (Thus, in principle, each person makes a free selection, or choice, as to whether the person will accept the office and its terms.)
5. Candidates [for offices in the bureaucracy] are selected on the basis of technical qualifications. In the most rational case, this is tested by examination or guaranteed by diplomas certifying technical training, or both. They are appointed, not elected.
6. [The employees] are remunerated by fixed salaries in money, for the most part with a right to pensions . . . The salary scale is primarily graded according to rank in the hierarchy.

7. The [position] is treated as the sole, or at least the primary, occupation of the incumbent.
8. It constitutes a career. There is a system of "promotion" according to seniority or to achievement, or both. Promotion is dependent on the judgment of superiors.
9. The official works entirely separated from ownership of the means of administration and without appropriation of his position.
10. The worker is subject to strict and systematic discipline and control in the conduct of the office.

Weber (p. 334) says that the Roman Catholic church, the modern army, and large-scale capitalistic enterprise, along with certain "charitable organization, or any number of other types of private enterprises, servicing ideal or material ends are bureaucratic organizations."

Although bureaucracy is usually seen in terms of pragmatic necessity as the most efficient way to organize any large group of people to get any big job done, inherent in its very being are certain dysfunctional characteristics which vitally affect its operations. Social workers are often forced to conclude that the relationship between bureaucracy and efficiency is complex, questionable, and perhaps, at its worst, inverse.

To quote from a recent book, *Overcoming Mismanagement in the Human Services* (Weissman, 1973, p. vii), bearing on some of the problems of bureaucracy:

> A very unhappy social worker, after receiving a poor evaluation from a supervisor, once wrote: "Social welfare like all Gaul is divided into three parts. The first has until recently been inhabited by the Hierarchae, which may account for the fact that the field has been subject to unsteadiness. The second by the Supervisii, which explains why too many of the most able no longer work with those in need of help. They are in conference. And the last by the Reformae, who believe the populace is anxious to substitute social change for sex."
>
> Had the worker been more dispassionate, this social worker might have pointed out that social welfare is also inhabited by thousands of hard-working, dedicated people who spend their lives under adverse situations with some of the most unhappy and unlucky people in the world and still manage to do a lot more good than bad.

Wilensky and Lebeaux (1958, p. 243) describe the limitations of social work bureaucracy as follows:

> Along with its gains, efficiency, reliability, precision, fairness—come what many students have called its pathologies: timidity, delay, officiousness, red tape, exaggeration of routine, limited adaptability. The agency as a means, a mechanism —the agency—for carrying out welfare policy becomes an end in itself. Between the altruist with the desire to help and the client with the need lies the machine, with its own "needs." These needs can result in an emphasis on technique and method, on organizational routines and records, rather than on people and service.

Barbara Lerner (1972, pp. 169–170), a psychologist, is concerned with this last limitation of bureaucracy when she writes:

> Bureaucratic means are intrinsically unsuited to the achievement of ultimate mental health ends because they are standardized means—the whole point of breaking up tasks into component parts and component parts into subcomponents

is to standardize procedures—and standardized procedures are rational only if one is striving to produce a standard product. . . .

Each human being is a unique entity and wants to remain so. People who voluntarily seek treatment may do so because they want to achieve an ultimtae end, such as the realization of something like their full share of the universal human potential for adequate psychosocial functioning, but people want to achieve their own unique version of that end in their own unique way. . . .

Thus clients who come seeking aid come as unique individuals seeking aid which is individually tailored to the totality of their needs by a person who is in close enough contact with them to apprehend them and who has the freedom and flexibility to respond to them in a unique way.

Lerner (p. 171) goes on to say that the bureaucratically organized agency is organized around "abstract, standard parts: specific programs organized around specific problems that are dealt with by specific procedures," rather than around clients as unique personalities or around the concern of practitioners for their clients. She complains that clients are "then defined in terms of the particular problems around which programs are organized" and are "processed to and through those programs and subjected to the various procedures and techniques which constitute them" rather than seen in terms of their own goals and expectations.

Listening to Lerner, one becomes aware that the problems of professionals in bureaucracies are not restricted to social work. These problems occur in any organization staffed by personnel who spend a considerable number of years in developing a particular expertise. Weissman (1973, p. viii) points out:

Professionals share a desire for and expect a large degree of autonomy from organizational control; they want maximum discretion in carrying out their professional activities, free from organizational interference or confining procedures. In addition, professionals tend to look to other professionals to gain some measure of self-esteem, are not likely to be devoted to any one organization, and accept a value system that puts great emphasis on the client's interest.

Bureaucrats are different from professionals. They perform specialized and routine activities under the supervision of a hierarchy of officials. Their loyalty and career are tied up with their organization. Therefore, conflict results when professionals are required to perform like bureaucrats.

We would differ with the conclusion of this last quote and might repeat that famous quotation, "We have met the enemy and they is us." Professionals and bureaucrats are not two different sets of people. There are bureaucrats who are not professionals, but, increasingly in our society, given the advancement of group practices in medicine and law, there are few professionals who are not also bureaucrats. With regard to social work, we need to recognize that bureaucratic forms of organization are useful in social services, not because society is unmindful of what is wrong with this form, or because society is basically evil, but because there simply are not at this time any feasible, superior organization models that have properties as well suited to carrying out the very complex functions required of social services involving the cooperative contributions of large numbers of specialized individuals (Pruger, 1978).

For the foreseeable future, individual social workers will find it necessary to relate to a bureaucratic structure as the environment in which they will work.

Thus, it will not help either the worker or the client for the worker to see the bureaucracy as something bad that should be condemned at every turn. Rather, it must be understood as a reality—a complex system in which both worker and client are subsystems. Given this important fact of life—we need to learn to work within and to change bureaucracy rather than to simply make ourselves feel good by holding bureaucracy as bad (Pruger, 1978).

CONFLICTS BETWEEN THE BUREAUCRACY AND THE PROFESSIONAL

Practicing social workers have been confronted with the harsh reality of the conflict between their judgment as to the ideal interventive actions needed to move toward the client's goal and what is possible given the resources and parameters of the agency within which both they and the client are operating. Often the most sensitive and concerned workers find themselves discouraged and angered by the many unavoidable compromises they must make between their client's needs and those of their agency in particular and of society in general. Perhaps some of this frustration could be avoided, and workers could be more effective in bringing about change in agency functioning, if they understood better the bureaucracy within which they of necessity operate. Actually, social work has been a bureaucratic profession from its very beginning, and social workers employed in agencies are not only professionals but bureaucrats. Thus, while social work has struggled to synthesize bureaucratic and professional norms, it has not always recognized that a profession and a bureaucracy possess a number of norms that are opposed in principle.

Weissman (1973, p. vii) points out that one of the crucial problems of professionals who are working to change the bureaucratic structure is their lack of recognition of the difference between nonprofit and profit-making organizations. "Money serves as an alarm system in private enterprise: Ford sooner or later must respond to the tension caused by lack of Edsel sales." In nonprofit organizations the connection between the product produced and the revenues are indirect. Thus the alarm system that would bring change is severely flawed. Both professionals and agency executives may prefer to be judged by effort expended rather than by the success or failure of the effort. Weissman (p. 3) says that without an effective accountability system social agencies cannot solve their problems and administration has little need to seriously consider the views and ideas of lower-level staff since it will not be penalized if it does not.

In an earlier chapter, the importance of evaluation was discussed. This has been a long-standing problem in all professions. Who is to evaluate the professional? Against what standard is the professional's work to be judged? The present struggle of the physician against some kind of publicly supported health care is an example of the problem. Physicians have successfully maintained up until now that only they (or, in some cases, a jury of their peers that they pick) can be allowed to judge their work. Incidentally, this stance probably explains the growing number of malpractice suits, since patients are no longer content, when the results of treatment are negative, to accept the professional's judgment that the process of treatment was correct. So, too, in the social work bureaucracy the question of who shall evaluate the effectiveness of the work is a difficult one. Is it to be the worker, the supervisor, the executive, the board, or the general public? We have said that contracted goals are the appropriate outcome. It would follow that we hold goal achievement to be a decision of client and worker, not of the agency.

Weber (1947, pp. 333–334) held that what is central to bureaucracy is specialization and the standardization of tasks and the rational allocation or assignment of these tasks in accordance with an overall plan. Collective tasks may thus be broken down into component tasks which are means to a collective end. Two assumptions underlie such a concept. The first is that there is something approaching a clear, consistent, complete, and generally agreed-upon definition of the ultimate end toward which the organization is working, and the second is that the end is achievable through standardized means (Lerner, 1972, p. 167). When a social agency defines its function it usually states the ends it intends to pursue in general terms. However, these ends are usually expressed in such general terms (for example, "the support of healthy family life") that the extent to which they have been achieved cannot be measured; or the ends are expressed in programmatic terms, such as "crisis intervention," "aftercare program," "family therapy program," or "drug program," which often result in defining the client's problems in terms of programs rather than of the client's goals. And most of us would agree that we do not have standardized means to apply even if the client could fit within a standardized goal. We are simply not able to say in working with individual human beings, "If this, then that." There are too many variables in the situation of the unique human system. A profession works by applying principles and methods to resolve problems determined by unique client input and professional judgment rather than by employing standardized procedures toward some predetermined goal established by a hierarchical authority.

Another conflict between the bureaucratic structure and the professional is found in the orientation toward authority. The professional regards authority as residing in professional competence; the bureaucrat sees authority as residing in the office held. An important difference is found in the orientation toward the client, in that professionals orient themselves toward serving the best interests of the client while the bureaucrat seeks to serve the best interests of the organization. Professionals usually identify with their professional colleagues. They should find their identification from their professional association. Bureaucrats identify with their particular social stratum within the bureaucratic hierarchy. And lastly, there is a different orientation toward the method of exercising power. "The professional norm is to influence clients and peers by modes which are oriented toward the pole of free exchange while the bureaucratic norm is oriented toward the pole of coercion" supported by the invoking of sanctions (Morgan, 1962, p. 115).

TYPES OF BUREAUCRATS

In an empirical study of social work performance in large public agencies, Ralph Morgan (1962, pp. 116–125) identified and developed an anchoring description of four ideal types of role conceptions of social workers in a bureaucratic setting. His work is summarized below:

> *Functional bureaucrats* are professionals "who just happen to be working in a social agency." They seek interaction with and recognition from their professional peers both inside and outside the agency. "Such individuals by their skill,

good judgment, and technical efficiency often provide a type of service" that is recognized by the agency as being highly effective. As a result the agency overlooks certain violations of agency norms as the price it must pay for having such a competent professional on its staff.

Service bureaucrats are social workers who are oriented toward helping their clients but who recognize that they are a part of a bureaucracy. They integrate themselves "into the bureaucratic group while maintaining professional peer group ties." While they are still "ambivalent about their identification with their agency, they see in it the best means of attaining their goals of practicing" their profession, and as helping resources rather than as antagonists of their clients and themselves.

The *specialist bureaucrat* is a classification that Morgan says encompasses the largest group of social workers. This worker is interested in reconciling the "bureaucracy to humans and humans to the bureaucracy." Specialist buraucrats use the rules and regulations of the agency to guide their professional judgments. "While they recognize that agency directives are in general necessary, they also recognize the richness of the human situation that can never be fully encompassed by specific rules and regulations." They see the agency as authorizing them to use their professional discretion to protect the interests both of the agency and of its clients. They realize that the agency is a bureaucracy and therefore heir to all the dysfunctional characteristics of this form of human organization. They usually have the professional "courage to sacrifice bureaucratic norms when they interfere with their professional function." They have successfully, through understanding and professional judgment, adapted in practice to norms which in theory are essentially irreconcilable. In fact, they may see this constantly shifting adaptation as the very stuff of professional life.

The *executive bureaucrat* likes "to manage people, money, and materials. While functional bureaucrats are oriented toward their profession, service bureaucrats toward those they serve, specialist bureaucrats toward the profession and the bureaucracy, executive bureaucrats seem oriented primarily toward the exercise of power. While executive bureaucrats are innovators and do not consider themselves bound by a rigid application of rules and regulations [in fact, they may be daring bureaucratic infighters and risk takers], they tend not to appreciate innovations by their own subordinates." They lean toward enforcement of bureaucratic norms for others and run a disciplined agency.

Job bureaucrats are people, professional workers, who "have a substantial career investment in the bureaucracy. At the center of their attention is the security of their own career, and they seek to safeguard and advance it through a meticulous application of regulations and adherence to the norms of the organization." Effective job bureaucrats achieve their greatest success in supervisory or administrative positions. While they hold themselves firmly to official policies of the organization, they realize that the other professionals in their sections have a different orientation, and while they tend to supervise closely, they exercise sufficient "selective nonattention" to the less rigid way in which their subordinate professionals operate, that through the proper amount of "social slippage" the social work job gets done. The ineffective job bureaucrat is characterized by a rigid overcompliance with regulations and norms. Directives that originally were issued to accomplish a mission become ends in themselves, and the mission of social work, or even of the agency itself, become secondary considerations.

AGENCY BUREAUCRACY AND THE WORKER

No one ever meets a pure type in real life, so perhaps it is understandable that the authors are not willing to put themselves in any one of the classes listed.

But we suppose that we could probably be located somewhere between the service bureaucrat and the specialist bureaucrat. We do not believe that a worker who accepts a position as a member of an agency staff and who utilizes agency resources, no matter how unsatisfactory they may be, can act as though the worker were a private practitioner or without concern for agency policies and procedures. As a staff member, the worker is bound by the agency policies. If these policies are unacceptable, one must either work to change them, while remaining bound by them, or one must leave the agency and work for change outside it.

The first principle for workers who would give their clients maximum service is to understand the organization for which they work and to know how its structure and function were and are determined. If one is going to be actively involved in change, one needs to know what the possible points of intervention are. Three major factors affect the organization of agencies: their source of support, the source of their sanction or right to operate, and the areas of their concern. Agencies obviously cannot operate without a source of funds. As a rule an agency's funds come either from public tax funds or from private voluntary contributions, although agencies supported primarily by private contributions may utilize tax funds through various contracts and grants. Any agency's policy and structure, procedures, and flexibility will be determined by the source and adequacy of its funding. As a general rule, the funds are never adequate to the demands that workers wish to meet, so that difficult choices among real needs must usually be made.

The public tax-supported agency will usually operate within legislation and will be dependent on some legislative body (for example, county commissioners) for its broad policy and for the appropriation of public funds for its support. In some cases the board or commission of a public service may be appointed by an elected executive officer (that is, governor). Such agencies are usually administered by individuals who may be required to prove their competence by passing various tests. These administrators will determine procedures and more detailed policy issues within the broad legislation that established and maintains the agency.

Private agencies usually operate under the general policy directives of a board of directors. Such a board has three primary functions: it establishes the right of the agency to carry on its program and sanctions the agency's activities; it is responsible for the agency's overall policy; and it is responsible for fund raising. Until very recently almost all boards were composed of an elite group of members with little understanding of the realities of the lives of those for whom they developed programs. Boards almost always operate by consensus. Because the board members of private agencies are volunteers, the members who are constantly on the losing side of an issue soon drop out unless they have a deep commitment. In most situations the board hires the executive of the agency, and it often happens that the executive sees the job as keeping the board happy on the one hand and running the agency the executives' own way on the other. The executive usually controls staff access to the board and the flow of information to the board about the agency's work. So the worker's attempts to represent clients and their interests in policy and program matters are often unheard.

Some social work departments (such as the social service department of a school system, a hospital, a court, and so on) operate as part of a larger host agency. In this situation the financial support and policy-making processes will be determined by those of the host agency, which generally operate under a similar structure.

Agencies have both a function and a program. The program is the ways and means that an agency utilizes to carry out its function as defined by the community. For the practitioner, this distinction has some importance in that although an agency's function may remain constant, its program ought to be responsive to the changing needs of the times. Thus an agency whose function is the care and treatment of children may initially have cared largely for orphaned or dependent children but now may be concerned primarily with delinquent children.

Each agency has an organizational (bureaucratic) structure by which it delegates its responsibilities and tasks and stabilizes and systematizes its operations. The executive is the primary administrative officer. Officers have direct responsibility for the day-to-day functioning of the agency. Because they are usually responsible for getting the money to run the agency, this responsibility may occupy most of their time and thought. They are responsible for relationships with the board of directors or a public body. They are usually responsible for working with other agencies toward community social work goals and for the public relations functions of the agency.

Below the executive on the organization table of a large agency one may find a bewildering array of division directors, unit supervisors, consultants, and line supervisors. A small agency may have only three levels of hierarchy: the executive, the supervisors, and the workers. Line workers are more conscious of their relationship to their direct supervisor—a professional person who is usually held responsible for two functions that at some times and to some people seem contradictory: (1) helping workers to improve their skills both in the interests of getting the present job done at the best level possible and for the worker's and client's future benefit, and (2) administratively holding workers responsible for doing the job to certain standards and evaluating their performance relative to those standards.

Many articles in social work literature deal with the supervisory process and its problems. Supervisors, like workers, differ, and some may be more interested in their job security and tenure than in the client's needs for service or the worker's need for both support and learning opportunities. All beginning workers can use considerable help in increasing their awareness of themselves and their way of working, and in adding to their fund of knowledge about people, resources, and helping processes. And in a large agency with considerable work pressure and a constant scarcity of resources, all line workers need considerable support of their supervisors in dealing with the constant frustrations of the day-to-day job.

Harry Wasserman (1970) examined the work of professional social workers in a large public agency. He found that structural constraints rather than social work knowledge and skills dictated what the worker was able to offer in the client's life situations. In this instance, 8 of the 12 workers studied had left the agency after two years. Wasserman (p. 99) concluded that "the two principal feelings expressed by the 12 new professional social workers during the two-year period were frustration and fatigue," and that "they were exhausted by having day after day to face critical human situations with insufficient material, intellectual and emotional resources and support." Certainly supervisors cannot wave a magic wand and undo the effects of structural constraints on the worker's capacity to help, but a supervisor who cares about the worker's capacity to help and the worker's mental health can, through support and the offer of intellectual and emotional resources, make a great deal of difference in what the worker is able to do and in how the worker grows on the job.

Because of the constant strains and problems of the supervisor's job there has been some push in certain agenices to do away with supervision. Perhaps social work could develop a better form than the supervisory process, but one cannot do away with the supervisory function. Doing away with authority relationships does not necessarily change either people or structural constraints or result in more effective work. As long as personal needs, attitudes, and differing levels of commitment and skill are brought to a job, there is a need for leadership. As Weissman (p. 131) points out:

> The planning and management of an organization requires specific expertise. . . . there is an ongoing need to reconcile the dilemmas and strains of organizational life. . . . as long as there is concern for the effectiveness of an organization, there will be considerable strain between the needs of the individuals for self-actualization and the needs of organizations for achievement and efficiency.

Somehow these strains need to be reconciled and resolved if clients are to be effectively served. The question concerning the supervisor that is of critical importance for the worker is the supervisor's position on the list of roles that Morgan developed.

Perhaps the primary problem with supervision is not that it is not valuable, or not necessary, but that it has been used in such a way that agencies have avoided consideration of their effectiveness by focusing on the effectiveness of their employees. In most agencies, workers receive yearly evaluations on the anniversary of their joining the staff. Perhaps what is needed are set dates on which both the workers and the agency would be evaluated. In other words the agency needs to look at itself at the same time that it is looking at its workers. As Weissman (p. 58) writes:

> The environment in which the agency operates—physical, social, financial— affects the worker's efforts. To tell workers to refine their skills or work harder in order to be successful is to ignore the impact of environment. The caseload or lack of cooperation from other agencies, not diagnostic or therapeutic skills, may be at fault.
>
> Evaluating individuals at different times during the year solely in terms of their individual therapeutic skills makes it less likely that the agency will have to react as a system to the results of evaluation. The problems of each worker can be viewed idiosyncratically.
>
> . . . Through consultation with experienced workers, agencies should establish the areas of skill needing improvement and the basis upon which to judge improvement—recordings, observations, client queries, and the like. The worker should choose how to get help, whether through conferences with the supervisor, through taking courses, through peer supervision, or through consultation. Letting the worker decide reduces the dependency feelings which develop through forced supervision.
>
> A degree of arbitrariness will always exist unless an agency has some method

of appraising success with clients. Without agency standards of success and an evaluation of the worker's record, workers and supervisors are dependent on secondary data. Case presentation becomes more important than the people treated. The way one writes or speaks about a case becomes more important than the results achieved.

Weissman (p. 59) then goes on to discuss the accountability of the agency for evaluation of its job. (This is another side of the earlier argument made by the authors about the need for evaluative research and ways of evaluating services.) He says:

> The key to increasing the influence of lower level staff vis-à-vis their superiors lies in a board (or other body) that can hold the agency accountable. Where there is real accountability, the ideas and experience of all levels of staff become valuable, and the incompetence of individuals becomes a matter of serious concern.
>
> If a board discovers that 80 percent of the agency's clients feel they have not been helped by the agency, the incompetent supervisors have something to worry about.

CLIENT, WORKER, AND BUREAUCRACY

The procedures of bureaucracy as well as the limitations of policy may be frustrating to both the client and the worker. It is well to recognize that "red tape" was and is developed to assure that people with equal troubles receive equal help and resources. But often it really operates to reduce the client's access to services or to make an already complex situation more difficult and confusing. It is the worker's responsibility to act as the client's broker and advocate in dealing with the policies and procedures of the bureaucracy. These roles have been discussed earlier, but one last word will be added here.

If workers are to help the client cope with the problems of access to services in the most helpful way possible, it is critically important that they know with accuracy and understanding the policies and procedures of their agency and the way they operate. Workers are not always as careful and disciplined as they might be in getting a really workable grasp of this knowledge. *Paperwork* can become a very naughty word in the worker's language, but the capacity to handle paperwork efficiently, accurately, and with concern for deadlines and the client's time, is an absolute requirement of the worker who would be a skilled advocate and broker. The authors have worked in agencies where certain chief clerks made more important decisions about who got what than some workers because the clerks had mastered the paper flow and the workers were too impatient to do so. While paperwork can be irritating, the worker needs to understand that it is an attempt to establish procedures by which clients are assured equal service.

One of the authors of this book is old enough to have worked in public welfare before the Social Security Act took effect, when it was the responsibility of the local township to aid people in need of money. At that time paperwork was considerably lighter than it became after the agency was able to secure federal funds if it established certain procedures to assure people equal service and the right of appeal if they felt that they had been capriciously denied. However, at that time people were able to secure aid only if they were able to convince the worker and/or the supervisor that they were "worthy of aid." Sometimes this meant that they had supported the proper political candidate with the proper enthusiasm. This decision could not be challenged—there were no procedures to assure this, no paper on which the basis of the decision was recorded. But back to the present.

The worker needs to thoroughly understand the parameters of the policy of the agency and the authority available for interpretation. A policy is a broad statement. It has to be interpreted by some individual before it can be applied in the interests of another individual. Far too often, a worker will either ask the worker at the next desk what the agency does about such and such or give the supervisor a quick call.

Our position is that the worker starts with what the client and the worker have decided is needed as a resource in the problem solution. Next the worker is responsible for finding out exactly what the written statement of the policy says. Then the worker sits down and thinks long and hard about what that policy actually means and what all the different possible ways to interpret and apply it are. Next the plan made with the client is used to test the various interpretations. The interpretation is selected that will best enable the worker to help the client with what is needed for problem-solving. Workers then write down that interpretation of the policy and the way they would apply it to the client situation. If necessary, this statement may be submitted to the supervisor for approval, but in any case it needs to be made a part of the record of service to the client. Our view is that taking the quick and easy route of asking colleagues or supervisors about policy is not the proper way to perform one's role as an independent professional person; and our experience has been that following that course increases the likelihood of receiving a directive that limits what one can do. Others do not always want to do the hard headwork either, and when one is in doubt about a policy the easier thing is to say no. It is out of this way of functioning—the use of the traditional messages about policy that circulate on the office grapevine—that old patterns get stabilized and become harder and harder to change. By really knowing policy and by utilizing creative interpretations of policy, the worker can help keep the agency active as an ever-changing bureaucracy.

Several years ago one of the authors conducted a study to find out (1) whether clients were receiving aid they needed and (2) why or why not. In the agency under study, workers reported great discouragement with the limitations of agency policies and felt that these policies prevented them from really helping their clients. The study revealed that the average client of that agency was receiving less than half of the amount of services and resources to which the client was legally entitled under its policies. In other words, it was not the agency policies that were limiting client access to services, but rather the narrow and traditional way that workers and supervisors were interpreting the policies. In the year following the study, as workers were helped to assume active responsibility for broadly interpreting policy, the aid to their clients more than doubled in cost, yet no one in the agency or on its board reached out to stop this more expensive way of operating. The point being made is that service to the client is not limited to what one does when one sits with the client. Some of the most important work, and sometimes the work that is most difficult and requires the most self-discipline and commitment, is the work involved when the worker takes on the role of broker with the agency's programs and its bureaucracy. Social workers are often the kind of people who prefer to deal with people rather than with paper—yet dealing with paper is a part of everyone's life in today's world. So workers can often fail the client in real and hurtful ways if they do not have expert skills in dealing with paper. Operating contrary to traditional grapevine interpretations of policy may often involve the worker in uncomfortable confrontations with the agency colleagues and the supervisor. And it is not easy for an individual worker as part of a system to move contrary to the patterns and relationships in the system. However, if workers' interpretations conform to written policy they can usually prevail in the client's interests, which is what social work is all about.

One more word. If policy does not permit adequate service to clients, this needs to be adequately documented. Workers must assume the responsibility of documenting in some detail the problems they see. It may be difficult to open up board structure and policy so clients can make an impact, but it will never happen if workers only "gripe." They must present organized evidence of their position.

CHANGING THE BUREAUCRACY

An article by Edward J. Pawlak on organizational tinkering has been reproduced in this chapter (see Reading 15–1). More important than its title would indicate, it really relates to what is being discussed in this section; the focus is on tactics for "tinkering" with the organizational structures, rules, and policies in order to bring about bureaucratic change. Another author who has written some excellent articles on the social worker's activities within the bureaucratic structure is Robert Pruger (1973). The authors have borrowed some of Pruger's ideas to combine with their own thoughts in putting together this section.

The authors' first suggestion for change would be to be clear about what needs to be changed, about the difficulties that can be anticipated in bringing about the solution, and about the cost of both the problem and its solution (problem definition, goals, and plan). So often people not experienced in the complexity and the balances of the bureaucratic setting will take a drastic step to change the situation and will be completely overwhelmed by the unexpected repercussions that follow. Let us consider, for example, the worker that feels that clients are being poorly served by a policy. Unable to change anything, the worker resigns in anger and frustration. A newspaper reporter hears of the problem and asks the worker about it. Seeing an opportunity to use the power of public opinion and certain of the obvious virtue of the cause, the worker tells the reporter of the problems. However, many people in the community do not see the story as an attempt toward better service. They interpret it as an example of how poorly social workers administer public funds, and a strong community pressure develops to cut the funds of the agency, to set up more stringent rules and regulations for the social workers to follow, and to replace the social work director with a business manager who will see that rules are followed.

The second principle is to determine what factors and forces inside and outside the organization are keeping the problem alive. What the worker did not know in this example was that the executive and the board were as deeply concerned as the staff with certain policies but, given the power position of certain people in the community, they had made a decision that any attempt to change things would result in costly backlash. This is not to say that one does not take on an open fight in spite of the threat of backlash. It is to say that one should know the approximate force of that movement and have decided in advance how it would be met. The "freedom fighters" in the Civil Rights Movement are an example of this. They knew in advance something of the expected response to their activities and they not only seriously considered them, but drilled themselves in advance so they would not be taken unawares by sudden actions of the opposition.

The next point follows logically from the above. One should anticipate the difficulties of the solution. Almost any solution to a social problem brings other problems in its implementation. Be sure that the solution is not worse than the problem and know some ways of dealing with anticipated difficulties of the solution. Find out whether those who have the responsibility of deciding about the problem are simply unaware of it or are strongly invested in present policy or opposed to any movement because a clash of interests and values is involved. And this leads to point four, which is determine where in the organization the responsibility for formal decision-making in respect to the problem lies. Who formally makes the decision and who or what can influence this decision?

Timing one's efforts can be crucial. Agencies are more often open to change (as are individuals) when they are in periods of crisis, for example, when budgets are increasing or decreasing, when there are great decreases or increases in the number of clients served, when their performance reports are being questioned, or when new methods of dealing with the problem are being widely acclaimed.

The process by which change takes place must be understood, and it must be recognized that the initiation of change often requires a different approach than does the implementation of change. We have often seen workers fight a hard and bruising battle for the initiation of change only to lose the war because they were unwilling or unable to be an active part of its implementation. It is the changes in the way things are done that are the test of how the client will be served differently.

Consider whether change can be achieved more effectively in this situation by advocacy strategy, by collaborative strategy, or by both. Advocacy strategy employs an impressive array of tools, including the use of citizen groups, unions, and professional organizations to engage with the practitioner in litigation, picketing, bargaining, building pressure alliances, contriving for crises to occur, bringing sanctions to bear through external authorities, and perhaps by encouraging noncompliance with policy by workers and clients. Collaborative strategy may employ some of the techniques outlined by Patti and Resnick (1972). Here the change agent may provide facts about the nature of the problem, present alternative ways of doing things, try to develop an experimental project that involves different ways of doing things and get permission to implement it, seek to establish a committee to study the situation and make recommendations for change, attempt to improve the working climate of the agency so that individuals feel trusted and safe and thus can look beyond securing their own position to the task to be done, attempt to bring professional values and ethics to bear, use a logical argument to persuade, and point out what is really happening under the present policy. This last approach will require documentation of the results of present policy.

Pruger (1973) deals with the strategic concerns of the "good bureaucrat" in some ways similar to the above discussion and adds some additional factors. We have summarized his material as follows:

1. "One important property of a good bureaucrat is staying power." This means a recognition that things happen slowly in complex organizations but that whatever changes workers have in mind cannot be implemented if they do not stay in and with the organization.
2. "The good bureaucrat must somehow maintain a vitality of action and independence of thought." Organizational life tends to suppress vitality of action and independence of thought. Workers must resist such pressure.
3. "There is always room for insights and tactics that help the individuals preserve and enlarge the discretionary aspect of their activity and, by extension, their sense of personal responsibility."

And, these are tactics the good bureaucrat will employ:

1. "Understand legitimate authority and organizational enforcement." The inescapable degree of generality found in the regulatory policies and codes of the organization allows for considerable autonomy of the individuals if they just recognize it and use it. The organization's power to control is less than many realize, but if the limits of legitimate authority are recognized, the individuals may expand their discretionary limits.
2. "Conserve energy." Change agents should not thrash around and feel discouraged and unappreciated because they do not receive in a large organization the kind of support they receive from their friends. Also, as stated earlier, master the paper flow of the organization. This will not only help the client but will also remove from the worker's shoulders the weight of resentment and emotional turmoil one feels as one looks at the uncompleted statistical forms on the desk. Workers should describe what can be changed and work on it rather than spend valuable hours bemoaning what cannot be dealt with.
3. "Acquire a competence needed by the organization."
4. "Don't yield unnecessarily to the requirements of administrative convenience. Keep in mind the difference between that which serves the organizational mission and that which serves the organization." Rules, standards, and directives as to the way things should be done are meant to be means that serve ends. In organizations means tend to become ends so that a worker may be more concerned about turning in the mileage report than the results of the visit to a client. Ends and means should be kept clear.
5. Workers should remember that "The good bureaucrat is not necessarily the most beloved one."

We would like to stress that these skills in changing the bureaucracy or acting as an advocate for client groups involve the following knowledge and abilities. The knowledge of how individual human beings and social systems develop, grow, exist, change, and cope with problems; the knowledge of how individuals interact within small social systems such as the family or primary groups (knowledge of family development and interaction, knowledge of group process); knowledge of transactions within larger social systems (organizational behavior); knowledge of common human needs and the way culture affects how these needs are expressed are all critical knowledge bases necessary for effective planning for advocacy and institutional change. In addition, to carry through such plans, the workers will need self-awareness, especially in certain areas such as innate pushes toward the expression of competition and aggression, their own level of anger and the favorite ways of using it; they will need the capacity to use self in a disciplined way within the parameters of the plan; they will need a high level of communication skills and ability to use effectively the various skills outlined in Chapter 11.

THE PROFESSION AS A SYSTEM

Social work is a profession, as we discussed earlier. All professions can be viewed as social systems. Because the social work profession is a system within which every social worker functions, whether it is recognized or not, every social worker ought to understand something about it. The profession through society's assignment of its functions, sanctions to some extent the work of all people who call themselves social workers, or who occupy jobs that are classi-fied as social work positions.

In Chapter 2 we identified the six characteristics of a profession. Through-out the text we have discussed the high degree of generalized and specialized knowledge needed by the professional. The value systems underlying social work practice have also been discussed. We certainly have indicated the need for social workers to have a commitment to community and client interests in-stead of being primarily motivated by self-interest. In this chapter we would like to continue in a more organized way to look at the sixth system of profes-sional practice—the profession, itself, as a social system.

First, we need to consider the fact that the knowledge and skills possessed by professionals give them powerful control over persons and things. It is im-portant to society, which provides the professional the opportunity to secure this power, that it be used primarily in the community interests and that it not be used to advance professionals at the costs of the welfare of those who sup-port their acquisition of such knowledge. Thus, the community usually has some organized way of sanctioning the persons who may claim status and who may practice in the name of the profession. Also, the profession itself, in order to safeguard itself against self-aggrandizement of its members and assure that its function in society is fulfilled, supports the underlying value of community service.

In all professions, the community sanctions the individual's right to practice through some combination of the following elements: (1) completion of a cer-tain prescribed course of education; (2) proving a certain level of competency through an examination process administered by the profession; (3) the licens-ing and regulation of the practitioner through a license, registration, or certifica-tion administered by the state (usually through a board with professionals as members); and (4) employment by an organization authorized by the state to offer certain services. Thus, there exists licensing of teachers and doctors and the registration of nurses. There has been considerable pressure within the social work profession to license social workers. Those who would license social workers usually make the point that such licensing would benefit the client systems by defining standards of service and the competence necessary for practice. It would establish a public accountability that will protect both the client and the practitioner from inconsistent, biased judgment of effectiveness of help offered. It would establish a legal definition of social work and establish levels of social work practice which should operate to protect both the professional and the client. It would give social work status among other professional groups.

Because of the importance of this question to social work (approximately half the states do presently license social work practitioners), a reprint of a very comprehensive article on licensing, which is highly recommended by the authors, has been included with this chapter (see Reading 15–2). Since licensing has come slowly to social work, the National Association of Social Workers attempted some time ago to set some standards through the establishment of a restricted title. The title, "Certified Social Worker," has been registered with the federal government and can be used only by persons certified by the professional association, the National Association of Social Workers. In order to use this title, social workers have to possess an MSW degree (a master's degree in social work), have worked two years in practice following the earning of the MSW under supervision of another worker who is an ACSW, must be a member in good standing of the NASW, and must pass a professional examination. People who meet these requirements may call themselves a Certified Social Worker and use the letters ACSW (Academy of Certified Social Workers) after their name. The profession recommends that no one engage in private practice who is not a member of the Academy.

All professions are organized into some kind of professional association. These professional organizations serve three purposes: (1) increasing the adequacy of the performance of the individual practitioner; (2) policing the ranks of its membership to insure competent performance of the individual members; and (3) to protect the members' exclusive right to practice their profession. In social work, the professional association is the National Association of Social Workers, a national association operating through regional chapters in each state. It accepts for membership those persons who have a BA degree in social welfare or social work.

The admission of the BA worker to membership in the professional association was followed by the setting up of professional undergraduate courses in social work in universities and the implementation of an accreditation program of such work by the Council on Social Work Education, the organization that accredits professional social work programs in higher education.

Social work as an emergent profession has never had complete control of who could call themselves a social worker and who could do the job in the field. Generally, the social agencies were the ones who effectively decided who could be social workers in that the persons they hired to fill social work positions were entitled to call themselves social workers. Thus, the education, knowledge, and skill of agency employees filling social work positions, who were known to the public and clients as social workers, has varied widely. In general, the private agencies that have often served the middle class have generally insisted on MSW degrees for employment, while the public services have required only a BA (or less) degree. In an effort to deal with this, NASW has developed a statement of levels of social work practice complete with professional qualifications for each level.

Today, the National Association of Social Workers has identified six levels of social work practice. There are two levels—*the social service aide* and *the social service technician* that require less than a college degree in social work.

To carry the title *"social worker,"* the person should have a bachelor's degree in social work (BSW).

To be a *graduate social worker,* the person needs a master's degree from an accredited professional school in social work. This usually requires two academic years beyond the BA degree, although it may require less time if the person has a BSW degree. To be a *certified social worker,* one must possess a MSW, have two years of practice beyond the degree under careful supervision, and must pass an ACSW examination. To be a *social work fellow,* one must possess a PhD or DSW in social work and have either two years' experience in specialization or have passed the ACSW examination plus two further years of specialized practice.

It has long been held that the requisite knowledge to judge professional performance is available only to those who have themselves been trained in applying such knowledge. The professional knowledge and skill of the professional person is so different from general knowledge and skill that no one outside the profession can judge the professional. This is usually discussed under the rubric of professional autonomy. Thus, every profession has some means of the self-regulation of practice.

Generally, these "shoulds" of professional practice are stated in a formal code of ethics. However, as certain professionals may engage in unethical or incompetent behavior, and as the community becomes more and more dependent on professional knowledge, the community is increasingly demanding that the people served by the profession should have the right to judge professionals by the outcome of their service *as the public perceives it.* They are questioning whether it is possible for the operation to be a success if the patient dies. This stance may well mark some unrealistic perceptions of the capacity of professionals on the part of the community, but it also marks a realistic concern with the notion that clients do not have the capacity to know when they have been well served—that only professionals have the ability to judge the outcome of their actions.

Another element in this notion of autonomy is that professionals are supposed to be self-directing in their work. As used here, autonomy refers to the professional's control of the content and terms of the work. However, autonomy is not a simple criterion of who is to be considered professional—at least most people have never been willing to designate those wives and mothers who run their own households as being professional. This introduces the notion that when we speak of professionals, what we are really talking about is some kind of organized autonomy—not the autonomy of the individual practitioner. Thus, the more that a profession as a profession is able to exercise autonomy, the more it represents, and its members are controlled by, a hierarchy of institutionalized expertise (Friedson, 1970, pp. 71–92). The question of the professionalization of social work has been raised by many authors on the basis that social welfare organizations are usually considered bureaucratic, not professional organizations. Thus, there are professionals operating in organizations that are marked by the fact that authority is that of the administrative office held. This conflicts with the notion that in a profession the authority is that of expertise. This has already been discussed under bureaucracy but it should be noted that perhaps one of the problems of all professions is that the rigidity and conservatism in the professions are also enforced by the concept of autonomy.

Each profession has its own culture. The interactions of social and professional roles required by the professional activities and professional groups generate particular ways of thinking and acting, and a particular language, unique to the profession. This may be called a professional culture. The value system of the profession in interaction with the value system of the bureaucracy is an important part of the culture of social work. A critical aspect of all professional education and inservice training is the attempt to socialize the workers to the agency and profession. By this, it is generally meant the internalization of the values and culture of the profession so that the professional person is constrained to work in certain ways and to take certain positions.

One of the problems in the achievement of greater autonomy of the profession is found in the fact that when agencies hire people *who have less than the recognized professional training*, these workers do not have a well-integrated identification with their profession that will allow them to stand outside bureaucratic expectation. Instead, they tend to be socialized to the culture of the agency rather than the culture of the profession. Thus, they may first see themselves as public welfare employees rather than first identifying themselves as social workers. As these workers often cannot easily go elsewhere and find employment as social workers, they are tied to their position in the agency rather than their identification as a professional.

Sound internalization of professional values is critically important as protection to the client system since in the helping process workers must use themselves and their judgments. There is seldom any way that another can interfere in the process of action to protect the client in advance of the worker's action. Therefore, the only assurance people have that a professional person can be trusted with professional tasks is that the person acts on the basis of deeply internalized feelings and judgments that stem from professional values and knowledge. This value system and the feelings and actions that stem from it become a part of the culture of the profession. The ambiguous position of social work within society in terms of its multiple functions and purposes also contributes greatly to shaping the culture of social work.

Lydia Rapoport (1959) says that "no other profession is as self-examining and critically self-conscious as social work." While she relates some problems of the profession to its youth, she also attributes much stress to the profession's ambiguous position in society and to its multiple purposes and functions. Social work, concerned with the social functioning of people and the adequacy of the social institutions which affect human functioning, "seeks to embrace and implement some principles and values which may be essentially unpopular and uncongenial to the dominant social order." This particular role of the profession, as has been observed, results in its being seen as a minority group that is both tolerated and feared. From this come outright attacks and depreciation by the society that sanctions social work. In addition, the social views of the profession tend to isolate individual workers from other professional groups.

One problem of social work is that the tasks it is expected to perform are unclear and that the responsibilities for which it is held to account are often contradictory. For example, many people expect the social worker to control every expenditure of the welfare client, but at the same time to further independent behavior on the part of welfare recipients. Both expectations cannot be satisfied—one or the other must be chosen. Social work is supposed to be working to produce social change, but the society of which social work is a part is totally unable to reach agreement as to the kinds of social change it will support.

Rapoport (1959) points out other sources of strain for social workers, some of which have been touched on earlier in this text. Among them are the following:

1. Being constantly confronted with the problems of human need, pain, and injustice;
2. The capacity for self-awareness and self-control required for the purposeful use of the social work relationship, and the need "to harmonize personal capacity and inclination with professional behavior and values;"
3. The institutional framework within which the social worker practices;
4. The opposing demands for "the maintenance of nearness and distance, of involvement and detachment, of rapport and objectivity;" and
5. The requirement for the tolerance of uncertainty, given our limited knowledge about human development and our difficulty in attempting to utilize what we do know.

RECAPITULATION

In this chapter we have moved from our focus on the interaction of client and worker for problem-solving to what it means for the worker to be a part of the action system of an agency and a profession. It is critically important for workers to understand the situation in which they work. We have tried to contribute to this understanding through a look at the nature of bureaucracy and professionalism; the conflicts between bureaucracy and professionalism; the worker and the client as operating within the parameters of agency policy; ways to bring about change in a bureaucracy; and the worker as a professional.

A LOOK FORWARD

We are now near the end of the text. Readers have two remaining things to look forward to (1) they have one more brief chapter which will try to summarize the text material; and (2) they should be looking forward to working with people and social systems, and perhaps testing whether the material in this book is really helpful in their practice. After all, that is why the authors wrote the text.

Reading
15–1 *Organizational tinkering**

Edward J. Pawlak

To tinker means to work at something in an experimental or makeshift way. Although clinicians' positions and roles in many social welfare organizations preclude them from pursuing ambitious organizational change, they still may be able to work at change in

* Copyright 1976, National Association of Social Workers, Inc. Reprinted by permission of author and publisher from *Social Work* 21:3 (September 1976), pp. 376–380.

modest, makeshift ways. And, despite the fact that clinical social work is usually practiced in an organizational and policy context, many clinicians are uninterested in acquiring the knowledge and skills that might facilitate intraorganizational tinkering on behalf of their practice or their clients. Others are overwhelmed, cynical, or disillusioned by their dealings with bureaucracy (Briar, 1968; Gottlieb, 1974, p. 34; Hanlan, 1971; Piliavin, 1968; Podell and Miller, 1974; Specht, 1968, pp. 42–43). Some front-line practitioners, however, have learned to tinker effectively (Hyman and Schreiber, 1974; Maher, 1974; Senna, 1974).

To help clinicians improve their talent in dealing with organizations, this article identifies tactics they can use to tinker with organizational structure, modes of operation, rules, conventions, policy, and programs. The specific tactics discussed are tinkering with bureaucratic succession and rules, the white paper or position paper, demonstration projects, modification of board composition, bypassing, influencing grant reviews, leaking information, and protest by resignation.

Although the author takes a partisan stand on behalf of clinicians, it does not follow that managers are necessarily the villains. However, some of the tactics identified here are directed toward those administrators who cause clinicians to harbor severe misgivings about the organization.

This article stems not only from the author's observation of and experience with organizational tinkering, but also from the contributions of others who have addressed similar themes (Bennis, 1969; Brager, 1968; Martin, 1971; Patti and Resnick, 1972; Specht, 1968, pp. 42–52; Weissman, 1973, pp. 57–131). It warns clinicians to bear in mind the pitfalls and dilemmas of organizational tinkering—that it takes place in a political climate and in a structure of authority, norms, and sanctions (Epstein, 1968; Green, 1966; Nader, Petkas and Blackwell, 1972; Patti, 1974; Weisband and Franck, 1975).

Bureaucratic succession

Bureaucratic succession usually refers to a change in leadership at the highest levels of an organization. Here, however, the author uses the broader concept that includes changes in leadership at all levels in the hierarchy. (Gouldner, 1954, pp. 59–104; Levenson, 1961). Bureaucratic succession must be called to the attention of clinicians because it is an opportunity to influence intraorganizational change. For clinicians to exert influence during this phase of organizational transition, it is essential that they understand certain features of organizational life that frequently accompany succession.

Prior to an administrator's departure, organizations usually go into a period of inaction. Most staff members are aware of the lame-duck character of this phase of organizational life, when any major change is avoided until the new administrator takes office. There are, however, ways in which clinicians take advantage of this period. They can, for example, (1) suggest criteria for the selection of a successor, (2) seek membership on the search committee, (3) prepare a position paper for the new administrator, (4) propose a revision in the governance structure to enhance participatory management, (5) organize fellow subordinates to propose changes that had been unacceptable to the outgoing administrator, or (6) propose the formulation of a task force to facilitate transition.

The "first one hundred days" is another critical phase of bureaucratic succession that should be examined for the opportunities it offers. Although new administrators tend to be conservative about implementing changes until they are more familiar with the organization, they still are interested in developing and in making their own mark. This three-month period, therefore, provides opportunities to orient and shape the perceptions of new administrators who, until they acquire their own intelligence about the organization, are both vulnerable and receptive to influence.

The following case illustrates how practitioners can tinker with organizational hierarchy by taking advantage of a resignation.

The resignation of a clinician who had served as director of staff development in a child welfare agency provided the staff with an opportunity to influence the transformation of the position into that of administrative assistant. The agency had recently undergone rapid growth in staff size, resources, and diversity, without an accompanying increase in the administrative staff. Thus, the clinician's resignation became the occasion for examining whether the position should be modified to serve such administrative staff functions as program development and grant management.

Bureaucratic succession, therefore, provides an opportunity for an organization to take pause; to examine its mission, structure, policies, practices, accomplishments, and problems; and to decide what it wants to become. It is incumbent upon practitioners to participate in these processes and to take advantage of the structure of influence during that vulnerable phase.

Rules

Rules are features of organizations that, by their nature, invite tinkering. They act as mechanisms of social control and standardization, provide guidelines for decision-making, limit discretion, and structure relationships between persons and units within the organizational structure and between separate organizations (Perrow, 1972, pp. 23–32). There are two types of rules—formal and informal. Formal rules are derived from law or are determined administratively or collectively. Informal rules—which may be as binding as formal ones—are practices that have been routinized so that they have become organizational conventions or traditions. Rules vary in specificity, in their inherent demand for compliance, in the manner in which compliance is monitored, and in their sanctions for a lack of compliance.

Clinicians can tinker with rules either by the kind of interpretations they apply to

them or by using their discretion, as is permitted with an ambiguous or general rule. Rules do not necessarily eliminate discretion, but they may eliminate alternatives that might otherwise be considered (Thompson, 1967, p. 120). Gottlieb (1974, p. 8) describes them as follows:

Rules are not necessarily static. They appear to be a controlling force working impersonally and equally, but they vary both in adherence and enforceability and are used variously by staff in their adaptation to the "welfare bind."

Hanlan (1967, p. 93) suggests that "in public welfare there exists an informal system that operates without invoking the formal administrative machinery of rules." The author overheard the director of a community action program encourage new workers "to err on the side of generosity in determining eligibility for programs." A vocational rehabilitation counselor reported that he had had many teeth fixed by liberally interpreting a rule that provided dental care for only those clients whose appearance and dental problems would otherwise have prevented them from being considered for employment involving public contact. This shows that one can tinker with the manner in which rules are interpreted and enforced.

Another way of tinkering with rules is to avoid what Gottlieb (1974, p. 8) calls "rule interpretations by agents of the system alone." She goes on to report that welfare workers encouraged clients to seek help in interpreting rules enforced by the National Welfare Rights Organization (NWRO). It is generally known that legal-aid clinics have been called on to give a legal interpretation of welfare rules and rules governing commitment to mental hospitals.

A supervisor for public assistance eligibility once reported that a thorough knowledge of all the rules enables the welfare worker to invoke one rule over another in order to help clients get what they need. This observation is supported by Gottlieb (1974, p. 32), who points out that rules allow for exceptions and that many NWRO members know the rules better than the workers and thus can challenge their interpretations. In his study of regulatory agencies, Nader (1972) suggests that rules not only are opportunities for action but are potential obstacles as well and that major effort is frequently required to persuade the agency to follow its own rules.

Another way of dealing with rules is to avoid asking for an interpretation. One agency administrator has suggested that personnel should not routinely ask for rulings and urges them to use their own discretion. He commented: "If you invoke authority, you put me in a position where I must exercise it. If I make a decision around here, it becomes a rule."

These ways of tinkering with rules suggest that clinicians should examine the function of rules, discern the latitude they are allowed in interpreting them, and exercise discretion. Although the foregoing examples are primarily taken from welfare settings, the principles outlined can be applied to traditional clinical settings.

Indirect influence

Too often, clinicians rely on the anecdotal or case approach to influence change in an organization. Such an approach is too easily countered by the rejoinder that exceptional cases do not require a change in policy but should be handled as exceptions. The white paper, or position paper, is a much ignored means of tinkering with organizations.

A white paper is a report on a specific subject that emanates from a recent investigation. A position paper is a statement that sets forth a policy or a perspective. The first is usually more carefully reasoned and documented; the second may be argued instead of reasoned. Both white papers and position papers provide opportunities for social documentation and for formulating a compelling case. Such statements strive for logic and are characterized by their use of both quantitative and qualitative data. As the following

example shows, by virtue of their character and quality, both position papers and white papers demand a specific response.

A student social worker wrote a position paper identifying the number of teenage pregnancies, the number of associated medical problems, and the high rate of venereal disease among adolescents. She argued for the redirection of the original planned parenthood proposal from the main office to satellite clinics in public housing developments and schools. The paper was well received and spurred the executive to obtain funding from the housing authority.

Lindblom (1970) has characterized decision-making in organizations as "disjointed incrementalism." Simon (1957) indicates that organizations "satisfice"—that is, they make decisions that are good enough. Uncertainties in the environment, the inability to scan all alternatives, and the unknown utility of a solution or decision all preclude optimal decision-making. If organizations were to try to comprehend all the information and contingencies necessary before making a rational decision, the complexity would be overwhelming. Thus, organizations are reluctant to make changes on a large scale because this could lead to large-scale and unpredictable consequences. Resistance to change, therefore, may often be attributed to structure rather than to a malevolent or unsympathetic administrator. This calls attention to organizational structure and processes, but does not mean that the values and roles of administrators are to be ignored.[1]

Given this perspective of organizational behavior, clinicians may consider approaching innovation incrementally and on a small scale by first gaining authorization for a demonstration project.[2] A demonstration project may be bounded by the duration of time or the proportion of the budget or staff time that is devoted to it. The problem with

---

[1] For a useful discussion on organizational resistance to change, *see* Patti (1974).

[2] For a negative view of demonstration grants, *see* Pratt (1974).

demonstration projects is that the people for whom the demonstration is being carried out are not always specified, nor are they always kept abreast of developments. Often there is a failure to articulate the ramifications and consequences of a successful or unsuccessful demonstration. Practitioners must develop a strategy of demonstration—a means of diffusing innovation throughout the organization or into other organizations and of obtaining commitments from the administration when the demonstration is complete. The following is an example of the commitment one social worker obtained.

A social worker met with a group of suspended or expelled junior high school students after class to discuss their problems. Realizing that she needed to have a chance to intervene directly in their school behavior, she persuaded the agency supervisor, the principal, and the classroom teacher to develop a pilot project—"the opportunity class"—to be used as a last resort before expulsion. When the project was organized, the social worker remained in the classroom for several periods at least two days each week. She handled the acting-out behavior problems while the teacher continued classroom instruction. Eventually the teacher acquired skill in handling students who were acting out. The class continued without the social worker's presence, and some students returned to a regular classroom while others were expelled.

Agency board committees are typically composed of elected members and the executive director of the agency. In addition, in some agencies, one or two staff members may also serve on the committee or occasionally attend meetings to make reports. One strategy of tinkering with the composition of the committee and the kind of information and influence it receives is to promote the idea that nonboard and nonstaff members with certain expertise be included on the committee. For example, a psychiatrist and a local expert on group treatment with children might be recruited to join a case services committee in order to provide legitimation to innovations that board members were grudgingly resisting.

Bypassing refers to a process whereby practitioners avoid taking proposals for change or grievances to their immediate superiors but seek instead a hearing or decision from a higher level in the hierarchy. In an enlightened organization, this form of bypassing is acceptable and even encouraged; government workers, in fact, are entitled to it as part of "due process." Bypassing is risky, however, in that it can discredit the judgment of the complainants if the matter is trivial or if it appears that it could have been resolved at a lower level in the hierarchy. Bypassing also places the administration in a vulnerable situation because if the tactic is justified, it reflects poorly on the judgment of the superior and the administrators who hired them. This may lead to questions of nonretention or spur a desired resignation. A successful instance of bypassing is described in the following example:

When a clinician's complaints concerning the physical plant and security of a youth home went unheeded by the director, he demanded to meet with the executive committee of the board. The director admitted that his own sense of urgency differed from that of his staff, but arranged for the meeting. The executive committee approved some of the recommendations for change and authorized that they be implemented as soon as possible.

Agencies often write grant applications for funds to support their programs. A critical phase of the application process occurs at a public review of the grant application when the funding agency invites comment or a letter of support from the agency or from interested parties. If clinicians are dissatisfied with a particular program, and if it is an important matter, they can provide the agency issuing the grant with dissenting information, testify at the review of the grant application, or respond from the standpoint of an "expert witness." In any event, the grant-review process may be an opportunity to voice concern about an agency's program and to influence the advisory group to give conditional approval or disapproval. As is shown in the following example, clinicians may attempt to influence the review process indirectly—by encouraging an expert third party to raise questions about the grant application—or directly.

A social worker was asked to serve as a technical reviewer for a volunteer program for young offenders in a regional planning advisory group. The program was modeled after an existing program in another part of the state. The documents supporting the application contained a manual that described the role of the volunteer. It suggested that a volunteer should report any violations of parole to the corrections authority but should not reveal this action to the offender. In seeming contradiction, it emphasized that the volunteer should be a "friend" of the offender. The social worker informed the advisory group of this provision and of his strenuous objection to it. The director of the program had failed to read the manual thoroughly and was unaware of the statement. The advisory group approved the program on the condition that the volunteer not serve as an informer and demanded that the staff codify the conditions under which it may be morally imperative for the volunteer to reveal the offender's behavior.

Social workers are often asked and frequently do endorse a program or a grant application perfunctorily, without having read the proposal. In other instances, programs and grants are endorsed in spite of strong reservations. Notwithstanding the pressures toward reciprocity that exist among agencies, such exchanges of professional courtesy are questionable.

Social workers should take advantage of requests for endorsement or participation in the grant-review process, particularly if they believe that certain aspects of a proposal or program are questionable. The desire for professional endorsement also underlies agency efforts to recruit clinicians for board membership or as paid consultants. Refusal of such offers is a way of "making a statement" about a program.

Radical tactics

Leaking information, or the covert release of information about an organization, is a tactic that should be used only in grave

matters after all other remedies within the organization have been exhausted. The third party to whom the informant gives the information has to verify it and the credibility of the informant, since this person is not willing to put one's character and job on the line. However, until "blowing the whistle" becomes an accepted institutionalized value, and until protections are legislated, it is likely that members of organizations will continue to act like "guerillas in a bureaucracy" (Nader, Petkas, and Blackwell, 1972, pp. 15, 25–33; Needleman and Needleman, 1974).

Clinicians who anticipate the need to leak information would be well advised to seek counsel, for discovery could result in liability damages. They are obliged to have a thorough, accurate, and verifiable account of the objectionable situation. As the ethics of leaking information have not been well formulated, clinicians need to consider carefully the professional, moral, and legal standards that support such action (Nader, Petkas, and Blackwell, 1972, pp. vii, 1–8, 29–30, 225–230). One way in which the clinician may choose to attack the problem is shown as follows.

The clinician in a foregoing example who was concerned about the physical plant and security of a youth home notified the state monitor about the condition of the home. At the next site visit, the monitor raised questions about the residents' access to balconies and the roof and about the staff-client ratio on weekends.

Resignation in protest, or public defection, is another tactic that should be used only when a clinician experiences unbearable misgivings and finds it both morally and professionally imperative to reveal them publicly. The major problem is that the organization has the financial and operational resources to counter the protest, but the employee has none. Also, with few exceptions, resignation in protest has a history of aversive consequences for the protester (Weisband and Franck 1975).

A resignation in protest may also discredit the agency. Therefore, prospective protesters must be prepared to have their observations and conclusions verified and their judgment subjected to public review and scrutiny. In addition, the protester must realize that future employers will wonder whether such history of protestation will continue. An example follows.

When his concerns went unheeded by the board, a clinician resigned in protest. Moreover, he informed the board and the director that he would discourage any professional worker from accepting employment at the agency. He was effective in discouraging local professionals from accepting employment at the agency unless firm commitments were made to modify policies and practices that were detrimental to clients.

The theory of escalation urges protesters to begin by using conventional and formal means to express grievances and influence change. Only after these have been exhausted, and traditional means have encountered failure and resistance, should they engage in a series of escalations to such unconventional or radical forms of protest as boycotting, "palace revolts," picketing, leaking information, and the like. The essential point of this strategy is that protesters should not begin by engaging in the most radical and abrasive strategy. To document the intransigence of the bureaucracy, change must be approached incrementally. If this is not done, the bureaucracy may point to the failure to follow administrative due process. The protester's etiquette and failure to go through channels then become the bone of contention, and the protester becomes the object of protest (Nader, Petkas, and Blackwell, 1972, pp. 16–25; Needleman and Needleman, 1974, pp. 285–289, 335–339; Weisband and Franck, 1975, pp. 55–94).

As a condition of employment and as a professional right and responsibility, clinicians should have the opportunity to bring their insights into the plans and programs of the organization they work for. Such participation requires that clinicians acquire skill in dealing with organizations. It is hoped that the participation of clinicians in organizational activity will promote responsive service delivery systems and satisfactory work climates.

At the risk of appearing to be a "double agent," the author plans to write a second article to advise administrators on how to cope with the tinkering of clinicians. After all, organizational power—whether in the hands of clinicians or administrators—"must be insecure to some degree if it is to be more responsible" (Nader, Petkas, and Blackwell 1972, p. 15).

Reading

15–2 Public regulation of social work*

David A. Hardcastle

A major contemporary movement in social work's efforts to attain recognition as a full profession is the move toward public regulation. The National Association of Social Workers, for example, has taken strong action to further this objective, as illustrated

* Copyright 1977, National Association of Social Workers, Inc. Reprinted by permission of author and publisher from *Social Work* 22:1 (January 1977), pp. 14–20.

in the following resolution approved by its 1969 Delegate Assembly:

Resolved: That the various combinations of Chapters, working in concert at a state level, be authorized to pursue licensing of Social Work practice within each state. . . (*NASW News*, 1974, 1975a, 1975b, 1975c, 1976).

The public or legal regulation of a profession occurs when the public, through formal legislation and the regulatory or legal powers of the state, defines and regulates professional behavior and conduct. Although the regulated profession may be involved in formulating the definitions and in the processes of regulation, it is the mandate and sanction of the state that ultimately defines the profession. Social work currently has some form of public regulation in Arkansas, California, Colorado, Delaware, Idaho, Illinois, Kansas, Kentucky, Louisiana, Maine, Maryland, Michigan, New York, Oklahoma, Puerto Rico, Rhode Island, South Carolina, South Dakota, Utah, and Virginia.

This article analyzes the conceptual foundation of legal regulation, and develops a classificatory scheme of legal regulation according to its major variables. It also analyzes and classifies existing legal regulations according to the variables.

PROFESSIONALISM

There is general consensus on the attributes of a profession, and they have been well discussed by Greenwood (1966) and Feldstein (1971), among others. Basically, these attributes are (1) a systematic and defined theory or a system of abstract propositions, (2) defined and specialized skills, (3) a regulatory code of ethics governing conduct, (4) a supportive professional culture or community with normative standards, values, and symbols, (5) professional authority which holds that professional behavior can only be evaluated by professional peers, and (6) the sanction of the community to exercise such authority.

The second point—defined and specialized skills—should be a basic prerequisite for public regulation of an occupational activity. These skills describe the activity to be regulated. However, they are not sufficient alone to transform an occupation into a profession nor do they provide all the prerequisites for public regulation.

According to Wilensky (1970), two additional elements are necessary for each transformation. The first element is technical expertise based on systematic knowledge and doctrine acquired through formal training. The neophyte practitioner must have this training to gain the formal knowledge and skills and the implicit or tacit knowledge, values, and norms of the craft. It is the latter —the tacit knowledge, values, and norms— that provide the basis for what is commonly referred to as the "art" of social work. The second critical element is the acquisition of the regulatory norms by the occupational category, which are needed to limit conduct and behavior. Essential to and inherent in the regulatory norms are the following factors: (1) other professionals, rather than clients or "outsiders," must make judgments of competence and appropriate professional conduct, and (2) service must be the primary motive for the activity. It is the ideal of service or of a "calling," with the practitioner standing above the sordid considerations of the marketplace, that separates the professions from occupations (MacIver, 1966, p. 51; Parsons, 1951, pp. 314–315; 1954, pp. 38–43). Although "service calling" does not exclude other motives, it does place service as the dominant and central motive.

Public or legal regulation of a profession and its activity indicates that the profession has received the sanction and mandate of the public. Wilensky (1970, pp. 489–490) holds that a benchmark of professional development, although not necessarily an integral part of its natural history, is attained when occupations engage in political action to gain the support of public law for the protection of their job territory and their sustaining code of ethics. Legal protection is an expedient of an occupation "on the make." It enhances status, protects jobs, and restricts jobholding to those who meet certain requirements, and protects the public from incompetence—that is, from practice by persons without the requisite technology, tacit knowledge, or normative behavior (Committee on the Study of Competence, 1968, p. iii).

Public regulation, therefore, implicitly recognizes the authority of peer judgments, in that the regulatory board is generally composed of professional peers; it also provides explicit community sanctions for the exercise of professional authority. But public regulation per se does not establish an occupational activity as a profession. In contemporary society most occupational activities are regulated in some manner, and many are directly regulated through formal statute. Wilensky (1970, pp. 484–487), for example, reports that egg graders are regulated in Indiana, well diggers in Maryland, and horseshoers in Illinois. Friedman (1962, p. 139) reports that, as early as 1938, North Carolina regulated 600 occupational activities ranging from medicine to dealing in scrap tobacco. During its 1974 session, when the Kansas legislature was considering a social work regulation bill, it was also considering a bill to license timber harvesters.

Purposes of regulation

The NASW 1975 policy statement (p. 15), by action of the Delegate Assembly, sets forth the following four purposes for the public regulation of social work:

1. Establishing a public, legal definition of the profession which recognizes the differential levels of social work practice.
2. Protecting consumer and clientele rights and raising standards of service competence of practitioners in both agency and independent practice.
3. Establishing a public accountability in the delivery of social services based on professional standards rather than inconsistent, private standards of performance, and that protects the practitioner in the performance of social work tasks.
4. Provide a basis for the development and enhancement of the profession within the context of other social institutions and professions.

The public justification for legal regulation is more general and succinct and is made on a twofold basis: the protection of the public and the development and protection of the profession.

It is assumed that the vendor engages in activities so complex that they require knowledge, skill, and technology for judgment beyond that reasonably expected for an independent evaluation by a consumer. The state therefore provides an a priori evaluation for the consumer. It is also assumed that the vendor's behavior has an irreversible impact on the consumer. If the vendor does not have the requisite knowledge, skills, and technology, the consumer may suffer severe and irreversible harm. However, as the Virginia statute (1975) states, "the potential for harm is recognizable and not remote or dependent on tenuous arguments." A third assumption is the "neighborhood effect" of the activity, in which the impact of the vendor's behavior clearly extends beyond the vendor and consumer and affects the general public. Examples of neighborhood effect may be found in the area of physical safety, within such fields as architecture, engineering, and public health, and perhaps social planning, community organization, and education.

The development and protection of the profession is inherent in the protection of the public, although distinct from it. Through its regulatory powers, the state can impose entry requirements and standards for maintaining performance. Tests of continued competence and the updating of knowledge and skill can be imposed. Although these standards are designed to protect the public, they also protect the competent professional from the deleterious neighborhood impact of charlatans practicing under the umbrella of the profession.

Less altruistic reasons for an occupational activity to promote legal regulation are imbedded in the potential for protection of the job market that such regulation affords. Depending on the restrictiveness of the entry for requirements, it has the potential of limiting the supply of the service in relation to the demand for the service. Although rational justification for restrictions can be made on the grounds of protecting the public, if they limit supply in relation to demand, the tendency will be to drive prices up. The potential of legal regulation to provide market control to the vendors or practitioners is related to the degree to which the vendors control the regulatory boards. Friedman (1962) cites a 1956 study indicating that 75 percent of the regulatory boards were controlled by persons who had a direct economic interest in the regulated activity. Indeed, it is generally a hallmark of full professional status when the vendors control the licensing process utilizing the regulatory powers of the state.

The potential of public regulation to provide revenue for states cannot be overlooked. Licensing fees and occupational taxes, like the charges for the sale of liquor licenses in certain states, can be a viable source of revenue. The example of North Carolina with its regulations and fee collections for over 600 occupational and economic activities cannot be ignored. In Kansas, 20 percent of the registration fees of social workers go into the state's general fund while 80 percent are used to defray the cost of regulation.

Categories of regulation

Public regulation can be parsimoniously classified into three categories according to the state's use of its regulatory powers to enforce its definitions and regulations to protect the public. These three categories are registration, certification, and licensure.

Registration. This is the state's listing or registry of persons identifying themselves with the activity. Registration provides a self-identified listing of vendors to potential users. The state's utilization of its regulatory powers is limited. There may be specific requirements for registration, such as the possession of certain educational credentials and the payment of fees, but unregistered vendors do not usually draw punitive measures from the state unless they claim registration. It is up to the market—the client, the agency, the payee—to determine the worth of the registered vendor over the unregistered vendor. This form of public regulation

exercises the least degree of regulatory power and the least interference with the activity of the marketplace.

Certification. This is the warranting by the state that the persons certified have attained a specified level of knowledge and skills. Like registration, certification does not prohibit uncertified persons from engaging in the behavior; it merely prevents their use of "certified" or a similar descriptive term with their title. Registration is a requisite of certification. The latter does further in that it requires that the state make a judgment as to the competence of the vendor. Certification thus provides the public with an a priori judgment of the competence of those using a term such as "certified" with their title. The state defines competence and may test for it, but does not enforce its definition of competence over the activity, only over the use of the title. Consumers and vendors have the choice as to whether they wish to use—and meet—the state's definition of competence. The unregulated vendor can engage in the activity if consumers can be found who are willing to purchase the service.

Licensure. This is the third and strongest form of legal regulation. It is a mechanism by which the state decrees that persons may not engage in particular economic activities and behaviors except under specific conditions set forth by the authority of the state and under its regulatory powers. Licensure states explicitly the requirements for knowledge and skills, describes how these are to be obtained and demonstrated, and uses the state's regulatory powers to enforce the definition of standards and behaviors. Licensure protects both the title and job activity. It defines the requirements of those who perform the services and limits the activities to those who meet its definition. For example, individuals may use an accountant who is not certified to monitor and record their fiscal affairs or they may use an unregistered architect to design their homes, but their surgery, whether for a fee or free, must be performed by a state-approved practitioner. Licensure combines registration and certification with control (Agostinelli, 1973; Friedman, 1962, pp. 137–161; Hardcastle, 1973; Levy, 1973a; Sheafor, 1973; Weinberger and Weinberger, 1974; Wilensky, 1970, pp. 483–501).

Regulation of social work

As mentioned earlier, 19 states and Puerto Rico have some form of public regulation of social work. The legislation for public regulation in 18 of these states and Puerto Rico, as well as the NASW Model Licensing Act, were analyzed and classified according to their potential for the protection of the public and the development of the profession (National Association of Social Workers, 1973). (Delaware's legislation was passed after the completion of this study and is therefore not included in the analysis. Several other states may also have enacted some legal regulation of social work by the time this article appears.)

Protection of the public. Each act of public regulation was analyzed in terms of its potential to protect the public. The stronger the potential for public protection, the more likely is public regulation to approach licensure.

Criteria used to examine the legislation for protection of the public aimed to determine whether the legislative acts contained the following:

1. Definitions and specifications of knowledge, skills, and values required for practice.
2. Entry requirements specified in terms of credentials, experience, and examinations.
3. Standards differentiating the knowledge and skills required for the various levels of practice—when these levels of practice are specified, especially if they are arranged in a hierarchy.
4. Utilization of regulatory powers to protect the public definitions and requirements for social work practice.
5. The functional exclusiveness of the definition.
6. Inclusion of the protection of confidentiality.
7. The degree to which "grandfathering" or the waiving of competence examinations for contemporary practitioners is avoided.
8. Requirements for demonstrations of continuing competence, such as reexaminations for competence and requirements for continuing education.

Two of the criteria may need elaboration. "Utilization of regulatory powers" refers to the degree to which the legislation prohibits unregulated persons from engaging in the activity. In other words, does the statute regulate functions and actions or merely restrict the use of certain titles? True licensure requires functional exclusiveness.

"Grandfathering" refers to the practice of automatically granting to the contemporary practitioner the credentials of the public regulations. Under grandfathering the practitioner meets the requirements for regulation upon applying and paying fees. The degree to which existing practitioners are grandfathered is critical for the protection of the public. If it is assumed that regulation is necessary to protect the public, the need for public protection must relate to current practitioners as well as future practitioners. Grandfathering, however, could allow current practitioners to practice for perhaps 30 to 40 years, untouched by requirements for updating knowledge or for testing of skills.

Certain issues of recertification are related to grandfathering. Without recertification, two tenuous assumptions must be made before any substantial client protection can be inferred: (1) social work knowledge and skills once acquired are mastered for life and (2) the profession is not generating new knowledge or skills so that social work knowledge and skills are static and will not change over the worker's life.

Regulation with extensive grandfathering and without meaningful recertification offers little protection to the client beyond that available without regulation. The current body of professionals and any future group who pass their entry examinations may have an expectancy of approximately 30 to 40 years of practice life. If so, regulation with grandfathering will have an approximate 20-year "half-life"; 20 years will elapse before the profession is half certified if one assumes a constant rate of entry into it and attrition from those leaving it. Under the same assumptions of entry and attrition without meaningful recertification for any future point beyond 20 years, only half the profession will have had a testing of competence within a 20-year span.

Table 1 summarizes the review of the regulations by the foregoing criteria. No state's legal regulations meet the criteria for full licensure. No state uses its regulatory powers to enforce its definition of social work practice for persons regulated by the legislation. Persons in all states may engage in the economic activity and behaviors without being regulated as social workers. However, they cannot claim the regulated title in the performance of the activity.

Development of the profession. The second area for analysis was the potential for the development of the profession means that the state, not the profession, assumes regulatory control, legislation can contain mechanisms to promote the development of the profession and of competent professionals. Criteria for analysis included the following:

1. *Exclusiveness of claim to professional praxis*

   Exemptions allowed for other professions

   Exemptions allowed for social workers employed under certain auspices

   Title protection

   Protection of functions

   Clear criteria for knowledge, skill, and function for differentiating between levels of social work if levels are used

TABLE 1
Classification of the legal regulations of the social work profession in 18 states and Puerto Rico and in the Model Licensing Act of the National Association of Social Workers (NASW)

Classification	*States, Puerto Rico, and NASW model*
Licensure: Full use of regulatory powers to enforce functional exclusiveness, credentials requirements for entry, examination of knowledge and skills	None
Strong certification: Use of regulatory powers for title protection, credentials requirements for entry, entry examination of knowledge and skills, and at least one other major criterion, such as continuing education, to protect the public	Colorado Idaho Illinois Kansas Kentucky Maryland South Dakota Utah NASW
Weak certification: Use of regulatory powers to protect preface to title, credentials requirements for entry, and entry examination, but no other major criteria to protect the public	California Louisiana Maine New York Oklahoma Virginia
Registration: Use of regulatory powers to protect preface only, credentials for entry examination, but no entry examination on knowledge or skills and no other major criteria to protect the public	Arkansas Michigan Puerto Rico Rhode Island South Carolina

2. *Recertification requirements for professional growth*

   Periodic examinations of knowledge and skills

   Continuing education including definitions of what is required

3. *Professional authority and autonomy*

   Composition of the regulatory board and proportion of social work professionals

   Autonomy of the board

   Decision-making power of the board

   Autonomy of practice and degree of dependence on controls external to the profession

4. *Reciprocity in terms of allowance for interstate transfer of requirements*

The criteria under the third category are critical. They determine whether the regulated professional is an autonomous professional or is limited to carrying out practice activity as a professional under the auspices of an agency.

According to Greenwood (1966), Parsons (1951, 1954) and other students of professions, the mark of a profession is strong reliance on peers for professional authority and for judgments of professional competence. The requiring of judgment-making by agency personnel in positions of control within an agency's organizational structure —that is, supervisors—is aprofessional. Essentially it substitutes bureaucratic and administrative judgments for professional ones. It does not further the profession but promotes the agency and discourages professional functioning independent of bureaucratic systems. Meaningful public regulation should curtail the need for bureaucratic regulation, not enlarge it.

Utilizing the major criteria to justify public regulation for the protection of clients and the public and for the development of the profession, it appears that public regulation of social work falls short.

Impact on protection

No state uses its regulatory powers to define and regulate functional behaviors for the social work profession. In short, licensure does not exist for social work. Only five states protect the unadorned title of "social worker." The remaining states, following the NASW Model Licensing Act, protect the title of social worker only when prefaced by "registered," "certified," or a similar term. Although 75 percent of the states require entry examinations, all but three have liberal grandfathering exclusions, exclusions for related professions, or exclusions from regulation allowed to some social workers because of the auspices of their employment. Recertification requirements are limited to payment of fees with the exception of continuing education required by four states and the NASW Model Licensing Act. Although certification can be revoked, this is done for negative behavior—"thou shalt nots." Recertification does not depend on positive behavior—"thou shalts."

Eighty percent of the legal regulations and the NASW Model Licensing Act specify more than one practice level. None specify functional or behavioral differences between the levels. The major differences relate to educational preparation and occasionally to differences in experience and auspices. Private practice as a regulated social work activity is permitted only for the upper levels.

In summary, protection of the public or clients is little improved by the current body of legal regulations over what existed without legal regulation. With the exception of the entry examination, the states, Puerto Rico, and the NASW Model Licensing Act appear to be certifying only that the professional has met baseline educational requirements associated with a specific title.

Impact on the profession

Again, the contemporary body of legal regulations appears to do little to promote the development of the profession. Almost all states, either specifically or by implication, exclude from regulation "other professions performing similar functions," whether or not these professions are regulated by other statutes. Approximately 40 percent ex-

TABLE 2
Potential of public regulations to promote the development of the social work profession, classified by states and the Model Licensing Act of the National Association of Social Workers (NASW)

Criteria	States, Puerto Rico, and NASW model
1. Exclusiveness of claim to professional praxis	
Exemption of related professions from regulation	California, Colorado, Kansas, Kentucky, Louisiana, Maryland, New York, South Dakota, Utah, Virginia, and NASW Model (others do not specify)
Exemption from regulation of social workers employed under specific auspices	California, Kansas, Kentucky, Louisiana, Maryland, Rhode Island, and Virginia
Protection of prefaced title, such as "certified social worker" or "registered social worker"	All
Protection of unadorned title of "social worker"	Illinois, Maryland Maine, South Dakota, and Utah
Protection of functions	None
Explicit criteria of knowledge and skills	None (not applicable in Louisiana, New York, Rhode Island, and South Carolina—which limit legal regulation to MSW degree)
2. Recertification requirements based on professional growth	
Periodic reexamination of knowledge and skills	None
Continuing education required	Colorado, Kansas, and South Dakota (and Kentucky at board option)
3. Professional authority and autonomy	
Social workers a majority on regulatory board	All except Arkansas and Colorado
Autonomous board	All except Kansas and NASW model
Board with decision-making powers	All except Kansas and NASW model
Practice defined as autonomous and independent of nonprofessional controls	California, Idaho, Illinois, Louisiana, Maine, New York, Oklahoma, Puerto Rico, Rhode Island, South Carolina, South Dakota, and Utah
4. Reciprocity between states	Colorado, Idaho, Illinois, Kansas, Kentucky, Maryland, Michigan, New York, South Dakota, Virginia, and NASW model

clude social workers who are employed under certain auspices. Only five states protect the unadorned title of social worker. Even NASW's Model Licensing Act does not protect it.

Although 80 percent of the legal regulations specify levels of practice, they do not explicitly mention differentials in knowledge and skills, nor are career ladders present.

Movement between levels is generally by meeting the next requirement for academic degrees. Notable exceptions are the requirements of experience for autonomous clinical practice and Michigan's experience continuum.

Registration or certification is generally for life, contingent on the periodic payment of fees. No state monitors the maintenance and upgrading of knowledge and skills, except for the requirement of continuing education in four states. It appears unlikely that legal regulation will provide motivation for professional development beyond that existing without it.

On the criteria related to professional authority and autonomy, the legal regulations grade higher. All but two states have regulatory boards composed primarily of social workers. The boards are autonomous and have decision-making powers, with the odd exceptions of the regulatory board in Kansas, which is advisory to the Secretary of Social and Rehabilitation Services, and the board recommended in the NASW Model Licensing Act, which would be advisory to a regulatory agency.

When the statutes contain levels of practice, the autonomy of the professional and the profession is a critical factor. Autonomous practice in the multilevel statutes is limited to the upper level of practice. Practitioners at lower levels can engage in the practice activity, but generally only under the auspices and supervision of an agency. The agency supervisor need not be a professional social worker or even a professional. Qualifications required for private practice may include supervision by an appropriately certified social worker. The point is not subtle. The practice of professionals in the field of social work, except for a limited number of elites at the upper level of practice, remains under the control of agencies, that is, under aprofessional or nonprofessional control. If this situation is justified on the basis that the lower levels lack the requisite knowledge and skills for autonomous peer-regulated practice, can their status as professionals be simultaneously advocated? This is not an argument against agencies as delivery systems or against administrative supervision and direction. Nor is it an argument against differentiated practice. It is an argument against the inconsistency of requiring by legal regulation that the majority of the activities of the profession be carried on within the confines of an agency in order to be called professional social work practice.

Slightly over half the states allow for reciprocity with states having similar requirements in their legal regulations. To some degree, the free movement of social workers throughout the country may be inhibited because of the lack of reciprocity between the states. However, this restriction probably has a minimal effect since the legal regulations are relatively flaccid.

Conclusions

Overall, the existing legal regulations and the provisions of the NASW Model Licensing Act appear to this author to have little potential for the protection of the public, the development of the profession, and greater impact on the profession than exists without legal regulation. The status quo is not significantly altered. According to Briggs (1975, p. 15) the basic difficulty seems to lie in the uncertainty and lack of preciseness in the definitions of knowledge and skills and the inability or unwillingness of those formulating the legal regulations to include and develop meaningful standards.

If those associated with social work are unable or unwilling to define more precisely the basic competence, knowledge, and skills of the profession, the assumption that they can test and differentiate these appears dubious. However, if they can define more precisely the requisite knowledge and skills, yet fail to test and monitor them, fail to exclude the incompetents and persons with less than full professional attributes from professional practice, and neglect to require periodic reexamination, then it is an unethical profession.

The profession appears to want the status and protection of public recognition without the costs. The dangers of weak legal regulations are that they may preempt stronger ones in that the weak regulations offer the semblance of public protection and development of the profession without their substance.

Social work, as a liberal profession, has the implicit obligation to resist arbitrary and meaningless public regulation as a bogus status-accruing device. Restrictions, even on a limited basis, are contentious if not offset by the strong and obvious potential for protecting the public and developing the profession.

Selected annotated bibliography

Beck, Walter E. "Agency Structure Related to the Use of Staff," *Social Casework* 50:6 (June 1969), pp. 341–346.
Greater clarity and flexibility in determining agency goals and setting priorities will affect the attitudes of staff and agency's usefulness to clients.

Billingsley, Andrew. "Bureaucratic and Professional Orientation Patterns in Social Casework," *Social Service Review* 38:4 (December 1964), pp. 400–407.
This study of 100 social workers (predominantly MSWs) in a family agency and a protective agency reviews four patterns of orientation—professionals, bureaucrats, conformists, and innovators—in relation to professionals and bureaucratic norms.

Cumming, Elaine. *Systems of Social Regulation.* New York: Atherton Press, 1968.
Cumming describes the complex relationships among social agencies as revealed by movement of clients around the system. She discusses how workers see their roles in the system, how areas of service interact and overlap, and how agencies change over a five-year span. This book will acquaint students at some depth with the organization of the network of "human services" in a middle-sized community.

Daedalus. *The Professions* (Fall 1963).
This issue of *Daedalus* contains several interesting and stimulating articles on the development, functioning, and place of the professions. Students will especially want to read Barber's article, "Some Problems in the Sociology of the Professions."

Feldstein, Donald. "Do We Need Professions in Our Society?" *Social Work* 16:4 (October 1971), pp. 5–12.
Feldstein discusses the conflict between professionalization and consumerism in our society. He feels that this basic conflict is an especially difficult one for social work in that the profession itself espouses a value of democracy and openness. The evolution and nature of the concepts profession and professionalization are well developed.

Freedman, Joel. "One Social Worker's Fight for Mental Patients' Rights," *Social Work* 16:4 (October 1971), pp. 92–95.
This is an account of a social worker who left an agency in order to continue a campaign to improve conditions for clients.

Green, A. D. "The Professional Worker in the Bureaucracy," *Social Service Review* 40:1 (March 1966), pp. 71–83.
Green's article is an excellent discussion of social workers' problems and conflicts in attempting to remain professional within a bureaucratic structure. It attempts to delineate some areas of conflict that are distinctive to the social work professional in contrast to other professionals who also operate in such structures. This is an article every student should read and ponder.

Greenwood, Ernest. "The Attributes of a Profession," *Social Work* 2:3 (July 1957), pp. 45–55.
This very basic article on the attributes of a profession is a classic that has been quoted extensively by other authors in writing about the profession of social work. It should be on every student's reading list.

Pruger, Robert. "The Good Bureaucrat," *Social Work* 18:4 (July 1973), pp. 26–32.
Social work is almost entirely an organization-based profession; social workers should develop skills to negotiate the bureaucratic environment rather than attempt to escape from it. Basic to this is an understanding of legitimate authority and organizational enforcement, acquisition of a competence needed by the organization, and a determination not to yield unnecessarily to the requirements of administrative convenience.

Segal, Brian. "Planning and Power in Hospital Social Service," *Social Casework* 51:7 (July 1970), pp. 399–405.
Segal's article is a case study of the way the social service staff of a hospital went about gaining power in the bureaucratic and professional structure through developing a technical monopoly.

Wasserman, Henry. "The Professional Social Worker in a Bureaucracy," *Social Work* 16:1 (January 1971), pp. 89–96.

Wasserman discusses findings from a study of new employees in a welfare agency. The social worker is powerless and sees the supervisor as incompetent, and administrator is only concerned about financial accountability. In response to the pressures of the bureaucracy, the workers develop defenses that result in their treating clients as objects and in the minimizing of their client contact.

Weissman, Harold H. *Overcoming Mismanagement in the Human Services.* San Francisco: Jossey-Bass, 1973.

This slim book is packed with interesting case studies of existing problems in particular service organizations and offers notions of effective changes that can be brought about in them. The authors feel that it should be on every social worker's reading list.

CHAPTER **16**

Conclusions

Through these chapters and the selection of readings, we have attempted to share our perspective on social work practice. That perspective can be developed and adapted by workers regardless of the setting or relational system in which they choose to practice. In this brief conclusion we reemphasize three recurring themes of the book. These themes are central to this model of practice.

SOCIAL WORK AS A PROBLEM-SOLVING PROCESS

The focus of social work practice is on the relationship between individuals and their environment. A social worker's activities are directed first toward defining and then toward resolving problems that develop in this interaction. This formulation does not specify or limit the social problems which may be subject to social work attention. The problem may be within the individual or the environment, or, as is frequently the case, it may stem from the nature of the person-situation interaction. Also inherent in the problem-solving theme is the notion that the problem has been felt or experienced by some person or group who wish to have it resolved. The experiencing of stress from a problem (either internal or external to the individual) provides the impetus or motivation for the client to become involved with the social worker in a problem-solving endeavor.

SOCIAL WORK AS A CLIENT-WORKER RELATIONSHIP

All aspects of problem solving are undertaken by the worker and client in partnership developed within and affected by the emotional climate of the relationship. The partnership nature of the process extends to decision making as to the nature of the problem and the desired objectives as well as the actual change efforts. This partnership aspect of the work permits operationalization of the concepts of individualization and client self-determination demanding accurate understanding of the irrational elements of the feeling developed on part of both worker and client. The worker is not perceived as an expert in what is best for the client but rather as an expert in facilitating a problem-solving process and in mobilizing resources to assist this process. Partnership implies joint input from worker and client—joint decision making and joint intervention. Participation on the part of the worker is as essential as participation on the part of the client.

SOCIAL WORK AS A RATIONAL PROCESS

Problem solving is a rational process in which worker and client jointly define the problem, specify objectives, and work toward the accomplishment of the objectives. Evaluation is the component of this process that provides feedback loops enabling the client-worker partnership to redefine the problem, goals, or intervention plan. The evaluation feedback loops provide a dynamic, systemic quality to the process. The worker, throughout the process, has the responsibility of maintaining a rational stance toward problem solving involving explicit problem definition, specific goals, and a rational plan to accomplish the goals. While all of these components may be changed on the basis of experience and evaluation, whenever activity is being undertaken with a client, the worker is responsible for the clarity of the joint agreement concerning specific problems, goals, and means.

THE BEGINNING

Through this book we have set forth principles in the areas of problem solving, partnership, and rational process which may serve as useful guides to the worker. These principles, however, will be applied in unique, ever-changing client situations. Their application requires the exercise of professional judgment. Such judgment involves the ability to make decisions and engage in actions guided by a set of principles. It is developed from continuous experience and learning.

We hope that the reader's beginning practice will be more exciting, less frustrating, and more positive than the experiences of this worker, who, after two social work jobs, decided to seek other employment:

> I asked when she first became interested in social work. She said that in her senior year in college she decided she would like to be a social worker. She felt she wanted to go into social work so she could help people help themselves and that helping people was her main reason for wanting to be a social worker.
>
> I asked whether she had expectations about the duties of the social worker. She said that she felt she could remake people's lives. I asked her to elaborate a little more on this and she said that she felt she could help people adjust to their problems in order to have healthy personalities. I asked her what she found when she started work, and she said that when she got her position she found she couldn't remake people's lives because she had a lot of paperwork and reports dealing with her clients. She said she could not change people's patterns of behavior as easily as she thought she could. These behavior patterns are so incorporated into their lives that it is difficult to change their set behaviors. She didn't have enough time to do all that she wanted to help the clients and had to limit her time so that she could interview all her clients, which was a difficult job. Usually AFDC mothers were especially hard to interview because they would change residence about four times a month. She said that only later at the private agency (her second job) was she able to give more time to her clients.
>
> I asked her what kind of people she dealt with at the private agency. She said she took care of adoptions and unwed mothers and that she really liked it better than the public welfare because she had more time with her clients. But she said that this was where she realized something would have to change. I

asked her to elaborate, and she said that many times she just didn't have answers for all the problems of her clients. When a client was really open with her, she felt that many times she didn't know quite how to handle the situation. She said she could not go running to a supervisor in the middle of an interview asking what to do now. She said that these certain moments could not be recaptured at any time. She decided that she needed more education, but she didn't know whether she wanted to take two more years of school.

Obviously this worker had little concept of partnership and perceived herself as being responsible for finding the solution to the clients' problems (remaking their lives) and for being the sole change agent. Perceiving herself as the sole expert, she became anxious when she did not have immediate answers to client questions. While it is probably fortunate that this particular person chose to leave social work, we may at times experience similar dilemmas.

As our experience and professional maturity increases, we will find less need to define ourselves as the expert holder-of-solutions-to-the-client-problems and will be increasingly able to acknowledge gaps in knowledge (knowledge on the part of both client and worker) and to engage the client in a joint quest for the necessary information. No worker is expected to know everything; disillusionment and disaster await those who think they do. What is required is the ability to involve clients, professional colleagues, supervisors and others in comfortably and jointly seeking out the information required for rational problem solving.

If you are seriously pursuing social work, you are about to embark on a journey requiring outstanding self-discipline. Earlier we used the analogy of the figure skater and noted that the truly creative use of self in a spontaneous way occurs only after hours and hours of discipline and practice. The ability to engage spontaneously and comfortably in a partnership for problem solving with clients does not come naturally, but it develops with self-discipline, with learning, with experience, and with practice. We have found the challenge exciting and rewarding and we hope that you will enter the profession with both a sureness of what you are doing and a tentativeness which permits change as new information comes to light.

Reference list

Abbott, Edith. *Social Welfare and Professional Education.* Chicago: University of Chicago Press, 1931.

Agostinelli, Anthony J. "The Legal Regulation of Social Work Practice." Mimeographed. Washington, D.C.: National Association of Social Workers, 1973.

Aguilar, Ignacio. "Initial Contracts with Mexican-American-American Families." *Social Work* 17:3 (May 1972), pp. 66–70.

Aguilera, Donna C., and Messick, Janice M. *Crisis Intervention: Theory and Methodology.* St. Louis, Mo.: C. V. Mosby, 1974.

Akers, Ronald L. "Economic Status and Delinquent Behavior: A Retest," *Journal of Research on Crime and Delinquency* 1 (January 1964), pp. 38–46.

Alberti, Robert E., and Emmons, Michael L. *Your Perfect Right: A Guide to Assertive Behavior.* San Luis Obispo, Calif.: Impact, 1974.

Alexander, Franz. "Extratherapeutic Experiences." In Franz Alexander and Thomas M. French (Eds.), *Psychoanalytic Therapy: Principles and Applications.* New York: Ronald Press, 1946, pp. 35–50.

Alinsky, Saul. *Reveille for Radicals.* New York: Random House, 1946.

———. "On Means and Ends." In Fred Cox et al. *Strategies of Community Organization.* Itasca: Ill.: Peacock Publishers, 1970, pp. 199–208.

Allport, Gordon W. "The Open System in Personality Theory," *Journal of Abnormal and Social Psychiatry* 61 (November 1960), pp. 301–311.

———. *Personality and Social Encounter.* Boston: Beacon, 1964.

———. "Linguistic Factors in Prejudice," in Paul A. Escholz, Alfred F. Rosa, and Virginia P. Clark (Eds.), *Language Awareness.* New York: St. Martin's Press, 1974, pp. 108–109.

American Association of Social Workers. *Social Casework—Generic and Specific: A Report of the Milford Conference, Studies in the Practice of Social Work,* no. 2. New York: AASW, 1929.

Annas, George J. *The Rights of Hospital Patients: The Basic A.C.L.U. Guide to a Hospital Patient's Rights—An American Civil Liberties Union Handbook.* New York: Avon, 1975.

Aptekar, Herbert H. *The Dynamics of Casework and Counseling.* New York: Riverside Press, 1955.

———. *An Intercultural Exploration: Universals and Differences in Social Work Values, Functions and Practice.* New York: Council on Social Work Education, 1966.

———. "A Review of *Theory for Social Work Practice,* by Ruth Smalley," *Journal of Education for Social Work* 3 (Fall 1967), pp. 99–105.

Arcaya, Jose. "The Multiple Realities Inherent in Probation Counseling," *Federal Probation* 37 (December 1973), pp. 58–63.

Argyris, Chris. *Interpersonal Competence and Organizational Effectiveness.* Homewood, Ill.: Irwin-Dorsey, 1962.

———. *Organization and Innovation.* Homewood, Ill.: Irwin, 1965a.

———. "Exploration in Interpersonal Competence—I," *Journal of Applied Behavioral Science* 1 (January-February-March 1965b), pp. 59–83.

———. "Exploration in Interpersonal Competence—II," *Journal of Applied Behavioral Science* 1 (July-August-September 1965c), pp. 255–269.

———. "Interpersonal Barriers to Decision Making," *Harvard Business Review* (March-April 1966), pp. 84–97.

———. "Conditions for Competence Acquisition and Therapy," *Journal of Applied Behavioral Science* 4 (April, May, June 1968), pp. 147–177.

Aries, Philippe. *Centuries of Childhood.* New York; Vintage Books, 1971.

Atherton, Charles. "The Social Assignment of Social Work," *Social Service Review* 43 (December 1969), pp. 421–429.

Audette, D., and Garwick, G. "Interviewer Procedures for Scoring the Goal Attainment Follow-up Guide." Unpublished Project Report, Program

Evaluation Resource Center, Minneapolis, Minnesota, 1973.

Auerswald, Edger H. "Interdisciplinary versus Ecological Approach," *Family Process* 7 (September 1968), pp. 202–215.

Austin, Lucille N. "Trends in Differential Treatment in Social Casework," *Social Casework* 29 (June 1948), pp. 203–211.

Axinn, June. "The Components of an Optimal Social Service Delivery System." Mimeographed. Philadelphia: University of Pennsylvania School of Social Work, 1970.

Babcock, Charlotte G. "Social Work as Work," *Social Casework* 34:10 (December 1953), pp. 415–422.

Backner, Burton L. "Counseling Black Students: Any Place for Whitey?" *Journal of Higher Education* 41:8 (November 1970), pp. 630–637.

Baer, Betty L., and Federico, Ronald C. *Educating the Baccalaureate Social Worker.* Cambridge, Mass.: Ballinger, 1978.

Bailey, Betty Jo, and Pinsky, Sidney. "1964 Voter Registration Drive." Unpublished report. New York, Mobilization for Youth, 1965.

Bailey, Walter C. "Correctional Outcome: An Evaluation of 100 Reports," *Journal of Criminal Law, Criminology and Police Science* 57 (June 1966), pp. 153–160.

Baker, Ron. "Toward Generic Social Work Practice—A Review and Some Innovations," *British Journal of Social Work* 5:2 (Summer 1975), pp. 205–209.

Baldwin, A. L.; Kalhorn, J.; and Breese, F. H. "Patterns of Parent Behavior," *Psychology Monographs* 58:3 (September 1945), pp. 1–75.

Baldwin, James Mark. *The Individual and Society; or, Psychology and Sociology.* Boston: Richard G. Badger, The Gorham Press, 1911.

Bales, Robert F., and Strodtbeck, Fred. "Phases in Group Problem-Solving," *Journal of Abnormal and Social Psychology* 46 (October 1951), pp. 485–495.

Bandler, Bernard. "The Concept of Ego-Supportive Psychotherapy." In Howard J. Parad and Roger R. Miller (Eds.), *Ego-Oriented Casework: Problems and Perspectives.* New York: Family Service Association of America, 1963, pp. 27–44.

Bandler, Louise S. "Casework with Multiproblem Families." In *Social Work Practice, 1964.* New York: Columbia University Press, 1964, pp. 158–171.

Bandura, Albert. "Behavioral Psychology," *Scientific American* 216:3 (March 1967), pp. 78–86.

Banfield, Edward. *The Unheavenly City: The Nature and the Future of Our Urban Crisis.* Boston: Little, Brown, 1970.

Banks, George P. "The Effects of Race on One-to-One Helping Interviews," *Social Science Review* 45 (June 1971), pp. 137–146.

Banta, H. David, and Fox, Renee C. "Role Strains of a Health Care Team in a Poverty Community," *Social Science and Medicine* 6 (December 1972), pp. 697–722.

Barber, Bernard. "Social-Class Differences in Educational Life Chances," *Teachers College Record* 63 (November 1961), pp. 102–113.

———. "Some Problems in the Sociology of the Professions," *Daedalus* 92:4 (Fall 1963), pp. 669–688.

Bardill, Donald R. "A Relationship-Focused Approach to Marital Problems," *Social Work* 11 (July 1966), pp. 70–77.

Barrett, Franklin L., and Perlmutter, Felice. "Black Clients and White Workers: A Report from the Field," *Child Welfare* 50:1 (January 1972), pp. 19–24.

Bartlett, Harriett M. "Toward Clarification and Improvement of Social Work Practice," *Social Work* 3:2 (April 1958), pp. 3–9.

———. "The Generic-specific Concept in Social Work Education and Practice." In Alfred J. Kahn, (Ed.), *Issues in American Social Work.* New York: Columbia University Press, 1959, pp. 159–190.

———. "The Place and Use of Knowledge in Social Work Practice," *Social Work* 9 (July 1964), pp. 36–46.

———. *The Common Base of Social Work Practice.* New York: National Association of Social Workers, 1970, pp. 63–152.

Bartollas, Clemens. "Sisyphus in a Juvenile Institution," *Social Work* 19:5 (September 1975), pp. 364–378.

Bartollas, Clemens; Dinitz, Simon; and Miller, Stuart J. *Victimization: The Exploitation Paradox of a Juvenile Institution.* New York: Sage Halsted Press, 1976.

Bateson, Gregory; Jackson, Don D.; Haley, Jay; and Weakland, John H. "A Note on the Double Bind—1962," *Family Process* 2 (1963), pp. 154–161.

Baxter, J. "Goal Attainment Score Conversion Key for Equally Weighted Scales." Unpublished Project Report, Program Evaluation Resource Center, Minneapolis, Minnesota, 1973.

Beall, Lynette. "The Corrupt Contract: Problems in Conjoint Therapy with Parents and Children," *American Journal of Orthopsychiatry* 42 (January 1972), pp. 77–81.

Beck, Aaron T. *Depression: Clinical, Experimental and Theoretical Aspects.* New York: Harper & Row, 1967.

———. *The Diagnosis and Management of Depression.* Philadelphia: University of Pennsylvania Press, 1973.

Beck, Bertram M. "Community Control: A Distraction, Not an Answer," *Social Work* 14 (October 1969), pp. 14–20.

Beck, Walter E. "Agency Structure Related to the Use of Staff," *Social Casework* 50 (June 1969), pp. 341–346.

Becker, Howard A., and Geer, Blanche. "Latent Culture: A Note on Theory of Latent Roles," *Administrative Science Quarterly* (September 1960), pp. 304–313.

Bell, Daniel. "Twelve Modes of Prediction: A Preliminary Sorting of Approaches in the Social Sciences," *Daedalus* 33:3 (1964), pp. 845–873.

Bell, Winifred. *Aid to Dependent Children.* New York: Columbia University Press, 1965.

Bendix, Reinhard. "Bureaucracy and the Problem of Power," in Robert Merton, Alisa Gray, Barbara Hockey, and Hanan C. Sebren, (Eds.), *Reader in Bureaucracy.* Glencoe, Ill.: Free Press, 1952, pp. 114–134.

Benjamin, Alfred. *The Helping Interview.* New York: Houghton Mifflin, 1969.

Benne, Kenneth D.; Bennis, Warren G.; and Chin, Robert. "General Strategies for Effecting Changes in Human Systems." In Warren G. Bennis, Kenneth D. Benne, and Robert Chin (Eds.), *The Planning of Change.* New York: Holt, Rinehart & Winston, 1969, pp. 32–62.

Bennett, Ivy B. "The Use of Ego Psychology Concepts in Family Service Intake," *Social Casework* 54:5 (May 1973), pp. 290–294.

Bennis, Warren. *Changing Organizations.* New York: McGraw-Hill, 1966.

———. "Post-Bureaucratic Leadership," *Trans-Action* 6 (July-August 1969), pp. 44–52.

———. "When to Resign," *Esquire* (June 1972), pp. 143–145, 188–190.

Bennis, Warren; Benne, Kenneth D.; and Chin, Robert (Eds.), *The Planning of Change.* New York: Holt, Rinehart & Winston, 1969.

Bennis, Warren, and Sheppard, H. "A Theory of Group Development," *Human Relations* 9 (November 1956), pp. 415–537.

Berelson, Bernard, and Steiner, Gary A. *Human Behavior: An Inventory of Scientific Findings.* New York: Harcourt, Brace & World, 1964.

Berger, P. *Invitation to Sociology.* New York: Doubleday, 1963.

Bergson, Henri. *The Two Sources of Morality and Religion.* Translated by R. Ashley Audra and Cloudesley Brereton, with the assistance of W. Horsfall Carter. New York: Doubleday, 1954.

Berkowitz, Sidney J. "Curriculum Models for Social Work Education." In *Modes of Professional Education.* Tulane Studies in Social Welfare. New Orleans: School of Social Work, Tulane University, 1969, pp. 228–234.

Bernstein, Barton E. "Malpractice: An Ogre on the Horizon," *Social Work* 23:3 (March 1978), pp. 106–112.

Bernstein, Saul. "Self-determination: King of Citizen in the Realm of Values?" *Social Work* 5:1 (January 1960), pp. 3–9.

Berschied, Ellen, and Walster, Elaine. *Interpersonal Attraction.* Reading, Mass.: Addison-Wesley, 1969.

Bettelheim, Bruno. *The Informed Heart.* New York: Avon, 1971.

Betz, Barbara J. "The Problem-Solving Approach and Therapeutic Effectiveness," *American Journal of Psychotherapy* 20 (January 1966), pp. 45–56.

Bibring, E. "The Mechanism of Depression." In P. Greenacre (Ed.), *Affective Disorders: Psychoanalytic Contributions to Their Study.* New York: International Universities Press, 1961, pp. 13–48.

Biddle, Bruce J., and Thomas, Edwin J. *Role Theory: Concepts and Research.* New York: Wiley, 1966.

Biddle, William W., and Biddle, L. J. *The Community Development Process: The Rediscovery of Local Initiative.* New York: Holt, Rinehart & Winston, 1965.

Bieri, James et al. "Sex Differences in Perceptual Behavior," *Journal of Personality* 26 (March 1958), pp. 1–12.

Biestek, Feliz. *The Casework Relationship.* Chicago: Loyola University Press, 1957.

Billingsley, Andrew. "Bureaucratic and Professional Orientation Patterns in Social Casework," *Social Service Review* 38 (December 1964), pp. 400–407.

Bisno, Herbert. "A Theoretical Framework for Teaching Social Work Methods and Skills with Particular Reference to Undergraduate Social Welfare Education," *Journal of Education for Social Work* 5:2 (Fall 1969), pp. 5–17.

Blair, Glen M.; Jones, R. Stewart; and Simpson, Ray H. *Educational Psychology.* New York: Macmillan, 1954.

Blanchard, Phyllis. "Tommy Nolan," in Helen Witmer (Ed.), *Psychiatric Interviews with Children.* New York: Commonwealth Fund, 1946, pp. 59–92.

Blau, Peter M. *Orientations Toward Clients in a Public Welfare Agency.* New York: Wiley, 1974.

Blau, Peter. *Approaches to the Study of Social Structure.* London: Basic Books, 1976.

Blau, Peter, and Scott, W. Richard. *Formal Organizations.* San Francisco: Chandler, 1962, pp. 232–234.

Blauner, Robert. "Negro Culture: Myth or Reality?" Paper presented at the Southern Regional Sociological Society Meeting, Atlanta, Georgia, 1968.

Bloch, Julia. "The White Worker and the Negro Client in Psychotherapy," *Social Work* 13:2 (April 1968), pp. 36–42.

Bloom, Martin. *Paradox of Helping: Introduction to the Philosophy of Scientific Practice.* New York: Wiley, 1975.

Bloom, Martin, and Black, Stephen R. "Evaluating One's Own Effectiveness and Efficiency," *Social Work* 22 (March 1976), pp. 130–136.

Blum, Arthur; Miranda, Magdalena; and Meyer, Maurice. "Goals and Means for Social Change." In John Turner (Ed.), *Neighborhood Organiza-*

tion for Community Action. New York: National Association of Social Workers, 1968, pp. 106–120.

Boehm, Werner W. "The Nature of Social Work," *Social Work* 3:2 (April 1958), pp. 10–19.

——. "Toward New Models of Social Work Practice," In *Social Work Practice 1967.* New York: Columbia University Press, 1967, pp. 3–18.

——. *Objectives of the Social Work Curriculum of the Future, The Comprehensive Report of the Curriculum Study.* vol. I. New York: Council on Social Work Education, 1959a.

——. *The Social Casework Method in Social Work Education, the Comprehensive Report of the Curriculum Study,* vol. X. New York: Council on Social Work Education, 1959b.

——. Ed., *Social Work Curriculum Study,* 12 vols. New York: Council on Social Work Education, 1959c.

Bormann, E., and Bormann, N. *Effective Small Group Communication.* Minneapolis: Burgess Publishing, 1976.

Bott, E. *Family and Social Network.* London, Tavistock Publications, 1957.

Bowlby, John. *Grief and Mourning in Infancy and Early Childhood.* New York: International Universities Press, 1960.

Bowlby, J. "A Note on Mother-Child Separation as a Mental Health Hazard," *British Journal of Medical Psychology* 31 (Summer 1972), pp. 38–59.

Bowles, Dorcas. "Making Casework Relevant to Black People: Approaches, Techniques, Theoretical Implications," *Child Welfare* 48:8 (October 1969), pp. 468–475.

Bradley, Trudy. *An Exploration of Caseworkers' Perception of Adaptive Applications.* New York: Child Welfare League of America, 1966.

Brager, George. "Organizing the Unaffiliated in a Low-Income Area," *Social Work* 8 (April 1963), pp. 34–40.

——. "Institutional Change: Perimeters of the Possible," *Social Work* 12 (January 1967), pp. 59–60.

——. "Advocacy and Political Behavior," *Social Work* 13:2 (April 1968), pp. 5–15.

——. "Helping vs. Influencing: Some Political Elements of Organizational Change." Paper presented at the National Conference on Social Welfare, San Francisco, 1975.

Brager, George A., and Jorcin, Valerie. "Bargaining: A Method in Community Change," *Social Work* 14:4 (October 1969), pp. 73–83.

Brandwein, A. Ruth. "The Social Situation of Divorced Mothers and Their Families," *Journal of Marriage and the Family* 36:3 (August 1974), pp. 498–514.

Brechenser, Donn M. "Brief Psychotherapy Using Transactional Analysis," *Social Casework* 53:3 (March 1972), pp. 173–176.

Brecher, Edward M. *The Sex Researchers.* Boston: Little, Brown, 1969.

Brennan, William C., and Khinduka, Shanti K. "Role Expectations of Social Workers and Lawyers in Juvenile Court," *Crime and Delinquency* 17 (April 1971), pp. 191–201.

Brenner, C. *An Elementary Textbook in Psychoanalysis.* Garden City, N.J.: Doubleday, 1955.

Briar, Scott. "The Current Crisis in Social Casework." In *Social Work Practice, 1967.* New York: Columbia University Press, 1967a, pp. 19–91.

——. "The Social Worker's Responsibility for the Civil Rights of Clients," *New Perspectives* 1:1 (Spring 1967b), pp. 6, 90.

——. "The Casework Predicament," *Social Work* 13:1 (January 1968), pp. 5–12.

——. "The Age of Accountability," *Social Work* 18:1 (January 1973), pp. 2, 114.

Briar, Scott et al. "Social Casework: Past, Present and Future," *Social Work* 13:1 (January 1968), pp. 5–59.

Briar, Scott, and Miller, Henry. *Problems and Issues in Social Casework.* New York: Columbia University Press, 1971, pp. 30–185.

Brieland, Donald. "Black Identity and the Helping Person," *Children* 16:5 (September-October 1969), pp. 170–176.

Brieland, D.; Briggs, T.; and Leuenberger, P. *The Team Model of Social Work Practice.* Syracuse, N.Y.: Syracuse University Press, 1973.

Briggs, T. "An Overview of Social Work Teams." In D. Brieland et al. (Eds.), *The Team Model of Social Work Practice.* Syracuse: Syracuse University Press, 1973.

Briggs, Thomas L. "A Critique of the N.A.S.W. Manpower Statement," *Journal of Education for Social Work* 11 (Winter 1975), pp. 9–15.

Brill, N. *Teamwork: Working Together in the Human Services.* Philadelphia: Lippincott, 1976.

Brintnall, J. "P.E.P. Newsletter Compendium." Unpublished Project Report, Program Evaluation Resource Center, Minneapolis, Minnesota, 1973.

Brown, Leonard N. "Social Worker's Verbal Acts and the Development of Mutual Expectations with Beginning Client Groups." Ph.D. dissertation, Columbia University School of Social Work, 1971.

Brown, Luna B. "Race as a Factor in Establishing a Casework Relationship," *Social Casework* 31 (March 3, 1950), pp. 91–97.

Brown, R. "Models of Attitude Change." In Brown, Roger; Galantor, Eugene; Hess, Eckhard H.; and Mandler, George (Eds.), *New Directions in Psychology.* New York: Holt, Rinehart & Winston, 1962, pp. 1–82.

Brown, Robert A. "The Technique of Ascription." Ph.D. dissertation, University of Southern California, 1971.

——. "Feedback in Family Interviewing," *Social Work* 18:5 (September 1973), pp. 52–59.

Brown, Wilfred. *Explorations in Management.* New York: Wiley, 1960.

Brownfain, J. "The APA Professional Liability Insurance Program," *American Psychologist* 26 (July 1971), pp. 648–651.

Browning, Robert M., and Stover, Donald O. *Behavior Modification in Child Treatment.* New York: Aldine-Atherton Press, 1971.

Bruner, Jerome S.; Goodnow, Jacqueline; and Austin, George A. *A Study of Thinking.* New York: Wiley, 1962, vol. 7.

Bryant, Eugene C.; Gardner, Issac; and Goldman, Morton. "References on Racial Attitudes as Affected by Interviewers of Different Ethnic Groups," *Journal of Social Psychology* 70 (October 1966), pp. 95–100.

Bryde, John F. *Modern Indian Psychology.* Vermillion, S.D.: University of South Dakota Institute of Indian Studies, 1971.

Buber, M., and Rogers, C. "Transcription of Dialogue Held." Unpublished manuscript, Ann Arbor, University of Michigan, 1957.

Buchanan, Garth N., and Wholey, Joseph S. "Federal Level Evaluation," *Evaluation* 1:1 (Fall 1972), pp. 17–22.

Buchanan, Scott. *The Doctrine of Signatures: A Defense of Theory in Medicine.* London: Kegan, Paul, Trench, Trubner, 1938.

Buckley, Walter. *Sociology and the Modern Systems Theory.* Englewood Cliffs, N.J.: Prentice-Hall, 1971.

———. (Ed.) *Modern Systems Research for the Behavioral Scientist.* Chicago: Aldine, 1968.

Burns, Crawford E. "White Staff, Black Children: Is There a Problem?" *Child Welfare* 50:2 (February 1971), pp. 90–96.

Burns, Mary E., and Glasser, Paul H. "Similarities and Differences in Casework and Group Work Practice," *Social Service Review* 37 (December 1963), pp. 416–428.

Burnstein, E. "Interpersonal Strategies as Determinants of Behavioral Interdependence." In Judson Mills (Ed.), *Experimental Social Psychology.* New York: Macmillan, 1969, pp. 390–396.

Burton, Arthur. *What Makes Behavior Change Possible?* New York: Brunner/Mazel, 1976.

Buxbaum, Edith. "Technique of Terminating Analysis," *International Journal of Psychoanalysis* 31:3 (1950), pp. 184–190.

Byler, William. "The Destruction of American Indian Families." In Steve Unger (Ed.), *The Destruction of American Indian Families.* New York: Association on American Indian Affairs, 1977, pp. 1–75.

Byrne, Don. "Attitudes and Attraction." In Leonard Berkowitz (Ed.), *Advances in Experimental Social Psychology.* New York: Academic Press, 1969, vol. 4, pp. 36–89.

Caine, Lynn. *Widow.* New York: Morrow, 1974.

California Legislature. *California Welfare: A Legislative Program for Reform.* Sacramento, Calif.: Assembly Office of Research, 1969.

Calnek, Maynard. "Racial Factors in the Counter-Transference: The Black Therapist and the Black Client," *American Journal of Orthopsychiatry* 40:1 (January 1970), pp. 39–46.

Cannon, Walter B. *Wisdom of the Body.* New York: Norton, 1932.

Caplon, Gerald. *Principles of Preventive Psychiatry.* New York: Basic Books, 1964.

———. "Crisis Intervention in Time of War." Paper presented at a workshop at the University of Haifa, Haifa, Israel, 1974.

Carkhuff, Robert B. *The Art of Helping: An Introduction to Life Skills.* Amherst, Mass.: Human Resource Development Press, 1973.

Carkhuff, Robert R., and Pierce, Richard. "Differential Effects of Therapist's Race and Social Class upon Depth of Self-Exploration in the Initial Clinical Interview," *Journal of Consulting Psychology* 31 (December 1967), pp. 632–634.

Carmichael, Stokely, and Hamilton, Charles. *Black Power.* New York: Random House, 1968.

Carp, Francis M. *Factors in Utilization of Services by Mexican-American Elderly.* Palo Alto, Calif.: American Institute for Research, 1968.

Carr-Saunders, Alexander M. "Metropolitan Conditions and Traditional Professional Relations." In Robert M. Fisher (Ed.), *The Metropolis in Modern Life.* New York: Doubleday, 1955, pp. 279–287.

Carr-Saunders, A. M., and Wilson, P. A. *The Professions.* Oxford, England: Clarendon Press, 1933.

Carson, R. C., and Heine, R. W. "Similarity and Success in Therapeutic Dyads," *Journal of Consulting Psychology* 26:1 (February 1962), pp. 38–43.

Carter, Genevieve W. "Social Work Community Organization Methods and Processes." In Walter A. Friedlander (Ed.), *Concepts and Methods of Social Work.* Englewood Cliffs, N.J.: Prentice-Hall, 1958.

Cartwright, D. "Achieving Change in People: Some Applications of Group Dynamics Theory," *Human Relations* 4:4 (Fall 1957), pp. 381–392.

Cartwright, D., and Zander, A. (Eds.). *Group Dynamics: Research and Theory.* New York: Harper & Row, 1968.

Cassidy, Patrick. "The Liability of Psychiatrists for Malpractice," *University of Pittsburgh Law Review* 36 (1974), pp. 108–137.

Chaiklin, Harris. "A Social Service Team for Public Welfare." In *Social Work Practice, 1970.* New York: Columbia University Press, 1970, pp. 103–113.

Chambers, Clarke A. "A Historical Perspective on Political Action vs. Individualized Treatment." In Paul E. Weinberger (Ed.), *Perspectives on Social Welfare.* New York: Macmillan, 1969, pp. 89–106.

Chase, Stuart. "How Language Shapes Our Thoughts." In J. Burl Hogins and Robert E. Yarker (Eds.), *Language: An Introductory Reader*. New York: Harper & Row, 1969.

Chin, Robert. "The Utility of Systems Models and Developmental Models for Practitioners." In Warren G. Bennis, Kenneth D. Benne, and Robert Chin (Eds.), *The Planning of Change*. New York: Holt, Rinehart & Winston, 1961, pp. 201–215.

Clapp, Raymond F. "Spanish Americans of the Southwest," *Welfare in Review* 4 (January 1966), pp. 1–12.

Clark, Kenneth B. *The Dark Ghetto: Dilemmas of Social Power*. New York: Harper & Row, 1965.

Clark, Margaret, and Mendelson, M. "Mexican-American Aged in San Francisco: A Case Description," *The Gerontologist* 9 (Summer 1969), pp. 90–95.

Cleveland, Harlan. "The Case for Bureaucracy," *The New York Times Magazine*, CXIII:38, 627, October 27, 1963. Section 6, p. 19.

Cloward, Richard A., and Epstein, Irwin. "Private Social Welfare's Disengagement from the Poor: The Case of Family Adjustment Agencies." In Mayer N. Zald (Ed.), *Social Welfare Institutions: A Sociological Reader*. New York: Wiley, 1965, pp. 623–644.

Cohen, Nathan E. (Ed.). *Social Work and Social Problems*. New York: National Association of Social Workers, 1964.

Cohen, Neil A. "The Public Welfare Department's Separation into Social Service and Income Maintenance Divisions: Its Impact on Role Conflict Perceptions and Job Orientations Among non-M.S.W. Welfare Workers." Ph.D. dissertation, School of Applied Social Sciences, Case Western Reserve University, 1973.

Commission on Social Work Practice. National Association of Social Workers. "Working Definition of Social Work Practice," *Social Work* 3:2 (April 1958), pp. 5–8.

Committee on the Study of Competence. *Guidelines for the Assessment of Professional Practice in Social Work*. New York: National Association of Social Workers, 1968.

Community Chests and Councils of America. *A Geographical Approach to Community Planning*. New York: Community Chests and Councils of America, 1951.

Condie, C. David; Hanson, Janet A.; Long, Nanci E.; Moss, Denna K.; and Kane, Rosalie A. "How the Public Views Social Work," *Social Work* 23 (January 1978), pp. 47–53.

Cooper, Shirley. "A Look at the Effect of Racism on Clinical Work," *Social Casework* 54:2 (February 1978), p. 78.

Cormican, Elin J., and Cormican, John D. "The Necessity of Linguistic Sophistication for Social Workers," *Journal of Education for Social Work* 13:1 (Spring 1977), pp. 18–22.

Cormican, John D. "Breaking Language Barriers Between the Patient and His Doctor," *Geriatrics* 30 (December 1975), pp. 104–110.

————. "Linguistic Subculture and Social Work Practice," *Social Casework* 57 (November 1976), p. 591.

————. "Linguistic Issues in Interviewing," *Social Casework* 59 (March 1978), pp. 145–152.

Coser, Lewis. *The Functions of Social Conflict*. Glencoe, Ill.: The Free Press, 1956.

Costin, Lela B. "School Social Work Practice: A New Model," *Social Work* 20 (March 1975), pp. 135–139.

Coyle, Grace L. *Group Work with American Youth*. New York: Harper & Row, 1948.

Cozby, Paul C. "Self-Disclosure: A Literature Review," *Psychological Bulletin* 79 (February 1973), pp. 73–91.

Cronbach, Lee. *Educational Psychology*. New York: Harcourt Brace, 1954.

Croxton, Tom A. "The Therapeutic Contract in Social Treatment." In Paul Glasser, Rosemary Sarri and Robert Vinter (Eds.), *Individual Change through Small Groups*. New York: Free Press, 1975, pp. 169–183.

Cumming, Elaine. *Systems of Social Regulation*. New York: Atherton Press, 1968.

Cumming, John, and Cumming, Elaine. *Ego and Milieu: Theory and Practice of Environmental Therapy*. New York: Atherton Press, 1962.

Curry, Andrew E. "The Negro Worker and the White Client: A commentary on the Treatment Relationship," *Social Casework* 45:3 (March 1964), pp. 131–136.

Dalton, Gene W. "Influence and Organizational Change." In Gene W. Dalton et al. (Eds.), *Organizational Change and Development*. Homewood, Ill.: Irwin-Dorsey, 1970, pp. 250–258.

Davenport, Judith, and Reims, Nancy. "Theoretical Orientation and Attitudes Toward Women," *Social Work* 23:4 (July 1978), pp. 306–311.

David, Morton D. *Game Theory*. New York: Basic Books, 1970.

Davidoff, Donald. "The Malpractice of Psychiatrists," *Duke Law Journal* (Summer 1966), pp. 693–697.

Davidoff, Paul. "Advocacy and Pluralism in Planning," *Journal of the American Institute of Planners* 31 (November 1965), pp. 331–338.

Davis, Gary A. *Psychology of Problem Solving: Theory and Practice*. New York: Basic Books, 1973.

Davis, Gerald J. "Practice Forum: Client Autobiography," *Child Welfare* 51 (May 1972), pp. 310–311.

Davis, James A. *Undergraduate Career Decisions*. Chicago: Aldine, 1965.

Davis, Sheldon A. "An Organic Problem-Solving Method of Organizational Change." In Warren G. Bennis, Kenneth D. Benne and Robert Chin

(Eds.), *The Planning of Change.* New York: Holt, Rinehart & Winston, 1969, pp. 357–371.

De Geynt, Willy. "Health Behavior and Health Needs in Urban Indians in Minneapolis," *Health Service Reports* 88 (April 1973), pp. 360–366.

Deloria, Vine, Jr. *Custer Died for Your Sins: An Indian Manifesto.* New York: Macmillan, 1969.

Densmore, Frances. *Chippewa Customs.* Minneapolis, Minn.: Ross and Haines, 1970.

De Schweinitz, Karl, and De Schweinitz, Elizabeth. *Interviewing in the Social Services.* London: National Institute for Social Work Training, 1962.

Deutsch, Karl W. "Toward a Cybernetic Model of Man and Society." In Walter Buckley (Ed.), *Modern Systems Research for the Behavioral Scientist.* Chicago: Aldine, 1969, pp. 387–400.

Deutsch, M. "Conflicts: Productive and Destructive," *Journal of Social Issues* 24 (1969), pp. 7–43.

Deutsch, Morton. *The Resolution of Conflict.* New Haven: Yale University Press, 1973.

Dewald, Paul. *Psychotherapy: A Dynamic Approach.* New York: Basic Books, 1971.

Dewey, John. *How We Think* (Revised ed.). New York: Heath, 1933.

Deykin, Eva Y.; Weissman, Myrna M.; and Klerman, Gerald L. "Treatment of Depressed Women," *British Journal of Social Work* 1 (Fall 1971), pp. 277–291.

Dillick, Sidney. *Community Organization for Neighborhood Development—Past and Present.* New York: Morrow, 1953.

Dillon, Carolyn. "The Professional Name Game," *Social Casework* 50 (June 1969), pp. 337–340.

Dinnerstein, Dorothy. *The Mermaid and the Minotaur.* New York: Harper & Row, 1976.

Dohrenwend, Barbara S.; Williams, J. A.; and Weiss, Carol H. "Interviewer Biasing Effects, Toward a Reconciliation of Findings," *Public Opinion Quarterly* 33 (Spring 1969), pp. 121–129.

Dohrenwend, B. S.; Colombotos, John; and Dohrenwend, B. P. "Social Distance and Interviewer Effects," *Public Opinion Quarterly* 32:3 (Fall 1968), pp. 410–422.

Dollard, John. *Criteria for the Life History.* New Haven, Conn.: Yale University Press, 1935.

Dreyfus, Edward A. "The Search for Intimacy," *Adolescence* 2 (March 1967), pp. 25–40.

Dubey, Sumati. "Blacks' Preference for Black Professionals, Businessmen, and Religious Leaders," *Public Opinion Quarterly* 34:1 (Spring 1970), pp. 113–116.

Duhl, Frederick. "Intervention, Therapy, and Change." In William Gray, Frederick Duhl, Nicholas D. Rizzo (Eds.), *General Systems Theory and Psychiatry,* Boston: Little, Brown, 1969.

Dumont, Matthew. *The Absurd Healer.* New York: Viking, 1968.

Duncan, Starkey, Jr. "Nonverbal Communication," *Psychological Bulletin.* 72 (1969), pp. 118–137.

Durkheim, Emile. *Suicide,* John A. Spaulding and George Simpson, Translators. New York: The Free Press, 1951.

Duvinage, Thelma. "Accommodation Attitudes of Negroes to White Caseworkers and Their Influence on Casework," *Smith College Studies in Social Work* 9:3 (March 1939), pp. 264–302.

Dyer, W. *Team Building: Issues and Alternatives.* Reading, Mass.: Addison-Wesley, 1977.

Eaton, Joseph W. "Science, 'Art' and Uncertainty in Social Work," *Social Work* 3 (July 1958), pp. 3–10.

———. "A Scientific Basis for Helping." In Alfred J. Kahn (Ed.), *Issues in American Social Work.* New York: Columbia University Press, 1959, pp. 270–292.

Edelson, Marshall. *The Termination of Intensive Psychotherapy.* Springfield, Ill.: Charles C Thomas, 1963.

Edenburg, Golda M.; Zinberg, Norman; and Kelman, Wendy. *Clinical Interviewing and Counseling: Principles and Techniques.* New York: Appleton-Century-Crofts, 1975.

Edson, Jean B. "How to Survive on a Committee," *Social Work* 22 (May 19.7), pp. 224–226.

Ehrlich, Paul. *The Population Bomb.* New York: Ballantine, 1967.

Empey, Lamar, and Erickson, Maynard L. "Hidden Delinquency and Social Status," *Social Forces* 44 (June 1966), pp. 546–554.

Engel, G.; Reichsman, F.; and Segal, H. "A Study of an Infant with Gastric Fistula in Behavior and the Rate of Total Hydrochloric Acid Secretion," *Psychosomatic Medicine* 18:5 (October 1956), pp. 374–398.

Epstein, Irwin. "Social Workers and Social Action," *Social Work* 13 (April 1968), pp. 101–108.

Erikson, Erik H. *Childhood and Society.* New York: Norton, 1950.

———. *Identity and the Life Cycle, Psychological Issues.* Monograph no. 1. New York: International Universities Press, 1959.

———. "Inner and Outer Space: Reflections on Womanhood," *Daedalus* 93 (Spring 1964a), pp. 582–606.

———. *Insight and Responsibility: Lectures on the Ethical Implications of Psychoanalytic Insight.* New York: Norton, 1964b.

Etzioni, Amitai. "Power as a Societal Force." In Marvin Olsen (Ed.), *Power in Societies.* New York: Macmillan, 1970.

Ewalt, Patricia L., and Kutz, Janice. "An Examination of Advice Giving as a Therapeutic Intervention," *Smith College Studies* 47:1 (November 1976), pp. 3–9.

Eysenck, Hans. "The Effects of Psychotherapy," in H. Eysenck (Ed.), *Handbook of Abnormal Psychology.* New York: Basic Books, 1961.

Eysenck, H. J. *The Structure of Human Personality*. London: Methuen, 1953.

Ezriel, H. "Notes on Psychoanalytic Group Therapy: II Interpretation and Research," *Psychiatry* 15 (May 1952), pp. 119–126.

Falk, Julia S. *Linguistics and Language*. Lexington, Mass.: Xerox College Publishing, 1973, pp. 214–225.

Family Service Association of America. *The Use of Group Techniques in the Family Agency: Three Papers from the FSAA Biennial Meeting, Washington, D.C., April 1959*. New York: Family Service Assn. of America, 1959.

Family Service Highlights. "Non-White Families Are Frequent Applicants for Family Service," *Family Service Highlights* 25:5 (May 1964), pp. 140–144.

Fanon, Frantz. *The Wretched of the Earth*. New York: Grove Press, 1965.

Fanshel, David. "The Exit of Children from Foster Care: An Interim Research Report," *Child Welfare* 50 (February 1971), pp. 65–81.

Fantl, Berta. "Casework in Lower Class Districts," *Mental Hygiene* 45 (July 1961), pp. 425–438.

Feldstein, Donald. "Do We Need Professions in Our Society?" *Social Work* 16 (October 1971), pp. 5–12.

Ferguson, Charles K. "Concerning the Nature of Human Systems and the Consultant's Role," *Journal of Applied Behavioral Science* 4 (1968), pp. 179–193.

Ferguson, Elizabeth A. *Social Work: An Introduction*. Philadelphia: Lippincott, 1963.

Fibush, Esther, and BeAlva Turnquest. "A Black and White Approach to the Problem of Racism," *Social Casework* 51:10 (October 1970), pp. 459–466.

Fiedler, Fred. "A Comparison of Therapeutic Relationships in Psychoanalytic, Non-Directive and Adlerian Therapy," *Journal of Consulting Psychology* 14 (December 1950), pp. 436–445.

Fierman, Louis B. (Ed.) *Effective Psychotherapy: The Contribution of Hellmuth Kaiser*. New York: Free Press, 1965.

Filley, Alan. *Interpersonal Conflict Resolution*. Glenview, Ill.: Scott, Foresman, 1975.

Finch, Wilbur A., Jr. "Education and Jobs: A Study of the Performance of Social Service Tasks in Public Welfare." D.S.W. dissertation, School of Social Welfare, University of California at Berkeley, 1975.

Finch, Wilbur A., Jr. "Social Workers versus Bureaucracy," *Social Work* 21:5 (September 1976), pp. 370–374.

Fine, Sidney A., and Wiley, Wretha W. *An Introduction to Functional Job Analysis*. Kalamazoo, Mich.: W.E. Upjohn Institute for Employment Research, 1971.

Firestein, Stephen. "Termination of Psychoanalysis of Adults: A Review of the Literature," *Journal of the American Psychoanalytic Association* 20 (December 1974), pp. 873–894.

Fisher, Joel. "Is Casework Effective? A Review," *Social Work* 18 (January 1973), pp. 5–20.

Fleming, Joan, and Benedek, Therese. *Psychoanalytic Supervision*. New York: Grune and Stratton, 1966, pp. 174–175.

Flexner, Abraham. "Is Social Work a Profession?" In *Proceedings of the National Conference of Charities and Correction*. Chicago: Hildmen Printing Co., 1915, pp. 576–590.

Forder, Anthony. "Social Work and System Theory," *British Journal of Social Work* 6 (Spring 1976), pp. 23–42.

Foster, Marion G., and Pearman, William A. "Social Work, Patient Rights and Patient Representatives," *Social Casework* 59:2 (February 1978), pp. 89–101.

Fox, Evelyn; Nelson, Marion; and Bolman, William. "The Termination Process: A Neglected Dimension in Social Work," *Social Work* 14:4 (October 1969), pp. 53–63.

Fraley, Yvonne L. "A Role Model for Practice," *Social Service Review* 43:2 (June 1969), pp. 145–154.

Francis, W. Nelson. *The Structure of American English*. New York: Ronald Press, 1958, pp. 517–522.

Frank, Jerome D. "Expectation and Therapeutic Outcome—The Placebo Effect and the Role Induction Interview." In Jerome D. Frank (Ed.), *Effective Ingredients of Successful Psychotherapy*. New York: Brunner/Mazel, 1978, pp. 1–35.

Frank, Jerome D. et al. *Effective Ingredients of Successful Psychotherapy*. New York: Brunner/Mazel, 1978.

———. *Persuasion and Healing*. New York: Schocken Books, 1961.

———. *Persuasion and Healing—A Comparative Study of Psychotherapy*. Baltimore, Md.: Johns Hopkins University Press, 1972.

Frank, Lawrence K. "The Interdisciplinary Frontiers in Human Relations Studies," *Journal of Human Relations* 2:4 (Fall 1954), pp. 89–92.

———. "Research for What?" *Journal of Social Issues* Kurt Lewin Memorial Award Issue, Supplement Series, No. 10 (1957).

Freedman, Alfred M.; Kaplan, Harold I.; and Sadok, Benjamin. *A Comprehensive Textbook on Psychiatry*. Baltimore, Md.: Williams and Wilkins, 1975.

Freedman, Joel. "One Social Worker's Fight for Mental Patients' Rights," *Social Work* 16 (October 1971), pp. 92–95.

Freeman, Howard, and Sherwood, Clarence. *Social Research and Social Policy*. Englewood Cliffs, N.J.: Prentice-Hall, 1970.

French, J., and Raven, M. "The Basis of Social Power." In D. Cartwright (Ed.), *Studies in Social Power*. Ann Arbor: University of Michigan, 1959.

French, Thomas M. *The Integration of Behavior: Basic Postulates.* Chicago: University of Chicago Press, 1952.

Freud, Sigmund. "Analysis, Terminal and Interminable." In *Collected Papers.* vol. 5. London, England: Hogarth Press, 1950a, pp. 316–357.

———. "Mourning and Melancholia." In *Collected Papers.* vol. 5. London: Basic Books, 1950b, pp. 152–172.

———. *Civilization and Its Discontents.* New York: Norton, 1961, pp. 23–24.

Frey, Louise. "Support and the Group," *Social Work* 7:4 (October 1962), pp. 35–42.

Frey, Louise, and Edenberg, Golda M. *Helping, Manipulation and Magic.* New York: National Association of Social Workers, 1978.

Frey, Louise, and Meyer, Marguerite. "Exploration and Working Agreement in Two Social Work Methods." In Saul Bernstein (Ed.), *Explorations in Group Work.* Boston: Boston University School of Social Work, 1965, pp. 2–11.

Friedman, Milton. *Capitalism and Freedom,* Chicago: University of Chicago Press, 1962.

Friedson, Eliot. "Dominant Professions, Bureaucracy and Client Services." In William R. Rosengran and Mark Lefton (Eds.), *Organizations and Clients.* Columbus, Ohio: Charles E. Merrill, 1970a, p. 74.

———. *Professional Dominance: The Social Structure of Medical Care.* New York: Aldine-Atherton Press, 1970b.

———. *Professions of Medicine: A Study of the Sociology of Applied Knowledge.* New York: Dodd, Mead, 1970c.

Fromm, Erich. *The Art of Loving.* New York: Harper & Bros., 1956.

———. *The Revolution of Hope—Toward a Humanized Technology.* New York: Bantam Books, 1968.

Gambrill, Eileen D.; Thomas, Edwin J.; and Carter, Robert D. "Procedure for Sociobehavioral Practice in Open Settings," *Social Work* 16 (January 1971), pp. 51–62.

Gambrill, Eileen D., and Wiltse, Kermit T. "Foster Care: Plans and Actualities," *Public Welfare* 32 (Spring 1974), pp. 12–21.

Garcia, Alejandro. "The Chicano and Social Work," *Social Casework* 52 (May 1971), pp. 274–278.

Garland, James A.; Jones, Hubert E.; and Kolodny, Ralph L. "A Model for Stages of Development in Social Work Groups." In Saul Bernstein (Ed.), *Explorations in Group Work.* Boston: Boston University School of Social Work, 1968, pp. 12–53.

Garrett, Annette. *Interviewing: Its Principles and Methods* (2d ed., revised by Elinor P. Zaki and Margret M. Mangold). New York: Family Service Association of America, 1972.

Gartner, Alan. "Four Professions: How Different,

How Alike," *Social Work* 20 (September 1975), pp. 353–358.

Garvin, Charles. "Complementarity of Role Expectations in Groups: The Member-Worker Contract." In *Social Work Practice, 1969.* New York: Columbia University Press, 1969, pp. 127–145.

———. "The Selection of Theory for Social Work Practice with Individuals." Mimeographed Ann Arbor, Mich.: University of Michigan, 1972.

Garwick, G. "Guide to Goals, One." Unpublished project report, 1972.

———. "Programmed Instruction in Goal Attainment Scaling." Unpublished project report, Program Evaluation Resource Center, Minneapolis, Minnesota, 1973.

Garwick, G., and Brintnall, J. "Tables for Calculating the Goal Attainment Score." Unpublished project report, 1973.

Gauldner, Alvin. "The Norm of Reciprocity," *American Sociological Review* 25 (April 1960), pp. 161–168.

Geer, James H.; Davison, Gerald C.; and Gatchel, Robert I. "Reduction of Stress in Humans through Nonverdical Perceived Control of Aversive Stimulation," *Journal of Personality and Social Psychology* 16 (1970), pp. 731–738.

Germain, Carel. "Social Study: Past and Future," *Social Casework* 49 (July 1968), pp. 403–409.

———. "Casework and Science: An Historical Encounter." In Robert W. Roberts and Robert Nee (Eds.), *Theories of Casework.* Chicago: 1971, pp. 3–33.

———. "The Ecological Perspective in Casework Practice," *Social Casework* 54 (June 1973), pp. 223–230.

Ghali, Sonia Badillo. "Culture Sensitivity and the Puerto Rican Client." Mimeographed, New York University, School of Social Work, 1966.

Giordano, Peggy C. "The Client's Perspective in Agency Evaluation," *Social Work* 22 (January 1977), pp. 34–39.

Gibb, L. P.; Bradford, J. R.; and Benne, D. D. (Eds.) *T-Group Theory and Laboratory Method: Innovation in Reeducation.* New York: Wiley, 1964.

Gilder, George F. *Naked Nomads: Unmarried Men in America.* New York: Quadrangle Press, 1974.

Gillis, John S. "Social Influence Therapy, The Therapist as Manipulator," *Psychology Today* 8:7 (December 1974), pp. 91–92.

Ginsburg, Mitchell A. "Changing Values in Social Work," Paper presented at the 16th Annual Program Meeting of the Council on Social Work Education, Minneapolis, Minnesota, January 23–26, 1968.

Gitterman, Alex. "Group Work in the Public Schools." In William Schwartz and Serapio Zalba (Eds.), *The Practice of Group Work.* New York: Columbia University Press, 1971, pp. 45–56.

Gitterman, Alex, and Schaeffer, Alice. "The White Professional and the Black Client," *Social Casework* 53 (May 1972), pp. 280–291.

Gladwin, Thomas. "Social Competence and Clinical Practice," *Psychiatry* 30 (February 1967), pp. 33–37.

Glaser, Barney A., and Strauss, Anselm L. *The Discovery of Grounded Theory: Strategies for Qualitative Research.* Chicago: Aldine, 1967.

Gochros, Jean. "Recognition and Use of Anger in Negro Clients," *Social Work* 11:1 (January 1966), pp. 28–38.

Goff, Regina M. "Some Educational Implications of Rejection on Aspiration Levels of Minority Group Children," *Journal of Experimental Education* 23 (December 1954), pp. 179–183.

Golan, Naomi. "When is a Client in Crisis?" *Social Casework* 50 (July 1969), pp. 389–394.

Golan, Naomi, and Gruschka, Ruth. "Integrating the New Immigrant: A Model for Social Work Practice in Transitional States," *Social Work* 18 (April 1971), pp. 82–87.

Goldberg, Gale, and Middleman, Ruth. *Social Service Delivery: A Structural Approach to Social Work Practice.* New York: Columbia University Press, 1974.

Goldberg, Phillip. "Are Women Prejudiced Against Women?" *Trans-Action* 5:4 (April 1968), pp. 28–30.

Goldberg, Stanley B. "Family Tasks and Reactions in the Crisis of Death," *Social Casework* 54 (July 1973), pp. 398–405.

Golding, William. *Free Fall.* New York: Harcourt, Brace, 1960.

Goldner, Fred H., and Ritti, R. R. "Professionalization as Career Immobility." In Oscar Grusky and George A. Miller (Eds.), *The Sociology of Organizations.* New York: Free Press, 1970, pp. 466–473.

Goldstein, Howard. *Social Work Practice: A Unitary Approach.* Columbia, S.C.: University of South Carolina Press, 1973.

Goode, W. J. *The Family.* Englewood Cliffs, N.J.: Prentice-Hall, 1964.

Goodman, James A. "Preface." In James A. Goodman (Ed.), *Dynamics of Racism.* Washington, D.C.: National Association of Social Workers, 1974, pp. ix–xiii.

Goodman, Nelson. *Fact, Fiction and Forecast* (2d ed.). Indianapolis, Ind.: Bobbs Merrill, 1965.

Good Tracks, Jimm G. "Native American Noninterference," *Social Work* 8:6 (November 1973), pp. 30–34.

Gordon, William E. "A Critique of the Working Definition," *Social Work* 7:4 (October 1962), pp. 3–13.

———. "Knowledge and Value: Their Distinction and Relationship in Clarifying Social Work Practice," *Social Work* 10:3 (July 1965), pp. 32–39.

———. "Basic Constructs for an Integrative and Generative Conception of Social Work." In Gordon Hearn (Ed.), *The General Systems Approach: Contributions Toward an Holistic Conception of Social Work.* New York: Council of Social Work Education, 1969, pp. 5–11.

Gottlieb, Naomi. *The Welfare Bind.* New York: Columbia University Press, 1974.

Gottleib, Werner, and Stanley, Joe H. "Mutual Goals and Goal-Setting in Casework," *Social Casework* 48 (October 1967), pp. 471–477.

Gottman, John M., and Leiblum, Sandra R. *How to Do Psychotherapy and How to Evaluate It: A Manual for Beginners.* New York: Holt, Rinehart & Winston, 1974.

Gould, Karolyn. *Where Do We Go From Here?— A Study of the Roads and Roadblocks to Career Mobility for Paraprofessionals Working in Human Service Agencies.* New York: National Committee on Employment of Youth, 1969, pp. 5–6.

Gouldner, Alvin. *Patterns of Industrial Bureaucracy.* Glencoe, Ill.: Free Press, 1954.

———. "The Norm of Reciprocity," *American Sociological Review* 25 (April 1960): 161–168.

Green, A. D. "The Professional Worker in the Bureaucracy," *Social Service Review* 40 (March 1966), pp. 71–83.

———. "Professional Role Orientations and Conflict Strategies," *Social Work* 15:6 (October 1970), pp. 87–92.

Greenhill, Laurence. "Making It." In Andrew Ferber, Marilyn Mendelsohn, and Augustus Napier (Eds.), *The Book of Family Therapy.* New York: Science House, 1972, pp. 507–531.

Greenwood, Ernest. "Attributes of a Profession," *Social Work* 2 (July 1957), p. 55.

———. "Research on the Clarification of Casework Concepts: A Review of and Commentary on the Nolan Study." Unpublished manuscript, University of California at Berkeley, 1965.

———. "The Elements of Professionalization." In Howard W. Vollmer and Donald L. Mills (Eds.), *Professionalization.* Englewood Cliffs: N.J.: Prentice-Hall, 1966.

Grier, William. "When the Therapist is Negro: Some Effects on the Treatment Process," *American Journal of Psychiatry* 123:12 (June 1967), pp. 1587–1592.

Gross, Neal; Masson, Ward; and McEachern, Alexander W. *Explorations in Role Analysis.* New York: Wiley, 1958.

Grosser, Charles F. "Community Development Programs Serving the Urban Poor," *Social Work* 10:3 (July 1965), pp. 18–21.

———. "Changing Theory and Changing Practice," *Social Casework* 50 (January 1969), pp. 16–21.

Guerin, Philip J., and Pendagast, Eileen G. "Evaluation of Family System and Genogram." In Philip T. Guerin (Ed.), *Family Therapy: Theory and Practice.* New York: Halsted Press, 1976.

Gump, Janice P. "Sex-Role Attitudes and Psychological Well-Being," *Journal of Social Issues* 28 (Spring 1972), pp. 79–92.

Gurin, Arnold. "The Community Organization Curriculum Development Project: A Preliminary Report," *Social Service Review* 42 (December 1968), pp. 421–434.

Guttentag, Marcia. "Group Cohesiveness, Ethnic Organization and Poverty," *Journal of Social Issues* 26:2 (Spring 1970), pp. 105–132.

Hale, James, and Podell, Gayle R. "Medical Malpractice in New York," *Syracuse Law Review* 27 (Spring 1976), pp. 657–805.

Haley, Jay. *Strategies of Psychotherapy.* New York: Grune & Stratton, 1963.

Hall, J. *Conflict Management Survey,* Kansas City: Teleometrics, 1969.

Halleck, Helen L. "Life Stress and Family Systems." Master's thesis, University of North Carolina, Chapel Hill, 1975.

Halleck, Seymour L. "The Criminal's Problem with Psychiatry," *Psychiatry* 23:4 (November 1960), pp. 346–399.

———. *The Politics of Therapy.* New York: Science Press, 1971.

———. "Family Therapy and Social Change." Paper presented at the 100th Anniversary Symposium, Jewish Family Service, New York, October 29, 1975.

Hallowell, A. Irving. "Ojibway Personality and Acculturation." In Paul Bohannon and Fred Plog (Eds.), *Beyond the Frontier.* New York: Natural History Press, 1967.

Hallowitz, David. "The Problem-Solving Component in Family Therapy," *Social Casework* 51 (February 1970), pp. 67–75.

Hallowitz, David; Bierman, Ralph; Harrison, Grace P.; and Stulberg, Burton. "The Assertive Counseling Component of Therapy," *Social Casework* 48 (November 1967), pp. 543–548.

Halmos, Paul. *Faith of the Counsellors.* New York: Schocken, 1966.

Halverson, Charles F., and Shore, Roy E. "Self-Disclosure and Interpersonal Functioning," *Journal of Consulting and Clinical Psychology* 33 (April 1969), pp. 213–217.

Hamilton, Gordon. *Psychotherapy in Child Guidance.* New York: Columbia University Press, 1947.

———. *Theory and Practice of Social Casework* (2d ed.). New York: Columbia University Press, 1951.

Hanlan, Archie. "Counteracting Problems of Bureaucracy in Public Welfare," *Social Work* 12 (July 1967), pp. 88–94.

———. "Casework Beyond Bureaucracy." *Social Casework* 52 (April 1971), pp. 195–198.

Hardcastle, David A. "Licensing Senate Bill No. 6 and Social Work," *The Kansas Conference Key* 22 (December 1973), pp. 1–4.

Hardman, Dale. "The Constructive Use of Authority," *Crime and Delinquency* 6 (July 1960), pp. 245–254.

———. "The Matter of Trust," *Crime and Delinquency* 15 (April 1969), pp. 203–218.

Harlow, H. "The Nature of Love," *The American Psychologist* 13 (1958), pp. 673–685.

Harris, Dale B. "Values and Standards in Educational Activities," *Social Casework* 39 (February-March 1958), pp. 159–167.

Harris, Marjorie. "Tort Liability of the Psychotherapist," *University of San Francisco Law Review* 8 (Winter 1973), pp. 405–436.

Harrison, Bennett. "Education and Underemployment in the Urban Ghetto," *American Economic Review* 62 (December 1972), pp. 296–812.

Hartford, Margaret E. *Groups in Social Work.* New York: Columbia University Press, 1971.

Hartman, Ann. "Anomie and Social Social Casework," *Social Casework* 50 (March 1969), pp. 131–137.

———. "To Think About the Unthinkable," *Social Casework* 51:4 (October 1970), pp. 467–474.

———. "The Generic Stance in the Family Agency," *Social Casework* 55:4 (April 1974), pp. 199–208.

———. "Diagrammatic Assessment of Family Relationships," *Social Casework* 59:8 (October 1978), pp. 465–476.

Hartman, Henry L. "Interviewing Techniques in Probation and Parole," *Federal Probation* 27:1 (March 1963), pp. 14–19.

Hartmann, Heinz. *Ego Psychology and the Problem of Adaptation.* New York: International Universities Press, 1958.

Hatcher, Hayes A. *Correctional Casework and Counseling.* Englewood Cliffs, N.J.: Prentice-Hall, 1978.

Hearn, Gordon. *Theory Building in Social Work.* Toronto: University of Toronto Press, 1958.

——— (Ed.). *The General Systems Approach: Contributions Toward an Holistic Conception of Social Work.* New York: Council on Social Work Education, 1969.

Heidegger, Martin. *Discourse on Thinking.* New York: Harper Torchbooks, 1966.

Hersey, John. *The Wall.* New York: Alfred A. Knopf, 1950.

Hersey, P., and Blanchard, K. "Leader Effectiveness and Adaptability Description (LEAD)." In W. Pfeiffer and J. Jones (Eds.), *The 1976 Annual Handbook for Group Facilitators.* Ann Arbor, Mich.: University Associates, 1976.

Hesse, Mary. "Models and Analogy in Science," *Encyclopedia of Philosophy* 5 (1967), pp. 354–359.

Hiatt, Harold. "The Problem of Termination of Psychotherapy," *American Journal of Psychotherapy* 19:4 (October 1965), pp. 607–615.

Hiroto, Donald S. "Locus of Control and Learned Helplessness," *Journal of Experimental Psychology* 102 (1974), pp. 187–193.

Hollingshead, August M. "Class Differences in Family Stability," *Annals of the American Academy of Political and Social Science* 272 (November 1950), pp. 39–46.

Hollis, Florence. *Casework: A Psychosocial Therapy.* New York: Random House, 1964.

———. "Casework and Social Class," *Social Casework* 46:10 (October 1965), pp. 463–471.

———. "Profile of Early Interviews in Marital Counseling," *Social Casework* 49 (January 1968), pp. 35–43.

———. "The Psycho-Social Approach to the Practice of Casework." In Robert W. Roberts and Robert H. Nee (Eds.), *Theories of Social Casework.* Chicago: University of Chicago Press, 1970, pp. 35–45.

Hooker, Carl E. "Learned Helplessness," *Social Work* 21:4 (May 1976), pp. 194–198.

Houston, Kent B. "Control over Stress, Locus of Control and Response to Stress," *Journal of Personality and Social Psychology* 21 (1972), pp. 244–255.

Huffaker, Clair. *Nobody Loves a Drunken Indian.* New York: David McKay, 1967.

Hughes, Everett C. "Professions." In Kenneth S. Lynn (Ed.), *The Professions in America.* Boston: Houghton Mifflin, 1965, pp. 1–14.

Hunt, Linda; Harrison, Kenneth; and Armstrong, Michael. "Integrating Group Dynamics Training and the Education and Development of Social Work Students," *British Journal of Social Work* 4:4 (Winter 1974), pp. 405–424.

Hush, Howard et al. "Relevant Agency Programs for the Large Urban Community," *Social Casework* 51 (April 1970), pp. 199–208.

Hyman, Herbert H. *Interviewing in Social Research.* Chicago: University of Chicago Press, 1954.

———. "The Value Systems of Different Classes: A Social Psychological Contribution to the Analysis of Stratification." In Reinhard Bendix and Seymour M. Lipset (Eds.), *Class, Status, and Power.* Glencoe: The Free Press, 1953, pp. 263–270.

Hyman, Irwin, and Schreiber, Karen. "The School Psychologist as Child Advocate," *Children Today* 3 (March-April 1974), pp. 21–33, 36.

Ittelson, William, and Cantril, Hadley. "Perception: A Transactional Approach." In Floyd Matson and Ashley Montagu (Eds.), *The Human Dialogue.* New York: Free Press, 1967, pp. 207–213.

Jackel, Merl M. "Clients with Character Disorders." In Francis J. Turner (Ed.), *Differential Diagnosis and Treatment.* New York: Free Press, 1976, pp. 200–201.

Jakubowski-Spector, Patricia. "Facilitating the Growth of Women through Assertive Training," *The Counseling Psychologist* 4 (1973), pp. 75–85.

Janchill, Sister Mary Paul. "Systems Concepts in Casework Theory and Practice," *Social Casework* 50:2 (February 1969), pp. 74–82.

Jandt, Fred. *Conflict Resolution Through Communication.* New York: Harper & Row, 1973.

Jenkins, David H. "Five Field Analyses Applied to a School Situation." In Warren Bennis, Kenneth Benne, and Robert Chin (Eds.), *The Planning of Change.* New York: Holt, Rinehart & Winston, 1964, pp. 238–244.

Johns, Ray, and De Marche, David F. *Community Organizations and Agency Responsibility.* New York: Association Press, 1951.

Johnson, D., and Johnson, F. *Joining Together: Group Theory and Group Skills.* Englewood Cliffs, N.J.: Prentice-Hall, 1975.

Johnson, Wendell. "Being Understanding and Understood: Or How to Find a Wandered Horse," *ETC* 8:3 (Spring 1951), pp. 171–179.

Johnston, Norman. "Sources of Distortion and Deception in Prison Interviewing," *Federal Probation* 20:1 (January 1956), pp. 43–48.

Jones, Howard (Ed.) *Towards a New Social Work.* Boston: Routledge and Kegan Paul, 1975.

Jourard, Sidney M., and Lasakow, Paul. "Some Factors in Self-Disclosure," *Journal of Abnormal and Social Psychology* 56 (February 1958), pp. 91–98.

Jung, C. C. *The Undiscovered Self.* New York: Mentor Books, 1959.

Kadushin, Alfred. "Prestige of Social Work— Facts and Factors," *Social Work* 3 (April 1958), pp. 37–43.

———. "The Knowledge Base of Social Work." In Alfred J. Kahn (Ed.), *Issues in American Social Work.* New York: Columbia University Press, 1959, pp. 39–80.

———. *The Social Work Interview.* New York: Columbia University Press, 1972.

Kagan, Jerome. *Change and Continuity in Infancy.* New York: Wiley, 1971.

Kagan, Jerome, and Moss, Howard. *Birth to Maturity: A Study in Psychological Development.* New York: Wiley, 1962.

Kahle, Joseph H. "Structuring and Administering a Modern Voluntary Agency," *Social Work* 14 (October 1969), pp. 20–28.

Kahler, Erich. *The Tower and the Abyss: An Inquiry into the Transformation of the Individual.* New York: George Braziller, 1957.

Kahn, Alfred J. "The Nature of Social Work Knowledge." In Cora Kasius (Ed.), *New Directions in Social Work.* New York: Harper and Bros., 1954, pp. 210–215.

———. "Trends and Problems in Community Organization," in *Social Work Practice 1964.* New York: Columbia University Press, 1964, pp. 9–19.

——— (Ed.) *Shaping the New Social Work.* New York: Columbia University Press, 1973.

Kahn, Robert, and Connell, Charles. *The Dynamics of Interviewing.* New York: Wiley, 1957.

Kami, Michael J. "Planning for Change with New Approaches," *Social Casework* 51 (April 1970), pp. 209–210.

Kammerman, Shelia B.; Dulgaff, Ralph; Getzel, George; and Nelson, Judith. "Knowledge for Practice: Social Service in Social Work," in Alfred J. Kahn (Ed.), *Shaping the New Social Work.* New York: Columbia University Press, 1973, pp. 97–146.

Kane, R. "The Interprofessional Team as a Small Group," *Social Work in Health Care* 1:1 (Fall 1975), pp. 19–32.

Kaplan, Abraham. *The Conduct of Inquiry: Methodology for Behavioral Science.* San Francisco: Chandler, 1964.

Kaplan, David. "Observations on Crisis Theory and Practice," *Social Casework* 49:3 (March 1968), pp. 151–155.

Katz, Daniel, and Kuhn, Robert L. *The Social Psychology of Organization.* New York: Wiley, 1966.

Keith-Lucas, Alan. "Ethics in Social Work." In *Encyclopedia of Social Work.* New York: National Association of Social Workers, 1971, vol. 1, pp. 324–328.

———. *The Giving and Taking of Help.* Chapel Hill, N.C.: University of North Carolina Press, 1972.

Keller, Gordon N. "Bicultural Social Work and Anthropology," *Social Casework* 53 (October 1972), pp. 455–465.

Keller, Suzanne. "The Social World of the Slum Child: Some Early Findings," *American Journal of Orthopsychiatry* 33 (October 1963), pp. 823–831.

Kelman, Norman. "Goals of Analytic Therapy: A Personal Viewpoint," *American Journal of Psychoanalysis* 14 (1954), pp. 105–114.

Kendall, Katherine A. *Social Work Values in an Age of Discontent.* New York: Council on Social Work Education, 1970.

Keniston, Kenneth. *Young Radicals.* New York: Harcourt, Brace & World, 1968.

Kidneigh, John C. "A Note on Organizing Knowledge." In *Modes of Professional Education.* Tulane Studies in Social Welfare. New Orleans: School of Social Work, Tulane University, 1969, vol. 11, pp. 153–160.

Kiev, Ari. *Magic, Faith and Healing.* New York: Free Press, 1964.

Kim, Bok-Lim C. "Casework with Japanese and Korean Wives of Americans," *Social Casework* 53:5 (May 1972), pp. 273–279.

Kincaid, Mary Lou. "Identity and Therapy in the Black Community," *Personnel and Guidance Journal* 47 (May 1969), pp. 884–890.

Kinsey, Alfred C. *Sexual Behavior in the Human Male.* Philadelphia: W. B. Saunders Co., 1948.

Kiresuk, T. J., and Sherman, R. E. "Goal Attainment Scaling: A General Method for Evaluating Comprehensive Community Mental Health Programs," *Community Mental Health Journal* 4 (1968), 443–453.

Klein, Alan F. *Social Work Through Group Process.* Albany, N.Y.: State University of New York at Albany, 1970.

Klein, Melanie. "A Contribution to the Psychogenesis of Manic-Depressive States." In *Contributions to Psychoanalysis.* London, England: Hogarth Press, 1948, pp. 282–310.

Klenk, Robert W., and Ryan, Robert M. *The Practice of Social Work* (2d ed.). Belmont, Calif.: Wadsworth, 1974.

Klockars, Carl B. "A Theory of Probation Supervision," *The Journal of Criminal Law, Criminology and Police Science* 63 (1972), pp. 550–557.

Klugman, David J.; Litman, Robert E.; and Wold, Carl L. "Suicide: Answering the Cry for Help," *Social Work* (October 1965), pp. 43–50.

Kochman, Thomas. "Rapping in the Black Ghetto," *Transaction* 6:4 (February 1969), pp. 26–34.

Koestler, Arthur. *The Ghost in the Machine.* New York: Macmillan, 1968.

Konopka, Gisela. *Group Work in the Institutions.* New York: Morrow, 1954.

———. *Edward C. Lindeman and Social Work Philosophy.* Minneapolis: University of Minnesota Press, 1958, chap. 9.

———. "Social Group Work: A Social Work Method," *Social Work* 5 (October 1960), pp. 53–61.

———. *Social Group Work: A Helping Process.* Englewood Cliffs, N.J.: Prentice-Hall, 1963).

Kooy, G. A. "Social Systems and Problems of Aging." In Richard Williams et al. (Eds.), *Processes of Aging.* New York: Atherton Press, 1963, vol. 2, pp. 43–60.

Kronenfeld, Daniel. "Community Organization and Welfare." Unpublished report, New York, *Mobilization for Youth,* 1965.

Kropotkin, P. *Mutual Aid, a Factor of Evolution.* New York: Knopf, 1925.

Krupp, George. "Maladaptive Reactions to the Death of a Family Member," *Social Casework* 53 (July 1972), pp. 425–426.

Krush, Thaddeus P.; Bjork, John W.; Sindell, Peter S.; and Nelle, Joanna. "Some Thoughts on the Formulation of Personality Disorders: Study of an Indian Boarding School Population." In *Hearings Before the Special Subcommittee on Indian Education of the Committee on Labor and Public Welfare, United States Senate. Part 5.* Washington, D.C.: U.S. Government Printing Office, 1969.

Kubie, S. L. *Practical and Theoretical Aspects of Psychoanalysis.* New York: Praeger, 1961.

Kuhn, Alfred. *The Logic of Social Systems.* San Francisco: Jossey-Bass, 1974.

Lamm, Maurice. *The Jewish Way in Death and Mourning.* New York: Jonathan David Publishers, 1969.

Latham, Joseph, Jr. "Torts—Duty to Act for Protection of Another—Liability of Psychotherapist for Failure to Warn of Homicide Threatened by Patient," *Vanderbilt Law Review* 28 (April 1975).

Lathrope, D. E. "A General Systems Approach in Social Work Practice." In Gordon Hearn (Ed.), *The General Systems Approach: Contributions Toward an Holistic Conception of Social Work.* New York: Council on Social Work Education, 1969, pp. 45–62.

Lazarus, Arnold A. "Learning Theory and the Treatment of Depression," *Behavior Research and Therapy* 6 (1968), pp. 83–89.

Leader, Arthur. "The Role of Intervention in Family-Group Treatment," *Social Casework* 45:6 (June 1964), pp. 327–337.

———. "Denied Dependency in Family Therapy," *Social Casework* 57:10 (December 1976), pp. 634–643.

Le Barre, Weston. *The Ghost Dance—The Origin of Religion.* New York: Dell, 1970.

Lee, Porter R. "Social Work: Cause or Function," *Proceedings of the National Conference of Social Work, 1929.* Chicago: University of Chicago Press, 1929, pp. 3–20.

Lefcourt, H. M. "Belief in Personal Control: Research and Implications," *Journal of Individual Psychology* 22 (1966), pp. 185–195.

Leifer, Ronald. "The Medical Model as Ideology," *International Journal of Psychiatry.* New York: Science House, 1970–71, vol. 9, pp. 13–21.

Leopold, E. "Hidden Strengths in the Disorganized Family: Discovery Through Extended Home Observations." Paper presented at meeting of American Orthopsychiatry Association, 1969.

———. "Rebound Children and Their Families A Community Survey Conducted by the Rebound Children and Youth Project." Mimeographed, New York: Rebound Children and Youth Project, 1968.

Lerman, Paul. "Delinquents without Crime." In David Gottlieb (Ed.), *Children's Liberation.* Englewood Cliffs, N.J.: Prentice-Hall, 1973, pp. 103–124.

Lerner, Barbara. *Therapy in the Ghetto.* Baltimore, Md.: Johns Hopkins Press, 1972.

Lessor, Richard, and Lutkus, Anita. "Two Techniques for the Social Work Practitioner," *Social Work* 16 (January 1971), pp. 5–6.

Leuenberger, P. "Team Dynamics and Decision Making." In D. Brieland et al. (Eds.), *The Model of Social Work Practice.* Syracuse: Syracuse University Press, 1973.

Levenson, Bernard. "Bureaucratic Succession." In Amitai Elzioni (Ed.), *Complex Organizations.* New York: Holt, Rinehart & Winston, 1961, pp. 362–365.

Levine, Irving M. "Ethnicity and Mental Health: A Social Conservation Approach." Paper presented at White House Conference on Ethnicity and Mental Health, Washington, D.C., June 1976.

Levinson, Daniel J. *The Seasons of a Man's Life.* New York: Alfred A. Knopf, 1978.

Levinson, Hilliard L. "Termination of Psychotherapy: Some Salient Issues." Article based on paper presented at the Illinois Society for Clinical Social Work, Chicago, Ill., October 28, 1975.

Levy, Charles S. "Social Worker and Client as Obstacles to Client Self-Determination," *Journal of Jewish Communal Service* 39 (Summer 1963), pp. 416–419.

———. "Values and Planned Change," *Social Casework* 54:10 (October 1972), pp. 488–493.

——— "The Legal Regulation of Social Work: The Board View." Mimeographed, Evanston, Ill., The National Clearinghouse for Legal Services, June 13, 1973a.

———. "The Value Base of Social Work," *Journal of Education for Social Work* 9:1 (Winter 1973b), pp. 34–42.

Levy, Leon H. *Psychological Interpretation.* New York: Holt, Rinehart & Winston, 1963.

Lewin, Kurt. "Formalization and Progress in Psychology." In Darwin Cartwright (Ed.), *Theory in Social Science: Selected Theoretical Papers.* New York: Harper & Brothers, 1951.

Lewinsohn, Peter M.; Weinstein, Malcolm S.; and Show, David A. "Depression: A Clinical-Research Approach." In Richard D. Rubin and Cyril M. Franks (Eds.), *Advances in Behavior Therapy.* New York: Academic Press, 1969, pp. 231–240.

Lewinsohn, Peter, and Libet, Julian. "Pleasant Events, Activity, Schedules and Depression," *Journal of Abnormal Psychology* 79 (1972), pp. 291–295.

Lewis, Harold. "Morality and the Politics of Practice," *Social Casework* 53:7 (July 1972), pp. 404–417.

———. "Reasoning in Practice," *Smith College Studies* 46 (November 1975), pp. 3–15.

Lewis, Ronald. "But We Have Been Helping Indians for a Long Time." Unpublished research. Milwaukee: University of Wisconsin School of Social Work, 1977.

Lewis, Ronald, G., and Mon Keung Ho. "Social Work with Native Americans," *Social Work* 20 (September 1975), pp. 379–382.

Lewis, Oscar. *La Vida: A Puerto Rican Family in the Culture of Poverty.* New York: Random House, 1966.

Liberman, Bernard. "The Role of Mastery in Psychotherapy: Maintenance of Improvement and Prescriptive Change." In J. Frank et al. (Eds.), *Effective Ingredients in Successful Psychotherapy*. New York, Brumer/Mazel, 1978, pp. 35–73.

Libet, Julian, and Lewinsohn, Peter. "Concept of Social Skill with Special Reference to the Behavior of Depressed Persons," *Journal of Consulting and Clinical Psychology* 40 (1973), pp. 304–312.

Liebow, Elliot. *Tally's Corner*. Boston: Little, Brown, 1967.

Lindblom, Charles E. "The Science of Muddling Through." In Fred Cox et al. (Eds.), *Strategies of Community Organization*. Itasca, Ill.: Peacock Publishers, 1970.

Lindemann, Erich. "Symptomatology and Management of Acute Grief," *American Journal of Psychiatry* 101 (September 1944), pp. 1–11.

Linton, Ralph. *The Study of Man*. New York: Appleton Century Co., 1936.

Lippitt, R. *Training in Community Relations: A Research Exploration*. New York: Harper & Brothers, 1949.

Lippitt, Ronald; Watson, Jeanne; and Westley, Bruce. *The Dynamics of Planned Change*. New York: Harcourt, Brace, 1958.

Lippitt, R.; Hooyman, G.; Sashkin, M.; and Kaplan, J. *Resourcebook for Planned Change*. Ann Arbor, Mich.: Human Resources Development Associates, 1978.

Lipton, Douglas; Martinson, Robert; and Wilks, Judith. *The Effectiveness of Correctional Treatment—A Survey of Treatment Evaluation Studies*. Springfield: Praeger Publishers, 1975.

Lipton, Samuel. "The Last Hour," *Journal of the American Psychoanalytic Association* 9 (May 1961), pp. 325–330.

Litwak, Eugene, and Meyer, Henry J. "The Administrative Style of the School and Organizational Tasks." In Fred M. Cox et al. (Eds.), *Strategies of Community Organization*. Itasca, Ill.: Peacock Publishers, 1970, pp. 78–91.

Lloyd, Gary A. "Integrated Methods and the Field Practice Course," *Social Work Education Reporter* 16 (June 1968), pp. 39–42.

Locklear, Herbert H. "American Indian Myths," *Social Work* 17 (May 1972), pp. 72–80.

London, Perry. *The Modes and Morals of Psychotherapy*. New York: Holt, Rinehart & Winston, 1964.

Lutz, Werner A. *Concepts and Principles Underlying Social Casework Practice in Medical Care and Rehabilitation Settings*. Monograph 3. Washington, D.C.: National Association of Social Workers, Medical Social Work Section, 1956.

Maas, Henry S. Group Research Project. Berkeley: School of Social Welfare, University of California, 1963. Hectograph.

———. "Socio-Cultural Factors in Psychiatric Services for Children," *Smith College Studies in Social Work* 25:2 (February 1955), pp. 1–90.

———. "The Role of Numbers in Clubs of Lower-Class and Middle-Class Adolescents," *Child Development* 25 (December 1954), pp. 241–251.

Maas, Henry S., and Engler, Richard E. *Children in Need of Parents*. New York: Columbia University Press, 1959.

Maccoby, Eleanor. *The Development of Sex Differences*. Palo Alto, Calif.: Stanford University Press, 1966.

MacIver, Robert. "Professional Groups and Cultural Norms." In Howard W. Vollmer and Donald L. Mills (Eds.), *Professionalization*. Englewood Cliffs, N.J.: Prentice-Hall, 1966.

Madsen, William. *The Mexican-American of South Texas*. New York: Holt, Rinehart & Winston, 1964.

Mager, Robert F. *Goal Analysis*. Belmont, Calif.: Fearon, 1972.

Maheffey, Mary Ann. "Lobbying and Social Work," *Social Work* 17 (January 1972), pp. 3–11.

Maher, Thomas F. "Freedom of Speech in Public Agencies," *Social Work* 19 (November 1974), pp. 698–703.

Mahoney, Stanley C. *The Art of Helping People Effectively*. New York: Association Press, 1967.

Maldonado, David, Jr. "The Chicano Aged," *Social Work* 21:3 (May 1975), pp. 213–216.

Malone, C. "Safety First: Comments On the Influence of External Danger in the Lives of Children of Disorganized Families," *American Journal Orthopsychiatry* 36:3 (1966), pp. 3–12.

Maluccio, Anthony N. "Action as a Tool in Casework Practice," *Social Casework* 55:1 (January 1974), pp. 30–36.

Maluccio, Anthony N., and Marlow, Wilma D. "The Case for the Contract," *Social Work* 9 (January 1974), pp. 28–37.

Marckwardt, Albert H. "Regional Variations." In J. Burl Hogins and Robert E. Yarber (Eds.), *Language: An Introductory Reader*. New York: Harper & Row, 1969, pp. 142–155.

Margulies, Rebecca Zames, and Blau, Peter M. "America's Leading Professional Schools," *Change* 5:9 (November 1973), pp. 21–27.

Marris, Peter, and Rein, Martin. *Dilemmas of Social Reform*. New York: Atherton Press, 1969.

Martin, Carl. "Beyond Bureaucracy." *Child Welfare* 1 (July 1971), pp. 384–388.

Martinson, Robert. "What Works?—Questions and Answers about Prison Reform," *The Public Interest* 35 (1974), pp. 22–94.

Maruyama, Magoroh. "The Second Cybernetics: Deviation-Amplifying Mutual Causal Processes." In Walter Buckley (Ed.), *Modern Systems Research for the Behavioral Scientist*. Chicago: Aldine, 1968, pp. 304–313.

Maslow, A. H. *Motivation and Personality.* New York: Harper & Row, 1954.

———. *Toward a Psychology of Being.* Princeton, N.J.: Van Nostrand, 1962.

———. "Self-Actualization and Beyond." In James F. Bugental (Ed.), *Challenges of Humanistic Psychology.* New York: McGraw-Hill, 1967.

Mass, Amy Iwasaki. "Asians as Individuals: The Japanese Community," *Social Casework* 57:3 (March 1976), pp. 160–164.

Matson, Floyd W. *The Broken Image: Man, Science and Society.* New York: George Braziller, 1964.

Maurer, Adoh. "Corporal Punishment," *American Psychologist* 29 (August 1974), pp. 614–626.

May, Rollo. "Contributions of Existential Psychotherapy." In Rollo May, Earnest Angel, and Henry F. Ellenberger (Eds.), *Existence: A New Dimension in Psychiatry and Psychology.* New York: Basic Books, 1958, pp. 37–91.

May, Rollo. "Love and Will," *Psychology Today,* 3 (August 1969), pp. 17–64.

Mayer, John E., and Timms, Noel. "Clash in Perspective Between Worker and Client," *Social Casework* 50 (January 1969), pp. 32–40.

———. *The Client Speaks: Working Class Impressions of Casework.* New York: Atherton Press, 1972.

McClelland, David C. *The Achieving Society.* New York: Van Nostrand, 1961.

———. *Motivating Economic Achievement.* New York: Free Press, 1969.

McCormick, Mary J. "Social Advocacy: A New Dimension in Social Work," *Social Casework* 51 (January 1970), pp. 3–11.

McGlothlin, William J. *Patterns of Professional Education.* New York: Putnam, 1960.

McIsaac, Hugh, and Wilkinson, Harold. "Clients Talk About Their Caseworkers," *Public Welfare* 23:2 (July 1965), pp. 147–154.

McLoed, Donna L., and Meyer, Henry J. "A Study of Values of Social Workers." In Edwin Thomas (Ed.), *Behavioral Science for Social Workers.* New York: Free Press, 1967, pp. 401–416.

McPheeters, Harold L. and Ryan, Robert M. *A Core of Competence for Baccalaureate Social Welfare and Curricular Implications.* Atlanta, Ga.: Southern Regional Education Board, 1971.

Mead, George Herbert. *Mind, Self and Society.* Chicago: University of Chicago Press, 1934.

Mead, Margaret. *Coming of Age in Samoa.* New York: Morrow, 1971.

Mechanic, David. "Sources of Power of Lower Participants in Complex Organizations," *Administrative Science Quarterly* 7 (December 1962), pp. 349–364.

Meehl, Paul F., and McClosky, Herbert. "Ethical and Political Aspects of Applied Psychology," *Journal of Abnormal Social Psychology* 42 (January 1947), pp. 91–98.

Meenaghan, Thomas. "What Means 'Community,'" *Social Work* 17:6 (November 1972), pp. 94–98.

Meenaghan, Thomas M., and Mascari, Michael. "Consumer Choice, Consumer Control in Service Delivery," *Social Work* 16:5 (October 1971), pp. 50–57.

Meier, Elizabeth. "Interactions between the Person and His Organizational Situation: A Basic for Classification in Casework," *Social Casework* 46 (November 1965), pp. 542–549.

Menninger, Karl. *Theory of Psychoanalytic Treatment.* New York: Harper & Row, 1964.

———. *The Crime of Punishment.* New York: Viking, 1968.

Merakeon, Stephen. "Tort Law: California's Expansion of the Duty to Warn," *Washburn Law Journal* 15 (Fall 1976), pp. 499–501.

Merton, Robert K. *Social Theory and Social Structure.* Glencoe, Ill.: Free Press, 1957.

Merton, Robert K., and Nisbet, Robert A. (Eds.). *Contemporary Social Problems.* New York: Harcourt, Brace & World, 1961.

Meyer, Carol H. *Social Work Practice: A Response to the Urban Crisis.* New York: Free Press, 1970.

———. "Direct Services in Old and New Concepts." In Alfred J. Kahn (Ed.), *Shaping the New Social Work.* New York: Columbia University Press, 1973, pp. 26–54.

———. "Individualizing the Multi-Problem Family." In Francis J. Turner (Ed.), *Differential Diagnosis and Treatment.* New York: Free Press, 1976a, pp. 595–603.

———. *Social Work Practice* (2d ed.). New York: Free Press, 1976b.

Meyer, Henry J. "Sociological Comments." In Charles Grosser, William E. Henry, and J. G. Kelly (Eds.), *Non-Professionals in the Human Services.* San Francisco: Jossey Bass, 1969, pp. 40–56.

Meyerhoff, Howard L., and Meyerhoff, Barbara. "Field Observations of Middle-Class Gangs," *Social Forces* 42 (March 1964), pp. 328–336.

Meyerson, Erma T. "The Social Work Image or Self-Image?" *Social Work* (July 1959), pp. 67–71.

Michael, Donald. *The Unprepared Society.* New York: Basic Books, 1968.

Michell, Kenneth. "Clinical Relevance of the Boundary Functions of Language," *Bulletin of the Menninger Clinic* 40 (November 1976), pp. 641–654.

Miller, Gerald, and Simons, Herbert (Eds.). *Perspectives on Communication in Social Conflict.* Englewood Cliffs, N.J.: Prentice-Hall, 1974.

Miller, Henry. "Value Dilemmas in Social Casework," *Social Work* 13 (January 1968), pp. 27–33.

Miller, Roger. "Student Research Perspectives on Race," *Smith College Studies in Social Work* 41:1 (November 1970), pp. 1–23.

Miller, Stuart C. "Ego Autonomy in Sensory Deprivation, Isolation, and Stress," *The International Journal of Psychoanalysis* 43:8 (January-February 1962), pp. 1–20.

Miller, Walter B. "Lower-Class Culture as a Generating Milieu of Gang Delinquency," *Journal of Social Issues* 12:2 (April 1958), pp. 5–19.

———. "Implications of Urban Lower-Class Culture for Social Workers," *Social Service Review* 33 (September 1959), pp. 219–236.

Miller, William R., and Seligman, Martin E. P. "Depression and the Perception of Reinforcement," *Journal of Abnormal Psychology* 82 (1973), pp. 62–73.

Minuchin, S. et al. *Families of the Slums: An Exploration of Their Structure and Treatment.* New York: Basic Books, 1967.

———. "Family Therapy: Technique or Theory." In J. Masserman (Ed.), *Science and Psychoanalysis.* New York: Grune & Stratton, 1969, vol. 14, pp. 179–187.

Minuchin, S., and Montalvo, B. "Techniques for Working With Disorganized Low Socioeconomic Families," *American Journal of Orthopsychiatry* 37:5 (1967), pp. 880–887.

Miranda, Manuel R. *Psychotherapy with the Spanish-Speaking: Issues in Research and Service Delivery.* Spanish-Speaking Mental Health Center, Los Angeles, California, 1976.

Mizio, Emelicia. "White Workers—Minority Client," *Social Work* 17 (May 1972), pp. 82–86.

———. "Impact of External Systems of the Puerto Rican Family," *Social Casework* 55 (February 1974), pp. 76–83.

———. "Impact of External Systems on Puerto Rican Family," *Social Casework* 55 (February 1974), pp. 76–83.

Mookin, Robert H. "Foster Care: In Whose Best Interest?" *Harvard Educational Review* 43 (November 1973), pp. 599–638.

Montalvo, Braulio. "Home-School Conflict and the Puerto Rican Child," *Social Casework* 55 (February 1974), pp. 100–110.

Morales-Darta, Jose. *Religion and Psychotherapy.* New York: Vintage Press, 1976.

Morgan, Ralph. "Role Performance in a Bureaucracy." In *Social Work Practice, 1962.* New York: Columbia University Press, 1962, pp. 115–125.

Morris, W., and Sashkin, M. *Organizational Behavior in Action: Skill Building Experiences.* St. Paul: West Publishing, 1976.

Morris, Robert, and Rein, Martin. "Emerging Patterns in Community Planning." In *Social Work Practice, 1963.* New York: Columbia University Press, 1963, pp. 174–175.

Morris, Robert, and Binstock, Alfred. *Feasible Planning for Social Change.* New York: Columbia University Press, 1967.

Mowrer, O. Hobart. *The Crisis in Psychiatry and Religion.* Princeton, N.J.: D. Van Nostrand, 1964.

———. *The New Group Therapy.* Princeton, N.J.: D. Van Nostrand, 1964.

Mullen, Edward. "Casework Communication," *Social Casework* 49 (December 1968), pp. 546–551.

Mullen, Hugh, and Songiuliano, Iris. *The Therapist's Contribution to the Treatment Process.* Springfield, Ill.: Charles C Thomas, 1964.

Multon, Ruth. "Some Effects of the New Feminism," *The American Journal of Psychiatry* 134 (January 1977), pp. 1–6.

Murphy, Campbell. *Community Organization Practice.* Boston: Houghton Mifflin Co., 1954.

Murphy, Gardner. *Human Potentialities.* New York: Basic Books, 1958.

Murphy, Lois. B. *The Widening World of Childhood.* New York: Basic Books, 1962.

Murray, Henry A., and Kluckhohn, Clyde. "Outline of a Conception of Personality." In C. Kluckhohn and H. A. Murray (Eds.), *Personality in Nature, Society and Culture* (2d ed.). New York: Alfred A. Knopf, 1953.

Myrdal, Gunnar. *An American Dilemma.* New York: Harper & Row, 1948.

Nader, Ralph; Peter J. Petkas; and Kate Blackwell. *Whistle-Blowing.* New York: Grossman Publishers, 1972.

Nagel, Ernest. *Logic Without Metaphysics.* Glencoe, Ill.: The Free Press, 1967.

Nagelberg, Leo. "The Meaning of Help in Psychotherapy," *Psychoanalysis and the Psychoanalytic Review* 46 (Winter 1959), pp. 49–60.

Natanson, Maurice (Ed.). *Philosophy of the Social Sciences: A Reader.* New York: Random House, 1963.

National Advisory Commission on Civil Disorders. *Report of the National Advisory Commission on Civil Disorders.* New York: Bantam Books, 1968.

National Association of Social Workers. "Working Definition of Social Work Practice." *Social Work* 3:2 (April 1958), pp. 5–9.

———. "New Policy Statement on Licensing Issued," *NASW News* 19 (September 1974), p. 12.

———. "The 1975 NASW Delegate Assembly Actions: Professional Issues; Legal Regulation of Social Work Practice Policies for a Continuing Effort," *NASW News* 20 (July 1975a), pp. 15–17.

———. "NASW Celebrates 20th Anniversary; Assembly Passes Reorganization Plan," *NASW News* 20 (July 1975b), pp. 1, 10.

———. "Legislative Moves Toward Licensure Continue Unabated," *NASW News* 20 (September 1975c), p. 12.

———. "Licensing Movement for Social Workers Growing in Both Size and Complexity," *NASW News* 21 (January 1976), p. 8.

———. "Committee Statement on the Role of the Caseworker in a Group Work Agency." Mimeographed. Chicago, 1958.

———. *Values in Social Work: A Re-examination.* Monograph 9. Regional Institute Program, N.A.S.W. New York: National Association of Social Workers, 1967.

———. *Legal Regulations of Social Work Practice.* Washington, D.C.: N.A.S.W., 1973.

———. *Encyclopedia of Social Work.* John B. Turner (Editor-in-Chief). New York: N.A.S.W, 1977.

———. "Special Issue on Conceptual Frameworks," *Social Work* 22:5 (September 1977).

———. "The Psychiatric Social Worker as Leader of a Group," *Report of the Committee on Practice.* Mimeographed. New York: n.d.

Native American Research Group. *Native American Families in the City.* San Francisco: Institute for Scientific Analysis, 1975.

Needleman, Martin L., and Needleman, Carolyn Emerson. *Guerrillas in the Bureaucracy.* New York: Wiley, 1974.

Neiman, Lionel J., and Hughes, James W. "The Problem of the Concept of Role—A Re-Survey of the Literature." In Herman D. Stein and Richard A. Cloward (Eds.), *Social Perspectives on Behavior.* Glencoe, Ill.: Free Press, 1959, pp. 77–85.

Newman, Edward, and Turem, Jerry. "The Crisis of Accountability," *Social Work* 19 (January 1974), pp. 5–16.

New York Times. Editorial, November 11, 1964.

Nitzberg, Harold, and Kahn, Marvin W. "Consultation with Welfare Workers in a Mental Health Clinic," *Social Work* 7:3 (July 1962), pp. 84–94.

Nooney, James B., and Polansky, Norman A. "The Influence of Perceived Similarity and Personality on Verbal Accessibility," *Merrill-Palmer Quarterly* 8 (January 1962), pp. 33–40.

Northen, Helen. *Social Work with Groups.* New York: Columbia University Press, 1969.

O'Connell, Patricia. "Family Developmental Tasks," *Smith College Studies in Social Work* 42 (June 1972), pp. 203–210.

O'Connor, Gerald. "Toward a New Policy in Adult Corrections," *Social Service Review* 46:4 (December 1972), pp. 581–596.

Olsen, Katherine M., and Olsen, Marvin E. "Role Expectations and Perceptions for Social Workers in Medical Settings," *Social Work* 12 (July 1967), pp. 70–78.

Oppenheimer, Martin, and Lakey, George. *A Manual for Direct Action.* Chicago: Quadrangle Books, 1965.

Oren, Anne Winslow, and Kidneigh, John C. "A Note on Social Work Values," *Minnesota Welfare* 13 (Fall 1961), pp. 26–31.

Ortiz, Carlos Buitrago. *Esperonza.* Tucson, Ariz.: University of Arizona Press, 1973.

Otis, Jack. "Liberty, Social Work, and Public Policy Development," *The Social Welfare Forum 1976.* Columbia University Press, 1976, pp. 36–46.

Overmier, Bruce, and Seligman, Martin E. P. "Efforts of Inescapable Shock upon Subsequent Escape and Avoidance Learning," *Journal of Comparative and Physiological Psychology* 63 (1967), pp. 23–33.

Overton, Alice. "Establishing the Relationship," *Crime and Delinquency* 11 (July 1965), pp. 229–238.

Overton, Alice, and Tinker, Katherine. *Casework Notebook.* St. Paul, Minn.: Greater St. Paul Community Chest and Councils, 1957.

Oxley, Genevieve B. "The Caseworker's Expectations in Client Motivation," *Social Casework* 47:7 (July 1966), pp. 432–437.

Oxley, Genevieve B. "A Life-Model Approach to Change," *Social Casework* 52 (December 1971), pp. 627–633.

Packard, Vance A. *A Nation of Strangers.* New York: David McKay, 1972.

Padula, Helen, and Munro, Marion. "Thoughts on the Nature of the Social Work Profession," *Social Work* 4 (October 1959), pp. 98–104.

Palgi, Phyllis. "Death, Mourning and Bereavement in Israel," *Israel Annals of Psychiatry and Related Disciplines* 9 (1973), pp. 73–86.

Panter, Ethel. "Ego Building Procedures that Foster Social Functioning," *Social Casework* 47:3 (March 1966), pp. 142–143.

Parad, Howard J. (Ed.). *Crisis Intervention: Selected Readings.* New York: Family Service Association of America, 1965.

Parloff, Morris B.; Iflund, B.; and Goldstein, N. "Communication of 'Therapy Values' between Therapist and Schizophrenic Patients." Paper presented before the American Psychiatric Association, Chicago, 1957.

Parsons, Talcott. *The Structure of Social Action.* New York: McGraw-Hill, 1937.

———. *The Social System.* Glencoe, Ill.: Free Press, 1951.

———. *Essays in Sociological Theory* (rev. ed.). Glencoe, Ill.: Free Press, 1954.

———. *Max Weber: The Theory of Social and Economic Organization.* New York: Free Press, 1964.

Patterson, Gerald R. *Families: Applications of Social Learning to Family Life.* Champaign, Ill.: Research Press, 1971.

Patti, Rino J. "Organizational Resistance and Change: The View from Below," *Social Service Review* 48 (September 1974), pp. 367–383.

Patti, Rino J., and Resnick, Herman. "Changing the Agency from Within," *Social Work* 17:4 (July 1972), pp. 48–57.

Pavenstedt, Eleanor. *The Drifters: Children of Disorganized Lower-Class Families.* Boston: Little, Brown, 1967.

Payne, James E. "Ombudsman Roles for Social Workers," *Social Work* 17:1 (January 1972), pp. 94–100.

Payne, Stanley. *The Art of Asking Questions.* Princeton, N.J.: Princeton University Press, 1951.

Perils, Leo. "Poets, Prophets and Practitioners: A Labor Leader Speaks Out," *Social Work Education Reporter* 15 (June 1967), p. 16.

Perlman, Helen Harris. *Social Casework: A Problem-Solving Process.* Chicago: University of Chicago Press, 1957.

———. "Intake and Some Role Considerations," *Social Casework* 41 (April 1960), pp. 171–176.

———. "The Role Concept and Social Casework: Some Explorations," *Social Service Review* 35:4 (December 1961), pp. 370–381.

———. "The Role Concept and Social Casework: Some Explorations II," *Social Service Review* 36:1 (March 1962a), pp. 17–31.

———. *So You Want to Be a Social Worker.* New York: Harper & Bros., 1962b.

———. "Social Casework." In *Encyclopedia of Social Work,* New York: National Association of Social Workers, 1965, p. 706.

———. "Casework Is Dead," *Social Casework* 48:1 (January 1967a), pp. 22–25.

———. "Self-Determination: Reality or Illusion?" N.A.S.W. Regional Institute IX. *Values in Social Work: A Re-examination.* New York: National Association of Social Workers, 1967b, pp. 51–67.

———. *Persona.* Chicago: University of Chicago Press, 1968.

———. "The Problem-Solving Model in Social Casework." In Robert W. Roberts and Robert H. Nee (Eds.), *Theories of Social Casework.* Chicago: University of Chicago Press, 1970, pp. 129–181.

———. *Perspectives on Social Casework.* Philadelphia: Temple University Press, 1971.

———. "In Quest of Coping," *Social Casework* 56:4 (April 1975), pp. 213–225.

Perrow, Charles. *Complex Organizations: A Critical Essay.* Glenview, Ill.: Scott, Foresman, 1972.

Pers, Jessica et al. "Somebody Else's Children: A Report on the Foster Care System in California." Childhood and Government Project, School of Law, University of California at Berkeley, 1974.

Peter, Laurence J., and Hull, Raymond. *The Peter Principle.* New York: Morrow, 1969.

Petro, Olive, and French, Betty. "The Black Client's View of Himself," *Social Casework* 53 (October 1972), pp. 466–474.

Pfeiffer, W., and Jones, J. *The 1971 Annual Handbook for Group Facilitators.* Ann Arbor, Mich.: University Associates, 1971.

Pfouts, Jane H., and Rader, Gordon H. "Influence of Interviewer Characteristics on the Interview," *Social Casework* 43 (December 1962), pp. 548–552.

Phillips, Helen V. *Essentials of Social Group Work Skill.* New York: Association Press, 1957.

Pincus, Allen, and Minahan, Anne. *Social Work Practice: Model and Method.* Itasca, Ill.: Peacock Publishers, 1973.

———. "Toward a Model for Teaching a Basic First Year Course in Methods of Social Work Practice." New York: Council on Social Work Education, 1970, pp. 34–58.

Pilivin, Irving. "Restructuring the Provision of Social Services," *Social Work* 13:1 (January 1968), pp. 34–41.

Plant, Marcus L. "Recent Developments in Medicolegal Areas," *ALIABA Course Materials Journal* 1 (March 1976), pp. 41–43.

Podell, Lawrence, and Miller, Ronald. *Professionalism in Public Social Services,* vol. 1, no. 2 "Study Series." New York: Human Resources Administration, 1974.

Polansky, Norman A. "The Concept of Verbal Accessibility," *Smith College Studies in Social Work* 36 (October 1956), pp. 4–6.

———. *Ego Psychology and Communication.* Chicago: Aldine-Atherton, 1971.

Polansky, Norman A.; Borgman, Robert D.; and de Saix, Christine. *Roots of Futility.* San Francisco: Jossey-Bass, 1972.

Pollack, Otto. "Image of the Social Worker in the Community and the Profession," *Social Work* 6 (April 1961), pp. 106–112.

Polya, G. *How to Solve It.* Princeton, New Jersey: Princeton University Press, 1957.

Porter, Lyman W.; Lowler, Edward E., III, and Hockman, J. R. *Behavior in Organizations.* New York: McGraw-Hill, 1975.

Portner, Doreen Lindsay. "Personality Development in Deaf Children," *Social Work* 22:1 (January 1977), pp. 54–57.

Powers, Edwin, and Witmer, Helen. *An Experiment in the Prevention of Delinquency: The Cambridge-Somerville Youth Study.* New York: Columbia University Press, 1951.

Pratt, George E. "The Demonstration Grant is Probably Counterproductive," *Social Work* 19 (July 1974), pp. 486–489.

Program Evaluation Project Report, 1969–1973. "Four Ways to Goal Attainment,'" *Evaluation,* Special Monograph, #1, Minneapolis: Program Evaluation Project, 1973.

Pruger, Robert. "The Good Bureaucrat," *Social Work* 18:4 (July 1973), pp. 26–32.

———. "Bureaucratic Functioning as a Social Work Skill." In Betty L. Baer and Ronald C. Frederico (Eds.), *Educating the Baccalaureate Social Worker.* Cambridge, Mass.: Ballinger, 1978, pp. 149–167.

Pumphrey, Muriel W. "The Teaching of Values and Ethics in Social Work Education." In Werner Baehm (Ed.), *Social Work Curriculum Study* vol. 13. New York: Council on Social Work Education, 1959.

Pumphrey, Ralph, and Pumphrey, Muriel. *The Heritage of American Social Work.* New York: Columbia University Press, 1961.

Purcell, Francis. "The Helping Professions and Problems of the Brief Contact." In Frank Reissman, Jerome Cohen, and Arthur Pearl (Eds.), *Mental Health of the Poor.* New York: Free Press, 1964, pp. 431–440.

Purcell, Francis, and Specht, Harry. "The House on Sixth Street," *Social Work* 10:4 (October 1965), pp. 69–76.

Rabkin, J. et al. "Delinquency and the Lateral Boundary of the Family." In P. Graubard (Ed.), *Children Against the Schools.* Chicago: Follett Educational Corp., 1969.

Rainwater, Lee. *And the Poor Get Children.* Chicago: Quadrangle Books, 1960.

Rapoport, Anatol. "Foreword." In Walter Buckley (Ed.), *Modern Systems Research for the Behavioral Scientist.* Chicago: Aldine, 1968, xiii.

Rapoport, Lydia. "In Defense of Social Work: An Examination of the Stress of the Profession." Lecture, June 16, 1959 at School of Social Welfare, University of California at Berkeley.

———. "In Defense of Social Work: An Examination of the Stress of the Profession," *Social Service Review* 34 (March 1960), pp. 62–74.

———. "Creativity in Social Work," *Smith College Studies in Social Work* 38:3 (June 1968), pp. 139–161.

———. "Crisis Intervention as a Mode of Brief Treatment." In Robert W. Roberts and Robert Nee (Eds.), *Theories of Social Casework*, Chicago: University of Chicago Press, 1970.

Raven, Bertram H., and Rietsema, Jan. "The Effects of Varied Clarity of Group Goal and Group Path Upon the Individual and His Relationship to His Group." In Dorwin Cartwright and Alvin Zander (Eds.), *Group Dynamics: Research and Theory.* Evanston, Ill.: Row, Peterson and Co., 1960, pp. 395–413.

Red Horse, John G., and Feit, Marvin. "Urban Native American Preventive Health Care." Paper presented at the American Public Health Association Meeting, Miami Beach, Florida, October, 1976.

Redl, Fritz, and Wineman, David. *The Aggressive Child.* Glencoe: The Free Press, 1967.

Reid, William J. "Target Problems, Time Limits, Task Structure." *Journal of Education for Social Work* 8:2 (Spring 1972), pp. 58–68.

Reid, William, and Epstein, Laura. *Task Centered Practice.* New York: Columbia University Press, 1977.

Reid, William J., and Shyne, Ann W. *Brief and Extended Casework.* New York: Columbia University Press, 1969.

Reilly, A., and Jones, J. "Team Building." In W. Pfeiffer and J. Jones (Eds.), *The 1974 Annual Handbook for Group Facilitators.* Ann Arbor, Mich.: University Associates, 1974.

Rein, Martin. "Social Work in Search of a Radical Profession," *Social Work* 15:2 (April 1970), pp. 13–33.

"Report of Twenty-Six Principals of District 1–4." Mimeographed. New York: City of New York, 1964.

Reynolds, Bertha C. *Unchartered Journey.* New York: Citadel Press, 1963.

Rich, John. *Interviewing Children and Adolescents.* New York: St. Martin's Press, 1968.

Richmond, Mary E. *Friendly Visiting among the Poor: A Handbook for Charity Workers.* New York: Macmillan, 1899.

———. *Social Diagnosis.* New York: Russell Sage Foundation, 1917.

Riessman, Frank. *The Culturally Deprived Child.* New York: Harper and Row, 1962.

———. "Strategies and Suggestions for Training Non-professionals." In Bernard Guerney (Ed.), *Psychotherapeutic Agents—New Roles for Non-professionals, Parents and Teachers.* New York: Holt, Rinehart & Winston, 1969, pp. 151–169.

Ripple, Lillian (Ed.). *Innovations in Teaching Social Work Practice.* New York: Council on Social Work Education, 1970.

———. "Problem Identification and Formulation." In Norman A. Polansky (Ed.), *Social Work Research.* Chicago: University of Chicago Press, 1960, pp. 24–47.

Ripple, Lillian, and Alexander, Ernestina. "Motivation, Capacity and Opportunity as Related to Casework Service: Nature of the Client's Problem," *Social Service Review* 30:1 (March 1956), pp. 38–54.

Ripple, Lillian; Alexander, Ernestina; and Polemis, Bernice. *Motivation, Capacity and Opportunity: Studies in Casework Theory and Practice.* Chicago, School of Social Service Administration, University of Chicago, 1964.

Robbins, William. "Termination: Problems and Techniques," *Journal of the American Psychoanalytic Association* 23 (January 1975), pp. 166–176.

Roberts, Robert W., and Nee, Robert H. (Eds.). *Theories of Social Casework.* Chicago: University of Chicago Press, 1970.

Robinson, Sally. "Is There a Difference?" *Nursing Outlook* 15 (November 1967), pp. 34–36.

Robison, James, and Smith, Gerald. "The Effectiveness of Correctional Programs," *Crime and Delinquency* 17 (January 1971), pp. 67–80.

Rogers, Carl. "Characteristics of a Helping Relationship." In Donald L. Avila, Arthur W. Combs, and William W. Purkey (Eds.), *The*

Helping Relationship Sourcebook. Boston: Allyn and Bacon, Inc., 1971, pp. 2–18.

———. "Client-Centered Therapy." In C. H. Patterson (Ed.), *Theories of Counseling and Psychotherapy.* New York: Harper & Row, 1966, pp. 378–413.

———. "The Therapeutic Relationship: Recent Theory and Research." In Floyd Matson and Ashley Montagu (Eds.), *The Human Dialogue.* New York: Free Press, 1967, pp. 246–259.

———. "Some Personal Learnings about Interpersonal Relationships." Filmed lecture produced by Academic Communications Facility, University of California at Los Angeles, n.d.

Romero, D. P. "Biases in Gender-Role Research," *Social Work* 22 (May 1977), pp. 214–218.

Rose, Arnold M. (Ed.). *Human Behavior and Social Processes.* Boston: Houghton Mifflin, 1962.

Rose, Sheldon D. "In Pursuit of Social Competence," *Social Work* 20 (January 1975), pp. 33–39.

Rosen, Aaron, and Liberman, Dina. "The Experimental Evaluation of Interview Performance of Social Workers," *Social Science Review* 46:3 (September 1972), pp. 395–412.

Rosenthal, David. "Changes in Some Moral Values Following Psychotherapy," *Journal of Consulting Psychology* 19 (December 1955), pp. 431–436.

Ross, Alan O. "Interruptions and Termination of Treatment." In Mary R. Haworth (Ed.), *Child Psychotherapy.* New York: Basic Books, 1964, pp. 290–292.

Ross, Murray G. *Community Organization.* New York: Harper & Brothers, 1955.

Rothblatt, Henry B., and Leroy, David H. "Avoiding Psychiatric Malpractice," *California Western Law Review* 9 (Winter 1973), pp. 260–272.

Rothman, Jack. "An Analysis of Goals and Roles in Community Organization Practice," *Social Work* 9 (April 1964), pp. 24–31.

———. "Three Models of Community Organization Practice," in *Social Work Practice, 1968.* New York: Columbia University Press, 1968, pp. 16–47.

Rubel, Arthur P. *Across the Tracks—Mexican-Americans in Texas City.* Austin, Texas: University of Texas Press, 1966.

Rubin, Gerald K. "Helping a Clinic Patient Modify Self-Destructive Thinking," *Social Work* 7:1 (January 1962), p. 76–80.

Rubin, Lillian. *Worlds of Pain.* New York: Basic Books, 1976.

Rubington, Earl, and Weinberg, Martin S. *Deviance: The Interactionist Perspective.* New York: Macmillan, 1968.

Ruddock, Ralph. *Roles and Relationships.* London: Routledge and Kegan Paul, 1969.

Ruiz, Pedro, and Langrod, John. "The Role of Folk Healers in Community Mental Health Services," *Community Mental Health Journal* 12 (Winter 1976), pp. 392–398.

Russell, Bertrand. "On Marriage." In Arlene S. and Jerome H. Skolnick (Eds.), *Family in Transition.* Boston: Little, Brown, 1971, pp. 284–285.

Ryan, William. *Blaming the Victim.* New York: Vintage Press, 1971.

Sabey, Francine. *The Nonprofessional Revolution in Mental Health.* New York: Columbia University Press, 1970.

Sachs, Wulf. *Black Hamlet.* Boston: Little, Brown, 1947.

Sager, Clifford J.; Brayboy, Thomas L.; and Waxenberg, Barbara R. *The Black Ghetto Family in Therapy—A Laboratory Experience.* New York: Grove Press, Inc., 1970.

Salomon, Elizabeth L. "Humanistic Values and Social Casework," *Social Casework* 48:1 (January 1967), pp. 26–33.

Sander, Irwin. "Professional Roles in Planned Change." In Robert Morris (Ed.), *Centrally Planned Change: Prospects and Concepts.* New York: National Association of Social Workers, 1964, pp. 102–116.

Satir, Virginia. *Conjoint Family Therapy: A Guide to Therapy and Technique.* Palo Alto, Calif.: Science and Behavior Books, 1964.

Sattler, Jerome A. "Racial Experimenter Effects in Experimentation, Testing, Interviewing and Psychotherapy," *Psychological Bulletin* 73:2 (February 1970), pp. 137–160.

Sauer, John. "Psychiatric Malpractice—A Survey," *Washburn Law Journal* 11 (Spring 1972), pp. 460–469.

Schachter, Stanley. *The Psychology of Affiliation.* Palo Alto, Calif.: Stanford University Press, 1959.

Schapler, James H., and Galinsky, Maida J. "Goals in Social Group Work Practice: Formulation, Implementation and Evaluation." In Paul Glasser, Rosemary Sarri, and Robert Vinter (Eds.), *Individual Change Through Small Groups.* New York: Free Press, 1974, pp. 126–148.

Schein, E., and Bennis W. *Personal and Organizational Change Through Group Methods: The Laboratory Approach.* New York: Wiley, 1965.

Scherz, Frances H. "Multiple-Client Interviewing: Treatment Interpretations," *Social Casework* 43 (March 1962), pp. 234–240.

———. "Theory and Practice of Family Therapy." In Robert W. Roberts and Robert Nee (Eds.), *Theories of Social Casework.* Chicago: University of Chicago Press, 1970, pp. 219–264.

Scheunemann, Yolanda R., and French, Betty. "Diagnosis as the Foundation of Professional Service," *Social Casework* 35:3 (March 1974), pp. 135–141.

Schiff, Sheldon K. "Termination of Therapy: Problems in a Community Psychiatric Outpatient Clinic," *Archives of General Psychiatry* 6:1 (January 1962), pp. 77–82.

Schindler, Ralph. "Malpractice—Another New Dimension of Liability—A Critical Analysis," *Trial Lawyer Guide* 20 (1976), pp. 129–151.

Schneiderman, Leonard. "A Social Action Model for the Social Work Practice," *Social Casework* 46 (October 1965), pp. 490–493.

Schorr, Alvin. *Explorations in Social Policy.* New York: Basic Books, 1968.

Schrag, Peter, and Divoky, Diane. *The Myth of the Hyperactive Child.* New York: Pantheon Books, 1975.

Schubert, Margret. *Interviewing in Social Work Practice.* New York: Council on Social Work Education, 1971.

Schulman, Lawrence. "Scapegoats, Group Workers and Preemptive Intervention," *Social Work* 12 (April 1967), pp. 37–43.

Schutz, Alfred. *The Problem of Multiple Realities: Collected papers.* The Hague: Martinus Nijoff, 1971, vol. 1.

Schutz, W. *The Interpersonal Underworld.* Palo Alto, Calif.: Science and Behavior Books, 1966.

Schwartz, Morris S., and Schwartz, Charlotte G. *Social Approaches to Mental Patient Care.* New York: Columbia University Press, 1964.

Schwartz, William. "Group Work and the Social Scene." In Alfred J. Kahn (Ed.), *Issues in American Social Work.* New York: Columbia University Press, 1959, pp. 110–137.

———. "Toward a Strategy of Group Work Practice," *Social Science Review* 36 (September 1962), pp. 268–279.

———. "Private Troubles and Public Issues: One Social Work Job or Two?" In *Social Welfare Forum,* 1969 (New York: Columbia University Press, 1969, pp. 22–43.

———. "On the Case of Groups in Social Work Practice," In William Schwartz and Serapio R. Zalba (Eds.), *The Practice of Group Work.* New York: Columbia University Press, 1971a, pp. 3–24.

———. "Social Group Work: The Interactionist Approach." In Robert Morris (Ed.), *Encyclopedia of Social Work.* New York: National Association of Social Workers, 1971b, pp. 1252–1263.

Scriven, Michael. "Unpredictability in Human Behavior." In B. Wolman (Ed.), *Scientific Psychology.* New York: Basic Books, 1965, pp. 412–424.

Seabury, Brett. "Arrangement of Physical Space in Social Work Settings," *Social Work* 16 (October 1971), pp. 43–49.

———. "The Contract: Uses, Abuses, and Limitations," *Social Work* 21 (January 1976), pp. 16–21.

Segal, Brian. "Planning and Power in Hospital Social Service," *Social Casework* 51 (July 1970), pp. 339–405.

Seiden, Anne. "Overview: Research on the Psychology of Women, I., Gender Differences and Sexual Reproductive Life," *American Journal of Psychiatry* 133 (September 1976), pp. 995–1007.

Selby, Lola G. "Supportive Treatment: The Development of a Concept and a Helping Method," *Social Service Review* 30:4 (December 1956), pp. 400–414.

Seligman, Martin E. P. "Depression and Learned Helplessness." In Raymond J. Friedman and Martin M. Katz (Eds.), *The Psychology of Depression: Contemporary Theory and Research.* New York: Halstead Press, 1974, pp. 83–107.

———. *Helplessness: On Depression, Development, and Death.* San Francisco: W. H. Freeman, 1975.

Seligman, Martin E. P., and Maier, Steve F. "Failure to Escape Traumatic Shock," *Journal of Experimental Psychology* 74 (1967), pp. 1–9.

Seligman, Martin E. P.; Maier, Steve F.; and Solomon, Richard L. "Unpredictable and Uncontrollable Aversive Events." In Robert F. Brush (Ed.), *Aversive Conditioning and Learning.* New York: Academic Press, 1971, pp. 347–400.

———. "Pavlovian Fear Conditioning and Learned Helplessness." In A. Campbell Byron, and Russell M. Church (Eds.), *Punishment and Aversive Behavior.* New York: Appleton-Century-Crofts, 1969, pp. 299–342.

Seligman, Michele. "The Interracial Casework Relationship," *Smith College Studies in Social Work* 39:1 (November 1968), p. 84.

Senna, Joseph J. "Changes in Due Process of Law," *Social Work* 19 (May 1974), pp. 319–324.

Sharp, Roland, and Wetzel, Ralph. *Behavior Modification in the Natural Environment.* New York: Academic Press, 1969.

Shapiro, Arthur K. "A Contribution to a History of the Placebo Effect," *Behavioral Science* 5 (April 1960), pp. 110–135.

Sharttuck, Gerald, and Marrin, John M. "New Professional Work Roles and Their Integration into a Social Agency Structure," *Social Work* 14 (July 1969), pp. 13–20.

Sheafor, Bradford W. "Why License Social Work?" *The Kansas Conference Key* 22 (November 1973), pp. 5–6.

Sherif, Muzafer. *The Psychology of Social Norms.* New York: Harper Bros., 1936.

Sherman, Murray H.; Ackerman, Nathan; Sherman, Stanford M.; and Mitchell, Celia. "Non-Verbal and Reenactment of Conflict in Family Therapy," *Family Process* 4 (March 1965), pp. 133–162.

Shevrin, Howard, and Shectman, Fredrick. "The Diagnostic Process in Psychiatric Evaluations," *Bulletin of the Menninger Clinic* 37 (September 1973), pp. 451–495.

Shireman, Joan, and Watson, Kenneth W. "Adoption of Real Children," *Social Work* 17 (July 1972), pp. 29–39.

Shonick, Helen. "The Crisis in Social Work, Points and Viewpoints," *Social Work* 17 (July 1972), pp. 102–104.

Short, James S., and Nye, F. Ivan. "Reported Behavior as a Criterion of Deviant Behavior," *Social Problems* 5:3 (Winter 1957), pp. 207–313.

Shyne, Ann. "What Research Tells Us About Short-Term Cases in Family Agencies," *Social Casework* 38 (May 1957), pp. 223–231.

———. "An Experimental Study of Casework Methods," *Social Casework* 46 (November 1965), pp. 535–541.

———. (Ed.). *Use of Judgments as Data in Social Work Research.* New York: National Association of Social Workers, 1959.

Siggins, Lorraine D. "Mourning: A Critical Review of the Literature," *International Journal of Psychiatry* 3 (May 1967), pp. 418–432.

Silverman, Marvin. "Children's Rights and Social Work," *Social Service Review* 51:1 (March 1977a), pp. 171–178.

Silverman, Phyllis R. "Services to the Widowed: First Steps in a Program of Preventive Intervention," *Community Mental Health Journal* 3 (Spring 1967), pp. 37–44.

———. "A Reexamination of the Intake Procedure," *Social Casework* 51 (December 1970), pp. 625–634.

Simmons, J. L. *Deviants.* Berkeley, Calif.: Glendessary Press, 1969.

Simon, Bernece. "Borrowed Concepts: Problems and Issues for Curriculum Planning," *Health and Disability Concepts in Social Work Education.* Proceedings of a Workshop Conference, School of Social Work, University of Minnesota, Minneapolis, Minnesota (April 1964), pp. 31–42.

Simon, Herbert. "Comments on the Theory of Organization," *American Political Science Review* 46:3 (1952), p. 1130–1139.

———. *Administrative Behavior* (2d ed.). New York: Macmillan, 1957a.

———. *Models of Man, Social and Rational.* New York: Wiley, 1957b.

Simpson, Richard L., and Simpson, Ida Harper. "Women and Bureaucracy in the Semi-Professions." In Amitai Etzioni (Ed.), *The Semi-Professions and Their Organization: Teachers, Nurses, Social Workers.* New York: Free Press, 1969, pp. 196–265.

Singer, Erwin. *Key Concepts in Psychotherapy.* New York: Basic Books, 1970.

Singer, Jerome L. "The Importance of Daydreaming," *Psychology Today* 11:1 (April 1968) pp. 18–27.

Sinick, Daniel. "Two Anxiety Scales Correlated and Examined for Sex Differences," *Journal of Clinical Psychology* 12 (October 1956), pp. 394–395.

Sinsheimer, Robert. "The Existential Casework Relationship," *Social Casework* 50 (February 1969), pp. 67–73.

Siporin, Max. *Introduction to Social Work Practice.* New York: Macmillan, 1975.

Skinner, B. F. *Beyond Freedom and Dignity.* New York: Knopf, 1971.

Slater, Philip. "Parental Role Differentiation." In Rose L. Caser (Ed.), *The Family: Its Structure and Functions.* New York: St. Martin's Press, 1964.

Slovenko, Ralph. "Psychotherapy and Confidentiality," *Cleveland State Law Review* 24 (Winter 1975), pp. 375–396.

Smaldino, Angelo. "The Importance of Hope in the Casework Relationship," *Social Casework* 56:6 (June 1975), pp. 328–333.

Smalley, Ruth E. *Theory for Social Work Practice.* New York: Columbia University Press, 1967.

———. "General Characteristics of the Functional Approach: A Brief Statement of the Origins of this Approach." In Robert W. Roberts and Robert H. Nee (Eds.), *Theories of Social Casework.* Chicago: University of Chicago Press, 1970, pp. 79–128.

Smith, Clagett. *Conflict Resolution: Contributions of the Behavior Sciences.* Notre Dame: University of Notre Dame Press, 1971.

Sobey, Francine. *The Nonprofessional Revolution in Mental Health.* New York: Columbia University Press, 1970.

Solnit, A. J. "Problems of Termination in Child Analysis: A Panel Discussion as Reported by Robert Kohemon," *Journal of the American Academy of Child Psychiatry* 17 (January 1969), pp. 191–205.

Solomon, L. "Team Development: A Training Approach." In W. Pfeiffer and J. Jones (Eds.), *The 1977 Annual Handbook for Group Facilitators.* Ann Arbor, Mich.: University Associates, 1977.

Sotomayor, Marta. "Mexican-American Interaction with Social Systems," *Social Casework* 5 (May 1971), pp. 316–322.

———. "Language, Culture, and Ethnicity in Developing Self-concept," *Social Casework* 58 (April 1977), pp. 195–203.

Specht, Harry. "Social Policy Formulation: The Role of the Social Caseworker." In *Social Work Practice, 1967.* New York: Columbia University Press, 1967, pp. 72–94.

———. "Casework Practice and Social Policy Formulation," *Social Work* 13 (January 1968), pp. 42–52.

———. "Disruptive Tactics," *Social Work* 14 (April 1969), pp. 5–15.

———. "The Deprofessionalization of Social Work," *Social Work* 17 (March 1972), pp. 3–15.

Specht, Harry, and Riessman, Frank. *Some Notes on a Model for an Integrated Social Work Approach to Social Problems.* New York: Mobilization for Youth, 1963.

Speck, Ross V. "Psychotherapy of the Social Network of a Schizophrenic Family," *Family Procedure* 6 (1967), pp. 208–214.

———. "Psychotherapy of Family Social Networks." Paper presented at the Family Therapy Symposium, Medical College of Virginia, Richmond, 1967a.

———. "The Politics and Psychotherapy of Mini- and Micro-Groups." Paper presented at Congress on Dialectics of Liberation, London, 1967b.

———. "NASW Membership: Characteristics, Deployment, and Salaries," *Personnel Information* 12 (May 1969), p. 1.

Stamm, Alfred M., and Olans, J. "The Social Network of the Family of a Schizophrenic: Implications for Social and Preventive Psychiatry." Paper presented at the Annual Meeting of the American Orthopedic Association, March 1967.

Stamm, Alfred M., and Morong, E. "Home-Centered Treatment of the Social Network of Schizophrenic Families: Two Approaches." Paper presented at Annual Meeting of the American Psychiatric Association, 1967.

Stamm, Isabel L. "Ego Psychology in the Emerging Theoretical Base of Casework." In Alfred J. Kahan (Ed.), *Issues in American Social Work*. New York: Columbia University Press, 1959, pp. 80–109.

Start, Frances B. "Barriers to Client-Worker Communication at Intake," *Social Casework* 40 (April 1954), pp. 177–183.

Stein, Herman D. "Organizational Theory—Implications for Administration Research." In Leonard S. Kogan (Ed.), *Social Science Theory and Social Work Research*. New York: National Association of Social Workers, 1960, pp. 81–95.

———. "The Concept of the Social Environment in Social Work Practice," *Smith College Studies in Social Work* 30 (June 1960), pp. 187–210.

Stein, Irma D. *Systems Theory, Science and Social Work*. Metuchen, N.J.: Scarecrow Press, 1974.

Stein, Theodore J. "A Content Analysis of Social Caseworkers and Client Interaction in Foster Care." D.S.W. dissertation, School of Social Welfare, University of California at Berkeley, 1974.

Stein, Theodore J., and Gambrill, Eileen D. "Foster Care: The Use of Contracts," *Public Welfare* 32:4 (Fall 1974), pp. 20–25.

Stewart, John (Ed.). *Bridges Not Walls: A Book about Interpersonal Communication*. Reading, Mass.: Addison-Wesley, 1973.

Stock, Richard O. "Societal Demands on the Voluntary Agency," *Social Casework* 50 (January 1969), pp. 27–31.

Stoller, Robert. *Splitting*. New York: Delta, 1973.

Stone, Alan A. "The Tarasoff Decisions: Suing Psychotherapists to Safeguard Society," *Harvard Law Review* 90 (December 1976), pp. 358–378.

Stouffer, Samuel A. "Some Observations on Study Design," *American Journal of Sociology* (January 1950), pp. 356–359.

Stover, Carl F. "Changing Patterns in the Philosophy of Management," *Public Administration Review* 18 (Winter 1978), pp. 21–27.

St. Pierre, C. Andre. "Motivating the Drug Addict in Treatment," *Social Work* 16:1 (January 1971), pp. 80–88.

Strange, Richard J., and Ricco, Anthony C. "Counselee Preferences for Counselors: Some Implications for Counselor Education," *Counselor Education and Supervision* 10 (Fall 1970), pp. 39–45.

Strean, Herbert. *Social Casework*. Metuchen, N.J.: Scarecrow Press, 1971.

———. "Casework with Ego-Fragmented Parents," *Social Casework* 49 (April 1968), p. 226.

Strong, E. K., Jr. *Vocational Interests of Men and Women*. Palo Alto, Calif.: Stanford University Press, 1943.

Stuart, Richard B. "Behavioral Contracting within the Families of Delinquents," *Journal of Behavioral Therapy and Experimental Psychiatry* 2:1 (March 1971), pp. 1–12.

Studt, Elliot. *A Conceptual Approach to Teaching Materials*. New York: Council on Social Work Education, 1965.

———. "Social Work Therapy and Implications for the Practice of Methods," *Social Work Education Reporter* 16 (June 1968), pp. 22–24.

Stumpf, Jack. "Community Planning and Development." In *Encyclopedia of Social Work*. New York: National Association of Social Workers, 1965, p. 194.

Suchman, Edward A. *Evaluative Research*. New York: Russell Sage Foundation, 1967.

———. "Action for What? A Critique of Evaluative Research." In Carole H. Weiss (Ed.), *Evaluating Action Programs*. Boston: Allyn & Bacon, 1972, pp. 52–84.

Sumati Dubey. "Blacks' Preference for Black Professionals, Businessmen, and Religious Leaders," *Public Opinion Quarterly* 34:1 (Spring 1970), pp. 113–116.

Sundel, Martin; Radin, Norma; and Churchill, Sallie R. "Diagnosis in Group Work." In Paul Glasser, Rosemary Sarri and Robert Vinter (Eds.), *Individual Change Through Small Groups*. New York: Free Press, 1974.

Sutton-Smith, Brian, and Rosenberg, Benjamin G. "Sex Differences in the Longitudinal Prediction of Adult Personality." Paper presented before the Society for Research in Child Development, Philadelphia, 1973.

Szasz, Thomas S. *The Myth of Mental Illness: Foundations of a Theory of Personal Conduct*. New York: Harper and Row, 1961.

———. *Psychiatric Justice*. New York: Macmillan, 1965.

Taber, Merlin A., and Vattano, Anthony J. "Clinical and Social Orientations in Social Work: An

Empirical Study," *Social Service Review* 44:1 (March 1970), pp. 34–43.

Taber, Richard H. "A Systems Approach to the Delivery of Mental Health Services in Black Ghettos," *American Journal of Orthopsychiatry* 40 (July 1970), pp. 702–709.

———. "Providing Mental Health Services to a Low Socio-Economic Black Community Without Requiring that People Perceive Themselves as Patients: An Ecological System Approach to a Community Group." Paper presented at 46th Annual Meeting of the American Orthopsychiatric Association, New York, 1969.

Tarshis, Carl Barry. "Liability for Psychotherapy," *University of Toronto Faculty Law Review* 30 (August 1972), pp. 75–87.

Tedeschi, James et al. *Conflict, Power and Games.* Chicago: Aldine, 1973.

Tessler, Richard C. "Clients Reaction to Initial Interviews: A Study of Relationship Formation." Ph.D. dissertation, University of Wisconsin, 1972.

———. "Clients Reaction to Initial Interviews: Determinants of Relationship-Centered and Problem-Centered Satisfaction," *Journal of Counseling Psychology* 22 (May 1975), pp. 187–191.

Tessler, Richard C., and Polansky, Norman A. "Perceived Similarity: A Paradox in Interviewing," *Social Work* 20:5 (September 1975), pp. 359–362.

Tharp, Roland G., and Wetzel, Ralph J. *Behavior Modification in the Natural Environment.* New York: Academic Press, 1969.

Thomas, Edwin J. "Behavioral Modification and Casework." In Robert W. Roberts and Robert H. Nee (Eds.), *Theories of Social Casework.* Chicago: University of Chicago Press, 1970, pp. 181–219.

———. *Behavior Modification Procedure: A Sourcebook.* Chicago: Aldine, 1974.

Thomas, Gloria. "Final Report of the Temporary Foster Care Project." Mimeographed. Lansing: Mich.: Department of Social Services, Division of Youth Services, 1978.

Thompson, James D. *Organizations in Action.* New York: McGraw-Hill, 1967.

Thornton, Jerry W., and Jacobs, Paul D. "Learned Helplessness in Human Subjects," *Journal of Experimental Psychology* 87 (1971), pp. 367–372.

Thursz, Daniel. "The Arsenal of Social Action Strategies: Options for Social Workers," *Social Work* 16 (January 1971), pp. 27–34.

Tighe, T. J., and Elliot, R. "A Technique for Controlling Behavior in Natural Life Settings," *Journal of Applied Behavior Analysis* 1 (Summer 1965), pp. 84–101.

Tillich, Paul. "The Philosophy of Social Work," *Social Service Review* 36:1 (March 1962), pp. 13–16.

Toch, Hans. "The Care and Feeding of Typolo-gies and Labels," *Federal Probation* 34:3 (September 1970), pp. 15–19.

Toffler, Alvin. *Future Shock.* New York: Random House, 1970.

Toren, Nina. "Semi-Professionalism and Social Work: A Theoretical Perspective." In Amitai Etzioni (Ed.), *The Semi-Professions and Their Organizations: Teachers, Nurses, Social Workers.* New York: Free Press, 1969, p. 166.

Towle, Charlotte. *Common Human Needs.* New York: National Association of Social Workers, 1965.

Towley, Louis. As quoted in Frank J. Bruno, *Trends in Social Work, 1874–1956.* New York: Columbia University Press, 1957, p. 22.

Townsend, Orville. "Vocational Rehabilitation and the Black Counselor: The Conventional Training Situation and the Battleground Across Town," *Journal of Rehabilitation* 36:6 (November-December 1970), pp. 26–31.

Tropp, Emanuel. "The Group: In Life and in Social Work," *Social Casework* 49 (May 1968), pp. 267–274.

Trecker, Harleigh B. *Group Process in Administration* (2d ed.). New York: Woman's Press, 1950.

———. *Social Group Work—Principles and Practices* (rev. ed.). New York: Whiteside, 1955, pp. 23–35.

———. "Approaching the Concept of Change in Education for Social Work," School of Social Work, Virginia Commonwealth University, 1974a. Mimeographed.

———. "Three Problematic Concepts: Client, Help, Worker," *Social Casework* 55:1 (January 1974b), pp. 19–29.

———. "A Developmental Theory." In Robert W. Roberts and Helen Northen (Eds.), *Theories of Social Work with Groups.* New York: Columbia University Press, 1976, pp. 198–238.

Truax, Charles B., and Carkhall, Robert. "Concreteness: A Neglected Variable in Research in Psychotherapy," *Journal of Clinical Psychology* 20 (April 1964), pp. 264–267.

———. *Toward Effective Counseling and Psychotherapy: Training and Practice.* Chicago: Aldine, 1967.

Truax, Charles. B., and Mitchell, Kevin M. "Research on Certain Interpersonal Skills in Relation to Process and Outcome." In Allen E. Bergin and Sol L. Garfield (Eds.), *Handbook for Psychotherapy and Behavior.* New York: Wiley, 1971, pp. 299–342.

Trungpa, Chogyam. *Born in Tibet.* Baltimore, Md.: Penguin Books, 1971.

Tucker, Gregory. "A Study of Verbal Accessibility in Hospitalized Paranoid Schizophrenics in Response to Two Styles of Interviewing." Ph.D. dissertation, Case Western Reserve University, 1972.

Turner, Ralph H. "Role-Taking: Process versus Conformity." In Arnold Rose (Ed.), *Human Behavior and Social Processes*. Boston: Houghton Mifflin, 1962, pp. 20–40.

Twente, Esther S. "Aging, Strength, and Creativity," *Social Work* 10:4 (July 1965), pp. 105–110.

Tyler, Inez, M. and Thompson, Sophie D. "Cultural Factors in Casework Treatment of a Navajo Mental Patient," *Social Casework* 46:4 (April 1965), pp. 215–220.

Tyler, Ralph. "Distinctive Attributes of Education for the Professions," *Social Work Journal* 33 (April 1952), pp. 54–69.

Udry, J. Richard. *The Social Context of Marriage*. Philadelphia: J. B. Lippincott, 1966.

Uesugi, Thomas K., and Vinachke, W. Edgar. "Strategy in a Feminine Game," *Sociometry* 26 (March 1963), pp. 75–88.

Ullman, Alice, and Davis, Milton. "Assessing the Medical Patient's Motivation and Ability to Work," *Social Casework* 46 (April 1965), pp. 195–202.

Ullman, Leonard P., and Krasner, Leonard. *A Psychological Approach to Abnormal Behavior*. Englewood Cliffs, N.J.: Prentice-Hall, 1969, pp. 414–428.

U.S. Department of Health, Education and Welfare, *Report of the President's Advisory Commission on Civil Disorders*, 1968.

U.S. Department of Health, Education and Welfare. *Secretary's Commission on Medical Malpractice Report*. Pubn. No. 05–72–88.

Vattano, Anthony. "Power to the People: Self-Help Groups," *Social Work* 17 (July 1972), pp. 7–15.

Vesper, Sue. "Casework Aimed at Supporting Marital Role Reversal." Paper presented at the Centennial Staff Institute, St. Louis, 1960.

Vickers, Geoffrey. "Is Adaptability Enough?" *Behavioral Science* 4 (1959), pp. 219–234.

Vickery, Anne. "A Systems Approach to Social Work Intervention: Its Uses for Work with Individuals and Families," *British Journal of Social Work* 4:4 (Winter 1974), pp. 389–403.

Vigilante, Joseph L. "The Future: Sour or Rosy? Points and Viewpoints," *Social Work* 17 (July 1972), pp. 3–4, 102–104.

Vinter, Robert. "The Social Structure of Social Service." In Alfred J. Kahn (Ed.), *Issues in American Social Work*. New York: Columbia University Press, 1959, pp. 242–269.

———. "The Essential Components of Social Work Practice." In Robert D. Vinter (Ed.), *Readings in Group Work Practice*. Ann Arbor, Mich.: Copers Publishers, 1967a, pp. 1–7.

———. "Approach to Group Work Practice." In Robert D. Vinter (Ed.), *Readings in Group Work Practice*. Ann Arbor, Mich.: Copers Publishers, 1967b.

———. "Analysis of Treatment Organizations." In

Yeheskel Hasenfeld and R. A. English (Eds.), *Human Service Organizations*. Ann Arbor, Mich.: University of Michigan Press, 1974, pp. 33–50.

Vogel, E., and Bell, N. "The Emotionally Disturbed Child as the Family Scrapegoat," in E. Vogel and N. Bell (Eds.), *A Modern Introduction to the Family*. New York: Free Press, 1968, pp. 382–397.

Von Bertalanffy, Ludwig. "The Theory of Open Systems in Physics and Biology," *Science* 3 (January 1950), pp. 23–29.

Von Bertalanffy, Ludwig. "General Systems Theory and Psychiatry." In Silvano Arieti (Ed.), *American Handbook of Psychiatry*. New York: Basic Books, 1966, pp. 705–721.

———. *General System Theory*. New York: Braziller, 1968.

Vontross, Clemmont. "Cultural Barriers in Counseling Relationships," *Personnel and Guidance Journal* 48 (September 1969), pp. 11–16.

———. "Counseling Blacks," *Personnel and Guidance Journal* 48 (May 1970), pp. 713–719.

———. "Racial Differences: Impediments to Rapport," *Journal of Consulting Psychology* 18 (1971), pp. 7–13.

Voss, Harwin L. "Socio-economic Status and Reported Delinquent Behavior," *Social Problems* 13 (Winter 1966), pp. 314–324.

Vygotsky, Lee Semenovich. *Thought and Language*. Cambridge, Mass.: The Massachusetts Institute of Technology Press, 1962.

Wade, Alan. "The Social Worker in the Political Process," in *Social Welfare Forum, 1966*. New York: Columbia University Press, 1966, pp. 52–67.

Walton, Richard. *Interpersonal Peace Making*. Reading, Mass.: Addison-Wesley, 1969.

Warren, Roland. "Types of Purposive Social Change at the Community Level." In Ralph M. Kramer and Harry Specht (Eds.), *Readings in Community Organization Practice*. Englewood Cliffs, N.J.: Prentice-Hall, 1969, pp. 205–222.

——— (Ed.). *Perspectives on the American Community*. Chicago: Rand McNally, 1966.

Wasserman, Harry. "Early Careers of Professional Workers in a Public Child Welfare Agency," *Social Work* 15:3 (July 1970), pp. 98–101.

———. "The Professional Social Worker in a Bureaucracy," *Social Work* 16 (January 1971), pp. 89–96.

Watson, James D. *The Double Helix*. New York: Atheneum, 1968.

Watzlawick, Paul; Weakland, John; and Fich, Richard. *Change: Principle of Problem Formation and Problem Resolution*. New York: Norton, 1974.

Weber, Max. *The Theory of Social and Economic Organization*. New York: Free Press, 1964.

Weinberg, Jon. "Counseling Recovering Alcoholics," *Social Work* 18:4 (July 1973), pp. 84–93.

Weinberger, Paul. "Assessing Professional Status in Social Welfare," *Personnel Information* 10 (July 1967), pp. 44–47.

Weinberger, Paul E., and Weinberger, Dorothy Z. "Legal Regulations in Perspective." In Paul E. Weinberger (Ed.), *Perspectives on Social Welfare: An Introductory Anthology.* New York: Macmillan, 1974, pp. 439–453.

Weiner, Hyman. "Towards Techniques for Social Change," *Social Work* 6 (April 1961), pp. 26–35.

———. "Social Change and Group Work Practice," *Social Work* 9 (July 1964), pp. 106–112.

Weiner, Rae B. "Adolescent Problems: Symptoms of Family Dysfunctioning," *Social Casework* 47 (June 1966), pp. 373–377.

Weisband, Edward, and Franck, Thomas M. *Resignation in Protest.* New York: Grossman Publishers, 1975.

Weiss, Carol H. *Validity of Interview Responses of Welfare Mothers—Final Report.* New York: Bureau of Applied Social Research, Columbia University, 1968.

Weissman, Harold H. *Overcoming Mismanagement in the Human Services.* San Francisco: Jossey-Bass, 1973.

Wheelis, Allen. "The Place of Action in Personality Change," *Psychiatry* 13 (May 1950), pp. 135–148.

White, Alfred. *The Apperceptive Mass of Foreigners as Applied to Americanization, The Mexican Group, 1923.* University of California, Berkeley, 1971.

White, Robert W. "Motivation Reconsidered: The Concept of Competence," *Psychological Review* 66 (1960), pp. 297–334.

———. *Ego and Reality in Psychoanalytic Theory.* New York: International Universities Press, 1963.

Whitehead, Alfred North. *The Aims of Education and Other Essays.* New York: Macmillan, 1929.

Whitehouse, Frederick A. "Professional Teamwork," *Social Welfare Forum, 1957.* New York: Columbia University Press, 1957, pp. 148–157.

Whittaker, James K. "Models of Group Development: Implications for Group Work Practice," *Social Service Review* 44 (September 1970), pp. 308–322.

———. *Social Treatment: An Approach to Interpersonal Helping.* Chicago: Aldine, 1974.

Wholey, Joseph S.; Scanlon, John W.; Duffy, Hugh G.; Fukumoto, James S., and Vogt, Leona M. *Federal Evaluation Policy: Analyzing the Effects of Public Programs.* Washington, D.C.: Urban Institute, 1971.

Wholey, Joseph S. "Evaluability Assessment." In L. Rutman (Ed.), *Evaluation Research Methods: A Basic Guide.* Beverly Hills: Sage Publications, 1977.

Wickenden, Elizabeth. "The Indigent and Welfare Administration." In *The Extention of Legal Services to the Poor.* Washington, D.C.: U.S. Department of Health, Education and Welfare, 1964.

Wilensky, Harold L. "The Professionalization of Everyone." In Oscar Grusky and G. A. Miller (Eds.), *The Sociology of Organizations.* New York: Free Press, 1970.

Wilensky, Harold L., and Lebeaux, Charles N. *Industrial Society and Social Welfare.* New York: Russell Sage Foundation, 1958.

William, Arnold. "Race and Ethnicity," *American Journal of Sociology* 77 (September 1971), pp. 211–227.

Williston, Samuel. *A Treatise on the Law of Contract* (3d ed.). Mt. Kisco, N.Y.: Baker, Voorhis, 1957.

Winston, Henry. *Strategy for a Black Agenda.* New York: International Publishers, 1973.

Wise, H.; Beckhand, R.; Rubin, I.; and Kyte, A. *Making Health Teams Work.* Cambridge, Mass.: Ballinger, 1974.

Wofford, Harris J. (Ed.). *Embers of the World: Conversations with Scott Buchanan.* Santa Barbara, Calif.: Center for the Study of Democratic Institutions, 1970.

Womack, William M. "Negro Interviewers and White Patients: The Question of Confidentiality and Trust," *Archives of General Psychiatry* 16:6 (June 1967), pp. 689–691.

Worthy, Morgan; Garz, Albert L.; and Kahn, Gay M. "Self-Disclosure as an Exchange Process," *Journal of Personality and Social Psychology* 13 (January 1969), pp. 59–63.

Yalom, Irvin. *The Theory and Practice of Group Psychotherapy.* New York: Basic Books, 1970.

Yamamato, Joe et al. "Factors in Patient Selection," *American Journal of Psychiatry* 123:5 (November 1967), pp. 630–636.

Zander, Alvin; Cohen, Arthur; and Stotland, Ezra. *Role Relations in the Mental Health Profession.* Ann Arbor, Mich.: Institute for Social Research, University of Michigan, 1957.

Zweig, Franklin. "The Social Worker as Legislative Ombudsman," *Social Work* 14 (January 1969), pp. 25–33.

Zweig, Franklin M., and Morris, Robert. "The Social Planning Design Guide: Process and Proposal," *Social Work* 11 (April 1966), pp. 13–21.

Index

This book has been set linotype in 10/12 Caledonia. Chapter numbers are 12 and 30 point Goudy Bold and chapter titles are 18 point Goudy Bold. Reading numbers are 11 point Caledonia Bold italic and 14 point Goudy Bold italic, and reading titles are 14 point Goudy Bold italic. The size of the maximum type area is 33½ by 50½ picas.